T0143323

Deep Learning for Multimedia Processing Applications

Deep Learning for Multimedia Processing Applications is a comprehensive guide that explores the revolutionary impact of deep learning techniques in the field of multimedia processing. Written for a wide range of readers, from students to professionals, this book offers a concise and accessible overview of the application of deep learning in various multimedia domains, including image processing, video analysis, audio recognition, and natural language processing.

Divided into two volumes, Volume Two delves into advanced topics such as convolutional neural networks (CNNs), recurrent neural networks (RNNs), and generative adversarial networks (GANs), explaining their unique capabilities in multimedia tasks. Readers will discover how deep learning techniques enable accurate and efficient image recognition, object detection, semantic segmentation, and image synthesis. The book also covers video analysis techniques, including action recognition, video captioning, and video generation, highlighting the role of deep learning in extracting meaningful information from videos.

Furthermore, the book explores audio processing tasks such as speech recognition, music classification, and sound event detection using deep learning models. It demonstrates how deep learning algorithms can effectively process audio data, opening up new possibilities in multimedia applications. Lastly, the book explores the integration of deep learning with natural language processing techniques, enabling systems to understand, generate, and interpret textual information in multimedia contexts.

Throughout the book, practical examples, code snippets, and real-world case studies are provided to help readers gain hands-on experience in implementing deep learning solutions for multimedia processing. *Deep Learning for Multimedia Processing Applications* is an essential resource for anyone interested in harnessing the power of deep learning to unlock the vast potential of multimedia data.

Uzair Aslam Bhatti was born in 1986. He received a PhD degree in information and communication engineering from Hainan University, Haikou, Hainan, in 2019. He completed his postdoctoral from Nanjing Normal University, Nanjing, China, in implementing Clifford algebra algorithms in analyzing the geospatial data using artificial intelligence (AI). He is currently working as an associate professor in the School of Information and Communication Engineering at Hainan University. His areas of specialty include AI, machine learning, and image processing. He is serving as a guest editor of various journals including *Frontier in Plant Science, Frontier in Environmental Science, Computer Materials and Continua, Plos One, IEEE Access,* etc., and has reviewed many IEEE Transactions and Elsevier journals.

Jingbing Li is a doctor, professor, doctoral supervisor, and the vice president of the Hainan Provincial Invention Association. He has been awarded honorary titles of Leading Talents in Hainan Province, Famous Teaching Teachers in Hainan Province, Outstanding Young and Middle-aged Backbone Teachers in Hainan Province, and Excellent Teachers in Baosteel. He has also won the second prize of the Hainan Provincial Science and Technology Progress Award three times (the first completer twice, the second completer once). He has obtained 13 authorized national invention patents, published 5 monographs, such as medical image digital watermarking, and published more than 80 SCI/EI retrieved academic papers (including 22 SCI retrieved papers) as the first author or corresponding author. He has presided over two projects of the National Natural Science Foundation of China and five projects of Hainan Province's key research and development projects and Hainan Province's international scientific and technological cooperation projects.

Dr. Mengxing Huang is the dean of the School of Information at Hainan University. He has occupied many roles, such as the leader of the talent team of "Smart Service", the chief scientist of the National Key R&D Program, a member of the Expert Committee of Artificial Intelligence and Blockchain of the Science and Technology Committee of the Ministry of Education, the executive director of the Postgraduate Education Branch of the China Electronics Education Society, and the Computer Professional Teaching Committee of the Ministry of Education, among others. His main research areas include big data and intelligent information processing, multi-source information perception and fusion, artificial intelligence and intelligent services, etc. In recent years, he has published more than 230 academic papers as the first author and corresponding author, obtained 36 invention patents authorized by the state and 96 software copyrights, published 4 monographs, and translated 2 books. He won first prize and second prize of the Hainan Provincial Science and Technology Progress Award as the first person who completed it, and he won two Hainan Provincial Excellent Teaching Achievement Awards and the Excellent Teacher Award. He has presided over and undertaken more than 30 national, provincial, and ministerial-level projects, such as national key research and development plan projects, national science and technology support plans, and National Natural Science Foundation projects.

Sibghat Ullah Bazai completed his undergraduate and graduate studies in computer engineering at the Balochistan University of Information Technology, Engineering, and Management Sciences (BUITEMS) in Quetta, Pakistan. He received his PhD (IT) in cybersecurity from Massey University in Auckland, New Zealand, in 2020. As part of his research, he is interested in applying cybersecurity, identifying diseases with deep learning, automating exams with natural language processing, developing local language sentiment data sets, and planning smart cities. Sibghat is a guest editor and reviewer for several journals' special issues in MDPI, Hindawi, CMC, PlosOne, Frontier, and others.

Muhammad Aamir received a bachelor of engineering degree in computer systems engineering from Mehran University of Engineering & Technology Jamshoro, Sindh, Pakistan, in 2008; a master of engineering degree in software engineering from Chongqing University, China, in 2014; and a PhD degree in computer science and technology from Sichuan University, Chengdu, China, in 2019. He is currently an associate professor at the Department of Computer, Huanggang Normal University, China. His main research interests include pattern recognition, computer vision, image processing, deep learning, and fractional calculus.

Deep Learning for Multimedia Processing Applications

Volume Two:
Signal Processing and Pattern Recognition

Edited by
Uzair Aslam Bhatti, Jingbing Li, Mengxing Huang,
Sibghat Ullah Bazai, and Muhammad Aamir

CRC Press
Taylor & Francis Group
Boca Raton London New York

CRC Press is an imprint of the
Taylor & Francis Group, an **informa** business

Designed cover image: Uzair Aslam Bhatti

First edition published [2024]
by CRC Press
2385 Executive Center Drive, Suite 320, Boca Raton, FL 33431

and by CRC Press
4 Park Square, Milton Park, Abingdon, Oxon, OX14 4RN

CRC Press is an imprint of Taylor & Francis Group, LLC

© 2024 selection and editorial matter, Uzair Aslam Bhatti, Jingbing Li, Mengxing Huang, Sibghat Ullah Bazai, & Muhammad Aamir; individual chapters, the contributors

ISBN: 978-1-032-62334-4 (hbk)
ISBN: 978-1-032-64618-3 (pbk)
ISBN: 978-1-032-64626-8 (ebk)

DOI: 10.1201/9781032646268

Typeset in Minion
by MPS Limited, Dehradun

Contents

ZIAUR RAHMAN, MUHAMMAD AAMIR, KANZA GULZAR, JAMEEL AHMED BHUTTO, MUHAMMAD ISHFAQ, ZAHEER AHMED DAYO, AND KHALID HUSSAIN MOHAMMADANI

MUHAMMAD HAROON, SAUD ALTAF, KANZA GULZAR, AND MUHAMMAD AAMIR

MOHSIN RAZA SIYAL, MANSOOR EBRAHIM, SYED HASAN ADIL, KAMRAN RAZA, AND NADEEM QAZI

9.5   CONCLUSIONS   206

CHAPTER 10 ■ Application of Machine Learning to Urban Ecology   209

  MIR MUHAMMAD NIZAMANI, GHULAM MUHAE-UD-DIN, QIAN ZHANG,
  MUHAMMAD AWAIS, MUHAMMAD QAYYUM, MUHAMMAD FARHAN,
  MUHAMMAD JABRAN, AND YONG WANG

10.1   INTRODUCTION   209

    10.1.1   Brief Background of Urban Ecology   209

    10.1.2   The Importance of Machine Learning in Urban Ecology   210

    10.1.3   Objectives of the Chapter   211

10.2   INTRODUCTION TO MACHINE LEARNING   211

    10.2.1   Types of Machine Learning Techniques   213

    10.2.2   How Machine Learning Can Benefit Urban Ecology   213

10.3   OVERVIEW OF URBAN ECOLOGICAL DATA SOURCES   214

    10.3.1   Preprocessing and Data Fusion Techniques   214

10.4   APPLICATIONS OF MACHINE LEARNING IN URBAN
       ECOSYSTEM SERVICES   215

    10.4.1   Urban Green Space Identification and Monitoring   215

    10.4.2   Biodiversity Assessment and Conservation   216

    10.4.3   Urban Heat Island Detection and Mitigation   217

    10.4.4   Air Quality Monitoring and Prediction   218

    10.4.5   Flood Risk Assessment and Management   219

10.5   APPLICATIONS OF MACHINE LEARNING IN URBAN
       LANDSCAPE PLANNING AND DESIGN   220

    10.5.1   Landscape Connectivity and Fragmentation Analysis   220

    10.5.2   Green Infrastructure Planning   221

    10.5.3   Urban Greening and Rewilding Strategies   222

    10.5.4   Urban Form Optimization for Ecological Resilience   223

    10.5.5   Evaluation of Landscape Design Alternatives   224

10.6   MACHINE LEARNING FOR SOCIO-ECOLOGICAL SYSTEMS IN
       URBAN ENVIRONMENTS   225

    10.6.1   Analyzing Human-Nature Interactions   226

    10.6.2   Environmental Justice and Equitable Access to Green Spaces   227

    10.6.3   Public Engagement and Decision-Making Support   228

    10.6.4   Community-Based Ecological Monitoring and Management   229

CHAPTER 12 ▪ Application of GIS and Remote-Sensing Technology in
Ecosystem Services and Biodiversity Conservation 284

MIR MUHAMMAD NIZAMANI, QIAN ZHANG, GHULAM MUHAE-UD-DIN,
MUHAMMAD AWAIS, MUHAMMAD QAYYUM, MUHAMMAD FARHAN,
MUHAMMAD JABRAN, AND YONG WANG

MUHAMMAD AKRAM, WAJID HASSAN MOOSA, AND NAJIBA

Contributors

Muhammad Aamir
College of Computer Science
Huanggang Normal University
Huanggang, China

Anuj Abraham
Technology Innovation Institute
Abu Dhabi, United Arab Emirates

Syed Hasan Adil
Faculty of Engineering, Sciences and
    Technology
Iqra University
Karachi, Pakistan

Raza Muhammad Ahmad
School of Cyberspace Security
Hainan University
Haikou, China

Shakeel Ahmed
College of Material Sciences
Hainan University
Haikou, China

Muhammad Akram
Faculty of Information and
    Communication Technology
Balochistan University of Information
    Technology, Engineering and
    Management Sciences
Quetta, Pakistan

Irfan Ali
Department of Computer Science
University of Agriculture Faisalabad
Faisalabad, Pakistan

Saud Altaf
University Institute of Information
    Technology
Pir Mehr Ali Shah Arid Agriculture
    University
Rawalpindi, Pakistan

Muhammad Nouman Arshad
Department of Computer Science
University of Agriculture Faisalabad
Faisalabad, Pakistan

Muhammad Awais
Institute of Plant Sciences, Faculty of
    Natural Sciences
University of Sindh
Jamshoro, Pakistan

Uzair Aslam Bhatti
School of Information and
    Communication Engineering
and
State Key Laboratory of Marine Resource
    Utilization in the South China Sea
Hainan University
Haikou, China

Jameel Ahmed Bhutto
College of Computer Science
Huanggang Normal University
Huanggang, China

Ahmed Mateen Buttar
Department of Computer Science
University of Agriculture Faisalabad
Faisalabad, Pakistan

Zaheer Ahmed Dayo
College of Computer Science
Huanggang Normal University
Huanggang, China

Mansoor Ebrahim
Faculty of Engineering, Sciences
  and Technology
Iqra University
Karachi, Pakistan

Muhammad Farhan
Department of Plant Pathology
Agricultural College
Guizhou University
Guiyang, China

Gagandeep
Computer Science and Engineering
CT Group of Institutions
Jalandhar, India

Yazeed Yasin Ghadi
Department of Computer Science
Al Ain University
Al Ain, United Arab Emirates

Kanza Gulzar
University Institute of Information
  Technology
Pir Mehr Ali Shah Arid Agriculture
  University
Rawalpindi, Pakistan

Muhammad Haroon
University Institute of Information
  Technology
Pir Mehr Ali Shah Arid Agriculture
  University
Rawalpindi, Pakistan

Mengxing Huang
School of Information and
  Communication Engineering
Hainan University
Haikou, China

Muhammad Ishfaq
College of Computer Science
Huanggang Normal University
Huanggang, China

Nasir Ishfaq
College of Information and
  Communication Engineering
Hainan University
Haikou, China

Muhammad Jabran
State Key Laboratory for Biology of Plant
  Diseases
Institute of Plant Protection
Chinese Academy of Agricultural Sciences
Beijing, China

Muhammad Sajid Khan
Wales Institute for Digital Information
University of South Wales
Cardiff, United Kingdom

Bui Huy Khoi
Industrial University of Ho Chi Minh City
Ho Chi Minh City, Vietnam

Kirti
School of Computer Science and
    Engineering
Lovely Professional University
Jalandhar, India

Abdullah Lakhan
Department of Cyber Security
Dawood University of Engineering and
    Technology
Karachi, Sindh, Pakistan

Nguyen Ngoc Lam
Industrial University of Ho Chi Minh City
Ho Chi Minh City, Vietnam

Jingbing Li
School of Information and
    Communication Engineering
and
State Key Laboratory of Marine Resource
    Utilization in the South China Sea
Hainan University
Haikou, China

Nguyen Ngoc Long
Industrial University of Ho Chi Minh City
Ho Chi Minh City, Vietnam

Khalid Hussain Mohammadani
College of Computer Science
Huanggang Normal University
Huanggang, China

Wajid Hassan Moosa
Faculty of Information and
    Communication Technology
Balochistan University of Information
    Technology Engineering and
    Management Sciences
Quetta, Pakistan

Ghulam Muhae-Ud-Din
Department of Plant Pathology
Agricultural College
Guizhou University
Guiyang, China

Najiba
Faculty of Information and
    Communication Technology
Balochistan University of Information
    Technology Engineering and
    Management Sciences
Quetta, Pakistan

Saqib Ali Nawaz
School of Information and
    Communication Engineering
Hainan University
Haikou, China

Mir Muhammad Nizamani
Department of Plant Pathology
Agricultural College
Guizhou University
Guiyang, China

Shitala Prasad
Computer Science & Engineering, School
    of Mathematics & Computer Science
Indian Institute of Technology Goa
Goa, India

Muhammad Qayyum
School of Economics and Statistics
Guangzhou University
Guangzhou, China

Nadeem Qazi
School of Architecture, Computing and
    Engineering
University of East London
London, UK

Ziaur Rahman
College of Computer Science
Huanggang Normal University
Huanggang, China

Kamran Raza
Faculty of Engineering, Sciences and
    Technology
Iqra University
Karachi, Pakistan

Tayyab Rehman
Institute of Avionics Engineering
Air University
Islamabad, Pakistan

Muhammad Malook Rind
Department of Computer Science
Sindh Madressatul Islam University
Karachi, Sindh, Pakistan

Anwar Ali Sathio
Department of CS&IT
Benazir Bhutto
    Shaheed University
Karachi, Sindh, Pakistan
and
Department of Computer Science
Sindh Madressatul Islam University
Karachi, Sindh, Pakistan

Muhammad Anwar Shahid
University of Windsor
Windsor, Canada

Mohsin Raza Siyal
Faculty of Engineering, Sciences and
    Technology
Iqra University
Karachi, Pakistan

Noshina Tariq
Institute of Avionics Engineering
Air University
Islamabad, Pakistan

Hafiz Gulfam Ahmad Umar
Department of Computer Science & IT
Ghazi University
Dera Ghazi Khan, Pakistan

Yong Wang
Department of Plant Pathology
Agricultural College
Guizhou University
Guiyang, China

Andrew Ware
Wales Institute of Digital Information
University of South Wales
Cardiff, United Kingdom

Haili Zhang
Hainan Key Laboratory for Sustainable
    Utilization of Tropical Bioresources
Hainan University
Haikou, China

Qian Zhang
Department of Plant Pathology
Agricultural College
Guizhou University
Guiyang, China

Qin Zhou
Hainan Key Laboratory for Sustainable
    Utilization of Tropical Bioresources
Hainan University
Haikou, China

## CHAPTER 1

A Review on Comparative Study of Image-Denoising in Medical Imaging

Nasir Ishfaq

College of Information and Communication Engineering, Hainan University, Haikou, China

1.1 INTRODUCTION

Medical imaging is a vital instrument for clinical diagnosis and research, as it provides a non-invasive conception of the human body's internal frameworks and processes. Noise may have many different types, including Gaussian noise, Poisson noise, blurred noise, speckle noise, and salt-and-pepper noise (Kumar & Nachamai, 2017). It is created by a variety of variables, some of which are external to the transmission system and some of which are ambient. In recent years, the technique of noise reduction has emerged as an increasingly significant consideration in medical imaging applications (Zhou et al., 2021). Consequently, image-denoising has become an essential task in medical imaging, as it aims to remove undesirable noise while conserving image details and structures.

Recently, various methods have been proposed like a median filter, wavelet-based denoising, total variation, and deep learning like convolutional neural networks (CNNs) (Mohan et al., 2021). These are the traditional methods that are used to remove the noise.

There have been many different ideas put up for doing autonomous analysis of digital medical data for the goals of screening, diagnosing, and treating patients (Remeseiro & Bolon-Canedo, 2019; Aamir et al., 2023). Noise has negative effects within the realm of diagnostic imaging, which can lower the accuracy of diagnoses and analyses (Karimi, Dou, Warfield, & Gholipour, 2020). Denoising is a pre-processing technique that is used to clean up medical pictures while protecting the confidentiality of data and images (Vimala et al., 2023).

The use of these methodologies may successfully accomplish good outcomes, cater to the real requirements of medical diagnosis, and significantly increase the efficiency of medical imaging. Increasing the reliability of medical diagnoses is a valuable use of this concept (Li, Zhao, Lv, & Li, 2021).

DOI: 10.1201/9781032646268-1

However, there is still a need for a full comparative analysis of these many noise reduction approaches. The goal of this research would be to determine the benefits and/or drawbacks of each method, as well as to provide direction for its implementation in certain medical imaging tasks (Guan et al., 2021).

In recent years, a variety of methods for image-denoising have been presented. These techniques range from conventional signal-processing methods to deep learning-based approaches. Recent advances in deep learning-based signal processing have gained popularity (Gampala, Kumar, Sushama, & Raj, 2020). In this chapter, we compare and contrast different imaging methods and discuss their many uses in the field of medical diagnostics.

1.1.1 Evaluation of Image-Denoising Techniques

Visual artifacts such as noise or distortion can be removed by using the image-denoising technique. Measures like the peak signal-to-noise ratio (PSNR) and the structural similarity index (SSIM) are employed with other assessment indicators to prove their effectiveness (Ahmed, El-Behaidy, & Youssif, 2021). The peak signal-to-noise ratio, or PSNR, describes the ratio of the maximum signal power to the amount of corrupting noise that will affect how accurately the signal is represented (Ahmad, Rahebi, Vurdu, & Eljali). An SSIM is easy to use, has a wide range of applications, and is considered a reliable and valid technique for measuring digital images. Newer measurement tools, such as SSIM, are designed from the perspectives of luminance, contrast, and structure to more accurately replicate the human visual system (Setiadi, 2021).

The images X-ray, MRI, and ultrasound were evaluated. Gaussian noise was added to the images with a standard deviation (σ) of 10, to the original images. We have compared the PSNR values of noisy and denoised photos using different techniques in order to better understand the benefits that may be noted from using denoised images rather than noisy ones.

1.1.1.1 Evaluation Metrics

Mean squared error (MSE), peak signal-to-noise ratio (PSNR), and mean absolute error (MAE) are just a few of the objective picture quality metrics that take pixel error into account. SSIM examines the structural differences between the original and distorted versions of a picture. Additionally, it compares regional patterns of pixels with normalized brightness and contrast. But SSIM is unable to assess the quality of photos with significant blur.

The following are the formulas for determining PSNR and SSIM:

The PSNR (dB) is calculated as:

$$\text{PSNR} = 1 \log_{10}\left(\frac{MAX_I^2}{\sqrt{MSE}}\right) \tag{1.1}$$

$$\text{SSIM} = \frac{\left(2\mu_x\mu_y + c_1\right)(2\sigma + c_2)}{\left(\mu_x^2 + \mu_y^2 + c_1\right)(\sigma_x^2 + \sigma_y^2 + c_2)} \tag{1.2}$$

MAX_I, in this case, denotes the image's highest pixel value. Image size is divided by all squared change differences in order to calculate the mean squared error (MSE) and SSIM is the structural similarity index, whereas μ_x and μ_y represent the means of the original and denoised pictures, respectively; σ_x and σ_y represent the standard deviations of the original and denoised images, respectively; σ_{xy} represents the covariance between the original and denoised images; and c_1 and c_2 are constants that prevent division by zero.

1.1.2 Image-Denoising Techniques

Image-denoising methods may be broken down into three broad categories: signal and image processing-based techniques, conventional methods, and deep learning-based techniques (Das, Diya, Meher, Panda, & Abraham, 2022). Conventional methods include wavelet-based denoising (Hidayat & Winursito, 2021), median filter (Batson & Royer, 2019), and total variation (Kim et al., 2018). An artificial neural network that uses convolutions to learn the denoising function directly from the training data, such as convolutional neural networks (CNNs), generative adversarial networks (GANs), or an autoencoder, is one of the deep learning-based methods (Li, Hsu, Xie, Cong, & Gao, 2020). The purpose of the DL method is to construct feature representations from unprocessed data. Methods for accomplishing this task include an unsupervised training strategy to process feature learning, followed by a classification procedure that contains CNNs, GANs, and autoencoders (Ahmad, Sun, You, Palade, & Mao, 2022).

Here, we provide an overview of the image-denoising techniques that we assess in our comparative study. We categorize these techniques into traditional and deep learning-based methods and describe their underlying principles and characteristic.

1.1.2.1 Traditional Image-Denoising Techniques

Traditional image-denoising techniques are based on mathematical models and statistical analysis of the image signals and noise (Wang, Li, Wang, Yu, & Wang, 2021). We describe the following traditional denoising methods.

1.1.2.1.1 Wavelet-Based Denoising   Wavelet-based denoising breaks the image down into many frequencies sub-bands using wavelet transforms and applies a thresholding function to each sub-band to remove noise while preserving edges and structures (Bnou, Raghay, & Hakim, 2020). Wavelet-based methods are among the most widely used techniques for image-denoising. These methods decompose the image into different frequency bands using a wavelet transform and then apply a thresholding function to remove the noise in each band (Aamir et al., 2018). The most common wavelet-based methods include the discrete wavelet transform (DWT) and the stationary wavelet transform (SWT) (Deeba, Kun, Dharejo, & Zhou, 2020).

Figure 1.1 demonstrates how the LR picture was processed using the DWT and SWT decomposition techniques as a wavelet approximation of the related HR image.

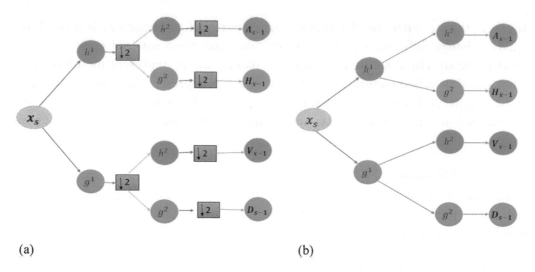

FIGURE 1.1 Wavelet decomposition: (a) DWT decomposition, (b) SWT decomposition (Deeba et al., 2020).

In our study, we have computed the PSNR and SSIM values for wavelet-based denoising on X-ray, MRI, and ultrasound images with Gaussian noise with a standard deviation of 10 using MatLab.

We applied wavelet denoising technique to X-ray, MRI, and ultrasound images. Figure 1.2 shows the comparisons of images. The PSNR and SSIM values obtained from the experiment are shown in Table 1.1.

1.1.2.1.2 Median Filter   Median filter denoising techniques are simple yet effective in removing noise from images. Median filters are non-linear filters that swap out picture pixels for the middle value between their neighbors (Danso et al., 2021). Because of its success in maintaining image edges and features, this method has found widespread use in medical imaging.

Our study utilized the median filter technique to denoise X-ray, MRI brain, and ultrasound abdominal images with Gaussian noise that had a standard deviation of 10. The denoising results are presented in Table 1.2, which shows that the median filter technique significantly improved the PSNR and SSIM values for all three types of medical images. Specifically, the PSNR values for X-ray, MRI brain, and ultrasound abdominal images increased by 0.22 dB, 0.01 dB, and 0.91 dB, respectively, while the SSIM values increased by 0.01, 0.06, and 0.03, respectively. The denoising results are consistent with the values obtained from our study, which showed that the PSNR values for X-ray, MRI brain, and ultrasound abdominal images were 30.79 dB, 30.86 dB, and 30.24 dB, respectively. In addition, the correspondent SSIM values for X-ray, MRI brain, and ultrasound abdominal images were 0.6981, 0.6966, and 0.7074, respectively. The median filter may enhance denoising performance while still accurately retaining edge details (Goyal, Dogra, Agrawal, Sohi, & Sharma, 2020). In medical imaging, it is important to maintain the details of images to obtain sufficient information for accurate diagnosis.

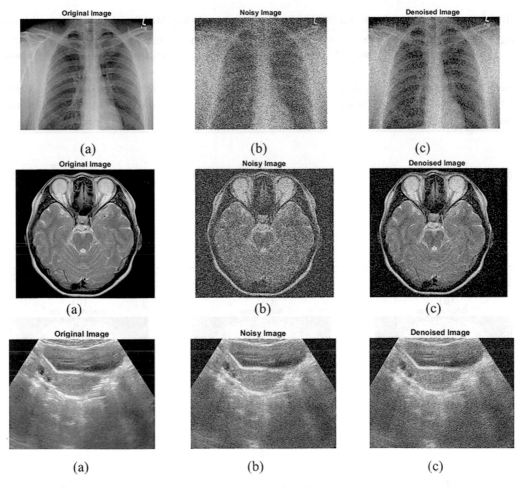

FIGURE 1.2 Visual comparisons of wavelet-based denoising results on three different images, X-ray, MRI, and ultrasound, distorted by standard deviation ten, adding white Gaussian noise: (a) original image, (b) noisy image, (c) denoised image.

TABLE 1.1 Wavelet-Based PSNR and SSIM Values for Denoising X-Ray, MRI Brain, and Ultrasound Images

Image type	Technique	PSNR (db)-original	PSNR (db)-Gaussian noise ($\sigma = 10$)	PSNR (db)-denoised	SSIM-original	SSIM-Gaussian noise ($\sigma = 10$)	SSIM-denoised
X-ray	Wavelet-based	21.62	9.20	28.83	0.2440	0.0176	0.9732
MRI brain	Wavelet-based	22.23	9.17	30.06	0.2867	0.0237	0.9683
Ultrasound	Wavelet-based	21.86	9.11	28.75	0.2869	0.0278	0.9685

If compared to other denoising techniques such as wavelet-based and deep learning-based techniques, removing Gaussian noise from medical pictures using a median filter has been shown to be less effective. But still, the median filter has its advantages, in terms of its speed and simplicity. The hybrid median filter is an enhanced variant of the

TABLE 1.2   Median Filter PSNR and SSIM Values for Denoising X-Ray, MRI Brain, and Ultrasound Images

Image type	Technique	PSNR (db)-original	PSNR (db)-Gaussian noise (σ = 10)	PSNR (db)-denoised	SSIM-original	SSIM-Gaussian noise (σ = 10)	SSIM-denoised
X-ray	Median Filter	30.79	14.35	29.94	0.6981	0.4433	0.9053
MRI brain	Median Filter	30.86	14.34	30.16	0.6966	0.4535	0.9012
Ultrasound	Median Filter	30.24	14.10	29.97	0.7074	0.4755	0.8972

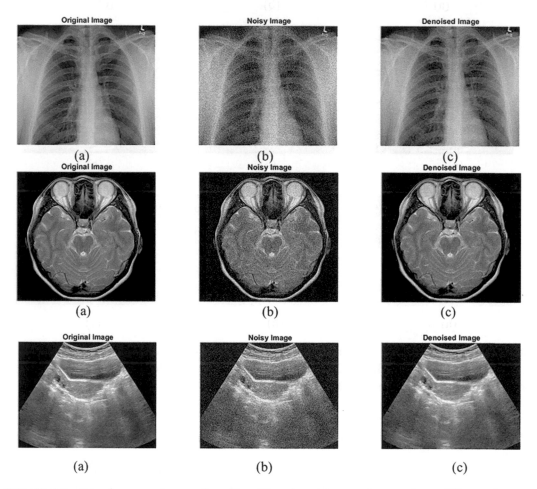

FIGURE 1.3   Visual comparisons of median filter denoising results on three different images, X-ray, MRI, and ultrasound, distorted by standard deviation ten, adding white Gaussian noise: (a) original image, (b) noisy image, (c) denoised image.

median filter that is capable of more effective noise suppression (Seetharaman, Tharun, & Anandan, 2021) (Figure 1.3).

1.1.2.1.3 Total Variation   Total variation denoising is a technique for reducing noise that was created to keep the edges of the original signal intact. Total variation is characterized in terms of an optimization problem, which is different from the way a traditional low-pass

TABLE 1.3 Total Variation PSNR and SSIM Values for Denoising X-Ray, MRI Brain, and Ultrasound Images

Image type	Technique	PSNR (db)-original	PSNR (db)-Gaussian noise ($\sigma = 10$)	PSNR (db)-denoised	SSIM-original	SSIM-Gaussian noise ($\sigma = 10$)	SSIM-denoised
X-ray	Total Variation	19.49	7.87	26.78	0.1813	0.0158	0.9784
MRI brain	Total Variation	20.20	8.04	27.62	0.2240	0.0199	0.9746
Ultrasound	Total Variation	19.75	7.84	26.88	0.2297	0.0204	0.9723

filter (Mustafa et al., 2020). The purpose of this section is to discuss and commute the PSNR and SSIM analysis of total variation technique on X-ray, MRI, and ultrasound images, along with other comparisons with other denoising techniques.

We have applied the total variation technique to X-ray, MRI brain, and ultrasound images added with Gaussian noise with a standard deviation (σ) of 10, using Matlab. Values of PSNR and SSIM, which we obtained from the experiment using Matlab, are shown in Table 1.3 (Figure 1.4).

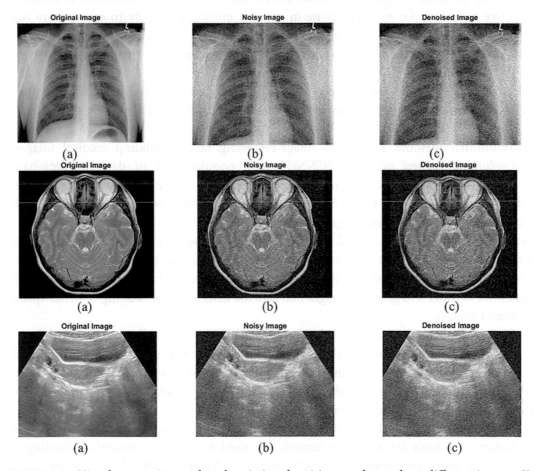

FIGURE 1.4 Visual comparisons of total variation denoising results on three different images, X-ray, MRI, and ultrasound, distorted by standard deviation ten, adding white Gaussian noise: (a) original image, (b) noisy image, (c) denoised image.

Table 1.3 evaluates that values of PSNR of total variation techniques are lower compared to other denoising techniques such as the wavelet-based denoising technique and median filter, which we commuted earlier. Similarly, SSIM values obtained by total variation denoising are lower in comparison with the wavelet-based denoising technique and median filter denoising techniques.

In the area of diagnostic imaging, several strategies for noise reduction were widely utilized. The goal of these techniques was to cut down on the amount of noise component that was present in medical images. Although the previous techniques – such as median, wavelet-based denoising technique, and median filter – were successful in suppressing the noise, the edge data was still compromised. Total variation (TV) noise reduction technology was created and is now being studied to solve this issue (Seo et al., 2016). It is a powerful technique that preserves edges and fine details while removing noise. However, the main disadvantage of total variation denoising is that it tends to produce images with staircase artifacts, which can be visually unappealing.

Compared to wavelet-based and median filter denoising techniques, total variation denoising produces images with lower PSNR and SSIM values. However, it is still an effective technique for reducing noise in medical images, especially in cases where edge preservation is critical. It is also worth noting that total variation denoising can be used in conjunction with other denoising techniques to further improve image quality.

1.1.2.1.4 Deep Learning-Based Deep learning-based denoising techniques use artificial neural networks to learn the denoising function directly from the training data (Bera & Biswas, 2021). Deep learning-based methods have shown superior performance compared to traditional methods in various image-denoising tasks, including medical imaging. Convolutional neural networks (CNNs) are a popular type of deep learning-based denoising method that uses convolutional layers to learn the spatial features of the image (Zeng, Zhang, Han, Gong, & Zhang, 2019). Generative adversarial networks (GANs) have also been employed for image-denoising tasks, which have shown promising results in generating high-quality denoised images (Fuentes-Hurtado, Sibarita, & Viasnoff, 2023). These networks consist of a generator network that generates the denoised image and a discriminator network that distinguishes between the denoised and original images. The generator is trained to generate images that fool the discriminator, leading to better-quality denoised images.

One of the advantages of deep learning-based denoising methods is their ability to learn the underlying features of the image and generalize well to unseen data (Roy et al., 2019). However, in order to train well, they need a significant quantity of labeled data, which may not always be available in medical imaging. Traditional denoising methods may still be helpful in such cases (Figure 1.5).

Table 1.4 shows that PSNR and SSIM values achieved by the deep learning-based technique are high for all three images, we used in this experiment, indicating its efficacy in reducing noise. The results obtained by using the deep learning-based technique are much better compared to results obtained by wavelet-based and median filter denoising techniques. These findings show consistency with previous studies,

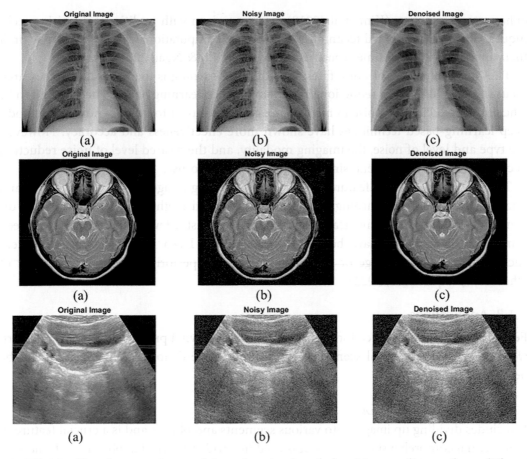

FIGURE 1.5 Visual comparisons of deep learning-based denoising results on three different images, X-ray, MRI, and ultrasound, distorted by standard deviation ten, adding white Gaussian noise: (a) original image, (b) noisy image, (c) denoised image

TABLE 1.4   DL-Based PSNR and SSIM Values for Denoising X-Ray, MRI Brain, and Ultrasound Images

Image type	Technique	PSNR (db)-original	PSNR (db)-Gaussian noise ($\sigma = 10$)	PSNR (db)-denoised	SSIM-original	SSIM-Gaussian noise ($\sigma = 10$)	SSIM-denoised
X-ray	Deep Learning-Based	28.81	11.22	30.09	0.9352	0.5732	0.9221
MRI brain	Deep Learning-Based	28.50	11.08	30.29	0.7980	0.5088	0.9121
Ultrasound	Deep Learning-Based	28.21	11.00	30.27	0.9161	0.5429	0.92

which show the effectiveness and accuracy of deep learning-based techniques over traditional denoising techniques.

Although deep learning has promising performance, it still has some flaws. It is challenging to create these vast data sets containing medical images of rare dangerous conditions in general practice, while deep learning needs a lot of data to reduce over-fitting and enhance performances (Kim et al., 2019). In comparison with traditional denoising techniques, deep learning-based techniques have higher computational costs, which may limit their application in real-time scenarios (Chai, Zeng, Li, & Ngai, 2021).

The implementation of noise filtering with deep learning is the most current research focus in the field of noise reduction. In our study, deep learning has also been found to be efficient in reducing the noise in medical images. In contrast to other denoising methods, deep learning-based techniques have shown more effectiveness and accuracy. However, the type and level of noise, the imaging modality, and the desired level of noise reduction decide to choose which denoising technique is better to use.

To improve and create features from already existing images in computer vision and image processing, deep learning has become a standard method. Computer-assisted diagnostics, radionics, and medical image analysis are just a few of the areas where deep learning (DL) methods have been successfully used. Deep neural networks are very successful in a broad range of applications, often outperforming humans in terms of efficiency (Yaqub et al., 2022).

1.1.3 Applications

For medical imaging applications, image-denoising is a vital processing step. In this part, we quickly go over several scenarios when using image-denoising algorithms might be beneficial.

1.1.3.1 Image Segmentation

It includes dividing up images into various segments and objects and is a crucial feature of many visual comprehension systems. It is used in a wide variety of applications. Denoising has the potential to improve accuracy in a number of different areas, including feature extraction and identification, noise reduction, and image segmentation and recognition. Various image-denoising methods have been utilized to increase image segmentation accuracy in medical imaging applications. Using a deep wavelet auto-encoder model (Abd El Kader et al., 2021), it identified and classified tumors that provide great precision, quick response, and little loss using MRI brain image segmentation methods.

1.1.3.2 Image Registration

During image registration, two images are geometrically aligned at different times, from different perspectives, and/or by different sensors (Tong et al., 2019). Different imaging circumstances result in the current disparities between images. Image registration has the potential to remove noise more effectively than other methods. The quality of each cross-correlation profile was able to be improved after the image-denoising process and, as a result, the accuracy of image registration was able to be attained by minimizing the amount of noise that was present throughout the registration process. For instance, to enhance the registration of cardiac magnetic resonance imaging (MRI) pictures, the NLML (non-local maximum likelihood) estimation technique, which is a competent non-local concept-based denoising algorithm, drew stimulus from non-local means (NLM) (Upadhya, Talawar, & Rajan, 2017).

1.1.3.3 Feature Extraction

An essential step in segmentation is feature extraction since each image has its own set of features that require an extraction (Saman & Jamjala Narayanan, 2019). To obtain processing results for medical image feature extraction, large amounts of data are analyzed, helping doctors to determine the case more accurately. There are several methods for extracting features including texture features, co-occurrence matrix, Gabor features, and wavelet transforms; decision boundary features are extracted using a minimum noise fraction transform; nonparametric weighted features are extracted using a spectrum (Soomro et al., 2022). Principal component analysis, linear discriminant analysis, and independent component analysis are three methods that may be used in order to minimize the number of features. A combination of feature extraction and feature reduction algorithms results in precise systems that are computationally efficient and use fewer features.

1.1.3.4 Examples

Table 1.5 shows examples of medical imaging image-denoising approaches. Each strategy improves picture segmentation and registration accuracy.

Equation (1.3) shows a possible formulation for the non-local means denoising algorithm used by (Haskins et al., 2019):

$$\hat{u}(x) = \frac{1}{Z(x)} \int_\Omega u(y) w(x, y) \, dy, \tag{1.3}$$

where $w(x, y)$ is a weight function that relies on the distance between pixels $(x) f(y)$ and $Z(x)$, is a normalization constant, $\hat{u}(x)$ is the denoised picture, and $u(y)$ is the noisy input image.

In general, the image-denoising technique is a crucial aid in medical imaging applications, enabling health professionals to get reliable and accurate results from medical images. For example, MRI is a powerful diagnostic technique in clinical applications. Denoising techniques that are equipped with the appropriate data sets for training are able to differentiate between aberrant and normal tumor areas and accurately identify the regions as either benign tumors, malignant tumors, or healthy brains (Gurbină, Lascu, & Lascu, 2019). The denoising model can successfully reduce noise in ultrasound images while maintaining the structures (Yancheng, Zeng, Dong, & Wang, 2023).

TABLE 1.5   Examples of Image-Denoising Techniques in Medical Imaging Applications

Application	Technique	Example
Image Segmentation	Median filtering and wavelet-based denoising	Improved segmentation of MR brain images (Khorram & Yazdi, 2019)
Image Registration	Non-local means denoising	Improved registration of cardiac MRI images (Haskins et al., 2019)
Feature Extraction	Median filtering and total variation denoising	Improved accuracy of feature extraction for breast ultrasound images (Virmani & Agarwal, 2020)

TABLE 1.6   Applications of Image-Denoising Techniques in Medical Imaging

Application	Denoising methods	Benefits
MRI imaging	Wavelet-based denoising	Improved image quality and tumor detection
Ultrasound imaging	Non-local means denoising	Improved fatal and cardiac structure visualization
CT Imaging	Total variation denoising	Improved image quality and reduced radiation dose
PET imaging	Anisotropic diffusion denoising	Improved image quality and tracer uptake quantification
Image segmentation	Median filtering	Improved segmentation accuracy and reduced noise artifacts
Image registration	Gaussian filtering	Improved alignment accuracy and reduced image distortion
Feature extraction	Non-linear filtering	Improved feature quantification and tissue characterization

Recent applications of image-denoising techniques in medical imaging have been summarized in Table 1.6, along with the corresponding denoising methods used and the benefits achieved.

With a growing demand for high-quality medical imaging, the development and improvement of denoising techniques are anticipated to continue to play an important role in the advancement of medical imaging.

1.1.4 Comparison

In Table 1.7, original values of PSNR (dB) and SSIM can be seen with Gaussian noise added with standard deviation (σ) 10 and the corresponding denoised images using different techniques (wavelet-based, median filter, total variation, and deep learning-based).

TABLE 1.7   A Comparison of Denoising Techniques for Medical Images: X-Ray, MRI, and Ultrasound Images

Image type	Denoising technique	PSNR (dB) - original	PSNR (dB) - Gaussian noise (σ = 10)	PSNR (db) - denoised	SSIM - original	SSIM - Gaussian noise (σ = 10)	SSIM - denoised
X-ray	Wavelet-based	21.62	9.20	28.83	0.2440	0.0176	0.9732
X-ray	Median filter	30.79	14.35	29.94	0.6981	0.4433	0.9053
X-ray	Total variation	19.49	7.87	26.78	0.1813	0.0158	0.9784
X-ray	Deep learning-based	28.81	11.22	30.09	0.9352	0.5732	0.9221
MRI	Wavelet-based	22.23	9.17	30.06	0.2867	0.0237	0.9683
MRI	Median filter	30.86	14.34	30.16	0.6966	0.4535	0.9012
MRI	Total variation	20.20	8.04	27.62	0.2240	0.0199	0.9746
MRI	Deep learning-based	28.50	11.08	30.29	0.7980	0.5088	0.9121
Ultrasound	Wavelet-based	21.86	9.11	28.75	0.2869	0.0278	0.9685
Ultrasound	Median filter	30.24	14.10	29.97	0.7074	0.4755	0.8972
Ultrasound	Total variation	19.75	7.84	26.88	0.2297	0.0204	0.9723
Ultrasound	Deep learning-based	28.21	11.00	30.27	0.9161	0.5429	0.9200

The wavelet-based denoising approach generated denoised X-ray pictures with a PSNR value of 28.83 (dB) and an SSIM value of 0.9732, whereas the median filter technique produced denoised X-ray images with a PSNR value of 29.94 (dB) and an SSIM value of 0.9053. The total variation approach yielded a PSNR value of 26.78 (dB) and an SSIM value of 0.9784, while the deep learning-based technique yielded a PSNR value of 30.09 (dB) and an SSIM value of 0.9221. Both of these results are much better than those obtained by the total variation technique. In general, the approach that was based on deep learning provided the best PSNR value, whereas the technique that was based on wavelets produced the highest SSIM value.

The wavelet-based denoising approach generated denoised MRI pictures with a PSNR value of 30.06 (dB) and an SSIM value of 0.9683, whereas the median filter technique produced denoised MRI images with a PSNR value of 30.16 (dB) and an SSIM value of 0.9012. Based on the total variation approach, a PSNR of 27.62 (dB) and SSIM value of 0.9746 were obtained, whereas a PSNR of 30.29 (dB) and SSIM of 0.9121 were obtained using a deep learning-based approach. The PSNR value obtained with the deep learning-based approach was higher, while the SSIM value obtained with the wavelet-based denoising approach was higher. In general, deep learning provided better PSNR results than total variation.

In comparison, the wavelet-based denoising approach produced denoised images with a PSNR value of 28.75 (dB) and SSIM value of 0.9685 for ultrasound images, whereas the median filter technique produced a PSNR value of 29.97 (dB) and SSIM value of 0.8972 for ultrasound images. With the total variation approach, the PSNR value was 26.88 (dB) and the SSIM was 0.9723, while with the deep learning-based approach, the PSNR was 30.27 (dB) and the SSIM was 0.9200. Both values were much higher than the values obtained by the total variation technique. In general, the approach that was based on deep learning provided the best PSNR value, whereas the technique that was based on wavelets produced the highest SSIM value.

The results indicate that the deep learning-based approach is the most successful at denoising all three different kinds of pictures, followed by the wavelet-based technique for X-ray and ultrasound images. In general, the deep learning-based technique is the most effective. In terms of SSIM, the effectiveness of the median filter approach for X-ray pictures is comparable to that of the deep learning-based technique although not quite as successful as the latter. When it comes to denoising all three different kinds of photos, the total variation approach is not nearly as successful as the other two procedures.

It is important to note that the addition of Gaussian noise to the first provided images has a considerable influence on the PSNR and SSIM values, causing them to decrease significantly across the board for all image processing methods and types of images. The significance of denoising techniques for enhancing image quality in noisy conditions is brought into focus by this point.

Overall, the analysis indicates that, depending on the individual application and objectives, both the deep learning-based approach and the median filter methodology are feasible options for image-denoising in medical imaging. The median filter outperformed the deep learning-based strategy in terms of SSIM findings, but it wasn't as effective in terms of PSNR. The best denoising method will be determined in practice by a variety of variables, including the intended trade-off between image qualities and processing efficiency.

1.2 CONCLUSION

Our research emphasizes the value of deep learning-based denoising methods for medical imaging. Future research might evaluate the efficacy of these methods on other kinds of medical images or investigate the usage of additional denoising models based on deep learning.

In general, our findings show that, for both PSNR and SSIM, deep learning-based denoising algorithms surpass more conventional ones like wavelet-based denoising, median filtering, and total variation denoising. This shows that denoising methods based on deep learning provide a viable way to raise the quality of medical images.

It is crucial to remember that the effectiveness of these procedures might change based on the unique properties of the processed medical pictures. A further study is needed to evaluate these techniques for medical image-denoising.

The denoising images of medical imaging is an integral part of the interpretation process, and different methods are available for handling the issue of image noise. A variety of traditional image-denoising methods have been successfully applied to medical imaging applications, including median filtering and wavelet-based denoising. DnCNN- and GAN-based methods for denoising medical images have shown improved accuracy, and these methods may completely alter medical image analysis.

Besides denoising, the use of deep learning approaches in combination with denoising improves image registration and feature extraction, which are important processes in medical image analysis. Through deep learning-based image registration, noise that interferes with the matching of points on the images can be removed, which can improve image registration accuracy. Various medical applications use feature extraction techniques, including the detection and classification of lung nodules.

Future research could explore the use of deep learning techniques for other applications in medical image analysis, such as image segmentation, object detection, and image reconstruction. With the continued advancements in deep learning and medical imaging technology, we can expect to see significant improvements in the accuracy and efficiency of medical image analysis in the years to come.

REFERENCES

Aamir, Muhammad, Rahman, Ziaur, Ahmed Abro, Waheed, Aslam Bhatti, Uzair, Ahmed Dayo, Zaheer, & Ishfaq, Muhammad (2023). Brain tumor classification utilizing deep features derived from high-quality regions in MRI images. *Biomedical Signal Processing and Control*, 85, 10498810.1016/j.bspc.2023.104988.

Aamir, Muhammad, Pu, Yi-Fei, Rahman, Ziaur, Tahir, Muhammad, Naeem, Hamad, & Dai, Qiang (2018). A Framework for Automatic Building Detection from Low-Contrast Satellite Images. *Symmetry*, 11, 310.3390/sym11010003.

Abd El Kader, I., Xu, G., Shuai, Z., Saminu, S., Javaid, I., Ahmad, I. S., & Kamhi, S. (2021). Brain tumor detection and classification on MR images by a deep wavelet auto-encoder model. *Diagnostics*, *11*(9), 1589.

Ahmad, B., Sun, J., You, Q., Palade, V., & Mao, Z. (2022). Brain tumor classification using a combination of variational autoencoders and generative adversarial networks. *Biomedicines*, *10*(2), 223.

Ahmad, T., Rahebi, J., Vurdu, C., & Eljali, E. Full reference image quality assessment method based on wavelet features and edge intensity. *International Journal of Engineering Research and Development*, *14*(3).

Ahmed, A. S., El-Behaidy, W. H., & Youssif, A. A. (2021). Medical image denoising system based on stacked convolutional autoencoder for enhancing 2-dimensional gel electrophoresis noise reduction. *Biomedical Signal Processing and Control*, *69*, 102842.

Batson, J., & Royer, L. (2019). *Noise2self: Blind denoising by self-supervision.* Paper presented at the International Conference on Machine Learning.

Bera, S., & Biswas, P. K. (2021). Noise conscious training of non local neural network powered by self attentive spectral normalized Markovian patch GAN for low dose CT denoising. *IEEE Transactions on Medical Imaging*, *40*(12), 3663–3673.

Bnou, K., Raghay, S., & Hakim, A. (2020). A wavelet denoising approach based on unsupervised learning model. *EURASIP Journal on Advances in Signal Processing*, *2020*(1), 1–26.

Chai, J., Zeng, H., Li, A., & Ngai, E. W. (2021). Deep learning in computer vision: A critical review of emerging techniques and application scenarios. *Machine Learning with Applications*, *6*, 100134.

Danso, S., Liping, S., Deng, H., Odoom, J., Appiah, E., Etse, B., & Liu, Q. (2021). Denoising terahertz image using non-linear filters. *Computer Engineering and Intelligent Systems*, *12*(2).

Das, P. K., Diya, V., Meher, S., Panda, R., & Abraham, A. (2022). A systematic review on recent advancements in deep and machine learning based detection and classification of acute lymphoblastic leukemia. *IEEE Access*, *10*.

Deeba, F., Kun, S., Dharejo, F. A., & Zhou, Y. (2020). Wavelet-based enhanced medical image super resolution. *IEEE Access*, *8*, 37035–37044.

Fuentes-Hurtado, F., Sibarita, J. B., & Viasnoff, V. (2023). CLIDiM: Contrastive learning for image denoising in microscopy. arXiv preprint arXiv:2303.15214.

Gampala, V., Kumar, M. S., Sushama, C., & Raj, E. F. I. (2020). Deep learning based image processing approaches for image deblurring. *Materials Today: Proceedings*. 10.1016/j.matpr.2020.11.076.

Goyal, B., Dogra, A., Agrawal, S., Sohi, B. S., & Sharma, A. (2020). Image denoising review: From classical to state-of-the-art approaches. *Information Fusion*, *55*, 220–244.

Guan, Yurong, Aamir, Muhammad, Rahman, Ziaur, Ali, Ammara, Abro, Waheed Ahmed, Dayo, Zaheer Ahmed, Bhutta, Muhammad Shoaib, & Hu, Zhihua (2021). A framework for efficient brain tumor classification using MRI images. *Mathematical Biosciences and Engineering*, *18*, 5790–581510.3934/mbe.2021292.

Gurbină, M., Lascu, M., & Lascu, D. (2019). *Tumor detection and classification of MRI brain image using different wavelet transforms and support vector machines.* Paper presented at the 2019 42nd International Conference on Telecommunications and Signal Processing (TSP).

Haskins, G., Kruecker, J., Kruger, U., Xu, S., Pinto, P. A., Wood, B. J., & Yan, P. (2019). Learning deep similarity metric for 3D MR–TRUS image registration. *International Journal of Computer Assisted Radiology and Surgery*, *14*, 417–425.

Hidayat, R., & Winursito, A. (2021). A modified MFCC for improved wavelet-based denoising on robust speech recognition. *International Journal of Intelligent Engineering and Systems*, *14*(1), 12–21.

Karimi, D., Dou, H., Warfield, S. K., & Gholipour, A. (2020). Deep learning with noisy labels: Exploring techniques and remedies in medical image analysis. *Medical Image Analysis*, *65*, 101759.

Khorram, B., & Yazdi, M. (2019). A new optimized thresholding method using ant colony algorithm for MR brain image segmentation. *Journal of Digital Imaging, 32*, 162–174.

Kim, K., Wu, D., Gong, K., Dutta, J., Kim, J. H., Son, Y. D., … Li, Q. (2018). Penalized PET reconstruction using deep learning prior and local linear fitting. *IEEE Transactions on Medical Imaging, 37*(6), 1478–1487.

Kim, M., Yun, J., Cho, Y., Shin, K., Jang, R., Bae, H. J., & Kim, N. (2019). Deep learning in medical imaging. *Neurospine, 16*(4), 657.

Kumar, N., & Nachamai, M. (2017). Noise removal and filtering techniques used in medical images. *Oriental Journal of Computer Science and Technology, 10*(1), 103–113.

Li, M., Hsu, W., Xie, X., Cong, J., & Gao, W. (2020). SACNN: Self-attention convolutional neural network for low-dose CT denoising with self-supervised perceptual loss network. *IEEE Transactions on Medical Imaging, 39*(7), 2289–2301.

Li, Y., Zhao, J., Lv, Z., & Li, J. (2021). Medical image fusion method by deep learning. *International Journal of Cognitive Computing in Engineering, 2*, 21–29.

Mohan, E., Rajesh, A., Sunitha, G., Konduru, R. M., Avanija, J., & Ganesh Babu, L. (2021). A deep neural network learning-based speckle noise removal technique for enhancing the quality of synthetic-aperture radar images. *Concurrency and Computation: Practice and Experience, 33*(13), e6239.

Mustafa, Z. A., Abrahim, B. A., Omara, A., Mohammed, A. A., Hassan, I. A., & Mustafa, E. A. (2020). Reduction of speckle noise and image enhancement in ultrasound image using filtering technique and edge detection. *Journal of Clinical Engineering, 45*(1), 51–65.

Remeseiro, B., & Bolon-Canedo, V. (2019). A review of feature selection methods in medical applications. *Computers in Biology and Medicine, 112*, 103375.

Roy, Y., Banville, H., Albuquerque, I., Gramfort, A., Falk, T. H., & Faubert, J. (2019). Deep learning-based electroencephalography analysis: A systematic review. *Journal of Neural Engineering, 16*(5), 051001.

Saman, S., & Jamjala Narayanan, S. (2019). Survey on brain tumor segmentation and feature extraction of MR images. *International Journal of Multimedia Information Retrieval, 8*, 79–99.

Seetharaman, R., Tharun, M., & Anandan, K. (2021). *A novel approach in hybrid median filtering for denoising medical images.* Paper presented at the IOP Conference Series: Materials Science and Engineering.

Seo, K., Kim, S. H., Kang, S. H., Park, J., Lee, C. L., & Lee, Y. (2016). The effects of total variation (TV) technique for noise reduction in radio-magnetic X-ray image: Quantitative study. *Journal of Magnetics, 21*(4), 593–598.

Setiadi, D. R. I. M. (2021). PSNR vs SSIM: Imperceptibility quality assessment for image steganography. *Multimedia Tools and Applications, 80*(6), 8423–8444.

Soomro, T. A., Zheng, L., Afifi, A. J., Ali, A., Soomro, S., Yin, M., & Gao, J. (2022). Image segmentation for MR brain tumor detection using machine learning: A review. *IEEE Reviews in Biomedical Engineering, 16*, 70–90.

Tong, X., Ye, Z., Xu, Y., Gao, S., Xie, H., Du, Q., … Luan, K. (2019). Image registration with Fourier-based image correlation: A comprehensive review of developments and applications. *IEEE Journal of Selected Topics in Applied Earth Observations and Remote Sensing, 12*(10), 4062–4081.

Upadhya, A. H., Talawar, B., & Rajan, J. (2017). GPU implementation of non-local maximum likelihood estimation method for denoising magnetic resonance images. *Journal of Real-Time Image Processing, 13*, 181–192.

Vimala, B. B., Srinivasan, S., Mathivanan, S. K., Muthukumaran, V., Babu, J. C., Herencsar, N., & Vilcekova, L. (2023). Image noise removal in ultrasound breast images based on hybrid deep learning technique. *Sensors, 23*(3), 1167.

Virmani, J., & Agarwal, R. (2020). Deep feature extraction and classification of breast ultrasound images. *Multimedia Tools and Applications, 79*(37–38), 27257–27292.

Wang, C., Li, M., Wang, R., Yu, H., & Wang, S. (2021). An image denoising method based on BP neural network optimized by improved whale optimization algorithm. *EURASIP Journal on Wireless Communications and Networking, 2021*(1), 1–22.

Yancheng, L., Zeng, X., Dong, Q., & Wang, X. (2023). RED-MAM: A residual encoder-decoder network based on multi-attention fusion for ultrasound image denoising. *Biomedical Signal Processing and Control, 79*, 104062.

Yaqub, M., Jinchao, F., Arshid, K., Ahmed, S., Zhang, W., Nawaz, M. Z., & Mahmood, T. (2022). Deep learning-based image reconstruction for different medical imaging modalities. *Computational and Mathematical Methods in Medicine, 2022*.

Zeng, Y., Zhang, M., Han, F., Gong, Y., & Zhang, J. (2019). Spectrum analysis and convolutional neural network for automatic modulation recognition. *IEEE Wireless Communications Letters, 8*(3), 929–932.

Zhou, S. K., Greenspan, H., Davatzikos, C., Duncan, J. S., Van Ginneken, B., Madabhushi, A., … Summers, R. M. (2021). A review of deep learning in medical imaging: Imaging traits, technology trends, case studies with progress highlights, and future promises. *Proceedings of the IEEE, 109*(5), 820–838.

## CHAPTER 2

Remote-Sensing Image Classification

A Comprehensive Review and Applications

Uzair Aslam Bhatti[1,2], Jingbing Li[1,2], Saqib Ali Nawaz[1],
Mengxing Huang[1], Raza Muhammad Ahmad[3], and
Yazeed Yasin Ghadi[4]

[1]*School of Information and Communication Engineering, Hainan University, Haikou, China*
[2]*State Key Laboratory of Marine Resource Utilization in the South China Sea, Hainan University, Haikou, China*
[3]*School of Cyberspace Security, Hainan University, Haikou, China*
[4]*Department of Computer Science, Al Ain University, Al Ain, UAE*

2.1 INTRODUCTION

Image classification, object detection in industrial production, medical image analysis, action recognition, and remote sensing are just a few examples of the many uses for deep learning and computer vision [1]. Satellite photos are the most common way geographers get their hands on new data, and civil engineers use satellite image analysis for all sorts of things [2–6]. There is a pressing need for effective methods of data extraction in order to manage the ever-increasing volume of the data gleaned from satellite sources. With the use of rudimentary image categorization, this massive collection of satellite photos may be sorted into meaningful orders. Feature extraction is the first step of a multi-step process that culminates in the classification of satellite pictures. Designing a method for classifying the desired images is the first stage in the image classification process. The photographs are then pre-processed in various ways, such as by grouping similar images together, improving them, resizing them, etc. The third stage is picking out the relevant parts of the photos and then creating the first clusters. The photos are then classified using an algorithm, and any necessary adjustments are made in the post-algorithm (or postprocessing) stage [7–10]. Figure 2.1 shows the significance of applications of deep learning in remote sensing.

Image classification is a fundamental task in computer vision that involves assigning a class label to an image based on its visual content. Image classification has numerous applications,

DOI: 10.1201/9781032646268-2

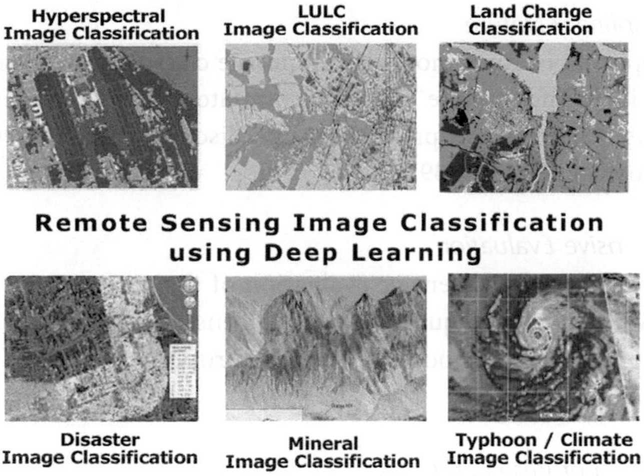

FIGURE 2.1   Remote-sensing image processing using deep learning.

including object recognition, face recognition, and medical image analysis. Traditionally, image classification has been performed using handcrafted features and machine learning algorithms such as support vector machines (SVMs) and random forests [11–18].

Deep learning, a subfield of machine learning, has revolutionized image classification in recent years. Deep learning algorithms, such as convolutional neural networks (CNNs), recurrent neural networks (RNNs), and deep belief networks (DBNs), have shown remarkable performance on a variety of image classification tasks [19–26]. These algorithms are based on hierarchical architectures that learn increasingly abstract features from the input data, leading to highly discriminative representations for classification. Deep learning-based image classification has been applied to various domains, including natural images, medical images, and remote-sensing images. In the context of remote sensing, image classification is essential for resource management, environmental monitoring, disaster response, and national security. Remote-sensing image classification involves the identification and labeling of different land cover types, such as forests, crops, water bodies, and urban areas, using remotely sensed data [27–37]. As image classification is a fundamental task in computer vision, deep learning algorithms have revolutionized image classification by achieving state-of-the-art performance on a variety of tasks. Deep learning-based remote-sensing image classification is critical for decision making and resource management in various fields and has the potential to make a significant impact on global challenges such as climate change and sustainable development.

2.1.1 Need for This Survey

There is a need for a survey of deep learning applications for remote-sensing image classification for several reasons:

2.1.1.1 Rapidly Evolving Field

Deep learning has revolutionized the field of remote-sensing image classification in recent years, and new techniques and applications are constantly emerging. A survey can provide an up-to-date overview of the state of the art in this field [38].

2.1.1.2 Multidisciplinary Nature

Deep learning applications for remote-sensing image classification are relevant to a wide range of fields, including remote sensing, computer vision, machine learning, and geospatial analysis. A survey can provide an interdisciplinary perspective and promote collaboration across these fields [39].

2.1.1.3 Comprehensive Evaluation

A survey can provide a comprehensive evaluation of the performance of different deep learning algorithms and techniques for remote-sensing image classification, helping researchers and practitioners choose the most appropriate approach for their specific application.

2.1.1.4 Identification of Research Gaps

A survey can help identify research gaps and challenges in deep learning-based remote-sensing image classification, which can inform future research directions and stimulate new developments in this field [40].

2.1.1.5 Practical Applications

A survey can highlight practical applications of deep learning-based remote-sensing image classification, demonstrating its potential impact on various fields, such as agriculture, environmental monitoring, disaster management, and national security.

In summary, a survey of deep learning applications for remote-sensing image classification is necessary to provide an up-to-date overview of the state of the art in this field, evaluate the performance of different techniques, identify research gaps and challenges, promote interdisciplinary collaboration, and highlight practical applications.

2.1.2 Need for Remote-Sensing Image Classification

There is a need for deep learning applications for remote-sensing image classification for the following reasons:

2.1.2.1 Rapidly Expanding Data Sources

Remote-sensing data sources are expanding rapidly, including hyperspectral and LiDAR data, which provide high-resolution and multi-dimensional information. A survey can help evaluate the performance of deep learning algorithms for these new data sources [41].

2.1.2.2 Optimization of Deep Learning Algorithms

Deep learning algorithms require optimization for remote-sensing applications due to differences in image characteristics, such as atmospheric and geometric distortions. A survey can provide insights into the optimization of deep learning algorithms for remote-sensing image classification [42].

2.1.2.3 Transferability of Models

Transferability of deep learning models is important for their application to different geographic locations, data sets, and imaging platforms. A survey can provide insights into the transferability of deep learning models for remote-sensing image classification [43].

2.1.2.4 Standardization of Evaluation Metrics

There is a lack of standardization in the evaluation metrics used for deep learning-based remote-sensing image classification, making it difficult to compare results across studies. A survey can provide an overview of the different evaluation metrics used and recommend standardization for future studies [44].

2.1.2.5 Integration of Multi-Source Data

Remote-sensing image classification can benefit from the integration of multi-source data, such as remote sensing and ground-based data. A survey can provide insights into the integration of multi-source data for deep learning-based remote-sensing image classification [45].

In summary, a survey of deep learning applications for remote-sensing image classification is needed to evaluate the performance of deep learning algorithms for new and expanding data sources, optimize algorithms for remote-sensing applications, evaluate the transferability of models, recommend standardization of evaluation metrics, and provide insights into the integration of multi-source data.

2.1.3 Significance of Remote-Sensing Image Classification

Studying deep learning-based remote-sensing image classification is important for a variety of reasons, including:

2.1.3.1 Improved Accuracy

Deep learning algorithms have been shown to outperform traditional machine learning algorithms in remote-sensing image classification tasks. This improved accuracy can lead to better decision making and more reliable results [46].

2.1.3.2 Automation

Deep learning algorithms can be trained to automatically detect and classify features in remote-sensing imagery, reducing the need for manual labeling and increasing the efficiency of image analysis [47].

2.1.3.3 Scalability

Deep learning algorithms can handle large data sets, making it possible to analyze and classify vast amounts of remote-sensing imagery, which would be impractical or impossible with manual methods.

2.1.3.4 Generalizability

Deep learning algorithms can generalize from training data to new and unseen data, making them applicable to a wide range of remote-sensing applications and environments [48].

2.1.3.5 Interdisciplinary Applications

Deep learning-based remote-sensing image classification has applications in many fields, such as environmental science, agriculture, urban planning, and disaster management, making it an essential area of study for interdisciplinary research.

2.1.3.6 Innovation

Deep learning-based remote-sensing image classification research is driving innovation in the development of new algorithms and techniques, leading to advancements in computer vision, artificial intelligence, and data science.

2.1.3.7 Addressing Complex Problems

Deep learning-based remote-sensing image classification can help address complex problems, such as monitoring and assessing changes in land cover and land use, identifying and tracking natural disasters, and evaluating the impacts of climate change.

2.1.3.8 Improved Understanding

Studying deep learning-based remote-sensing image classification can lead to a better understanding of how neural networks work and how they can be optimized for different remote-sensing applications.

2.1.3.9 Career Opportunities

Deep learning-based remote-sensing image classification is a rapidly growing field, and studying it can lead to career opportunities in academia, industry, and government [49].

Studying deep learning-based remote-sensing image classification is important because it can lead to improved accuracy, automation, scalability, generalizability, interdisciplinary applications, innovation, addressing complex problems, improved understanding, and career opportunities. With the continued advancement of deep learning techniques, their potential impact on remote-sensing applications will only continue to grow.

2.1.4 Research Gap for Deep Learning-Based Remote-Sensing Image Classification

Although deep learning-based remote-sensing image classification has shown promising results in recent years, there are still some research gaps and challenges that need to be addressed. Here are some of the key research gaps in this area:

2.1.4.1 Limited Training Data

Deep learning algorithms require large amounts of labeled data to achieve high accuracy, but collecting and labeling ground truth data for remote-sensing imagery can be time-consuming and expensive, especially for rare or complex land cover types.

2.1.4.2 Transferability of Models

Deep learning models trained on one data set or location may not generalize well to other data sets or locations due to differences in image quality, environmental conditions, and land cover types.

2.1.4.3 Interpretability

Deep learning models are often considered black boxes, meaning that it can be difficult to understand how they arrive at their decisions. This can be problematic in some applications, such as environmental monitoring, where transparency and interpretability are important.

2.1.4.4 Class Imbalance

In some remote-sensing applications, such as rare species detection or anomaly detection, there may be significant class imbalance, where one or more classes are underrepresented in the data set. This can lead to bias and reduced accuracy in the classification results.

2.1.4.5 Limited Understanding of Uncertainty

Deep learning models provide a point estimate of the class label for each pixel or object, but they do not provide information on the uncertainty associated with the classification. This can be problematic in applications where uncertainty is important, such as in disaster response or risk assessment.

2.1.4.6 Limited Application to Hyperspectral Data

While deep learning has shown promising results in multispectral remote-sensing image classification, its application to hyperspectral data is still relatively limited due to challenges such as high dimensionality and limited training data.

2.1.4.7 Limited Application to Small-Scale Features

Deep learning-based remote-sensing image classification has shown promising results in identifying and classifying large-scale land cover types, but its application to small-scale features such as individual trees, crops, or buildings is still challenging.

Addressing these research gaps will require the development of new methods and techniques, as well as collaboration across disciplines and industries.

2.2 DEEP LEARNING ARCHITECTURES FOR REMOTE-SENSING IMAGE CLASSIFICATION

Deep learning architectures have significantly improved the performance of remote-sensing image classification tasks. Several popular deep learning models are commonly used in this field:

2.2.1 Convolutional Neural Networks (CNNs)

CNNs are widely used for remote-sensing image classification due to their ability to automatically learn hierarchical feature representations from input data. These networks consist of multiple layers, including convolutional layers, pooling layers, and fully connected layers. Popular CNN architectures include VGG, ResNet, Inception, and DenseNet [50–59].

2.2.2 Fully Convolutional Networks (FCNs)

FCNs are an adaptation of CNNs for semantic segmentation tasks, where the goal is to assign a class label to each pixel in an image. FCNs replace the fully connected layers in a CNN with convolutional layers, allowing them to generate dense pixel-wise output maps for classification. This property makes FCNs well suited for remote-sensing image classification tasks [60–63].

2.2.3 U-Net

U-Net is a specialized CNN architecture for semantic segmentation, particularly effective for biomedical image segmentation. It features an encoder-decoder structure with skip connections, which help the network recover fine-grained spatial information. Due to its effectiveness in segmentation tasks, U-Net has been adopted for remote-sensing image classification as well [64].

2.2.4 SegNet

SegNet is another encoder-decoder architecture designed specifically for semantic segmentation tasks. It uses pooling indices from the encoder to upsample feature maps in the decoder, reducing the number of parameters and computational complexity. SegNet has been successfully applied to remote-sensing image classification tasks [65].

2.2.5 DeepLab

DeepLab is a series of CNN-based semantic segmentation models that incorporate atrous (or dilated) convolutions and spatial pyramid pooling modules to capture multi-scale contextual information. DeepLab models, such as DeepLabv3 and DeepLabv3+, have been used for remote-sensing image classification tasks [66,67].

2.2.6 Gated Recurrent Units (GRUs) and Long Short-Term Memory (LSTM) Networks

These recurrent neural network (RNN) architectures are designed to model temporal dependencies in sequential data. They can be used in combination with CNNs or FCNs to handle multi-temporal remote-sensing images for classification tasks that require temporal context, such as land use and land cover change detection.

2.2.7 Autoencoders

Autoencoders are unsupervised deep learning models that learn to reconstruct input data through a bottleneck layer. They can be used for feature extraction and dimensionality reduction in remote-sensing image classification tasks, with the extracted features then used as input for a supervised classification model [68].

2.2.8 Generative Adversarial Networks (GANs)

GANs consist of two neural networks – a generator and a discriminator – that compete against each other. While GANs are primarily used for generating realistic synthetic images, they can also be adapted for remote-sensing image classification tasks by incorporating a classification component, such as a CNN, into the discriminator.

2.2.9 Capsule Networks (CapsNets)

CapsNets are a type of deep learning architecture that attempts to address some limitations of traditional CNNs, particularly their inability to model spatial hierarchies and viewpoint invariance. CapsNets use dynamic routing algorithms to learn the relationships between low-level and high-level features, potentially making them more robust for remote-sensing image classification tasks [69].

2.2.10 Attention-Based Mechanisms

Attention mechanisms, such as self-attention and spatial attention, have been incorporated into deep learning models to improve their performance by selectively focusing on relevant features or regions in the input data. These mechanisms can be integrated with CNNs or RNNs to enhance their ability to capture contextual information and dependencies in remote-sensing images [70].

2.2.11 Graph Convolutional Networks (GCNs)

GCNs extend traditional CNNs to handle non-Euclidean data, such as graphs, by operating on adjacency matrices and node feature matrices. They can be applied to remote-sensing image classification tasks where the data exhibits irregular, non-grid structures or requires the integration of additional contextual information, such as elevation data or social factors [71].

2.2.12 Siamese Networks

Siamese networks are a type of deep learning architecture designed for learning similarity measures between input pairs. They can be used for change detection in remote-sensing images by training a model to learn the differences between two co-registered images acquired at different times.

2.2.13 3D Convolutional Neural Networks (3D-CNNs)

3D-CNNs extend traditional 2D convolutional layers to operate on volumetric data, allowing them to capture spatial and spectral dependencies simultaneously. They can be used for remote-sensing image classification tasks that involve hyperspectral data, which consists of hundreds of contiguous spectral bands [72–76].

These additional deep learning architectures, along with the previously mentioned models, demonstrate the wide variety of approaches that can be applied to remote-sensing image classification tasks. By leveraging these advanced techniques and adapting them to the unique challenges of remote-sensing data, researchers and practitioners continue to push the boundaries of performance and applicability in this domain.

2.3 DIFFERENCES IN DEEP LEARNING ARCHITECTURES FOR REMOTE-SENSING IMAGE CLASSIFICATION

Deep learning methods have been widely used for remote-sensing image classification tasks, and there are several differences between the different methods. Here are some of the key differences:

2.3.1 Architecture

Different deep learning methods use different architectures, such as convolutional neural networks (CNNs), recurrent neural networks (RNNs), and deep belief networks (DBNs). Each architecture has its own strengths and weaknesses, depending on the specific application and type of data.

2.3.2 Input Data

Different deep learning methods use different types of input data, such as multispectral, hyperspectral, and synthetic aperture radar data. Each type of data has different characteristics and requires different pre-processing and feature extraction techniques.

2.3.3 Training Strategy

Different deep learning methods use different training strategies, such as supervised, unsupervised, or semi-supervised learning. The choice of training strategy depends on the availability of labeled data and the desired level of accuracy.

2.3.4 Transfer Learning

Some deep learning methods use transfer learning, which involves transferring knowledge learned from one data set or task to another data set or task. Transfer learning can improve the performance of deep learning methods, especially in cases where training data is limited.

2.3.5 Optimization

Different deep learning methods use different optimization algorithms, such as stochastic gradient descent or Adam. Optimization algorithms affect the speed and accuracy of training and the generalization ability of the model.

2.3.6 Interpretability

Different deep learning methods have different levels of interpretability, with some methods providing more interpretable results than others. Interpretability is important for applications where transparency and understanding of the decision-making process are critical.

In summary, deep learning methods differ in their architecture, input data, training strategy, transfer learning, optimization, and interpretability. The choice of deep learning method depends on the specific application, available data, desired level of accuracy, and interpretability requirements.

2.4 REMOTE-SENSING DATA SOURCES AND CHARACTERISTICS

The previous model used in this conversation is unavailable. We've switched you to the latest default model.

Remote-sensing data can be collected from a variety of platforms, including satellites, aircraft, and unmanned aerial vehicles (UAVs). These platforms use various types of sensors to capture data, such as multispectral, hyperspectral, and synthetic aperture radar (SAR). Here are some key characteristics of each type of remote-sensing platform and sensor:

2.4.1 Satellites

Satellites are the most common platform for remote sensing, with a range of sensors designed for different applications. Some common satellites used for remote sensing include Landsat, Sentinel, MODIS, and ASTER. These satellites collect data at various spatial and temporal resolutions, from 10 m to 30 m for Landsat and Sentinel to 90 m for MODIS [77].

2.4.2 UAVs

UAVs are increasingly used for remote-sensing applications due to their flexibility and low cost. They can capture data at higher spatial resolutions than satellites and aircraft, typically ranging from 1 cm to 10 cm. UAVs are particularly useful for capturing data in areas where access is restricted or for monitoring small-scale features such as crops, buildings, or infrastructure [78].

2.4.3 Multispectral Sensors

Multispectral sensors capture data across several broad bands of the electromagnetic spectrum, typically visible and near-infrared bands. They can provide information on vegetation health, land cover types, and water quality. Some common multispectral sensors include Landsat, Sentinel-2, and MODIS.

2.4.4 Hyperspectral Sensors

Hyperspectral sensors capture data across narrow and contiguous spectral bands, providing high spectral resolution data. They can be used to identify and map specific materials, minerals, and vegetation species. Hyperspectral sensors are typically used in research and applications that require detailed spectral information, such as mineral exploration, environmental monitoring, and precision agriculture [79–83].

2.4.5 Synthetic Aperture Radar (SAR)

SAR is an active remote-sensing technology that uses radar to detect and map surface features, even in darkness or through clouds. SAR data can be used to generate high-resolution images of the Earth's surface, including topography, land cover, and changes in the Earth's surface caused by human or natural processes.

In addition to these platforms and sensors, remote-sensing imagery has several key characteristics that affect its quality and suitability for various applications:

2.4.6 Spatial Resolution

Spatial resolution refers to the size of the smallest feature that can be detected in an image. It is typically measured in meters and can range from tens of meters for satellite data to centimeters for UAV data [84].

2.4.7 Spectral Resolution

Spectral resolution refers to the number and width of spectral bands captured by the sensor. Multispectral sensors typically have fewer spectral bands than hyperspectral sensors, but they capture data across broad bands of the electromagnetic spectrum [85].

2.4.8 Temporal Resolution

Temporal resolution refers to the frequency at which data is collected over a given area. It can range from daily or weekly for some satellite data to hourly or even sub-hourly for UAV data [86–91].

2.4.9 Radiometric Resolution

Radiometric resolution refers to the sensitivity of the sensor to the intensity of the electromagnetic radiation captured. Higher radiometric resolution enables the detection of smaller differences in reflectance or emission, allowing for more accurate classification of surface features [92–96].

Understanding the characteristics of remote-sensing data sources and imagery is crucial for selecting the appropriate platform and sensor for a given application and for ensuring the quality and reliability of the data.

2.5 APPLICATION OF DEEP LEARNING IN REMOTE SENSING

Deep learning has numerous applications in remote sensing, which is the science of acquiring and interpreting data from remote sensors [97]. Some of the most prominent applications of deep learning in remote sensing include the following.

2.5.1 Land Cover Classification

Land cover classification involves identifying and mapping different types of land cover, such as forests, water bodies, agricultural land, and urban areas. Deep learning can be used to automatically classify pixels in remote-sensing images into different land cover classes, improving the accuracy and efficiency of the classification process (Table 2.1).

Land cover classification is the process of assigning land cover types to pixels or regions in remote-sensing imagery. This task is critical for various applications such as land-use planning, natural resource management, and environmental monitoring. Traditional machine learning techniques such as support vector machines (SVMs) and random forests (RFs) have been used for land cover classification tasks, but in recent years, deep learning approaches have gained popularity due to their ability to extract meaningful features from high-dimensional data. Deep learning models such as convolutional neural networks (CNNs) have shown promising results in land cover classification tasks. CNNs can

TABLE 2.1   Land Cover Classification Using DL

Study	Method/algorithm	Data set	Results
[98]	Shared and specific feature learning (S2FL) model	• HS-MS Houston2013 • Heterogeneous HS-SAR Berlin • Heterogeneous HS-SAR-DSM Augsburg	OA > 70% AA > 40% Kappa > 0.56
[99]	• K-nearest neighbor (KNN) • Random forest (RF) • Support vector machine (SVM) • Artificial neural network (ANN)	• ASTER GDEMV2 data • Landsat-8 Operational Land Imager	OA is: ANN (97.16%), RF (96.92%), SVM (96.20%), KNN (93.98%)
[100]	Deep convolutional neural networks (CNNs)	• Gaofen-2, • Gaofen-1, J • ilin-1, • Ziyuan-3, • Sentinel-2A, and • Google Earth platform data	OA > 95% Kappa > 0.90
[101]	Random forest, SVM, and KNM	• Google Earth platform data	OA ranging from 77.66% to 89.80%
[102]	Hidden Markov model (HMM)	• Landsat Images	OA: 77.9% ± 1.4%
[103]	• CNN • RF • 3NN • SVM	• Indian Pines • Pavia University • Salinas • San Francisco	OA > 95% Kappa > 0.90

automatically learn features from input data, making them ideal for tasks where the feature extraction process is challenging or time-consuming. These models consist of multiple convolutional layers that extract increasingly complex features from the input data, followed by fully connected layers that perform classification. Another deep learning model that has been used for land cover classification is recurrent neural networks (RNNs). RNNs can model sequences of data, making them suitable for time series data, such as satellite images over time. Long short-term memory (LSTM) networks, a type of RNN, have shown promising results in land cover classification tasks. Transfer learning is another approach that has been used for land cover classification. Transfer learning involves using a pre-trained deep learning model on a large data set to extract features that can be used for a smaller data set. This approach can save time and computational resources and improve the performance of the model. In addition to the above approaches, data augmentation techniques such as rotation, flipping, and cropping can improve the robustness of deep learning models and prevent overfitting.

In an effort to find a practical means of mapping LULC patterns, the RS community has approached the issue from a wide variety of angles. These investigations, which span from traditional statistical methods to advanced machine learning (ML) techniques, have all contributed to better answers to this issue. Maximum-likelihood classifier (MLC) [104], distance measure [105], clustering [106], and logistic regression [107] are some examples of the more conventional approaches of classifying RS data. At the turn of the century, increasingly sophisticated techniques have been utilized for LULC mapping.

These include decision trees [108], k-nearest-neighbors (kNNs) [109], random forests (RFs) [110], neural networks [111], and support vector machines (SVMs) [112]. In 2016, research was conducted to determine the current state of supervised algorithms for LULC classification [113]. It has been observed that SVM, kNN, and RF all outperform more common classifiers, with SVM being the most effective. Recently, deep learning (DL) approaches have surpassed previous achievements in several areas, including image recognition [114]. High performance has been achieved in many computers vision tasks [115] thanks to the ability of DL models to automatically learn useful representations of raw input data with many degrees of abstraction. Recent research shows that DL performs better than SVM techniques [116,117]; thus, it's no surprise that it's been successfully used to LULC classification recently. Many DL architectures, including convolutional neural networks (CNNs) [118,119], stacked autoencoders (SAEs) [120], and deep belief networks (DBNs) [121], have been studied for their potential application to RS tasks. Recent polls have found that CNNs are the most popular model utilized because they get the best results on average [122].

2.5.2 Vegetation Monitoring

Vegetation monitoring is an essential task for various applications, such as crop yield estimation, forest management, and environmental monitoring. Remote sensing is a widely used technique for vegetation monitoring, where satellite or aerial imagery is used to extract information about vegetation properties such as vegetation cover, biomass, and growth patterns. In recent years, deep learning techniques have been applied to remote-sensing data for vegetation monitoring tasks, providing accurate and efficient solutions. Convolutional neural networks (CNNs) are a popular deep learning technique used for vegetation monitoring. CNNs can extract meaningful features from high-dimensional remote-sensing data, such as multispectral imagery, which are used to classify vegetation types and detect changes in vegetation cover over time. CNNs can also be used to estimate vegetation biomass and predict crop yields by analyzing the relationships between the spectral properties of the vegetation and the ground truth measurements. Recurrent neural networks (RNNs), particularly long short-term memory (LSTM) networks, are another type of deep learning technique used for vegetation monitoring. RNNs can model time series data and can be used to analyze the temporal changes in vegetation cover over time. This approach is particularly useful for monitoring vegetation growth patterns, identifying areas of deforestation or degradation, and predicting vegetation growth in response to climate and weather patterns. Transfer learning is another technique used for vegetation monitoring using deep learning. Transfer learning involves using a pre-trained deep learning model on a large data set, such as ImageNet, to extract features that can be used for a smaller data set, such as vegetation monitoring. This approach can save time and computational resources and improve the performance of the model. In addition to the above techniques, data augmentation and fusion techniques can improve the performance and robustness of deep learning models for vegetation monitoring. Data augmentation involves generating additional training data by applying transformations such as rotation, flipping, and cropping to the original data. Data fusion involves combining multiple sources of remote-sensing data, such as multispectral imagery and LiDAR data, to improve the accuracy of vegetation monitoring.

Deep learning can be used to classify vegetation types and monitor changes in vegetation cover over time, which is important for understanding and predicting ecological processes, as well as for land management and conservation. Phenological factors generated from remote sensing have been used to forecast crop yields in recent research [123,124]. Date information for phenological periods is included in the set of variables used to track crop development. Dates help evaluate whether or not each phenological stage coincides with optimal growing circumstances [125] and how an early or late phenological stage can affect crop development [126], especially in the face of rapid climate change. Indicators of the effects of climate change include shifts in flowering and fruiting times, as well as the duration of the growing season [127]. The plant breeding community is also interested in creating crops with a longer "stay-green" time, which would extend the grain-fill period and slow the pace of senescence [128–130].

2.5.3 Urban Land-Use Classification

Urban land classification is an essential task for various applications such as urban planning, infrastructure development, and environmental monitoring. Remote sensing is a widely used technique for urban land classification, where satellite or aerial imagery is used to extract information about urban land cover types such as buildings, roads, and vegetation. In recent years, deep learning techniques have been applied to remote-sensing data for urban land classification, providing accurate and efficient solutions [131].

Important for urban planning and administration, deep learning can categorize urban land use such as residential, commercial, and industrial zones. Urban planning, government policymaking, and monitoring urbanization all benefit from an accurate classification of urban land use [132]. Recent improvements in computer and remote-sensing technology have made readily available high-quality, high-resolution remote-sensing picture data that can serve as vital sources for land-use classification. Classifications based on a single land cover, category, or item. Although scene classification is a more challenging task than classification schemes based on individual categories or objects, it offers benefits such as the ability to differentiate given land-use scene images into predefined semantically meaningful categories and the provision of advanced interpretations of remote-sensing images [133]. Remote-sensing applications such as land resource management, urban development and planning, Earth observation, and wildlife conservation are where researchers have concentrated their efforts to reap the benefits of land-use scene-based classification [134]. Nonetheless, the varied land-use landscapes are greatly influenced by human and societal activities. Most of the information conveyed by a land-use scenario is based on the different types of land cover or ground objects that it includes. Manual categorization is rarely practical and appropriate due to the difficulties involved in explaining the finer points of characteristics and offering effective and efficient categories. Land-use scene categorization, especially automated classification, remains a challenge in high-resolution remote-sensing images [135].

2.5.4 HSI Remote Sensing

Classifying HSIs is seen as inherently nonlinear [136], and the first approach by linear-transformation-based statistical techniques like principal component analytical methods, such as principal component analysis (PCA) [137] and independent component analysis (ICA) [138]; the discriminant analytical methods, such as linear [139] and fisher [140]; wavelet transforms [141]; and composite [142], probabilistic [143], and generalized [144] kernel methods, failed. Their analysis was still restricted to geographic data. They noted that the complexity introduced by the use of feature extractor approaches aided by some fundamental random classifiers in terms of resources (money, physical space, and time) is not warranted because the results are not accurate enough. Researchers grew interested in using the latest emerging but not tiresome computer-based methods for HSI categorization after the success of the more traditional methodical approaches. It has been suggested by recent research that the last decade has been the most dynamic in terms of computer-based technology, particularly with the advent of machine learning. Machine learning (ML) is a sophisticated computational tool that mimics the way the human brain thinks. By maintaining abstraction, it only represents what is actually a complex system. As a result, it can simplify matters and get insights from the mountain of HS data in order to unearth the concealed discriminative features, both spectro- and geo- [145]. As a result, it is able to overcome all obstacles and accurately determine which class each object in the target HSI data belongs to. As a result, they operate as stand-alone methods that accomplish the task at hand.

HSI (hyperspectral imaging) data sets consist of high-dimensional images where each pixel contains a spectrum of electromagnetic radiation reflected or emitted from the Earth's surface. These images have hundreds of spectral bands, which capture detailed information about the material composition and reflectance properties of the objects in the scene. HSI data sets are commonly used in remote sensing for various applications, such as land cover classification, mineral mapping, and environmental monitoring.

HSI data sets are typically collected using sensors mounted on aircraft or satellites. The sensors capture data in the visible, near-infrared, and short-wave infrared regions of the electromagnetic spectrum. The spectral resolution of HSI data sets can range from a few to several hundred bands, depending on the sensor used. HSI data sets can be processed and analyzed using various techniques, including feature extraction, dimensionality reduction, and classification. Feature extraction techniques involve extracting meaningful features from the high-dimensional HSI data, such as texture, shape, and spectral features. Dimensionality reduction techniques involve reducing the number of spectral bands in the data while preserving the relevant information. Classification techniques involve assigning each pixel in the HSI data set to a land cover or material class based on the extracted features or reduced spectral bands.

HSI data sets used for classification tasks typically include ground truth labels that indicate the land cover or material class of each pixel in the image. These ground truth labels are used to train and validate classification models, such as machine learning or deep learning models. Examples of HSI data sets commonly used for land cover classification include the Indian Pines data set, the Pavia University data set, the Salinas data set, and the Houston data set. These data sets contain HSI data with different spatial and spectral resolutions, captured using different sensors, and covering different geographic regions. In conclusion, HSI data sets consist of high-dimensional images with hundreds of spectral bands, capturing detailed information about the material composition and reflectance properties of the Earth's surface. These data sets are commonly used in remote sensing for various applications, including land cover classification. HSI data sets can be processed and analyzed using various techniques, including feature extraction, dimensionality reduction, and classification, and typically include ground truth labels for training and validation.

2.6 CHALLENGES FOR DEEP LEARNING METHODS FOR RS IMAGE PROCESSING

With the advent of deep learning, large quantities of remotely sensed data can now be mined and analyzed. The study of RS image categorization relies heavily on convolutional neural networks (CNNs), a subset of deep learning models. The purpose of this work was to provide a comprehensive overview of the current state of the art in CNN-based deep learning for RS image categorization. Objects in RS photos are more complex, making feature extraction more challenging than with computer vision images. As a result, there are several academic works dedicated to solving the problems of CNN-based RS picture categorization. They have made significant strides in RS image categorization using a CNN model, training data, and training methodologies [146–151]. While these findings are important, they only scratch the surface of what may be learned about RS image classification using a convolutional neural network. We review a number of concerns that need to be thought about and researched in depth, including the fact that RS picture categorization is still experiencing unprecedented and considerable obstacles.

Remote-sensing image classification is the process of assigning a class label to each pixel or segment in an image, typically acquired from satellites or aerial platforms. Despite the advances in deep learning techniques for remote-sensing image classification, several challenges still exist:

2.6.1 High Spatial and Spectral Variability

Remote-sensing images can exhibit significant variability in terms of spatial resolution, spectral range, and imaging conditions. This variability can pose challenges in designing a classification algorithm that is robust and accurate across different data sets.

2.6.2 Limited Annotated Data

Obtaining accurate and large-scale ground truth annotations for remote-sensing images can be expensive, time-consuming, and labor-intensive. This limited availability of labeled data can hinder the training of deep learning models, leading to overfitting and reduced generalization capabilities.

2.6.3 Class Imbalance

Some classes of objects or land cover types may be underrepresented in the training data, leading to class imbalance. This can result in biased classification performance, with the model favoring the majority class at the expense of minority classes.

2.6.4 Intra-Class Variability

Remote-sensing images often contain high intra-class variability due to changes in the appearance of objects or land cover types across different geographic locations, seasons, and imaging conditions. This can make it challenging for classification algorithms to correctly identify and distinguish between different instances of the same class.

2.6.5 Spectral Mixing and Shadow Effects

In high-resolution remote-sensing images, spectral mixing occurs when a single pixel contains multiple land cover types or objects, leading to mixed spectral signatures. Additionally, shadow effects can further complicate the classification process, as they can cause objects or land cover types to appear differently.

2.6.6 Sensor Noise and Atmospheric Interference

Remote-sensing images are often affected by sensor noise, atmospheric interference, and other artifacts that can degrade the image quality and introduce additional challenges in the classification process.

2.6.7 Computational Complexity

Deep learning models, particularly those with complex architectures, can be computationally expensive to train and deploy. This may pose challenges in terms of processing large volumes of remote-sensing data, especially in real-time or near-real-time applications.

2.6.8 Adaptability and Generalization

Developing a classification model that can adapt to different remote-sensing data sets and generalize well to new, unseen data remains a significant challenge. This includes handling changes in imaging conditions, geographic locations, and land cover types.

Addressing these challenges often involves employing advanced deep learning techniques, data augmentation, transfer learning, and other methodologies to improve the performance and robustness of remote-sensing image classification models.

2.7 LIMITATIONS

While remote-sensing image classification has shown great potential for various applications, there are some limitations that need to be considered:

2.7.1 Dependence on Image Quality

The quality of the remote-sensing imagery is crucial for accurate classification. Factors such as low spatial or spectral resolution, noise, atmospheric interference, and cloud cover can negatively affect the classification results [151].

2.7.2 Temporal Variability

Changes in land cover and object appearances due to seasonal variations, natural disasters, or human interventions can affect the accuracy of classification models if they are not designed to account for these temporal changes [152].

2.7.3 Generalization and Transferability

Classification models often struggle to generalize to new, unseen data, especially when there are differences in imaging conditions, sensor characteristics, or geographic locations. This may require additional fine-tuning or adaptation of the model for each new data set [153].

2.7.4 Scalability

Processing and analyzing large volumes of remote-sensing data can be computationally intensive, particularly when using deep learning models with complex architectures. This may impose limitations on the scalability of classification approaches, especially for real-time or near-real-time applications [154].

2.7.5 Interpretability

Deep learning models, while achieving high classification accuracy, are often considered "black boxes" due to their complex architectures and lack of interpretability. This can make it difficult to understand the underlying reasons for the classification results, which is particularly important in certain applications where explainability is required [155,156].

2.7.6 Labeling Challenges

Obtaining accurate and comprehensive ground truth annotations for remote-sensing images can be time-consuming, expensive, and labor-intensive. This limitation can impact the quality of training data and the performance of classification models [155].

2.7.7 Privacy Concerns

The high-resolution nature of some remote-sensing imagery may raise privacy concerns, particularly in urban areas where individuals or private property may be identifiable. This can impose limitations on the use and dissemination of remote-sensing data for classification tasks.

2.7.8 Legal and Policy Constraints

There may be legal and policy constraints on the use of remote-sensing data for certain applications, particularly when dealing with sensitive areas, national security concerns, or cross-border issues [157].

Despite these limitations, remote-sensing image classification continues to advance through the development of new techniques, algorithms, and data sources. Researchers and practitioners are constantly working to address these challenges and improve the overall performance and applicability of remote-sensing image classification methods.

2.8 CONCLUSION

Remote-sensing image classification has numerous applications in various fields, including agriculture, forestry, land-use planning, disaster management, environmental monitoring, and national security. By analyzing remote-sensing imagery and extracting information on land cover types and changes over time, remote-sensing image classification can help decision makers make informed and timely decisions for better resource management, food security, disaster response, and climate change adaptation. Deep learning-based remote-sensing image classification has emerged as a promising approach to improve the accuracy and efficiency of remote-sensing image classification. It has the potential to automate the process of image analysis, handle large and complex data sets, and generalize well to new and unseen data. By leveraging the power of deep neural networks, researchers can achieve high accuracy in image classification and extract valuable information from remote-sensing data. However, there are still some research gaps and challenges in deep learning-based remote-sensing image classification, such as limited training data, interpretability, and transferability of models. Addressing these challenges will require interdisciplinary collaboration and the development of new methods and techniques.

In conclusion, remote-sensing image classification and deep learning-based remote-sensing image classification have significant potential for various applications. By improving our understanding of Earth's surface features and processes, we can make better decisions for sustainable development, environmental conservation, and global security.

2.8.1 Future Work

Remote-sensing image classification plays a crucial role in understanding and managing Earth's resources, environment, and human activities. Its importance cannot be overstated, as it provides valuable information for a wide range of applications, with significant potential for future growth and innovation:

2.8.1.1 Environmental Monitoring and Management

Remote-sensing image classification contributes to the monitoring and assessment of land cover and land use changes, deforestation, desertification, wetland loss, and urban sprawl. This information is vital for making informed decisions about sustainable resource management, conservation efforts, and climate change mitigation strategies.

2.8.1.2 Agriculture and Food Security

Accurate classification of agricultural land and crop types enables precision farming, irrigation planning, and yield estimation. It supports global food security by helping optimize agricultural production, monitor crop health, and assess the impacts of natural disasters or climate change on crop yields.

2.8.1.3 Disaster Response and Recovery

Remote-sensing image classification can be used to assess the extent of damage after natural disasters, such as floods, earthquakes, wildfires, and hurricanes. This information is invaluable for prioritizing response efforts, allocating resources, and planning long-term recovery and reconstruction.

2.8.1.4 Urban Planning and Development

High-resolution remote-sensing images can be used to classify urban features such as buildings, roads, and green spaces. This data informs urban planning decisions, infrastructure development, and the monitoring of urban growth to ensure sustainable and resilient cities.

2.8.1.5 Water Resource Management

Remote-sensing image classification aids in monitoring water bodies, estimating water quality, and assessing the impacts of human activities on water resources. This information is crucial for managing water resources effectively and ensuring their long-term sustainability.

2.8.1.6 Climate Change Research

By providing detailed information on land cover and land use changes, remote-sensing image classification contributes to climate change research, allowing scientists to better understand the relationships between human activities, land surface processes, and climate change.

2.8.1.7 National Security and Defense

Remote-sensing image classification can support national security and defense applications by identifying and monitoring critical infrastructure, assessing the impacts of natural or human-made disasters, and detecting changes in land use or land cover that might indicate potential security threats.

The potential for future growth and innovation in remote-sensing image classification is immense. Advances in deep learning techniques, improved sensor technology, increased data availability, and the integration of multi-source data promise to revolutionize the field. These developments will enable more accurate, efficient, and timely classification, benefiting various applications and stakeholders worldwide. The continued expansion and refinement of remote-sensing image classification techniques will undoubtedly have a profound impact on our ability to understand, manage, and protect our planet.

FUNDING

This work was supported in part by Key Research Project of Hainan Province under Grant ZDYF2021SHFZ093; the Natural Science Foundation of China under Grants 62063004 and 62162022; the Hainan Provincial Natural Science Foundation of China under Grants 2019RC018, 521QN206, and 619QN249; the Major Scientific Project of Zhejiang Lab 2020ND8AD01; and the Scientific Research Foundation for Hainan University (No. KYQD(ZR)-21013).

REFERENCES

1. Cui, W., Liu, J., Li, J., Fang, Y., Xiao, X., Bhatti, U. A., & Nawaz, S. A. (2021). A robust zero watermarking algorithm for medical images based on Tetrolet-DCT. In *Cyberspace Safety and Security: 12th International Symposium, CSS 2020, Haikou, China, December 1–3, 2020, Proceedings 12* (pp. 109–119). Springer International Publishing.

2. Yi, D., Liu, J., Li, J., Zhou, J., Bhatti, U. A., Fang, Y., & Nawaz, S. A. (2021). A robust digital watermarking for medical images based on PHTs-DCT. In *Cyberspace Safety and Security: 12th International Symposium, CSS 2020, Haikou, China, December 1–3, 2020, Proceedings 12* (pp. 95–108). Springer International Publishing.

3. Xiao, X., Liu, J., Li, J., Fang, Y., Zeng, C., Hu, J., & Bhatti, U. A. (2021). A zero-watermarking algorithm for medical images based on Gabor-DCT. In *Cyberspace Safety and Security: 12th International Symposium, CSS 2020, Haikou, China, December 1–3, 2020, Proceedings 12* (pp. 144–156). Springer International Publishing.

4. Fang, Y., Liu, J., Li, J., Yi, D., Cui, W., Xiao, X., … & Bhatti, U. A. (2021). A novel robust watermarking algorithm for encrypted medical image based on Bandelet-DCT. In *Innovation in Medicine and Healthcare: Proceedings of 9th KES-InMed 2021* (pp. 61–73). Springer Singapore.

5. Yi, D., Li, J., Fang, Y., Cui, W., Xiao, X., Bhatti, U. A., & Han, B. (2021). A robust zero-watermarking algorithm based on PHTs-DCT for medical images in the encrypted domain. In *Innovation in Medicine and Healthcare: Proceedings of 9th KES-InMed 2021* (pp. 101–113). Springer Singapore.

6. Xiao, X., Li, J., Yi, D., Fang, Y., Cui, W., Bhatti, U. A., & Han, B. (2021). Robust zero watermarking algorithm for encrypted medical images based on DWT-Gabor. In *Innovation in Medicine and Healthcare: Proceedings of 9th KES-InMed 2021* (pp. 75–86). Springer Singapore.

7. Cui, W., Liu, J., Li, J., Fang, Y., Yi, D., Xiao, X., … & Han, B. (2021). A zero watermarking scheme for encrypted medical images based on Tetrolet-DCT. In *Innovation in Medicine and Healthcare: Proceedings of 9th KES-InMed 2021* (pp. 87–99). Springer Singapore.

8. Nawaz, S. A., Li, J., Bhatti, U. A., Mehmood, A., Ahmed, R., & Ul Ain, Q. (2020). A novel hybrid discrete cosine transform speeded up robust feature-based secure medical image watermarking algorithm. *Journal of Medical Imaging and Health Informatics*, *10*(11), 2588–2599.

9. Bhatti, U. A., Yu, Z., Yuan, L., Zeeshan, Z., Nawaz, S. A., Bhatti, M., … & Wen, L. (2020). Geometric algebra applications in geospatial artificial intelligence and remote sensing image processing. *IEEE Access*, *8*, 155783–155796.

10. Ahmad, R. M., Yao, X., Nawaz, S. A., Bhatti, U. A., Mehmood, A., Bhatti, M. A., & Shaukat, M. U. (2020, June). Robust image watermarking method in wavelet domain based on SIFT features. In *Proceedings of the 2020 3rd International Conference on Artificial Intelligence and Pattern Recognition* (pp. 180–185). IEEE.

11. Shoukat, M. U., Bhatti, U. A., Yiqiang, Y., Mehmood, A., Nawaz, S. A., & Ahmad, R. (2020, June). Improved multiple watermarking algorithm for medical images. In *Proceedings of the 2020 3rd International Conference on Artificial Intelligence and Pattern Recognition* (pp. 152–156).

12. Nawaz, S. A., Li, J., Bhatti, U. A., Mehmood, A., Shoukat, M. U., & Bhatti, M. A. (2020). Advance hybrid medical watermarking algorithm using speeded up robust features and discrete cosine transform. *PLoS One*, *15*(6), e0232902.

13. Bhatti, U. A., Yu, Z., Li, J., Nawaz, S. A., Mehmood, A., Zhang, K., & Yuan, L. (2020). Hybrid watermarking algorithm using clifford algebra with Arnold scrambling and chaotic encryption. *IEEE Access*, *8*, 76386–76398.

14. Huang, S., Huang, M., Zhang, Y., Chen, J., & Bhatti, U. (2020). Medical image segmentation using deep learning with feature enhancement. *IET Image Processing*, *14*(14), 3324–3332.
15. Nawaz, S. A., Li, J., Bhatti, U. A., Li, H., Han, B., & Mehmood, A. (2020, February). Improved watermarking algorithm based on SURF and SVD with wavelet transformation against geometric attacks. In *Proceedings of the 2020 3rd International Conference on Image and Graphics Processing* (pp. 49–56).
16. Bhatti, U. A., Yuan, L., Yu, Z., Nawaz, S. A., Mehmood, A., Bhatti, M. A., ... & Xiao, S. (2021). Predictive data modeling using sp-kNN for risk factor evaluation in urban demographical healthcare data. *Journal of Medical Imaging and Health Informatics*, *11*(1), 7–14.
17. Nawaz, S. A., Li, J., Bhatti, U. A., Li, H., Han, B., Mehmood, A., ... & Zhou, J. (2020). A robust color image zero-watermarking based on SURF and DCT features. In *Artificial Intelligence and Security: 6th International Conference, ICAIS 2020, Hohhot, China, July 17–20, 2020, Proceedings, Part II 6* (pp. 650–660). Springer Singapore.
18. Nawaz, S. A., Li, J., Bhatti, U. A., Shoukat, M. U., & Mehmood, A. (2020). Advance watermarking algorithm using SURF with DWT and DCT for CT images. In *Innovation in Medicine and Healthcare: Proceedings of 8th KES-InMed 2020* (pp. 47–55). Springer Singapore.
19. Nawaz, S. A., Li, J., Liu, J., Bhatti, U. A., Zhou, J., & Ahmad, R. M. (2020). A feature-based hybrid medical image watermarking algorithm based on SURF-DCT. In *Advances in Natural Computation, Fuzzy Systems and Knowledge Discovery: Volume 2* (pp. 1080–1090). Springer International Publishing.
20. Bhatti, U. A., Huang, M., Wu, D., Zhang, Y., Mehmood, A., & Han, H. (2019). Recommendation system using feature extraction and pattern recognition in clinical care systems. *Enterprise Information Systems*, *13*(3), 329–351.
21. Liu, J., Li, J., Ma, J., Sadiq, N., Bhatti, U. A., & Ai, Y. (2019). A robust multi-watermarking algorithm for medical images based on DTCWT-DCT and Henon map. *Applied Sciences*, *9*(4), 700.
22. Liu, J., Li, J., Chen, Y., Zou, X., Cheng, J., Liu, Y., & Bhatti, U. A. (2019). A robust zero-watermarking based on SIFT-DCT for medical images in the encrypted domain. *Computers, Materials & Continua*, *61*(1), 363–378.
23. Dai, Q., Li, J., Bhatti, U. A., Cheng, J., & Bai, X. (2019). An automatic identification algorithm for encrypted anti-counterfeiting tag based on DWT-DCT and Chen's Chaos. In *Artificial Intelligence and Security: 5th International Conference, ICAIS 2019, New York, NY, USA, July 26–28, 2019, Proceedings, Part III 5* (pp. 596–608). Springer International Publishing.
24. Liu, Y., Li, J., Liu, J., Bhatti, U. A., Chen, Y., & Hu, S. (2019). Watermarking algorithm for encrypted medical image based on DCT-DFRFT. In *Innovation in Medicine and Healthcare Systems, and Multimedia: Proceedings of KES-InMed-19 and KES-IIMSS-19 Conferences* (pp. 105–114). Springer Singapore.
25. Dai, Q., Li, J., Bhatti, U. A., Chen, Y. W., & Liu, J. (2019). SWT-DCT-based robust watermarking for medical image. In *Innovation in Medicine and Healthcare Systems, and Multimedia: Proceedings of KES-InMed-19 and KES-IIMSS-19 Conferences* (pp. 93–103). Springer Singapore.
26. Wu, X., Li, J., Bhatti, U. A., & Chen, Y. W. (2019). Logistic map and contourlet-based robust zero watermark for medical images. In *Innovation in Medicine and Healthcare Systems, and Multimedia: Proceedings of KES-InMed-19 and KES-IIMSS-19 Conferences* (pp. 115–123). Springer Singapore.

27. Liu, J., Li, J., Zhang, K., Bhatti, U. A., & Ai, Y. (2019). Zero-watermarking algorithm for medical images based on dual-tree complex wavelet transform and discrete cosine transform. *Journal of Medical Imaging and Health Informatics, 9*(1), 188–194.

28. Wu, D., Huang, M., Zhang, Y., Bhatti, U. A., & Chen, Q. (2018). Strategy for assessment of disaster risk using typhoon hazards modeling based on chlorophyll-a content of seawater. *EURASIP Journal on Wireless Communications and Networking, 2018*, 1–12.

29. Huang, M., Han, H., Wang, H., Li, L., Zhang, Y., & Bhatti, U. A. (2018). A clinical decision support framework for heterogeneous data sources. *IEEE Journal of Biomedical and Health Informatics, 22*(6), 1824–1833.

30. Chen, Q., Huang, M., Wang, H., Zhang, Y., Feng, W., Wang, X., ... & Bhatti, U. A. (2018, May). A feature preprocessing framework of remote sensing image for marine targets recognition. In *2018 OCEANS-MTS/IEEE Kobe Techno-Oceans (OTO)* (pp. 1–5). IEEE.

31. Bhatti, U. A., Huang, M., Wang, H., Zhang, Y., Mehmood, A., & Di, W. (2018). Recommendation system for immunization coverage and monitoring. *Human Vaccines & Immunotherapeutics, 14*(1), 165–171.

32. Wang, L., Li, J., Cheng, J., Bhatti, U. A., & Dai, Q. (2018). DOS attacks intrusion detection algorithm based on support vector machine. In *Cloud Computing and Security: 4th International Conference, ICCCS 2018, Haikou, China, June 8–10, 2018, Revised Selected Papers, Part V 4* (pp. 286–297). Springer International Publishing.

33. Han, H., Huang, M., Zhang, Y., & Bhatti, U. A. (2018). An architecture of secure health information storage system based on blockchain technology. In *Cloud Computing and Security: 4th International Conference, ICCCS 2018, Haikou, China, June 8-10, 2018, Revised Selected Papers, Part II 4* (pp. 578–588). Springer International Publishing.

34. Xiao, T., Li, J., Liu, J., Cheng, J., & Bhatti, U. A. (2018). A robust algorithm of encrypted face recognition based on DWT-DCT and Tent map. In *Cloud Computing and Security: 4th International Conference, ICCCS 2018, Haikou, China, June 8-10, 2018, Revised Selected Papers, Part II 4* (pp. 508–518). Springer International Publishing.

35. Bhatti, U. A., Hashmi, M. Z., Sun, Y., Masud, M., & Nizamani, M. M. Artificial intelligence applications in reduction of carbon emissions: Step towards sustainable environment. *Frontiers in Environmental Science, 11*, 425.

36. Nawaz, S. A., Li, J., Bhatti, U. A., Shoukat, M. U., & Ahmad, R. M. AI based object detection latest trends in remote sensing, multimedia and agriculture applications. *Frontiers in Plant Science*, 4273.

37. Bhatti, U. A., Huang, M., Zhang, Y., & Feng, W. (2017). Research on the smartphone based eHealth systems for strengthing healthcare organization. In *Smart Health: International Conference, ICSH 2016, Haikou, China, December 24–25, 2016, Revised Selected Papers* (pp. 91–101). Springer International Publishing.

38. Viitaniemi, V., & Laaksonen, J. (2008). Techniques for image classification, object detection and object segmentation. In *Visual Information Systems. Web-Based Visual Information Search and Management: 10th International Conference, VISUAL 2008, Salerno, Italy, September 11–12, 2008. Proceedings 10* (pp. 231–234). Springer Berlin Heidelberg.

39. Brownlee, J. (2019). *Deep learning for computer vision: Image classification, object detection, and face recognition in Python.* Machine Learning Mastery.

40. Kuznetsova, A., Rom, H., Alldrin, N., Uijlings, J., Krasin, I., Pont-Tuset, J., ... & Ferrari, V. (2020). The open images data set v4: Unified image classification, object detection, and visual relationship detection at scale. *International Journal of Computer Vision, 128*(7), 1956–1981.

41. Druzhkov, P. N., & Kustikova, V. D. (2016). A survey of deep learning methods and software tools for image classification and object detection. *Pattern Recognition and Image Analysis, 26*, 9–15.

42. Wang, X., Bai, X., Liu, W., & Latecki, L. J. (2011, June). Feature context for image classification and object detection. In (pp. 961–968). IEEE. CVPR 2011.

43. Szegedy, C., Toshev, A., & Erhan, D. (2013). Deep neural networks for object detection. *Advances in Neural Information Processing Systems*, 26, 1–15.

44. Cheng, G., Han, J., Zhou, P., & Guo, L. (2014). Multi-class geospatial object detection and geographic image classification based on collection of part detectors. *ISPRS Journal of Photogrammetry and Remote Sensing*, 98, 119–132.

45. Dhillon, A., & Verma, G. K. (2020). Convolutional neural network: A review of models, methodologies and applications to object detection. *Progress in Artificial Intelligence*, 9(2), 85–112.

46. Wu, X., Sahoo, D., & Hoi, S. C. (2020). Recent advances in deep learning for object detection. *Neurocomputing*, 396, 39–64.

47. Obeso, A. M., Benois-Pineau, J., Vázquez, M. S. G., & Acosta, A. Á. R. (2022). Visual vs internal attention mechanisms in deep neural networks for image classification and object detection. *Pattern Recognition*, 123, 108411.

48. Song, Z., Chen, Q., Huang, Z., Hua, Y., & Yan, S. (2011, June). Contextualizing object detection and classification. In (pp. 1585–1592). IEEE. CVPR 2011.

49. Athira, M. V., & Khan, D. M. (2020, July). Recent trends on object detection and image classification: A review. In *2020 International Conference on Computational Performance Evaluation (ComPE)* (pp. 427–435). IEEE.

50. Pathak, A. R., Pandey, M., & Rautaray, S. (2018). Application of deep learning for object detection. *Procedia Computer Science*, 132, 1706–1717.

51. Khan, F. S., Anwer, R. M., Van De Weijer, J., Bagdanov, A. D., Vanrell, M., & Lopez, A. M. (2012, June). Color attributes for object detection. In *2012 IEEE Conference on Computer Vision and Pattern Recognition* (pp. 3306–3313). IEEE.

52. Khan, F. S., Anwer, R. M., Van De Weijer, J., Bagdanov, A. D., Vanrell, M., & Lopez, A. M. (2012, June). Color attributes for object detection. In *2012 IEEE Conference on Computer Vision and Pattern Recognition* (pp. 3306–3313). IEEE.

53. Kang, K., Ouyang, W., Li, H., & Wang, X. (2016). Object detection from video tubelets with convolutional neural networks. In *Conference on Computer Vision and Pattern Recognition* (pp. 817–825). Proceedings of the IEEE.

54. Xu, H., Yao, L., Zhang, W., Liang, X., & Li, Z. (2019). Auto-FPN: Automatic network architecture adaptation for object detection beyond classification. In *International Conference on Computer Vision* (pp. 6649–6658). Proceedings of the IEEE/CVF.

55. Zhou, P., Ni, B., Geng, C., Hu, J., & Xu, Y. (2018). Scale-transferrable object detection. In *Conference on Computer Vision and Pattern Recognition* (pp. 528–537). Proceedings of the IEEE.

56. Schneiderman, H., & Kanade, T. (2004). Object detection using the statistics of parts. *International Journal of Computer Vision*, 56(3), 1–20.

57. Sharma, N., Jain, V., & Mishra, A. (2018). An analysis of convolutional neural networks for image classification. *Procedia Computer Science*, 132, 377–384.

58. Fuchs, K., Grundmann, T., & Fleisch, E. (2019, October). Towards identification of packaged products via computer vision: Convolutional neural networks for object detection and image classification in retail environments. In *Proceedings of the 9th International Conference on the Internet of Things* (pp. 1–8).

59. Li, M., Zang, S., Zhang, B., Li, S., & Wu, C. (2014). A review of remote sensing image classification techniques: The role of spatio-contextual information. *European Journal of Remote Sensing*, 47(1), 389–411.

60. Tuia, D., Ratle, F., Pacifici, F., Kanevski, M. F., & Emery, W. J. (2009). Active learning methods for remote sensing image classification. *IEEE Transactions on Geoscience and Remote Sensing*, 47(7), 2218–2232.

61. Maggiori, E., Tarabalka, Y., Charpiat, G., & Alliez, P. (2016). Convolutional neural networks for large-scale remote-sensing image classification. *IEEE Transactions on Geoscience and Remote Sensing, 55*(2), 645–657.

62. Tuia, D., Volpi, M., Copa, L., Kanevski, M., & Munoz-Mari, J. (2011). A survey of active learning algorithms for supervised remote sensing image classification. *IEEE Journal of Selected Topics in Signal Processing, 5*(3), 606–617.

63. Song, J., Gao, S., Zhu, Y., & Ma, C. (2019). A survey of remote sensing image classification based on CNNs. *Big Earth Data, 3*(3), 232–254.

64. Comber, A., Fisher, P., Brunsdon, C., & Khmag, A. (2012). Spatial analysis of remote sensing image classification accuracy. *Remote Sensing of Environment, 127*, 237–246.

65. Roli, F., & Fumera, G. (2001, January). Support vector machines for remote sensing image classification. In *Image and Signal Processing for Remote Sensing VI* (Vol. 4170, pp. 160–166). SPIE.

66. Hamida, A. B., Benoit, A., Lambert, P., & Amar, C. B. (2018). 3-D deep learning approach for remote sensing image classification. *IEEE Transactions on Geoscience and Remote Sensing, 56*(8), 4420–4434.

67. Aamir, M., Rahman, Z., Dayo, Z. A., Abro, W. A., Uddin, M. I., Khan, I., Imran, A. S., Ali, Z., Ishfaq, M., Guan, Y., & Hu, Z. (2022, July 1). A deep learning approach for brain tumor classification using MRI images. *Computers and Electrical Engineering, 101*, 108105.

68. Aamir, M., Pu, Y. F., Rahman, Z., Tahir, M., Naeem, H., & Dai, Q. (2018 December 21). A framework for automatic building detection from low-contrast satellite images. *Symmetry, 11*(1), 3.

69. Aamir, M., Rahman, Z., Abro, W. A., Tahir, M., & Ahmed, S. M. (2019, October 1). An optimized architecture of image classification using convolutional neural network. *International Journal of Image, Graphics and Signal Processing, 10*(10), 30.

70. Aamir, M., Pu, Y. F., Rahman, Z., Abro, W. A., Naeem, H., Ullah, F., & Badr, A. M. (2018). A hybrid proposed framework for object detection and classification. *Journal of Information Processing Systems, 14*(5), 1176–1194.

71. Aamir, M., Pu, Y. F., Abro, W. A., Naeem, H., & Rahman, Z. (2017, June 5). A hybrid approach for object proposal generation. In *International Conference on Sensing and Imaging* (pp. 251–259). Springer, Cham.

72. Aamir, M., Rahman, Z., Pu, Y. F., Abro, W. A., & Gulzar, K. (2019). Satellite image enhancement using wavelet-domain based on singular value decomposition. *International Journal of Advanced Computer Science and Applications, 10*(6), 1–16.

73. Aamir, M., Rahman, Z., Abro, W. A., Bhatti, U. A., Dayo, Z. A., & Ishfaq, M. (2023). Brain tumor classification utilizing deep features derived from high-quality regions in MRI images. *Biomedical Signal Processing and Control, 85*, 104988.

74. Guan Y., Aamir M., Hu Z., Abro W. A., Rahman Z., Dayo Z. A., & Akram S. (2021, April 1). A region-based efficient network for accurate object detection. *Traitement du Signal, 38*(2), 1–20.

75. Guan Y., Aamir M., Hu Z., Dayo Z. A., Rahman Z., Abro W. A., & Soothar P. (2021, June 1). An object detection framework based on deep features and high-quality object locations. *Traitement du Signal, 38*(3), 1–10.

76. Romero, A., Gatta, C., & Camps-Valls, G. (2015). Unsupervised deep feature extraction for remote sensing image classification. *IEEE Transactions on Geoscience and Remote Sensing, 54*(3), 1349–1362.

77. Liu, P., Choo, K. K. R., Wang, L., & Huang, F. (2017). SVM or deep learning? A comparative study on remote sensing image classification. *Soft Computing, 21*, 7053–7065.

78. Li, Y., Zhang, H., Xue, X., Jiang, Y., & Shen, Q. (2018). Deep learning for remote sensing image classification: A survey. *Wiley Interdisciplinary Reviews: Data Mining and Knowledge Discovery, 8*(6), e1264.

79. Maggiori, E., Tarabalka, Y., Charpiat, G., & Alliez, P. (2016, July). Fully convolutional neural networks for remote sensing image classification. In *IEEE International Geoscience and Remote Sensing Symposium (IGARSS)* (pp. 5071–5074). IEEE.

80. Cai, W., & Wei, Z. (2020). Remote sensing image classification based on a cross-attention mechanism and graph convolution. *IEEE Geoscience and Remote Sensing Letters, 19*, 1–5.

81. Bazi, Y., & Melgani, F. (2009). Gaussian process approach to remote sensing image classification. *IEEE Transactions on Geoscience and Remote Sensing, 48*(1), 186–197.

82. Hong, D., Gao, L., Yokoya, N., Yao, J., Chanussot, J., Du, Q., & Zhang, B. (2020). More diverse means better: Multimodal deep learning meets remote-sensing imagery classification. *IEEE Transactions on Geoscience and Remote Sensing, 59*(5), 4340–4354.

83. Stumpf, A., Lachiche, N., Malet, J. P., Kerle, N., & Puissant, A. (2013). Active learning in the spatial domain for remote sensing image classification. *IEEE Transactions on Geoscience and Remote Sensing, 52*(5), 2492–2507.

84. Qayyum, M., Yuyuan, Y., Bhatti, U. A., & Shijie, L. (2023). Evaluation of the one belt and one road (OBOR) in economic development and suggestions analysis based on SWOT analysis with weighted AHP and entropy methods. *Multimedia Tools and Applications, 82*(10), 14985–15006.

85. Li, D., Li, J., Bhatti, U. A., Nawaz, S. A., Liu, J., Chen, Y. W., & Cao, L. (2023). Hybrid encrypted watermarking algorithm for medical images based on DCT and improved DarkNet53. *Electronics, 12*(7), 1554.

86. Bhatti, U. A., Tang, H., Wu, G., Marjan, S., & Hussain, A. (2023). Deep learning with graph convolutional networks: An overview and latest applications in computational intelligence. *International Journal of Intelligent Systems, 2023*, 1–19.

87. Hasnain, A., Sheng, Y., Hashmi, M. Z., Bhatti, U. A., Ahmed, Z., & Zha, Y. (2023). Assessing the ambient air quality patterns associated to the COVID-19 outbreak in the Yangtze River Delta: A random forest approach. *Chemosphere, 314*, 137638.

88. Aamir, M., Bazai, S., Bhatti, U. A., Dayo, Z. A., Liu, J., & Zhang, K. (2023, January). Applications of machine learning in medicine: Current trends and prospects. In *2023 Global Conference on Wireless and Optical Technologies (GCWOT)* (pp. 1–4). IEEE.

89. Chen, H., Zhang, Y., Bhatti, U. A., & Huang, M. (2023). Safe decision controller for autonomous driving based on deep reinforcement learning in nondeterministic environment. *Sensors, 23*(3), 1198.

90. Fan, Y., Li, J., Bhatti, U. A., Shao, C., Gong, C., Cheng, J., & Chen, Y. (2023). A multi-watermarking algorithm for medical images using inception V3 and DCT. *CMC-Computers Materials & Continua, 74*(1), 1279–1302.

91. Aamir, M., Bhatti, M. A., Bazai, S. U., Marjan, S., Mirza, A. M., Wahid, A., … & Bhatti, U. A. (2022). Predicting the environmental change of carbon emission patterns in South Asia: A deep learning approach using BiLSTM. *Atmosphere, 13*(12), 2011.

92. Li, D., Chen, Y. W., Li, J., Cao, L., Bhatti, U. A., & Zhang, P. (2022). Robust watermarking algorithm for medical images based on accelerated-KAZE discrete cosine transform. *IET Biometrics, 11*(6), 534–546.

93. Gong, C., Liu, J., Gong, M., Li, J., Bhatti, U. A., & Ma, J. (2022). Robust medical zero-watermarking algorithm based on Residual-DenseNet. *IET Biometrics, 11*(6), 547–556.

94. Bhatti, U. A., Nizamani, M. M., & Mengxing, H. (2022). Climate change threatens Pakistan's snow leopards. *Science, 377*(6606), 585–586.

95. Galvan, L. P. C., Bhatti, U. A., Campo, C. C., & Stanojevic, S. Toward sustainable development: The nexus between CO_2 emission, economic growth, trade openness, and the middle-income trap in Latin American countries. *Frontiers in Environmental Science, 1003*, 1–29.

96. Bhatti, U. A., Zeeshan, Z., Nizamani, M. M., Bazai, S., Yu, Z., & Yuan, L. (2022). Assessing the change of ambient air quality patterns in Jiangsu Province of China pre-to post-COVID-19. *Chemosphere, 288*, 132569.

97. Bhatti, U. A., Yu, Z., Hasnain, A., Nawaz, S. A., Yuan, L., Wen, L., & Bhatti, M. A. (2022). Evaluating the impact of roads on the diversity pattern and density of trees to improve the conservation of species. *Environmental Science and Pollution Research, 29*, 1–11.

98. Hong, D., Hu, J., Yao, J., Chanussot, J., & Zhu, X. X. (2021). Multimodal remote sensing benchmark data sets for land cover classification with a shared and specific feature learning model. *ISPRS Journal of Photogrammetry and Remote Sensing, 178*, 68–80.

99. Ge, G., Shi, Z., Zhu, Y., Yang, X., & Hao, Y. (2020). Land use/cover classification in an arid desert-oasis mosaic landscape of China using remote sensed imagery: Performance assessment of four machine learning algorithms. *Global Ecology and Conservation, 22*, e00971.

100. Tong, X. Y., Xia, G. S., Lu, Q., Shen, H., Li, S., You, S., & Zhang, L. (2020). Land-cover classification with high-resolution remote-sensing images using transferable deep models. *Remote Sensing of Environment, 237*, 111322.

101. Phan, T. N., Kuch, V., & Lehnert, L. W. (2020). Land cover classification using Google Earth Engine and random forest classifier—The role of image composition. *Remote Sensing, 12*(15), 2411.

102. Hermosilla, T., Wulder, M. A., White, J. C., & Coops, N. C. (2022). Land cover classification in an era of big and open data: Optimizing localized implementation and training data selection to improve mapping outcomes. *Remote Sensing of Environment, 268*, 112780.

103. Carranza-García, M., García-Gutiérrez, J., & Riquelme, J. C. (2019). A framework for evaluating land use and land cover classification using convolutional neural networks. *Remote Sensing, 11*(3), 274.

104. Rogan, J., Franklin, J., & Roberts, D. A. (2002). A comparison of methods for monitoring multitemporal vegetation change using Thematic Mapper imagery. *Remote Sensing of Environment, 80*, 143–156.

105. Du, Q., & Chang, C. I. (2001). A linear constrained distance-based discriminant analysis for hyperspectral image classification. *Pattern Recognition, 34*, 361–373.

106. Kal-Yi, H. (2002). A synergistic automatic clustering technique (SYNERACT) for multi-spectral image analysis. *Photogrammetric* Engineering & Remote Sensing, *68*, 33–40.

107. Etter, A., McAlpine, C., Wilson, K., Phinn, S., & Possingham, H. (2006). Regional patterns of agricultural land use and deforestation in Colombia. *Agriculture, Ecosystems & Environment, 114*, 369–386.

108. Xu, M., Watanachaturaporn, P., Varshney, P. K., & Arora, M. K. (2005). Decision tree regression for soft classification of remote-sensing data. *Remote Sensing of Environment, 97*, 322–336.

109. Samaniego, L., Bardossy, A., & Schulz, K. (2008). Supervised classification of remotely sensed imagery using a modified k-NN technique. *IEEE Transactions on Geoscience and Remote Sensing, 46*, 2112–2125.

110. Gislason, P., Benediktsson, J., & Sveinsson, J. (2006). Random forests for land cover classification. *Pattern Recognition Letters, 27*, 294–300.

111. Mas, J., & Flores, J. (2008). The application of artificial neural networks to the analysis of remotely sensed data. *International Journal of Remote Sensing, 29*, 617–663.

112. Melgani, F., & Bruzzone, L. (2004). Classification of hyperspectral remote-sensing images with support vector machines. *IEEE Transactions on Geoscience and Remote Sensing, 42*, 1778–1790.

113. Khatami, R., Mountrakis, G., & Stehman, S. V. (2016). A meta-analysis of remote sensing research on supervised pixel-based land-cover image classification processes: General guidelines for practitioners and future research. *Remote Sensing of Environment*, *177*, 89–100.

114. He, K., Zhang, X., Ren, S., & Sun, J. (2015). Deep residual learning for image recognition. arXiv, arXiv:1512.03385.

115. Li, Y., Zhang, H., Xue, X., Jiang, Y., & Shen, Q. (2018). Deep learning for remote sensing image classification: A survey. *Wiley Interdisciplinary Reviews: Data Mining and Knowledge Discovery*, *8*, e1264.

116. Kussul, N., Lavreniuk, M., Skakun, S., & Shelestov, A. (2017). Deep learning classification of land cover and crop types using remote sensing data. *IEEE Geoscience and Remote Sensing Letters*, *14*, 778–782.

117. Ding, J., Chen, B., Liu, H., & Huang, M. (2016). Convolutional neural network with data augmentation for SAR target recognition. *IEEE Geoscience and Remote Sensing Letters*, *13*, 364–368.

118. Romero, A., Gatta, C., & Camps-Valls, G. (2016). Unsupervised deep feature extraction for remote sensing image classification. *IEEE Transactions on Geoscience and Remote Sensing*, *54*, 1349–1362.

119. Castelluccio, M., Poggi, G., Sansone, C., & Verdoliva, L. (2015). Land use classification in remote sensing images by convolutional neural networks. arXiv, arXiv:1508.00092.

120. Li, W., Fu, H., Yu, L., Gong, P., Feng, D., Li, C., & Clinton, N. (2016). Stacked autoencoder-based deep learning for remote-sensing image classification: A case study of African land-cover mapping. *International Journal of Remote Sensing*, *37*, 5632–5646.

121. Chen, Y., Zhao, X., & Jia, X. (2015). Spectral–spatial classification of hyperspectral data based on deep belief network. *IEEE Journal of Selected Topics in Applied Earth Observations and Remote Sensing*, *8*, 2381–2392.

122. Guo, Y., Fu, Y., Hao, F., Zhang, X., Wu, W., Jin, X., Bryant, C. R., & Senthilnath, J. (2021). Integrated phenology and climate in rice yields prediction using machine learning methods. *Ecological Indicators*, *120*, 106935.

123. Shammi, S. A., & Meng, Q. (2020). Use time series NDVI and EVI to develop dynamic crop growth metrics for yield modeling. *Ecological Indicators*, 107124.

124. Vina, A., Gitelson, A. A., Rundquist, D. C., Keydan, G., Leavitt, B., & Schepers, J. (2004). Monitoring maize (Zea Mays L.) phenology with remote sensing. *Agronomy Journal*, *96*, 1139–1147.

125. Ahmad, S., Abbas, Q., Abbas, G., Fatima, Z., Atique-ur-Rehman Naz, S., Younis, H., Khan, R. J., Nasim, W., & Habib ur Rehman, M. (2017). Quantification of climate warming and crop management impacts on cotton phenology. *Plants*, *6*, 7.

126. He, L., Jin, N., & Yu, Q. (2020). Impacts of climate change and crop management practices on soybean phenology changes in China. *Science of the Total Environment*, *707*, 135631–135638.

127. Harris, K., Subudhi, P., Borrell, A., Jordan, D., Rosenow, D., Nguyen, H., Klein, P., Klein, R., & Mullet, J. (2007). Sorghum stay-green QTL individually reduce post-flowering drought-induced leaf senescence. *Journal of Experimental Botany*, *58*, 327–338.

128. Christopher, J. T., Veyradier, M., Borrell, A. K., Harvey, G., Fletcher, S., & Chenu, K. (2014). Phenotyping novel stay-green traits to capture genetic variation in senescence dynamics. *Functional Plant Biology*, *41*, 1035–1048.

129. Gaju, O., Allard, V., Martre, P., Le Gouis, J., Moreau, D., Bogard, M., Hubbart, S., & Foulkes, M. J. (2014). Nitrogen partitioning and remobilization in relation to leaf senescence, grain yield and grain nitrogen concentration in wheat cultivars. *Field Crops Research*, *155*, 213–223.

130. Jozdani, S. E., Momeni, M., Johnson, B. A., & Sattari, M. (2018). A regression modelling approach for optimizing segmentation scale parameters to extract buildings of different sizes. *International Journal of Remote Sensing, 39*, 684–703.

131. Dietterich, T. G. (2000). An experimental comparison of three methods for constructing ensembles of decision trees: Bagging, boosting, and randomization. *Machine Learning, 40*, 139–157.

132. Ma, L., Li, M., Ma, X., Cheng, L., Du, P., & Liu, Y. (2017). A review of supervised object-based land-cover image classification. *ISPRS Journal of Photogrammetry and Remote Sensing, 130*, 277–293.

133. Zhu, X. X., Tuia, D., Mou, L., Xia, G., Zhang, L., Xu, F., & Fraundorfer, F. (2017). Deep Learning in remote sensing: A comprehensive review and list of resources. *IEEE Geoscience and Remote Sensing Magazine, 5*, 8–36.

134. Boualleg, Y., Farah, M., & Farah, I. R. (2019). Remote sensing scene classification using convolutional features and deep forest classifier. *IEEE Geoscience and Remote Sensing Letters*, 1–5.

135. Lv, X., Ming, D., Chen, Y., & Wang, M. (2019). Very high resolution remote sensing image classification with SEEDS-CNN and scale effect analysis for superpixel CNN classification. *International Journal of Remote Sensing, 40*, 506–531.

136. Zhong, Y., Wang, X., Wang, S., & Zhang, L. (2021). Advances in spaceborne hyperspectral remote sensing in China. *Geo-spatial Information Science, 24*(1), 95–120.

137. Paoletti, M. E., Haut, J. M., Plaza, J., & Plaza, A. (2019). Deep learning classifiers for hyperspectral imaging: A review. *ISPRS Journal of Photogrammetry and Remote Sensing, 158*, 279–317.

138. Jia, S., Zhan, Z., Zhang, M., Xu, M., Huang, Q., Zhou, J., & Jia, X. (2020). Multiple feature-based superpixel-level decision fusion for hyperspectral and LiDAR data classification. *IEEE Transactions on Geoscience and Remote Sensing, 59*(2), 1437–1452.

139. Song, W., Li, S., Kang, X., & Huang, K. (2016, July). Hyperspectral image classification based on KNN sparse representation. In *2016 IEEE International Geoscience and Remote Sensing Symposium (IGARSS)* (pp. 2411–2414). IEEE.

140. Abbasi, B., Arefi, H., Bigdeli, B., Motagh, M., & Roessner, S. (2015). Fusion of hyperspectral and lidar data based on dimension reduction and maximum likelihood. *The International Archives of Photogrammetry, Remote Sensing and Spatial Information Sciences, 40*(7), 569.

141. Zhao, C., Zhao, H., Wang, G., & Chen, H. (2020). Improvement SVM classification performance of hyperspectral image using chaotic sequences in artificial bee colony. *IEEE Access, 8*, 73947–73956.

142. Li, X., Ding, M., & Pižurica, A. (2019). Deep feature fusion via two-stream convolutional neural network for hyperspectral image classification. *IEEE Transactions on Geoscience and Remote Sensing, 58*(4), 2615–2629.

143. Gong, J., Yang, X., Han, D., Zhang, D., Jin, H., & Gao, Z. (2007, November). Research and evaluation of Beijing-1 image fusion based on Imagesharp algorithm. In *Second International Conference on Space Information Technology* (Vol. 6795, p. 67952L). International Society for Optics and Photonics.

144. Niande, J., Yaonan, W., & Jianxu, M. (2008). Research on remote sensing image fusion based on Curvelet transform. *Chinese Journal of Scientific Instrument, 29*(1), 61.

145. Yokoya, N., Yairi, T., & Iwasaki, A. (2011). Coupled nonnegative matrix factorization unmixing for hyperspectral and multispectral data fusion. *IEEE Transactions on Geoscience and Remote Sensing, 50*(2), 528–537.

146. Hasnain, A., Sheng, Y., Hashmi, M. Z., Bhatti, U. A., Hussain, A., Hameed, M., … & Zha, Y. (2022). Time series analysis and forecasting of air pollutants based on prophet forecasting model in Jiangsu province, *China Frontiers in Environmental Science, 1044.*

147. Gong, C., Li, J., Bhatti, U. A., Gong, M., Ma, J., & Huang, M. (2021). Robust and secure zero-watermarking algorithm for medical images based on Harris-SURF-DCT and chaotic map. *Security and Communication Networks, 2021*, 1–13.

148. Aamir, M., Li, Z., Bazai, S., Wagan, R. A., Bhatti, U. A., Nizamani, M. M., & Akram, S. (2021). Spatiotemporal change of air-quality patterns in Hubei province—A pre-to post-COVID-19 analysis using path analysis and regression. *Atmosphere, 12*(10), 1338.

149. Bhatti, U. A., Yu, Z., Chanussot, J., Zeeshan, Z., Yuan, L., Luo, W., ... & Mehmood, A. (2021). Local similarity-based spatial–spectral fusion hyperspectral image classification with deep CNN and Gabor filtering. *IEEE Transactions on Geoscience and Remote Sensing, 60*, 1–15.

150. Nawaz, S. A., Li, J., Bhatti, U. A., Bazai, S. U., Zafar, A., Bhatti, M. A., ... & Shoukat, M. U. (2021). A hybrid approach to forecast the COVID-19 epidemic trend. *PLoS One, 16*(10), e0256971.

151. Hasnain, A., Hashmi, M. Z., Bhatti, U. A., Nadeem, B., Wei, G., Zha, Y., & Sheng, Y. (2021). Assessment of air pollution before, during and after the COVID-19 pandemic lockdown in Nanjing, China. *Atmosphere, 12*(6), 743.

152. Bhatti, U. A., Yan, Y., Zhou, M., Ali, S., Hussain, A., Qingsong, H., ... & Yuan, L. (2021). Time series analysis and forecasting of air pollution particulate matter (PM 2.5): An SARIMA and factor analysis approach. *IEEE Access, 9*, 41019–41031.

153. Bhatti, U. A., Ming-Quan, Z., Qing-Song, H., Ali, S., Hussain, A., Yuhuan, Y., ... & Nawaz, S. A. (2021). Advanced color edge detection using clifford algebra in satellite images. *IEEE Photonics Journal, 13*(2), 1–20.

154. Zeeshan, Z., Bhatti, U. A., Memon, W. H., Ali, S., Nawaz, S. A., Nizamani, M. M., ... & Shoukat, M. U. (2021). Feature-based multi-criteria recommendation system using a weighted approach with ranking correlation. *Intelligent Data Analysis, 25*(4), 1013–1029.

155. Bhatti, U. A., Marjan, S., Wahid, A., Syam, M. S., Huang, M., Tang, H., & Hasnain, A. (2023). The effects of socioeconomic factors on particulate matter concentration in China's: New evidence from spatial econometric model. *Journal of Cleaner Production, 417*, 137969.

156. Zhang, Yu, Chen, Jing, Ma, Xiangxun, Wang, Gang, Bhatti, Uzair Aslam, & Huang, Mengxing (2024). Interactive medical image annotation using improved Attention U-net with compound geodesic distance. *Expert Systems with Applications, 237*, 121282. 10.1016/j.eswa.2023.121282.

157. Bhatti, Uzair Aslam, Huang, Mengxing, Neira-Molina, Harold, Marjan, Shah, Baryalai, Mehmood, Tang, Hao, Wu, Guilu, & Bazai, Sibghat Ullah (2023). MFFCG – Multi feature fusion for hyperspectral image classification using graph attention network. *Expert Systems with Applications, 229*, 120496. 10.1016/j.eswa.2023.120496.

## CHAPTER 3

Deep Learning Framework for Face Detection and Recognition for Dark Faces Using VGG19 with Variant of Histogram Equalization

Kirti[1] and Gagandeep[2]

[1]*School of Computer Science and Engineering, Lovely Professional University, Jalandhar, India*
[2]*Computer Science and Engineering, CT Group of Institutions, Jalandhar, India*

3.1 INTRODUCTION

Recent trends in artificial intelligence have upgraded the standard of living of humans by making almost each task automatic. Due to its collaborative discipline, computer vision is at its peak. There are manifold subject areas of computer vision, such as: 1) machine vision, 2) medical, and 3) military applications, etc. [1]. Machine vision is one of the most salient from the aforementioned areas for detection purpose. The highbrow issue of machine vision is recognition. Face detection and recognition has emerged as one of the most crucial subjects because of its enactment in almost every field: 1) social platform, 2) security purpose, and 3) identification, etc. Face detection and recognition is a two-step process, as the name says. Face detection [2–5] is to locate the faces from the image. Face recognition is practicable only after the detection phase. There are various state-of-the-art algorithms based on machine and deep learning that exist in the literature. The best algorithm to detect and recognize faces is a convolutional neural network [6]. There is an abundance of deep learning models that exist in the literature, but the most prominent are as follows: (a) VGG-Face, (b) GOOGLeNet, (c) AlexNnet, (d) ZFnet, and (e) ResNet, etc. [7]. Even with the proper advancement in face detection and recognition, the issue of detecting the dark faces still persists.

The rest of this chapter is systematized as follows: Section 3.2 elucidates the brief of literature and the related work. Section 3.3.1 explicates the overview of convolutional

DOI: 10.1201/9781032646268-3

neural network. In Section 3.3.2, histogram equalization has been discussed. Section 3.3.3 depicts how the data set has been collected. Section 3.3.4 describes the methodology that has been used. In Section 3.4, experimental discussions and results are given. At the end, in Section 3.5, future scope and the conclusion of the hybridized technique have been explicated.

3.2 LITERATURE REVIEW

Lots of work has been already done in the field of face detection and recognition using deep learning. Figure 3.1 demonstrates the number of documents published from year 2005 to 2019 to detect and recognize the face using deep learning and convolutional neural network. That data is collected from the citation and abstract database bestowed by Elsevier's Scopus.

The authors [8] have scrutinized that in comparison to dark faces, people with white faces are more distinguishable. According to [9], measurement spacing is the most salient approach to detect faces in an image. The authors in [10], introduced an implicit algorithm using gabor features to detect faces with refined efficacy. The authors [11] deployed a model that uses face variants to spot the faces in the image. The authors [12] established an original parser that uses a mapping approach from faces to labels. The authors in [13] wield an intelligent denoising encoder based on an iterative stack in amalgamation with a deep neural network to recognize faces. The authors in [14] propounded a scheme to comprehend the issue of detecting the faces from multiple perspectives. The authors in [15] fabricated a model based on deep learning that is task-contrived. The authors in [16] propounded a model based on a convolutional network that wields an SIAMESE network to refine the accuracy of detecting faces. The authors in [17] overcame the issues of acute occlusion of faces as well as face position from different perspective by deploying the model rooted on deep learning. The deployed model wields a scoring approach to improve the model. The authors in [18] established an image characteristic to fasten the face-detecting process. The authors in [19] deployed a deep learning model that is task constrained. The authors in [20] wield 3D rendering to originate pose-specific features of a convolutional neural network. The authors in [21] wield the blend of the two most prominent neural networks: (a) convolutional and (b) bi-directional LSTM (long short-term memory). To uplift the accuracy of a convolutional neural network, the author presented a cascaded configured framework as well as mining scheme for hard samples.

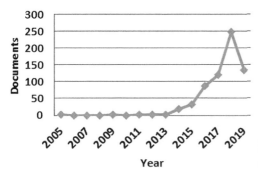

FIGURE 3.1 Documents published per year on face detection and recognition using deep learning.

Then the R-CNN [22,23] came into existence, but the accuracy as well as the time complexity was not impressive to detect and recognize faces. The author in [24] exploited faster R-CNN to refine the efficacy for face detection. The authors in [25] proffered novel scheme for face spoofing detection rooted upon local binary pattern. To ameliorate the efficacy of the state-of-the-art approaches, the authors in [26] practiced the amalgamation of diverse schemes: (a) hard mining, (b) training the model at multi-scale, (c) merging of features, and (d) fine-tuning the parameters. The authors in [27] wield a classifier named sparse representation for face identification.

Even after the enormous advancement in the area of face detection and recognition, one significant challenge still remains, the challenge of detecting dark faces. The challenge was first addressed in [28]. To label the faces, the authors in [28] have wield the Fitzpatrick skin type classification strategy. The authors have classified the pilot parliament benchmark in two groups: (a) more relevant to white faces and (b) more relevant to dark faces. According to the authors, the accuracy is quite low for dark females and there is a huge gap between the accuracy of white males and dark females.

3.3 MATERIAL AND TECHNIQUES

3.3.1 Convolutional Neural Network

Deep learning is a sub-category of machine learning; the name itself describes the method used by multiple layers to find out the essential features from the input image. Lower layers may detect the edges while the higher layers detect objects. Deep learning is based on the artificial neural network, especially a convolutional neural network (CNN) [6]. As is clear from the name CNN, it practices a convolution operation on multiple input layers instead of simple matrix multiplication. CNN comprises multiple layers of three types: (a) input layer, (b) output layer, and (c) hidden layers. Here, hidden layers refer to a sequence of convolutional layers that convolve with a dot product that is further succeeded by RELU [29] layer followed by pooling layers and fully connected layers. The CNN model is divided into two phases: (a) feature learning and (b) classification. Phase 1 includes convolution, pooling, and RELU layer. On the other hand, phase 2 incorporates fully connected and normalization layers. Figure 3.2 demonstrates the working of a CNN model.

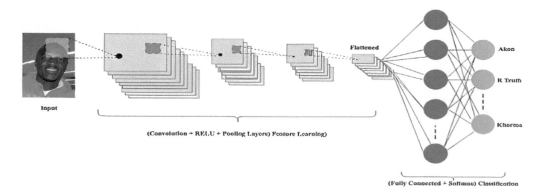

FIGURE 3.2   Working of CNN model.

3.3.2 Histogram Equalization

Histogram equalization (HE) [30,31] is an image enhancement technique to amplify the contrast of the images. It is one of the popular methods due to its efficacy and simplicity in diverse applications. It utilizes the histogram of the image and provides recommended results when the image comprises dark and bright objects. Adaptive histogram equalization (AHE) is a modified version of a former method that creates the multiple local histograms of an image and thus improves the contrast of the image in local regions that lead to enhanced edges as well. But there is one limitation of AHE that it over-intensifies the noise of an image. To overcome this limitation, there was the existence of another modified version of HE that is a contrast-limited adaptive histogram equalization (CLAHE) to reduce the over-intensification of noise of an image.

3.3.3 Data Set

To apply the hybridized technique to detect and recognize dark complexion faces, the most important component is a data set. The authors have faced the problem of how to gather the data for dark complexion faces. Therefore, the authors have constructed a new data set. The data set is collected by downloading the pictures of famous personalities with a dark complexion from the Internet. The famous personalities involve the cricketers, actors, actresses, wrestlers, and singers named Akon, Bravo, Dewanda Wise, Booker T, Kharma, Kofi Kingston, etc. The data set involves 1,645 images in total in which 1,515 and 530 images have been used as training and validation sets, respectively. The data set comprises 60% of images of dark males and 40% images of dark females. There are 13 classes in the developed data set in which 9 classes are for dark males and 6 classes are for dark females. The data set that supports the findings of this chapter is available from the corresponding author, [Kirti], upon reasonable request. Figure 3.3 shows the sample images of the constructed data set.

FIGURE 3.3   Sample images from classification data set of dark faces.

3.3.4 Proposed Framework

In this chapter, the authors have applied some pre-processing techniques on a constructed data set. The steps the authors have followed to detect and recognize the dark faces are shown in Figure 3.4.

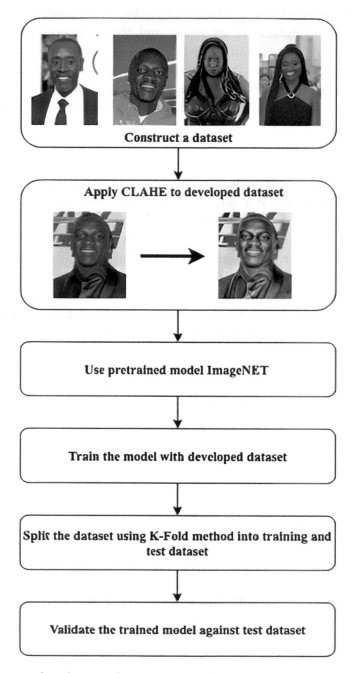

FIGURE 3.4   Steps used to detect and recognize dark faces.

1. The first and foremost step to develop the deep learning framework for dark face detection and recognition is to construct a data set of dark faces. The images from the data set are then fed to the model. Assume image I is of M × N × 3 resolution, where M is the number of columns while N is the number of rows and 3 represents the number of channels of RGB image.

2. To overcome the issue of racial biasness [28] by accurately detecting and recognizing the dark faces, apply the contrast-limited adaptive histogram equalization (CLAHE) to a constructed data set. It enhances the original images of a data set, say I, by using the following steps. It divides the image I into different parts based on the spatial information that is not overlapping each other. Based on the spatial information, this computes the histogram for each part. It then computes the contrast-limited histogram of an image using equations (3.1) and (3.2).

$$CL_n = Avg_n \times Clip_n \tag{3.1}$$

$$Avg_n = \frac{M_n \times N_n}{Gray_n} \tag{3.2}$$

In equation (3.1), CL_n represents the contrast-limited value of each part, n represents the total number of pixels, and Avg_n represents the average of the total pixels. In equation (3.2), M_n and N_n symbolizes the pixel column wise and row wise, respectively, and $Gray_n$ represents the number of intensity level of an image I.

3. After the pre-processing step, a pretrained model such as imageNET has been used to train the model to extract the features of the developed data set of dark faces.

4. After pretraining the model, train it with a CNN model and split the data set constructed using the K-fold method into a training, testing, and validation data set.

5. At last, after training, the trained model validates the proposed framework against a testing and validation data set.

3.4 EXPERIMENT AND RESULTS

3.4.1 Evaluation Parameter

To assess the efficiency of proposed framework, accuracy is used as the evaluation metric. Accuracy can be expressed as the proportion of total number of precise classification of detected and recognized images to total number of images in a data set. Accuracy for classification can be expressed in the form of equation (3.3).

$$Accuracy = \frac{T_P + T_N}{T_P + T_N + F_P + F_N} \times 100 \tag{3.3}$$

where T_N are precise predicted negative pixels and T_p are precise predicted positive pixels. F_p are uncorrected predicted positive pixels, and F_N can be expressed as the uncorrected predicted negative pixels that are actually true.

3.4.2 Experimental Setup

The authors have used the JupyterHub platform to deploy the model for dark face detection and recognition. The aforementioned platform yields high-speed GPU computing, which is necessitated to train the VGG19 model. There exist few parameters that are a must to be fine-tuned for the desired accuracy. There is no specific technique for fine-tuning. The authors have set the image size of (224, 224, 3). The epochs are set to 40. The total count of iterations is 2,000 and the batch size is set to 30. The overall data set comprises 1,630 images and 13 classes. The training set involves 70% of the data set, i.e., 1,515 images, and 30% of the data set, i.e., 530 images. The dropout is set to 0.1 and 'adam' is used for optimization The hyperparameters fine-tuning has been performed and Table 3.1 represents the parameters that acquired the best results upon the constructed data set of dark faces.

3.4.3 Results and Analysis

For qualitative and quantitative analysis, the accuracy of the model has been used. The authors have implemented the general VGG19 model and VGG19 model with CLAHE. The accuracy for both aforementioned models has been acquired for critical analysis of their efficiency. Table 3.2 represents the training and testing accuracy acquired using both VGG19 and VGG19 with CLAHE, respectively.

TABLE 3.1 Parameters Used to Implement the CNN Model

Parameter	Value
Epoch	40
Batch size	30
Image size	(224,224,3)
Iterations	2000
Activation function	ReLU, Softmax
Optimizer	Adam
Dropout	0.2
Learning rate	0.1

TABLE 3.2 Accuracy Given by VGG19 and VGG19 with CLAHE

Method	Accuracy	
	Training	Testing
VGG19	100	71.64
VGG19 with CLAHE	100	72.02

TABLE 3.3 Accuracy Given by VGG19 with and without CLAHE on Dark Male and Female Data Sets Separately

Method	Accuracy on dark male data set (60%)		Accuracy on dark female data set (40%)	
	Training	Testing	Training	Testing
VGG19	100	70.79	100	73.07
VGG19 with CLAHE	100	72.96	100	74.61

It can be discerned from Table 3.2 that the accuracy of the model was enhanced after its amalgamation with CLAHE. The accuracy of the model increases after enhancing the data set by applying CLAHE at the pre-processing step. To critically analyze the proposed framework's efficiency, the authors have also acquired the accuracy by splitting the data set into dark male and dark female data sets separately. Table 3.3 represents the training and testing accuracy acquired using both the VGG19 as well as the VGG19 with CLAHE for dark male and female data sets, respectively.

For qualitative analysis of the proposed framework model, graphical representation of the accuracy acquired using both VGG19 and VGG19 in amalgamation to CLAHE is shown in Figure 3.5 and Figure 3.6.

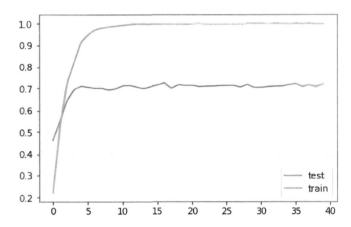

FIGURE 3.5 Accuracy acquired using the proposed framework.

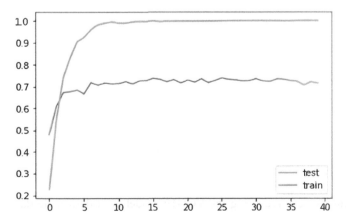

FIGURE 3.6 Accuracy acquired using the VGG19 model.

From Figure 3.5, it can be seen that the training accuracy is 100% for the constructed data set after applying CLAHE at the pre-processing step. On the other hand, the test accuracy for the constructed data set is 72.02%. Figure 3.6 shows the accuracy acquired using VGG19 on a constructed data set of dark faces.

The accuracy acquired after splitting the data set into a dark male data set and dark female data set is represented graphically. Figure 3.7 and Figure 3.8 show the accuracy acquired using a proposed framework and VGG19 on a dark male data set.

It can be seen from Figure 3.7 and Figure 3.8 that the training accuracy remains 100% for the dark male data set, employing both a proposed framework and VGG19 model, but the test accuracy increases after applying CLAHE at the pre-processing step. Figure 3.9 and Figure 3.10 show the accuracy acquired using a proposed framework and VGG19 on a dark female data set.

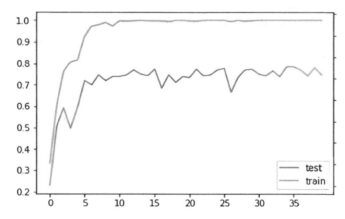

FIGURE 3.7   Accuracy acquired using a proposed framework on a dark male data set.

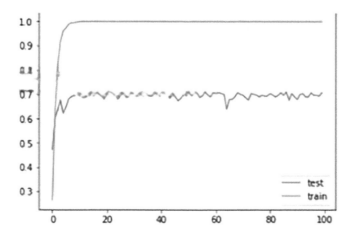

FIGURE 3.8   Accuracy acquired using the VGG19 model on a dark male data set.

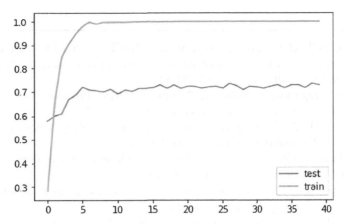

FIGURE 3.9   Accuracy acquired using a proposed framework on the dark female data set.

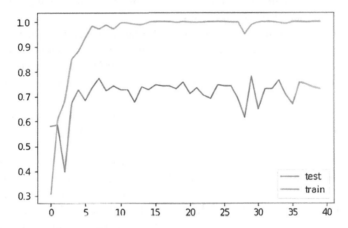

FIGURE 3.10   Accuracy acquired using the proposed framework on the dark female data set.

3.5 CONCLUSION

The motive of this chapter is to solve a global issue of racial biasness in the face detection and recognition domain. Even though a huge advancement has been made in this domain, the major issue of dark complexion detection still persists. The authors have constructed a new data set that comprises dark complexion faces of famous personalities. Then the authors have employed the VGG19 model and VGG19 model in amalgamation with CLAHE. The VGG19 in amalgamation with CLAHE delivered recommended results in comparison to VGG19. Still there is a scope to improve the accuracy for dark face detection and recognition. The researcher can blend the VGG19 with other variants of histogram equalization. Different pre-processing techniques, like the difference of Gaussian, gamma correction, etc., can also be employed to enhance the accuracy.

REFERENCES

[1] Pajares, G., Tellaeche, A., BurgosArtizzu, X. P., & Ribeiro, A. (2007). Design of a computer vision system for a differential spraying operation in precision agriculture using Hebbian learning. *IET Computer Vision*, *1*(3), 93–99.

[2] Ali, A. S. O., Sagayan, V., Malik, A., & Aziz, A. (2016). Proposed face recognition system after plastic surgery. *IET Computer Vision*, *10*(5), 344–350.

[3] Hassaballah, M., & Aly, S. (2015). Face recognition: Challenges, achievements and future directions. *IET Computer Vision*, *9*(4), 614–626.

[4] Xu, Y., Zhou, X., Chen, S., & Li, F. (2019). Deep learning for multiple object tracking: A survey. *IET Computer Vision*, *13*(4), 355–368.

[5] Zaman, F. H. K. (2020). Locally lateral manifolds of normalised Gabor features for face recognition. *IET Computer Vision*, *14*(4), 122–130

[6] Zhao, X., Meng, C., Feng, M., Chang, S., & Zeng, Q. (2017). Eye feature point detection based on single convolutional neural network. *IET Computer Vision*, *12*(4), 453–457.

[7] Taheri, S., & Toygar, Ö. (2018). Animal classification using facial images with score-level fusion. *IET Computer Vision*, *12*(5), 679–685.

[8] Malpass, R. S., & Kravitz, J. (1969). Recognition for faces of own and other race. *Journal of Personality and Social Psychology*, *13*(4), 330.

[9] Nixon, M. (1985). Eye spacing measurement for facial recognition. In applications of digital image processing VIII . *International Society for Optics and Photonics*, *575*, 279–285.

[10] Xiaohua, L., Lam, K. M., Lansun, S., & Jiliu, Z. (2009). Face detection using simplified Gabor features and hierarchical regions in a cascade of classifiers. *Pattern Recognition Letters*, *30*(8), 717–728.

[11] Taffar, M., & Benmohammed, M. (2011). Generic face invariant model for face detection. In Image Processing and Communications Challenges 3 (pp. 43–51). Springer, Berlin, Heidelberg.

[12] Luo, P., Wang, X., & Tang, X. (2012, June). Hierarchical face parsing via deep learning. In 2012 IEEE Conference on Computer Vision and Pattern Recognition (pp. 2480–2487). IEEE.

[13] Zhang, Y., Liu, R., Zhang, S., & Zhu, M. (2013, November). Occlusion-robust face recognition using iterative stacked denoising autoencoder. In International Conference on Neural Information Processing (pp. 352–359). Springer, Berlin, Heidelberg.

[14] Zhang, C., & Zhang, Z. (2014, March). Improving multiview face detection with multi-task deep convolutional neural networks. In IEEE Winter Conference on Applications of Computer Vision (pp. 1036–1041). IEEE.

[15] Zhang, Z., Luo, P., Loy, C. C., & Tang, X. (2014, September). Facial landmark detection by deep multi-task learning. In European Conference on Computer Vision (pp. 94–108). Springer, Cham.

[16] Wang, W., Yang, J., Xiao, J., Li, S., & Zhou, D. (2014, November). Face recognition based on deep learning. In International Conference on Human Centered Computing (pp. 812–820). Springer, Cham.

[17] Yang, S., Luo, P., Loy, C. C., & Tang, X. (2015). From facial parts responses to face detection: A deep learning approach. In Proceedings of the IEEE International Conference on Computer Vision (pp. 3676–3684).

[18] Li, Y., Sun, B., Wu, T., & Wang, Y. (2016, October). Face detection with end-to-end integration of a convnet and a 3D model. In European Conference on Computer Vision (pp. 420–436). Springer, Cham.

[19] Zhang, Z., Luo, P., Loy, C. C., & Tang, X. (2015). Learning deep representation for face alignment with auxiliary attributes. *IEEE Transactions on Pattern Analysis and Machine Intelligence*, *38*(5), 918–930.

[20] AbdAlmageed, W., Wu, Y., Rawls, S., Harel, S., Hassner, T., Masi, I., ... & Nevatia, R. (2016, March). Face recognition using deep multi-pose representations. In 2016 IEEE Winter Conference on Applications of Computer Vision (WACV) (pp. 1–9). IEEE.

[21] Jaiswal, S., & Valstar, M. (2016, March). Deep learning the dynamic appearance and shape of facial action units. In 2016 IEEE Winter Conference on Applications of Computer Vision (WACV) (pp. 1–8). IEEE.

[22] Girshick, R. (2015). Fast R-CNN. In Proceedings of the IEEE International Conference on Computer Vision (pp. 1440–1448).

[23] Ren, S., He, K., Girshick, R., & Sun, J. (2015). Faster R-CNN: Towards real-time object detection with region proposal networks. In Advances in Neural Information Processing Systems (pp. 91–99).

[24] Jiang, H., & Learned-Miller, E. (2017, May). Face detection with the faster R-CNN. In 2017 12th IEEE International Conference on Automatic Face & Gesture Recognition (FG 2017) (pp. 650–657). IEEE.

[25] Li, L., Feng, X., Xia, Z., Jiang, X., & Hadid, A. (2018). Face spoofing detection with local binary pattern network. *Journal of Visual Communication and Image Representation*, *54*, 182–192.

[26] Sun, X., Wu, P., & Hoi, S. C. (2018). Face detection using deep learning: An improved faster RCNN approach. *Neurocomputing*, *299*, 42–50.

[27] Cheng, E. J., Chou, K. P., Rajora, S., Jin, B. H., Tanveer, M., Lin, C. T., ... & Prasad, M. (2019). Deep sparse representation classifier for facial recognition and detection system. *Pattern Recognition Letters*, *125*, 71–77.

[28] Buolamwini, J., & Gebru, T. (2018, January). Gender shades: Intersectional accuracy disparities in commercial gender classification. In Conference on Fairness, Accountability and Transparency (pp. 77–91).

[29] Godin, F., Degrave, J., Dambre, J., & De Neve, W. (2018). Dual rectified linear units (DReLUs): A replacement for tanh activation functions in quasi-recurrent neural networks. *Pattern Recognition Letters*, *116*, 8–14.

[30] Singh, K., & Kapoor, R. (2014). Image enhancement using exposure based sub image histogram equalization. *Pattern Recognition Letters*, *36*, 10–14.

[31] Stoel, B. C., Vossepoel, A. M., Kroon, H. M., & Kool, L. S. (1990). Interactive histogram equalization. *Pattern Recognition Letters*, *11*(1990), 247–254.

## CHAPTER 4

A 3D Method for Combining Geometric Verification and Volume Reconstruction in a Photo Tourism System

Muhammad Sajid Khan and Andrew Ware

Wales Institute of Digital Information, University of South Wales, Cardiff, United Kingdom

4.1 INTRODUCTION

Structure from motion (SfM) is currently the most active area of 3D vision research with application areas, including digital tourism, medical imaging, the film industry, computer games, and image reconstruction. SfM enables the construction of 3D models from multiple 2D images. SfM builds a three-dimensional model of stationary objects or sceneries for digital tourism out of a series of 2D images. The series of pictures may come from the Internet or be part of an individual set of photos.

Existing digital tourism systems make use of two main characteristics. The first is the geometric structure, and the second is the camera pose motion. Both are estimated simultaneously during the central part of the SfM process. These characteristics enable the construction of 3D models from multiple 2D images, not necessarily acquired during the same period or with the same camera. Nonetheless, a dense correlation between pixels or portions of the same scene captured from different viewpoints is necessary for the majority of current 3D structure and scene flow estimate algorithms.

The unstructured 2D images are first organized so that all similar images are grouped and then sequenced, ready for feature correspondence to be carried out using a method for feature detection and matching.

In the method outlined here, feature matching is performed using the k-nearest neighbor technique. Features in each image are matched with all features in the other 2D images, enabling a tree of matching elements to be constructed. The seed-and-expand approach [1] can be used to match stereo pictures with excellent accuracy and resilience. An estimate of the fundamental matrix is then used to perform camera calibration,

DOI: 10.1201/9781032646268-4

mapping camera coordinates to real-world coordinates facilitating comprehensive models with good accuracy.

The algorithm used for 3D reconstruction is an extension of bundle adjustment [2]. The extension reduces the processing time required to render the 2D images as a 3D model, which leads to a better user experience. An explanation of the extension is the focus of this chapter, which is organized as follows: review of existing systems, methodology, volume reconstruction, experiments, and results and analysis provide an evaluation and draw conclusions concerning the new implementation.

4.2 LITERATURE REVIEW

Noah Snavely et al. [3] present a system to explore unordered 2D images using a 3D interface. The system uses image-based modeling to provide realistic renderings in 3D of a set of 2D images. The implementation was evaluated using several data sets, including one containing 120 2D images of the Great Wall of China and another containing 197 2D images of Prague [4].

A hybrid real-time implementation of the bundle adjustment algorithm was presented by Choudhary et al. [5]. Bundler is a solution for unordered picture collections that uses structure from motion (SfM) (for instance, images from the Internet). Bundler creates a 3D reconstruction of the camera and (sparse) scene geometry as an output from a series of photos, image features, and image matches. A few photos at a time, the algorithm gradually reconstruct the scene. Bundle adjustments use CPU and GPU processors to conduct various portions of the computation in parallel, allowing the processing of several 2D images.

A good summary of open-source software for 3D reconstruction and dense point cloud matching from 2D photos may be found in a review study by Zacharek et al. [6]. In their article, they discuss the applications of dense point clouds, patch-based multi-view stereo (PMVS), and clustering views for multi-view stereo (CMVS) in visual SfM and bundler for open street map (OSM). They also examine incremental SfM and offer a helpful review of visual, OSM bundler/PMVS2, and automated reconstruction cloud (ARC3D).

The sequential processes in SfM and incremental SfM differ from the aforementioned open-source programs, as demonstrated by Zacharek et al. By identifying feature correspondence and estimating camera parameters prior to executing the reconstruction, the SfM techniques enable 3D reconstruction from a set of 2D images. OSM bundler and visual SfM output, however, are fairly similar.

Pierre Moulon et al. [7] developed the Python photogrammetry toolbox (PPT) to resolve 3D-view issues associated with the unorganized images used in global structure from motion systems. The PPT automates the process's steps to two commands, facilitating graphical and command-line interfaces. Global calibration was used to ensure the accuracy and scalability, and the reconstruction process stablizes the structure and outliers' free geometry.

Gao Yi et al. [8] discuss the basic principle of SfM, which enables the construction of a 3D point cloud using at least two camera views. The process of SfM implementation is also summarized. The paper reports test results on seven data sets (Trevi Fountain, Sistine Chapel Ceiling, Harmandir Sahib, Colosseum, Notre Dame Facade, Stonehenge, and Statue of Liberty), which show that there are unresolved issues in terms of robustness and correctness of the 3D models produced.

Wilson et al. [9] present a method for outlier filtering and introduce a simple averaging scheme that resolves problems associated with SfM 3D camera translation (point observation) using averaging epipolar geometry. The bundle correction is only carried out once by global SfM algorithms, which also compute camera positions from the epipolar geometry graph (EG). The epipolar geometry outliers are, however, more easily detected by matrix-based approaches [10].

In [11], geometry constraints from multi-view reconstructions are a part of Luo et al.'s innovative local descriptor learning approach. The authors analyze the suggested descriptor using three data sets.

A summary of the most recent 3D reconstruction techniques is given by Kordelas et al. in their publication [12]. The study's first method, which uses laser scanner technology to first eliminate superfluous data, enables quick, high-resolution, and accurate 3D reconstruction. For interactive 3D reconstruction, RGB-D cameras are advised by Zollhöfer et al. [13]. Although Gherardi et al. [14] provide a mechanical structure and motion pipeline capable of enhancing productivity while using uncalibrated images. Adaptive community-based structure from motion (CSfM) for 3D reconstruction is suggested by Hanian Cui et al. [15] in other related studies, which increases robustness and effectiveness. The epipolar geometry is partitioned into many communities using CSfM, and parallel reconstruction is carried out for each community.

While incremental SfM provides robustness and accuracy, efficiency and scalability were still unresolved issues for which Hanian Cui et al. [15] proposed batched incremental SfM as a solution. This approach involves two nested loops; the inner loop tracks the triangulation, while the outer loop facilitates camera registration. The approach is more efficient, robust, and scalable when used for large-scale 3D reconstruction. As pairwise feature matching is an essential part of the 3D reconstruction, insufficient matches can break the completeness of the 3D model. Hanian Cui et al. proposed a progressive SfM approach to handle the completeness issues of a 3D model.

The results of these experimental approaches were better than many state-of-the-art methods regarding accuracy, completeness, robustness, and computational efficiency. The Photo Tourism project looked into the issue of taking unstructured photos and reconstructing 3D points from them (such as those from online image searches). With the aid of several data sets, the system was assessed (i.e., Prague, a set of 197 photographs; Great Wall of China, a collection of 120 photos; Notre Dame, a group of 597 pictures). Across all data sets, the average reprojection error was 1.516 pixels. When the system's camera count increases, the SfM implementation becomes complex.

SIFT GPU [16] and multicore bundle adjustment are used by the visual SfM project for quick feature matching and reconstruction. The 750-picture Notre Dame data set was

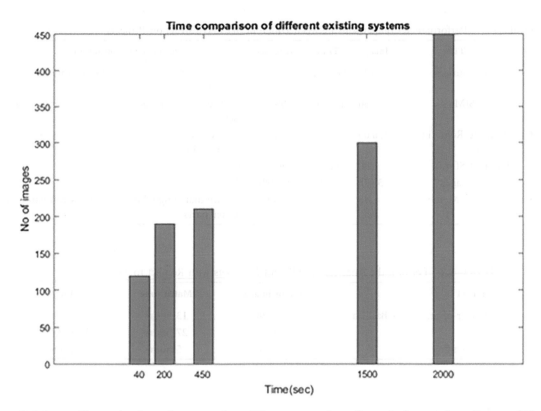

FIGURE 4.1   Shows the time taken to perform 3D reconstruction of a particular number of images [3].

rebuilt in 150 seconds. With more photos, feature matching takes longer to complete. The input pictures for the efficient structure from motion with weak position and orientation priors (a quick and scalable reconstruction method that depends on robust bundle correction and global rotation registration) are obtained from GPS/IMU sensors. The system needed 190 seconds to reconstruct the model after being tested on a data set of 200 images. By using the view selection method, the matching effort is decreased from $O(n2)$ to $O(nd)$. Finally, we display the system's experimental findings; 48 photos are used to evaluate our strategy. Our results proved better than visual SfM in computational time and accuracy (Figure 4.1).

A sea of images is a collection of pictures captured every few inches over a large area (the dense sampling approach is used to capture, render, and manage images taken within large indoor environments). The system has been tested in a variety of locations, including a library, a museum, and an office. Pose optimization for the office data set, which has 3,475 images, takes 25 minutes; for the library data set, which has 1,947 images, 20 minutes; and for the museum data set, which has 9,832 images, 30 minutes. The error model for the museum calculated the minimum pose error bound to be 0.0011 times the environment's diagonal, with an accuracy of 99.89% and an error bound of 2.4 cm. Table 4.2, constructed similar to Table 4.1, reports the numeric results of different data sets regarding the time taken during reconstruction.

TABLE 4.1   Performance Comparisons between Different 3D Reconstruction Projects

S.#	Title	Images	Time	Accuracy	Performance/limitations
1	Photo Tourism	120	Few hrs	98%	It becomes slow as the number of images increases
2	Visual SfM	50	120 sec	99%	Feature matching becomes slow for large data sets
3	Building Rome in a Day	150,00	21 hrs	$O(n2)$	It depends on the number of images & job distribution
4	Efficient SfM	200	190 sec	$O(nd)$	N.S
5	Sea of Images	3,475	25 min	99.89%	N.S
6	Proposed Method	48	30 sec	99.90%	Feature matching takes less time as compared to other parts

TABLE 4.2   Perform the Analysis of Different Data Sets with Respect to Time

Data set	No. of images	Match time	Time
Interior of St. Peter's Basilica	150,00	13 hours	8 hours
Venice	250,000	27 hours	38 hours
Dubrovnik	57,845	5 hours	7.5 hours

4.3 METHOD

This section introduces a methodology that reduces the processing time of the feature matching step of SfM by combining existing systems. The method reduces the computation time and improves the quality of the 3D model converting from 2D standard data set images. The main issue is the slow processing of the SfM concern with the feature matching step. Our system demonstrates successful results on standard data sets, the main reason is consuming more computation time. This chapter introduces a system to enhance the quality of a 3D model for user experience to reduce these difficulties during 3D reconstruction (UX).

First, the methodology involves using a pre-processing technique that removes unnecessary data [17–19]. In the second step, 2D feature extraction of calibrated images is performed using the SIFT algorithm. In the third step, features are matched before; the fourth step, geometric verification, confirms whether matches accurately correspond to 3D points in a scene. The object's volume in the scene is reconstructed in the fifth step. In the sixth stage, triangulation is utilized to determine a tracked picture coordinate in three dimensions across two or more photos. Finally, the seventh step produces the output using bundle adjustment. The process flow through the steps is shown in Figure 4.2.

4.3.1 Processing

After loading the 2D images into the system, they are pre-processed to quicken the 3D reconstruction steps. In order to speed up processing and handle image size and focal length, pre-processing eliminates unnecessary information from the photos, such as

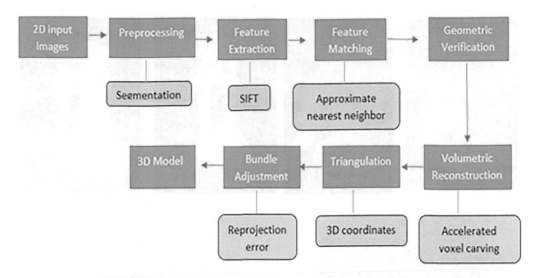

FIGURE 4.2   The 3D method to combine geometric verification and volume reconstruction for the photo tourism system.

images with inadequate lighting that cannot be used for 3D reconstruction. Segmentation of the input data sets is achieved using a threshold method that enables the selection of the object of interest and removes raw data. A black pixel is substituted for a pixel whose intensity I (i,j) is below the threshold, while a white pixel is substituted for a pixel whose intensity I (i,j) is above the threshold.

4.3.2 Feature Extraction

The second phase is feature extraction, in which the SIFT method is used to extract features from 2D images. SIFT is both scale- and feature-invariant. It looks for image scaling and location at the initial step of computation. To determine position, scale, and contrast, a thorough model is fitted as shown in Figure 1.3. Images of various scales are convolved by SIFT using a Gaussian filter, and the difference of the Gaussian-blurred images is then calculated. The peaks and minima of the Gaussian (difference of Gaussians) difference at various scales are then used to represent key locations. A DoG picture is specifically provided by:

$$D(x, y, \sigma) = L(x, y, k_i\sigma) - L(x, y, k_j\sigma) \tag{4.1}$$

In this case, L(x, y, and k) represents the outcome of scaling the original image I(x, y) with the Gaussian blurring G(x, y, and k) at scale $k\sigma$ (Figure 4.3).

$$L(x, y, k\sigma) = G(x, y, k\sigma) * I(x, y) \tag{4.2}$$

4.3.3 Feature Matching

To identify which photographs, represent typical elements of the scene, feature extraction is utilized to extract features from the input 2D images. Two distinct

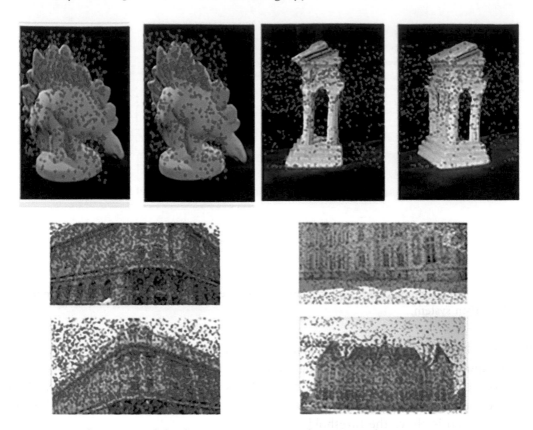

FIGURE 4.3 The output of the feature extraction uni data set: castle.

photographs can depict the same aspect of a scene if they share a common description. Pre-processing reduces computation time at this stage compared to not pre-processing. A pre-processing of calibrated images in feature matching takes less time than processing of uncalibrated images. The match feature function, which returns the indexes of the matching features in the two input feature sets, is used to match features. A binary feature (an object for holding binary feature vectors) or a matrix must be used as the input feature. The matching between photos is determined using the approximate closest neighbor method. It locates the point in the supplied set that is most near a supplied point. The following definitions apply to the nearest neighbor (NN) search problem.

Get the S point that is closest to q with a collection S of point in area M and a query point q ∈ M.

4.3.4 Geometric Verification

The potentially overlapping image pairings are verified geometrically in the fourth phase. It is used to find matches that are precise correspondences of 3D points in a scene, such as in Figure 4.4, and to identify those matches. Matching simply determines if the matches share something in common because it is based solely on appearance. By calculating a transformation that uses projective geometry to map feature locations between images, SfM

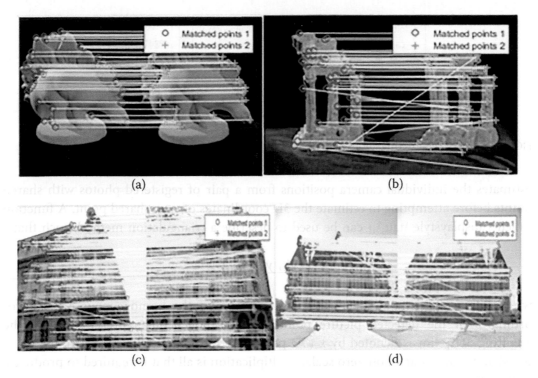

FIGURE 4.4   Matched features output courtesy of (a) dinoring, (b) templering, (c) uni data set, (d) castle.

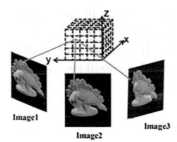

FIGURE 4.5   Geometric verification of dinoring data set.

validates the matches. Corresponding features may not always translate to the same scene point. To lower the error, geometric verification is carried out (Figure 4.5).

4.3.5 Volumetric Reconstruction

A method known as volumetric reconstruction is based on carving a bounding volume with the use of a color similarity criterion. The technique is made to take advantage of the video card's hardware-accelerated features. It is used to reassemble the volume that each object in the scene took up. As in Figure 4.6, it makes use of rapid voxel carving.

4.3.6 Triangulation

Three-way comparison is the sixth phase. By specifying the 3D coordinates of additional points added during the 3D reconstruction process, it creates a dense point cloud. It

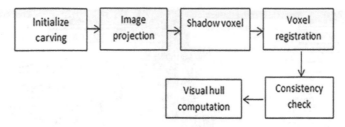

FIGURE 4.6   Accelerated voxel carving.

estimates the individual camera positions from a pair of registered photos with shared points before attempting to estimate the 3D coordinates of each shared point. A function called {\displaystyle \tau \,} can be used to describe a triangulation method, such that

$$x \sim \tau (y'_1, y'_2, C_1, C_2) \tag{4.3}$$

where y'_1, y'_2, the camera matrices are C_1, C_2, and the homogeneous are the co-ordinates of the detected picture points. The homogeneous representation of the resulting 3D point is denoted by x (3D point). As homogeneous vectors are involved, the sign denotes that a non-zero scalar multiplication is all that is required to produce a vector that is equal to x.

4.3.7 Bundle Adjustment

The final stage, bundle adjustment (BA), minimizes these mistakes by preventing inaccurate camera posture estimation. Since errors could have been produced in the preceding step, bundle adjustment can help prevent errors. It is a sort of quality improvement for 3D reconstruction. Bundle adjustment reduces the overall reprojection error for every 3D point and camera parameter, in particular

$$\min_{a_j, b_i} \sum_{i=1}^{n} \sum_{j=1}^{m} v_{ij} d \left(Q(a_j, b_i), x_{ij} \right)^2 \tag{4.4}$$

where $Q(a_j, b_i)$ is the predicted projection of point i on image j and $d(x, y)$ denotes the Euclidean distance between the image points.

4.4 EXPERIMENTS

4.4.1 Data Set Description

We have evaluated our system on several data sets, as in Figure 4.7 (a) shows a dinoring data set (a set contains 48 images) taken from the Vision Middlebury website, (b) shows a uni data set (a set contains eight images), (c) shows a castle data set (a set contains 11 images) by "Chateau de Sceaux", Sceaux castle France photographer.

We compared our results as in Figure 4.8 with visual SfM, as in Figure 4.9, which shows that our model's output is more detailed fully than their model.

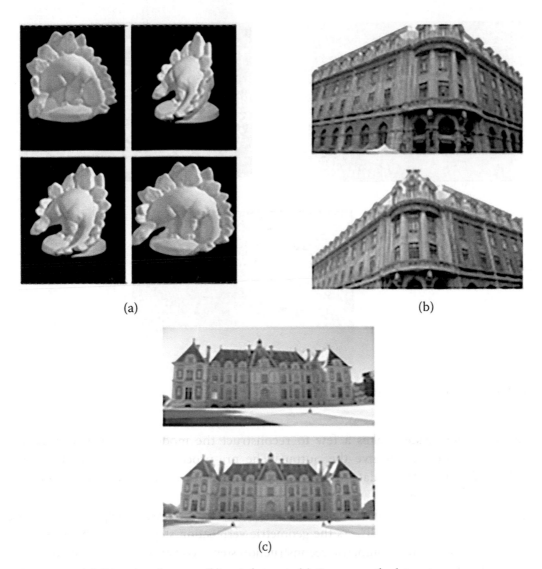

FIGURE 4.7   (a) Dinoring data set, (b) uni data set, (c) Sceaux castle data set.

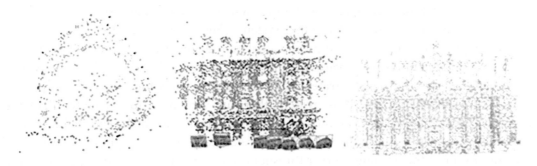

FIGURE 4.8   Result of visual SfM.

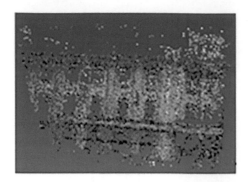 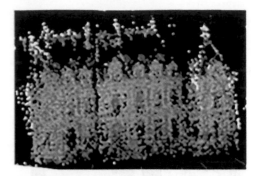

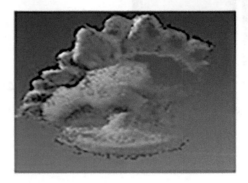

FIGURE 4.9 The output of the proposed system.

Secondly, their system takes a few to reconstruct the model. However, our system takes a few minutes to give the output. The pre-processing time depends on the quality of images of the data sets (less relevant images result in a more significant pre-processing error).

The geometric verification and volumetric reconstruction steps help generate more relevant and complete results. As the geometric verification step corrects the location of points in 3D space, the volumetric reconstruction step reconstructs the volume occupied by the object.

4.5 RESULTS AND ANALYSIS

The proposed method is compared with other systems to verify the results and show the error occurrence rate is lower than other systems (Figures 4.10 and 4.11).

The graph above compares the mean calculation error of our proposed system and other current systems utilizing various numbers of images [15]. The yellow line (which represents our system) demonstrates that our computation's total error is lower than that of the current system. It is evident that our system performs better than the current system. Every pair of photos has its initial error calculated, and if the error is not smaller than the minimum value, it is recalculated. A pair of photos is deleted if they do not meet the minimum error threshold. This computation with repeated errors produces reliable results.

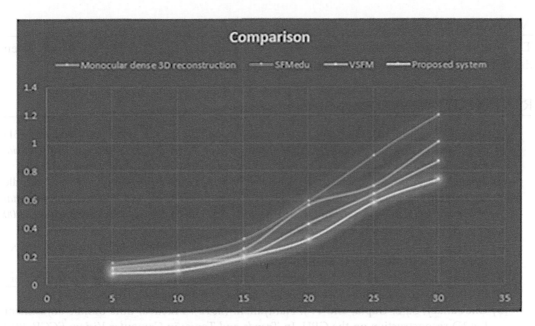

FIGURE 4.10 Comparison of the durations of the current and proposed systems.

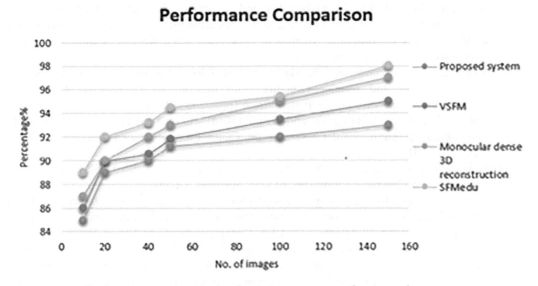

FIGURE 4.11 Performance comparison of existing systems and proposed system.

4.6 CONCLUSION

This chapter introduces a reconstruction system that improves key challenges identified when using existing 3D reconstruction methodologies. The system increases the quality of the 3D model and decreases the response time of 3D reconstruction. The 3D model produced by the new system is more dense and more complete than the existing systems. However, work is required to further reduce computation time. Moreover, in cases where input images contain distortion, this can lead to inappropriate 3D models.

ACKNOWLEDGMENTS

The authors' home institutions have expressed their gratitude for the assistance given during the collaborative work mentioned in the publication.

REFERENCES

[1] Wu, P., Y. Liu, M. Ye, and J. Li. (2016, September 22). Fast and adaptive 3D reconstruction with extensively high completeness. *IEEE Transactions on Multimedia*, 19(2): 266–278.

[2] Triggs B., P. F. McLauchlan, R. I. Hartley, and A. W. Fitzgibbon. (1999). Bundle adjustment—A modern synthesis. In *Vision Algorithms: Theory and Practice: International Workshop on Vision Algorithms Corfu, Greece, September 21–22, 1999 Proceedings 2000* (pp. 298–372). Springer, Berlin, Heidelberg.

[3] Snavely, N., S. M. Seitz, and R. Szeliski. (2006). Photo tourism: Exploring photo collections in 3D. In *ACM Siggraph 2006 Papers* (pp. 835–846).

[4] Snavely, N., S. M. Seitz, and R. Szeliski. (2008, November 1). Modeling the world from internet photo collections. *International Journal of Computer Vision*, 80(2): 189–210.

[5] Choudhary, S., S. Gupta, and P. J. Narayanan. (2012). Practical time bundle adjustment for 3D reconstruction on the GPU. In *Trends and Topics in Computer Vision: ECCV 2010 Workshops, Heraklion, Crete, Greece, September 10–11, 2010, Revised Selected Papers, Part II 11* (pp. 423–435). Springer, Berlin, Heidelberg.

[6] Zachareka, M., P. Delisa, M. Kedzierskia, and A. Fryskowskaa. (2017). Generating accurate 3D models of architectural heritage structures using low-cost camera and open source algorithms. *The International Archives of Photogrammetry, Remote Sensing and Spatial Information Sciences*, 42: 99.

[7] Moulon, P., P. Monasse, and R. Marlet. (2013). Global fusion of relative motions for robust, accurate and scalable structure from motion. In *Proceedings of the IEEE International Conference on Computer Vision* (pp. 3248–3255).

[8] Gao, Y., L. Jianxin, Q. Hangping, and W. Bo. (2014). Survey of structure from motion. In *Proceedings of International Conference on Cloud Computing and Internet of Things* (pp. 72–76). IEEE.

[9] Wilson, K., and N. Snavely. (2014). Robust global translations with 1DSfM. In *European Conference on Computer Vision* (pp. 61–75). Springer, Cham.

[10] Zach, C. (2008). Fast and high-quality fusion of depth maps. In *Proceedings of the International Symposium on 3D Data Processing, Visualisation and Transmission (3DPVT)*, vol. 1, no. 2, Atlanta, GA, USA: Georgia Institute of Technology.

[11] Luo, Z., T. Shen, L. Zhou, S. Zhu, R. Zhang, Y. Yao, T. Fang, and L. Quan. (2018). GeoDesc: Learning local descriptors by integrating geometry constraints. In *Proceeding of the European Conference on Computer Vision (ECCV)* (pp. 168–183).

[12] Kordelas, G., J. P. M. Agapito, J. V. Hernandez, and P. Daras. (2010). State-of-the-art algorithms for complete 3D model reconstruction. "Engage" summer school. In *Proceedings of the Engage Summer School* (p. 115, vol. 1315). Zermatt, Switzerland.

[13] Zollhöfer, M., M. Nießner, S. Izadi, C. Rehmann, C. Zach, M. Fisher, C. Wu, A. Fitzgibbon, C. Loop, C. Theobalt, and M. Stamminger. (2014 July 27). Real-time non-rigid reconstruction using an RGB-D camera. *ACM Transactions on Graphics (ToG)*, 33(4): 1–2.

[14] Gherardi, R., M. Farenzena, and A. Fusiello. (2010, June 13). Improving the efficiency of hierarchical structure-and-motion. In *2010 IEEE Computer Society Conference on Computer Vision and Pattern Recognition* (pp. 1594–1600). IEEE.

[15] Cui, H., S. Shen, W. Gao, and Z. Hu. (2015). *Fusion of auxiliary imaging information for robust, scalable and fast 3D reconstruction.* Springer.

[16] Aamir, M., Y. F. Pu, Z. Rahman, W. A. Abro, H. Naeem, F. Ullah, and A. M. Badr. (2018). A hybrid proposed framework for object detection and classification. *Journal of Information Processing Systems,* 14(5): 1176–1194.

[17] Aamir, M., Z. Rahman, Y. F. Pu, W. A. Abro, and K. Gulzar. (2019). Satellite image enhancement using wavelet-domain based on singular value decomposition. *International Journal of Advanced Computer Science and Applications,* 10(6).

[18] Aamir, M., Y. F. Pu, Z. Rahman, M. Tahir, H. Naeem, and Q. Dai. (2018, December 21). A framework for automatic building detection from low-contrast satellite images. *Symmetry,* 11(1): 3.

[19] Aamir, M., Z. Rahman, Z. A. Dayo, W. A. Abro, M. I. Uddin, I. Khan, A. S. Imran, Z. Ali, M. Ishfaq, Y. Guan, Z. Hu. (2022, July 1). A deep learning approach for brain tumor classification using MRI images. *Computers and Electrical Engineering,* 101: 108105.

## CHAPTER 5

Deep Learning Algorithms and Architectures for Multimodal Data Analysis

Anwar Ali Sathio[1,2], Muhammad Malook Rind[2], and Abdullah Lakhan[3]

[1]*Department of CS&IT, Benazir Bhutto Shaheed University, Karachi, Sindh, Pakistan*
[2]*Department of Computer Science, Sindh Madressatul Islam University, Karachi, Sindh, Pakistan*
[3]*Department of Cyber Security, Dawood University of Engineering and Technology, Karachi, Sindh, Pakistan*

5.1 INTRODUCTION TO MULTIMODAL DATA ANALYSIS

Multimodal data refers to data represented in multiple modes, such as text, speech, images, and videos. Each method provides a different perspective or piece of information about the data and, when analyzed together, can provide a more comprehensive understanding of the phenomenon being studied. Multimodal data analysis has roots in several disciplines, including linguistics, psychology, and computer science. Over the years of evolution, new technologies emerged and recognized the potential benefits of combining data from various sources. Today, multimodal data analysis using deep learning is used in multiple fields [1,2], including healthcare, education, and social sciences. Multimodal data analysis poses several challenges, dealing with missing data and managing large data sets, such as the need for sophisticated tools. And the different schemes used to integrate and analyze data from various sources. However, multimodal data analysis is applied for many applications [3,4] to gain insights into complex situations, make more accurate predictions, and identify patterns.

Common applications of multimodal data analysis: following are the multimodal data analysis application areas:

- **Healthcare:** analyzing patient data from multiple sources to make better diagnoses and treatment decisions.

DOI: 10.1201/9781032646268-5

- **Education:** analyzing student data from multiple sources to improve learning outcomes.

- **Social sciences:** analyzing data from social media, interviews, and surveys to gain insights into human behavior.

- **Robotics:** analyzing sensor data from multiple sources to improve robot performance and decision making [4–6].

- **Marketing:** analyzing customer data from multiple sources to identify patterns and trends and make better marketing decisions.

Multimodal data analysis techniques use various methods for different problem solutions; such problems may be data fusion, machine learning, and natural language processing. The data fusion integrates data from multiple sources (image, text, etc.) into a single data set. Where machine learning algorithms training analyzes the data to make predictions, in natural language processing, we may use it to analyze and process the natural language data. We can reduce ethical concerns by getting permission for personal data protection when operating for analysis purposes, applying proper references, and formal permission procedures.

Future directions and trends in multimodal data analysis: we know that technology will not stop advancing; there are possibilities to expand the analysis techniques. Emerging trends like augmented and virtual reality, wearable devices' data, and deep learning techniques are in the market so analysis methods will remain in the research domains [1,5]. This is why the research field has a good potential to develop as a multimodal data analysis tool. That is why it is expanding and accessible to everyone, including general users, experts, educators, and professionals.

5.2 OVERVIEW OF DEEP LEARNING ALGORITHMS AND ARCHITECTURES

Deep learning, the subclass of machine learning, benefits classifications. Clustering can be defined as "a subclass of machine learning using artificial neural networks (ANNs) to understand and discover the hidden patterns from complex data sets." Deep learning has two primary areas: 1) neural networks (multiple layers) and 2) significant data volumes with complex issues. As we know, deep learning is a subclass of machine learning that concentrates on developing algorithms and can learn from big, complex data [4,7]. In deep learning, we build ANNs independently without explicit programming for the best outcomes. Figure 5.1 shows the area specification of deep learning [8,9]. Deep learning models are layered modeling in which interconnected nodes process and transform data to produce the best results. The deep model is vital in classifying and clustering supervised learning research fields. Such applications included computer vision, NLP, and speech recognition. We can achieve a state-of-the-art performance – with some popular deep learning frameworks when using Python libraries: TensorFlow, PyTorch, and Keras. Following are the various types of ANNs; we describe these in detail to understand the functionalities of multiple models [5,10].

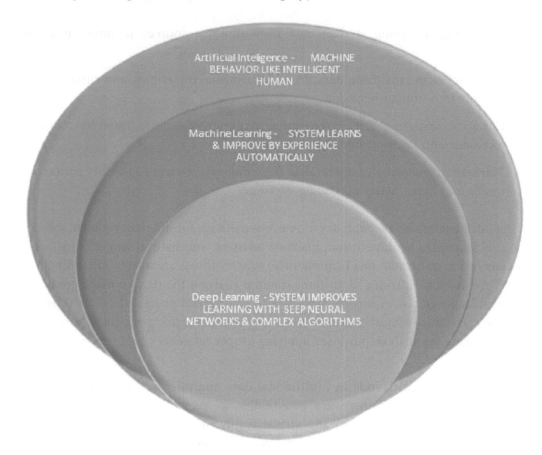

FIGURE 5.1   Shows deep learning and AI association.

A. Types of neural networks

Deep learning is nothing but a concept of supervised learning, as ANNs are the basic architecture of neural networks and have many types, each having unique architecture and purposes. The three commonly used ANNs model architectures are as follows:

1. **The Convolutional Neural Networks (CNNs):** the CNNs are a subtype of ANNs, networks designed for image processing to analyze the images and various grid-like data. Layers perform convolution operations by the CNN model and extract the features from input data sources. In the CNNs, we apply for classification and clustering data cases specially designed for image and video recognition success-fully. Figure 5.2 shows the architecture of a CNN [11–13].

2. **The Recurrent Neural Networks (RNNs):** in the RNNs, we see the connections between nodes forming a loop, which allows feedback and memory concepts in the networks. When dealing with sequential data, the RNNs are a better option for various applications like language modeling and speech recognition. Figure 5.3 shows the architecture of RNN [14].

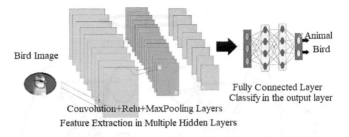

FIGURE 5.2   Shows the architecture of CNN.

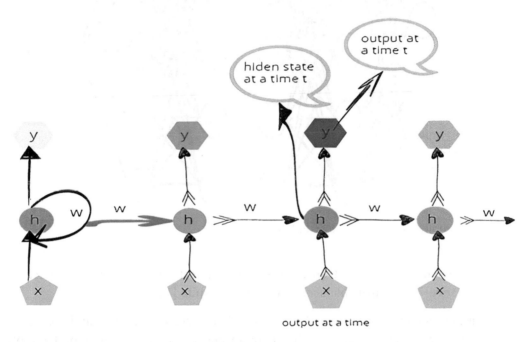

FIGURE 5.3   Shows the architecture of RNN.

3. **The Feedforward Neural Networks (FFNN):** the FFNN is a network of various layers with interconnected nodes. In model processing, it receives input from the previous layer and only sends its output to the next layer. The FFNNs are such types of models that help to solve classification and regression problems. Figure 5.4 shows the architecture of FFNN [15].

The field of deep learning is still an emerging topic of research, so many other types of deep neural networks are also very effective. Each type of network has its potential strength and weaknesses and is suitable for various problem solutions. Every kind of neural network has several categories; some are critical and listed below:

1. **AlexNet** – its ANN model was introduced by Alex Krizhevsky, Ilya Sutskever, and Geoffrey Hinton in 2012; eight layers in the proposed model, composed of five convolutional layers and three fully connected layers for processing. Initially, the

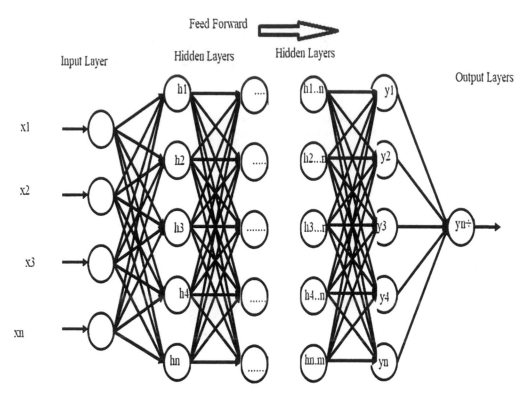

FIGURE 5.4 Shows the architecture of FFNN.

AlexNet model was used on a large-scale data set and got state-of-the-art performances at a reasonable accuracy ratio in results [16].

2. **An autoencoder** – is also an ANN model that learns to compress and reconstruct data. The model autoencoder has two: an encoder and a decoder part for processing data. In the encoder part, the model takes the input and compresses it into a lower-dimensional image. In contrast, the decoder takes the compressed representation and reconstructs the original data of images or various data types in the other part. These network models usually are used to compress and reduce the dimensionality of the data [17].

3. **A bidirectional recurrent neural network (BRNN)** – is a type of ANN that processes the sequential data types only to forward and backward directions. BRNN network captures all inputs (past/future) contextual information, making it useful for speech recognition and NLP problems [18,19].

4. **A deep belief network (DBN)** – the DBNs are ANNs consisting of numerous layers of restricted Boltzmann machines (RBMs), each layer able to learn compression of input data, which is then to be used as input for the next layer in the model. The model of DBNs is designed for unsupervised machine learning goals with the ability of clustering and feature extraction from given data.

5. **A gated recurrent unit (GRU)** – is a type of RNN; it is beneficial to sequential data processing. GRU models use a gating mechanism to update and forget last-time step data, which also allows capturing long-term dependencies in the input data processing [20,21].

6. **Inception model** – it is the CNN model to reduce the dimensionality with 1×1 convolutions introduced in 205. In this scheme, various parallel convolutional layers accomplished varying filter sizes, which allowed extracting features at different scales. The inception model also reduces the number of parameters and improves computational efficiency in the dimensionality reduction process [22].

7. **LeNet – family (LeNet-1, LeNet-4, LeNet-5)** – is the LeNet model Yann LeCun introduced, a type of CNN architecture in the 1990s. LeNet model architecture has various convolutional and subsampling layers, followed by one or more fully connected layers. The LeNet model can achieve good results on handwritten digit recognition tasks, and its design has influenced many subsequent CNN architectures [14,23].

8. **Long short-term memory (LSTM)** – LSTM model is an RNN architecture that addresses the vanishing gradient problem in standard RNN model processing during backpropagation. The LSTM model was introduced by Hochreiter and Schmidhuber in 1997; it has an additional memory cell that allows them to maintain information over a long time. That property of the LSTM model makes it ideal for many applications like speech recognition, language translation, image captioning, etc. [24].

9. **Multi-layer perceptron (MLP)** – the MLP model is an FFNN with many layers of perceptron; each perceptron computes a weighted sum of its inputs and applies a non-linear activation function to produce its output in the hidden layers. The MLP models are commonly used in different applications of pattern recognition, image processing, and speech recognition [25,26].

10. **Residual network (ResNet)** – ResNet model is a deep learning ANN architecture introduced in 2015 and addresses the problem of vanishing gradients by submitting residual connections. In the model's connections, it allows the network to skip over layers and pass information directly to later layers so that the model possibly trains intense networks with hundreds of layers in processing complex data [27,28].

11. **Restricted Boltzmann machines (RBMs)** – are generative ANN architectures of a visible and hidden layer. The model learns a probability distribution over the input data and can be used for dimensionality reduction, feature learning, collaborative filtering, etc. The RBM architectural model gets training by the mechanism of a contrastive divergence algorithm [29,30].

12. **Visual geometry group (VGG)** – the VGG is a CNN architecture introduced by Simonyan and Zisserman in 2005. The VGG model has multiple layers with 3×3

TABLE 5.1   Comparative Analysis for Gaps Identifications of the Various Deep Neural Network Algorithms

Deep learning algorithms	Architectures used	Components	References
Convolutional Neural Network (CNN)	Feature extraction by convolutional layers.	Consists of convolutional pooling and fully connected layers.	[11]
Recurrent Neural Network (RNN)	Process sequential data.	Consists of recurrent and fully connected layers.	[14]
Autoencoder	Learns a compressed representation of input data.	Encoder network, decoder network.	[32]
Deep Belief Network (DBN)	To learn hierarchical representations of input data.	RBMs, fully connected layers.	[33,34]
Restricted Boltzmann Machine (RBM)	A generative model seeks a compressed representation of input data.	Visible units, hidden units.	[29]
Variational Autoencoder (VAE)	Uses a probabilistic encoder and decoder – to improve the capability of learning for input data.	Encoder network, decoder network, latent space.	[35]
Generative Adversarial Network (GAN)	A generator, and a discriminator, to learn a compressed input data representation.	Generator network, discriminator network.	[36]
Multimodal Deep Embedded Clustering (MDEC)	A clustering algorithm that can be used for multimodal data analysis.	Encoder network, clustering layer, modality-specific branches.	[3,37]
Deep Convolutional Embedded Clustering (DCEC)	Type of DCNN gets to learn from a compressed representation of input data.	Convolutional layers, pooling layers, clustering layer.	[32,38]

convolutional filters, extended by max pooling and fully connected layers. The VGG model is primarily known for image classification due to its high accuracy ratio and perfect feature extraction in many computer vision applications. The VGG model has two numerous variant models, i.e., VGG16 and VGG19, for the classification of images [31]. The comprehensive detailed survey has been added for deep neural network algorithms with components in Table 5.1.

5.2.1 Pre-Processing of the Multimodal Data

The method of pre-processing for multimodal data has several steps to ensure the data is adequately prepared for usage to test the models in deep learning's neural networks [39]. In the initial processing mechanism of any deep learning model, first, we must clean the data by removing noise. Secondly, normalize the data to ensure that all data features remain on the same scaling pattern. Moreover, in the feature extraction process, we must transform the data into suitable data presentation in a network. In feature extraction, we apply principal component analysis (PCA) or independent component analysis (ICA) to analyze the data. After the initial stage, we split the data set into training and testing sets, pre-processing to evaluate the model accuracy [40].

A. Data cleaning and pre-processing

In the deep learning architecture, we must remove any noise or irrelevant data from the data set before getting model processing and preparing it for further evaluation model analysis process. The deep model processing assures the data normalization, feature scaling, and outlier removal so that the data shall be clean and consistent for further processing of the data modalities.

B. Feature extraction and representation for each modality

In deep neural networks, feature extraction is essential, and it involves identifying relevant features from the raw data. And feature representation consists of encoding the features in a useful way for machine learning algorithms. We must extract features for various data models separately, such as image features extracted through CNNs models [41]. At the same time, text can be represented using word embeddings or bag-of-words representations.

In deep neural architectures, we can measure the features by two factors, one is PCA, and the other is ICA; these are explained below.

- **Principal Component Analysis (PCA)**

  The feature extraction and dimensionality reduction analysis method is PCA, which is generally used to get model performance analysis. The PCA transforms the data into a new coordinate system where each successive dimension captures the maximum variance. The PCA method reduces features to retain most of the original information, allowing the model to get more efficient and practical training.

- **Independent Component Analysis (ICA)**

  The ICA separates the multidimensional signal into independent, non-Gaussian components. The ICA method uses pre-processing to extract relevant features from the multimodal data (audio and video signals or text and image data). The ICA method is very useful for extracting statistically independent components with a more meaningful interpretation of the data [42–44]. The ICA is empirically applied to each modality separately or combines data to extract elements of the essential features. These elements positively impact a neural network, where it learns more efficiently for data representations. ICA is a valuable tool for pre-processing multimodal data in deep neural networks.

C. Techniques for combining multiple modalities

In the deep neural networks' architecture, these techniques combine multiple modalities, which may be classified into early, late, and hybrid fusion. The subclass of early fusion combines the raw data from different modalities into a single set. Second, late fusion involves learning other representations for each modality that are combined later. The last one is hybrid fusion, which combines both schemes early in the pipeline process. These techniques are effective for better performance of various models' data representations, such as multimodal autoencoders or deep neural networks.

5.2.2 The Training Process of Deep Learning Models on Multimodal Data

A. Training process

In the deep neural networks model, the training process has the following steps for training a custom-build model:

a. **Data pre-processing:** in this process, we must get the alignment and the same format; more consists of stages like data cleaning, normalization, and feature extraction for data analysis.

b. **Model selection:** the important aspect of deep learning is to select an appropriate model to handle the data, as we know that the CNNs model is adequate for images, the RNNs model is helpful for sequential data, and transformers well for text data separately [45–47].

c. **Model architecture:** it's directly related to the data types and the problem's complexity; designing the model's architecture according to given data models is not easy. First, specify the number of layers required, then choose the size of the hidden layers, then select the activation function to apply in the selected deep neural model; it shall complete the whole process.

d. **Model training:** when we finalize the model architecture, we train the model using multimodal data. In that process, first, we define what loss function to be applied and then optimize the modeled algorithm by minimizing the loss function. We minimize the loss function by updating the model parameters through an iterative procedure in the model training process.

e. **Model evaluation:** in the deep neural model evaluation, we can evaluate after the assessment of the model at both phases, training and testing the model separately with many metrics like accuracy, precision, recall, confusion matrix, and F1-score.

f. **Fine-tuning:** we usually face many problems when using complex data; we can solve these issues when model evaluation results are unsatisfactory. Then we can adjust the hyperparameters again and again. If results remain unchanged or unsatisfactory, then we must retry another deep model architecture until successful, satisfactory results.

g. **Deployment:** we can deploy only the model by getting a comparative analysis of the model results to solve real-world problems.

B. Training strategies for multimodal data

As explained below, several training strategies can be employed when training deep learning models on multimodal data, including joint, parallel, and serial training.

1. **Joint Training:** in this training approach, all modalities are combined into a single model, which then trains by a single loss function. We get effective results when the data modalities remain highly correlated and contain complementary information.

2. **Parallel Training:** in this training approach, we train models separately for each modality and get outputs combinedly with these models for predictions. This model training approach is only effective when we have modalities with relatively independent and different statistical properties.

3. **Serial Training:** in this training approach, we use one modality to be applied for pre-train processing, and afterward, other modalities are incorporated into the model for fine-tuning. This model training approach will be effective only when one modality contains more information than the others or has different time scales.

C. Regularization techniques

In deep models, regularization techniques are essential for preventing overfitting data issues. And this can improve the model performance; two main regularization techniques are mentioned below.

1. **Dropout:** this technique can be used during the model training phase; some neurons drop out randomly by process, which helps prevent overfitting by forcing the network to learn more robust representations.

2. **Batch normalization:** in the technique, we normalize the inputs to each layer and get optimization of the network more stable mode. It can also reduce overfitting by preventing internal covariate shifts.

D. Hyperparameter tuning

The concept of hyperparameter tuning, in which we select the optimal values; various techniques to achieve this need grid search, random search, and Bayesian optimization methods. In the hyperparameters tuning model, we must focus on the learning rate, batch size, and the number of hidden layers essential for fine-tuning. It's important to tune these hyperparameters carefully, as they impact the model's performance directly.

5.2.3 Deep Learning Methods and Blockchain Technology Consortium

Blockchain technology has been a trendy research topic in recent years. Blockchain is a distributed ledger technology useful for secure and transparent data transactions removing the role of intermediaries. The combination of these two technologies has the potential impact. It makes a powerful tool for various current applications in the sectors such as finance, healthcare, automation, pervasive computing fields, and logistics [48,49]. We explore the role of deep learning methods and blockchain technology in the existing frameworks for multimodal data analysis and problem solutions [7,50]. A blockchain technology consortium is a group of organizations working to create a shared blockchain infrastructure. The organizations relate to different industries and fields of interest, and their collaboration leads to contributing innovations. The cooperation of deep learning methods enhances blockchain technologies' capabilities by enabling better data analysis, prediction, and decision-making support in many applications to secure transactional data processing [51,52].

One potential application of deep learning with blockchain technology is fraud detection and mitigation. Deep learning's trained models must detect patterns in large data sets and identify fraudulent global transactions. Deep learning and blockchain technology are very effective methodologies to get better results of the transparency and immutability to notify the fraudulent activities identification and prevention in real time. The world will be a global village due to the usage of the Internet; business communications increase day by day, and these collaborative frameworks are helpful in the financial and business industry, where fraud is a significant threat to every transaction. The second potential application of deep learning in a blockchain technology consortium is an increase in supply chain [7,53] management systems globally. Deep learning algorithms can analyze data from various sources, including IoT-based systems, and provide real-time insights into data transactions in the supply chain systems. These frameworks will help identify inefficiencies, predict demand, and improve logistics management systems. The transparency of blockchain can also provide traceability of products throughout the supply chain, ensuring that these products are good sources ethically and sustainably. Deep learning can also be used with blockchain frameworks to improve healthcare systems by analyzing large data sets to identify patterns and predict health outcomes trustfully. The use of blockchain can ensure the privacy and security of patient data while providing a transparent and immutable record of medical procedures and results. Integrating deep learning methods and blockchain technology frameworks has the great potential to create a powerful tool for various global-level distributed applications in multiple sectors. In the future, as these collaborative frameworks and technologies continue to evolve, we expect to see more innovative applications that leverage their combined potential in broad fields.

A. Deep learning interoperability with blockchain technology

Blockchain technology is distributed and already capable of interoperability mechanisms with heterogeneous environments. Interoperability is a critical factor in integrating different technologies in the case of deep learning and blockchain technology, which refers to the ability of these two technologies to get together seamlessly for transaction data processing subject areas. Deep learning can enhance the capabilities of blockchain technology by providing better data analysis and prediction. The interoperability mechanism between deep learning and blockchain technology can be achieved through smart contracts. Smart contracts are self-executing contracts with the terms of the agreement between two parties being directly written into code for building trust and transparency by all means [7]. They can be used to facilitate and verify the negotiation and performance of a contract. In the case of heterogeneous environments, smart contracts can be used to automate the processing of data analysis and predictions to optimize the running of systems smoothly. Smart contract codes are easy to program and execute deep learning algorithms on a blockchain network. This enables the data to be analyzed securely and the results to be stored on the blockchain immutable and transparently for future usage. It will help the business and ensure processing secure and tamper-proof design. Additionally, smart contracts can be used to ensure that the results of the deep learning process are only accessible to authorized parties in the networks. Adapting these technologies' collaborative work will enhance a great level performances of the network systems globally, and also, we can expect to see more innovations with combined potential works.

B. Deep learning and cross-border blockchain technology frameworks

The blockchain is now moving towards emerging models like the cross-border mechanism to maximize the usage of the technology in heterogeneous environments where transactions may involve a range of complexities, including multiple intermediaries, varying regulations, and currency conversions. Cross-border blockchain technology is a peer-to-peer (P2P) mechanism with the potential for cross-border transactional data. It provides a secure and transparent platform for peer-to-peer transactions in homo- and hetero-geneous network systems. The collaborative work of deep learning and cross-border blockchain systems can enhance the capabilities of better data analysis and prediction. The model of this paradigm will be very popular because Internet businesses shall be trendy and capture the whole market and business hubs. Therefore, we see the future of these collaboration applications. The blockchain has the string security and immutability mechanism where deep learning algorithms will enhance the optimization, predictions, and data analysis well. The ANNs shall play a vital role as agent-based systems to help the cross-border blockchain remove the role of intermediaries to establish the P2P connections for fast transactions between two nodes or devices in a heterogeneous environment. The deep ANN models can be trained for cross-border transactions to analyze vast amounts of data, including financial data, social media data, and other relevant information. This information helps to get better performance of the models to identify patterns, predict outcomes, and decision making. We use the collaborative mechanism for analyzing data related to exchange rates, political instability, and trade policies to predict the impact on cross-border transactions. We can establish cross-border frameworks through smart contracts that automate cross-border transactions, eliminating the need for intermediaries and reducing transaction costs. These frameworks are decentralized to exchange the data or amount that enables cross-border transactions without currency conversions. Today, political systems around the globe have been facing a lot of terrorism schemes; we can apply it to remove the two factors: trust and authenticity of the legal works. For example, one potential application of deep learning in cross-border blockchain technology (CBBT) is anti-money laundering (AML) compliance; it helps prevent illicit activities and ensure compliance with regulations locally and internationally.

C. Applications of deep cross-border blockchain technologies

Many applications exist globally that present the scope of the deep cross-border block-chain technologies (DCBBT); some of them we have stated below.

1. **E-commerce business:** DCBBT mechanism is a very effective and efficient system to handle big data and secure transactions. In cross-border communication, we observe different modes, such as business-to-business (B2B), business-to-consumer (B2C), and consumer-to-consumer (C2C) business models [54,55].

2. **Supply chain management:** DCBBT helps create a transparent and secure supply chain network and enables stakeholders to track the movement of goods, reduce fraud, improve efficiency, etc. Deep algorithms can analyze logistics, transportation, and inventory systems data for better decisions [56].

3. **Healthcare:** in the healthcare systems, health-related records are vital in all dimensions, such as patients' electronic health records and management's databases. The DCBBT helps create a secure, transparent healthcare network in heterogeneous cross-border environments. DCBBT enables patients to access their medical records securely, reducing the risk of data breaches, and can utilize the data everywhere globally. And, deep learning algorithms are very effective in analyzing medical data, enabling better diagnosis and treatment [50,56–58].

4. **Finance:** the concept of DCBBT basically relates to financial sectors, where we need more security and trust for transactions. The DCBBT enables P2P network transaction systems to cut off the middleman's role to reduce overall costs. The consortium of the DCBBT model helps analyze financial data and enables better risk management and investment decisions globally [53,55].

5. **Real estate:** DCBBT also plays a vital role in creating a secure and transparent real estate network system. DCBBT enables stakeholders to track property ownership and transfer, reducing fraudulent documentation. DCBBT model helps to analyze real estate data, enabling better pricing and supporting elements for decisions.

6. **Voting:** DCBBT helps create a secure and transparent voting system using neural networks. It enables voters to cast their votes securely, reducing the risk of fraud, and can also be used to analyze voting data for better decision making.

DCBBT has a wide range of applications across different industries; such applications leverage the capabilities of collaborative works with deep learning and blockchain technology to create secure and transparent networks for better decision making.

D. Deep learning and cross-border blockchain integration

The integration of deep learning and cross-border blockchain technology can revolutionize various businesses and industries through secure and transparent networks; see

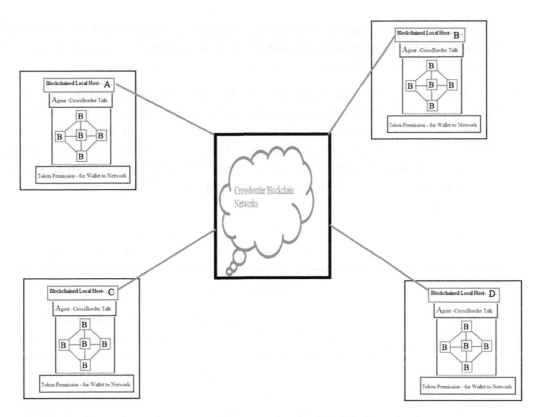

FIGURE 5.5   Shows the architecture of the cross-border blockchain technology.

the architecture in Figure 5.5. It automates complex processing and provides data insights through data analysis tools. This integration offers several benefits, including enhanced data security, automation of complex processes, handling of big data, cumulative decision making, and enabled network intelligence. Deep learning and blockchain technology offer several benefits, including enhanced data security, automation of complex processes, handling of big data, cumulative decision making, and enabled network intelligence. Technologies continue to emerge we see more innovative applications come from their combined potential networks.

The following are some examples to describe the vital role of the various applications of deep learning in multimodal data:

- **Speech recognition:** it is a very vital application that has been used in today's applications, such as Google assistants and artificial intelligence-based APIs in many search engines, to handle communications problems. The multimodal deep learning techniques enhance the speech recognition systems' accuracy by combining audio and visual data, such as lip movements, gestures, facial movements, and facial expressions, to get the input source for analysis [59].

- **Image data acquisitions:** it has an efficient impact in the field of automation and robotics to get the image data to transform into information with multimodal deep learning; we generate natural language descriptions of images by combining visual features with language models, gesture extractions, face expressions in videos, and identifying the objects from a list of unidentified data objects [60], etc.

- **Healthcare:** we know that health-related data are multimodal types, and deep learning can play a vital role in enhancing the accuracy of results. These collaborations may keep electronic health records (EHRs) safe and useable for future purposes in many healthcare applications. These applications effectively impact human health and economic effects when we use them in various sectors, such as diagnosis and treatment planning, by combining medical images, patient records, and other data sources [50].

- **Autonomous driving:** the world's future is trending toward automation and robotics, so multimodal data with deep learning plays a vital role in enhancing accuracy and overall performance. Many autonomous driving applications combining visual, lidar, and radar data will improve object detection and tracking [32,61].

- **Show and tell:** in 2015, introduced an image-captioning system. Its deep multimodal learning architecture combines CNN with the LSTM network to generate the lexical semantic data to describe the images. CNN is useful for feature image extractions, whereas the LSTM technique is very effective for generating text sentences from images like object character recognition (OCR). The system used a large data set of image-caption pairs with parameters BLEU and METEOR for performance analysis [59].

- **Speech2Face:** a system presented in 2019 using CNN and RNN, it takes an input speech signal to generate a facial image of the speaker. CNN is a specialized technique to extract features from any data. The RNN is a very effective method to generate a sequence of facial features from given speech signal data. Speech2Face application proved its potential performance power over other applications in virtual assistants, live communications, etc. [20,36,62].

- **Neural machine translation (NMT):** a system introduced by Sutskever et al. (2014); they combine RNN and an attention mechanism to handle the problem solutions for language translations as an interpreter. The RNN technique of deep learning applies to encode the input sentence into a fixed-length vector. In contrast, the attention mechanism aligns the input sentence with the output sentence for translations of sentences. This application has been applied in many online translating tools today [63–65].

- **ChatGPT-4 multimodal transformation model:** ChatGPT-4 is an artificial intelligence chatbot released by openai.com; many other vendors like Microsoft released the versions [66,67].

- **Google multimodal neural machine translation:** Google developed application systems combining CNN for impressions and RNN for decoding text with images with high accuracy in Google assistants (APIs) [63].

- **Microsoft emotion recognition:** Microsoft also developed an emotion recognition system that uses deep learning techniques (CNN and RNN collaborate to process the audio-visual data processing models) to recognize facial expressions and speech patterns in the tool [20].

- **Brain2Pix:** in the Brain2Pix, MIT researchers use the deep learning method GAN with EEG data to generate images from brain signals to generate the images data for mental health analysis [68], [69].

- **Facebook multimodal word embeddings:** Facebook developed a multimodal word embedding system by CNN and RNN, which combines various data inputs such as text, images, and audio to generate more accurate word embeddings by applying the models combinedly [60].

1. Hands-On Practice

We can understand the deep learning architectures with various model implementations for hands-on practice with Python, which will help users understand better. The following implementation deep models in Python tool 3.0 are to be tested with any platform such as Anaconda, ipython, Jupiter or VS code, etc. To get started with Python practice, we need to have some basic knowledge of Python programming and be familiar with deep learning Python tools such as TensorFlow, Keras, PyTorch, etc.

The following are the steps we must follow to start practicing with Python for deep learning models:

1. Set up your environment – in Python, we need to set up your environment by installing Python and the necessary deep learning libraries such as TensorFlow, Keras, and PyTorch.

2. Choose a data set – after environmental setup in Python 3.0 and above version, we need to choose a standard and open-sourced data set and work with the deep learning models publicly available through Internet sources such as Kaggle, UCI repositories, etc.

3. Before starting the model training, we must pre-process the data, such as resizing images, normalizing pixel values, extracting audio features, etc. Many Python libraries like OpenCV can also do this processing for images, etc., which can also be installed in the setup.

4. Build a deep learning model – after the pre-processing step, we have to build a deep learning model; as every model has a specific area task and data set, we choose a particular type of model such as CNN for image classification, RNN for sequence prediction, etc. Many tutorials and examples are available online on websites such as GitHub for building deep learning models in Python using libraries such as TensorFlow, Keras, and PyTorch.

5. Train and evaluate the model – after building the deep learning custom model for a specific task, we must train it on pre-processed data. This we achieve typically by splitting data into training and validation data sets and using backpropagation to update the model parameters. Then we evaluate the model performance on training and testing data sets separately with metrics, such as accuracy or mean squared error, confusion metrics, etc.

6. Fine-tune and optimize the model – after getting a custom-built model, we can fine-tune and optimize it for better performance by adding or removing some hyperparameters, such as learning rate or regularization strength, or using techniques such as transfer learning to leverage pre-trained models.

With the right tools and techniques, Python can be a powerful tool for working with multimodal data and developing advanced deep learning models in diversified applications.

We added the following critical implementations of different deep learning models in Python for getting started and better understanding:

A. CNN deep learning model using Python with Keras library

```
# First, we will import the necessary libraries:
import numpy as np
import tensorflow as tf
from tensorflow import keras
from sklearn.metrics import confusion_matrix, f1_score

# Next, we will load the dataset and split it into training and testing sets:

# Load dataset
# X_train and X_test should be numpy arrays containing the images
# y_train and y_test should be numpy arrays containing the corresponding labels
X_train, y_train = ...
X_test, y_test = ...

# Normalize pixel values to be between 0 and 1
X_train = X_train / 255.0
X_test = X_test / 255.0

# Split training set into training and validation sets
# This will be used for early stopping during training
X_train, X_val = X_train[:-1000], X_train[-1000:]
y_train, y_val = y_train[:-1000], y_train[-1000:]

# Next, we will define the CNN model:
```

```
# Define the model
  model = keras.models.Sequential ([
    keras.layers.Conv2D(32, (3, 3), activation='relu', input_shape=X_train.shape[1:]),
    keras.layers.MaxPooling2D((2, 2)),
    keras.layers.Conv2D(64, (3, 3), activation='relu'),
    keras.layers.MaxPooling2D((2, 2)),
    keras.layers.Conv2D(128, (3, 3), activation='relu'),
    keras.layers.MaxPooling2D((2, 2)),
    keras.layers.Flatten(),
    keras.layers.Dense(64, activation='relu'),
    keras.layers.Dense(10, activation='softmax')])

# Compile the model
model.compile(optimizer='adam',
        loss='sparse_categorical_crossentropy',
        metrics=['accuracy'])

# Next, we will train the model and use early stopping to prevent overfitting:

# Train the model
history = model.fit(X_train, y_train, epochs=10, batch_size=32,
            validation_data=(X_val, y_val),
            callbacks=[keras.callbacks.EarlyStopping(patience=3)])

# After training, we can evaluate the model on the testing set:
# Evaluate the model on the testing set
test_loss, test_acc = model.evaluate(X_test, y_test)

# Print the testing accuracy
print('Testing accuracy:', test_acc)

# We can also calculate the confusion matrix and F1 score:
# Predict the labels for the testing set
y_pred = model.predict(X_test)
y_pred = np.argmax(y_pred, axis=1)

# Calculate the confusion matrix
cm = confusion_matrix(y_test, y_pred)
print('Confusion matrix:')
print(cm)

# Calculate the F1 score
f1 = f1_score(y_test, y_pred, average='weighted')
print('F1 score:', f1)
```

In this example, we are building a CNN model for binary classification using the Keras Sequential API.

1. We start by defining the input shape of our data, which is 224 × 224 RGB images.

2. We then add two convolutional layers with 32 and 64 filters, each followed by a max pooling layer.

3. The output of the convolutional layers is flattened and passed through a fully connected layer with 128 units and a ReLU activation function.

4. We add a dropout layer for regularization and an output layer with a sigmoid activation function for binary classification.

5. To train the model, we use the appropriate method of the model object, passing in our training and validation data, along with the number of epochs and batch size for training. In this example, x_train and x_test are NumPy arrays containing our image data, and y_train and y_test are NumPy arrays containing the corresponding labels (0 or 1).

6. Before training the model, we must pre-process data and load it into these arrays. This is a simple CNN deep learning model; the specific architecture and hyperparameters we choose will depend on our task and data set. We may experiment with different architectures and hyperparameters to achieve the required performance.

B. Implementation of a primary convolutional neural network (CNN-VGG16, VGG19, ResNet50) model with detailed features

```
# CNN - VGG16, VGG19 and ResNet50 models implementations.
# import libraries

import os
import cv2
import numpy as np
import matplotlib.pyplot as plt
from sklearn.model_selection import train_test_split
from sklearn.metrics import classification_report
from tensorflow.keras.models import Sequential
from tensorflow.keras.layers import Dense, Dropout, GlobalAveragePooling2D,
Activation
from tensorflow.keras.applications import VGG16, VGG19, ResNet50
from tensorflow.keras.preprocessing.image import ImageDataGenerator
from tensorflow.keras.utils import to_categorical
from sklearn.preprocessing import LabelEncoder, OneHotEncoder
```

```python
#from tensorflow.keras.datasets import YOUR_LUNG_CANCER_DATASET
# Specify the directory containing the images
image_directory = 'BloodCancer'

# Initialize empty lists to store images and labels
images = []
labels = []

# Iterate over each file in the directory
for filename in os.listdir(image_directory):
    if filename.endswith('.tiff'):
        # Read the image file
        image = cv2.imread(os.path.join(image_directory, filename))
        # Convert the image to the desired format if needed
        image = cv2.cvtColor(image, cv2.COLOR_BGR2RGB)
        # Append the image to the list
        images.append(image)
        # Extract the label from the filename or directory structure if applicable
        label = filename.split('.')[0]
# Example: extracting the label from "cat.jpg"
        labels.append(label)

# Preprocess and prepare the data
labels = np.array(labels)
num_classes = len(np.unique(labels))
print(labels)
```

output--- of the above cell
['Sample_10' 'Sample_100' 'Sample_1000' 'Sample_101' 'Sample_102'
 'Sample_103' 'Sample_104' 'Sample_105' 'Sample_106' 'Sample_107'
 'Sample_108' 'Sample_109' 'Sample_11' 'Sample_110' 'Sample_111'
 'Sample_112' 'Sample_113' 'Sample_114' 'Sample_115' 'Sample_116'
 'Sample_117' 'Sample_118' 'Sample_119' 'Sample_12' 'Sample_120'
 'Sample_121' 'Sample_122' 'Sample_123' 'Sample_124' 'Sample_125'
 'Sample_126' 'Sample_127' 'Sample_128' 'Sample_129' 'Sample_13'
 'Sample_130' 'Sample_131' 'Sample_132' 'Sample_133' 'Sample_134'
 'Sample_135' 'Sample_136' 'Sample_137' 'Sample_138' 'Sample_139'
 'Sample_14' 'Sample_140' 'Sample_141' 'Sample_142' 'Sample_143'
 'Sample_144' 'Sample_145' 'Sample_146' 'Sample_147' 'Sample_148'
 'Sample_149' 'Sample_15' 'Sample_150' 'Sample_151' 'Sample_152'
 'Sample_153' 'Sample_154' 'Sample_155' 'Sample_156' 'Sample_157'
 'Sample_158' 'Sample_159' 'Sample_16' 'Sample_160' 'Sample_161'
 'Sample_162' 'Sample_163' 'Sample_164' 'Sample_165' 'Sample_166'

...
'Sample_982' 'Sample_983' 'Sample_984' 'Sample_985' 'Sample_986'
'Sample_987' 'Sample_988' 'Sample_989' 'Sample_99' 'Sample_990'
'Sample_991' 'Sample_992' 'Sample_993' 'Sample_994' 'Sample_995'
'Sample_996' 'Sample_997' 'Sample_998' 'Sample_999']

```
#_------------------------------------------------------------------------------
# Convert string labels to numerical values
label_encoder = LabelEncoder()
numerical_labels = label_encoder.fit_transform(labels)

# Apply one-hot encoding
onehot_encoder = OneHotEncoder(sparse=False)
label_l = onehot_encoder.fit_transform(numerical_labels.reshape(-1, 1))

print(label_l)
label_l.shape
```

output-----------
[[1. 0. 0 ... . 0. 0. 0.]
 [0. 1. 0 ... . 0. 0. 0.]
 [0. 0. 1 ... . 0. 0. 0.] ...
 [0. 0. 0 ... . 1. 0. 0.]
 [0. 0. 0 ... . 0. 1. 0.]
 [0. 0. 0 ... . 0. 0. 1.]]
(999, 999)

```
#-----------------------------------------------
### Normalize pixel values between 0 and 1 and convert to RGB
images = np.array(images)
image_i = images.astype('float32') / 255
#image_i = np.repeat(np.expand_dims(images, axis=3), 3, axis=3)
image_i.shape
```

output----------------------------
(999, 64, 64, 3)
```
#_____
# Split the dataset into training and validation sets
x_train, x_val, y_train, y_val = train_test_split(image_i, label_l, test_size=0.2,
random_state=42)
x_train.shape
x_val.shape
```

```
output--------------
(200, 64, 64, 3)
```

```
# Data augmentation
datagen = ImageDataGenerator(
    rotation_range=20,
    width_shift_range=0.2,
    height_shift_range=0.2,
    shear_range=0.2,
    zoom_range=0.2,
    horizontal_flip=True,
    vertical_flip=True
)
datagen.fit(x_train)

# Data augmentation
datagen = ImageDataGenerator(
    rotation_range=20,
    width_shift_range=0.2,
    height_shift_range=0.2,
    shear_range=0.2,
    zoom_range=0.2,
    horizontal_flip=True,
    vertical_flip=True
)
datagen.fit(x_val)

# Load pre-trained models
input_shape = (64, 64, 3)
vgg16 = VGG16(weights='imagenet', include_top=False, input_shape=input_shape)
vgg19 = VGG19(weights='imagenet', include_top=False, input_shape=input_shape)
resnet50 = ResNet50(weights='imagenet', include_top=False, input_shape=input_shape)

# Build custom models
model1 = Sequential()
model1.add(vgg16)
model1.add(GlobalAveragePooling2D())
model1.add(Dense(128))
model1.add(Activation('relu'))
model1.add(Dropout(0.5))
model1.add(Dense(num_classes))
model1.add(Activation('softmax'))
```

```
model2 = Sequential()
model2.add(vgg19)
model2.add(GlobalAveragePooling2D())
model2.add(Dense(128))
model2.add(Activation('relu'))
model2.add(Dropout(0.5))
model2.add(Dense(num_classes))
model2.add(Activation('softmax'))

model3 = Sequential()
model3.add(resnet50)
model3.add(GlobalAveragePooling2D())
model3.add(Dense(128))
model3.add(Activation('relu'))
model3.add(Dropout(0.5))
model3.add(Dense(num_classes))
model3.add(Activation('softmax'))

# Compile models
model1.compile(loss='categorical_crossentropy', optimizer='adam', metrics=
['accuracy'])
model2.compile(loss='categorical_crossentropy', optimizer='adam', metrics=
['accuracy'])
model3.compile(loss='categorical_crossentropy', optimizer='adam', metrics=
['accuracy'])

# Train models
batch_size = 32
epochs = 10

history1 = model1.fit(datagen.flow(x_train, y_train, batch_size=batch_size),
            steps_per_epoch=len(x_train) // batch_size,
            epochs=epochs,
            validation_data=(x_val, y_val))

#-------------------------- output--------------------------------------------
Epoch 1/10
24/24 [=====================] - 107 s 4 s/step - loss: 6.9565 - accuracy:
0.0026 - val_loss: 6.9277 - val_accuracy: 0.0000e+00
  Epoch 2/10
24/24 [=====================] - 102 s 4 s/step - loss: 6.9159 - accuracy:
0.0013 - val_loss: 6.9479 - val_accuracy: 0.0000e+00
  Epoch 3/10
```

24/24 [======================] - 102 s 4 s/step - loss: 6.9044 - accuracy: 0.0000e+00 - val_loss: 7.0179 - val_accuracy: 0.0000e+00
Epoch 4/10
24/24 [======================] - 99 s 4 s/step - loss: 6.8902 - accuracy: 0.0000e+00 - val_loss: 7.1823 - val_accuracy: 0.0000e+00
Epoch 5/10
24/24 [======================] - 104 s 4 s/step - loss: 6.8561 - accuracy: 0.0026 - val_loss: 7.6520 - val_accuracy: 0.0000e+00
Epoch 6/10
24/24 [======================] - 98 s 4 s/step - loss: 6.8480 - accuracy: 0.0026 - val_loss: 7.7079 - val_accuracy: 0.0000e+00
Epoch 7/10
24/24 [======================] - 100 s 4 s/step - loss: 6.8188 - accuracy: 0.0013 - val_loss: 8.0330 - val_accuracy: 0.0000c+00
Epoch 8/10
...
Epoch 9/10
24/24 [======================] - 100 s 4 s/step - loss: 6.7930 - accuracy: 0.0026 - val_loss: 8.3655 - val_accuracy: 0.0000e+00
Epoch 10/10
24/24 [======================] - 103 s 4 s/step - loss: 6.7880 - accuracy: 0.0000e+00 - val_loss: 8.4479 - val_accuracy: 0.0000e+00

```
#_____

_____
```

```
history2 – model2.fit(datagen.flow(x_train, y_train, batch_size=batch_size),
          steps_per_epoch=len(x_train) // batch_size,
          epochs=epochs,
          validation_data=(x_val, y_val))
```

```
# -----——----------------output-----------------------------------------------
--------------------
```
Epoch 1/10
24/24 [======================] - 161 s 7 s/step - loss: 7.1554 - accuracy: 0.0013 - val_loss: 6.9704 - val_accuracy: 0.0000e+00
Epoch 2/10
24/24 [======================] - 177 s 7 s/step - loss: 6.9069 - accuracy: 0.0000e+00 - val_loss: 6.9560 - val_accuracy: 0.0000e+00
Epoch 3/10
24/24 [======================] - 189 s 8 s/step - loss: 6.8909 - accuracy: 0.0013 - val_loss: 7.1664 - val_accuracy: 0.0000e+00
Epoch 4/10

24/24 [=======================] - 181 s 8 s/step - loss: 6.8871 - accuracy: 0.0013 - val_loss: 7.3641 - val_accuracy: 0.0000e+00
Epoch 5/10
24/24 [=======================] - 185 s 8 s/step - loss: 6.8613 - accuracy: 0.0026 - val_loss: 7.2950 - val_accuracy: 0.0000e+00
Epoch 6/10
24/24 [=======================] - 177 s 7 s/step - loss: 6.8221 - accuracy: 0.0000e+00 - val_loss: 7.9442 - val_accuracy: 0.0000e+00
Epoch 7/10
24/24 [=======================] - 171 s 7 s/step - loss: 6.8042 - accuracy: 0.0000e+00 - val_loss: 7.9601 - val_accuracy: 0.0000e+00
Epoch 8/10
...
Epoch 9/10
24/24 [=======================] - 186 s 8 s/step - loss: 6.7843 - accuracy: 0.0000e+00 - val_loss: 8.4795 - val_accuracy: 0.0000e+00
Epoch 10/10
24/24 [=======================] - 232 s 10 s/step - loss: 6.7754 - accuracy: 0.0000e+00 - val_loss: 8.3270 - val_accuracy: 0.0000e+00

```
#
```

```
history3 = model3.fit(datagen.flow(x_train, y_train, batch_size=batch_size),
            steps_per_epoch=len(x_train) // batch_size,
            epochs=epochs,
            validation_data=(x_val, y_val))
```

Epoch 1/10
24/24 [=======================] - 213 s 7 s/step - loss: 7.0735 - accuracy: 0.0000e+00 - val_loss: 104.1608 - val_accuracy: 0.0000e+00
Epoch 2/10
24/24 [=======================] - 181 s 8 s/step - loss: 6.9199 - accuracy: 0.0000e+00 - val_loss: 6.9369 - val_accuracy: 0.0000e+00
Epoch 3/10
24/24 [=======================] - 188 s 8 s/step - loss: 6.8981 - accuracy: 0.0000e+00 - val_loss: 6.9564 - val_accuracy: 0.0000e+00
Epoch 4/10
24/24 [=======================] - 139 s 6 s/step - loss: 6.8858 - accuracy: 0.0026 - val_loss: 8.5120 - val_accuracy: 0.0000e+00
Epoch 5/10
24/24 [=======================] - 126 s 5 s/step - loss: 6.8362 - accuracy: 0.0000e+00 - val_loss: 6.9932 - val_accuracy: 0.0000e+00

```
Epoch 6/10
24/24 [=======================] - 111 s 5 s/step - loss: 6.8044 - accuracy:
0.0013 - val_loss: 7.0090 - val_accuracy: 0.0000e+00
Epoch 7/10
24/24 [=======================] - 119 s 5 s/step - loss: 6.7556 - accuracy:
0.0000e+00 - val_loss: 7.0247 - val_accuracy: 0.0000e+00
Epoch 8/10
...
Epoch 9/10
24/24 [=======================] - 118 s 5 s/step - loss: 6.6357 - accuracy:
0.0026 - val_loss: 7.8606 - val_accuracy: 0.0000e+00
Epoch 10/10
24/24 [=======================] - 112 s 5 s/step - loss: 6.6068 - accuracy:
0.0000e+00 - val_loss: 64.7426 - val_accuracy: 0.0000e+00
```

#_____

_____

```
# Evaluate models on the test set
score1 = model1.evaluate(x_val, y_val, verbose=0)
score2 = model2.evaluate(x_val, y_val, verbose=0)
score3 = model3.evaluate(x_val, y_val, verbose=0)

print("Model 1 - Test Loss:", score1[0])
print("Model 1 - Test Accuracy:", score1[1])
print()
print("Model 2 - Test Loss:", score2[0])
print("Model 2 - Test Accuracy:", score2[1])
print()
print("Model 3 - Test Loss:", score3[0])
print("Model 3 - Test Accuracy:", score3[1])

# Visualize models accuracy and loss over epochs
plt.figure(figsize=(12, 4))
plt.subplot(1, 3, 1)
plt.plot(history1.history['accuracy'])
plt.plot(history1.history['val_accuracy'])
plt.title('Model 1 Accuracy')
plt.ylabel('Accuracy')
plt.xlabel('Epoch')
plt.legend(['Train', 'Validation'], loc='upper left')
plt.subplot(1, 3, 2)
plt.plot(history2.history['accuracy'])
```

```
plt.plot(history2.history['val_accuracy'])
plt.title('Model 2 Accuracy')
plt.ylabel('Accuracy')
plt.xlabel('Epoch')
plt.legend(['Train', 'Validation'], loc='upper left')
plt.subplot(1, 3, 3)
plt.plot(history3.history['accuracy'])
plt.plot(history3.history['val_accuracy'])
plt.title('Model 3 Accuracy')
plt.ylabel('Accuracy')
plt.xlabel('Epoch')
plt.legend(['Train', 'Validation'], loc='upper left')
plt.tight_layout()
plt.show()
```

The convolutional and pooling layers are:

- Convolution: output = activation (W * input + b)

  - Where W is the filter weights, b is the bias, input is the input feature map, * denotes the convolution operation, and activation is the activation function (in this case, ReLU).

- Max pooling: output = max_pool (input, pool_size)

  - Where input is the input feature map, max_pool is the max pooling operation, and pool_size is the size of the pooling window.

- The fully connected layers are standard dense layers with a ReLU activation function.

- The loss function is categorical cross-entropy, the optimizer is Adam with a learning rate of 0.001, and the metrics are accuracy.

For model training, we can use the appropriate method of the model object, passing in our training and validation data, along with the number of epochs and batch size for training.

C. RNN deep learning model for multimodal data in Python using the Keras library

```
# RNN implementations in Python
# First, we'll need to import the necessary libraries:
import numpy as np
import pandas as pd
```

```python
import matplotlib.pyplot as plt
from sklearn.metrics import classification_report, confusion_matrix
from keras.models import Sequential
from keras.layers import Conv2D, MaxPooling2D, Flatten, Dense, Dropout
from keras.optimizers import Adam
from keras.utils import to_categorical
from keras.datasets import mnist

# Next, we'll load the dataset. For this example, we'll use the MNIST dataset,
# which consists of handwritten digits.
(x_train, y_train), (x_test, y_test) = mnist.load_data()
# We'll preprocess the data by normalizing the pixel values and
# converting the labels to categorical format.
x_train = x_train.astype('float32') / 255
x_test = x_test.astype('float32') / 255
y_train = to_categorical(y_train)
y_test = to_categorical(y_test)
# We'll define the model architecture using the Sequential API of Keras.
model = Sequential()
model.add(Conv2D(32, (3, 3), activation='relu', input_shape=(28, 28, 1)))
model.add(MaxPooling2D((2, 2)))
model.add(Conv2D(64, (3, 3), activation='relu'))
model.add(MaxPooling2D((2, 2)))
model.add(Conv2D(128, (3, 3), activation='relu'))
model.add(Flatten())
model.add(Dense(64, activation='relu'))
model.add(Dropout(0.5))
model.add(Dense(10, activation='softmax'))
# We'll compile the model with an appropriate loss function, optimizer,
# and evaluation metric.
model.compile(optimizer=Adam(lr=0.001),
        loss='categorical_crossentropy',
        metrics=['accuracy'])
# We'll train the model on the training set and validate it on the validation set.
history = model.fit(x_train.reshape(-1, 28, 28, 1), y_train,
            validation_split=0.2, epochs=10, batch_size=128)
# We'll evaluate the model on the test set and
# print the classification report and #confusion matrix.
y_pred = np.argmax(model.predict(x_test.reshape(-1, 28, 28, 1)), axis=1)
y_true = np.argmax(y_test, axis=1)
print('Classification Report:\n', classification_report(y_true, y_pred))
print('Confusion Matrix:\n', confusion_matrix(y_true, y_pred))
# Finally, we'll plot the training and validation accuracy over epochs.
```

```
plt.plot(history.history['accuracy'])
plt.plot(history.history['val_accuracy'])
plt.title('Model Accuracy')
plt.xlabel('Epoch')
plt.ylabel('Accuracy')
plt.legend(['Train', 'Validation'], loc='lower right')
plt.show()
```

D. Feedforward neural network (FFNN) for multimodal data in Python using the Keras library

```
# Implementation of FFNN
# First, we'll need to import the necessary libraries:
import numpy as np
import pandas as pd
import matplotlib.pyplot as plt
from sklearn.metrics import classification_report, confusion_matrix, f1_score
from keras.models import Sequential
from keras.layers import Dense, Dropout
from keras.optimizers import Adam
from keras.utils import to_categorical

# Next, we'll load the sample dataset. For this example,
# we'll use the Iris dataset, which consists of measurements of flower petals and
sepals.
url = "https://archive.ics.uci.edu/ml/machine-learning-databases/iris/iris.data"
names = ['sepal-length', 'sepal-width', 'petal-length', 'petal-width', 'class']
dataset = pd.read_csv(url, names=names)

X = dataset.iloc[:,:-1].values
y = dataset.iloc[:, -1].values

y = np.where(y == 'Iris-setosa', 0, np.where(y == 'Iris-versicolor', 1, 2))

y = to_categorical(y, num_classes=3)

# We'll preprocess the data by normalizing the input features.
X = (X - np.mean(X, axis=0)) / np.std(X, axis=0)

# We'll define the model architecture using the Sequential API of Keras.
model = Sequential()
model.add(Dense(16, activation='relu', input_shape=(4,)))
model.add(Dropout(0.2))
```

```
model.add(Dense(8, activation='relu'))
model.add(Dropout(0.2))
model.add(Dense(3, activation='softmax'))
# We'll compile the model with an appropriate loss function, optimizer, and
evaluation metric.
model.compile(optimizer=Adam(lr=0.001),
        loss='categorical_crossentropy',
        metrics=['accuracy'])
# We'll train the model on the training set and validate it on the validation set.

history = model.fit(X, y, validation_split=0.2, epochs=50, batch_size=8)

# We'll evaluate the model on the test set and
# print the classification report, confusion matrix, #and F1 score.

y_pred = np.argmax(model.predict(X), axis=1)
y_true = np.argmax(y, axis=1)

print('Classification Report:\n', classification_report(y_true, y_pred))
print('Confusion Matrix:\n', confusion_matrix(y_true, y_pred))
print('F1 Score:', f1_score(y_true, y_pred, average='macro'))
# Finally, we'll plot the training and validation accuracy over epochs.
plt.plot(history.history['accuracy'])
plt.plot(history.history['val_accuracy'])
plt.title('Model Accuracy')
plt.xlabel('Epoch')
plt.ylabel('Accuracy')
plt.legend(['Train', 'Validation'], loc='lower right')
plt.show()
```

E. Gated Recurrent Unit (GRU) model for multimodal data in Python using the Keras library

```
# GRU Model implementation in Python
# First, we'll need to import the necessary libraries:
import numpy as np
import pandas as pd
import matplotlib.pyplot as plt
from sklearn.metrics import classification_report, confusion_matrix, f1_score
from keras.models import Sequential
from keras.layers import Dense, GRU, Dropout
from keras.optimizers import Adam
from keras.utils import to_categorical
```

```
# Next, we'll load the sample dataset. For this example,
# we'll use the IMDB movie review dataset,
# which consists of reviews labeled as positive or negative.
from keras.datasets import imdb

num_words = 10000
maxlen = 200
(X_train, y_train), (X_test, y_test) = imdb.load_data(num_words=num_words)
X_train = pad_sequences(X_train, maxlen=maxlen)
X_test = pad_sequences(X_test, maxlen=maxlen)
y_train = to_categorical(y_train, num_classes=2)
y_test = to_categorical(y_test, num_classes=2)
# We'll define the model architecture using the Sequential API of Keras.
model = Sequential()
model.add(Embedding(num_words, 32, input_length=maxlen))
model.add(GRU(32))
model.add(Dropout(0.2))
model.add(Dense(2, activation='softmax'))
# We'll compile the model with an appropriate loss function, optimizer, and
evaluation metric.
model.compile(optimizer=Adam(lr=0.001),
        loss='categorical_crossentropy',
        metrics=['accuracy'])

# We'll train the model on the training set and validate it on the validation set.
history = model.fit(X_train, y_train, validation_split=0.2, epochs=5, batch_
size=128)

# We'll evaluate the model on the test set and
# print the classification report, confusion matrix, and F1 score.
y_pred = np.argmax(model.predict(X_test), axis=1)
y_true = np.argmax(y_test, axis=1)
print('Classification Report:\n', classification_report(y_true, y_pred))
print('Confusion Matrix:\n', confusion_matrix(y_true, y_pred))
print('F1 Score:', f1_score(y_true, y_pred))
# Finally, we'll plot the training and validation accuracy over epochs.
plt.plot(history.history['accuracy'])
plt.plot(history.history['val_accuracy'])
plt.title('Model Accuracy')
plt.xlabel('Epoch')
plt.ylabel('Accuracy')
plt.legend(['Train', 'Validation'], loc='lower right')
plt.show()
```

F. Long short-term memory (LSTM) model for multimodal data in Python using the Keras library

```python
# Implementation LSTM (Long Short-Term Memory) network in Python
# First, we'll need to import the necessary libraries:

import numpy as np
import pandas as pd
import matplotlib.pyplot as plt
from sklearn.metrics import classification_report, confusion_matrix, f1_score
from keras.models import Sequential
from keras.layers import Dense, LSTM, Dropout
from keras.optimizers import Adam
from keras.utils import to_categorical
# Next, we'll load the sample dataset. For this example, we'll use
# the IMDB movie review dataset, which # consists of reviews labeled as positive
or negative.
from keras.datasets import imdb

num_words = 10000
maxlen = 200
(X_train, y_train), (X_test, y_test) = imdb.load_data(num_words=num_words)

X_train = pad_sequences(X_train, maxlen=maxlen)
X_test = pad_sequences(X_test, maxlen=maxlen)

y_train = to_categorical(y_train, num_classes=2)
y_test = to_categorical(y_test, num_classes=2)

# We'll define the model architecture using the Sequential API of Keras.
model = Sequential()

model.add(Embedding(num_words, 32, input_length=maxlen))
model.add(LSTM(32))
model.add(Dropout(0.2))
model.add(Dense(2, activation='softmax'))

# We'll compile the model with an appropriate loss function, optimizer, and
evaluation metric.

model.compile(optimizer=Adam(lr=0.001),
        loss='categorical_crossentropy',
        metrics=['accuracy'])
```

```
# We'll train the model on the training set and validate it on the validation set.

history = model.fit(X_train, y_train, validation_split=0.2, epochs=5, batch_
size=128)
# We'll evaluate the model on the test set and
#print the classification report, confusion matrix, and F1 score.
y_pred = np.argmax(model.predict(X_test), axis=1)
y_true = np.argmax(y_test, axis=1)

print('Classification Report:\n', classification_report(y_true, y_pred))
print('Confusion Matrix:\n', confusion_matrix(y_true, y_pred))
print('F1 Score:', f1_score(y_true, y_pred))

# Finally, we'll plot the training and validation accuracy over epochs.

plt.plot(history.history['accuracy'])
plt.plot(history.history['val_accuracy'])
plt.title('Model Accuracy')
plt.xlabel('Epoch')
plt.ylabel('Accuracy')
plt.legend(['Train', 'Validation'], loc='lower right')
plt.show()
```

G. Multi-layer perceptron (MLP) model for multimodal data in Python using the Keras library

```
# First, we'll need to import the necessary libraries:

import numpy as np
import pandas as pd
import matplotlib.pyplot as plt
from sklearn.metrics import classification_report, confusion_matrix, f1_score
from keras.models import Sequential
from keras.layers import Dense, Dropout
from keras.optimizers import Adam
from keras.utils import to_categorical

# Next, we'll load the sample dataset. For this example,
# we'll use the MNIST handwritten digit dataset.
from keras.datasets import mnist

(X_train, y_train), (X_test, y_test) = mnist.load_data()

X_train = X_train.reshape((X_train.shape[0], 784))
```

```python
X_test = X_test.reshape((X_test.shape[0], 784))

X_train = X_train.astype('float32') / 255
X_test = X_test.astype('float32') / 255

y_train = to_categorical(y_train, num_classes=10)
y_test = to_categorical(y_test, num_classes=10)

# We'll define the model architecture using the Sequential API of Keras.

model = Sequential()

model.add(Dense(256, activation='relu', input_shape=(784,)))
model.add(Dropout(0.2))
model.add(Dense(128, activation='relu'))
model.add(Dropout(0.2))
model.add(Dense(10, activation='softmax'))
# We'll compile the model with an appropriate loss function, optimizer, and
evaluation metric.

model.compile(optimizer=Adam(lr=0.001),
        loss='categorical_crossentropy',
        metrics=['accuracy'])
# We'll train the model on the training set and validate it on the validation set.

history = model.fit(X_train, y_train, validation_split=0.2, epochs=10, batch_
size=128)
# We'll evaluate the model on the test set and print the classification report,
confusion matrix, # and F1 score.
y_pred = np.argmax(model.predict(X_test), axis=1)
y_true = np.argmax(y_test, axis=1)

print('Classification Report:\n', classification_report(y_true, y_pred))
print('Confusion Matrix:\n', confusion_matrix(y_true, y_pred))
print('F1 Score:', f1_score(y_true, y_pred, average='weighted'))

# # Finally, we'll plot the training and validation accuracy over epochs.
plt.plot(history.history['accuracy'])
plt.plot(history.history['val_accuracy'])
plt.title('Model Accuracy')
plt.xlabel('Epoch')
plt.ylabel('Accuracy')
plt.legend(['Train', 'Validation'], loc='lower right')
plt.show()
```

5.3 CONCLUSION AND FUTURE DIRECTIONS

A. Summary of key takeaways

1. Multimodal deep learning involves combining multiple types of data, such as images, audio, and text, to increase the processing and performance of models.

2. Several strategies apply to joint, parallel, and serial training for models.

3. Regularization techniques help to improve the general performance of multimodal deep learning models.

4. Multimodal deep learning has applications in various domains, such as speech recognition, image captioning, healthcare, and autonomous driving.

5. Some examples of multimodal deep learning applications include Google Multimodal Neural Machine Translation, Microsoft Emotion Recognition, Brain2Pix, and Facebook Multimodal Word Embeddings.

B. Limitations and challenges of deep multimodal learning

1. Data availability: multimodal data is often tricky and expensive, making it challenging to train deep multimodal models.

2. Heterogeneity: multimodal data can have different statistical properties and distributions, making it challenging to design models that can effectively fuse information from other modalities.

3. Interpretability: these models may face complexity to interpret, and it is challenging to understand how they conclude.

4. Overfitting: when the input data is composed of significant parameters, models face an overfitting problem.

C. Future directions

1. Explain ability: developing methods to interpret and explain the decisions made by multimodal deep learning models is an important research direction.

2. Transfer learning: this learning helps to improve the model performance of multimodal data by leveraging pre-trained models for specific modalities.

3. Data augmentation: data augmentation techniques can help increase the size and diversity of multimodal data sets, making it easier to train deep multimodal models.

4. Reinforcement learning: this type of learning applies to optimize multimodal deep learning models for specific tasks in many applications.

5. Federated learning: in this learning, we can train models on distributed data sources to improve privacy and scalability factors.

6. Cross-border blockchain technology integration: in this domain, the collaborative frameworks will enhance the performance of global application transparency with max security arrangements in global transactional networks.

ABBREVIATIONS

Alex Net – 08 layered CNN model presented by Alex with collaboration
Artificial Intelligence – AI
Artificial Neural Networks – ANNs
Autoencoder (an unsupervised learning technique for neural networks)
Bidirectional RNN – a combination of two RNN
Convolutional Neural Networks – CNNs
Convolutions Independent Component analysis – ICA
Deep Belief Network – DBN
Deep Convolutional Embedded Clustering – DCEC
Electroencephalography – EEG
Feedforward Neural Networks – FFNNs
Gated Recurrent Units – GRUs
Generative Adversarial Networks – GANs
Graphics Processing Unit – GPU
Inception model – used for dimensionality reduction by 1×1
Long short-term memory – LSTM
Massachusetts Institute of Technology – MIT
Multi-layer perceptron – MLP
Multimodal Deep Embedded Clustering – MDEC
Natural Language Processing – NLP
Principal Component Analysis – PCA
Recurrent Neural Network – RNN
Recurrent Neural Networks – RNNs
Residual Networks – ResNet
Restricted Boltzmann Machine – RBM
Short-Term Long Memory – LSTM
The Networks – LeNet (CNN normally considered)
Variational Autoencoder – VAE
Visual geometry Group – VGG16/19 convolutional layered types

REFERENCES

[1] R. Sood, M. Vatsa, and R. Singh, "Multimodal Deep Learning," 2020. http://repository. iiitd.edu.in/xmlui/handle/123456789/916
[2] K. Sohn, W. Shang, and H. Lee, "Improved Multimodal Deep Learning with Variation of Information," *Advances in Neural Information Processing Systems*, vol. 27, Chicago, 2014.
[3] N. Srivastava and R. Salakhutdinov, "Multimodal Learning with Deep Boltzmann Machines," *Advances in Neural Information Processing Systems*, vol. 25, Chicago, 2012.

[4] N. Aranjuelo, L. Unzueta, I. Arganda-Carreras, and O. Otaegui, "Multimodal Deep Learning for Advanced Driving Systems," in *Lecture Notes in Computer Science (Including Subseries Lecture Notes in Artificial Intelligence and Lecture Notes in Bioinformatics)*, Springer Verlag, 2018, pp. 95–105. doi: 10.1007/978-3-319-94544-6_10.

[5] J. Summaira, X. Li, A. M. Shoib, S. Li, and J. Abdul, "Recent Advances and Trends in Multimodal Deep Learning: A Review," May 2021, [online]. Available: http://arxiv.org/abs/2105.11087

[6] T. Kim, B. Kang, M. Rho, S. Sezer, and E. G. Im, "A Multimodal Deep Learning Method for Android Malware Detection Using Various Features," *IEEE Transactions on Information Forensics and Security*, vol. 14, no. 3, pp. 773–788, March 2019. doi: 10.1109/TIFS.2018.2866319.

[7] H. Li, "Piano Automatic Computer Composition by Deep Learning and Blockchain Technology," *IEEE Access*, vol. 8, pp. 188951–188958, 2020. doi: 10.1109/ACCESS.2020.3031155.

[8] M. Aamir, Y. F. Pu, Z. Rahman, M. Tahir, H. Naeem, and Q. Dai, "A Framework for Automatic Building Detection From Low-Contrast Satellite Images," *Symmetry (Basel)*, vol. 11, no. 1, January 2019. doi: 10.3390/sym11010003.

[9] Y. Guan *et al.*, "An Object Detection Framework Based on Deep Features and High-Quality Object Locations," *Traitement du Signal*, vol. 38, no. 3, pp. 719–730, June 2021. doi: 10.18280/ts.380319.

[10] C. Cangea, P. Veličković, and P. Liò, "XFlow: Cross-Modal Deep Neural Networks for Audiovisual Classification," September 2017, [online]. Available: http://arxiv.org/abs/1709.00572

[11] A. O. Panhwar *et al.*, "Plant Health Detection Enabled CNN Scheme in IoT Network," *International Journal of Computing and Digital Systems*, vol. 12, no. 1, pp. 335–344, 2022. doi: 10.12785/ijcds/120127.

[12] N. Wu, X. Wang, B. Lin, and K. Zhang, "A CNN-Based End-to-End Learning Framework Toward Intelligent Communication Systems," *IEEE Access*, vol. 7, pp. 110197–110204, 2019. doi: 10.1109/ACCESS.2019.2926843.

[13] Y. Chen, S. Liu, X. Shen, and J. Jia, "Fast Point R-CNN." In *Proceedings of the IEEE/CVF International Conference on Computer Vision*, 2019, pp. 9775–9784.

[14] W. Yin, K. Kann, M. Yu, and H. Schuetze, "Comparative Study of CNN and Rnn for Natural Language Processing," 2017, arxiv.org, [online]. Available: https://arxiv.org/abs/1702.01923

[15] M. H. S. C. F. of Sciences University of and Undefined 2006, "A Brief Review of Feedforward Neural Networks," 2006, *dergipark.org.tr*, [online]. Available: https://dergipark.org.tr/en/pub/aupse/article/890416

[16] G. Klein *et al.*, "Opennmt: Neural Machine Translation Toolkit," *arxiv.org*, [online]. Available: https://arxiv.org/abs/1805.11462

[17] S. Chang, "Deep Clustering With Fusion Autoencoder," 2022, arXiv preprint arXiv:2201.04727.

[18] M. Schuster, K. K. P. I. Transactions on Signal, and Undefined 1997, "Bidirectional Recurrent Neural Networks," *ieeexplore.ieee.org*, vol. 45, no. 11, 1997, [online]. Available: https://ieeexplore.ieee.org/abstract/document/650093/

[19] O. Tilk and T. Alumäe, "Bidirectional Recurrent Neural Network with Attention Mechanism for Punctuation Restoration," *Researchgate.net*, 2016. doi: 10.21437/Interspeech.2016-1517.

[20] R. Rana, "Gated Recurrent Unit (GRU) for Emotion Classification from Noisy Speech," May 2016, [online]. Available: http://arxiv.org/abs/1612.07778

[21] J. Chung, C. Gulcehre, K. Cho, and Y. Bengio, "Empirical Evaluation of Gated Recurrent Neural Networks on Sequence Modeling," May 2014, [online]. Available: http://arxiv.org/abs/1412.3555

[22] W. Wang, Y. Huang, Y. Wang, and L. Wang, "Generalized Autoencoder: A Neural Network Framework for Dimensionality Reduction," *cv-foundation.org*, 2014, [online]. Available: https://www.cv-foundation.org/openaccess/content_cvpr_workshops_2014/W15/html/Wang_Generalized_Autoencoder_A_2014_CVPR_paper.html

[23] L. O. Chua, "CNN: A Vision of Complexity," *International Journal of Bifurcation and Chaos*, vol. 7, no. 10, pp. 2219–2425, 1997. doi: 10.1142/S0218127497001618.

[24] R. C. Staudemeyer and E. R. Morris, "Understanding LSTM – A Tutorial into Long Short-Term Memory Recurrent Neural Networks," May 2019, [online]. Available: http://arxiv.org/abs/1909.09586

[25] X. Hu and Y. Han, "A Novel Matrix Completion Model Based on the Multi-Layer Perceptron Integrating Kernel Regularization," *ieeexplore.ieee.org*, 2021, [online]. Available: https://ieeexplore.ieee.org/abstract/document/9420060/

[26] M. Riedmiller, "Multi Layer Perceptron: Machine Learning Lab," *ml.informatik.uni-freiburg.de*, 2014, [online]. Available: https://ml.informatik.uni-freiburg.de/former/_media/documents/teaching/ss12/ml/05_mlps.printer.pdf

[27] M. Abdi and S. Nahavandi, "Multi-Residual Networks: Improving the Speed and Accuracy of Residual Networks," May 2016, [online]. Available: http://arxiv.org/abs/1609.05672

[28] S. Targ, D. Almeida, and K. Lyman, "Resnet in Resnet: Generalizing Residual Architectures," May 2016, [online]. Available: http://arxiv.org/abs/1603.08029

[29] V. Upadhya and P. S. Sastry, "An Overview of Restricted Boltzmann Machines," *Journal of the Indian Institute of Science*, vol. 99, no. 2, pp. 225–236, May 2019. doi: 10.1007/s41745-019-0102-z.

[30] A. Fischer and C. Igel, "An Introduction to Restricted Boltzmann Machines," *Lecture Notes in Computer Science (Including Subseries Lecture Notes in Artificial Intelligence and Lecture Notes in Bioinformatics)*, vol. 7441, LNCS, pp. 14–36, 2012. doi: 10.1007/978-3-642-33275-3_2.

[31] A. Younis, L. Qiang, C. O. Nyatega, and M. J. Adamu, "Brain Tumor Analysis Using Deep Learning and VGG-16 Ensembling Learning Approaches,"*mdpi.com*, 2022, [online]. Available: https://www.mdpi.com/1734192

[32] X. Guo, X. Liu, E. Zhu, and J. Yin, "Deep Clustering with Convolutional Autoencoders," in *Lecture Notes in Computer Science (Including Subseries Lecture Notes in Artificial Intelligence and Lecture Notes in Bioinformatics)*, Springer Verlag, 2017, pp. 373–382. doi: 10.1007/978-3-319-70096-0_39.

[33] A. Mohamed, G. Dahl, and G. Hinton, "Deep Belief Networks for Phone Recognition," *cs.utoronto.ca*, 2009, [online]. Available: http://www.cs.utoronto.ca/~gdahl/papers/dbnPhoneRec.pdf

[34] Y. Hua, J. Guo, and H. Zhao, "Deep Belief Networks and Deep Learning," *ieeexplore.ieee.org*, 2015, [online]. Available: https://ieeexplore.ieee.org/abstract/document/7111524/

[35] T. Cemgil, S. Ghaisas et al., "The Autoencoding Variational Autoencoder," *proceedings.neurips.cc*, 2020, [online]. Available: https://proceedings.neurips.cc/paper/2020/hash/ac10ff1941c540cd87c107330996f4f6-Abstract.html

[36] D. Bunker, "Speech2Face: Reconstructed Lip Syncing with Generative Adversarial Networks," *dbunker.io*, 2017, [online]. Available: https://www.dbunker.io/docs/2017_Bunker_Speech2FaceProposal.pdf

[37] G. Castellano and G. Vessio, "Deep Convolutional Embedding for Digitized Painting Clustering," March 2020, [online]. Available: http://arxiv.org/abs/2003.08597

[38] A. Alqahtani, X. Xie, J. Deng, and M. W. Jones, "A Deep Convolutional Auto-Encoder With Embedded Clustering," *ieeexplore.ieee.org*. doi: 10.24963/ijcai.2017/243.

[39] M. Aamir, Y. F. Pu, W. A. Abro, H. Naeem, and Z. Rahman, "A Hybrid Approach for Object Proposal Generation," in *Lecture Notes in Electrical Engineering*, Springer Verlag, 2019, pp. 251–259. doi: 10.1007/978-3-319-91659-0_18.

[40] M. Aamir, Z. Rahman, W. Ahmed Abro, M. Tahir, and S. Mustajar Ahmed, "An Optimized Architecture of Image Classification Using Convolutional Neural Network," *International Journal of Image, Graphics and Signal Processing*, vol. 11, no. 10, pp. 30–39, October 2019. doi: 10.5815/ijigsp.2019.10.05.

[41] Y. Guan *et al.*, "A Framework for Efficient Brain Tumor Classification Using MRI Images," *Mathematical Biosciences and Engineering*, vol. 18, no. 5, pp. 5790–5815, 2021. doi: 10.3934/MBE.2021292.

[42] A. A. Sathio, "A Study on the Conceptual Frame Work of Data Warehousing in Health Sector in Pakistan: A Case Study of a Hospital System and Disease (Hepatitis C)," *International Journal of Computer (IJC)*, vol. 29, no. 1, pp. 59–81, September 2018. doi: https://www.researchgate.net/publication/324896538_A_Study_On_The_Conceptual_Frame_Work_Of_Data_Warehousing_In_Health_Sector_In_Pakistan_A_Case_Study_Of_a_Hospital_System_And_Disease_Hepatitis_C/citations.

[43] A. A. Sathio and A. M. Brohi, *The Imperative Role of Pervasive Data in Healthcare*, in M. S. Husain *et al.*, (Eds.), Cham: Springer, 2021, pp. 17–21. doi: 10.1007/978-3-030-77746-3_2

[44] A. A. Laghariet al. , "The Role of Software Configuration Management and Capability Maturity Model in System Quality," 2019, [online]. Available: https://www.researchgate.net/publication/337707282

[45] Y. Guan *et al.*, "A Region-Based Efficient Network for Accurate Object Detection," *Traitement du Signal*, vol. 38, no. 2, pp. 481–494, April 2021. doi: 10.18280/ts.380228.

[46] M. Aamir *et al.*, "A Hybrid Proposed Framework for Object Detection and Classification," *Journal of Information Processing Systems*, vol. 14, no. 5, pp. 1176–1194, 2018. doi: 10.3745/JIPS.02.0095.

[47] M. Aamir *et al.*, "A Deep Learning Approach for Brain Tumor Classification Using MRI Images," *Computers and Electrical Engineering*, vol. 101, July 2022. doi: 10.1016/j.compeleceng.2022.108105.

[48] R. Kumar, X. Zhang, W. Wang, R. U. Khan, J. Kumar *et al.*, "A Multimodal Malware Detection Technique for Android Iot Devices Using Various Features," *ieeexplore.ieee.org*, 2019, [online]. Available: https://ieeexplore.ieee.org/abstract/document/8721053/

[49] G. Simi Margarat *et al.*, "Early Diagnosis of Tuberculosis Using Deep Learning Approach for IoT Based Healthcare Applications," *Computational Intelligence and Neuroscience*, vol. 2022, 2022. doi: 10.1155/2022/3357508.

[50] R. Kumar, Arjunaditya, D. Singh, K. Srinivasan, and Y. C. Hu, "AI-Powered Blockchain Technology for Public Health: A Contemporary Review, Open Challenges, and Future Research Directions," *Healthcare (Switzerland)*, vol. 11, no. 1, MDPI, January 01, 2023. doi: 10.3390/healthcare11010081.

[51] J. Ngiam, A. Khosla, M. Kim, J. Nam, H. Lee, and A. Y. Ng, "Multimodal Deep Learning," in *Proceedings of the 28th International Conference on Machine Learning*, Chicago, 2011, pp. 689–696.

[52] S. R. Mary *et al.*, "Deep Learning Model for the Image Fusion and Accurate Classification of Remote Sensing Images," *Computational Intelligence and Neuroscience*, vol. 2022, pp. 1–9, November 2022. doi: 10.1155/2022/2668567.

[53] J. Wild, "Blockchain Believers Seek to Shake-up Financial Services," *longfinance.net*, 2015, [online]. Available: https://www.longfinance.net/media/documents/Blockchain_believers.pdf

[54] A. A. Loutfi *et al.,* "De-hyping Blockchain-Based Cross-Border Payment Solutions: A Quantitative Comparative Study of Decentralized Blockchain Infrastructures vs. Swift GPI1," *researchgate.net*, 2019, [online]. Available: https://www.researchgate.net/profile/Stefan-Suetterlin/publication/334139727_Team_learning_in_cybersecurity_exercises/links/5d1a241e299bf1547c8eec06/Team-learning-in-cybersecurity-exercises.pdf#page=68

[55] "Crossbordr Blockchain Technology - Google Scholar." [Online]. Available: https://scholar.google.com/scholar?hl=en&as_sdt=0%2C5&q=+crossbordr+blockchain+technology+&btnG=

[56] M. Supriya, and V. K. Chattu, "A Review of Artificial Intelligence, Big Data, and Blockchain Technology Applications in Medicine and Global Health," *Big Data and Cognitive Computing*, vol. 5, p. 41, 2021. doi: 10.3390/bdcc5030041.

[57] B. Mallikarjuna, G. Shrivastava, and M. Sharma, "Blockchain Technology: A DNN Token-Based Approach in Healthcare and Covid-19 to Generate Extracted Data," *Wiley Online Library*, 2022, [online]. Available: https://onlinelibrary.wiley.com/doi/abs/10.1111/exsy.12778

[58] A. A. Sathio, M. Ali Dootio, A. Lakhan, M. U. Rehman, A. Orangzeb Pnhwar, and M. A. Sahito, "Pervasive Futuristic Healthcare and Blockchain Enabled Digital Identities-Challenges and Future Intensions," in *Proceedings - 2021 International Conference on Computing, Electronics and Communications Engineering, iCCECE 2021*, Institute of Electrical and Electronics Engineers Inc., August 2021, pp. 30–35. doi: 10.1109/iCCECE52344.2021.9534846.

[59] O. V. Google, A. T. Google, S. B. Google, and D. E. Google, "Show and Tell: A Neural Image Caption Generator," *cv-foundation.org*, [online]. Available: https://www.cv-foundation.org/openaccess/content_cvpr_2015/html/Vinyals_Show_and_Tell_2015_CVPR_paper.html

[60] "Facebook Multimodal Word Embeddings - Google Scholar." [Online]. Available: https://scholar.google.com/scholar?hl=en&as_sdt=0%2C5&q=%E2%80%A2%09Facebook+Multimodal+Word+Embeddings&btnG=

[61] Y. Yang, I. G. Morillo, and T. M. Hospedales, "Deep Neural Decision Trees," June 2018, [online]. Available: http://arxiv.org/abs/1806.06988

[62] "Speech2Face - Google Scholar." [Online]. Available: https://scholar.google.com/scholar?hl=en&as_sdt=0%2C5&q=+%E2%80%A2%09Speech2Face&btnG=

[63] S. R. Laskar, A. F. U. R. Khilji, P. Pakray, and S. Bandyopadhyay, "Multimodal Neural Machine Translation for English to Hindi," *aclanthology.org*, pp. 109–113, 2020, [online]. Available: https://aclanthology.org/2020.wat-1.11/

[64] M. T. Luong, I. Sutskever, Q. V. Le, O. Vinyals , and W. Zaremba, "Addressing the Rare Word Problem in Neural Machine Translation," *arxiv.org*, 2015, [online]. Available: https://arxiv.org/abs/1410.8206

[65] S. Jean, K. Cho, R. Memisevic, and Y. Bengio, "On Using Very Large Target Vocabulary for Neural Machine Translation," *ACL-IJCNLP 2015 - 53rd Annual Meeting of the Association for Computational Linguistics and the 7th International Joint Conference on Natural Language Processing of the Asian Federation of Natural Language Processing, Proceedings of the Conference*, vol. 1, pp. 1–10, 2015, doi: 10.3115/v1/p15-1001.

[66] Y. Liu *et al.*, "Summary of ChatGPT/GPT-4 Research and Perspective Towards the Future of Large Language Models," *arxiv.org*, [online]. Available: https://arxiv.org/abs/2304.01852

[67] Y. Bang, S. Cahyawijaya, N. Lee, W. Dai *et al.*, "A Multitask, Multilingual, Multimodal Evaluation of ChatGPT on Reasoning, Hallucination, and Interactivity," *arxiv.org*, 2023, [online]. Available: https://arxiv.org/abs/2302.04023

[68] K. Seeliger, U. Güçlü, L. Le, Y. Güçlütürk, and M. van Gerven, "Brain2Pix: Fully Convolutional Naturalistic Video Reconstruction From Brain Activity," 2021, [online]. Available: https://pure.mpg.de/pubman/faces/ViewItemOverviewPage.jsp?itemId=item_3430706

[69] L. Le, L. Ambrogioni, K. Seeliger *et al.*, "Brain2Pix: Fully Convolutional Naturalistic Video Frame Reconstruction From Brain Activity," *pure.mpg.de*, 2022, [online]. Available: https://pure.mpg.de/pubman/faces/ViewItemOverviewPage.jsp?itemId=item_3478712

## CHAPTER 6

Deep Learning Algorithms

Clustering and Classifications for Multimedia Data

Anwar Ali Sathio[1,2], Muhammad Malook Rind[2], and Abdullah Lakhan[3]

[1]*Department of CS&IT, Benazir Bhutto Shaheed University, Karachi, Sindh, Pakistan*
[2]*Department of Computer Science, Sindh Madressatul Islam University, Karachi, Sindh, Pakistan*
[3]*Department of Cyber Security, Dawood University of Engineering and Technology, Karachi, Sindh, Pakistan*

6.1 INTRODUCTION

6.1.1 Deep Learning and Its Applications in Multimedia Data Analysis

Deep learning is a powerful tool for analyzing complex, particularly multimedia data (text, images, audio, and video). Deep learning algorithms are highly effective for clustering and classifying multimedia data, critically impacting different deep learning fields such as computer vision, natural language processing (NLP), and speech recognition applications [1]. This chapter will provide an overview of deep learning algorithms for clustering and classifying multimedia data, as the classification of deep learning justified in the Figure 6.1. We discussed several popular algorithms, their applications, current research directions, and future trends in the field. The chapter is intended for researchers and practitioners working in deep learning for multimedia data analysis, as well as graduate students and advanced undergraduates interested in learning about the latest developments in the field. Deep learning involves training neural networks to extract complex features and relationships from large data sets. Deep learning has significantly advanced multimedia data analysis, and one of the most prominent applications is image recognition. Convolutional neural networks (CNN) are very effective for recognizing objects, faces, [2], etc., and can extract features to classify images into various categories. Deep learning algorithms, such as recurrent neural networks (RNN) and long short-term memory (LSTM) approaches, provide good speech recognition application results. Natural language processing (NLP) is another area where deep learning has shown remarkable success. Deep learning-based NLP can understand the meaning of sentences,

DOI: 10.1201/9781032646268-6

Artificial Intelligence - MACHINE
BEHAVIOR LIKE INTELLIGENT
HUMAN

Machine Learning - SYSTEM LEARNS
& IMPROVE BY EXPERIENCE
AUTOMATICALLY

Deep Learning - SYSTEM IMPROVES
LEARNING WITH SEEP NEURAL
NETWORKS & COMPLEX ALGORITHMS

FIGURE 6.1   Shows AI and deep learning domain association.

generate human-like responses, and translate languages. NLP has applications in chat-bots, language translation, and sentiment analysis.

In summary, deep learning has revolutionized multimedia data analysis and has various applications in various domains. With large data sets and high-performance computing resources, deep learning-based approaches expect to advance.

6.1.2 Classification Algorithms in Deep Learning Can Be Broadly Classified into the Following Categories

1. **Supervised Learning:** Supervised learning algorithms use labeled training examples to predict output class labels or values based on input data. These algorithms learn to map the input data to the corresponding output labels; for instance, convolutional neural networks (CNNs), recurrent neural networks (RNNs), and deep belief networks (DBNs) are very effective in supervised learning [3,4].

2. **Unsupervised Learning:** The algorithms are designed to uncover patterns and structures in input data without any pre-existing knowledge of the output labels. These algorithms are typically employed for clustering, dimensionality reduction, and generative modeling. The studies showed the effectiveness of mentioned

approaches; for example, autoencoders, restricted Boltzmann machines (RBMs), and deep generative models like variational autoencoders (VAEs) and generative adversarial networks (GANs) proved their performance [3,4].

3. **Reinforcement Learning (RL):** This approach involves learning how to make decisions by interacting with an environment. In this technique, an agent learns to act in a setting to maximize a reward signal. Deep learning is a subdomain of machine learning that leverages artificial neural networks to model and solve intricate problems. By merging RL with deep learning, significant progress has been achieved in AI, particularly in robotics, gaming, and autonomous vehicles [5,6]. Some examples of frequently utilized RL algorithms in deep learning are described below:

1.1 **Q-learning:** This algorithm estimates the value of a particular action in a given state by Q-function, and the Q-values are updated based on the rewards received for different actions [7,8].

1.2 **Deep Q-Networks (DQN):** This is a DNN variant of Q-learning to model more complex and higher-dimensional state spaces while approximating the Q-function [7,8].

1.3 **Policy Gradient Methods:** These methods learn a policy that maps states to actions and use gradient descent to optimize the policy based on the rewards received.

1.4 **Actor-Critic Methods:** When methods combine policy gradient with value-based techniques like Q-learning, they shall improve the learnability with policy and value function to improve decision-making capabilities.

1.5 **Deep Deterministic Policy Gradient (DDPG):** This variant of actor-critic methods employs deep neural networks to approximate both the policy and the value function, making it useful for continuous control problems with continuous action spaces [7,8,9].

These DNN approaches are very effective and widely applied in multimedia (image, text, speech) applications that can classify the data easily.

6.1.3 Deep Learning for Clustering Multimedia Data

The act of grouping comparable data items according to their qualities is known as clustering. Clustering algorithms are frequently employed in multimedia data processing for applications such as picture segmentation, object detection, and audio recognition. Due to the large dimensionality and complexity of the data, clustering multimedia data poses difficulties. Numerous well-known algorithms have been created since deep learning techniques are adept at pressing multimedia data. Convolutional autoencoders are capable of both encoding and decoding pictures. With deep convolutional embedded clustering (DCEC), it is possible to efficiently learn a compressed representation of images that is beneficial for data clusters [10]. Another highly efficient methodology for multimodal clustering data is multimodal deep-embedded clustering (MDEC) [11–13]. Case studies have shown how well deep learning clusters multimedia data. For instance, one study clustered a sizable satellite image data set using convolutional autoencoders. According to the survey, convolutional autoencoders significantly impacted how images were grouped according to their geographic characteristics [14–16]. The best performance was achieved in a different investigation using DCEC to cluster a sizable data set of natural photos. These are just a few examples of the algorithms created for grouping multimedia data, and deep learning algorithms have shown significant promise in this regard. These algorithms work incredibly well for applications like object detection, speech recognition, and image segmentation. We anticipate that more reliable techniques for clustering multimedia data will be created as deep learning develops.

6.1.4 Types of Clustering

The following are the main types of clustering algorithms:

A. Density-based clustering groups data based on areas where the high concentrations data points, surrounded by low concentrations areas, identify these dense areas, and declare them as clusters. One advantage of this approach is that clusters can have any shape and are not limited to pre-defined conditions. Outliers are not assigned to any clusters and are ignored by this clustering algorithm [11].

B. Distribution-based clustering all those data cluster points as potential areas cluster belonging probability to a cluster. The algorithm identifies a center point, and the likelihood of a data point belonging to a cluster decreases as the distance from the center increases. If the data distribution is unknown, it may be advisable to use a different clustering algorithm [12].

C. Centroid-based clustering is a technique to separate data facts mapping on multiple central points. Each data center is assigned to a cluster by using a squared distance from its centroid; even though the method is vulnerable to initial parameters, it is also efficient and effective [17].

D. Hierarchical-based clustering is hierarchical structure data mapping, as a database or any taxonomies build a tree of clusters, which organizes the data from the top-down approach [17,18].

6.1.5 Classification of Clustering Algorithms in Deep Learning

In deep learning, clustering algorithms can be broadly categorized into two types:

A. Hard Clustering: Hard clustering algorithms partition the data into distinct clusters where each data point belongs to only one cluster. K-means is mainly used as a hard clustering deep algorithm [19–21]. The main objective of the clustering approach is to decrease the sum of squared distances between data points to their nearest centers. Hierarchical clustering and spectral clustering are other examples of hard clustering algorithms [11,22].

B. Soft Clustering: Soft clustering algorithms assign probabilities or weights to each data point, indicating their membership degree to each cluster. Soft clustering algorithms are useful when data points have fuzzy boundaries or belong to multiple clusters simultaneously. Some examples are the Gaussian mixture model (GMM) and fuzzy C-means, which could model data points as a mixture of Gaussian distributions [12,13].

Hard and soft clustering algorithms can be applied to various deep learning applications such as image segmentation, anomaly detection, and dimensionality reduction. The selection of the clustering algorithm depends on the data's nature and the application's objectives.

6.1.6 List of More Comprehensive Deep Learning Clustering Algorithms

1. Autoencoder-Based Clustering (ABC)

2. Boltzmann Machine (BM)

3. Convolutional Autoencoders

4. Deep Adaptive Clustering (DAC)

5. Deep Autoencoders

6. Deep Belief Network (DBN)

7. Deep Co-Clustering (DCC)

8. Deep Continuous Clustering (DCC)

9. Deep Embedded Clustering (DEC)

10. Deep Spectral Clustering (DSC)

11. Deep Subspace Clustering (DSC)

12. Generative Adversarial Network (GAN)

13. Hierarchical Temporal Memory (HTM)

14. Hopfield Network

15. K-Means Deep Clustering (K-Means DC)

16. Mean-Shift Deep Clustering (MS-DC)

17. Neural Gas Clustering (NGC)

18. Restricted Boltzmann Machine (RBM)

19. Self-Organizing Map (SOM)

20. Variational Autoencoder (VAE)

Convolutional autoencoders utilize convolutional layers instead of fully connected ones, enabling DNN to process image data. In contrast, DCEC is an unsupervised deep clustering algorithm that uses convolutional autoencoders to learn feature representations and cluster assignments jointly. Deep learning for multimodal data analysis (DLMDA) employs CNNs, RNNs, and autoencoders to learn representations for each modality and perform clustering. Deep multimodal clustering (DMC) is a type of DLMDA that handles various data types; similarly, deep multimodal similarity learning (DMSL) uses a siamese neural network to learn a similarity function between multimodal data to clustering. Multimodal deep clustering (MDC) leverages multiple autoencoders to learn feature representations for each modality and perform clustering. Multimodal deep embedded clustering (MDEC) utilizes deep autoencoders to learn feature representations for each modality and then combines them to perform clustering [23–26].

Although some of these algorithms, such as convolutional autoencoders, can be used for clustering multimedia data, they are not specific to multimodal data. It's important to note that other clustering algorithms may exist beyond those listed here; the field of deep learning is constantly evolving in research.

6.2 DEEP CLUSTERING ALGORITHM CHALLENGES AND THE MULTIMEDIA DATA

Deep clustering of multimedia data using methods is challenging for several reasons. Some of the critical challenges are:

1. **Top of form high-dimensional data:** Multimedia data is typically high-dimensional, meaning each data point has many features. For example, an image can have thousands or millions of pixels, each representing a feature. Applying clustering algorithms is challenging, as traditional methods can suffer from the curse of dimensionality.

2. **Nonlinear relationships:** Deep learning algorithms are well suited for capturing nonlinear relationships in data but applying these methods to multimedia data can still be challenging. For example, different images of the same object can have significant variations in lighting, orientation, and other factors, making it difficult to cluster them together.

3. **Lack of labeled data:** Clustering algorithms typically require labeled data to train the model, but labeling multimedia data can be time-consuming and expensive. In fact, there may be limited labeled data available for qualifying deep learning models for clustering.

4. **Scalability:** Deep learning models for clustering can be computationally intensive, mainly when working with large amounts of multimedia data. It is challenging to scale up these methods to handle big data.

5. **Interpretability:** Deep learning models can be difficult to interpret, making understanding challenging. Because specific data points are clustered, particularly problematic when working with multimedia data, as it can be hard to determine which features drive the clustering results.

6.2.1 Convolutional Autoencoders for Clustering Images

Convolutional autoencoders (CAEs) are neural networks that process images and learn to encode and decode images. Computer vision applications such as image denoising, super-resolution, and segmentation are commonly related to the computer vision field. One area where CAEs can be particularly useful is image clustering, an encoder component to extract features and group similar images into clusters in the neural networks [27,28]. This approach can effectively organize large image data sets and identify patterns or similarities between images [29].

CAEs method for image clustering has the following steps:

1. Train the CAE on an image data set to learn model encoding and decoding functions.

2. Extract the features from the encoder part of the trained CAE for each image in the data set.

3. Using any clustering algorithm, supposed k-means group the images based on their feature vectors.

4. Evaluate the quality of the clustering results using metrics such as the silhouette score or the Davies-Bouldin index.

Using convolutional autoencoders (CAEs) for image clustering can be highly effective, as these networks can learn meaningful representations of visual features within images – however, the accuracy of the clustering by the quality of the CAE to chosen clustering algorithm. In addition, selecting the optimal number of clusters is crucial and will depend on the specific data set and task. Therefore, careful consideration and evaluation of the CAE and clustering algorithm and appropriate selection of the number of clusters are essential for achieving accurate and reliable results in image clustering tasks.

6.2.2 Deep Convolutional Embedded Clustering for Clustering Images

Deep convolutional embedded clustering (DCEC) is a clustering algorithm that uses deep learning techniques to cluster images.

DCEC must combine the power of CNNs for feature extraction and clustering to similar group images, further classified into two:

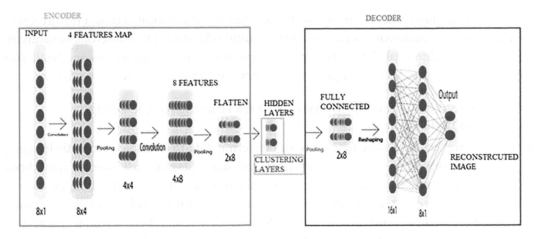

FIGURE 6.2   Shows the DCEC architecture.

I. A DCNN extracts high-level features from the image's data set; then, the CNN model is trained in an unsupervised manner using a reconstruction loss, which encourages the network to learn a compact representation of the images [30,31].

II. A clustering algorithm groups the images based on their feature representations. The clustering algorithm used in DCEC is based on the traditional k-means algorithm, but it is modified to consider the deep feature representations learned by CNN [2]. The DCEC algorithm is trained end-to-end, meaning the CNN and the clustering algorithm are trained together. During training, the CNN is optimized to produce feature representations well suited for clustering, while the clustering algorithm is optimized to group similar images together based on their feature representations.

Once trained, the DCEC model can use the clustering approach to cluster fresh images and classify them according to their attributes. Considering the intricate structure of image data and learning high-level feature representations suitable for clustering, DCEC is a reliable approach for grouping images, typical DCEC model has been showed in the Figure 6.2.

6.2.3 Multimodal Deep Embedded Clustering for Clustering Multimodal Data

Multimodal deep embedded clustering (MDEC) is a clustering method that blends deep learning with clustering to cluster multimodal data. Data with several modalities, like text, graphics, and audio, is called multimodal data. After training, MDEC is required to provide multimodal data representation. The CNN model combines clustering and reconstruction loss during training using a joint loss function. The reconstruction loss motivates the learned model to re-create the original multimodal data precisely, and the clustering loss motivates the available representation to group related data points together. After the neural network has been trained, the learned representation is clustered using a conventional clustering approach, like k-means.

To facilitate more efficient grouping, the learned representation acts as a feature space that captures the underlying structure of the multimodal data. On numerous benchmark data sets of multimodal data sets, various applications in computer vision, NLP, and multimedia analysis, MDEC outperformed other cutting-edge clustering algorithms.

6.2.4 Case Studies – The Effectiveness of Deep Learning for Clustering Multimodal Data

Deep learning techniques are new tools for clustering data that enable automatic learning of high-level representations from unstructured data. Several case studies have been carried out to show how well deep learning clusters multimedia data. Images, videos, audio, and text are just a few kinds of data that have been the subject of these studies' clustering research. For instance, in one study by Google researchers, a sizable image data set was clustered using deep learning. The photos were first clustered using k-means clustering after a deep neural network was trained to understand image representations. This study demonstrated that, on various image data sets, deep learning-based clustering outperformed conventional clustering techniques.

Another study, which concentrated on grouping video data, learned spatiotemporal representations from video frames using deep convolutional neural networks (DCNNs). The researchers discovered that deep learning-based clustering performed better on a sizable video data set than conventional clustering methods.

In a third study, MIT researchers used deep learning to cluster musical data. They clustered the musical data using the k-means technique after using DCNN to learn audio representations from music clips. The outcomes showed that deep learning-based clustering performed better on diverse music data sets than conventional clustering algorithms. Last, text data clustering has also been done using deep learning. In a study, Stanford University researchers employed a deep neural network to learn text representations before using k-means clustering to group news articles. This study demonstrated that deep learning-based clustering outperformed conventional clustering techniques on a sizable news data set.

These case studies show how deep learning has the potential to cluster multimedia data more effectively than conventional clustering techniques. As a result, deep learning has emerged as a promising study field in multimedia clustering and has the potential to enhance clustering performance in various applications.

6.3 DEEP LEARNING FOR CLASSIFICATION OF MULTIMEDIA DATA

Deep learning has significantly impacted the field of multimedia classification by providing superior performance on various multimedia data types, including images, videos, and audio. The CNNs, RNNs, and their variants have remarkable performance in multimedia classification. The following is a comprehensive list of deep learning classification algorithms:

1. Autoencoders

2. Capsule Network

3. Convolutional Neural Network (CNN)

4. Deep Belief Network (DBN)

5. Deep Residual Network (ResNet)

6. DenseNet

7. EfficientNet

8. Extreme Learning Machine (ELM)

9. Generative Adversarial Network (GAN)

10. Inception

11. Long Short-Term Memory (LSTM)

12. MobileNet

13. Multilayer Perceptron (MLP)

14. Radial Basis Function Network (RBFN)

15. Recurrent Neural Network (RNN)

16. ShuffleNet

17. SqueezeNet

18. Support Vector Machine (SVM)

19. Transformer Network

20. VGG

The list of popular deep classification algorithms is increasing day to day, but some essential algorithms are mentioned below:

A. **Convolutional Neural Networks (CNNs):** CNNs model showed in Figure 6.3 are a type of neural network that processes and classifies image data. The network is composed of a series of layers like convolutional and pooling layers to extract the features from the input data set of images. Then it uses these features to classify the image into one or more categories. Convolutional neural networks (CNNs) were designed by Yann LeCun, Yoshua Bengio, and colleagues in the 1990s, specifically for handwritten digit recognition. LeCun and his team developed a network architecture called LeNet-5, which used convolutional layers and max-pooling layers to extract features from handwritten digit images. LeNet-5 was revolutionary at the time, as it was the first successful application of deep learning to image recognition tasks. The network's high performance is marked on the MNIST, a popular benchmark data set for handwritten digit recognition. Since then, CNNs

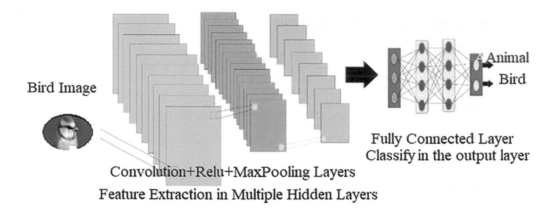

FIGURE 6.3 Shows the CNN architecture.

have evolved significantly, with many researchers developing new network architectures and training techniques to achieve even better performance on various computer vision tasks. CNNs are now widely applied in applications to solve many problems; for example, self-driving cars, facial recognition, and medical imaging [32–34]. CNNs solve problems in computer vision tasks, such as image recognition, object detection, and segmentation. The conceptual model of CNN is inspired by the structure of the visual cortex in the human brain, where neurons respond to specific regions of the visual field. The model of CNNs classified into convolutional, pooling, and fully connected layers. Firstly, the convolutional layer involves filters over the input image to extract features [35–37]. Then the pooling layer samples the convolutional layer's output, reducing the feature map's spatial size. The fully connected layer takes the flattened output of the pooling layer and produces the final classification of the images from a given data set. In the convolutional operation, the network must extract spatial features from the input images, and the network learns each filter pattern-wise during training in the input image. After applying many filters, the model learns to detect features such as edges, corners, and textures.

B. **Deep Belief Networks (DBNs)** were first presented in a 2006 paper titled "A Fast-Learning Algorithm for Deep Belief Nets" by Geoffrey Hinton, Simon Osindero, and Yee-Whye Teh. The DBN showed in Figure 6.4, is a deep learning approach

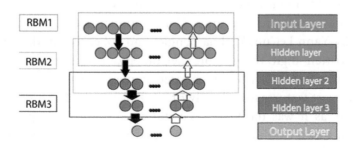

FIGURE 6.4 Shows the DBN architecture.

that consists of multiple layers of binary and continuous random variables. These neural networks have multiple layers of restricted Boltzmann machines and can be used for unsupervised learning and classification tasks. DBNs get trained in two-stage processes; one model is trained layer by layer using unsupervised model restricted Boltzmann machines (RBMs). With each layer, its hierarchical representation-based model for input data learns increasingly for abstract features. In the second stage, the model is trained using a supervised learning algorithm such as backpropagation. The fine-tuning setting adjusts the network weights to optimize a specific objective function, such as classification accuracy [38]. DBNs have many applications, including image and speech recognition, NLP, etc. The success of DBNs has led to significant research in deep learning, and they are one of the foundational architectures of modern deep learning.

C. **Generative Adversarial Networks (GANs):** The GAN model consists of a generator and a discriminator, which generates new data that resembles the training data. GANs model showed in Figure 6.5, can also be used for classification by training the discriminator to classify data into different categories. Generative adversarial networks (GANs) were first presented in a 2014 paper titled "Generative Adversarial Networks" by Ian Goodfellow and his colleagues at the University of Montreal. The paper proposed a novel approach to generative modeling that involved training two neural networks in a competitive setting [39,40]. The authors proposed a design using a game-theoretic approach to training the two networks, where the generator network learns to produce realistic data that can fool the discriminator network. The authors demonstrated the effectiveness of their approach on several image and handwriting data sets, showing that GANs could generate high-quality synthetic data that closely resembled real data. GANs are used for various applications, from image and video generation to text and audio

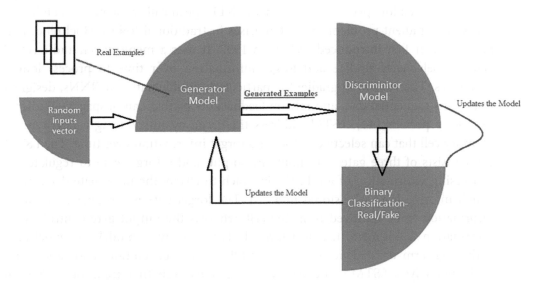

FIGURE 6.5   Shows the GANs architecture.

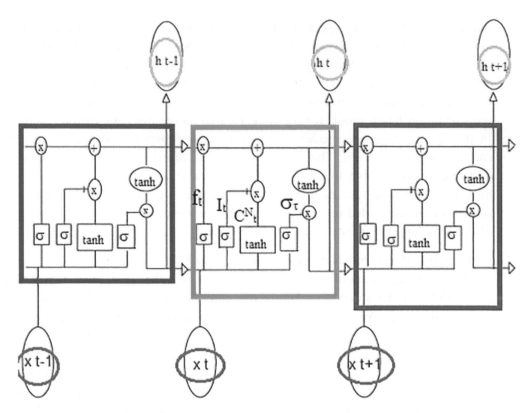

FIGURE 6.6 Shows the LSTM architecture.

synthesis. The success of GANs has spurred a large body of research on improving their training stability, scalability, and applicability to different types of data [41–43].

D. **Long Short-Term Memory (LSTM):** LSTM model showed in Figure 6.6, is a type of RNN applied for speech recognition and NLP specifically designed to handle the vanishing gradient problem that often arises in traditional RNNs. Hochreiter and Schmidhuber first introduced LSTMs in 1997. It uses a memory cell and a set of gates to selectively update and forget information over time to process longer sequences. The vanishing gradient is particularly problematic for RNNs, designed to process sequential data and rely on feedback loops that can propagate gradients over long periods [44]. LSTMs address this issue by introducing a new type of memory cell that can selectively store and forget information over time. The LSTM cell consists of three gates: an input, an output, and a forget gate to regulate the processing information of a cell. During each timestep, the input gate determines which information to be stored in a cell. The forget gate is responsible for what information to be removed from the cell, whereas the output gate controls what information is output to the next layer. LSTMs effectively model sequential data with long-term dependencies, such as NLP, speech recognition, and time series problem analysis. LSTM model performs more effectively than traditional RNNs in many applications' problems, including speech recognition, machine translation,

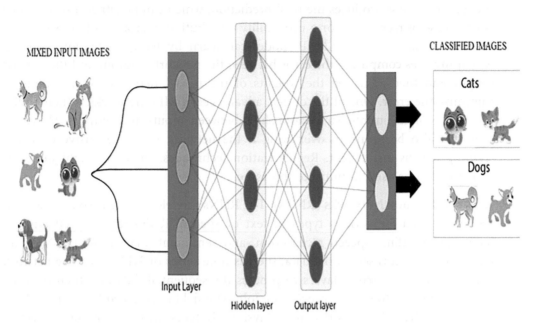

FIGURE 6.7   Shows the MLP architecture.

image captioning, and sentiment analysis. However, LSTMs can be computationally expensive and may suffer from overfitting if not appropriately trained. Several variations of LSTMs have been proposed to address these issues, such as the gated recurrent unit (GRU) and the peephole LSTM, which introduce additional mechanisms to improve the efficiency and effectiveness of the model.

E. **Multilayer Perceptron (MLP) Networks:** These neural networks have multiple layers of fully connected nodes and are commonly used for speech recognition and text classification tasks. The MLP network showed in Figure 6.7, was first introduced in a seminal paper by Paul Werbos in 1975, entitled; "Beyond Regression: New Tools for Prediction and Analysis in the Behavioural Sciences" [45]. In the study, Werbos proposed a backpropagation model to train a neural network with multiple layers and demonstrated that such networks could learn complex nonlinear relationships. However, it wasn't until the 1980s and 1990s that MLP networks gained widespread popularity, mainly due to the development of more efficient algorithms for training them. Today, MLP network models are the most used and vital components in deep learning applications. The MLP networks are artificial neural networks (ANNs) consisting of multiple layers with interconnected nodes or neurons [23,46,47]. This model network design effectively performs various tasks, including pattern recognition, classification, and linear regression. An MLP network model describes the input layer, receives the data input, and processes it to the first hidden layer. Each neuron in the hidden layer applies a nonlinear activation function to the input data doing processing to the next layer.

The process repeats for each subsequent hidden layer until the output layer reaches the target. Then it produces the final prediction, which can be either a scalar value (in the case of regression) or a probability distribution over a set of classes in the case of classification. The MLP model can learn by backpropagation training, which involves computing the error between the network's output and the desired output and then adjusting the weights of the model network's connections to minimize the error. One of the critical advantages of MLP networks is their ability to learn complex, nonlinear relationships between inputs and outputs. However, they can also be prone to overfitting if the network is too extensive or if the training data is insufficient. Regularization techniques, such as weight decay or dropout, can be used to mitigate this issue.

F. **Recurrent Neural Networks (RNNs):** The RNNs modeled in Figure 6.8 depend on sequential data for various types of text or speech. RNNs are very effective in language modeling, speech recognition, and sentiment analysis [48]. RNNs are designed to process sequential data, such as time series or NLP data. The network uses a series of recurrent layers to process the sequential data and then uses the final hidden state to make a prediction. John Hopfield introduced RNNs in 1982 in his paper "Neural Networks and Physical Systems with Emergent Collective Computational Abilities." However, it wasn't until the 1990s that RNNs gained widespread attention from machine learning researchers by developing more efficient models. The basic idea behind RNNs is to use feedback connections to allow the network to maintain a "memory" of previous inputs. The RNN makes them well suited to tasks such as time-series prediction, speech recognition, and

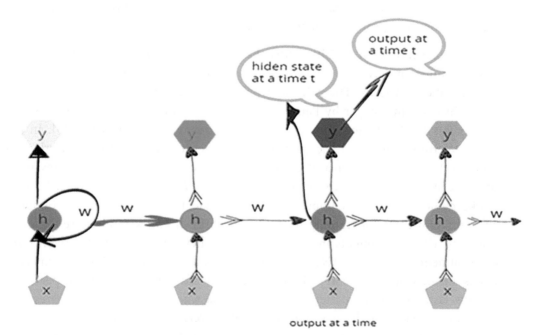

FIGURE 6.8   Shows the RNN architecture.

natural language processing. The critical challenge of RNNs model training is to vanish gradients, where the gradients are used to update the network weights. The concept has become very small and effectively "vanished" as they propagate backward through the network. To address this issue, various techniques such as LSTM (long short-term memory) and GRU (gated recurrent units) have been developed to allow RNNs to maintain longer-term dependencies [49,50]. Today, the RNN model is applicable in various applications, from speech recognition and NLP to image and video analysis. Still, it is a research area in the world.

G. **Residual Networks (ResNets):** These neural networks employ skip connections, allowing deeper networks can train more effectively, as an image classifier ResNets model showed in Figure 6.9, were first introduced by Kaiming He et al. in 2016, "Deep Residual Learning for Image Recognition" at an international conference [51,52]. The critical innovation of this network model is residual blocks, which allow the network to learn residual mappings rather than trying to learn the underlying mapping from input to output directly. The resulting data receives by adding skip connections that bypass one or more network layers. This model will allow the residual mapping more easily. Using residual blocks in the model ResNets network has various advantages, including improved training speed and better accuracy on deep networks. By allowing the network to learn residual mappings, ResNets can better handle the problem of vanishing gradients that can occur in deep networks.

H. **Support Vector Machines (SVMs):** SVMs are a popular machine learning algorithm, modeled in Figure 6.10 for classification. However, they can also be combined with deep learning techniques to improve performance using in-depth features as input. An SVM is not typically considered a deep learning method, a supervised machine learning algorithm that can be used for classification and regression tasks. SVM was introduced by Vapnik et al. in the 1990s [53,54]. On the other hand, deep learning is a subfield of machine learning that focuses on using neural networks with multiple layers to learn data representations. Deep learning is popular globally and has been used to achieve state-of-the-art results in many areas, including image recognition, NLP, and speech recognition. So, SVM is a robust network and widely used machine learning algorithm. It is not considered a deep learning method, but now deep learning methods usually refer to the model networks with many layers, which were not widely used until the mid-2000s.

I. **Deep Neural Decision Trees (DNDT):** DNDT showed in the Figure 6.11, is a machine learning approach model that combines the benefits of a decision tree model and neural networks. It was introduced in a research paper by Xiao Zhang et al. in 2017 [55–58]. The DNDTs are to perform classification tasks by recursively partitioning the input space into smaller and smaller regions. The algorithm uses decision trees to split the input space and uses a neural network to classify each region. Traditional decision trees define a series of rules to partition the input space

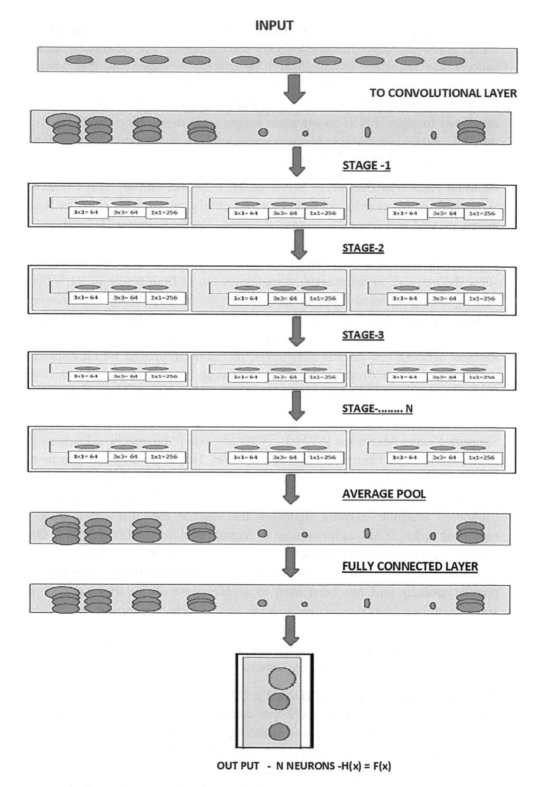

FIGURE 6.9   Shows the ResNet architecture.

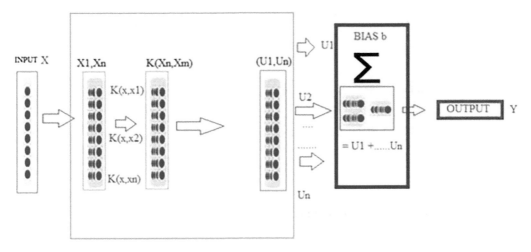

FIGURE 6.10   Shows the SVM architecture.

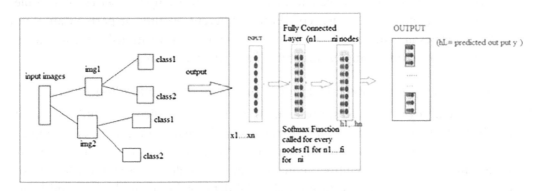

FIGURE 6.11   Shows the DNDT architecture.

into smaller regions, and a simple model fits into each region. In neural networks, a complex nonlinear model learns by combining simple units called neurons. However, decision trees suffer from high variance and low expressiveness, while neural networks may suffer from overfitting and lack of interpretability [57]. DNDT aims to overcome these limitations by learning a decision tree structure optimized for a neural network model. It partitions the input space using a binary tree structure, where each leaf node is associated with a neural network model that predicts the target output for the corresponding input region. The decision tree structure learns by a reinforcement learning approach, where the reward is based on the model's accuracy on the training data.

J. **Capsule Networks (CapsNets):** The CapsNets showed in the Figure 6.12, were introduced by Geoffrey Hinton et al. in 2017 as a novel approach to address the limitations of traditional neural networks in image recognition tasks [59,60]. The idea was to group neurons into capsules, where each capsule represents an instantiation parameter of a visual entity, such as an object or part of an object

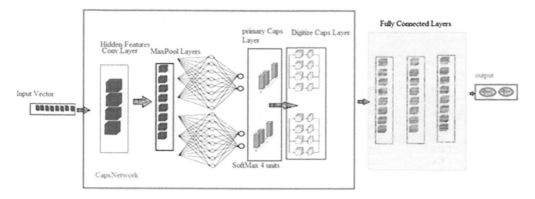

FIGURE 6.12   Shows the CapsNets architecture.

[61,62]. Capsule networks are a type of neural network designed to capture hierarchical relationships between features. The network uses a series of capsules, which are groups of neurons representing different features or parts of an object. The capsules are connected based on their hierarchical relationships, allowing the network to capture complex structures and patterns in the input data.

6.3.1 Incorporating Multimodal Data for Improving Classification Performance

Multimodal data involves images, texts, audio, and videos, which can enhance classification through the custom model and performance in many computer vision applications. One approach to incorporating multimodal data is through fusion models that combine information from multiple modalities into a single representation for classification. There are several ways to fuse multimodal data, including early, late, and hybrid fusion.

Early fusion combines the features from each modality into a single vector at the input level, which is then fed into a classification model, such as a neural network. This approach can be practical when complementary modalities provide specific information about the input. Each modality is processed separately in late fusion, and their outputs are later combined in the classification pipeline. For instance, in image classification, features extracted from an image and its corresponding text description can be combined after processing each modality separately. Late fusion is useful when the modalities provide redundant or complementary information. Hybrid fusion combines early and late fusion, integrating features from each modality at multiple levels. This approach can be more effective than early or late fusion when the modalities provide complementary and redundant information.

Incorporating multimodal data can improve the robustness of classification models by reducing the impact of noise or errors in a single modality. For example, including audio and visual data in speech recognition can enhance performance in noisy environments where the audio signal may be degraded. Multimodal data can improve classification performance by leveraging complementary and redundant information from multiple modalities.

6.4 BLOCKCHAIN TECHNOLOGY AND DEEP LEARNING ALGORITHMS IN THE CONTEXT OF MULTIMODAL DATA

Blockchain technology and deep learning algorithms combined to create a secure and efficient system for processing multimodal data. Here are some ways that blockchain technology can apply the tech in the context of deep learning algorithms:

I. **Data storage and sharing:** Blockchain technology provides a decentralized and secure way to store and share data, which can be particularly useful for large and complex multimodal data. Deep learning [63–66] algorithms can be trained on this data for more accurate and efficient analysis.

II. **Data provenance:** Blockchain technology can provide a way to track the origin and history of data, which is essential for ensuring the integrity of the data used in deep learning algorithms. This level can help prevent data tampering and ensure that the data is trustworthy [67].

III. **Privacy and security:** Blockchain technology can ensure the confidentiality and security of multimodal data in deep learning algorithms. This is particularly important when dealing with sensitive data such as medical records or financial information [68–71].

A. **Critical factors of distributed ledger technology (DLT):**

1. Decentralization: DLT is designed to be decentralized, meaning no central authority controls the system. Instead, it is distributed across a network of nodes, each maintaining a copy of the ledge [72].

2. Security: DLT is designed on cryptographic principles, which makes it highly secure. The data stored on the ledger is protected by a complex set of cryptographic algorithms that make it virtually impossible to tamper with [73].

3. Transparency: DLT provides a high degree of transparency; all transactions are recorded on the ledger and viewed by anyone on the network [74,75].

B. **Critical components of deep learning algorithms:**

1. Neural networks: Algorithms based on ANNs designed to mimic the behavior of the human brain. These networks setting up of interconnected nodes that process and transmit information.

2. Training data: Deep learning algorithms require much training data to learn from. This data is typically labeled, meaning it is classified or categorized somehow.

3. Optimization algorithms: Deep learning algorithms use optimization algorithms to adjust the weights and biases of the neural network. These

algorithms are designed to minimize the error between predicted and actual output [6,76,77].

In summary, combining blockchain technology with deep learning algorithms can provide a powerful tool for processing and analyzing multimodal data. The critical factors of DLT, including decentralization, security, and transparency, can help ensure the integrity and privacy of the data. In contrast, the essential components of deep learning algorithms, including neural networks, training data, and optimization algorithms, can help ensure accurate and efficient analysis.

6.4.1 Cross-Border Blockchain Technology and Deep Learning Methods

Cross-border blockchain technology refers to using blockchain technology to enable secure and decentralized transactions and data sharing across different borders and jurisdictions [78–81]. We define the cross-border blockchain as an emerging technology with the following key attributes:

1. A blockchain technology mechanism

2. That communicates across the border with another blockchain technology mechanism

3. With an independent P2P network-TCP covered

4. Wallet -Wallet cross-border without a middleman or intermediary barriers-communication

5. P-2-P -TCP global network- data communication

6. An independent entity of one P2P to talk with another entity of P2P networks without a middleman character.

7. Cross-border data, assets, or money transfer/exchange using wallet's token passing algorithm between two different systems/applications by permissioned consensus algorithm of every node and authentication of master (full) node of two various entities.

8. Digital identities security and management – transmissions between heterogeneous cross-border blockchain network applications.

These key points summarized the definition of cross-border blockchain technology and the conceptual model of the cross border blockchain in the Figure 6.13 as below:

Cross border blockchain – an emerging technology, a most secured way to transfer data, digital identities, money, or any digital assets with complete encryption methods and removing the intermediatory layer of granting permission for any transfer/share of digital assets data between two nodes, parties, networks, out of frontiers/countries in a minimum time.

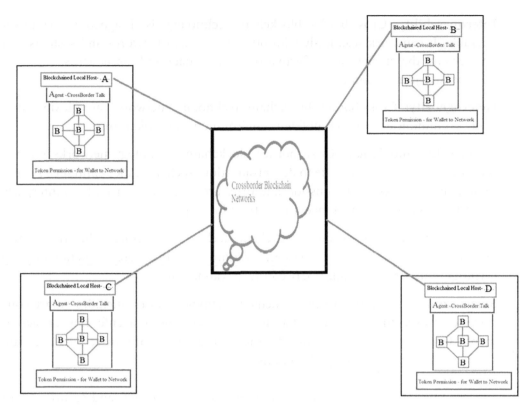

FIGURE 6.13   Shows the cross-border blockchain architecture.

6.4.2 Key Attributes of Cross-Border Blockchain Technology

The following are some suggested key attributes of cross-border blockchain technology:

1. **Decentralization:** Cross-border blockchain technology is designed to be decentralized, with no central controlling authority. Since it's distributed across a network of nodes, each maintains a copy of the ledger. This technique helps ensure the security and privacy of transactions and data across different borders and jurisdictions.

2. **Distributed capability:** Cross-border blockchain technology is fragmented into network nodes to ensure the secrecy and transparency of the validated data are not readable by unauthorized persons or nodes.

3. **Transparency:** Cross-border blockchain technology provides high clarity, as all transactions are recorded on the ledger and can be viewed by anyone on the network. This level helps ensure the integrity of the data and reduces the risk of fraud and other forms of criminal activity.

4. **Security:** Cross-border blockchain technology designed on cryptographic principles makes it highly secure. The data stored on the ledger is protected by a complex set of cryptographic algorithms that make it virtually impossible to tamper with.

5. **Interoperability:** Cross-border blockchain technology is designed to be inter-operable. It can work seamlessly with other blockchain networks and systems and help ensure the efficient and effective transfer of data and assets across different borders and jurisdictions.

6. **Heterogeneity:** Cross-border blockchain technology networks are flexible and easily communicate between different environments and platforms.

7. **Remove the middleman:** Cross-border blockchain technology networks remove the role of the middleman, due to decentralization, such as in the remittance system middleman and central permission authority are mandatory at both counterparts for any transactions, which take a long time for approval.

8. **Trust-building:** Cross-border blockchain technology ensures the trust level between stakeholders due to decentralization and distributed functionality by cryptographic strategies and smart contracts validation.

9. **Smart contracts:** Cross-border blockchain technology often includes smart contracts (self-executing contracts) that automate verifying and enforcing an agreement's terms and help ensure the efficiency and accuracy of transactions and data sharing across borders and jurisdictions.

Cross-border blockchain technology is a decentralized, transparent, and secure system enabling transactions and data sharing across different borders and jurisdictions. Its key attributes include decentralization, transparency, security, interoperability, and the use of smart contracts.

6.4.3 Cross-Border and Deep Learning Multimodal Blockchain Technology

Cross-border blockchain technology and deep learning methods process and analyze multimodal data across borders and jurisdictions [21,82]. Some ways these technologies apply in the context:

1. **Cross-border data sharing:** Blockchain technology can provide a secure and de-centralized way to share data across different borders and jurisdictions. It's imperative when dealing with sensitive data such as medical records or financial information, which may be subject to foreign laws and regulations in different countries. It can be trained on the given data for more accurate and efficient analysis [65,83,84].

2. **Multilingual processing:** Multimodal data often includes text, images, and other forms of content in multiple languages. Deep learning methods such as natural language processing (NLP) and computer vision process this data and extract meaningful insights. Blockchain technology can help ensure the accuracy and privacy of this data, regardless of the language or jurisdiction.

3. **Fraud detection:** Deep learning algorithms can detect fraud and other forms of criminal activity in multimodal data. Blockchain technology can provide a secure and transparent way to track the origin and history of this data, making it easier to detect and prevent fraudulent activity across different borders and jurisdictions.

4. **Supply chain management:** Blockchain technology can track the movement of goods and services across different borders and jurisdictions. Deep learning algorithms can analyze this data and provide insights into supply chain efficiency, product quality, and other factors. The DLT algorithms improve supply chain management and reduce business costs across borders.

6.4.4 Future Trends and Applications of the Blockchain and Deep Learning

Cross-border blockchain technology and deep learning methods can process and analyze multimodal data across borders and jurisdictions. These technologies can help ensure the security and privacy of sensitive data, detect fraud and other criminal activity, and improve supply chain management, among other applications.

Deep learning for multimedia data analysis is continuously progressing, and this section aims to provide an overview of the current research directions and future trends. One contemporary study area of interest is the design and development of algorithms capable of handling enormous volumes of multimedia data. Deep learning algorithms that can manage and analyze such data in a scalable manner have become increasingly necessary due to the expanding volume of multimedia data generated in numerous sectors, such as social media, e-commerce, and healthcare. To speed up the training and inference of deep learning models on enormous amounts of multimedia data, researchers are investigating methods including distributed learning, parallel processing, and GPU acceleration.

Integrating deep learning with AI tools like reinforcement learning and generative adversarial networks (GANs) is another area of research. The main goal of reinforcement learning is to teach agents how to interact with their environment and gain knowledge via feedback. At the same time, GANs are deep learning models that can generate realistic data samples, such as images and videos. Researchers are exploring how these technologies can be combined with deep learning to enhance multimedia data analysis. For instance, reinforcement learning can optimize the clustering and classification of multimedia data, while GANs can be used to generate synthetic data for training deep learning models [68,85,86].

A third research direction is developing deep learning algorithms that effectively handle multimodal data. Multimodal data contains information from different modalities, such as images, audio, and text. Researchers are exploring how deep learning algorithms can extract and fuse information from various modalities to enhance multimedia data analysis. For instance, deep learning models can be trained to generate captions for images or recognize objects in videos using visual and auditory cues.

Regarding future trends, one critical direction is developing explainable deep learning algorithms. Explainable AI refers to the ability of AI models to explain their decisions and actions, which is especially crucial in domains such as healthcare and finance, where decisions made by AI models can have significant consequences. Researchers are exploring how deep learning models can be designed to provide transparent and interpretable explanations for their outputs.

Designing deep learning algorithms that can handle spatiotemporal data is another potential development. Videos and sensor data are examples of spatiotemporal data, including space and time information. To manage spatiotemporal data, which is crucial for surveillance, transportation, and environmental monitoring applications, researchers are looking into how deep learning algorithms might be modified.

The field of deep learning for multimedia data analysis is rapidly growing, and new research directions and trends are constantly emerging. To manage multimodal and spatiotemporal data, researchers are investigating large-scale learning approaches and merging them with other AI technologies to create models that make sense. More powerful deep learning algorithms for analyzing multimedia data will appear as the area develops.

6.5 CONCLUSION

The chapter before thoroughly described how deep learning algorithms can be used to cluster and categorize multimedia data. The challenges offered by clustering multimedia data have shown incredible promise for deep learning algorithms. These deep learning methods are more potent for multimodal data, including multimodal deep embedded clustering, deep convolutional embedded clustering, and convolutional autoencoders. In numerous real-world applications, these algorithms successfully cluster multimedia data.

In the chapter, deep learning for multimedia data analysis was also discussed in terms of future trends and present research goals. Constructing explainable deep learning algorithms, integrating with other AI technologies, and building algorithms that can manage large-scale and multimodal data have all become required study fields due to the growth of multimedia data. These developments have significant consequences for both theory and practice, and they can potentially revolutionize several industries, including social media, healthcare, and finance. The chapter also discussed the difficulties of using deep learning algorithms for clustering and classification, including the size of the data sets and the interpretability of the complex representations that these algorithms learn to represent data. Therefore, academics and practitioners should focus on developing novel techniques for collecting and labeling massive data sets, novel approaches for understanding and visualizing deep learning algorithms, and novel applications. Consider the ethical ramifications of using deep learning algorithms as they are used more frequently, considering issues like bias and privacy. In conclusion, the development of deep learning for multimedia data analysis opens intriguing new research and application areas, and the field is expected to continue to develop.

ABBREVIATIONS

1. Autoencoder-Based Clustering (ABC)

2. Autoencoders

3. Boltzmann Machine (BM)

4. Capsule Network

5. Convolutional Autoencoders

6. Convolutional Neural Network (CNN)

7. Deep Adaptive Clustering (DAC)

8. Deep Autoencoders

9. Deep Belief Network (DBN)

10. Deep Belief Network (DBN)

11. Deep Co-Clustering (DCC)

12. Deep Continuous Clustering (DCC)

13. Deep Embedded Clustering (DEC)

14. Deep Residual Network (ResNet)

15. Deep Spectral Clustering (DSC)

16. Deep Subspace Clustering (DSC)

17. Densely Connected Convolutional Networks (DenseNet)

18. Efficient Net, a CNN, Improving Accuracy and Efficiency through AutoML and Model Scaling.

19. Extreme Learning Machine (ELM)

20. Generative Adversarial Network (GAN)

21. Generative Adversarial Network (GAN)

22. Hierarchical Temporal Memory (HTM)

23. Hopfield Network

24. Inception means implanting an idea into someone's subconscious mind through a dream.

25. K-Means Deep Clustering (K-Means DC)

26. Long Short-Term Memory (LSTM)

27. Mean-Shift Deep Clustering (MS-DC)

28. MobileNet, convolutional neural network

29. MobileNet-v2, a convolutional neural network that is 53 layers deep.

30. Multilayer Perceptron (MLP)

31. Neural Gas Clustering (NGC)

32. Radial Basis Function Network (RBFN)

33. Recurrent Neural Network (RNN)

34. Region-Based Convolutional Neural Network (R-CNN or RCNN)

35. Residual Neural Network-34 Layers (ResNet-34)

36. Residual Neural Network-50 Layers (ResNet-50)

37. Restricted Boltzmann Machine (RBM)

38. Self-Organizing Map (SOM)

39. ShuffleNet, CNN for mobile devices

40. SqueezeNet, CNN has 18 layers

41. Support Vector Machine (SVM)

42. Transformer Network

43. Variational Autoencoder (VAE)

44. Visual Geometry Group (VGG)

45. Visual Geometry Group, 16 layers (VGG-16)

46. Visual Geometry Group, 19 layers (VGG-19)

47. Visual Geometry Group, Deep Neural Network (VGGNet)

REFERENCES

[1] Z. Kastrati, F. Dalipi, A. S. Imran, K. P. Nuci, and M. A. Wani, "Sentiment Analysis of Students' Feedback with NLP and Deep Learning: A Systematic Mapping Study," *mdpi.com*, 2021, doi: 10.3390/app11093986.

[2] A. O. Panhwar *et al.*, "Plant Health Detection Enabled CNN Scheme in IoT Network," *International Journal of Computing and Digital Systems*, vol. 12, no. 1, pp. 335–344, 2022, doi: 10.12785/ijcds/120127.

[3] E. F. Morales and H. J. Escalante, "A Brief Introduction to Supervised, Unsupervised, and Reinforcement Learning," *Elsevier*, 2022, [Online]. Available: https://www.sciencedirect.com/science/article/pii/B9780128201251000178

[4] S. K. Chinnamgari, *R Machine Learning Projects: Implement Supervised, Unsupervised, and Reinforcement Learning Techniques Using R3.5*, 2019, [Online]. Available: https://books.google.com/books?hl=en&lr=&id=4dKDDwAAQBAJ&oi=fnd&pg=PP1&dq=deep+learning+supervised+unsupervised+reinforcement&ots=pxnLaGcToB&sig=MMafc1Uir2Eo0ZY6zuZbbbwIJkk

[5] Y. Li, "Deep Reinforcement Learning: An Overview," May 2017, [Online]. Available: http://arxiv.org/abs/1701.07274

[6] J. García and F. Fernández, "A Comprehensive Survey on Safe Reinforcement Learning," *Journal of Machine Learning Research*, vol. 16, no. 1, pp. 1437–1480, 2015.

[7] "Q-Learning Deep Q, Deep Deterministic Policy Gradient - Google Scholar," [Online]. Available: https://scholar.google.com/scholar?hl=en&as_sdt=0%2C5&q=Q-learning+deep+Q%2C+Deep+Deterministic+Policy+Gradient++&btnG=

[8] W. Shi, S. Song, C. Wu, and C. L. Philip Chen, "Multi Pseudo Q-Learning-Based Deterministic Policy Gradient for Tracking Control of Autonomous Underwater Vehicles," *ieeexplore.ieee.org*, 2018, [Online]. Available: https://ieeexplore.ieee.org/abstract/document/8594674/

[9] T. Tiong, I. Saad, K. T. K. Teo, and H. B. Lago, "Deep Reinforcement Learning with Robust Deep Deterministic Policy Gradient," *ieeexplore.ieee.org*, 2020, [Online]. Available: https://ieeexplore.ieee.org/abstract/document/9309539/

[10] A. Krizhevsky, I. Sutskever, and G. E. Hinton, "ImageNet Classification with Deep Convolutional Neural Networks," *Commun ACM*, vol. 60, no. 6, pp. 84–90, June 2017, doi: 10.1145/3065386.

[11] M. Abavisani and V. M. Patel, "Deep Multimodal Subspace Clustering Networks," *ieeexplore.ieee.org*, 2018, [Online]. Available: https://ieeexplore.ieee.org/abstract/document/8488484/

[12] X. Zhang, J. Mu, L. Zong, and X. Yang, "End-To-End Deep Multimodal Clustering," *ieeexplore.ieee.org*, 2020, [Online]. Available: https://ieeexplore.ieee.org/abstract/document/9102921/

[13] L. Zong, F. Miao, X. Zhang, and B. Xu, "Multimodal Clustering via Deep Commonness and Uniqueness Mining," *International Conference on Information and Knowledge Management, Proceedings*, pp. 2357–2360, May 2020, doi: 10.1145/3340531.3412103.

[14] A. A. Sathio, "A Study on the Conceptual Frame Work of Data Warehousing in Health Sector in Pakistan a Case Study of a Hospital System and Disease (Hepatitis C)," *International Journal of Computer (IJC)*, vol. 29, no. 1, pp. 59–81, September 2018, doi: https://www.researchgate.net/publication/324896538_A_Study_On_The_Conceptual_Frame_Work_Of_Data_Warehousing_In_Health_Sector_In_Pakistan_A_Case_Study_Of_a_Hospital_System_And_Disease_Hepatitis_C/citations.

[15] A. A. Sathio and A. M. Brohi, *The Imperative Role of Pervasive Data in Healthcare*, in M. S. Husain et al., (Eds.), Switzerland AG: Springer, Cham, 2021, pp. 17–21. doi: 10.1007/978-3-030-77746-3_2

[16] A. A. Laghari et al., "The Role of Software Configuration Management and Capability Maturity Model in System Quality," 2019. [Online]. Available: https://www.researchgate.net/publication/337707282

[17] R. Qi, A. Ma, Q. Ma, and Q. Zou, "Clustering and Classification Methods for Single-Cell RNA-Sequencing Data," *Briefings in Bioinformatics*, vol. 21, no. 4, Oxford University Press, pp. 1196–1208, July 10, 2019. doi: 10.1093/bib/bbz062.

[18] M. R. Karim et al., "Deep lEarning-Based Clustering Approaches for Bioinformatics," *Brief Bioinform*, vol. 22, no. 1, pp. 393–415, January 2021, doi: 10.1093/bib/bbz170.

[19] A. A. Sathio, M. ur R. Shaikh, A. O. Panhwar, M. A. Sahito, and A. Lakhan, "Recommended Employment Model for Silent Community using Smart Technology," *International Journal of Emerging Trends in Engineering Research*, vol. 9, no. 7, pp. 1030–1034, July 2021, doi: 10.30534/ijeter/2021/31972021.

[20] A. A. Sathio, M. ur R. Shaikh, A. O. Panhwar, M. A. Sahito, A. Lakhan, and R. Singh, "Implementation of ETL Tool for Data Warehousing for Non-Hodgkin Lymphoma (NHL) Cancer in Public Sector, Pakistan," *International Journal of Emerging Trends in Engineering Research*, vol. 9, no. 7, pp. 1003–1007, July 2021, doi: 10.30534/ijeter/2021/27972021.

[21] M. ur R. Shaikh, A. A. Sathio, A. Lakhan, A. O. Panhwar, M. A. Sahito, and A. Kehar, "Dynamic Content Enabled Microservice for Business Applications in Distributed Cloudlet Cloud Network," *International Journal of Emerging Trends in Engineering Research*, vol. 9, no. 7, pp. 1035–1039, July 2021, doi: 10.30534/ijeter/2021/32972021.

[22] M. Chegini, J. Bernard, P. Berger, A. Sourin, K. Andrews, and T. Schreck, "Interactive Labelling of a Multivariate Data Set for Supervised Machine Learning Using Linked Visualisations, Clustering, and Active Learning," *Visual Informatics*, vol. 3, no. 1, pp. 9–17, March 2019, doi: 10.1016/j.visinf.2019.03.002.

[23] J. Khatti and K. S. Grover, "CBR Prediction of Pavement Materials in Unsoaked Condition Using LSSVM, LSTM-RNN, and ANN Approaches," *International Journal of Pavement Research and Technology*, 2023, doi: 10.1007/S42947-022-00268-6.

[24] J. Khatti and K. S. Grover, "CBR Prediction of Pavement Materials in Unsoaked Condition Using LSSVM, LSTM-RNN, and ANN Approaches," *Springer*, 2023, [Online]. Available: https://link.springer.com/article/. doi:10.1007/s42947-022-00268-6

[25] N. Chaibi, B. Atmani, and M. Mokaddem, "Deep Learning Approaches to Intrusion Detection: A New Performance of ANN and RNN on NSL-KDD," *ACM International Conference Proceeding Series*, May 2020, doi: 10.1145/3432867.3432889.

[26] N. Chaibi, B. Atmani, and M. Mokaddem , "Deep Learning Approaches to Intrusion Detection: A New Performance of ANN and RNN on NSL-KDD," *dl.acm.org*, 2020, [Online]. Available: 10.1145/3432867.3432889

[27] X. Guo, X. Liu, E. Zhu, and J. Yin, "Deep Clustering with Convolutional Autoencoders," in *Lecture Notes in Computer Science (Including Subseries Lecture Notes in Artificial Intelligence and Lecture Notes in Bioinformatics)*, Springer Verlag, 2017, pp. 373–382. doi: 10.1007/978-3-319-70096-0_39.

[28] X. Guo *et al.*, "Deep Clustering with Convolutional Autoencoders," *Springer*, vol. 10635, LNCS, pp. 373–382, 2017, doi: 10.1007/978-3-319-70096-0_39.

[29] S. Chang, "Deep Clustering with Fusion Autoencoder," arXiv preprint arXiv:2201.04727. Chicago.

[30] Y. Bengio, Y. Lecun, and G. Hinton, "Deep Learning for AI," *Commun ACM*, vol. 64, no. 7, pp. 58–65, June 2021, doi: 10.1145/3448250.

[31] X. Guo, X. Liu, E. Zhu, and J. Yin, "Deep Clustering with Convolutional Autoencoders," in *Lecture Notes in Computer Science (Including Subseries Lecture Notes in Artificial Intelligence and Lecture Notes in Bioinformatics)*, Springer Verlag, 2017, pp. 373–382. doi: 10.1007/978-3-319-70096-0_39.

[32] M. Aamir, Z. Rahman, W. Ahmed Abro, M. Tahir, and S. Mustajar Ahmed, "An Optimized Architecture of Image Classification Using Convolutional Neural Network," *International Journal of Image, Graphics and Signal Processing*, vol. 11, no. 10, pp. 30–39, October 2019, doi: 10.5815/ijigsp.2019.10.05.

[33] M. Aamir, Z. Rahman, Y. F. Pu, W. A. Abro, and K. Gulzar, "Satellite Image Enhancement Using Wavelet-Domain Based on Singular Value Decomposition," 2019, [Online]. Available: www.ijacsa.thesai.org

[34] M. Aamir, Y. F. Pu, Z. Rahman, M. Tahir, H. Naeem, and Q. Dai, "A Framework for Automatic Building Detection from Low-Contrast Satellite Images," *Symmetry (Basel)*, vol. 11, no. 1, January 2019, doi: 10.3390/sym11010003.

[35] Y. Guan, *et al.*, "A Region-Based Efficient Network for Accurate Object Detection," *Traitement du Signal*, vol. 38, no. 2, pp. 481–494, April 2021, doi: 10.18280/ts.380228.

[36] M. Aamir *et al.*, "A Hybrid Proposed Framework for Object Detection and Classification," *Journal of Information Processing Systems*, vol. 14, no. 5, pp. 1176–1194, 2018, doi: 10.3745/JIPS.02.0095.

[37] Y. Guan *et al.*, "A Framework for Efficient Brain Tumor Classification Using MRI Images," *Mathematical Biosciences and Engineering*, vol. 18, no. 5, pp. 5790–5815, 2021, doi: 10.3934/MBE.2021292.

[38] Y. Hua, J. Guo, and H. Zhao, "Deep Belief Networks and Deep Learning," *ieeexplore.ieee.org*, 2015, [Online]. Available: https://ieeexplore.ieee.org/abstract/document/7111524/

[39] T. Iqbal and H. Ali, "Generative Adversarial Network for Medical Images (MI-GAN)," *Journal of Medical Systems*, vol. 42, no. 11, May 2018, doi: 10.1007/S10916-018-1072-9.

[40] T. Iqbal and H. Ali, "Generative Adversarial Network for Medical Images (MI-GAN)," *Springer*, 2018, [Online]. Available: https://link.springer.com/article/. doi: 10.1007/s10916-018-1072-9

[41] M. Aamir, Y. F. Pu, W. A. Abro, H. Naeem, and Z. Rahman, "A Hybrid Approach for Object Proposal Generation," in *Lecture Notes in Electrical Engineering*, Springer Verlag, 2019, pp. 251–259. doi: 10.1007/978-3-319-91659-0_18.

[42] M. Aamir *et al.*, "A Deep Learning Approach for Brain Tumor Classification Using MRI Images," *Computers and Electrical Engineering*, vol. 101, July 2022, doi: 10.1016/j.compeleceng.2022.108105.

[43] Y. Guan *et al.*, "An Object Detection Framework Based on Deep Features and High-Quality Object Locations," *Traitement du Signal*, vol. 38, no. 3, pp. 719–730, June 2021, doi: 10.18280/ts.380319.

[44] R. C. Staudemeyer and E. R. Morris, "Understanding LSTM – A Tutorial into Long Short-Term Memory Recurrent Neural Networks," May 2019, [Online]. Available: http://arxiv.org/abs/1909.09586

[45] M. Riedmiller, "Multi Layer Perceptron," *ml.informatik.uni-freiburg.de*, 2014, [Online]. Available: https://ml.informatik.uni-freiburg.de/former/_media/documents/teaching/ss12/ml/05_mlps.printer.pdf

[46] A. Javed, H. Larijani, A. Ahmadinia, and R. Emmanuel, "Comparison of the Robustness of RNN, MPC and ANN Controller for Residential Heating System," *ieeexplore.ieee.org*, 2014, [Online]. Available: https://ieeexplore.ieee.org/abstract/document/7034849/

[47] J. Khatti and K. S. Grover "CBR Prediction of Pavement Materials in Unsoaked Condition Using LSSVM, LSTM-RNN, and ANN Approaches," *Springer*, 2023, [Online]. Available: https://link.springer.com/article/. doi: 10.1007/s42947-022-00268-6

[48] W. Yin, K. Kann, M. Yu, and H. Schütze, "Comparative Study of CNN and RNN for Natural Language Processing," *arxiv.org*, 2017, [Online]. Available: https://arxiv.org/abs/1702.01923

[49] J. Chung, C. Gulcehre, K. Cho, and Y. Bengio, "Empirical Evaluation of Gated Recurrent Neural Networks on Sequence Modeling," May 2014, [Online]. Available: http://arxiv.org/abs/1412.3555

[50] R. Rana, "Gated Recurrent Unit (GRU) for Emotion Classification from Noisy Speech," May 2016, [Online]. Available: http://arxiv.org/abs/1612.07778

[51] M. Abdi and S. Nahavandi, "Multi-Residual Networks: Improving the Speed and Accuracy of Residual Networks," May 2016, [Online]. Available: http://arxiv.org/abs/1609.05672

[52] S. Targ, D. Almeida, and K. Lyman, "Resnet in Resnet: Generalizing Residual Architectures," May 2016, [Online]. Available: http://arxiv.org/abs/1603.08029

[53] P. Du, X. Ma, Z. Wang, Y. Mo, and P. Peng, "A Prediction Method of Missing Vehicle Position Information Based on Least Square Support Vector Machine," *Sustainable Operations and Computers*, vol. 2, no. January, pp. 30–35, 2021, doi: 10.1016/j.susoc.2021.03.003.

[54] J. Raja, P. Shanmugam, and R. Pitchai, "An Automated Early Detection of Glaucoma Using Support Vector Machine Based Visual Geometry Group 19 (VGG-19) Convolutional Neural Network," *Wireless Personal Communications*, vol. 118, no. 1, pp. 523–534, May 2021, doi: 10.1007/S11277-020-08029-Z.

[55] Y. Yang, I. G. Morillo, and T. M. Hospedales, "Deep Neural Decision Trees," June 2018, [Online]. Available: http://arxiv.org/abs/1806.06988

[56] M. Arifuzzaman, M. R. Hasan, T. J. Toma, S. B. Hassan, and A. K. Paul, "An Advanced Decision Tree-Based Deep Neural Network in Nonlinear Data Classification," *Technologies (Basel)*, vol. 11, no. 1, February 2023, doi: 10.3390/technologies11010024.

[57] Y. Yang, I. G. Morillo, and T. M. Hospedales, "Deep Neural Decision Trees," June 2018, [Online]. Available: http://arxiv.org/abs/1806.06988

[58] M. Arifuzzaman, M. R. Hasan, T. J. Toma, S. B. Hassan, and A. K. Paul, "An Advanced Decision Tree-Based Deep Neural Network in Nonlinear Data Classification," *Technologies (Basel)*, vol. 11, no. 1, February 2023, doi: 10.3390/technologies11010024.

[59] W. Zhao, J. Ye, M. Yang, Z. Lei, S. Zhang, and Z. Zhao, "Investigating Capsule Networks with Dynamic Routing for Text Classification," March 2018, [Online]. Available: http://arxiv.org/abs/1804.00538

[60] H. W. Fentaw and T. H. Kim, "Design and Investigation of Capsule Networks for Sentence Classification," *Applied Sciences (Switzerland)*, vol. 9, no. 11, June 2019, doi: 10.3390/app9112200.

[61] H. W. Fentaw and T. H. Kim, "Design and Investigation of Capsule Networks for Sentence Classification," *Applied Sciences (Switzerland)*, vol. 9, no. 11, June 2019, doi: 10.3390/app9112200.

[62] W. Zhao, J. Ye, M. Yang, Z. Lei, S. Zhang, and Z. Zhao, "Investigating Capsule Networks with Dynamic Routing for Text Classification," March 2018, [Online]. Available: http://arxiv.org/abs/1804.00538

[63] Y. Zhu, C. Huang, Z. Hu, A. Al-Dhelaan, and M. Al-Dhelaan, "Blockchain-Enabled Access Management System for Edge Computing," *Electronics*, vol. 10, no. 9, pp. 1–15, 2021.

[64] A. Dolgui et al., "Blockchain-Oriented Dynamic Modelling of Smart Contract Design and Execution in the Supply Chain," 2020, doi: 10.1080/00207543.2019.1627439.

[65] R. Neisse, G. Steri, and I. Nai-fovino, "A Blockchain-Based Approach for Data Accountability and Provenance Tracking", doi: 10.1145/3098954.3098958.

[66] M. Jurgelaitis et al., "Modelling Principles for Blockchain-Based Implementation of Business or Scientific Processes," *CEUR Workshop Proceedings: IVUS 2019 International Conference on Information Technologies: Proceedings of the International Conference on Information Technologies* (vol. 2470, pp. 43–47). Kaunas, Lithuania, April 25, 2019.

[67] A. Roehrs, C. André, R. Righi, V. Ferreira, J. Roberto, and D. C. Schmidt, "Analyzing the Performance of a Blockchain-Based Personal Health Record Implementation," *Journal of Biomedical Informatics*, vol. 92, no. March, p. 103140, 2019, doi: 10.1016/j.jbi.2019.103140.

[68] S. Pooja, L. K. Raju, U. Chhapekar, and C. B. Chandrakala, "Face Detection Using Deep Learning to Ensure a Coercion Resistant Blockchain-Based Electronic Voting," *Engineered Science*, vol. 16, pp. 341–353, 2021, doi: 10.30919/es8d585.

[69] M. A. Bouras, B. Xia, A. O. Abuassba, H. Ning, and Q. Lu, "IoT-CCAC: A Blockchain-Based Consortium Capability Access Control Approach For IoT," pp. 1–22, 2021, doi: 10.7717/peerj-cs.455.

[70] A. Ouaddah, A. A. Elkalam, and A. A. Ouahman, "FairAccess: A New Blockchain-Based Access Control Framework for the Internet of Things," no. February, pp. 5943–5964, 2017, doi: 10.1002/sec.1748.

[71] A. P. Joshi, M. Han, and Y. Wang, "A Survey on Security and Privacy Issues of Blockchain Technology," vol. 1, no. 2, pp. 121–147, 2018, doi: 10.3934/mfc.2018007.

[72] S. K. Krause, H. Natarajan, and H. L. Gradstein, *Distributed Ledger Technology (DLT) and Blockchain*. Washington, DC: World Bank Group.

[73] A. Roehrs, C. André, and R. Righi, "OmniPHR: A Distributed Architecture Model to Integrate Personal Health Records," *Journal of Biomedical Informatics*, vol. 71, pp. 70–81, 2017, doi: 10.1016/j.jbi.2017.05.012.

[74] "Dynamic Content Enabled Microservice for Business Applications in Distributed Cloudlet Cloud Network," *International Journal of Emerging Trends in Engineering Research*, vol. 9, no. 7, pp. 1035–1039, July 2021, doi: 10.30534/ijeter/2021/32972021.

[75] J. N. S. Rubí and P. R. de L. Gondim, "Interoperable Internet of Medical Things Platform for e-Health Applications," *International Journal of Distributed Sensor Networks*, vol. 16, no. 1, 2020, doi: 10.1177/1550147719889591.

[76] K. Upadhyay, R. Dantu, Y. He , S. Badruddoja , and A. Salau, "Auditing Metaverse Requires Multimodal Deep Learning," *ieeexplore.ieee.org*, 2022, doi: 10.1109/TPS-ISA5 6441.2022.00015.

[77] N. Aranjuelo, L. Unzueta, I. Arganda-Carreras, and O. Otaegui, "Multimodal Deep Learning for Advanced Driving Systems," in *Lecture Notes in Computer Science (Including Subseries Lecture Notes in Artificial Intelligence and Lecture Notes in Bioinformatics)*, Springer Verlag, 2018, pp. 95–105. doi: 10.1007/978-3-319-94544-6_10.

[78] Y. Petrushenko *et al.*, "The Opportunities of Engaging FinTech Companies into the System of Crossborder Money Transfers in Ukraine," *ceeol.com*, 2018, [Online]. Available: https://www.ceeol.com/search/article-detail?id=741970

[79] S. Islam, S. Badsha, S. Sengupta, and H. M. La, "Blockchain-Enabled Intelligent Vehicular Edge Computing," no. March, 2021, doi: 10.13140/RG.2.2.23175.32166.

[80] F. Corradini, A. Marcelletti, A. Morichetta, A. Polini, E. Scala, and F. Tiezzi, "Model-Driven Engineering for Multi-Party Business Processes on Multiple Blockchains," *Blockchain: Research and Applications*, vol. 2, no. 3, p. 100018, 2021, doi: 10.1016/j.bcra.2 021.100018.

[81] A. H. Sodhro *et al.*, "Towards Blockchain-Enabled Security Technique for Industrial Internet of Things Based Decentralized Applications," *Journal of Grid Computing*, vol. 18 pp. 615–628, 2020.

[82] A. A. Sathio, M. Ali Dootio, A. Lakhan, M. U. Rehman, A. Orangzeb Pnhwar, and M. A. Sahito, "Pervasive Futuristic Healthcare and Blockchain enabled Digital Identities-Challenges and Future Intensions," in *Proceedings 2021 International Conference on Computing, Electronics and Communications Engineering, iCCECE 2021*, Institute of Electrical and Electronics Engineers Inc., August 2021, pp. 30–35. doi: 10.1109/ iCCECE52344.2021.9534846.

[83] K. Gilani *et al.*, "A Survey on Blockchain-Based Identity Management and Decentralized Privacy for Personal Data to Cite This Version: A Survey on Blockchain-Based Identity Management and Decentralized Privacy for Personal Data," *2020 2nd Conference on Blockchain Research & Applications for Innovative Networks and Services (BRAINS)* (pp. 97–101). IEEE, September 2020.

[84] M. Supriya and V. K. Chattu, "A Review of Artificial Intelligence, Big Data, and Blockchain Technology Applications in Medicine and Global Health," *mdpi.com*, vol. 5, p. 41, 2021, doi: 10.3390/bdcc5030041.

[85] L. Guo, "Application of Blockchain Based on Deep Learning Algorithm in Enterprise Internet of Things System," *Mobile Information Systems*, vol. 2022, 2022, doi: 10.1155/2 022/9943452.

[86] P. Tagde *et al.*, "Blockchain and Artificial Intelligence Technology in e-Health," doi: 10.1 007/s11356-021-16223-0/Published.

## CHAPTER 7

A Non-Reference Low-Light Image Enhancement Approach Using Deep Convolutional Neural Networks

Ziaur Rahman[1], Muhammad Aamir[1], Kanza Gulzar[2],
Jameel Ahmed Bhutto[1], Muhammad Ishfaq[1],
Zaheer Ahmed Dayo[1], and Khalid Hussain Mohammadani[1]

[1]*College of Computer Science, Huanggang Normal University, Huanggang, China*
[2]*University Institute of Information Technology, Pir Mehr Ali Shah Arid Agriculture University, Rawalpindi, Pakistan*

7.1 INTRODUCTION

Research has shown that over 85% of the information people receive from the outside world has become an integral part of our daily lives. Among the various types of information, sound and images are the most direct and intuitive and can be used for a variety of purposes [1]. The human brain is highly efficient at perceiving, storing, and interpreting visual information, and a weighty percentage of the brain is dedicated to processing such information. Unlike the human brain, cameras cannot reliably capture and process visual details due to various factors such as irregular lighting, weather conditions, etc. [2]. In addition, in most cases, the image produced by a camera cannot be immediately stored in an application. Instead, it has to undergo several pre-processing steps depending on the specific task [3]. The basic pre-processing tasks aimed at improving image quality include brightness, color, contrast, and noise reduction [4]. Digital cameras are ubiquitous and are used in a wide range of fields, including surveillance, traffic monitoring, medicine, television programs, and social media, among others. Cameras assist human vision by capturing and presenting highly visible images to users in any environment. However, different lighting

DOI: 10.1201/9781032646268-7

conditions typically refer to poor lighting conditions such as cloudy, night, and indoor scenes [5,6]. In addition, image noise is inevitably introduced during the capture process due to the imaging equipment. Low-light images have inherently low illumination levels, which amplifies the noise introduced during the imaging process, making it more noticeable. It is essential to perform appropriate enhancement and discard noise in dim images. Recently, learning-based systems have been introduced to the field of dark image enhancement [1,5]. LLNet [7] represents the progressive application to boost the dark regions in dim images. Initially, they used of self-encoders idea to detect latent deep features and perform adaptive revivifying and denoising. Moreover, MBLLEN [8] developed an end-to-end neural network idea and used multi-module feature extraction to boost the visual quality. Most of these methods exploited the robust learning capabilities of learning networks. To achieve optimal enhancement results through learning, numerous paired data sets are fed into the network model. However, this method requires significant human and substantial sources to gather paired data sets and importantly it can initiate a reduction in the generalization capability of the network.

To address these issues, this chapter uses deep CNNs to extract illumination and reflectance components from low-light images. It combines the denoising effect of BM3D [9] with the optimization network of reflection components to enhance image detail information while suppressing image noise. Finally, a method for training images without reference is used, and a novel loss function called trend consistency is introduced to regulate the trend consistency of the output images. This approach partially overcomes the limitations that reference images impose on enhancement results.

7.2 LITERATURE REVIEW

Images acquired in low-light situations normally endure underexposure and low contrast, posing serious challenges for subsequent image processing. As a result, boosting contrast in dim image has become a diverse area of research in computer vision. In recent years, significant breakthroughs in low-light image enhancement have been achieved through histogram-based methods and the Retinex model offered by Land [10]. For instance, Pizer et al. [11] and Reza et al. [12] successively proposed the AHE and CLAHE procedures to highlight dim regions in dark photos, but the enhanced images often show color distortion. Jobson et al. [13] extended the use of Gaussian function to evaluate the reflectance part of the original input image. Their model is inadequate in its ability to lever noise in dark regions. Lin et al. [14] linearly weighted the sum of the pre-retinex model at several different scales; however, this scheme is constrained for backlit images. Fu et al. [15] suggested a fusion-based scheme for improving diverse contents in backlit images. Moreover, Ying et al. [16] purported a double exposure idea based on fusion scheme to attain accurate visual contents in dark images. Ren et al. [17] implied a dual operational idea that not only removes noise but enhances the dim region in low-light images via the Retinex model. Although these systems have made notable advancement in the domain of correcting dark image enhancement, the enhanced images still have insufficient brightness recovery and are prone to detail loss, indicating certain limitations.

Recently, with the surge of deep learning, it has outperformed traditional algorithms in object recognition [18,19], super-resolution reconstruction [20], and image denoising [21]. Some researchers have also applied deep learning to image enhancement, such as Li et al. [22], who combined the shallow LightenNet network and the Retinex model to achieve quality image outcomes. Panwar et al. [23] proposed a deep learning model to correct the visual features in dim images. However, the results of the model are inappropriate for backlit images.

7.3 MATERIAL AND TECHNIQUES

7.3.1 Retinex Theory

Based on the Retinex theory, this chapter designs a deep convolutional neural network. The Retinex theory suggests that an image (S) obtained by an image sensor can be regarded as the product of a reflection module (R) and an illumination module (Im). This can be formulated like this:

$$S = R \circ Im \qquad (7.1)$$

where $\circ$ represents element-wise multiplication. The R contains the intrinsic features of the image being captured, while the Im represents the distribution of light on the object being photographed. For images taken under normal natural igniting conditions, the light distribution must continuously change and retain most of the edge information [24]. In low-light enhancement methods that consider noise, it is believed that noise can be classified as additive noise, mainly existing in the R [25]. Therefore, it is necessary to conceal the noise contents in the extracted R to obtain a less noisy and more detailed texture:

$$\hat{S} = \hat{R} \circ Im \qquad (7.2)$$

For this purpose, the BM3D [9] denoising process is aligned into the optimization of the reflection component. Low-light image enhancement is achieved without reference images through the constraint of the loss function. Figure 7.1 indicates the general framework of the formed network. The overall network primarily comprises two slices:

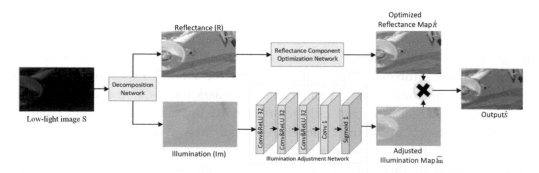

FIGURE 7.1 Overall framework of the network.

decomposition and optimization networks. The optimization network is further composed of a reflection part optimization network and an illumination part adjustment network. The input dim image S is first processed by the decomposition network to extract the illumination (Im) and the reflectance R. These two components are then fed individually into the illumination and reflectance optimization networks for optimization. Finally, the optimized components $\widehat{Im}$ and $\hat{R}$ are multiplied together to attain the final corrected image $\hat{S}$. The intended concepts of the decomposition and optimization networks are depicted separately below.

7.3.2 Decomposition Network

The decomposition network consists of two branches, with the upper branch used to extract the reflection component and the lower branch used to extract the illumination component, as shown in Figure 7.1. The task of the decomposition network is to extract the corresponding illumination and reflection components from the input dim image, which is an exceedingly ill-posed challenge. It is necessary to constrain the output of the network by a reasonable design of the loss function. Permitting the Retinex theory, the illumination part must have smooth characteristics, while the reflection part should preserve the texture detail characteristics of the input image as much as possible [26]. Therefore, the loss function for the initial reflectance component is

$$L_{rs}^{D} = \|\nabla R - \nabla S\|_1 \tag{7.3}$$

where ∇ represents the first-order difference operator, S is the input dark image, R characterizes the reflection part, and $\|\bullet\|_1$ signifies the $L1$ norm. The gradient is measured in both directions, i.e., horizontal and vertical directions, and the ultimate gradient calculation outcome is the sum of the results in both directions. This loss function measures the differences in boundary, texture, and other changing information. By minimizing it, the chapter forces the reflected component to be as realistic as possible to the original dim image. For the constraint of the illumination part, this chapter uses the formula from reference [27] to achieve the smoothing of the illumination, which is:

$$L_{is}^{D} = \frac{\nabla Im}{\max(|\nabla S|, \, \varepsilon)_1} \tag{7.4}$$

where ε represents a very small positive number (in this chapter, 0.0001), and $|\cdot|$ represents the absolute value. According to this loss function, when the pixel points to be calculated are located at the edge of the object in the image, the value calculated by this function will be smaller, i.e., the penalty will be smaller. When the position to be calculated is in a flatter area of the image, the penalty will become larger, thus achieving the smoothing of the illumination component. Since the illumination part and reflection component are disintegrated from the input dim image, corresponding

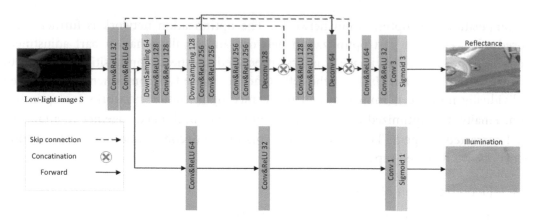

FIGURE 7.2 Overall framework of decomposition network.

to the Retinex, their product should be consistent with the input image, i.e., $S - R \circ Im$ the value tends to 0. To achieve this, the reconstruction loss function is constructed:

$$L_{\text{rec}}^{\text{D}} = \|S - (R + 0.0001) \circ (\text{Im} + 0.0001)\|_1 \tag{7.5}$$

To avoid excessive oscillation of parameters during backpropagation, R and Im are both added with 0.0001. The overall loss function for the decomposition network can be expressed as: (Figure 7.2)

$$L^{\text{D}} = 0.01 \times L_{\text{rs}}^{\text{D}} + 0.15 \times L_{\text{is}}^{\text{D}} + L_{\text{rec}}^{\text{D}} \tag{7.6}$$

where the weighting coefficients are determined through experiments.

7.3.3 Optimizing the Network

The optimization of the kernel size and stride in the downsampling layer, deconvolution layer, and concatenation layer of the network is consistent with the settings in the decomposition network. The network consists of a reflectance part optimization network and an illumination part adjustment network, where the illumination component adjustment network consists of a set of convolution layers with invariant sizes. The adjustment of the network parameters is realized by the entire loss function of the optimization network. The task of the reflection component optimization network is to further deepen the texture detail information in the reflectance part while dominating noise, as shown in Figure 7.3. After denoising using the BM3D algorithm [9], some of the detailed information in the image is lost. To address this issue, a convolutional network is applied to attain the strong texture information, thus compensating for the aforementioned defects to some extent. As shown in Figure 7.3, the denoised reflectance component is extracted at different sizes and fused into different convolutional levels of the network, thus increasing the textural contents of the reflectance part while suppressing noise. Since training the network using a non-reference image method lacks guidance from normally illuminated images for the

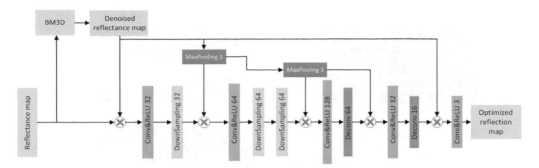

FIGURE 7.3   Optimization network for estimation of reflectance component.

network output, a reasonably designed loss function is needed to constrain the final enhancement result and allow the network to converge in the correct direction. Inspired by [28], the following three loss functions are designed.

7.3.3.1 Spatial Consistency Loss

In general, the constraint on the reflectance image is based on the close relation between the gradient image of the output reflectance image and the gradient image of the input image. The higher the matching contents, the closer the texture and edge information in the reflectance image are to the texture and edge information in the low-light input image [29]. However, for low-light images, since the texture details in the input low-light image are affected by both the illumination and reflection components, the gradient image values calculated from the low-light image are bound to be smaller than those of the gradient image of the normally illuminated image. Therefore, to allow the reflectance component to retain more detailed information, the gradient constraint on the reflectance component should be relaxed accordingly. To verify this idea, a pair of low-light and normally illuminated images are selected from the LOL data set [30]. At the same positions in Figures 7.4(b) and 7.4(d), the gradients of the corresponding 200 and 400 points (the red lines in Figure 7.4) are calculated, and the change trends at these 200 and 400 points are revealed in Figures 7.4(e) and 7.4(f). It can be seen from Figures 7.4(e) and 7.4(f) that the change trends of the normal and low-light images are consistent overall, with some fluctuations in the neighborhoods of certain pixels. The fluctuations in the neighborhoods of some pixels are caused by the low-light conditions, which blur the edges and other details of some objects. Although the illumination part of the dim image has changed compared to the normal illumination, the texture trend remains the same. If it is strictly required that the gradient of the dim image is wholly dependable with the gradient image of the normal illumination image, the gradient of the illumination component obtained by decomposing the dark image based on Retinex will have fluctuations in the details due to the smoother gradient of the low-light image and will not achieve the desired uniform illumination part. Based on the above considerations, the trend image calculation method is proposed based on the conventional image gradient image calculation:

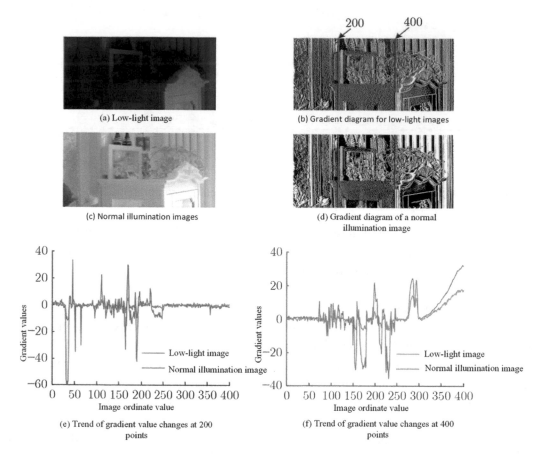

FIGURE 7.4 Gradient change trend at the same location of images under different illuminations.

$$\nabla_d f(x, y) = \begin{cases} t, & \nabla f_d(x, y) > 0 \\ 0, & \nabla f_d(x, y) = 0, d \in \{h, w\} \\ -t, & \nabla f_d(x, y) < 0 \end{cases} \qquad (7.7)$$

where $\nabla_d f(x, y)$ represents the image at (x, y) in a certain direction. The first-order gradient value of the image, represented by a certain direction of the image, including the vertical direction and the horizontal direction, is a variable that indicates that when the gradient is greater than 0 or less than 0, the change trend of the image is consistent, and only its sign needs to be considered. In this chapter, it is set to 5. As analyzed above, the ultimate enhancement outcomes are obtained by multiplying the adjusted illumination component and the reflection component, and its texture information may be somewhat lost. At the same time, to address the insufficient representativeness of global calculations for local areas, this chapter adopts local calculations in several random areas of the image. In concrete terms, the representation of a loss function is as indicated below:

$$L_{sp}^{on} = \frac{1}{K} \sum_{i=1}^{K} \sum_{j \in \aleph(i)} (|(\nabla \hat{S}_i - \nabla \hat{S}_j)| - |(\nabla S_i - \nabla S_j)|)^2 + \lambda \times |\nabla \hat{S} - \nabla S|_1 \qquad (7.8)$$

where K represents the number of randomly selected local areas (in this chapter K is set at 16), $\aleph(i)$ represents the set composed of the four neighborhoods (including the upper, lower, left, and right neighborhoods, where both the neighborhood size and the local area size are 4 × 4) $\overline{\nabla} S_i$ and $\overline{\nabla} S_i$ of the ith local area, and represents the average trend values at the same position of a given local area in the final output enhanced image $\hat{S}$ and input dim image S, respectively. In the grayscale space, $\hat{S}_j$ represents the average trend value in the jth neighborhood of the ith confined area in the enhanced result.

7.3.3.2 Exposure Control Loss

This chapter first converts the output enhanced image from RGB space to grayscale space and then randomly selects ten non-overlapping local areas in the grayscale image to limit the amount of exposure in the enhanced result. After normalization, the average pixel value of each local area tends to 0.6, and the loss function is:

$$L_{exp}^{on} = \frac{1}{N} \sum_{k=1}^{N} |Y_k - E| \qquad (7.9)$$

where N signifies the amount of randomly selected non-overlapping local areas (in this chapter N is set to 10, with an area size of 16 × 16), characterizes the average pixel value of the kth local area, and E denotes the exposure. The exposure level directs the average brightness, which is calculated by averaging the brightness values of all pixels in the image. Exposure level is divided into ten levels from 0 to 1. Among them, 1 represents normal exposure, while 0 represents extremely low illumination (in this document, it is set to 0.6).

7.3.3.3 Color Consistency Loss

To suppress color distortion in the improved result, the typical pixel value ratio of different channels in the enhanced image can be made to match the ratio in the dark image, and the typical loss function is:

$$L_{col}^{on} = \sum_{(p,q) \in \omega} (Y^p - Y^q)^2, \, \omega = \{(R, G), (R, B), (B, G)\}\} \qquad (7.10)$$

where $\omega = \{(R, G), (R, B), (B, G)\}$ represents the average pixel value of a certain channel, and p and q belong to one of the three RGB channels. The entire loss function of the proposed algorithm is:

$$L^{on} = L_{sp}^{on} + L_{exp}^{on} + 0.5 \times L_{col}^{on} \qquad (7.11)$$

7.4 EXPERIMENT AND RESULTS

7.4.1 Experimental Design

The experimental configurations are Windows 11, NVIDIA RTX 3070 GPUs, and 64 GB of RAM. Training epochs and initial learning rate are set to 0.002 and 200, respectively. The parameters of Adam are set to: b1 = 0.9, b2 = 0.999. The training sample image data set is from synthetic low light [20] with a total of 22,471 low-light images, of which 80% are used as the training data set and the rest as the test data set. Since the synthetic degraded images cannot fully represent real dim images, this chapter also collects 30 real dim images from mainstream dark image adjustment papers as a complementary test. The evaluation metrics are PSNR [31], SSIM [32], and NIQE [33], which together can comprehensively reflect the enhancement effect of enhanced images to some extent. PSNR is mainly used to measure the resemblance between the enhanced and the referenced image globally, with a higher value indicating a better enhancement effect; SSIM quantifies the sameness between the enhanced result and the source image in terms of structure, contrast, and brightness, with a higher rate indicating that the enhancement result is closer to the source image; NIQE is mainly used to evaluate the naturalness of the enhanced image, with a lower value indicating a better image enhancement effect, specifically by calculating the distance between the enhanced image feature model parameters and the pre-established model parameters. In order to verify the effectiveness of the proposed algorithm, experiments are carried out using both objective and subjective evaluations.

7.4.2 Subjective Evaluation

As shown in Figures 7.5 and 7.6, this chapter first presents the produced results of different algorithms on some images. In Figure 7.5, prior algorithms did not perform well in representing the structural details, but the processed result of proposed model can clearly

FIGURE 7.5 Visual results of backlit images.

FIGURE 7.6   Visual results of nighttime images.

adjust the overall visual quality. The final result of our scheme is distant to the reference image in terms of detail representation. Moreover, regarding the noise distribution around the edges in Figure 7.6, taking the processing result of LIME [34] as an example, its processing effect is obviously overexposed, and its noise suppression is poor. Although the processing result of RetinexGAN [35] did not have overexposure, the overall vividness and noise suppression of the image are inferior to the handling effect treatment of the proposed algorithm. Figure 7.7 illustrates the managing visual esthetics of different

FIGURE 7.7   Visual results of non-uniform images.

algorithms on real scenes. Compared with the produced enhanced results of Dong [36] and SRIE [37], the visual result of this chapter has no obvious contour phenomena and overall effect is brighter. LIME [34] achieved better visual results in terms of color and structural details; however, it achieved lower quantitative scores. The result of RetinexGAN [35] has a bright and clear visual effect, but the image shows obvious color distortion. In summary, the proposed algorithm achieves a balanced overall effect in terms of subjective perception, including image brightness enhancement, noise suppression, and color preservation.

7.4.3 Objective Evaluation

To further attest the efficiency of our algorithm, we chose the commonly used PSNR, SSIM, and NIQE as evaluation criteria in the sphere research of image enhancement. The values of all the indicators are the average values obtained on the test set, and the calculable values are shown in Table 7.1. As can be seen from Table 7.1, this chapter achieved the best scores in PSNR and SSIM, which shows that the proposed algorithm has achieved good results in preserving detailed information and verifies the efficacy of the trend consistency proposed in this chapter. Although the algorithm in this chapter did not achieve the optimal result in NIQE, it is relatively close to the more prominent results of RetinexGAN [35] and LIME [34], which indicates that the algorithm in this chapter also has some ability to preserve the naturalness of the image, but the color constraint of the output image needs further improvement. In summary, the algorithm in this chapter has achieved a good balance in improving image brightness, reducing noise interference, and maintaining image naturalness. Figure 7.8 shows the score distribution of PSNR, SSIM, and NIQE of the algorithm in this chapter on the test set. It can be seen from the figure that the algorithm in this chapter has higher scores for most of the images, confirming that the algorithm has strong robustness.

TABLE 7.1 Objective Evaluation Index Scores for the Results of the Prior and Proposed Algorithms

Metrics	LIME [34]	Dong [36]	SRIE [37]	RetinexGAN [35]	Ours
PSNR	15.9062	14.61	13.122	16.37	**16.41**
SSIM	0.5748	0.57	0.5059	0.57	**0.62**
NIQE	8.25	8.921	8.324	8.42	**7.721**

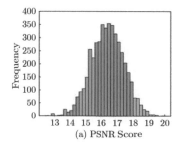
(a) PSNR Score

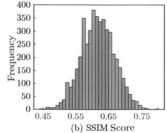
(b) SSIM Score

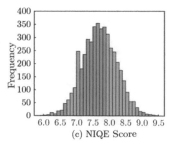
(c) NIQE Score

FIGURE 7.8 The distribution of scores for various indicators of the proposed algorithm on the test set.

TABLE 7.2   The Testing Results of Different Algorithms on the LOL Data Set

Metrics	LIME [34]	Dong [36]	SRIE [37]	RetinexGAN [35]	Ours
PSNR	16.920	15.21	11.8551	16.574	**17.863**
SSIM	0.731	0.681	0.69	0.751	**0.791**

7.4.4 Generalization Ability

To verify the generalization ability of our study, we randomly selected 30 images from the widely used LOL data set, and the specific outcomes are revealed in Table 7.2. The evidence in Table 7.2 shows that the proposed scheme accomplished the best results in SSIM and is relatively close to the optimal RetinexGAN [35] in PSNR. This shows that the proposed algorithm can still achieve better results on the LOL data set, confirming that our designed scheme has good generalization ability.

7.5 CONCLUSION

The method of computing the gradient maps is improved, and a trend-consistent loss is proposed and built in this study by examining the link between the gradient maps of images with normal illumination and dim illumination. To meet the noise suppression requirement, the denoising effect of BM3D is integrated into the reflection component optimization network. Finally, the enhancement results overcome the limitations of the reference images to some extent and achieve better enhancement effects by using training without reference images. The simulated findings' subjective and objective assessments show that the suggested method can improve extreme dim images' brightness and detail information while preserving the naturalness of the image. However, further research is needed to make the color of the output image more rich, as the color constraint of the output image is still insufficient.

REFERENCES

[1] Wang, Wencheng, Xiaojin Wu, Xiaohui Yuan, and Zairui Gao. "An experiment-based review of low-light image enhancement methods." *IEEE Access* 8 (2020): 87884–87917.

[2] Li, Mading, Jiaying Liu, Wenhan Yang, Xiaoyan Sun, and Zongming Guo. "Structure-revealing low-light image enhancement via robust retinex model." *IEEE Transactions on Image Processing* 27, no. 6 (2018): 2828–2841.

[3] Ying, Zhenqiang, Ge Li, Yurui Ren, Ronggang Wang, and Wenmin Wang. "A new low-light image enhancement algorithm using camera response model." In Proceedings of the IEEE International Conference on Computer Vision Workshops, pp. 3015–3022. 2017.

[4] Wang, Li-Wen, Zhi-Song Liu, Wan-Chi Siu, and Daniel PK Lun. "Lightening network for low-light image enhancement." *IEEE Transactions on Image Processing* 29 (2020): 7984–7996.

[5] Liu, Jiaying, Dejia Xu, Wenhan Yang, Minhao Fan, and Haofeng Huang. "Benchmarking low-light image enhancement and beyond." *International Journal of Computer Vision* 129 (2021): 1153–1184.

[6] Wang, Yufei, Renjie Wan, Wenhan Yang, Haoliang Li, Lap-Pui Chau, and Alex Kot. "Low-light image enhancement with normalizing flow." In Proceedings of the AAAI Conference on Artificial Intelligence, vol. 36, no. 3, pp. 2604–2612. 2022.

[7] Lore, Kin Gwn, Adedotun Akintayo, and Soumik Sarkar. "LLNet: A deep autoencoder approach to natural low-light image enhancement." *Pattern Recognition* 61 (2017): 650–662.

[8] Lv, Feifan, Feng Lu, Jianhua Wu, and Chongsoon Lim. "MBLLEN: Low-light image/video enhancement using CNNs." In BMVC, vol. 220, no. 1, p. 4. 2018.

[9] Hasan, Mahmud, and Mahmoud R. El-Sakka. "Improved BM3D image denoising using SSIM-optimized Wiener filter." *EURASIP Journal on Image and Video Processing* 2018 (2018): 1–12.

[10] Brainard, David H., and Brian A. Wandell. "Analysis of the retinex theory of color vision." *JOSA A* 3, no. 10 (1986): 1651–1661.

[11] Pizer, Stephen M., E. Philip Amburn, John D. Austin, Robert Cromartie, Ari Geselowitz, Trey Greer, Bart ter Haar Romeny, John B. Zimmerman, and Karel Zuiderveld. "Adaptive histogram equalization and its variations." *Computer Vision, Graphics, and Image Processing* 39, no. 3 (1987): 355–368.

[12] Reza, Ali M. "Realization of the contrast limited adaptive histogram equalization (CLAHE) for real-time image enhancement." *Journal of VLSI Signal Processing Systems for Signal, Image and Video Technology* 38 (2004): 35–44.

[13] Jobson, Daniel J., Zia-ur Rahman, and Glenn A. Woodell. "Properties and performance of a center/surround retinex." *IEEE Transactions on Image Processing* 6, no. 3 (1997): 451–462.

[14] Lin, Haoning, and Zhenwei Shi. "Multi-scale retinex improvement for nighttime image enhancement." *Optik* 125, no. 24 (2014): 7143–7148.

[15] Fu, Xueyang, Delu Zeng, Yue Huang, Yinghao Liao, Xinghao Ding, and John Paisley. "A fusion-based enhancing method for weakly illuminated images." *Signal Processing* 129 (2016): 82–96.

[16] Ying, Zhenqiang, Ge Li, and Wen Gao. "A bio-inspired multi-exposure fusion framework for low-light image enhancement." arXiv preprint arXiv:1711.00591 (2017).

[17] Ren, Xutong, Mading Li, Wen-Huang Cheng, and Jiaying Liu. "Joint enhancement and denoising method via sequential decomposition." In 2018 IEEE International Symposium on Circuits and Systems (ISCAS), pp. 1–5. IEEE, 2018.

[18] Guo, Weiya, Xuezhi Xia, and Wang Xiaofei. "A remote sensing ship recognition method based on dynamic probability generative model." *Expert Systems with Applications* 41, no. 14 (2014): 6446–6458.

[19] Shao, Xiaopeng, Hua Fan, Guangxu Lu, and Jun Xu. "An improved infrared dim and small target detection algorithm based on the contrast mechanism of human visual system." *Infrared Physics & Technology* 55, no. 5 (2012): 403–408.

[20] Ying, Changsheng, Peng Zhao, and Ye Li. "Low-light-level image super-resolution reconstruction based on iterative projection photon localization algorithm." *Journal of Electronic Imaging* 27, no. 1 (2018): 013026.

[21] Fu, Xueyang, Borong Liang, Yue Huang, Xinghao Ding, and John Paisley. "Lightweight pyramid networks for image deraining." *IEEE Transactions on Neural Networks and Learning Systems* 31, no. 6 (2019): 1794–1807.

[22] Li, Chongyi, Jichang Guo, Fatih Porikli, and Yanwei Pang. "LightenNet: A convolutional neural network for weakly illuminated image enhancement." *Pattern Recognition Letters* 104 (2018): 15–22.

[23] Panwar, Moomal, and Sanjay B.C. Gaur. "Inception-based CNN for low-light image enhancement." In Computational Vision and Bio-Inspired Computing: Proceedings of ICCVBIC 2021, pp. 533–545. Singapore: Springer Singapore, 2022.

[24] Wang, Liqian, Liang Xiao, Hongyi Liu, and Zhihui Wei. "Variational Bayesian method for retinex." *IEEE Transactions on Image Processing* 23, no. 8 (2014): 3381–3396.

[25] Ren, Xutong, Wenhan Yang, Wen-Huang Cheng, and Jiaying Liu. "LR3M: Robust low-light enhancement via low-rank regularized retinex model." *IEEE Transactions on Image Processing* 29 (2020): 5862–5876.

[26] Wang, Yang, Yang Cao, Zheng-Jun Zha, Jing Zhang, Zhiwei Xiong, Wei Zhang, and Feng Wu. "Progressive retinex: Mutually reinforced illumination-noise perception network for low-light image enhancement." In Proceedings of the 27th ACM International Conference on Multimedia, pp. 2015–2023. 2019.

[27] Zhang, Yonghua, Jiawan Zhang, and Xiaojie Guo. "Kindling the darkness: A practical low-light image enhancer." In Proceedings of the 27th ACM International Conference on Multimedia, pp. 1632–1640. 2019.

[28] Mao, Qinghua, Yufei Wang, Xuhui Zhang, Xiaoyong Zhao, Guangming Zhang, and Kundayi Mushayi. "Clarity method of fog and dust image in fully mechanized mining face." *Machine Vision and Applications* 33, no. 2 (2022): 30.

[29] Wei, Chen, Wenjing Wang, Wenhan Yang, and Jiaying Liu. "Deep retinex decomposition for low-light enhancement." arXiv preprint arXiv:1808.04560 (2018).

[30] Zhao, Lin, Shao-Ping Lu, Tao Chen, Zhenglu Yang, and Ariel Shamir. "Deep symmetric network for underexposed image enhancement with recurrent attentional learning." In Proceedings of the IEEE/CVF International Conference on Computer Vision, pp. 12075–12084. 2021.

[31] Sara, Umme, Morium Akter, and Mohammad Shorif Uddin. "Image quality assessment through FSIM, SSIM, MSE and PSNR—A comparative study." *Journal of Computer and Communications* 7, no. 3 (2019): 8–18.

[32] Wang, Zhou, Alan C. Bovik, Hamid R. Sheikh, and Eero P. Simoncelli. "Image quality assessment: From error visibility to structural similarity." *IEEE Transactions on Image Processing* 13, no. 4 (2004): 600–612.

[33] Mittal, Anish, Rajiv Soundararajan, and Alan C. Bovik. "Making a "completely blind" image quality analyzer." *IEEE Signal Processing Letters* 20, no. 3 (2012): 209–212.

[34] Guo, Xiaojie, Yu Li, and Haibin Ling. "LIME: Low-light image enhancement via illumination map estimation." *IEEE Transactions on Image Processing* 26, no. 2 (2016): 982–993.

[35] Ma, Tian, Ming Guo, Zhenhua Yu, Yanping Chen, Xincheng Ren, Runtao Xi, Yuancheng Li, and Xinlei Zhou. "RetinexGAN: Unsupervised low-light enhancement with two-layer convolutional decomposition networks." *IEEE Access* 9 (2021): 56539–56550.

[36] Dong, Xuan, Yi Pang, and Jiangtao Wen. "Fast efficient algorithm for enhancement of low lighting video." In ACM SIGGRAPH 2010 Posters, pp. 1–1, 2010.

[37] Fu, Xueyang, Delu Zeng, Yue Huang, Xiao-Ping Zhang, and Xinghao Ding. "A weighted variational model for simultaneous reflectance and illumination estimation." In Proceedings of the IEEE Conference on Computer Vision and Pattern Recognition, pp. 2782–2790, 2016.

## CHAPTER 8

Human Pose Analysis and Gesture Recognition

Methods and Applications

Muhammad Haroon[1], Saud Altaf[1], Kanza Gulzar[1], and Muhammad Aamir[2]

[1]*University Institute of Information Technology, Pir Mehr Ali Shah Arid Agriculture University, Rawalpindi, Pakistan*
[2]*College of Computer Science, Huanggang Normal University, Huanggang, China*

8.1 INTRODUCTION

This chapter presents a summary of the most recent research on human pose estimation and hand gesture recognition in a multi-sensing environment. This literature review covers the present state of research on the available sensors, processes, techniques, and challenges involved in human activity recognition (HAR).

Numerous applications now utilize HAR intended to enhance the overall user experience, with the selection of a recognition method being entirely based on the application's requirements. Researchers provide the most accurate activity recognition by combining a variety of sensors, techniques, and algorithms, suited to the needs of each applications because there is no single solution capable of solving all problems.

Activity recognition is a challenging task where adaptability is the major challenge. That is, the system cannot correctly classify information that is different from the information used to train the system. Environmental factors, the input sensor employed, the orientation of human movement, and the number of subjects performing the same activity are all potential causes of inconsistency that designers of human activity identification systems may want to account for in their work [1].

It is difficult to determine the beginning and ending of a human activity, making it a challenge for human posture and gesture detection systems to handle transition movements between different tasks [2]. In the event that the system is unable to differentiate between the end of one task and the beginning of another, it is possible that it will either make an error or fail to recognize the task at all.

DOI: 10.1201/9781032646268-8

In this field, significant research is required to establish trusted systems for recognizing activities performed by different signers; for instance, recognizing activities by those people who were not included in the training set. These systems are useful in real-world applications because a wide range of people may utilize them without requiring lengthy training for each new user.

There have been a number of review studies that have highlighted the existing research on human pose estimation and gesture recognition systems [3], but these studies have only looked at the research development as a whole. These studies include systems that utilize a single sensor or many sensors to detect gestures and estimate human position in a particular environment. In order to be practical in everyday life, a system for recognizing hand gestures and estimating human poses needs to be applicable to people everywhere.

In addition, this study explored a number of available data sets and existing methodologies for combining diverse types of input data for a unified decision-making system. As a whole, the work has the potential to serve as a thorough introduction to the study of human pose analysis and hand gesture identification in real time, thereby easing the way for additional research in this area.

Recent trends in artificial intelligence have upgraded the standard of living of humans by making almost each task automatic.

8.2 LITERATURE REVIEW

In this chapter, we conduct a systematic review of the literature on multisensor-based human pose analysis and gesture recognition with the intent of addressing the following questions: what sensor technologies are currently available, as well as what kinds of devices make use of human poses and hand gestures for interaction? What are the existing solutions in a single-sensing and multi-sensing environment? What kinds of feature extraction methods are there, and how are they utilized in pose and gesture recognition? To what extent do different recognition algorithms and data sets vary in their effectiveness? The recent research on the given field is discussed in detail to highlight the gaps, current advancements, methods, algorithm data sets, and limitations of the studies.

Detecting and identifying human activities can be accomplished using a wide variety of input devices and recognition techniques. The following are examples of some of the most commonly used approaches:

- Bodily attached sensor
- Computer vision
- Signal-based approaches
- Multi-sensing methods

8.2.1 Bodily Attached Sensors Based Methods

The most accurate and robust method of activity recognition is provided by sensors that are worn on or attached to the body. This method has many potential applications in fields as diverse as human-computer interface (HCI), activity monitoring, and patient monitoring. Recognition based on body-attached sensors has been made possible by the widespread availability of commercially accessible low-power sensors capable of capturing the data in a variety of settings. This improvement in user experience and satisfaction is made possible, largely, by artificial intelligence; now it makes a significant contribution to the further advancement of human activity recognition. This study further presents a detailed analysis of recent research to analyze the most recent advancements, emerging trends, and critical challenges in the bodily attached sensor. In addition, the chapter discussed future research directions and potential applications for human activity recognition based on artificial intelligence.

8.2.1.1 Commonly Used Methods

The review explored sensor-based methods for recognizing poses and gestures in 3D and 2D environments based on sensors attached to the body. Common methods to activity recognition are discussed, and criteria for assessing a recognition system are highlighted. The comparison of cutting-edge methods is presented, along with their relative performance and limitations.

8.2.1.1.1 Inertial Navigation System   The inertial sensors are featured in a technologically advanced inertial navigation system (INS). In the field of HAR, accelerometers, gyroscopes, and magnetometers are generally utilized [4]. For example, a multimodal approach using inertial sensors was proposed for in-home health monitoring and assessment [5]. Using the gradient descent method, the study first calculated the gyroscopic displacement and then subtracted that value through the gyroscopic data to arrive at real-time orientation data that was both accurate and reliable. To provide joint kinematics that are free of error, the authors [6] designed a new estimating approach that precisely integrates matching spots into the algorithm for inertial sensors. Joint kinematic error was eliminated by utilizing information gathered from all of the interconnected segments' accelerometers and gyroscopes.

Wearable accelerometers can be applied to improve patient medical assistance [7], calculate approximation of exercise-induced energy expenditure [8], gait estimation and gait analysis [9], fall detection [10], and identify usual daily activities [11]. Mainly due to their inexpensive price, compact size, and ability to interact with current sensor network infrastructures, accelerometers have become increasingly popular. In addition to evaluating the features of a fixed posture, they may show the dynamic range of a movement's frequency, intensity, and angle.

The study [12] developed a wearable a technology for recognizing gestures that utilize a three-axis accelerometer and numerous electromyography sensory inputs to provide information exchange via gestures in real time. The researcher [13] incorporated inertial motion sensors into driving gloves for use in measuring driver strain by tracking their grip on the steering wheel's directional axis. The findings of another study by [14] gait classification were carried out to test walking style by gathering information on foot movement with accelerometers and analyzing it with a decision tree. In a study [15], a method has been suggested for adjusting accelerometers and magnetometers in order to resolve for orthogonal inaccuracy and magnetic issues. A multi-sensor data fusion algorithm that includes matching filters and error checking for movement patterns relying on a conventional microcontroller has also been defined.

A gyroscope can estimate the velocity and direction of human movement at different angles, making it possible to classify activity into three distinct displacement levels: zero, mild, and high. Sleeping, sitting, and standing are all examples of activities that are considered zero-displacement activities since they do not need the body to be moved in any way. There are certain movements that are used to change positions, such as getting up from a seated position to a standing one or from lying down to sitting. Some of the most challenging activities to recognize are fast walking, jogging, climbing stairs, and other vigorous physical activities [16].

8.2.1.1.2 Biosensor-Based Methods   Human activity can be detected using biosensors, also known as physiological sensors. Some examples are the electroencephalogram (EEG) [17], the electrocardiogram (ECG) [18], the galvanic skin response (GSR), the heat sensors [19], and the electromyography (EMG) [20]. Electromyography (EMG)-based gesture classification has achieved widespread use in a variety of contexts, from personal computers, playing video games, and to highly autonomous robot wearable technology, medical instruments, and motorized prosthetics [21].

In order to improve recognition efficiency, the authors [22] designed a system for real-time ECG data processing and implemented a hybrid ECG technique for extracting features. A classification system for hand gestures by [23]. Input data from several sources was merged using the K-neighbor technique and non-linear dimensionality reduction. The use of cardiac based on a collection by wearable sensors, [24] developed an innovative method for the inter-beat interval (IBI) and heart rate variability are two examples of physiological features that can be accurately measured (HRV). Applying feature extraction processes, desired morphological features recovered from a variety of physiological data; for example, "R-peaks" of electrocardiograms (ECGs), cardiac output peaks, greatest slopes, and pulmonary artery pressure onsets (PPGs). Further, a fusion system has been developed to make use of the specific morphological aspects of mono physiological signals.

A force display system was developed [25], for patients undergoing upper limb rehabilitation can benefit from the use of wearable arm posture sensors and electromechanical sensors to learn how to apply accurate force. Samples on hand end pressure, hand position, and electromyography (EMG) data were collected using a controlled experimental environment, and an adequate fit for arm end pressure was determined using a generalized regression neural network as a sensor fusion technique. Assessment throughout evaluation revealed that the trained neural network for extended regression calculated the hand end pressure.

8.2.1.1.3 Pressure Transmitter-Based Methods   There are numerous pressure sensor types available to enable pressure transmission systems, such as force sensing resistors [26], bending sensors [27], barometric pressure sensors [28], and capacitive pressure sensors

[29] based on textiles. Textile-based sensors could greatly address a number of the deficiencies related with recently developed pressure monitoring devices.

The flexibility and ease of use offered by these sensors, as well as the relative efficiency with which they can be utilized, are undeniable benefits. These sensors offer sensing within the large and reliable body mapping including limb and other body parts. Human movement can be monitored by attaching the sensor to the knee joints like squatting if its maximum sensing pressure is greater than 20 kilopascals. When the sensor's detection limit is as low as 100 pa, it can be used to pick up on minute physiological activities like throat vibrations [30]. Attaching ultrathin piezoelectric sensors based on piezoelectric nanowires to the user's eyelids allows for the detection of eye movements and the calculation of the speed at which the eye moves to the left or right [31].

8.2.1.1.4 Computer Vision-Based Methods Due to advances in integrated circuit technology, the size of cameras has decreased to the point where they may be worn as vision sensors. The use of wide-viewing-angle cameras (WVSs) is growing in fields like activity tracking [32], telesurgery [33], and telepresence [34].

8.2.1.1.5 Flexible Real-Time Tracking-Based Methods Flexible real-time tracking-based methods include elaborate, rigid sensor architectures that can only measure strain at levels below 5%. Limitations on direct application may result from the computational complexity of data processing and the limited availability of motion information provided by the acquisition of just data on symmetric movement [35]. The energy consumption, complexity, and precision of wearable, adaptable sensors are superior to those of conventional sensing devices [36].

These advantages establish flexible sensors as a solid means of measuring the efficacy of human and robotic motion [37]. This makes them a great option for use in a variety of wearable devices. With polyvinylidene fluoride (PVDF) thin-film piezoelectric polymer sensing capabilities, [38] claimed to have successfully created a wearable gesture controller. As described by the authors, [39] multilayer graphene (MG) is attached to electro spun polyamide to provide a dynamic, moisture detector and array. This sensor can identify asthma by real-time tracking of breathing rate and a wireless alert system, and it offers a non-contact interface for medicine supply to bedridden patients.

In a study [40], a sensing glove and a motorized glove made from a soft and flexible material were developed to provide greater security and comfort than conventional, hard therapeutic tools. Moreover, because of the application of data mining, the sensing glove gestures identified with a degree of precision (93.32%). This study does not provide a comprehensive overview of flexible sensors, but it does discuss some of the possibilities for their use. In the developing field of information fusion, flexible, wearable sensors will play a crucial role.

8.2.1.2 Bodily Attached Smart Device-Based Methods

The review investigated different approaches to recognize human poses and gestures based on sensors that are worn to the human body and have the capability to process information in real time. Common approaches to activity recognition are reviewed, and criteria for evaluating a recognition system are focused. This article presents a comparison of cutting-edge approaches, together with an analysis of their respective performances and the challenges they address.

8.2.1.2.1 Hand Mounted-Based Methods   The smartphone has developed from a simple communications platform to a powerful sensing device in the recent decades. Smartphones have a wide variety of sensors for measuring temperature, humidity, ambient light, and motion in addition to the usual suspects like Wi-Fi, Bluetooth, accelerometers, magnetometers, barometers, gyroscopes, and proximity detectors. Smartphones could be beneficial for identifying human activity because they are so accessible and do not interfere with their users' daily lives [41].

In addition to being held in one's hand, a smartphone's portability also allows it to be tucked away in a coat or pants pocket. It is important to consider the smartphone's location while gathering information, as the accelerometers are responsible for axis-based motion tracking or the gyroscope establishes direction. Because of variations in clothes, body composition, and behavior, smartphone positioning can vary widely among respondents. In [42], a coordinate transformation and principal component analysis (CT-PCA) method is proposed for mitigating the effects of orientation, position, and subject variation, and online support vector machine (OSVM) based upgrading techniques for improving the model in real time through the web.

To compensate for the bias that using gyroscope input in the orientation estimation creates, the authors [43] presented a complementary filter (CFF) with a simple feedback mechanism. Researchers subsequently suggested an enhanced position estimation approach that uses a Kalman filter relying on quaternions in conjunction with calibration estimations derived using gradient descent. Authors assessed CFF and gradient descent, both types of initial rehabilitative training, evaluated their effectiveness.

These findings prove that CFF can quickly detect movement, with any mistakes brought on by the gyroscope information sharing being rapidly addressed by the feedback system. The multi-sensory capabilities of the smart watch are among its many impressive attributes. In earlier research [44], an eWatch system is coupled with multiple sensors. These sensors include a dual-axis accelerometer, a light sensor, a temperature sensor, and a microphone.

Facebook's Reality Lab has invented a magical bracelet that uses electromyography sensors to decipher motor nerve impulses from the spinal cord towards the hand. The Empatica E4 wristbands capture information from multiple sensors, which are then merged via sensor fusion and deep learning algorithms in order to analyze the user's exercise, resting, everyday life, jogging, bicycling, and strength exercises. Determine the user's actual energy usage and level of fitness [45].

It has been demonstrated by the authors [46] that using many wearable devices, as opposed to just one, can enhance bodily status categorization and activity levels. These devices include skin conductivity, temperature, accelerometer, volume of blood, and heartbeat (for example, accelerometer). Improving the dependability of information on strength training for precise decision making is dependent on the accuracy of usage assessments. In these methods, users are required to equip themselves with certain hardware in order to gather the information that is then utilized to predict human action. It can be suggested that such methods are intrusive to some degree. In addition, most methods only provide you broad strokes of data, and even that data can be unreliable because it is derived from subjective factors.

8.2.1.2.2 Head Mounted-Based Methods   A set of head-mounted smart glasses consists of a microprocessor, compact projection, detectors, lens, command center, and a storing unit. The medical, emergency, tourism, and other industries might all benefit from the versatility of smart glasses.

Sleeping phase categorization including an accuracy rate of above 95% is presented in [47], the study introduced a new EEG inside the form of earphones. In order to categorize essential emotions, we developed a machine learning-based support vector machine in-ear EEG wearable sensors. Validation of the approach is achieved via comparison to head EEG readings. There is a strong correlation between in-ear EEG signals and neighboring T7 and T8 scalp signals. Therefore, in-ear EEG can replace scalp EEG near the ears.

8.2.1.2.3 Torso Wearable-Based Methods   In recent research [48] with the k-nearest neighbor (KNN) algorithm, the recognition rate for nine motion modes (standing, sitting, running, walking, continuous squatting, up and down stairs, and up and down mountains) can reach 99.96%. The article [49] described the use of a specifically developed wearable lift-assist vest (WLAV) to reduce the burden on the erector spine muscle group during symmetric squat lifting exercises.

The device has numerous potential applications, including clinical research, illness prevention, and the rehabilitation of back muscles that have been overworked. The authors in [50] introduced a shirt equipped with dry electrodes to measure electromyographic activity in the upper body during physical activity. The gadget receives data from six distinct channels and transmits it to a computer via a Bluetooth device. Due to the system's ability to monitor EMG data in real time, it can assist coaches of both professional and amateur teams in refining their training techniques.

8.2.2 Computer Vision-Based Recognition Systems

This section offers an in-depth review of the present state of gesture recognition technology, covering topics such as the existing state of multi-sensing environments, feature extraction methods, algorithms, and data sets. With the potential for its application in the recognition of sign languages. Studies involving hand gesture recognition have a substantial impact on studies involving sign language recognition.

In an earlier work in computer vision-based sign language recognition [51], Japanese sign language was recognized. Because of developments in gesture recognition since then, studies of sign language recognition have become increasingly feasible. A more viable option is for aiding persons with disabilities in their daily communication needs. Over 200 different sign languages are currently used by about 70 million individuals worldwide, so the opportunity for sign language identification is enormous, as stated by the "World Federation of the Deaf" [52].

A proposed series of data points derived from hand skeletons to train a deep learning model for recognizing hand gestures is from [53]. The training procedure comprised a two-step technique involving a convolutional neural network and a long-term memory. A proposed technique obtained best results for small data sets and had unsatisfactory performance for large data sets because of computational complexities.

The technique of detecting and naming the signals made by the user is part of the gesture and sign language recognition. Converting these signs into meaningful words and expressions, the concepts of gesture recognition are the primary emphasis of this study, covering topics such smart sensors, gesture identification, extraction of features, and recognition, in which different strategies at every step are detailed and respective benefits are evaluated. This study uses state-of-the-art research done by the researchers over the decades, from earliest to recent time [51].

As stated earlier, that gesture recognition field is empowered by different data-capturing techniques. In an effort to simplify data collection and achieve the best possible recognition accuracy, researchers have employed a wide variety of sensors. Methods for recognizing gestures have been categorized in this study according to the sensors employed to collect the data for easy evaluation. Two of the three widely used approaches discussed in this literature review are vision sensor and wireless sensor-based approaches. The third widely used approach is the bodily attached sensor, which lies outside the scope of this study. Let us do an in-depth review on vision and wireless sensor-based approaches.

One of the earliest works [54] in the field, a method was developed to recover and interpret a person's 3D body structures, given at least six head feature points and a set of body joints on the picture plane, and the head geometry and joint-formed body segment lengths. First, head feature points and image projections are used to determine a transformation matrix. The matrix's camera location and orientation are extracted. Finally, the camera-cantered 3D head coordinates are obtained.

Advancements in human–computer interactions enabled computers to visually recognize the hand gesture. Sign language, medical help, and virtual reality are just few of the many fields that can benefit from gesture recognition. Background complexity, diversity of gestures, different interpretations, and space-time fluctuations all contribute to make gesture recognition a difficult process [54].

In a study [55], the author of this piece uses two different data sets to discuss four methods for categorizing static hand gestures. Differentiating hand positions requires first locating and then removing noise from pixels representing hands in every image. The outcomes demonstrated that the artificial neural network (ANN) performed effectively and that feature selection and data preparation are crucial when employing low-resolution images such as those used in this study.

A computer vision-based study [56] proposes a convolutional neural network to recognize hand gestures. The improvement of feature extraction was accomplished by the use of geometric filtering, outline formation, modular estimation, and edge detection during pre-processing. Different convolutional neural networks are trained and tested, compared to published architectures and other methods. All training metrics and convergence graphs are studied to validate the proposed approach. Convolutional neural networks recognize gestures in this research. The method uses geometric filtering, outline formation, modular estimation, and edge detection. Unlike previous designs and methodologies, training and testing use convolutional neural networks.

This section elaborates on the major contribution of researchers in recent years on vision-based identifying gestures and interpreting sign language. The study consists of important aspects in gesture recognition ranging from sensor type, algorithms for gesture detection, feature extraction, and classification [57]. As concluded by a survey, [58] states that to achieve the best outcomes, it is vital to choose an appropriate algorithm and useful data.

Vision-based gesture recognition involves single or multiple sensors for image capturing as an input containing single or multiple objects. As identified by a survey [59], the following sensors are commonly used to recognize gestures.

- Traditional cameras (CCD Sensor)

- Depth camera (Kinect Sensor)

- Stereovision cameras (3D Sensor)

- Infrared cameras (Night Vision Sensor)

- Leap motion sensor (Motion Sensor)

- Pan-Tilt-Zoom cameras (PTZ Sensors)

In the following subsections, sign language recognition focuses on the RGB image from the camera and the depth image from the Kinect sensor because these two sensor devices account for the majority of gesture recognition research.

8.2.2.1 RGB Camera-Based Systems
The traditional cameras are appealing, easy to use, and low-cost input devices for interaction. Cameras use binary numbers to represent the amount of light they receive, called a pixel. Digital cameras convert binary values to digital values in the form of bits ($28=256$ in grayscale). The larger the bit size means more accurate measurement of light, called "bit depth" (8, 10, 12 bits = 256, 1,024, and 4,096) [60].

Single- and triple-chip cameras are utilized to capture color images. Multicolor charge-coupled device (CCD) sensors with a single chip are common, inexpensive photographic technology. When compared to utilizing an algorithm to identify color, the three-chip color CCD sensors' ability to accurately reproduce colors applying individual luminance for each of the RGB channels is a clear advantage. High-resolution three-chip cameras feature reduced illumination sensitivity and are expensive [61].

Over the years, researchers have used such camera devices for machine learning frameworks and methods. The main advantage these cameras offer is the real-time input without requiring the user to wear or carry anything special. On the other hand, they do have some limitations and challenges associated with them. The challenge, however, is that designing camera-based interfaces is quite difficult [62]. The learning method is constrained by the steps of object detection, extraction of features, classification techniques, and classifiers. Variant illumination, background complexity, and movement of the hand affect the overall accuracy of the vision-based recognition system. The article [63] provides a complete assessment of cutting-edge 3D hand forms and posture estimation algorithms based on RGB-D cameras. To offer a comprehensive overview of recent advances, additionally discussed are the relevant RGB-D sensors, hand-based data, and an accuracy achieved.

In order to overcome the challenges and limitations, researchers have proposed numerous techniques. The authors [64] proposed a convolutional neural network and a stacked de-noising auto-encoder (SDAE) for ASL recognition based on images acquired as of (Thomas Moeslund's Gesture Recognition Database—PRIMA) a public database. A database of 2,060 images was created using a RGB camera sensor. A few letters, J and Z, are excluded in the data set due to their non-static nature. The acquired binary data were filtered utilizing a median filter. In order to remove noise before an algorithm is used to segment hand-occupied regions written and run in a MATLAB environment. Results show that the CNN achieved the accuracy of 91.33% and the third layer of SDAE achieved the highest accuracy of 92.83%. Missing alphabets in the database make the productivity of the proposed technique limited to some extent.

In another research work, [65] account for variables like context, lighting, and possible interference; an image-based dynamic hand motion detection method is presented. Applying the compact criterion, researchers updated the Kanade-Lucas-Tomasi feature tracking system and then applied it to the task of tracking the hands. Multiple classifications, including ANN, support vector machine (SVM), and K-nearest neighbor (KNN), are fused to create a classification fuzzy system. When compared with the results of using multiple independent classifications, classifier integration yields a statistically significant improvement (92.23%). Furthermore, the presented system works best with discrete movements; therefore, it will need to expand in the future to include dynamic sets of hand movements.

The study [66] is a review of available sign language gesture detection techniques. The review discussed the stage-wise techniques used in these processes. This paper also highlights the limitations that limit the efficiency and accuracy of sign language gesture recognition. In a review article, [67] presents texture feature extraction algorithms. Methods based on statistics, structures, morphs, models, graphs, training, and complexity are all in this category and provide an overview of the process, advantages, restrictions, and samples of implementation of each of the seven categories of methods. The review highlights two categories of methods for future study due to their exceptional performance.

Researchers in these studies [68,69] proposed a number of methods for recognizing hand gestures in signs using only visual information. Additionally, researchers [70,71] provide a comprehensive review of hand gesture approaches for compensating for light changes. In [72,73], researchers suggested real-time gesture recognition utilizing depth data under a variant complex background. The study [74] proposed a lightweight technique with a static background to recognize low-resolution images.

The author in [75] proposes a model for recognition using a multimodal neural network that can tell the difference among light variations and a person's gestures. The study [76] proposed the technique to combine two neural networks, ResC3D neural network, as well as convolutional LSTM (ConvLSTM) to improve the efficiency and the accuracy of the recognition system. The approach has been tested on three public data sets: Kinect Sheffield SKIG, ChaLearn LAP, isolated gesture (IsoGD), and EgoGesture data sets. The end-to-end nature of this concept, consequently, creates complications for implementing the proposed solution when applied to virtual action recognition. In research [77], the authors offer an event-based system that is built on a neuromorphic visualization device, an encoding procedure for feature extraction, and an adapted lightweight network for hand gesture classification. According to the research [78], the proposed descriptor uses three kinds of characteristics with varying scales to describe the hand form. The study then examined hand gesture recognition using an artificial neural network.

The study [79] recommends a multi-view features extraction method that incorporates hand shapes, distinct hand locations, and movements for optimal results. The research then presents a multi-view learning-based feature-combining framework that enhances the multisensory characteristics internally and externally to train a multi-class machine learning with the help of the suitably conjoined characteristic to recognize the various hand gesture movements into distinct categories with distinct meanings. As demonstrated in [79], one way to compensate for a scene's low ambient lighting is to balance it against incident illumination. The project presents a prototype ASL learning app. A long-short memory classifier that uses a KNN algorithm performs the classification. The categorization model uses inputs like sphere radius, finger angles, and finger distances. The model is trained on 2,600 samples, 100 per alphabet. The study utilizes the leap motion sensor that has the area of coverage limits.

As demonstrated in [80], the database contains information on the imaging hardware, the collecting technique, the database's organization, numerous possible uses for the database, and presented the extracted the data sets from the data set. This research compiled a collection of around 40,000 photographs of almost 70 individuals. Every individual photographed in 12 distinct stances, under 43 distinct lighting situations, and multiple distinct facial expressions. Another study [81] acquired a large data set with varying lighting conditions to test the remote photo plethysmography (RPG) model's performance. Additionally, this research presented a technique to measure a patient's heart rate remotely in bad lighting conditions. The incorporation of artificial intelligence has led to an increase in the recognition systems' level of precision. The study [82] presented a bidirectional neural network architecture that uses LSTM and GRU layers to create mutually historical and prospective frameworks. In this technique, multiple clustering algorithms are proposed.

8.2.2.2 Kinect Sensor-Based Systems

Studies of human motion recognition have been conducted for quite some time. Some examples of sensors used for human motion recognition include 2D color video, the

Kinect sensor's 3D skeleton data, and 3D motion capture technology. In a study, [83] proposed a low memory consumption technique using CNN and transfer learning for translation of ASL fingerspelling into a letter. The proposed method utilizes a Google pre-trained model named MobileNet V1 to train the data set from Surrey University.

In a review research, [84] studied human action recognition with Kinect images, along with their application areas. Analyze how Kinect has been implemented in fields like medicine, teaching, the sciences, automation, gesture recognition and identification, customer support, retailing, safe working conditions, and even three-dimensional modeling. For the technical side, explain Microsoft Kinect and its 2D iterations, the 3D imaging capabilities it employs, as well as the motion detection methods and its various applications. To highlight gesture recognition technologies, categorize gesture recognition approaches. Research studies can use these databases to enhance gesture recognition and other lower-level vision-based problems like categorization, object recognition, and pose analysis.

That might have an impact on image classification when it comes to sign language, representing the dialects in which they originally used. A recent research [85], this article describes a method for pattern identification using sEMG data from nine distinct gestures. The study [86] with Log-spiral codes with symmetric patterns were proposed in the novel method created to identify human hands and comprehend actions from video streams utilizing long spiral codes. The authors [86,87] recently introduced a two-dimensional convolutional neural network (CNN) they dubbed HDANet. That CNN is based on the transformer's self-attention algorithm and employs two-dimensional learning to identify the hyperspectral correlations between images. In a research [88], an approach towards identifying images from Oracle Bone Symbols into current Chinese characters is presented by a study that used a convolutional model that extracted the correlation in both glyph sets of symbols. This research shows the possibility to convert photographs of Oracle Bone Characters into more contemporary Chinese characters.

Similarly, in a study, the authors [89] describe a joint medical humanoid robots with surgical care that is controlled by arm movements as well as enhanced through an augmented reality-based operating rooms. Findings indicate that using arm movements to control the operating robot resulted in more precise syringe insertions. Researchers [90] have presented a finger identification method that provides depth to verify identities. To measure the patient's fingers, the technique first separates the hand. Earlier, [90] provided an in-depth analysis of methods for using hand gestures to mitigate the impact of lighting changes. K-NN, the classification algorithm presented in [91], and also the random forest classification algorithm described in [92] are among the most prevalent classifications commonly used in research.

The authors in [93] proposed a new identification system using a two-channel deep neural network that can detect gestures regardless of lighting conditions. This research identified seven classes of sign language movements by analyzing individual hands' appearance, form, and position. First, at the initialization phase, skin color was detected utilizing luminance within HSV space to generate a consistent data point. In this study, researchers used a classification SVM classifier to successfully categorize photos out of a database of 3,414 gestures matched with 37 Pakistani Sign Language letters. Researchers suggested an activity framework utilizing an embedded computer image device based on a biological, the embedding mechanism for pattern recognition, plus a modular approach to action classification. According to [94], the high-contrast and low-contrast photos can benefit from the optimization method for histogram equalization since the optimization algorithm maintains visual quality and resolution in both cases. This beta adjustment is dynamic with the optimization algorithm, which is used to determine the best possible beta coefficients.

According to [95], one way to handle the variant lighting is to balance it over the lighting that comes from outside. The computer system includes information on how to acquire the data set itself, as well as information regarding the actual camera equipment used, overall collection technique, the program's organization, and a number of its possible applications. More than 40,000 samples of 68 participants were compiled for the research. Each individual was recorded in 13 distinct stances, with 43 distinct lighting situations, and with 4 distinct facial gestures. In another study [81], to assess virtual optical plethysmography's effectiveness, a sizable database was gathered under a range of lighting conditions. Furthermore, the research suggests a low-light improvement technique for virtual cardiac measurement in dim environments.

Constructing high-resolution MR photos via lower-resolution ones is the goal of a latest analysis [96]. In order to address both the low- and high-frequency parts of an MR photograph, it actually constitutes a splitting approach. Increased filtering along a tensorizing GAN is used to diagnose hypertension and early dementia. This suggested approach utilizes the human mind's structural advantages via tensorizing a multiplayer videogame platform for three players. This proposed methodology uses initial MRI characteristics, thanks to the incorporation of high-order filtering inside the classification model. The study [97] proposed cutting-edge artificially intelligent algorithms for EMG gesture recognition categorization in order to comprehend the result of neural network models with accordance to biological mechanisms in order to identify arm motions by tracking and integrating coordinated muscle movements.

8.2.2.3 Wireless Sensor-Based Systems

The extensive acceptance of wireless communication has resulted in a surge in data transmission volume. Breakthroughs towards passively continuously monitoring activities have arisen because of the widespread of wireless connections. The objective of the research is to perform a review of the current research in the field motion tracking using signals to improve a comprehensive grasp of present autonomous sensor methods capable of providing recommendation for future approaches. Current studies on wireless gesture tracking are examined and compared by this study from seven different points of view, such as different wireless systems data, mathematical frameworks, channel filtering approaches, movement categorization, detection of features, classifying, and deployment. Increasing sensory possibilities in human activity recognition are expected. Seven obstacles to wireless human motion detection are identified in the study because of an examination of the published literature: reliability, non-coexistence of detecting and connectivity, security, different user motion detection, restricted field strength, difficult machine learning, and limitations of the current databases. In conclusion, the review includes four prospective future research trends. These include the development of new mathematical frameworks, the combination of monitoring and communication systems, the understanding of detecting by transmitters, and the construction of accessible data set to allow future wireless sensing possibilities on human activities.

The study [98] proposed a recognition network to perform a multi-person estimation with three observations and techniques. The study pointed out that the "insufficient designs" are the main cause of unsatisfactory performance of multi-stage pose estimation. The study defined the technique to aggregate features across different stages to strengthen the information flow and training phase. WiTrack2.0 is a method for determining the location of several individuals by using the reflected transmitted signal from human bodies in environments with a high number of interference paths. WiTrack2.0 locates stationary individuals by measuring current respiration. WiTrack2.0 was tested inside an office block. This simultaneously located up to five people with an average accuracy of 11.7 cm. WiTrack2.0 enables coarse body part tracking with a median inaccuracy of 12.5 for many users.

The research [99] examines recent methods for two-dimensional and three-dimensional posture estimation. Single-person and multi-person approaches are two basic pipelines. Proposed architectures divide each category into two groups. We also describe current data sets and performance indicators. Finally, we discuss the strategies' pros and cons.

The study [100] investigated the influence of several parameters on the quality of CSI data harvested from Wi-Fi signals. Their data visualization findings revealed the randomization and ineffectiveness of the obtained CSI samples. Using CSI as a case study, researchers performed tests to distinguish distinct activities or gestures. Their findings revealed that in typical environments like the lab and conference room, accurate segmentation is difficult to achieve, and important gesture elements were challenging to extract.

In a recent study, [101] introduced a context-aware strategy for 3D human skeletal tracking using RFID technology. The authors proposed Meta-Position after identifying the issue of RFID-based ambient tracking. This method incorporated RFID sensors with tags, which were readily adjustable to a variety of settings by fine-tuning. Multiple meta-learning methods (Reptile and MAML) were part of the Meta-Pose framework. An extensive evaluation was performed with data acquired from a Kinect 2.0 sensor. Meta-Pose was shown to be accurate and flexible by being compared to recent methods.

In Wi-Mose, [102] researchers combined the amplitude and channel state information (CSI) to rebuild 3D human poses. The study also developed an ANN to select only human pose information through CSI data to convert it to key-point coordinates. Wi-Mose achieved an average single joint displacement of 29.7 mm and a total system inaccuracy of 37.8 mm. A 21% and 10% improvement in accuracy over the baseline strategy was shown in the results section.

The study [103] analyzed received signal strength (RSSI) to set a threshold point. It incorporated the received signal variation with the range to identify extreme values using a low-pass filtering to exclude high-frequency information. The index weighted moving average filter to reduce "Saw tooth Wave" determined the extent to which the present value could be justified by reference to past data.

Recently, the authors [104] proposed WiFall, which is a non-intrusive fall detector. WiFall uses CSI to indicate activity. It can detect human falls without added hardware, environmental setup, or wearable devices. The study implemented WiFall on desktops with 802.11n NICs and analyzed its performance in three indoor environments with different Tx-Rx connection architectures. WiFall could accurately detect a single person's fall in our field. WiFall achieved 90% detection precision and 15% false alarms using a one-class SVM classifier in all testing scenarios. The random forest algorithm could detect falls with 94% accuracy and 13% false alarms.

About 78% of the research articles discuss vision-based methods, whereas only 22% discuss camera-based techniques for gesture recognition [59]. Device-based recognition widely uses vision sensors like cameras [105] and Kinect [106] to capture body poses in order to interpret the pose. Among both camera and Kinect technologies, Kinect is covering a large area of research as it provides more options to look at the human poses for improved accuracy and efficiency. On the other hand, device-free human pose received increased use of the signals generated by commercial hardware devices in order to complete the recognition task. These systems are categorized as radar-based [107,108], RSSI [109], CSI-based methods [110,111], and a combination of both CSI- and RSSI-based techniques [112].

Other useful techniques for device-free human pose estimation are explored in surveys [113,114]. CSI is important because it offers fine-grained signal information at the subcarrier level, which has wide applications in computer vision [115]. Recent research has combined Kinect-based data with wireless signal-based data to better recognize human poses [116]. A recent research by [117] introduced a method for estimating the 3D skeletal posture from a collection of joints based on the two-dimensional angle of arrival of signals reflected back from the human body. There was only one sensor that could provide 2D-AoA to identify moving limbs, so the participant was asked to face the sensor during evaluation. If multiple sensors deployed at right angles, the user can change orientations. While walking, the system may not work well. The study [118] explored the use of RFID tags for 3D human posture monitoring, with an emphasis on fine-tuning with a small number of data points and on meta-learning. In order to attain desirable results while fine-tuning, more time and money are required in collecting training data from bigger data sets.

In a recent study [119], the authors combined computer vision and RFID technology in multi-person scenarios to design a more advanced exercise monitoring system. This allowed them to track more information about the participants' workouts. This design was implemented in a smart exercise equipment application by the study using commercially available Kinect cameras and RFID devices. Three-dimensional (3D) position analysis, subject-adaptive monitoring, and significant rendering were all suggested in [120] the technology to utilize a distinctive cycle kinematic neural network to describe human poses in everyday life. The system was built with commercially available RFID readers and tags, and it was evaluated with an RFID-based comparative methodology.

In the paper [101], the author presented a vision-based, real-time human posture evaluation and tracking system. To estimate human positions in real-time based on RFID frequency data, the approach utilizes a multilayer kinetic network. For training this system, Kinect 2.0 machine vision input was used for classification. Due to the necessity of the original subject skeleton in the training phase, the proposed methodology was compromised when the subject was tested with an untrained subject or in a distinct standing position. In another study [121], a kinematic network was suggested as a way to train models without having to pair RFID and Kinect data. The subject-adaptive system that came out of it was made by learning how to turn sensor data into a skeletal system for each subject. When tested with a known subject, the efficiency of the model was a little lower than with the classical RFID pose tracking method. The study [122] proposed a new classification model for 3D human action recognition, one that could incorporate a user's anatomical data into the posture generation process for more accurate joints estimates. This method comprised nine distributed transmitters, and participants were required to perform actions in a fixed location. Consequently, the suggested technology was limited to particular applications and was not suited for everyday usage.

8.2.3 Pose and Gesture Recognition Using Multiple Sensors

Utilizing a combination of Wi-Fi and Kinect, the researchers [116] were able to identify human interaction in environments with obstruction, poor lighting, and different viewing directions. To begin, they developed a data set for the Wi-Fi-based activity recognition tool known as WiAR. They made a baseband decision model that took into account human behavior. The researchers maximized the temporal communication of nearby skeletal joints and established a connection among CSI and movement classifiers based on the skeletons. They investigated the use of forensic techniques and big data with regard to skeletal joints in order to enhance activity recognition in humans. They used commercial Wi-Fi hardware and put HuAc through its paces in three different environments. Using the WiAR data set, HuAc achieved an accuracy of 93%.

In a recent work [123], YouTube information contains live performance data of Indian classical dance, with both local and Internet monitoring sound and video. Using ten different dancing styles of classical dance and a range of postures, an individual's fingerprint can be used to develop data to a database. Dancing is one of ten different topics for which data is collected online via YouTube. In both scenarios, every dancing position is held for 60 seconds or for the duration of a movie. FPGA learning and eight distinct sample variables, all conducted by diverse subject sets. The last two examples for putting the taught FPGA to the challenge. In order to improve recognition accuracy, they have used a new FPGA design and their own testing data set. They attained a 90% classification performance by comparing the output on the same data set to another categorization model.

The study [124] demonstrated gesture identification utilizing numerous inertial measurement unit devices to acquire hand joint speed and orientation. The suggested gesture classification approach used convolutional network and temporal network to recognize various hand motions from IMU signals. Baseball referees' hand gestures, which include broad and subtle hand movements, were used to validate the suggested gesture detection system. The evaluation showed the suggested recognition model outperformed other works. Twenty independent participants found that a learning method based on action recognition significantly boosted the subjective decision-making ability of its users.

The authors [125] found the latest developments in body sensor systems and digital vision have made it possible to accurately measure unidentified hand and finger activities at 120 Hz. Due to finger occlusion by other hand parts, these novel sensors create hurdles for real-time gesture identification. They describe a multisensor approach that improves real-time computer vision gesture recognition position estimation. The artificial hand's measurements can be used to build a model to determine whose hand angles and postures lead to the greatest increases in posture estimation error. This method employs a classification algorithm to determine the optimal RFID skeletal posture at every time interval, yielding a sequence of steadily improving poses. The robotic hand does some pinching and tapping on the surface. This novel method improves upon the accuracy of pose estimates from a motion device by roughly 30% while still operating in real time. The solution surpasses the weighted sum of hand locations, according to assessments. An analysis of the classifier's efficiency shows that the amount of time spent offline training is negligible and that the setup provides 90.8% data set optimization. By evaluating skeleton locations from many perspectives, this approach enhances touchless exhibit interfaces in high-occlusion conditions.

The research [126] proposes a fusion of multiple sensors to recognize the real-time sign languages. The system interacts in state-space, not observation states, unlike traditional methods, that does not account for the connections between different modes of transportation. This method recognizes hearing-impaired people's dynamic isolated sign motions. The data set examined utilizing data fusion methods. CHMM achieves 90.80% recognition accuracy. The CHMM-based approach outperforms popular data fusion techniques.

The recent research [127] designed a system based on multiple motion sensors, each embedded with an accelerometer, gyroscope, magnetometer, a Kalman filter, multi-layer recurrent encoder, and skeleton-based decoder. Calibrating all the sensors increased the computational cost. The experimentation results failed to account for the spatial relationship between the available skeletons and hindered the capture of structural interdependence.

8.2.4 Data Fusion in a Multisensory Environment

The added sensors at times provide the information missed by one sensor. Several studies have demonstrated an enhancement in precision over single sensors. Using different sensory devices simultaneously for HAR in variant environments is a challenging task. Even though there are numerous approaches to fuse sensors data for activity recognition, nearly all researchers report using a unique arrangement of approaches to fuse data, making it clear that standardized practices and guidelines are needed [128]. This review part evaluates the numerous sensors data fusion strategies previously proposed for

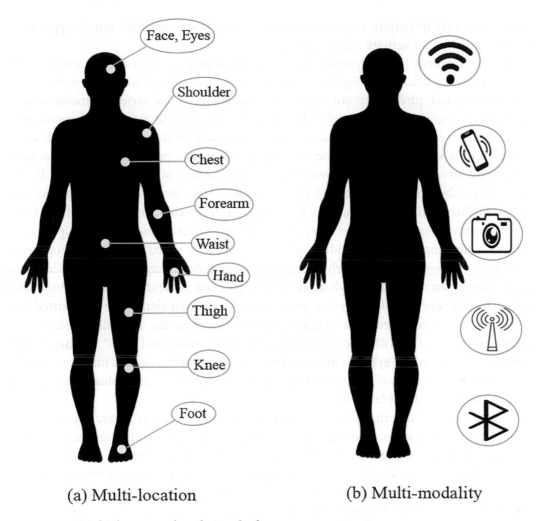

(a) Multi-location   (b) Multi-modality

FIGURE 8.1   Multiple sensor data fusion for human pose estimation systems.

human action recognition, assessing their merits and shortcomings and offering an overview of the state of the art. Using the categories in Figure 8.1, this section breaks down sensor fusion into subheadings based on the number of different types of data and the number of different locations at which those data were collected.

8.2.4.1 Multimodality Sensor Fusion

When multiple sensors are combined into one, it increases the reliability and decreases the uncertainty. The idea behind this is that one source can make up for the inaccuracies of another, which has many practical benefits, including increased accuracy and fault resilience. In some cases, accelerometers might not be effective in providing data on their own. In order to provide a more precise classification of activity, they must be combined with other sensors like Kinect [124], smart sensing devices [125], and ECG devices [81].

The study [3] was for a more thorough understanding of wearable sensor fusion, and the research team suggested taking a more holistic approach. This study offered a deeper insight into very important components of new stand-alone multiple sensor application domains for human activity identification.

Another research [118] suggested that recognition of a subject's actions was essential for numerous artificial intelligence-based activities, including those in the realms of athletics, medical, physical security, etc. It was beneficial to use various cameras at once for action recognition, as this could fill in gaps left by a single input and demonstrated reduced errors in the proposed studies. There was a need for standardized guidelines and norms in data stream integration because nearly all authors presenting multiple sensors for activity recognition used their own unique combination of fusion techniques. In this study, researchers organized the multiple sensors fusion methods for activity recognition, evaluated their performance and benefits, and considered the current state of the field.

In a recent research [129], the recognition system extracted and classified sign words. It was challenging to identify individual sign letters in a video. The study proposed a novel method that could accurately detect word boundaries in sign language videos. This framework extracted isolated indicators from videos using hand form and motion data and displayed superior efficiency than other works. Extracted signs were then sorted into categories and recognized by a Hidden Markov Model in the recognition stage. The algorithm achieved 95.18% accuracy for one-hand motions and 93.87 for two. When using head position and eye gaze information, the suggested framework improved by 2.24 and 2.9% on one and two hand gestures, respectively, over systems using solely manual features, based on 33 isolated signs.

The study [130] described the subjective vs. objective ways to measuring emotional responses that have various benefits. Subjective techniques (self and observers) were best for coarse-grained temporal emotion representations (e.g., rage, fear, valence, dominance) (tens of seconds to minutes). Objective techniques (sensors and software) were appropriate for measuring fine-grained behavioral/physiological responses (e.g., facial expressions, electro dermal activity) (milliseconds to seconds). Both strategies had pros and cons. Subjective techniques used people's knowledge and reasoning to create sophisticated, contextualized emotion judgments. They were limited by weariness, biases (e.g., social desirability bias), and inaccuracies (e.g., self-report memory reconstruction). Objective techniques were not affected by fatigue or biases and were more scalable, but had limited inference and reasoning capabilities, and only delivered behavioral/physiological responses.

In a multimodal system proposed by [131], two different sensors were used, each of which made frames at a different rate. To reduce the number of dimensions, PCA applied to the head pose feature vector before the features combined. By combining the hand and head pose feature vectors, a new feature vector was generated. For this research, researchers used a technique called independent Bayesian classifier combination (IBCC). The outcomes for both two- and one-handed signs were computed. In terms of performance, the data demonstrated a 95.18% success rate in identifying single-hand motions and a 93.87% success rate in identifying double-hand gestures. Researchers found that both manually entered and automated data contained additional, valuable information. It was also possible to use non-human features and other classifier combination strategies to enhance recognition results.

8.2.4.1.1 Environmental and Vision Sensors   Ambient sensors consist of acoustic, light, thermal, ultraviolet, and radar systems. These sensor nodes are used to monitor changes in the environment and recognize human activity in certain locations [3]. To accurately recognize the actions of multiple residents, researchers trained a multilayer perceptron classification using image data of movement in color space using input via PIR and temperature devices [132].

For indoor localization, the research [118] combined data from distributed environmental sensors with data from wearable sensors tracking human body activity. By combining the experimental data collected from multiple sensors, including an accelerometer, Doppler radar, and 3D sensor, [133] were able to overcome the performance limitation of using a single sensor, in particular for the classification of similar activities. Initial findings verifed that system performance could be enhanced by integrating data from various types of sensors. When compared against utilizing devices separately, the integration method improved accuracy of classification by 11.2%, and when compared to using accelerometers alone, it improved the classification accuracy by 16.9%.

Proposed are pressure detectors paired with accelerometer sensor, when used as part of an inertial navigation system for pedestrians, specifically to better estimate where the user is with relation to the ground during the stance phase of walking [134]. Wireless Internet Protocol, global positioning system coordinates, and mobile phones acceleration data were used to infer mobile behavior in [105]. A new information fusion approach was developed for training human gait behavior using data gathered by global positioning system and numerous kinematic devices placed by the user, with the goal of improving the reliability of the location estimation.

8.2.4.1.2 Vision and Wearable Sensors   Pose identification can be achieved with numerous methods due to the virtual tracking capabilities of sensors in image-sensor-based systems [135]. Based on their research, [135] in comparison to existing methods that focused on accelerometers or camera systems, it was found that using both data sources not only increased the classification performance but also decreased the amount of error rates. Researchers looked into the potential of combining visual and kinematic devices for HAR [136]. The study [137] first proposed has proven to be an invaluable resource for rehabilitation professionals. Motion states were identified using an embedded multiple accelerometer, global navigation satellite system, image sensor, and stopwatch.

Currently, the widely used depth cameras are the Kinect sensor and image sensors. Specifically for indoor body motion identification, the depth image provided by an image sensor is more accurate and tolerant to illumination changes than the image generated by a conventional camera. The combination of depth cameras and inertial sensors enhances the efficiency of detection since the latter give a thorough representation of whole-body movements, whereas the former records local movement features [138]. In a recent study [139], movement data was extracted by using inertial sensors to determine the object's motion characteristics and a depth camera to determine the object's true joint size and beginning orientation. This was done so that the golf swing posture could be analyzed and fixed.

With the help of a depth image and an inertial device worn by the musician, researchers were able to fuse multiple sources of data in [140]. A classification method was suggested that could properly recognize individual bow strokes in a traditional violinist performance. Data from a depth sensor and accelerometer sensor were used to create a database portraying violin bow action. Secondly, researchers transferred the depth image input to a three-dimensional form of points and the accelerometer sensor readings towards the rotation, tilt, and flip orientations, all in an effort to better understand and utilize the information provided by these sensors. Finally, the bow movement classification was performed in a range of methods to account for the advantages and disadvantages of different computational modeling and decision-level fusion approaches.

Data from the external accelerometers were utilized in a research to calculate four major statistical parameters, including mean, variance, standard deviation, and average deviation using angular velocity data [141] to create the feature vector. Nvidia presented the concept of negative lag classification, in which classification performed ahead of the gesture's completion, to address the time lag in the identification and tracking of complex body movements from multi-modal data input [141].

Nvidia presented a continuous 3-D deep neural network that could recognize and classify complex movements from multi-modal data input. As a result, the delay was drastically reduced, and the recognition was now practically instantaneous. The system was trained to make predictions about target class based on continuous gestures in data input with temporal classification.

8.2.4.2 Multi-Location Sensor Fusion

The ability to recognize multiple activities being performed at once by a human being is a significant obstacle. In certain instances, it is feasible to multitask, just like when jogging and brushing your hair or any variation combined. This is where a hierarchical approach comes in handy, by breaking down the tasks at hand into smaller, more manageable chunks.

For comprehensive motion capture, a number of speed sensors are attached on various parts of the body, including the neck, the arm, leg, the knee, and the torso [142]. According to an earlier research [143], arm wearable devices normally yield acceptable identification precision of over 85% for relatively simple actions like lying in bed, whereas the waistline tracker was selected from all classifications as the one that offered the maximum accuracy and recognition rates for lower-level activities such as eating and writing.

Environmental sensors can generate multiple variables depending on the medium the equipment is placed on, and the allocation of sensing information from various positions can be dissimilar, regardless of whether the participant is executing the same action [144]. A recent research looked at how human behavioral traits could be used to predict the consistency of data from various sensors [145]. They suggested that the improved behavioral recognition rate could be achieved by combining sensor data from various locations in order to more accurately reflect the characteristics of poses and efficiently collect relevant details from existing data.

Using accelerometers attached to ten different body regions, including the arms, ankles, and chest, [146] were able to conduct a thorough human activity recognition. Accelerometers and gyroscopes were used in a different study [147] in which devices were placed on the chest and forearm and provided the most accurate findings when applied to HAR. The results showed that the proposed methods of combining multiple sensors to detect, recognize, and classify a human activity performed better in terms of accuracy achieved.

8.2.5 Pose and Gesture Data Set

This section provides a summary of the data sets developed in the context of human pose and gesture recognition. The basic characteristics of the data sets are described, together with a detailed analysis of their overall strengths and weaknesses. Methods for design and application of data sets for gesture recognition are presented.

The absence of a comprehensive and significant data pool is one of the most frequently encountered obstacles that arises in the process of applying machine learning to projects involving gesture detection. In order for machine learning to function, users will be required to supply it with information that is needed to train our models. The set of data must be modified to suit your requirements, but there are several data sets that can be of great assistance.

In a study [148], HuAc combined Wi-Fi and Kinect to detect human activity in occlusion, low light, and diverse angles. The study designed a subcarrier-selection method based on human activity sensitivity. The focus was on improving the 3D connection between neighboring skeleton joints and establishing a bridge between CSI, and movement detection based on skeleton motion. They investigated CSI and crowdsourcing skeletal joints to improve human activity recognition and tested HuAc in three settings utilizing commercial Wi-Fi equipment. Using the WiAR data set, HuAc obtained 93% accuracy.

To test the efficacy of image-based machine learning techniques, several researchers used the initial MNIST collection, which featured images of handwritten characters [149]. The researchers for the collection of data set had created drop-in substitutes, which were difficult for machine learning and novel for practical uses. The name of a new drop-in version was Fashion-MNIST. Every photo was 28 pixels tall and 28 pixels wide, for a maximum of 784 pixels, and each symbolized a garment. The Zalando researchers made the stunning statement that "the majority of pairs of MNIST digits (i.e., the total of 784 pixels per example) can be discriminated fairly well by a single pixel."

The Sign Language data set was presented in the standard data file containing descriptions and number of pixels in separate fields to encourage the development of additional drop-in solutions [150]. Each of the 24 categories of alphabet within the ASL database reflected a different set of arm movements in American Sign Language (excluding J and Z, which require motion). Databases of hand gestures and associated citations were freely accessible to the researchers.

The survey conducted in [151] presented gesture-recognition data sets. The key data set properties were presented in an easy-to-access form. This document described the data set's strengths and weaknesses. Guidelines were offered for creating and selecting gesture data sets. This survey may help researchers generate or use gesture recognition data sets.

Video footage of people doing standard hand movements was recorded by a camera or a webcam, all of which have been precisely tagged, made up the 20BN-JESTER data set [152]. A sizable group of people worked together to compile the collection. Because of this, powerful machine learning models may be trained to recognize human hand motions. Corporate permits are offered upon request in addition to the free academic use.

This research [153] introduced the LeapGestRecog Dataset, a sign language recognition library constructed from a collection of near-infrared images captured through a Leap Motion sensor. This data set included ten distinct hand motions recorded by ten distinct participants: five men and five women.

The EgoGesture data set [154] is suitable for supervised learning due to its large sample population, high variance, and high validity. This collection contained over 24,000 gesture instances and 3,000,000 photos spanning geographic and color regions for 50 separate individuals. The team created 83 separate both dynamic and static gestures focusing on interfaces with wearable technologies and collected them in six diverse indoor and outdoor settings featuring a variety of backgrounds and illumination. Different sampling approaches were investigated, each yielding a somewhat different level of precision on the movement classification data set that had been subdivided, or on the real-time detecting and recognizing activities. The research also provided an overall evaluation of gathering the data from scene to scene.

The research [155] introduced a database of 44 healthy participants' sEMG signals from eight different hand gestures, with the goal of facilitating gesture recognition technology (including idle state). For the purpose of benchmarking classification methods and conducting experiments on the efficacy of different electrode designs, robustness enhancements, and armband localization settings for wearable sEMG-based HMIs, a publicly available EMG data set was made available. There was a lot of room for variation in the performance because it incorporated both a repeating and sequential gesture execution style, each with its own durational requirements. Using an RGB video stream and a depth camera, the data set offered a novel method for establishing gesture execution ground truth.

There are ten unique hand motions that captured infrared and stored in a library called the Hand Gesture Recognition Database [55]. The gestural archive was organized under ten subfolders (numbered 00–09) that each covered a certain theme. Every sub-directory contained its own set of gesture-specific subfolders. Kaggle intended to develop a vocabulary search that stored the titles of the motions needed to detect and assigned a numbered identification to every action. In addition, they constructed a vocabulary inverse search that revealed the action related to a specific identifier.

8.3 CONCLUSION

This chapter has outlined the details of proposed HAR methods for providing efficient and accurate recognition of human poses and gestures. The research features a literature review outlining the history of human pose and gesture recognition technologies, their uses, and typical system architectures. Discussed are existing methods to handle the multi-sensory input data, and the contribution of available data sets.

In terms of future improvement in 3D human pose estimation and gesture recognition, additional advancements could be researched to improve overall system operation. Future development would be extended toward the incorporation of complex depth images with more gesture angles in other languages at multiple angles and lighting conditions in outdoor environments. Future development could be extended toward the incorporation of complex depth images with more gesture angles in other languages (regional sign language) by using multiple high-resolution camera modules. Further complexity in recognition can be created to select more features at multiple angles and lighting conditions in outdoor environments.

This chapter analyzed RFID data variability and generalization concerns. The generalization issue could be reduced by expanding the training data set to include additional subjects and positions. Future study will continue to address the more general challenges of RFID-based pose monitoring systems. It is important to sample a larger data set of multiple objects with diverse poses in the different environments in order to obtain a level of performance in fine-tuning that is considered satisfactory. The 3D human posture estimation system that is built on a cloud-edge framework could potentially be enhanced with the addition of hybrid artificial intelligence approaches. Multiple human objects must be considered concurrently with additional poses and machine learning techniques.

It is important to sample a larger data set of multiple objects with diverse poses in the different environments in order to obtain a level of performance in fine-tuning that is considered to be satisfactory. The 3D human posture estimation system that is built on a cloud-edge framework could potentially be enhanced with the addition of hybrid artificial intelligence approaches.

REFERENCES

[1] Franslin, N.M.F., Ng, G.W.. (2022). Vision-based dynamic hand gesture recognition techniques and applications: A review. In: Proceedings of the 8th International Conference on Computational Science and Technology; 2022:125–138.

[2] Oudah, M., Al-Naji, A., Chahl, J. (2020). Hand gesture recognition based on computer vision: A review of techniques. *Journal of Imaging.* 6(8). doi:10.3390/JIMAGING6080073

[3] Qiu, S., Zhao, H., Jiang, N., et al. (2022). Multi-sensor information fusion based on machine learning for real applications in human activity recognition: State-of-the-art and research challenges. *Information Fusion.* 80(October 2021), 241–265. doi:10.1016/j.inffus.2021.11.006

[4] Li, J., Liu, X., Wang, Z., Zhao, H., Zhang, T., Qiu, S., Zhou, X., Cai, H., Ni, R., A.C. (2021). Real-time human motion capture based on wearable inertial sensor networks. *IEEE Internet of Things Journal.* 9(11), 8953–8966.

[5] Majumder, S., Deen, M.J. (2020). A robust orientation filter for wearable sensing applications. *IEEE Sensors Journal.* 20(23), 14228–14236.

[6] Weygers, I., Kok, M., De Vroey, H., Verbeerst, T., Versteyhe, M., Hallez, H., Claeys, K. (2020). Drift-free inertial sensor-based joint kinematics for long-term arbitrary movements. *IEEE Sensors Journal.* 20(14), 7969–7979.

[7] Harris, T.J., Owen, C.G., Victor, C.R., Adams, R., Ekelund, U., Cook, D.G. (2009). A comparison of questionnaire, accelerometer, and pedometer: Measures in older people. *Medicine and Science in Sports and Exercise.* 41(7), 1392–1402.

[8] Jee, H.C., Jeongwhan, L., Hyun, T.H., Jong, P.K., Jae, C.P., Kunsoo, S. (2005). Estimation of activity energy expenditure: Accelerometer approach. In Annual International Conference of the IEEE Engineering in Medicine and Biology - Proceedings. 7 VOLS, 3830–3833. doi:10.1109/IEMBS.2005.1615295

[9] Mayagoitia, J.C., Lötters, P.H., Veltink, H.H. (2002). Standing balance evaluation using a triaxial accelerometer. *Gait Posture.* 16(1), 55–59.

[10] Bourke, A.K., O'Brien, J.V., Lyons, G.M. (2007). Evaluation of a threshold-based tri-axial accelerometer fall detection algorithm. *Gait Posture.* 26(2), 194–199.

[11] Curone, G.M., Bertolotti, A., Cristiani, E.L., Secco, G.M. (2010). A real-time and self-calibrating algorithm based on triaxial accelerometer signals for the detection of human posture and activity. *IEEE Transactions on Information Technology in Biomedicine.* 14(4), 1098–1105.

[12] Lu, X., Chen, Q., Li, X., Zhang, P.Z. (2014). A hand gesture recognition framework and wearable gesture-based interaction prototype for mobile devices. *IEEE Transactions on Human-Machine Systems.* 42(2), 293–299.

[13] Lee, W.Y.C. (2016). Wearable glove-type driver stress detection using a motion sensor. *IEEE Transactions on Intelligent Transportation Systems.* 18(7), 1835–1844.

[14] Wang, C.W., Lin, Y.T.C., Yang, Y.J.H. (2012). Walking pattern classification and walking distance estimation algorithms using gait phase information. *IEEE Transactions on Biomedical Engineering.* 59(10), 2884–2892.

[15] Qiu, L., Liu, H., Zhao, Z., Wang, Y.J. (2018). Mems inertial sensors based gait analysis for rehabilitation assessment via multi-sensor fusion. *Micromachines.* 9(9), 442.

[16] Zhu, W.S. (2009). Multi-sensor fusion for human daily activity recognition in robot-assisted living. In: Proceedings of the 4th ACM/IEEE International Conference on Human Robot Interaction; 2009:303–304.

[17] Schirrmeister, J.T., Springenberg, L.D.J., Fiederer, M., Glasstetter, K., Eggensperger, M. (2017). Deep learning with convolutional neural networks for EEG decoding and visualization. *Human Brain Mapping.* 38(11), 5391–5420.

[18] Zhang, D., Zhou, X.Z. (2017). HeartID: A multiresolution convolutional neural network for ECG-based biometric human identification in smart health applications. *IEEE Access.* 5, 11805–11816.

[19] Fadhillah, Z.A.N., Afikah, N.E.N., Safiee, A.W., Asnida, A.K.M., Rafiq, M.H.R. (2018). Development of a low-cost wearable breast cancer detection device. In: 2nd International Conference on BioSignal Analysis, Processing and Systems, ICBAPS, IEEE; 2018:41–46.

[20] Batzianoulis, S., El-Khoury, E., Pirondini, M., Coscia, S.M. (2017). Billard, EMG-based decoding of grasp gestures in reaching-to-grasping motions. *Robotics and Autonomous Systems.* 91, 59–70.

[21] Gailey, P., Artemiadis, M.S. (2017). Proof of concept of an online EMG-based decoding of hand postures and individual digit forces for prosthetic hand control. *Frontiers in Neurology.* 8(7), 1–15.

[22] Zhang, R., Gravina, H., Lu, M., Villari, G.F. (2018). PEA: Parallel electrocardiogram-based authentication for smart healthcare systems. *Journal of Network and Computer Applications.* 117, 10–16.

[23] Rabin, M., Kahlon, S., Malayev, A.R. (2020). Classification of human hand movements based on EMG signals using nonlinear dimensionality reduction and data fusion techniques. *Expert Systems With Applications.* 149, 113–130.

[24] Aygun, H., Ghasemzadeh, R.J. (2019). Robust interbeat interval and heart rate variability estimation method from various morphological features using wearable sensors. *IEEE Journal of Biomedical and Health Informatics*. 24(8), 2238–2250.

[25] Xiong, C., Wu, H., Zhou, A., Song, L., Hu, X.P.L. (2018). Design of an accurate end-of-arm force display system based on wearable arm gesture sensors and EMG sensors. *Information Fusion*. 39, 178–185.

[26] Ngueleu, A.K., Blanchette, L., Bouyer, D., Maltais, B.J., McFadyen, H., Moffet, C.S.B. (2019). Design and accuracy of an instrumented insole using pressure sensors for step count. *Sensors*. 19(5), 984.

[27] Hegde, E.S. (2014). Smartstep: A fully integrated, low-power insole monitor. *Electronics*. 3(2), 381–397.

[28] Jacobs, D.P.F. (2015). Estimation of ground reaction forces and ankle moment with multiple, low-cost sensors. *Journal of NeuroEngineering and Rehabilitation*. 12(1), 1–12.

[29] Tabor, T., Agcayazi, A., Fleming, B., Thompson, A., Kapoor, M., Liu, M.Y., Lee, H., Huang, A., Bozkurt, T.K.G. (2021). Textile-based pressure sensors for monitoring prosthetic-socket interfaces. *IEEE Sensors*. 21(7), 9413–9422.

[30] Peng, K., Dong, C., Ye, Y., Jiang, S., Zhai, R., Cheng, D., Liu, X., Gao, J., Wang, Z.L.W. (2020). A breathable, biodegradable, antibacterial, and self-powered electronic skin based on all-nanofiber triboelectric nanogenerators. *Science Advances*. 6(26), 1–16.

[31] Rigas, H., Raffle, O.V.K. (2017). Hybrid ps-v technique: A novel sensor fusion approach for fast mobile eye-tracking with sensor-shift aware correction. *IEEE Sensors Journal*. 17(24), 8356–8366.

[32] Ozcan, S.V. (2015). Wearable camera-and accelerometer-based fall detection on portable devices. *IEEE Embedded Systems Letters*. 8(1), 6–9.

[33] Hussain, F.U.D., Farrukh, S., Su, Z., Wang, H.C. (2019). CMOS image sensor design and image processing algorithm implementation for total hip arthroplasty surgery. *IEEE Transactions on Biomedical Circuits and Systems*. 13(6), 1383–1392.

[34] Rae, G., Venolia, J.C., Tang, D.M. (2015). A framework for understanding and designing telepresence. In: Proceedings of the 18th ACM Conference on Computer Supported Cooperative Work & Social Computing; 2015:1552–1566.

[35] Choi, M.H., Kim, Y.S., Oh, S.H., Jung, J.H., Jung, H.J., Sung, H.W., Lee, H.M.L. (2017). Highly stretchable, hysteresis-free ionic liquid-based strain sensor for precise human motion monitoring. *ACS Applied Materials & Interfaces*. 9(2), 1770–1780.

[36] Berman, H.S. (2011). Sensors for gesture recognition systems. *IEEE Transactions on Systems, Man, and Cybernetics, Part C (Applications and Reviews)*. 43(2), 277–290.

[37] Dai, L.B., Huang, Y., Du, J., Han, J.K. (2021). Self-healing flexible strain sensors based on dynamically cross-linked conductive nanocomposites. *Composites Communications*. 24, 109–128.

[38] Van Volkinburg, G.W. (2017). Development of a wearable controller for gesture-recognition-based applications using polyvinylidene fluoride. *IEEE Transactions on Biomedical Circuits and Systems*. 11(4), 900–909.

[39] Lu, C., Jiang, G., Hu, J., Liu, B.Y. (2021). Flexible noncontact sensing for human–machine interaction. *Advanced Material. Published Online* 2021, 210–218.

[40] Chen, L., Gong, L., Wei, S.-C., Yeh, L., Da Xu, L., Zheng, Z.Z. (2020). A wearable hand rehabilitation system with soft gloves. *IEEE Transactions on Industrial Informatics*. 17(2), 943–952.

[41] Fu, L.W. (2003). Data dimensionality reduction with application to simplifying rbf network structure and improving classification performance. *IEEE Transactions on Systems, Man, and Cybernetics: Systems*. 33(3), 399–409.

[42] Chen, Q., Zhu, Y.C., Soh, L.Z. (2017). Robust human activity recognition using smartphone sensors via CT-PCA and online SVM. *IEEE Transactions on Industrial Informatics*. 13(6), 370–380.

[43] Yean, B.S., Lee, C.K., Yeo, C.H., Vun, H.L.O. (2017). Smartphone orientation estimation algorithm combining Kalman filter with gradient descent. *IEEE Journal of Biomedical and Health Informatics*. 22(5), 1421–1433.

[44] Maurer, A., Smailagic, D.P., Siewiorek, M.D. (2006). Activity recognition and monitoring using multiple sensors on different body positions. In: International Workshop on Wearable and Implantable Body Sensor Networks, IEEE; 2006:4.

[45] McCarthy, N., Pradhan, C., Redpath, A.A. (2016). Validation of the empatica E4 wristband. In: 2016 IEEE EMBS International Student Conference, ISC, IEEE; 2016:1–4.

[46] Sevil, M., Rashid, Z., Maloney, I., Hajizadeh, S., Samadi, M.R., Askari, N., Hobbs, R., Brandt, M., Park, L.Q. (2020). Determining physical activity characteristics from wristband data for use in automated insulin delivery systems. *IEEE Sensors Journal*. 20(21), 12859–12870.

[47] Nguyen, R., Alqurashi, Z., Raghebi, F., Banaei-Kashani, A.C., Halbower, T.V. (2017). LIBS: A lightweight and inexpensive in-ear sensing system for automatic whole-night sleep stage monitoring. *GetMobile: Mobile Computing and Communications*. 21(3), 31–34.

[48] Athavipach, S., Pan-Ngum, P.I. (2019). A wearable in-ear EEG device for emotion monitoring. *Sensors*. 19(18), 419–437.

[49] Yang, Q., Li, X., Wang, P., Di, H., Ding, Y., Bai, W., Dong, S.Z. (2021). Smart wearable monitoring system based on multi-type sensors for motion recognition. *Smart Materials and Structures*. 30(3), 311–332.

[50] Ataei, R., Abedi, Y., Mohammadi, N.F. (2020). Analysing the effect of wearable lift-assist vest in squat lifting task using back muscle EMG data and musculoskeletal model. *Physical and Engineering Sciences in Medicine*. 43(2), 651–658.

[51] Pino, Y., Arias, P.A. (2018). Wearable EMG shirt for upper limb training. In: 2018 40th Annual International Conference of the IEEE Engineering in Medicine and Biology Society, EMBC, IEEE; 2018:4406–4409.

[52] Federation. (2021). World Federation of the Deaf. Published 2021. https://wfdeaf.org/our-work/#what-we-do

[53] Lee, H.J., Chen, Z. (1985). Determination of 3D human body postures from a single view. *Computer Vision, Graphics and Image Processing*. 30(2), 148–168. doi:10.1016/0734-189X(85)90094-5

[54] Chakraborty, B.K., Sarma, D., Bhuyan, M.K., MacDorman, K.F. (2018). Review of constraints on vision-based gesture recognition for human–computer interaction. *IET Computer Vision*. 12(1), 3–15. doi:10.1049/iet-cvi.2017.0052

[55] Beddiar, D.R., Nini, B., Sabokrou, M., Hadid, A. (2020). Vision-based human activity recognition: A survey. *Multimedia Tools and Applications*. 79(41–42), 30509–30555. doi:10.1007/s11042-020-09004-3

[56] Pinto, R.F., Borges, C.D.B., Almeida, A.M.A., Paula, I.C. (2019). Static hand gesture recognition based on convolutional neural networks. *Journal of Electrical and Computer Engineering*. 2019. doi:10.1155/2019/4167890

[57] Hongyi, L., Wang, L. (2021). Latest developments of gesture recognition for human–robot collaboration. In: *Advanced Human-Robot Collaboration in Manufacturing*. Springer, Cham; 2021:43–68. doi:10.1007/978-3-030-69178-3_2

[58] Zhang, H.B., Zhang, Y.X., Zhong, B., et al. (2019). A comprehensive survey of vision-based human action recognition methods. *Sensors (Switzerland)*. 19(5), 1–20. doi:10.3390/s19051005

[59] Al-Shamayleh, A.S., Ahmad, R., Abushariah, M.A.M., Alam, K.A., Jomhari, N. (2018). A systematic literature review on vision based gesture recognition techniques. *Multimedia Tools and Applications. Published Online.* 2018, 1–64. doi:10.1007/s11042-018-5971-z

[60] Chouinard, J. (2019). The Fundamentals of Camera and Image Sensor Technology; 2019. https://www.visiononline.org/userassets/aiauploads/file/cvp_the-fundamentals-of-camera-and-image-sensor-technology_jon-chouinard.pdf

[61] Center, K. (2018). Imaging Electronics 101: Understanding Camera Sensors for Machine Vision Applications. Published 2018. Accessed February 9, 2021. https://www.edmundoptics.com/knowledge-center/application-notes/imaging/understanding-camera-sensors-for-machine-vision-applications/

[62] Fails, J., Olsen, D. (2003). A design tool for camera-based interaction. In: Proceedings of the Conference on Human Factors in Computing Systems - CHI '03; 2003:449. doi:10.1145/642611.642690

[63] Huang, L., Zhang, B., Guo, Z., Xiao, Y., Cao, Z., Yuan, J. (2021). Survey on depth and RGB image-based 3D hand shape and pose estimation. *Virtual Reality and Intelligent Hardware.* 3(3), 207–234. doi:10.1016/j.vrih.2021.05.002

[64] Oyedotun, O.K., Khashman, A. (2017). Deep learning in vision-based static hand gesture recognition. *Neural Computing and Applications.* 28(12), 3941–3951. doi:10.1007/s00521-016-2294-8

[65] Thomas Moeslund's gesture recognition database—PRIMA. http://www-prima.inrialpes.fr/FGnet/data/12-MoeslundGesture/database.html

[66] Singha, J., Roy, A., Laskar, R.H. (2018). Dynamic hand gesture recognition using vision-based approach for human–computer interaction. *Neural Computing and Applications.* 29(4), 1129–1141. doi:10.1007/s00521-016-2525-z

[67] Humeau-Heurtier, A. (2019). Texture feature extraction methods: A survey. *IEEE Access.* 7, 8975–9000. doi:10.1109/ACCESS.2018.2890743

[68] Khan, N.S., Abid, A., Abid, K. (2020). A novel natural language processing (NLP)-based machine translation model for english to Pakistan sign language translation. *Cognitive Computation.* 12(4), 748–765. doi:10.1007/s12559-020-09731-7

[69] Rezende, T.M., Almeida, S.G.M., Guimarães, F.G. (2021). Development and validation of a Brazilian sign language database for human gesture recognition. *Neural Computing and Applications.* 4. doi:10.1007/s00521-021-05802-4

[70] Al-Hammadi, M., Muhammad, G., Abdul, W., et al. (2020). Deep learning-based approach for sign language gesture recognition with efficient hand gesture representation. *IEEE Access.* 8, 192527–192542. doi:10.1109/ACCESS.2020.3032140

[71] Guo, L., Lu, Z., Yao, L. (2021). Human-machine interaction sensing technology based on hand gesture recognition: A review. *IEEE Transactions on Human-Machine Systems.* 51(4), 23–47.

[72] Vishwakarma, D.K. (2017). Hand gesture recognition using shape and texture evidences in complex background. In: Proceedings of the International Conference on Inventive Computing and Informatics (ICICI 2017); 2017:278–283.

[73] Vishwakarma, D.K., Grover, V. (2018). Hand gesture recognition in low-intensity environment using depth images. In: Proceedings of the International Conference on Intelligent Sustainable Systems, ICISS 2017 (ICISS):429–433. doi:10.1109/ISS1.2017.8389446

[74] Vishwakarma, D.K., Maheshwari, R., Kapoor, R. (2015). An efficient approach for the recognition of hand gestures from very low resolution images. In: Proceedings - 2015 5th International Conference on Communication Systems and Network Technologies, CSNT 2015. Published online; 2015:467–471. doi:10.1109/CSNT.2015.84

[75] Xiao, Y.W. (2020). A hand gesture recognition algorithm based on DC-CNN. *Multimedia Tools and Applications.* 79(13–14):9193–9205. doi:10.1007/s11042-019-7193-4

[76] Tang, X., Yan, Z., Peng, J., Hao, B., Wang, H., Li, J. (2021). Selective spatiotemporal features learning for dynamic gesture recognition. *Expert Systems with Applications.* 169(July 2020), 114499. doi:10.1016/j.eswa.2020.114499

[77] Chen, G., Xu, Z., Li, Z., et al. (2021). A novel illumination-robust hand gesture recognition system with event-based neuromorphic vision sensor. *IEEE Transactions on Automation Science and Engineering. Published Online.* 2021, 1–13. doi:10.1109/TASE.2020.3045880

[78] Huang, Y., Yang, J. (2021). A multi-scale descriptor for real time RGB-D hand gesture recognition. *Pattern Recognition Letters.* 144, 97–104. doi:10.1016/j.patrec.2020.11.011

[79] Lee, C.K.M., Ng, K.K.H., Chen, C.H., Lau, H.C.W., Chung, S.Y., Tsoi, T. (2021). American sign language recognition and training method with recurrent neural network. *Expert Systems with Applications.* 167. doi:10.1016/j.eswa.2020.114403

[80] Wang, Y., Ren, A., Zhou, M., Wang, W., Yang, X. (2020). A novel detection and recognition method for continuous hand gesture using FMCW radar. *IEEE Access.* 8, 167264–167275. doi:10.1109/ACCESS.2020.3023187

[81] Xi, L., Chen, W., Zhao, C., Wu, X., Wang, J. (2020). Image enhancement for remote photoplethysmography in a low-light environment. In: Proceedings - 2020 15th IEEE International Conference on Automatic Face and Gesture Recognition, FG 2020, (Fg):761–764. doi:10.1109/FG47880.2020.00076

[82] Onan, A. (2022). Bidirectional convolutional recurrent neural network architecture with group-wise enhancement mechanism for text sentiment classification. *Journal of King Saud University - Computer and Information Sciences.* 34(5), 2098–2117. doi:10.1016/j.jksuci.2022.02.025

[83] Kumar, D.A., Sastry, A.S.C.S., Kishore, P.V.V., Kumar, E.K. (2022). 3D sign language recognition using spatio temporal graph kernels. *Journal of King Saud University - Computer and Information Sciences.* 34(2), 143–152. doi:10.1016/j.jksuci.2018.11.008

[84] Lun, R., Zhao, W. (2015). A survey of applications and human motion recognition with Microsoft kinect. 29(2015). doi:10.1142/S0218001415550083

[85] Ceolini, E., Frenkel, C., Shrestha, S.B., et al. (2020). Hand-gesture recognition based on emg and event-based camera sensor fusion: A benchmark in neuromorphic computing. *Frontiers in Neuroscience.* 14(August), 1–15. doi:10.3389/fnins.2020.00637

[86] Nemati, H., Fan, Y., Alonso-fernandez, F. (2016). Hand detection and gesture recognition using symmetric patterns. *Studies in Computational Intelligence.* 642, 365–375.

[87] Zhang, Q., Feng, L., Liang, H., Yang, Y. (2022). Hybrid domain attention network for efficient super-resolution. *Symmetry.* 14(4). doi:10.3390/sym14040697

[88] Barsoum, E. (2019). Human motion anticipation and recognition from RGB-D. *Columbia University.* 11(2), 251–275.

[89] Wen, R., Tay, W.L., Nguyen, B.P., Chng, C.B., Chui, C.K. (2014). Hand gesture guided robot-assisted surgery based on a direct augmented reality interface. *Computer Methods and Programs in Biomedicine.* 116(2), 68–80. doi:10.1016/j.cmpb.2013.12.018

[90] Nguyen, B.P., Tay, W.L., Chui, C.K. (2015). Robust biometric recognition from palm depth images for gloved hands. *IEEE Transactions on Human-Machine Systems.* 45(6), 799–804. doi:10.1109/THMS.2015.2453203

[91] Chang, C.C., Lin, C.J. (2011). LIBSVM: A library for support vector machines. *ACM Transactions on Intelligent Systems and Technology.* 2(3). doi:10.1145/1961189.1961199

[92] Jin, Z., Shang, J., Zhu, Q., Ling, C., Xie, W., Qiang, B. (2020). RFRSF: Employee turnover prediction based on random forests and survival analysis. *Lecture Notes in Computer*

Science (Including Subseries Lecture Notes in Artificial Intelligence and Lecture Notes in Bioinformatics). 12343 LNCS, 503–515. doi:10.1007/978-3-030-62008-0_35

[93] Saqlain Shah, S.M., Abbas Naqvi, H., Khan, J.I., Ramzan, M., Zulqarnain, Khan, H.U. (2018). Shape based Pakistan sign language categorization using statistical features and support vector machines. *IEEE Access.* 6, 59242–59252. doi:10.1109/ACCESS.2018.2872670

[94] Mahmood, A., Khan, S.A., Hussain, S., Almaghayreh, E.M. (2019). An adaptive image contrast enhancement technique for low-contrast images. *IEEE Access.* 7, 161584–161593. doi:10.1109/ACCESS.2019.2951468

[95] Al Delail, B., Bhaskar, H., Zemerly, M.J., Werghi, N. (2018). Balancing incident and Ambient light for illumination compensation in video applications. In: Proceedings - International Conference on Image Processing, ICIP. IEEE; 2018:1762–1766. doi:10.11 09/ICIP.2018.8451378

[96] You, S., Lei, B., Wang, S., et al. (2022). Fine perceptive GANS for Brain MR image super-resolution in wavelet domain. *IEEE Transactions on Neural Networks and Learning Systems. Published Online.* 2022, 1–13. doi:10.1109/TNNLS.2022.3153088

[97] Gozzi, N., Malandri, L., Mercorio, F., Pedrocchi, A. (2022). XAI for myo-controlled prosthesis: Explaining EMG data for hand gesture classification. *Knowledge-Based Systems.* 240, 108053. doi:10.1016/j.knosys.2021.108053

[98] Adib, F., Kabelac, Z., Katabi, D., Nsdi, I. (2015). WiTrack2.0 multi-person localization via RF body reflections. In: Proceedings of the 12th USENIX Symposium on Networked Systems Design and Implementation (NSDI '15). Published online 2015. https://www.usenix.org/conference/nsdi15/technical-sessions/presentation/adib

[99] Ben Gamra, M., Akhloufi, M.A. (2021). A review of deep learning techniques for 2D and 3D human pose estimation. *Image and Vision Computing.* 114. doi:10.1016/j.imavis.2021.104282

[100] Cheng, H., Hei, X., Wu, D. (2018). An experimental study of harvesting channel state information of WiFi signals. In: 2018 IEEE International Conference on Consumer Electronics-Taiwan; 1–2.

[101] Yang, C., Wang, L., Wang, X., Mao, S. (2022). Environment adaptive RFID based 3D human pose tracking with a Meta-learning approach. *IEEE Journal of Radio Frequency Identification.* 7281(c), 1–13. doi:10.1109/JRFID.2022.3140256

[102] Wang, Y., Guo, L., Lu, Z., Wen, X., Zhou, S., Meng, W. (2021). From point to space: 3D moving human pose estimation using commodity WiFi. *IEEE Communications Letters.* 25(7), 2235–2239. doi:10.1109/LCOMM.2021.3073271

[103] Guo, L., Wang, L., Liu, J., et al. (2017). A novel benchmark on human activity recognition using WiFi signals. In: 2017 IEEE 19th International Conference on e-Health Networking, Applications and Services, Healthcom 2017. 2017-Decem; 1–6. doi:10.1109/HealthCom.2017.8210783

[104] Han, C., Wu, K., Wang, Y., Ni, L.M. (2014). WiFall: Device-free fall detection by wireless networks. INFOCOM. *2014 Proceedings IEEE.* 16(2), 271–279. doi:10.1109/INFOCOM.2 014.6847948

[105] Badiola-Bengoa, A., Mendez-Zorrilla, A. (2021). A systematic review of the application of camera-based human pose estimation in the field of sport and physical exercise. *Sensors.* 21(18). doi:10.3390/s21185996

[106] Lin, K.C., Ko, C.W., Hung, H.C., Chen, N.S. (2021). The effect of real-time pose recognition on badminton learning performance. *Interactive Learning Environments.* 0(0), 1–15. doi:10.1080/10494820.2021.1981396

[107] Xu, D., Qi, X., Li, C., Sheng, Z., Huang, H. (2021). Wise information technology of med: Human pose recognition in elderly care. *Sensors.* 21(21), 1–20. doi:10.3390/s21217130

[108] Ding, W., Guo, X., Wang, G. (2021). Radar-based human activity recognition using hybrid neural network model with multidomain fusion. *IEEE Transactions on Aerospace and Electronic Systems.* 57(5), 2889–2898. doi:10.1109/TAES.2021.3068436

[109] Oguchi, K., Maruta, S., Hanawa, D. (2014). Human positioning estimation method using received signal strength indicator (RSSI) in a wireless sensor network. *Procedia Computer Science.* 34, 126–132. doi:10.1016/j.procs.2014.07.066

[110] Hao, Z., Duan, Y., Dang, X., Liu, Y., Zhang, D. (2020). Wi-sl: Contactless fine-grained gesture recognition uses channel state information. *Sensors (Switzerland).* 20(14), 1–26. doi:10.3390/s20144025

[111] Kato, S., Fukushima, T., Murakami, T., et al. (2021). CSI2Image: Image reconstruction from channel state information using generative adversarial networks. *IEEE Access.* 9, 47154–47168. doi:10.1109/ACCESS.2021.3066158

[112] Yan, J., Ma, C., Kang, B., Wu, X., Liu, H. (2021). Extreme learning machine and AdaBoost-based localization using CSI and RSSI. *IEEE Communications Letters.* 25(6), 1906–1910. doi:10.1109/LCOMM.2021.3058420

[113] Liu, J., Teng, G., Hong, F. (2020). Human activity sensing with wireless signals: A survey. *Sensors (Switzerland).* 20(4). doi:10.3390/s20041210

[114] Wu, D., Zhang, D., Xu, C., Wang, H., Li, X. (2017). Device-free WiFi human sensing: From pattern-based to model-based approaches. *IEEE Communications Magazine.* 55(10), 91–97. doi:10.1109/MCOM.2017.1700143

[115] Yousefi, S., Narui, H., Dayal, S., Ermon, S., Valaee, S. (2017). A survey of human activity recognition using WiFi CSI. arXiv preprint arXiv:170807129. Published online 2017, 1–8. http://arxiv.org/abs/1708.07129

[116] Guo, L., Wang, L., Liu, J., Zhou, W., Lu, B. (2018). HuAc: Human activity recognition using crowdsourced WiFi signals and skeleton data. *Hindawi Journal of Wireless Communications and Mobile Computing.* Published online 2018. doi:10.1155/2018/6163475

[117] Yang, C., Wang, X., Mao, S. (2021). RFID-Pose: Vision-aided three-dimensional human pose estimation with radio-frequency identification. *IEEE Transactions on Reliability.* 70(3), 1218–1231.

[118] Yang, C., Wang, L., Wang, X., Mao, S. (2022). Meta-Pose: Environment-adaptive human skeleton tracking with RFID. In: IEEE GLOBECOM; 2022:1–6. doi:10.1109/globecom46510.2021.9685315

[119] Liu, Z., Liu, X., Li, K. (2020). Deeper exercise monitoring for smart gym using fused RFID and CV data. In: Proceedings - IEEE INFOCOM; 2020 July:11–19. doi:10.1109/INFOCOM41043.2020.9155360

[120] Yang, C., Wang, X., Mao, S. (2021). RFID-based 3D human pose tracking: A subject generalization approach. *Digital Communications and Networks.* (September). doi:10.1016/j.dcan.2021.09.002

[121] Yang, C., Wang, X., Mao, S. (2020). Subject-adaptive skeleton tracking with RFID. In: Proceedings - 2020 16th International Conference on Mobility, Sensing and Networking, MSN 2020. Published online 2020; 599–606. doi:10.1109/MSN50589.2020.00098

[122] Jiang, W., Xue, H., Miao, C., et al. (2020). Towards 3D human pose construction using wifi. In: Proceedings of the Annual International Conference on Mobile Computing and Networking, MOBICOM. Published online 2020; 295–308. doi:10.1145/3372224.3380900

[123] Ma, F. (2021). Action recognition of dance video learning based on embedded system and computer vision image. *Microprocessors and Microsystems.* 81(December 2020), 103779. doi:10.1016/j.micpro.2020.103779

[124] Pan, T.Y., Chang, C.Y., Tsai, W.L., Hu, M.C. (2021). Multisensor-based 3D gesture recognition for a decision-making training system. *IEEE Sensors Journal.* 21(1), 706–716. doi:10.1109/JSEN.2020.3012887

[125] Rossol, N., Cheng, I., Basu, A. (2016). A multisensor technique for gesture recognition through intelligent skeletal pose analysis. *IEEE Transactions on Human-Machine Systems.* 46(3), 350–359. doi:10.1109/THMS.2015.2467212

[126] Kumar, P., Gauba, H., Roy, P.P., Dogra, D.P. (2017). Coupled HMM-based multi-sensor data fusion for sign language recognition. *Pattern Recognition Letters.* 86, 1–8. doi:10.101 6/j.patrec.2016.12.004

[127] Wang, S., Wang, A., Ran, M., et al. (2022). Hand gesture recognition framework using a lie group based spatio-temporal recurrent network with multiple hand-worn motion sensors. *Information Sciences.* 606, 722–741. doi:10.1016/j.ins.2022.05.085

[128] Aguileta, A.A., Brena, R.F., Mayora, O., Molino-Minero-re, E., Trejo, L.A. (2019). Multi-sensor fusion for activity recognition—A survey. *Sensors (Switzerland).* 19(17), 1–41. doi:10.3390/s19173808

[129] Jebali, M., Dakhli, A., Jemni, M. (2021). Vision-based continuous sign language recognition using multimodal sensor fusion. *Evolving Systems.* Published online 2021. doi:10.1007/s12530-020-09365-y

[130] D'Mello, S.K., Bosch, N., Chen, H. (2018). Multimodal-multisensor affect detection. In: The Handbook of Multimodal-Multisensor Interfaces: Foundations, User Modeling, and Common Modality Combinations - Volume 2; 2018:167–202. doi:10.1145/3107990.3107998

[131] Tan, M., Gochoo, S.C., Huang, Y.H., Liu, S.H., Liu, Y.F.H. (2018). Multi-resident activity recognition in a smart home using RGB activity image and DCNN. *IEEE Sensors Journal.* 18(23), 9718–9727.

[132] Pham, D., Yang, W.S. (2018). A sensor fusion approach to indoor human localization based on environmental and wearable sensors. *IEEE Transactions on Automation Science and Engineering.* 16(1), 339–350.

[133] Shrestha, F., Fioranelli, J., Le Kernec, H., Heidari, M., Pepa, E., Cippitelli, E., Gambi, S.S. (2017). Multisensor data fusion for human activities classification and fall detection. In: 2017 IEEE Sensors; 2017:1–3.

[134] Anacleto, L., Figueiredo, A., Almeida, P.N. (2014). Localization system for pedestrians based on sensor and information fusion. In: 17th International Conference on Information Fusion, IEEE; 2014:1–8.

[135] Zhou, J., Guo, S.W. (2015). Motion recognition by using a stacked autoencoder- based deep learning algorithm with smart phones. In: International Conference on Wireless Algorithms, Systems, and Applications, Springer. Vol 164; 2015:778–787.

[136] Chen, R., Jafari, N.K. (2017). A survey of depth and inertial sensor fusion for human action recognition. *Multimedia Tools and Applications.* 76(3), 4405–4425.

[137] Wu, E.D., Lemaire, N.B. (2011). Change-of-state determination to recognize mobility activities using a BlackBerry smartphone. In: 2011 Annual International Conference of the IEEE Engineering in Medicine and Biology Society, IEEE; 2011:5252–5255.

[138] Hwang, K.R., Ko, S.B.P. (2021). Motion data acquisition method for motion analysis in golf. *Concurrency and Computation: Practice and Experience.* 3(2), 5215.

[139] Sun, B.Y., Liu, P.C.C. (2020). Deep learning-based violin bowing action recognition. *Sensors.* 20(20), 5732.

[140] Chen, H., Hao, R., Jafari, N.K. (2017). Weighted fusion of depth and inertial data to improve view invariance for real-time human action recognition. In: Real-Time Image and Video Processing International Society for Optics and Photonics; 2017:764–782.

[141] Narayana, P., Beveridge, J.R., Draper, B.A. (2018). Gesture recognition: focus on the hands. In: Proceedings of the IEEE Computer Society Conference on Computer Vision and Pattern Recognition; 2018:5235–5244. doi:10.1109/CVPR.2018.00549

[142] Chen, Z., Wang, A. (2017). Hierarchical method for human concurrent activity recognition using miniature inertial sensors. *Sensor Review.* 37(1), 101–109.

[143] Raj, A., Subramanya, D., Fox, J.B. (2008). Rao-blackwellized particle fil- ters for recognizing activities and spatial context from wearable sensors. In: *Experimental Robotics*, Springer; 2008:211–221.

[144] Wang, D., Wu, R., Gravina, G., Fortino, Y., Jiang, K.T. (2017). Kernel fusion based extreme learning machine for cross-location activity recognition. *Information Fusion*. 37, 1–9.

[145] Sun, J., Ye, T., Wang, S., Huang, J.L. (2020). Behavioral feature recognition of multi-task compressed sensing with fusion relevance in the Internet of Things environment. *Computer and Communications*. 157, 381–393.

[146] Janidarmian, A., Roshan Fekr, K., Radecka, Z.Z. (2017). A comprehensive analysis on wearable acceleration sensors in human activity recognition. *Sensors*. 17, 529.

[147] Nweke, Y.W., Teh, U.R., Alo, G.M. (2018). Analysis of multi-sensor fusion for mobile and wearable sensor based human activity recognition. In: Proceedings of the International Conference on Data Processing and Applications; 2018:22–26.

[148] Guo, L., Guo, S., Wang, L., et al. (2019). Wiar: A public data set for wifi-based activity recognition. *IEEE Access*. 7, 154935–154945. doi:10.1109/ACCESS.2019.2947024

[149] Escalera, S., Athitsos, V., Guyon, I. (2017). Challenges in multi-modal gesture recognition. *Journal of Machine Learning Research*. 17(2017), 1–60. doi:10.1007/978-3-319-57021-1_1

[150] Sarma, D., Bhuyan, M.K. (2021). *Methods, Databases and Recent Advancement of Vision-Based Hand Gesture Recognition for HCI Systems: A Review*. Vol 2. Springer Singapore; 2021. doi:10.1007/s42979-021-00827-x

[151] Ruffieux, S. , Lalanne, D. (2014). A survey of datasets for human gesture recognition. In: 2014. doi:10.1007/978-3-319-07230-2

[152] Ur Rehman, M., Ahmed, F., Khan, M.A., et al. (2022). Dynamic hand gesture recognition using 3D-CNN and LSTM networks. *Computers, Materials and Continua*. 70(3), 4675–4690. doi:10.32604/cmc.2022.019586

[153] Mantecón, T., del-Blanco, C.R., Jaureguizar, F., García, N. (2016). Hand gesture recognition using infrared imagery provided by leap motion controller. *Lecture Notes in Computer Science* (including subseries Lecture Notes in Artificial Intelligence and Lecture Notes in Bioinformatics). 10016 LNCS, 47-57. doi:10.1007/978-3-319-48680-2_5

[154] Zhang, Y., Cao, C., Cheng, J., Lu, H. (2018). EgoGesture: A new dataset and benchmark for egocentric hand gesture recognition. *IEEE Transactions on Multimedia*. 20(5), 1038–1050. doi:10.1109/TMM.2018.2808769

[155] Kaczmarek, P., Mánkowski, T., Tomczyński, J. (2019). PutEMG—A surface electromyography hand gesture recognition data set. *Sensors (Switzerland)*. 19(16). doi:10.3390/s19163548

Human Action Recognition Using ConvLSTM with Adversarial Noise and Compressive-Sensing-Based Dimensionality Reduction, Concise and Informative

Mohsin Raza Siyal[1], Mansoor Ebrahim[1], Syed Hasan Adil[1], Kamran Raza[1], and Nadeem Qazi[2]

[1]Faculty of Engineering, Sciences and Technology, Iqra University, Karachi, Pakistan
[2]School of Architecture, Computing and Engineering, University of East London, London, UK

9.1 INTRODUCTION

In recent years, compressive sensing has intrigued many researchers from computer vision, digital signal, and information theory communities. The motive of interest is because of many applications, such as data compression, medical imaging, storage, digital image processing, transmission, and more. Compressive sensing offers recovery of sparse signals with a smaller number of measurements required by Shannon sampling [1]. Tactically, CS has also been used for data compression in digital image processing.

This chapter is using the CS dimensionality reduction approach in the human action recognition problem. Human action recognition is an emerging field in computer vision because of the diverse applications, such as automated security surveillance, robotics, video information retrieval, and medical diagnoses. There are many approaches available for human action recognition and mostly the goal is to extract rich information features to achieve high accuracy. Usually, extracted features are characterized as very high dimensional vectors that cause low performance and high computational complexity issues; hence, not practical for real-time applications. It is because high-dimensional

DOI: 10.1201/9781032646268-9

features tend to be unable to uncover the inherent properties of data. Hence, to reduce dimensionality and computational complexity by extracting the intrinsic properties of data, dimensionality reduction methods are used in human action recognition. There are so many dimensionality reduction methods out there, including multidimensional scaling (MDS), isometric feature map (ISOMAP), local linear embedding (LLE), and the most popular one, principal component analysis (PCA) [2,3].

MDS is a linear dimensionality reduction method to locate a composition of points in a low dimensional space whose inter-point distances correspond to similarities or dissimilarities in higher dimensions [4]. MDS is equivalent to PCA under Euclidian distance. ISOMAP is a nonlinear dimensionality reduction method; instead of measuring Euclidean distance between points, it uses graph distance to estimate the geodesical distance. It preserves the global data structure; however, the computational complexity is high and very sensitive to noise. Similarly, LLE is also a nonlinear method that uses global optimization to approximate data by a group of linear patches. It connects these patches on a low-dimensional subspace by keeping local geometry properties and nearby relationships between patches preserved. PCA is the most used linear dimensionality reduction method that depicts the high-dimensional data to low-dimensional while preserving the maximal variance. However, these conventional methods are limited to generalization because they need to tune their parameters by learning through a training set. In this process, it is highly likely to degrade recognition accuracy because a large amount of information might be lost [5].

In this chapter, we propose a new approach to solve the human action recognition problem with the use of compressive sensing to reduce the dimensionality of data and Adversarial ConvLSTM to learn the sequential data [6]. To satisfy the restricted isometry property (RIP), compressive sensing with Gaussian random matrix mixture (CS-GRM<) uses the firefly optimized Gaussian distribution to construct the measuring matrix [7]. Additionally, CS-GRMM does not require a training process as it uses single matrix multiplication to map high-dimensional vector space into lower. For feature extraction and classification, we propose a novel approach with a fusion of convolutional neural networks, long short-term memory, and adversarial loss function to achieve better efficiency and accuracy. A convolutional neural network (ConvNet/CNN) is a deep learning algorithm that takes input images in the first layer or zero layers by assigning variable weights biases to calculate the difference between each input and send them through pooling and convolutional layers to a final fully connected layer, which will then distribute the output in probabilities [5,8]. ConvNet uses much less pre-processing than the conventional methods of classification [9]. It does not need to create the filters manually as it is in the case of primitive algorithms. LSTM is a type of recurrent network that uses feedback to learn about the previous output of the layers. It is used to learn sequential data like videos, where each frame has something to do with the previous. Here, the proposed model uses the combined effect of CNN and LSTM to achieve better classification with the ability to learn an entire sequence of data [10]. To improve the accuracy of training and to overcome issues like inter-class and multi-viewpoint, an adversarial loss function is proposed that generates the noise and feedback to learn [11–13]. This chapter also compares the PCA, LLE, and MDS approaches with the proposed model and other classification methods like convLSTM and classic SVM. A support vector machine (SVM) is the classification algorithm in which data points would plot in n-dimensional space where n is the number of features extracted from data [14].

The rest of the chapter is organized as follows: Section 9.2 explains the background theory regarding the CS and Adversarial ConvLSTM, respectively. In Section 9.3, the proposed model for action recognition is briefly explained. In Section 9.4, experimental results on benchmark action data sets are provided. Section 9.5 concludes the chapter.

9.2 BACKGROUND

Compressive sensing is the alternative approach to the Shannon-Nyquist sampling theorem. CS theory has two major principles: sparsity and incoherence. Let us assume that $\(x\)$ is the discrete signal in the measurement matrix RN with a matrix (NxN) and vector (y) in $(RM, M < < N)$ that contains the measurement of x that forms

$$y = \emptyset x \tag{9.1}$$

where measurement matrix (Φ) is equivalent to $(RMxN)$. x can be reconstructed from (y) with good probability, if satisfies the restricted isometry property (RIP) by having a constant $(\delta \varepsilon(0,1))$ takes all k-sparse vector in RN.

$$(1 - \delta)\|x\|_2^2 \leq \emptyset \|x\|_2^2 \leq (1 + \delta)\|x\|_2^2 \tag{9.2}$$

Generally, to evaluate the performance of matrix, it uses the coherence of matrix instead of (N/K) combination to avoid computational complexity.

$$\mu(\emptyset) = max_{1 \leq i \leq j \leq N} \frac{|(\emptyset_i, \emptyset_j))|}{\|\emptyset_i\|_2 \|\emptyset_j\|_2} \tag{9.3}$$

where (ϕ_i), (ϕ_j) are the inner products of (ϕ) into two columns.

Firefly is a meta-heuristic optimization technique inspired by flashing patterns and night fireflies [7]. The algorithm is based on three simple nature rules:

1. Every firefly shall be attracted to each other since they all are unisex.

2. All fireflies move randomly unless there is a firefly brighter than others. Attraction is directly proportional to brightness.

3. The brightness is determined by the landscape of the encoded objective function.

The brightness intensity $(I(r))$ varies from following the inverse square law:

$$I(r) = \frac{I_0}{r^2} \tag{9.4}$$

The movement of fireflies is based on the attractiveness principle. Following is the equation to determine the movement of a firefly

$$x_{ik} = x_{ik} + \beta_{o}^{e^{-\gamma \cdot r_{ij}^2}} \cdot (x_{ik} - x_{jk}) + \alpha S_k \left(rand_{ik} - \frac{1}{2} \right) \tag{9.5}$$

where firefly j is more attracted to firefly I, k is range of dimension of problem. (α) is the scaling parameter, $(rand_{ik})$ is the 0–1 random number, and (S_k) is also an scaling parameter.

A convolutional neural network is the type of deep neural network. The basic structure of ConvNet is based on multiple layers such as input, convolutional, pooling, and fully connected layer. Unlike conventional method, ConvNet requires fewer pre-processing stages. Generally, convolution could be discrete or continuous and can be written mathematically as:

Continuous convolution

$$y(t) = \int_{-\infty}^{\infty} f(p)g(t - \tau)d\tau = f(t) \times g(t) \tag{9.6}$$

where $(y(t))$, (t) and (τ) are variables, while $(f(t))$ and $(g(t))$ are continuous functions.

Discrete convolution

$$y(n) = \sum_{i=\infty}^{\infty} f(i)g(n - i) = f(n) \times g(n) \tag{9.7}$$

where $(y(n))$ is the output, (n) and (i) are the variables, and $(f(n))$ and $(g(n))$ are discrete functions. The convolutional layer contains the kernel or filters that result in an activation function for feature extraction. The output of the feature map is passed through the pooling layer, which down-samples the feature maps in patches. In a fully connected layer, each node is connected to the back and front layers. Finally, the output layer acts as the classifier, where all the results are distributed among nodes through softmax.

9.3 PROPOSED MODEL

The idea is constructed from the Gaussian mixture model, which is the probabilistic model that represents the part of the overall population in a normally distributed way. It says a Gaussian distribution generates all the data points and it does not require knowing which part that data point belongs. We design a novel measurement matrix with a Gaussian random matrix (GRM).

It is very important for a measuring matrix to satisfy RIP. Given the Gaussian mixture distribution:

$$p \left(\varnothing_{ij} = sum_{l=1}^{k} w_l N \left(\varnothing_{ij} 0, \frac{1}{KMw_l} \right) \right) \tag{9.8}$$

where w_l is the weight of the Gaussian distribution at l^{th} and it ranges from 0 to 1. Also, it has 1 and 0 for variance and mean, respectively. It can be noted that $y = \phi_{GM} x$ represents dimensionality reduction, which is loss. Subsequently, if it meets the RIP conditions, compressed low-dimensional space can hold the high-dimensional space.

Satisfying RIP:

$$
\begin{aligned}
E\left((\phi i.\ x^2)\right) &= E\left(\left(\sum_{j=1}^{N} \phi_{ij} x_j\right)^2\right) \\
&= E\left(\sum_{j=1}^{N} \left(\phi_{ij}\right)^2 + \sum_{u=1}^{N}\sum_{v=1}^{N} 2x_u x_v \phi_{iu} \phi_{iv}\right) \\
&= \sum_{j=1}^{N} x_j^2 E\left(\phi_{ij}^2\right) + \sum_{u=1}^{N}\sum_{v=1}^{N} 2x_u x_v E(\phi_{iu}) E(\phi_{iv}) \\
&= \sum_{j=1}^{N} x_j^2 \left(\sum_{l=1}^{k} \frac{w_1}{kMw_1}\right) \\
&= \frac{1}{M}\sum_{j=1}^{N} x_j^2 = \left(\frac{\|x\|_2^2}{M}\right)
\end{aligned}
$$

Finally,

$$
E\left(\|\varnothing_{GM} x\|_2^2\right) = \sum_{i=1}^{M} E\left((\varnothing i.\ x^2)\right) = M \times \left(\frac{\|x\|_2^2}{M}\right) = \|x\|_2^2 \tag{9.9}
$$

where $(\|\varnothing_{GM} x\|_2^2)$ is the random variable and $(\phi_i.\ x)$ is a random Gaussian mixture k-component. Additionally, ϕ_{GM} is the weight that is optimized by the firefly algorithm.

The proposed method consists of six components: (1) data layer, (2) compressive sensing, (3) feature learning, (4) sequential learning, (5) Softmax (probabilities), and (6) output (Figure 9.1).

9.3.1 Data Layer

In the data layer, the classic KTH and UCF-101 data set is used as the input to compressive sensing for dimension reduction [15,16]. The UCF101 data set has almost 13,000 videos compiled from 101 classes including playing yo-yo, dancing, putting on makeup, archery, and more.

The KTH data set is performed by 25 individuals and it has 600 25fps videos with 6 human action classes, such as running, walking, jogging, hand waving, and clapping (Figure 9.2).

For KTH, there are 600 videos with 25 fps with a total duration of 3 hours and 9 minutes that give 11,340 seconds of total length (Table 9.1). In order to get total processing frames (tpf), multiply the length of the total video in seconds (tvls) with fps:

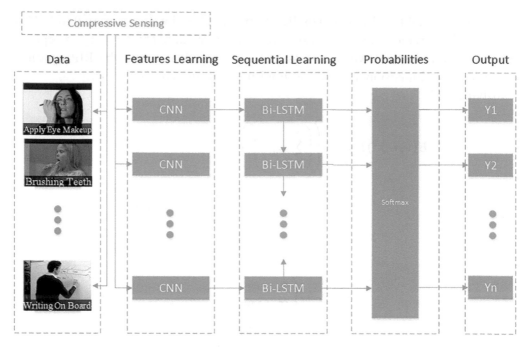

FIGURE 9.1   Proposed model: Adversarial ConvLSTM with CS.

$$\text{Total Processing frames} = tvls \times fps$$
$$\text{Total Processing frames} = 11340 \times 25$$
$$\text{Total Processing frames} = 283500$$

where the total pixels are calculated with the KTH spatial resolution of 160×120 pixels each frame:

$$\text{Total pixels} = pixelsperframe \times totalprocessingframes$$
$$\text{Total pixels} = 19200 \times 283500$$
$$\text{Total pixels} = 5.44 \text{ billions}$$

For UCF101, there are 13,320 videos with 25 fps and a total duration of 1,600 minutes which gives 96,000 seconds. To get total processing frames (tpf), multiply the multiply total videos length in seconds (tvls) with fps:

$$\text{Total Processing frames} = tvls \times fps$$
$$\text{Total Processing frames} = 96000 \times 25$$
$$\text{Total Processing frames} = 2400000$$

where the total pixels are calculated with the UCF101 spatial resolution of 320×240 pixels each frame.

FIGURE 9.2   Example frames for two data sets: (a) UCF101 and (b) KTH.

TABLE 9.1   Statistics of Data Sets: KTH and UCF101

	KTH	UCF-101
Number of videos	600	13,320
Frame per second	25	25
Total video length (min)	189	1,600
Mean clip length (Sec)	19	7
Min clip length (Sec)	08	01
Max clip length (Sec)	59	71
Total frames to process	283,500	2,400,000
Total Pixels	5.44b	184.32b

$$\text{Total pixels} = pixelsperframe \times totalprocessingframes$$
$$\text{Total pixels} = 76800 \times 2400000$$
$$\text{Total pixels} = 184.32 \text{ billions}$$

While looking at the statistics, they explain the need for a compression algorithm before processing the huge data. It has been very effective to reduce the dimensionality before training the model in the past as well. However, it has always been a challenge to extract the feature information from the compressed data. Here, the compression method plays a vital role, not just to reduce the dimension but in such a way the highly concerned features are not affected by it.

9.3.2 Compressive Sensing

The proposed method uses compressive sensing with a Gaussian random matrix (CS-GRM) along with the firefly optimized Gaussian distribution to construct the measuring matrix. A single matrix multiplication is used to map high-dimensional vector space into lower, which does not require a training process.

Compressive sensing is further divided into three parts: (1) high-dimensional data, (2) measurement matrix, and (3) low-dimensional data. In high-dimensional data, feature extraction from raw video data is performed and converted into low-dimension data using single matrix multiplication (Figure 9.3).

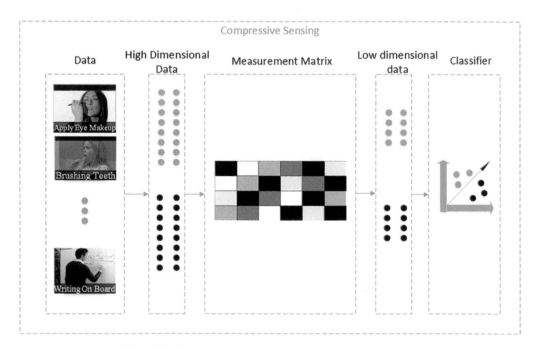

FIGURE 9.3 Proposed model: Compressive sensing section.

9.3.3 Feature Learning

Feature learning or feature extraction is performed in the first layer of the convolution. It is between the convolution activation function and the last pooling layer. Convolution maintains the relationship between image data and pixels using a kernel as a matrix.

9.3.4 Sequential Learning

The proposed method uses adversarial ConvLSTM to solve this time series classification problem. Output from the last pooling layer of feature learning is flattened into a single row, which then becomes an input for a linear network. This method uses a batch normalization method before the non-linear function, which can speed up the training process. For learning nonlinear elements, the method uses ReLU as activation functions [17]. Also, the method uses the adversarial loss function (GANs) in place of the usual cross-entropy.

9.3.5 Softmax

Softmax or logistic function is the type of activation function with an output range from 0 to 1. It is used for categorizing the output into probabilities.

9.3.6 Output Layer

The output layer is the final layer of the classification in which the result is categorically distributed. The number of stages is equal to the number of classes.

9.4 RESULTS AND DISCUSSION

This research uses the two data sets, KTH and UFC-101, to evaluate the proposed method. To demonstrate the efficiency and effectiveness of the proposed method, we use PCA, singular value decomposition (SVD), locally linear embedding (LLE), and multi-dimensional scaling (MDS) as dimension reduction methods to compare with the proposed compressive sensing method.

The KTH data set is more challenging than UFC-101 because it is performed by 25 individuals who give us various viewpoints, scales, and locations. It consists of 600 videos with basic activities like walking, running, jogging, boxing, waving, and clapping. However, UFC-101 consists of 101 classes gathered from social media websites, which give a large variety of activities to classify (Figure 9.4).

9.4.1 SVM Classifier

The first experiment is performed with classic SVM along with different dimension reduction methods. It can be noticed that SVM as a classifier and compressive sensing as dimensionality reduction perform much better than the other methods in Kth data sets (Figure 9.5); however, for UCF-101, SVD tops the other methods due to a large number of frames with a variation in colors (Figure 9.6 and Table 9.2).

It can be noticed from Figure 9.6 that under the small dimensions proposed, the CS method is performing more stably than the other methods.

FIGURE 9.4   Classification results.

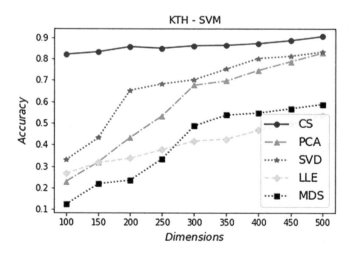

FIGURE 9.5   Comparison of SVM method with all dimension reduction methods and Kth data set.

It can also be observed that the CS method does not fall under the lower range of dimensions, where other methods fall drastically. The reason for this is the lower coherence of the measurement matrix tends to improve classification speed and recognition strength.

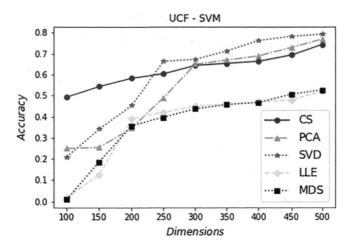

FIGURE 9.6   Comparison of SVM method with all dimension reduction methods and UCF data set.

TABLE 9.2   SVM Results Comparison with Different Dimension Reduction Methods

DR methods	KTH (accuracy)	UCF-101
PCA	82.6	77.0
SVD	83.2	79.2
LLE	53.7	51.9
MDS	58.8	52.6
CS	90.5	85.3

9.4.2 ConvLSTM Classifier

Similarly, the experiment is performed with the convLSTM classification method that uses the fusion of convolution and LSTM for sequential learning. It sends the part of the output to the first pooling layer and keeps using the feedback to learn subsequent frames in order. The problem with SVM is resolved with the use of ConvLSTM and it can be observed that the CS method performs must better than PCA and other methods with both data sets (Table 9.3). It can also be seen that with both data sets the CS method has more stability with a low range of dimensions (Figure 9.7, Figure 9.8).

TABLE 9.3   ConvLSTM Results Comparison with Different Dimension Reduction Methods

DR methods	KTH (accuracy)	UCF-101
PCA	82.6	77.0
SVD	83.2	79.2
LLE	53.7	51.9
MDS	58.8	52.6
CS	90.5	85.3

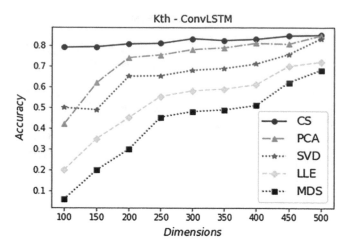

FIGURE 9.7   Comparison of ConvLSTM method with all dimension reduction methods and KTH data set.

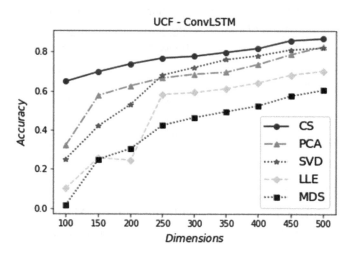

FIGURE 9.8   Comparison of ConvLSTM method with all dimension reduction methods and UCF data set.

9.4.3 ConvLSTM with GANs

The proposed method uses the adversarial loss function instead of classic methods. The use adversarial loss function, which creates different noises to accommodate results to learn random variations in the data, solves the problem of variation in viewpoint and scale. It can be observed that the proposed method with adversarial ConvLSTM with CS outperformed all the other methods (Table 9.4).

It can also be seen that even with 100 dimensions, CS has 79.2% accuracy and the other methods have less than 50%, which indicates that even with smaller dimensions, this method keeps the accuracy stable and reasonable (Figure 9.9, Figure 9.10).

TABLE 9.4 ConvLSTM with GANs Comparison with Different Dimension Reduction Methods

DR methods	KTH (accuracy)	UCF-101
PCA	82.6	77.0
SVD	83.2	79.2
LLE	53.7	51.9
MDS	58.8	52.6
CS	90.5	85.3

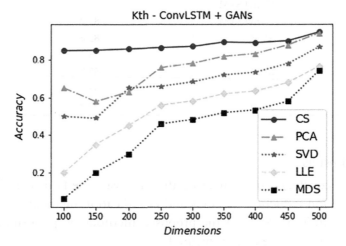

FIGURE 9.9 Comparison of ConvLSTM-GANs method with all dimension reduction methods using KTH data set.

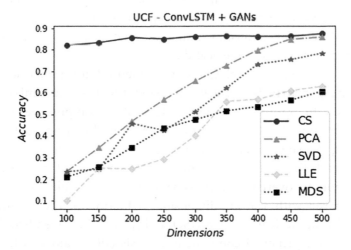

FIGURE 9.10 Comparison of ConvLSTM-GANs method with all dimension reduction methods using UCF data set.

TABLE 9.5   All Results Compared with Different Dimension Reduction Methods

DR methods	Classifier	KTH (accuracy)	UCF-101
PCA	ConvLSTM – GANs	94.3	85.8
SVD	ConvLSTM – GANs	86.8	78.2
LLE	ConvLSTM – GANs	76.6	62.9
MDS	ConvLSTM – GANs	74.2	60.5
CS	ConvLSTM – GANs	94.8	86.3
PCA	ConvLSTM	84.9	82.6
SVD	ConvLSTM	83.4	82.1
LLE	ConvLSTM	72.1	70.2
MDS	ConvLSTM	68.2	60.5
CS	ConvLSTM	87.2	86.8
PCA	SVM	82.6	77.0
SVD	SVM	83.2	79.2
LLE	SVM	53.7	51.9
MDS	SVM	58.8	52.6
CS	SVM	90.5	85.3

9.4.4 Overall Results

This experiment concluded by comparing the proposed method with different combinations of dimension reduction methods and classification methods.

It can be seen in Table 9.5 that the proposed methods outperformed other classification and dimensionality reduction methods.

9.5 CONCLUSIONS

Human action recognition is a fascinating field and many researchers from computer vision and machine learning communities are working on this progressively. The idea is because of its distinct applications, including automated security surveillance, robotics, video information retrieval, and medical diagnoses.

This chapter proposed a novel CS-GRMM method for dimension reduction, in which a measuring matrix is constructed using the Gaussian mixture. The firefly algorithm is used to optimize the parameters of a compressive-sensing Gaussian random matrix mixture. CS-GRMM results in the low-dimension data providing high dimensions using the single matrix multiplication, which does not require additional training. Along with that, adversarial ConvLSTM is proposed, which uses the adversarial loss function to overcome various viewpoint and scale issues. The proposed method is compared with various dimension reduction methods, multidimensional scaling (MDS), isometric feature map (ISOMAP), local linear embedding (LLE), and the most popular one principal component analysis (PCA) along with two classifiers, SVM and convLSTM. The results indicate the CS-GRMM with adversarial ConvLSTM outperformed all the other methods.

SUPPLEMENTARY MATERIALS

This chapter uses the two data sets, KTH and UCF-101, to evaluate the proposed method.

ACKNOWLEDGMENTS

This section is optional and may recognize those individuals who provided help during the research and preparation of the manuscript. The author would like to acknowledge the technical and administrative support of Iqra University, Pakistan and University of East London, UK.

The author(s) declare(s) that there is no conflict of interest regarding the publication of this chapter.

REFERENCES

1. J. B. Tenenbaum, V. De Silva, and J. C. Langford, "A global geometric framework for nonlinear dimensionality reduction," *Science*, vol. 290, no. 5500, pp. 2319–2323, 2000, doi: 10.1126/science.290.5500.2319.
2. I. K. Fodor, "A survey of dimension reduction techniques," *Library*, vol. 18, no. 1, pp. 1–18, 2002, doi: 10.2172/15002155.
3. J. Ye, H. Hu, G. J. Qi, and K. A. Hua, "A temporal order modeling approach to human action recognition from multimodal sensor data," *ACM Trans. Multimed. Comput. Commun. Appl.*, vol. 1, no. 1, pp. 1–22, 2016, doi: 10.1145/3038917.
4. M. C. Hout, M. H. Papesh, and S. D. Goldinger, "Multidimensional scaling," *Wiley Interdiscip. Rev. Cogn. Sci.*, vol. 4, no. 1, pp. 93–103, 2013, doi: 10.1002/wcs.1203.
5. A. Krizhevsky, I. Sutskever, and G. E. Hinton, "Imagenet classification with deep convolutional neural networks. In advances in neural information," *Adv. Neural Inf. Process. Syst.*, vol. 60, no. 6, pp. 1097–1105, 2012.
6. J. Yamato, J. Ohya, and K. Ishii, "Recognizing human action in time-sequential images using hidden Markov model," *Comput. Vis. Pattern Recognit.*, pp. 379–385, 1992, doi: 10.1109/CVPR.1992.223161.
7. X. S. Yang, "Firefly algorithms for multimodal optimization," *Lect. Notes Comput. Sci. (including Subser. Lect. Notes Artif. Intell. Lect. Notes Bioinformatics)*, vol. 5792 LNCS, pp. 169–178, 2009, doi: 10.1007/978-3-642-04944-6_14.
8. R. Gupta, A. Y. S. Chia, and D. Rajan, "Human activities recognition using depth images," *Proc. 21st ACM Int. Conf. Multimed.*, pp. 283–292, 2013, doi: 10.1145/2502081.2502099.
9. L. Palafox and H. Hashimoto, "Human action recognition using wavelet signal analysis as an input in 4W1H," *2010 8th IEEE Int. Conf. Ind. Informatics*, pp. 679–684, 2010, doi: 10.1109/INDIN.2010.5549660.
10. K. He, X. Zhang, S. Ren, and J. Sun, "Deep residual learning for image recognition," *Proc. IEEE Comput. Soc. Conf. Comput. Vis. Pattern Recognit.*, vol. 2016-December, pp. 770–778, 2016, doi: 10.1109/CVPR.2016.90.
11. M. Ramanathan, W. Y. Yau, and E. K. Teoh, "Human action recognition with video data: Research and evaluation challenges," *IEEE Trans. Human-Machine Syst.*, vol. 44, no. 5, pp. 650–663, 2014, doi: 10.1109/THMS.2014.2325871.
12. K. P. Chou et al., "Robust feature-based automated multi-view human action recognition system," *IEEE Access*, vol. 3536, no. c, pp. 1–1, 2018, doi: 10.1109/ACCESS.2018.2809552.

13. D. Anguita, A. Ghio, L. Oneto, X. Parra, and J. L. Reyes-Ortiz, "Human activity recognition on smartphones using a multiclass hardware-friendly support vector machine," *Lect. Notes Comput. Sci. (including Subser. Lect. Notes Artif. Intell. Lect. Notes Bioinformatics)*, vol. 7657 LNCS, pp. 216–223, 2012, doi: 10.1007/978-3-642-35395-6_30.

14. D. Anguita, A. Ghio, L. Oneto, X. Parra, and J. L. Reyes-Ortiz, "A public domain dataset for human activity recognition using smartphones," *Eur. Symp. Artif. Neural Networks, Comput. Intell. Mach. Learn.*, no. April, pp. 24–26, 2013. ISBN 978-2-87419-081-0.

15. S. Ji, M. Yang, and K. Yu, "3D convolutional neural networks for human action recognition," *PAMI*, vol. 35, no. 1, pp. 221–231, 2013, doi: 10.1109/TPAMI.2012.59.

16. K. Soomro, A. R. Zamir, and M. Shah, "UCF101: A dataset of 101 human actions classes from videos in the wild," *CoRR*, no. November, 2012. http://arxiv.org/abs/1212.0402

17. A. F. Agarap, "Deep learning using rectified linear units (ReLU)," no. 1, pp. 2–8, 2018. arXiv preprint arXiv:1803.08375.

## CHAPTER 10

Application of Machine Learning to Urban Ecology

Mir Muhammad Nizamani[1], Ghulam Muhae-Ud-Din[1],
Qian Zhang[1], Muhammad Awais[2], Muhammad Qayyum[3],
Muhammad Farhan[1], Muhammad Jabran[4], and Yong Wang[1]

[1]*Department of Plant Pathology, Agricultural College, Guizhou University, Guiyang, China*
[2]*Institute of Plant Sciences, University of Sindh, Jamshoro, Pakistan*
[3]*School of Economics and Statistics, Guangzhou University, Guangzhou, China*
[4]*State Key Laboratory for Biology of Plant Diseases, Institute of Plant Protection, Beijing, China*

10.1 INTRODUCTION

10.1.1 Brief Background of Urban Ecology

Urban ecology is an interdisciplinary field of study that focuses on the complex interactions between living organisms, their environments, and the built environment within
urban ecosystems (McIntyre et al., 2008). As cities continue to grow and expand, understanding the dynamics of urban ecosystems has become increasingly important for
promoting sustainable development and enhancing the quality of life for urban residents.
Urban ecology combines principles from ecology, landscape ecology, environmental
science, geography, and urban planning to examine the ecological, social, and economic
aspects of urban environments (Wu, 2014).

In recent years, the rapid urbanization and increasing complexity of urban ecosystems
have necessitated innovative approaches to better comprehend, manage, and design
sustainable urban environments (Bai et al., 2016). The study of urban ecology encompasses various aspects, such as the distribution and function of green spaces, the
provision of ecosystem services, biodiversity conservation, urban heat island effects, air
and water quality, and the relationships between human populations and urban ecosystems (Leal Filho et al., 2020; Cheng et al., 2020). Urban ecology seeks to identify and
address the challenges that arise from the unique characteristics of urban environments,
including the high density of human populations, the prevalence of impervious surfaces,
altered hydrological cycles, and the presence of diverse and often competing land uses
(Bolund & Hunhammar, 1999; Cerreta et al., 2020). By integrating knowledge from

DOI: 10.1201/9781032646268-10

various disciplines, urban ecology aims to develop holistic solutions that balance the needs of human societies with the conservation and enhancement of urban ecosystems (Maes et al., 2019).

A key aspect of urban ecology is the concept of socio-ecological systems, which recognizes that human populations and ecosystems are interconnected and interdependent (Heymans et al., 2019; Caniglia et al., 2021). Socio-ecological systems research in urban environments seeks to understand how human behavior, social structures, and institutions influence and are influenced by urban ecosystems. This chapter also explores the distribution and accessibility of urban green spaces and ecosystem services, addressing issues of environmental justice and equity. Machine learning has emerged as a promising tool for advancing urban ecology research and practice, as it can analyze and model complex relationships between biotic, abiotic, and anthropogenic factors within urban socio-ecological systems (Blanco et al., 2021). The integration of machine learning techniques in urban ecology can contribute to the development of more sustainable, resilient, and biodiverse urban environments by informing effective urban planning, design, and management strategies.

Overall, urban ecology is a vital field of study that helps us understand the complex dynamics of urban ecosystems and develop strategies to create sustainable and livable cities. By combining interdisciplinary knowledge and harnessing the power of innovative tools like machine learning, urban ecology researchers and practitioners can contribute to the enhancement of both human well-being and the ecosystems in which they reside.

10.1.2 The Importance of Machine Learning in Urban Ecology

With the rapid advancement of technology and the increasing availability of large data sets, machine learning has emerged as a powerful tool for analyzing and modeling complex urban ecological systems. Machine learning techniques can help researchers and urban planners identify patterns, predict trends, and optimize interventions in urban ecosystems. By employing machine learning algorithms, urban ecology can benefit from data-driven insights, leading to more efficient and effective decision-making processes in urban planning and management. Machine learning algorithms can analyze vast amounts of data from various sources, such as satellite imagery, remote sensing, social media, and environmental monitoring systems, to uncover hidden patterns and relationships within urban ecosystems (Yuan et al., 2020). This ability to process and analyze large data sets allows researchers and practitioners to better understand the intricate interactions between biotic, abiotic, and anthropogenic factors in urban environments.

Predictive modeling using machine learning techniques can forecast the impacts of different urban planning and design scenarios on ecosystems and the provision of ecosystem services. This enables urban planners and managers to evaluate the potential consequences of their decisions, assess the trade-offs between different alternatives, and ultimately choose the most sustainable and beneficial options for urban landscapes (Caldow et al., 2015). Moreover, machine learning can optimize interventions in urban ecosystems by identifying the most effective locations, configurations, and designs for green infrastructure, habitat restoration, and other ecological enhancements. This helps ensure that urban ecological interventions are targeted and tailored to maximize their effectiveness and overall benefits.

By harnessing the power of machine learning, urban ecology can not only gain valuable insights into the functioning of urban ecosystems but also facilitate more informed, data-driven decision-making processes in urban planning and management (Bibri & Krogstie, 2020). This, in turn, can contribute to the creation of more sustainable, resilient, and biodiverse urban environments that enhance the well-being of both human societies and the ecosystems they inhabit.

10.1.3 Objectives of the Chapter

This chapter aims to provide an overview of the applications of machine learning in urban ecology, exploring its potential in various aspects of urban ecological research and practice. The chapter will cover the following key topics:

The relevance of machine learning to urban ecology

Urban ecological data sources and pre-processing techniques

Applications of machine learning in urban ecosystem services

Applications of machine learning in urban landscape planning and design

Machine learning for socio-ecological systems in urban environments

Challenges and future directions in the application of machine learning to urban ecology (Figure 10.1).

By examining these topics, the chapter will demonstrate the potential of machine learning to advance our understanding of urban ecological systems and support sustainable urban development.

10.2 INTRODUCTION TO MACHINE LEARNING

Machine learning (ML) is a subset of artificial intelligence that focuses on the development of algorithms and models that enable computers to learn from and make predictions or decisions based on data. ML techniques can automatically identify patterns in complex data, learn from those patterns, and adapt their performance over time. This ability to learn and adapt makes machine learning particularly well-suited for analyzing and modeling complex systems, such as urban ecosystems.

There are three main types of machine learning: supervised learning, unsupervised learning, and reinforcement learning.

Supervised learning: In supervised learning, algorithms are trained on labeled data, which includes both input data and the corresponding correct output. The goal of supervised learning is to learn a mapping from inputs to outputs, such that the algorithm

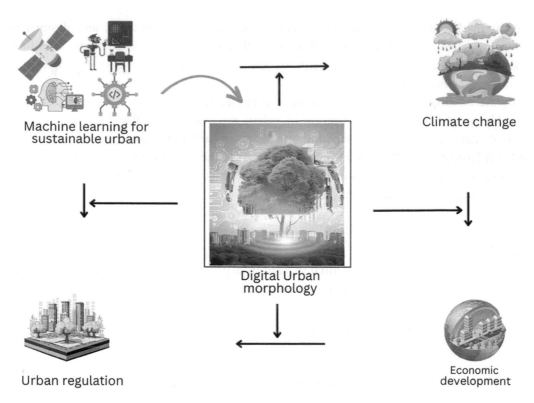

FIGURE 10.1   Application of machine learning to urban ecology.

can make accurate predictions for new, unseen data. Supervised learning is commonly used for tasks such as classification, where an algorithm predicts which category an input belongs to, and regression, where an algorithm predicts a continuous numerical value (Ayodele, 2010).

Unsupervised learning: Unlike supervised learning, unsupervised learning involves training algorithms on unlabeled data, meaning that the data does not come with pre-defined output labels. The goal of unsupervised learning is to identify patterns or structures within the data, such as clusters, without any prior knowledge of the output. Common unsupervised learning tasks include clustering, where an algorithm groups similar data points together, and dimensionality reduction, where an algorithm reduces the number of variables in a data set while preserving its essential features (Sarker, 2021).

Reinforcement learning: Reinforcement learning is a type of machine learning in which an algorithm, or agent, learns by interacting with an environment through trial and error to maximize a reward signal. In reinforcement learning, the agent receives feedback in the form of rewards or penalties after taking actions and uses this feedback to adjust its behavior in order to achieve its objective. Reinforcement learning is particularly well-suited for tasks that involve decision making over time, such as game playing, robot control, and resource allocation (Arulkumaran et al., 2017).

By leveraging these various types of machine learning techniques, researchers and practitioners can develop powerful models and algorithms that can analyze, predict, and optimize complex systems, such as urban ecosystems, leading to more informed decision making and improved outcomes.

10.2.1 Types of Machine Learning Techniques

Several machine learning techniques are particularly relevant to urban ecology, including:

a. Regression: Used to model the relationship between a dependent variable and one or more independent variables, regression techniques can be employed to predict continuous outcomes, such as urban temperature or air quality levels (Ayodele, 2010; Bhatti 2022a).

b. Classification: A technique used to categorize data into predefined classes, classification can be useful for tasks like species identification, land use classification, or predicting the presence of specific ecological features (Ayodele, 2010).

c. Clustering: An unsupervised learning technique that groups similar data points together, clustering can be applied to identify patterns in urban ecosystems, such as the distribution of green spaces or habitat types (Ayodele, 2010).

d. Deep learning: A subfield of machine learning based on artificial neural networks, deep learning can be particularly effective at processing large-scale and high-dimensional data, such as satellite imagery, for tasks like image classification and object detection (Ayodele, 2010).

e. Decision trees and random forests: These techniques involve recursively splitting the data into subsets based on specific features, enabling the identification of complex relationships and interactions among variables in urban ecological systems (Ayodele, 2010).

10.2.2 How Machine Learning Can Benefit Urban Ecology

Machine learning has the potential to significantly advance urban ecology in several ways:

a. Analyzing large-scale and high-dimensional data: ML can efficiently process and analyze large volumes of multidimensional data, such as satellite images and remote-sensing data, enabling the study of urban ecological patterns and processes at various spatial and temporal scales (Chen et al., 2021).

b. Predictive modeling: ML can help model complex urban ecological systems, allowing for the prediction of future changes in response to various drivers, such as climate change, urbanization, and land use alterations (Franklin et al., 2016).

c. Identifying patterns and relationships: ML can automatically identify patterns and relationships among variables, revealing new insights into the functioning of urban ecosystems and the factors that shape their structure and dynamics (Zhong et al., 2021).

d. Decision support and optimization: ML can be applied to optimize urban planning and management strategies, such as green infrastructure development, biodiversity conservation, and urban heat island mitigation, by providing data-driven insights and recommendations (Rolnick et al., 2022).

e. Integrating interdisciplinary data: ML can facilitate the integration of data from diverse sources and disciplines, fostering a more comprehensive understanding of the complex socio-ecological systems within urban environments (Frank et al., 2017).

10.3 OVERVIEW OF URBAN ECOLOGICAL DATA SOURCES

Urban ecological research relies on diverse data sources to understand and analyze the complex interactions between biotic, abiotic, and anthropogenic factors within urban environments. Some key data sources include:

a. Satellite and aerial imagery: High-resolution images from satellites and aerial platforms provide valuable information on land cover, land use, vegetation, and urban structures (Huang et al., 2020; Wang et al., 2020).

b. Remote-sensing data: This includes data from multispectral and hyperspectral sensors, LiDAR (light detection and ranging), and radar, which can be used to assess various urban ecological parameters such as vegetation health, surface temperature, and topography (Klemas, 2011).

c. Social media and crowdsourced data: Platforms like Twitter, Flickr, and OpenStreetMap can provide insights into human-nature interactions, public perceptions of urban ecology, and the distribution of urban green spaces (Song et al., 2020).

d. In situ measurements: Field-based measurements of vegetation, soil, water, and air quality parameters, as well as biodiversity surveys, contribute to a more detailed understanding of urban ecosystems (Lausch et al., 2017).

e. Socioeconomic data: Census data, land use planning documents, and environmental impact assessments can provide information on demographic and land use patterns that influence urban ecological processes (Buyantuyev & Wu, 2010).

10.3.1 Preprocessing and Data Fusion Techniques

Given the diverse and often heterogeneous nature of urban ecological data, pre-processing and data fusion techniques are essential to ensure data quality, compatibility, and comparability. Some common pre-processing and data fusion steps include the following:

a. Data cleaning: Removing errors, inconsistencies, and missing values from data sets to improve data quality and reliability (Arora et al., 2017).

b. Georeferencing and spatial alignment: Ensuring that all spatial data are referenced to a common coordinate system and have consistent spatial resolutions, which facilitates the integration and analysis of data from different sources (Klein et al., 2015).

c. Temporal alignment: Ensuring that all data sets have consistent temporal resolutions, such as daily, monthly, or yearly intervals, which enables the examination of urban ecological dynamics over time (Gebbert et al., 2014).

d. Data normalization and transformation: Applying mathematical transformations to data to ensure comparability and facilitate the integration of data from different sources (Quackenbush, 2002).

e. Feature extraction and selection: Identifying relevant features and variables from large and complex data sets, which can help reduce data dimensionality and improve the efficiency and accuracy of machine learning algorithms (Hira & Gillies, 2015).

f. Data fusion: Combining data from multiple sources to create a comprehensive, integrated data set that can be used for urban ecological analysis and modeling. Data fusion techniques can include overlay analysis, data assimilation, and statistical modeling approaches (Arsenault et al., 2018).

By employing these pre-processing and data fusion techniques, urban ecological researchers and practitioners can ensure the quality and consistency of their data sets, which in turn supports more accurate and reliable analyses and modeling using machine learning algorithms.

10.4 APPLICATIONS OF MACHINE LEARNING IN URBAN ECOSYSTEM SERVICES

Urban ecosystem services are the benefits that humans derive from the ecological processes and functions of urban ecosystems. Machine learning can be employed to assess, monitor, and optimize these services, leading to more sustainable and resilient urban environments. Some key applications of machine learning in urban ecosystem services include the following.

10.4.1 Urban Green Space Identification and Monitoring

Machine learning algorithms, particularly deep learning techniques such as convolutional neural networks (CNNs), have demonstrated remarkable success in the analysis of high-resolution satellite and aerial imagery. These techniques can be employed to identify, classify, and monitor urban green spaces, providing valuable information for urban ecology research and practice (Van Herzele et al., 2003).

Identification and classification of urban green spaces: CNNs can automatically detect and differentiate various types of urban green spaces, such as parks, gardens, street trees, and green roofs, from satellite and aerial images areas (Wu & Biljecki, 2021). This capability enables researchers and practitioners to create detailed maps of urban green spaces, which can be used to assess the overall green coverage and the spatial distribution of green spaces within urban.

Monitoring urban green spaces over time: By analyzing time-series satellite and aerial imagery, machine learning algorithms can track changes in urban green spaces over time, such as the expansion or loss of green areas, the growth or decline of vegetation, and the effects of urban development on green spaces (Labenski et al., 2022; Zhang et al., 2022). This information can help urban planners and managers evaluate the effectiveness of existing policies and interventions aimed at promoting urban greenery, as well as identify emerging trends and issues that require attention.

Assessing the quality of urban green spaces: In addition to identifying and classifying green spaces, machine learning algorithms can also be used to evaluate their quality (Xia et al., 2021). For instance, algorithms can analyze factors such as the diversity and health of vegetation, the presence of water bodies, and the connectivity of green spaces, providing insights into the ecological value and functionality of urban greenery.

Informing urban planning and management strategies: The information obtained from ML analysis of satellite and aerial imagery can be used to inform urban planning and management strategies aimed at enhancing urban greenery (Xia et al., 2021). For example, the identification of areas with low green space coverage or poor-quality green spaces can guide targeted interventions to improve the availability, distribution, and quality of urban green spaces. Additionally, the monitoring of green spaces over time can help urban planners and managers evaluate the success of their strategies and make data-driven adjustments to achieve their goals.

By leveraging ML techniques such as CNNs to analyze high-resolution satellite and aerial imagery, researchers and practitioners in urban ecology can gain valuable insights into the state and dynamics of urban green spaces. These insights can, in turn, inform the development and implementation of effective urban planning and management strategies that promote sustainable, resilient, and biodiverse urban environments.

10.4.2 Biodiversity Assessment and Conservation

Machine learning can indeed be applied to automate the identification and classification of species using data from remote sensing, acoustic monitoring, and camera traps, among other sources. By facilitating the rapid assessment of biodiversity in urban environments, machine learning can help prioritize conservation efforts, monitor the effectiveness of restoration projects, and guide the development of urban habitats that support diverse flora and fauna (Trivedi et al., 2016). Some applications of machine learning in this context include the following:

Remote-sensing data analysis: Machine learning algorithms can analyze data from satellite imagery, LiDAR, and other remote sensing sources to identify and map different land cover types, vegetation types, and habitats (Maurya et al., 2021). This information can be used to assess the distribution and connectivity of habitats within urban environments, identify areas of high biodiversity value, and guide habitat restoration and conservation efforts.

Acoustic monitoring: Machine learning algorithms, particularly deep learning techniques such as convolutional neural networks (CNNs), can analyze audio recordings from urban environments to identify and classify species based on their vocalizations (Hidayat et al., 2021). This can be particularly useful for monitoring avian, amphibian, and bat species in urban areas, providing valuable information on their presence, abundance, and distribution.

Camera trap image analysis: Machine learning algorithms can be used to automatically analyze images from camera traps placed in urban environments, identifying and classifying species based on their appearance (Gomez et al., 2016). This can be a valuable tool for monitoring the presence and distribution of various wildlife species, such as mammals and birds, in urban habitats.

Species distribution modeling: Machine learning can also be employed to model species distributions in urban environments based on environmental variables and species occurrence data (Cha et al., 2021). These models can help predict the presence and abundance of species in different urban habitats, identify potential areas for habitat restoration or creation, and assess the potential impacts of urban development on biodiversity.

Monitoring restoration projects: Machine learning can be used to track the progress and effectiveness of urban habitat restoration projects by analyzing changes in vegetation structure, species composition, and other ecological indicators over time (Reif & Theel, 2017). This information can help guide adaptive management strategies to maximize the ecological benefits of restoration efforts.

By leveraging machine learning techniques to automate the identification and classification of species in urban environments, researchers and practitioners can gain valuable insights into urban biodiversity patterns and dynamics. These insights can, in turn, inform the development and implementation of effective conservation, restoration, and urban planning strategies that promote biodiverse and resilient urban ecosystems.

10.4.3 Urban Heat Island Detection and Mitigation

Urban heat islands (UHIs) are indeed areas within cities where temperatures are significantly higher than in surrounding rural areas, primarily due to factors such as increased impervious surfaces, reduced vegetation cover, and the release of anthropogenic heat. Machine learning techniques can be employed to analyze remote-sensing data, such as land surface temperature and land cover, to identify and monitor UHI patterns (Deilami et al., 2018). By understanding the drivers and distribution of UHIs, urban planners and managers can develop targeted interventions to reduce urban heat and mitigate the adverse effects of UHIs on human health, energy consumption, and the environment.

Analyzing remote-sensing data: Machine learning algorithms can be used to process and analyze remote-sensing data, such as satellite imagery, to extract relevant information on land surface temperature, land cover, and other factors related to UHI formation (Khalil et al., 2021). For example, ML techniques can identify and quantify impervious surfaces, vegetation cover, and building density within urban areas, which can then be correlated with land surface temperature data to better understand the drivers of UHI patterns.

Identifying and monitoring UHI patterns: By analyzing remote-sensing data, ML techniques can help identify and monitor UHI patterns within cities, including the spatial distribution of hotspots and their temporal dynamics (Kesavan et al., 2021). This information can be used to assess the vulnerability of different urban areas to UHI effects and prioritize interventions to mitigate urban heat.

Developing targeted interventions: With a better understanding of the drivers and distribution of UHIs, urban planners and managers can develop targeted interventions to reduce urban heat, such as:

a. Increasing tree canopy cover: Planting trees and promoting the growth of urban forests can help reduce UHI effects by providing shade, reducing impervious surfaces, and facilitating evaporative cooling (He et al., 2022).

b. Implementing green roofs and walls: Green roofs and walls can help reduce UHI effects by providing insulation, increasing evapotranspiration, and reducing the heat absorbed and emitted by building surfaces (He et al., 2022).

c. Employing cool building materials: Using materials with high reflectivity and low thermal conductivity in building construction and pavement can help reduce the absorption and emission of heat, thereby mitigating UHI effects (He et al., 2022).

d. Enhancing urban design: Urban design strategies, such as incorporating open spaces, optimizing building orientation, and promoting natural ventilation, can help reduce the impacts of UHIs on urban environments (He et al., 2022).

By leveraging ML techniques to analyze remote-sensing data and better understand the drivers and distribution of UHIs, urban planners and managers can develop and implement targeted interventions that reduce urban heat, improve human comfort and health, and promote more sustainable and resilient urban environments.

10.4.4 Air Quality Monitoring and Prediction

Machine learning algorithms can indeed be applied to model and predict air quality in urban areas using data from various sources, such as air quality monitoring stations, remote-sensing platforms, and traffic and meteorological data. These models can offer valuable insights for urban planners, policymakers, and public health officials, enabling them to develop effective strategies for improving air quality and mitigating the adverse effects of air pollution on human health and the environment.

Identifying pollution hotspots: Machine learning algorithms can analyze air quality data, along with other relevant factors such as land use, traffic patterns, and meteorological conditions, to identify areas within cities where air pollution levels are consistently high (Ma et al., 2020). Identifying these hotspots can help prioritize interventions to reduce emissions and improve air quality in the most affected areas.

Assessing the impacts of urban planning and transportation policies: Machine learning models can be used to evaluate the potential effects of various urban planning and transportation policies on air quality, such as the implementation of congestion pricing, the promotion of public transportation, and the establishment of low-emission zones (Rivasplata, 2013). By predicting the consequences of these policies on air pollution levels, policymakers can make more informed decisions about which strategies are likely to be most effective in improving air quality.

Providing real-time air quality forecasts: Machine learning algorithms can also be employed to develop real-time air quality forecasting models that predict pollutant concentrations over short time horizons (e.g., hours or days) (Zhang et al., 2020). These forecasts can be used to inform public health interventions, such as issuing air quality alerts, advising vulnerable populations to limit outdoor activities during periods of poor air quality, and implementing temporary measures to reduce emissions from industrial and transportation sources.

Identifying and understanding complex relationships: Machine learning techniques can help uncover complex, nonlinear relationships between air quality, meteorological factors, and urban characteristics that may be difficult to identify using traditional statistical methods (Ma et al., 2020). This improved understanding can contribute to the development of more accurate and reliable air quality models and predictions.

By applying ML algorithms to model and predict air quality in urban areas, researchers, policymakers, and public health officials can gain a deeper understanding of the factors that contribute to air pollution and develop more effective strategies for improving air quality and protecting public health.

10.4.5 Flood Risk Assessment and Management

Machine learning techniques, such as decision trees, random forests, and artificial neural networks, can indeed be employed to assess flood risk in urban areas by modeling the relationships between environmental, hydrological, and land use factors (Chen et al., 2021). These models can provide valuable insights for urban planners and managers in the development of flood mitigation strategies and support more informed decision-making processes.

Modeling flood risk: Machine learning algorithms can be used to model flood risk in urban areas by analyzing various factors that contribute to flooding, such as rainfall intensity, soil characteristics, topography, land use, and drainage infrastructure (Rahman et al., 2021). By identifying the most significant factors influencing flood risk and quantifying their relationships, these models can help predict the likelihood and severity of flooding under different conditions.

Flood mitigation strategies: Based on the insights gained from ML models, urban planners and managers can develop targeted flood mitigation strategies (Munawar et al., 2021), such as:

a. Implementing green infrastructure: Green infrastructure, such as rain gardens, bioswales, and permeable pavements, can help reduce surface runoff and enhance infiltration, thereby reducing flood risk in urban areas.

b. Improving stormwater management systems: Machine learning models can help identify areas with inadequate stormwater management infrastructure, guiding the implementation of improvements to existing systems or the development of new infrastructure to reduce flood risk.

c. Enhancing urban design: Urban design strategies, such as increasing open space, preserving natural drainage corridors, and elevating buildings in flood-prone areas, can help reduce flood risk and minimize the impacts of flooding on urban environments.

Identifying vulnerable areas: Machine learning techniques can be used to analyze spatial patterns of flood risk, helping urban planners and managers identify areas most vulnerable to flooding (Eini et al., 2020; Nizamani et al., 2023). This information can be used to prioritize investments in flood mitigation infrastructure and inform land use planning decisions to minimize exposure to flood hazards.

Evaluating the effectiveness of flood mitigation measures: Machine learning models can also be employed to evaluate the effectiveness of implemented flood mitigation measures by analyzing changes in flood risk over time (Mosavi et al., 2018). This information can help guide adaptive management strategies and inform the allocation of resources to maximize the benefits of flood mitigation efforts.

By employing ML techniques to assess flood risk in urban areas, urban planners and managers can develop more effective flood mitigation strategies, enhance the resilience of urban environments to flooding, and reduce the social, economic, and environmental impacts of flood events.

10.5 APPLICATIONS OF MACHINE LEARNING IN URBAN LANDSCAPE PLANNING AND DESIGN

Machine learning can play a significant role in informing and enhancing urban landscape planning and design by facilitating data-driven decision making, optimizing interventions, and evaluating the potential impacts of design alternatives (Liu, 2022). Some key applications of ML in urban landscape planning and design include the following.

10.5.1 Landscape Connectivity and Fragmentation Analysis

Machine learning techniques can indeed be used to analyze landscape connectivity and fragmentation, which are critical for maintaining biodiversity and ecosystem functionality in urban areas. By examining land use and land cover data, as well as species movement patterns, ML algorithms can provide valuable insights for urban planners, conservationists, and policymakers, enabling them to develop more effective conservation strategies and green infrastructure networks.

Analyzing land use and land cover data: Machine learning algorithms can be employed to process and analyze land use and land cover data from various sources, such as satellite imagery, aerial photography, and GIS databases (Yuan, 2008). This analysis can help identify different habitat types, levels of fragmentation, and the degree of connectivity within urban environments.

Modeling species movement patterns: Machine learning techniques can be used to model species movement patterns based on habitat preferences, dispersal capabilities, and landscape features (Garzon et al., 2006). These models can help identify critical habitat corridors and areas of high ecological value, which are essential for maintaining viable populations and promoting species persistence in urban areas.

Informing conservation strategies: The insights gained from machine learning analyses of landscape connectivity and fragmentation can be used to inform the development of conservation strategies, such as the establishment of protected areas, the restoration of degraded habitats, and the creation of habitat corridors (Albani Rocchetti et al., 2021). By prioritizing areas of high ecological value and connectivity, these strategies can help maintain biodiversity and ecosystem functionality within urban environments.

Guiding green infrastructure networks: Machine learning can also support the planning and design of green infrastructure networks, which aim to enhance ecological connectivity within urban areas by linking patches of green space, such as parks, gardens, and green roofs (Gulshad et al., 2022). By identifying critical habitat corridors and areas of high ecological value, ML can help guide the placement and design of green infrastructure components to maximize their contribution to landscape connectivity and overall urban ecosystem health.

Evaluating the effectiveness of conservation and green infrastructure efforts: Machine learning models can be used to assess the effectiveness of implemented conservation strategies and green infrastructure networks by analyzing changes in landscape connectivity and fragmentation over time (Meerow, 2019). This information can help guide adaptive management strategies and inform the allocation of resources to maximize the ecological benefits of conservation and green infrastructure efforts.

By leveraging ML techniques to analyze landscape connectivity and fragmentation in urban areas, urban planners, conservationists, and policymakers can develop more effective strategies for conserving biodiversity and promoting ecosystem functionality within increasingly urbanized landscapes.

10.5.2 Green Infrastructure Planning

Machine learning can indeed support the planning and design of green infrastructure in urban environments. Green infrastructure components, such as parks, green roofs, rain gardens, and bioswales, provide a range of ecosystem services that are critical for maintaining the quality of life and sustainability in urban areas (Mauree et al., 2019). By analyzing spatial data on urban green spaces, land use, and environmental conditions, machine learning algorithms can optimize the location, configuration, and functionality of green infrastructure components, thereby enhancing their ability to provide services such as stormwater management, air quality improvement, and urban heat island mitigation.

Analyzing spatial data: Machine learning algorithms can be employed to process and analyze spatial data from various sources, such as satellite imagery, aerial photography, and GIS databases (Tehrany et al., 2019). This analysis can help identify the distribution and characteristics of existing green spaces, impervious surfaces, and other relevant features in urban environments.

Optimizing location and configuration: Machine learning techniques can be used to optimize the location and configuration of green infrastructure components based on factors such as land use, environmental conditions, and the need for specific ecosystem services (Labib, 2019). For example, machine learning can help determine the most effective locations for rain gardens and bioswales to maximize their contribution to stormwater management, or identify areas where green roofs would have the most significant impact on mitigating urban heat islands.

Enhancing functionality: Machine learning algorithms can also be used to design green infrastructure components that are tailored to the specific environmental conditions and requirements of urban areas (Marando et al., 2022). By analyzing data on factors such as soil type, vegetation, and climate, ML can help optimize the selection of plant species, substrate materials, and other design elements to maximize the functionality of green infrastructure components in terms of providing ecosystem services.

Assessing performance and impact: Machine learning models can be employed to evaluate the performance and impact of green infrastructure components on various ecosystem services, such as stormwater management, air quality improvement, and urban heat island mitigation (Meerow, 2019). This information can help guide adaptive management strategies and inform the allocation of resources to maximize the benefits of green infrastructure efforts.

Integrating multiple objectives: Machine learning techniques can support the integration of multiple objectives in the planning and design of green infrastructure, such as enhancing biodiversity, providing recreational opportunities, and improving aesthetics.

Integrating multiple objectives: Machine learning techniques can support the integration of multiple objectives in the planning and design of green infrastructure, such as enhancing biodiversity, providing recreational opportunities, and improving aesthetics (Wang et al., 2020). By considering various objectives simultaneously, machine learning can help develop green infrastructure networks that are both ecologically functional and socially desirable.

By leveraging ML techniques to support the planning and design of green infrastructure in urban environments, urban planners and policymakers can develop more effective strategies for providing ecosystem services, enhancing urban sustainability, and improving the quality of life for urban residents.

10.5.3 Urban Greening and Rewilding Strategies

Machine learning techniques can indeed be employed to identify and prioritize areas for urban greening and rewilding efforts, which aim to restore or enhance natural habitats within urban environments. By analyzing data on land use, biodiversity, and ecosystem services, ML algorithms can help identify suitable locations for habitat restoration, species reintroduction, and the creation of new green spaces, thereby contributing to more biodiverse and resilient urban ecosystems.

Identifying suitable locations: Machine learning algorithms can process and analyze large volumes of spatial data from various sources, such as satellite imagery, aerial photography, and GIS databases, to identify suitable locations for urban greening and rewilding efforts (Yousefi et al., 2021). By considering factors such as land use, habitat quality, and the availability of green spaces, machine learning can help prioritize areas that have the greatest potential for ecological restoration and improvement.

Assessing biodiversity and ecosystem services: Machine learning techniques can be used to analyze data on biodiversity, such as species richness and habitat diversity, as well as the provision of ecosystem services, such as carbon sequestration, air quality improvement, and stormwater management (Watson et al., 2019; Nizamani et al., 2021). By considering the relationships between land use, biodiversity, and ecosystem services, ML algorithms can help identify areas where urban greening and rewilding efforts are likely to have the greatest impact on enhancing urban ecosystems.

Prioritizing interventions: Machine learning algorithms can be employed to prioritize urban greening and rewilding interventions based on multiple criteria, such as ecological, social, and economic factors (Ye et al., 2019a). For example, ML can help identify areas where habitat restoration or species reintroduction efforts are likely to have the greatest benefits in terms of enhancing biodiversity, providing recreational opportunities, and improving local property values.

Evaluating the effectiveness of interventions: Machine learning techniques can also be used to evaluate the effectiveness of urban greening and rewilding efforts by analyzing changes in biodiversity, ecosystem services, and other relevant indicators over time (Koh et al., 2022). This information can help guide adaptive management strategies and inform the allocation of resources to maximize the ecological, social, and economic benefits of urban greening and rewilding efforts.

Integrating stakeholder input and preferences: Machine learning techniques can support the integration of stakeholder input and preferences in the planning and prioritization of urban greening and rewilding efforts (Hernandez-Santin et al., 2023). By considering factors such as public opinion, community needs, and local cultural values, ML can help develop urban greening and rewilding strategies that are both ecologically effective and socially acceptable.

By employing ML techniques to identify and prioritize areas for urban greening and rewilding efforts, urban planners, conservationists, and policymakers can develop more effective strategies for restoring and enhancing natural habitats within urban environments, contributing to more biodiverse, resilient, and sustainable urban ecosystems.

10.5.4 Urban Form Optimization for Ecological Resilience

Machine learning can indeed be applied to optimize urban form and design for ecological resilience, considering factors such as climate change adaptation, natural hazard mitigation, and the provision of ecosystem services. By modeling the relationships between urban form, land use, and ecological processes, ML algorithms can identify design strategies that maximize ecological benefits, minimize environmental impacts, and enhance the overall resilience of urban environments.

Modeling relationships between urban form and ecological processes: Machine learning algorithms can be employed to analyze large volumes of data on urban form, land use, and ecological processes, identifying patterns and relationships that can inform urban design strategies (Tekouabou et al., 2022). By considering factors such as building density, green space distribution, and transportation networks, ML can help determine how different urban forms influence ecological resilience.

Climate change adaptation: Machine learning techniques can be used to model the impacts of climate change on urban environments, such as increased temperatures, extreme weather events, and sea-level rise (Biesbroek et al., 2020). By analyzing data on climate projections, land use, and urban form, ML algorithms can identify urban design strategies that enhance adaptation to climate change, such as increasing green space connectivity, implementing green roofs, and designing flood-resistant infrastructure.

Natural hazard mitigation: Machine learning can also be applied to assess the vulnerability of urban areas to natural hazards, such as floods, landslides, and earthquakes (Wang et al., 2021). By modeling the relationships between urban form, land use, and hazard exposure, machine learning algorithms can help identify design strategies that minimize the risks associated with natural hazards, such as implementing green infrastructure for stormwater management or adopting land-use planning policies that restrict development in high-risk areas.

Provision of ecosystem services: Machine learning techniques can be used to optimize the provision of ecosystem services in urban environments, such as air quality improvement, carbon sequestration, and stormwater management (Lu et al., 2022). By analyzing data on urban form, land use, and environmental conditions, ML algorithms can identify design strategies that maximize the provision of ecosystem services, such as creating urban forests, enhancing green space connectivity, or implementing permeable pavements.

Evaluating and optimizing urban design strategies: Machine learning algorithms can be employed to evaluate the effectiveness of different urban design strategies in enhancing ecological resilience, based on multiple criteria, such as ecological, social, and economic factors (Li et al., 2022). By modeling the relationships between urban form, land use, and ecological processes, ML can help identify design strategies that strike the optimal balance between maximizing ecological benefits, minimizing environmental impacts, and meeting the needs of urban residents.

By leveraging ML techniques to optimize urban form and design for ecological resilience, urban planners and policymakers can develop more effective strategies for creating sustainable, resilient, and biodiverse urban environments that are better equipped to adapt to climate change, mitigate natural hazards, and provide essential ecosystem services.

10.5.5 Evaluation of Landscape Design Alternatives

Machine learning techniques can indeed be used to evaluate and compare the potential impacts of different landscape design alternatives on urban ecosystems and the provision of ecosystem services. By analyzing data on land use, environmental conditions, and socio-economic factors, ML algorithms can assess the trade-offs and synergies among design alternatives, informing the selection of the most sustainable and beneficial options for urban landscapes.

Analyzing landscape design alternatives: Machine learning algorithms can process and analyze data on various landscape design alternatives, taking into account factors such as land use, vegetation, infrastructure, and environmental conditions (Eslamirad et al., 2020). This analysis can help determine the potential impacts of different design alternatives on urban ecosystems and the provision of ecosystem services.

Assessing trade-offs and synergies: Machine learning techniques can be employed to assess the trade-offs and synergies among different landscape design alternatives, considering factors such as ecological, social, and economic benefits (Darvishi et al., 2022). For example, ML can help identify design alternatives that maximize the provision of ecosystem services, such as stormwater management or carbon sequestration, while minimizing negative impacts on biodiversity, water quality, or property values.

Evaluating potential impacts on ecosystem services: Machine learning algorithms can be used to model the potential impacts of different landscape design alternatives on the provision of various ecosystem services, such as air quality improvement, climate regulation, and recreational opportunities (Green et al., 2021). By considering the relationships between land use, environmental conditions, and ecosystem services, ML can help identify design alternatives that enhance the overall sustainability and resilience of urban landscapes.

Comparing design alternatives: Machine learning techniques can support the comparison of different landscape design alternatives based on multiple criteria, such as ecological, social, and economic factors (Lee & Chang, 2018). By modeling the relationships between landscape design, urban ecosystems, and the provision of ecosystem services, ML algorithms can help identify the most sustainable and beneficial options for urban landscapes.

Incorporating stakeholder preferences and input: Machine learning techniques can be used to incorporate stakeholder preferences and input into the evaluation and comparison of landscape design alternatives (Linkov et al., 2006). By considering factors such as public opinion, community needs, and local cultural values, ML can help develop landscape design strategies that are both ecologically effective and socially acceptable.

By employing machine learning techniques to evaluate and compare the potential impacts of different landscape design alternatives on urban ecosystems and the provision of ecosystem services, urban planners, landscape architects, and policymakers can make more informed decisions, selecting the most sustainable and beneficial options for urban landscapes. This data-driven approach can lead to the creation of more resilient, biodiverse, and livable urban environments that promote human well-being and ecological health.

By employing ML algorithms in these various aspects of urban landscape planning and design, researchers and practitioners can gain valuable insights and develop more effective strategies for creating sustainable, resilient, and ecologically vibrant urban environments.

10.6 MACHINE LEARNING FOR SOCIO-ECOLOGICAL SYSTEMS IN URBAN ENVIRONMENTS

Socio-ecological systems in urban environments encompass the complex interactions between human societies and urban ecosystems. Machine learning can help analyze these interactions and provide insights into the social, economic, and environmental dimensions of urban ecology. Key applications of ML for socio-ecological systems in urban environments include the following.

10.6.1 Analyzing Human-Nature Interactions

Machine learning can indeed be employed to study human-nature interactions in urban environments by analyzing data from social media platforms, surveys, and geotagged photographs (Toivonen et al., 2019). These analyses can reveal patterns of human use and perception of urban green spaces, identify areas of high recreational or cultural value, and provide insights into the drivers of human behavior in relation to urban ecosystems.

Analyzing social media data: Machine learning algorithms can be used to process and analyze large volumes of data from social media platforms, such as Twitter, Instagram, and Facebook, to understand how people interact with and perceive urban green spaces (Balaji et al., 2021). Techniques such as sentiment analysis and natural language processing can help identify positive or negative perceptions of specific green spaces, as well as the factors that influence these perceptions, such as safety, accessibility, or aesthetics.

Analyzing geotagged photographs: Machine learning can be employed to analyze geotagged photographs from platforms like Flickr or Google Street View to study the spatial distribution of human-nature interactions in urban environments (Kim et al., 2020). By processing visual data, ML algorithms can identify popular locations, the types of activities people engage in, and the characteristics of green spaces that attract visitors, such as the presence of water features, play areas, or particular vegetation types.

Analyzing survey data: Machine learning techniques can be used to analyze survey data on human-nature interactions in urban environments, such as questionnaires on green space use, preferences, and perceived benefits (Balaji et al., 2021). By identifying patterns and relationships in survey responses, ML can help reveal the factors that influence human behavior in relation to urban ecosystems, such as socio-demographic characteristics, environmental attitudes, or personal values.

Identifying areas of high recreational or cultural value: Machine learning algorithms can help identify areas of high recreational or cultural value within urban environments by analyzing data on green space use, preferences, and perceptions (Gosal et al., 2019). By considering factors such as visitation rates, recreational activities, and cultural significance, ML can support the prioritization of green spaces for conservation, enhancement, or development.

Informing urban planning and management: Insights from machine learning analyses of human-nature interactions can inform urban planning and management strategies aimed at enhancing the quality, accessibility, and attractiveness of urban green spaces (Ye et al., 2019b). By understanding how people interact with and perceive urban ecosystems, planners and managers can develop targeted interventions that promote human well-being, encourage the use of green spaces, and foster positive human-nature relationships.

By leveraging ML techniques to study human-nature interactions in urban environments, researchers, planners, and policymakers can gain valuable insights into the factors that drive human behavior in relation to urban ecosystems. This information can help guide the development of urban planning and management strategies that create more sustainable, resilient, and livable urban environments that support both human well-being and ecological health.

10.6.2 Environmental Justice and Equitable Access to Green Spaces

Machine learning has the potential to revolutionize the way we understand and address issues related to environmental justice and the equitable distribution of green spaces in urban areas (Anguelovski, 2013). By analyzing complex, multidimensional data sets, ML algorithms can uncover patterns and relationships that might otherwise remain hidden. This is particularly important when examining the distribution of green spaces, as these areas offer significant benefits to residents in terms of physical and mental health, social cohesion, and environmental quality.

To assess environmental justice and the equitable distribution of green spaces, ML models can be trained on various types of data, including the following:

Geographic Information System (GIS) data: This provides detailed spatial information about the location, size, and quality of green spaces within a given area (Pouya & Aghlmand, 2022). GIS data can also include information on other environmental features, such as water bodies and pollution levels, to give a more comprehensive picture of the urban environment.

Demographic data: Population data, including age, race, income, and education levels, can help identify which communities may be disproportionately affected by a lack of green space access or environmental hazards (Voelkel et al., 2018). This information can be used to ensure that marginalized groups are not left behind in urban planning and development efforts.

Socioeconomic variables: Data on factors such as housing, employment, and transportation can help determine the underlying causes of green space inequality and inform targeted interventions (Dai, 2011). For example, if an area with limited green space access is also characterized by low car ownership, public transit improvements or bike-sharing programs could be implemented to increase access to existing green spaces.

Once the relevant data has been collected and processed, ML algorithms can be employed for the following:

Identify areas of inequality: By analyzing spatial and demographic data, ML models can pinpoint specific neighborhoods or communities that lack sufficient green space access, helping to prioritize areas for intervention.

Evaluate the impact of potential interventions: ML algorithms can simulate the effects of various policy measures, such as the creation of new parks, the improvement of existing green spaces, or the implementation of transportation initiatives. This can help decision makers choose the most effective strategies to promote equitable distribution of urban ecosystem services.

Monitor progress over time: As urban landscapes evolve and new data becomes available, ML models can be continually updated to track changes in green space distribution and assess the effectiveness of implemented interventions. This allows for adaptive management and ongoing improvement of urban planning efforts.

Machine learning offers a powerful tool to help assess environmental justice and the equitable distribution of green spaces in urban areas. By examining large data sets and identifying areas of inequality, ML algorithms can inform targeted interventions that promote more equitable access to urban ecosystem services, ultimately improving the quality of life for all residents.

10.6.3 Public Engagement and Decision-Making Support

Machine learning has tremendous potential for enhancing public engagement and decision making in urban ecology. By leveraging advanced algorithms and large data sets, ML can offer valuable insights and recommendations that support a more inclusive, data-driven approach to addressing complex urban ecological challenges. Here are several ways in which ML can support this process:

Analyzing public opinion: Natural language processing (NLP) and sentiment analysis techniques can be used to mine large volumes of textual data, such as social media posts, news articles, and public comments, to gauge public opinion on various urban ecological issues (Ding et al., 2022). This can help identify trends, concerns, and priorities among different stakeholder groups.

Identifying key stakeholders: ML algorithms can help identify and classify key stakeholder groups, such as residents, businesses, environmental organizations, and government agencies (Balogun et al., 2021). By understanding the unique interests and concerns of these groups, decision makers can better tailor their engagement efforts and ensure that diverse perspectives are taken into account.

Modeling policy impacts: ML models can be employed to simulate the potential environmental, social, and economic impacts of different policy or management scenarios (Xiao et al., 2020). These models can provide valuable insights into the trade-offs and synergies associated with various approaches, helping to inform more balanced and equitable decision-making processes.

Optimizing resource allocation: ML can be used to optimize the allocation of resources, such as funding, personnel, and infrastructure, for urban ecological initiatives (Aviso et al., 2018). By analyzing historical data and predicting future trends, ML algorithms can help identify the most cost-effective and impactful strategies for addressing urban ecological challenges.

Enhancing public engagement: ML tools can be used to develop interactive platforms that enable more effective public participation in the decision-making process (O'connor et al., 2016). For example, ML algorithms can be integrated into online platforms to provide personalized recommendations for public engagement activities or generate visualizations that help users better understand complex urban ecological issues.

Monitoring and evaluation: ML techniques can be employed to track the progress of urban ecological initiatives, evaluate their effectiveness, and identify areas for improvement (Yigitcanlar et al., 2020). For example, remote-sensing and computer vision algorithms can be used to monitor changes in urban green spaces, biodiversity, and other ecological indicators over time.

Machine learning can play a significant role in supporting public engagement and decision making in urban ecology. By providing data-driven insights and recommendations, ML can help ensure that diverse perspectives and interests are considered, ultimately contributing to more sustainable, resilient, and livable urban environments.

10.6.4 Community-Based Ecological Monitoring and Management

Machine learning has the potential to significantly enhance community-based ecological monitoring and management efforts (McKay & Johnson, 2017). By leveraging ML algorithms, citizen scientists and local communities can more effectively analyze and interpret large, heterogeneous data sets, leading to more informed decisions and actions regarding urban ecological issues. Here are several ways in which ML can facilitate these efforts:

Data integration and pre-processing: ML techniques can be used to integrate and preprocess data from various sources, such as remote sensing images, geospatial data, and social media posts (Chaki et al., 2018). By automating data cleaning, normalization, and transformation tasks, ML can help streamline the data preparation process and ensure that community-based initiatives have access to high-quality, consistent data sets.

Automated data analysis: ML algorithms can automate the analysis of large, complex data sets collected by citizen scientists and local communities, enabling them to identify patterns, trends, and anomalies more quickly and accurately (Bergen et al., 2019). This can help reduce the barriers to entry for community-based initiatives and empower local stakeholders to contribute to urban ecological research and management more effectively.

Real-time monitoring: ML techniques can be employed to support real-time ecological monitoring, allowing communities to respond more rapidly to emerging issues or disturbances (Cai et al., 2020). For example, computer vision algorithms can be used to process images from camera traps or drones, enabling the automatic identification and tracking of species populations, habitat changes, or other ecological indicators.

Predictive modeling: ML models can be used to forecast future ecological conditions or the impacts of different management scenarios, helping communities make more informed decisions about the allocation of resources or the prioritization of conservation actions (Samal et al., 2021). For example, ML algorithms can be employed to predict the spread of invasive species, the risk of habitat fragmentation, or the effects of climate change on urban ecosystems.

Decision support tools: ML techniques can be integrated into decision support tools that help local stakeholders evaluate different management options and identify the most effective strategies for achieving their ecological objectives (Zhai et al., 2020). By providing data-driven insights and recommendations, ML can help ensure that community-based initiatives are guided by the best available evidence and that local perspectives are taken into account.

Capacity building and empowerment: ML can help build capacity and empower local communities by providing them with the tools and knowledge they need to effectively participate in ecological monitoring and management efforts (Chapman & Schott, 2020). By democratizing access to advanced data analysis techniques, ML can help level the playing field for community-based initiatives, enabling them to compete with larger, more well-funded organizations.

Machine learning can play a pivotal role in facilitating community-based ecological monitoring and management efforts by automating data processing and analysis tasks, reducing barriers to entry, and empowering local stakeholders to contribute to urban ecological research and management. By harnessing the power of ML, communities can more effectively address the complex, interconnected challenges facing urban ecosystems and work together to create more sustainable, resilient, and livable environments.

By leveraging machine learning techniques in these various aspects of socio-ecological systems in urban environments, researchers and practitioners can develop a more comprehensive understanding of the complex relationships between human societies and urban ecosystems, and work toward more sustainable, resilient, and inclusive urban environments.

10.7 CHALLENGES AND FUTURE DIRECTIONS

While ML offers significant potential for advancing urban ecology research and practice, there are several challenges and future directions to consider.

10.7.1 Data Quality and Availability

Indeed, ML algorithms are highly dependent on the quality and quantity of data available for analysis. In the context of urban ecology, data quality and availability can be affected by various factors, such as missing, inconsistent, or biased data (Vetrò et al., 2021). To overcome these challenges and ensure accurate analysis and modeling, several strategies can be employed:

Standardized data collection protocols: Developing and implementing standardized data collection and reporting protocols is crucial for ensuring data consistency and comparability across different studies, projects, and locations (Harvey, 1993). This includes the use of consistent data formats, metadata standards, and sampling methodologies. Standardization can also help reduce data entry errors and improve overall data quality.

Data sharing and collaboration: Encouraging collaboration among researchers, practitioners, and data providers can help improve data availability and quality (Tan, 2016). By sharing data sets and promoting open access to data resources, urban ecologists can leverage larger, more diverse data sets for analysis and modeling, helping to overcome issues associated with missing or biased data.

Data imputation and integration techniques: Machine learning and statistical techniques can be employed to address missing or inconsistent data by estimating missing values based on available information or by integrating data from multiple sources (Gudivada et al, 2017). For example, data imputation methods can be used to fill in gaps in time series data, while data fusion techniques can help combine data sets with different spatial or temporal resolutions.

Bias correction and sensitivity analysis: Analyzing and correcting for biases in data is essential for ensuring accurate and reliable results (Teutschbein & Seibert, 2012). This can involve applying bias-correction techniques, such as re-sampling or weighting methods, as well as conducting sensitivity analyses to assess the impact of potential biases on model performance.

Quality control and data validation: Implementing robust quality control and data validation processes can help identify and address data quality issues early in the analysis process (Pachouly et al., 2022). This may include automated data checks, expert review, or cross-validation against independent data sources.

Capacity building and training: Building capacity among researchers, practitioners, and data providers is essential for ensuring that data collection, management, and analysis practices are consistent and of high quality (Schmeller et al., 2017). This can involve providing training in data collection and analysis techniques, as well as promoting the use of standardized protocols and tools.

Crowdsourcing and citizen science: Engaging citizen scientists and local communities in data collection efforts can help increase data availability and diversity, particularly in areas where traditional data sources may be limited (Lee et al., 2020). To ensure data quality, crowdsourcing initiatives should be supported by appropriate training, guidance, and quality control measures.

By addressing data quality and availability challenges in urban ecology, researchers and practitioners can ensure that ML algorithms produce accurate and reliable insights, supporting more effective decision making and management of urban ecosystems.

10.7.2 Interpreting and Validating Machine Learning Models

The "black-box" nature of complex ML models, especially deep learning techniques, can make it challenging to understand and validate their underlying processes and predictions. Developing more interpretable and explainable machine learning (XAI) models is crucial for building trust in their applications and ensuring their responsible use in urban ecology. Here are some strategies to achieve this:

Feature importance analysis: Assessing the importance of different input features in machine learning models can help provide insights into the relationships between input variables and model predictions. Methods such as permutation importance, feature importance ranking from tree-based models, or LASSO regression can be employed to identify the most influential variables and their effects on model outputs.

Model visualization: Visualizing the structure and processes of machine learning models can help improve understanding and interpretability (Hohman et al., 2019). For example, decision tree models can be represented as flowcharts, while neural network architectures can be illustrated using node-link diagrams. Additionally, visualization techniques like partial dependence plots or individual conditional expectation (ICE) plots can help explore the relationships between input features and model predictions.

Surrogate models: Creating simpler, more interpretable models that approximate the behavior of complex models can help improve understanding of the underlying processes (Angione et al., 2022). For example, a decision tree or linear regression model can be trained to mimic the predictions of a more complex model, providing a more interpretable representation of the relationships between input variables and model outputs.

Local explanations: Generating local explanations for individual predictions can help improve interpretability and trust in machine learning models (ElShawi et al., 2021). Techniques like local interpretable model-agnostic explanations (LIME) (Recio-García et al., 2020) or Shapley additive explanations (SHAP) can be used to provide explanations for specific instances (Santos et al., 2021), helping users understand the factors driving individual model predictions.

Regularization and simplification: Applying regularization techniques or model simplification methods can help reduce model complexity and improve interpretability (Plumb et al., 2020). For example, L1 or L2 regularization can be used to penalize overly complex models, while model pruning or architecture search techniques can help identify simpler, more interpretable model structures.

Transparency and documentation: Providing clear and comprehensive documentation of the data, methods, and assumptions used in ML models is essential for building trust and facilitating model validation (Schuwirth et al., 2019). This includes providing details on data pre-processing, model training, hyperparameter tuning, and performance evaluation, as well as any limitations or uncertainties associated with model predictions.

User-centered design: Developing machine learning applications with a focus on user needs and requirements can help ensure that models are interpretable and actionable for decision makers (Celino, 2020). This may involve engaging users in the development process, designing intuitive interfaces and visualizations, and providing context-appropriate explanations and guidance.

By implementing these strategies, researchers and practitioners can develop more interpretable and explainable ML models for urban ecology applications, helping to build trust and ensure the responsible use of these powerful tools in decision-making and management processes (Bhatti et al., 2023a).

10.7.3 Integrating Cross-Disciplinary Knowledge

Urban ecology is an interdisciplinary field, and applying ML effectively in this context necessitates collaboration across disciplines and the development of techniques that can handle diverse data types and analytical approaches. To advance the field, several strategies can be employed:

Cross-disciplinary collaboration: Encouraging collaboration between researchers and practitioners from diverse disciplines, such as ecology, geography, urban planning, and social sciences, is crucial for addressing the complex challenges of urban ecology (Kingsland, 2019). This may involve organizing interdisciplinary workshops, conferences, or joint research projects that facilitate knowledge exchange and foster collaborative networks.

Shared language and frameworks: Developing a shared language and conceptual frameworks that span across disciplines can help facilitate communication and understanding among diverse stakeholders (Díaz et al., 2015). This may involve the development of standardized terminologies, taxonomies, or ontologies that capture the key concepts and relationships in urban ecology.

Multi-modal data integration: Developing machine learning techniques that can accommodate diverse data types, such as geospatial, remote sensing, socio-economic, and qualitative data, is essential for addressing the complex, interconnected issues in urban ecology (Xie et al., 2022). This may involve the development of multi-modal data fusion techniques or the use of unsupervised or semi-supervised learning approaches to handle heterogeneous data sources (Bhatti et al., 2023a).

Interdisciplinary training and education: Promoting interdisciplinary training and education programs that provide students and professionals with the skills and knowledge they need to work effectively across disciplines is essential for advancing the field of urban ecology (Annan-Diab & Molinari, 2017). This may involve the development of interdisciplinary degree programs, short courses, or online learning resources that cover the key concepts and methods from relevant disciplines.

Transdisciplinary research: Encouraging transdisciplinary research that integrates knowledge from multiple disciplines and stakeholders can help generate novel insights and solutions for urban ecological challenges (Polk, M., 2015). This may involve the development of participatory research methods, scenario planning exercises, or system dynamics models that facilitate the co-creation of knowledge and decision making.

Methodological innovation: Developing new machine learning techniques that can accommodate diverse analytical approaches and address the unique challenges of urban ecology is crucial for advancing the field (Azevedo, 2015). This may involve the development of novel algorithms, model architectures, or evaluation metrics that are specifically designed for urban ecological applications.

Open science and data sharing: Promoting open science and data sharing practices can help facilitate interdisciplinary collaboration and the development of new ML techniques (Himanen et al., 2019). This may involve the creation of open data repositories, data sharing platforms, or open-source software tools that enable researchers and practitioners to access and build upon each other's work.

By fostering cross-disciplinary collaboration and developing machine learning techniques that can accommodate diverse data types and analytical approaches, researchers and practitioners can advance the field of urban ecology and more effectively address the complex, interconnected challenges facing urban ecosystems.

10.7.4 Ethical Considerations

The ethical considerations associated with the use of ML in urban ecology. Addressing these concerns is essential for ensuring that machine learning applications are used responsibly and in a manner that promotes social and environmental equity (Cheng, 2022). Here are some strategies to address these ethical challenges:

Data privacy and protection: Developing and adhering to robust data privacy and protection guidelines is crucial for safeguarding the personal information of individuals whose data may be used in urban ecological studies. This includes obtaining informed consent, anonymizing data, and implementing strict access controls and data security measures. Additionally, compliance with relevant data protection regulations, such as the general data protection regulation (GDPR) in the European Union, is essential (Yuan & Li, 2019).

Algorithmic fairness and transparency: Ensuring that ML algorithms are fair and unbiased is important for preventing the reinforcement of existing social or environmental inequalities. This involves using techniques to detect and mitigate biases in data, as well as developing and employing algorithms that promote fairness and transparency. Techniques such as fairness-aware machine learning, adversarial training, and counterfactual reasoning can help address potential biases in model predictions (Mehrabi et al., 2021).

Ethical guidelines and frameworks: Developing and implementing ethical guidelines and frameworks specific to the use of machine learning in urban ecology can help ensure that these applications are used responsibly and in a manner that promotes social and environmental equity (Elias et al., 1997). This may involve establishing principles for responsible data collection, analysis, and use, as well as guidelines for stakeholder engagement, transparency, and accountability.

Stakeholder engagement and representation: Engaging diverse stakeholders, including marginalized or underrepresented groups, in the development and evaluation of ML applications can help ensure that these tools are used in a manner that is equitable and respects the rights and interests of all affected parties (Janevic et al., 2022). This may involve conducting participatory research, incorporating local knowledge, or using collaborative decision-making processes.

Ongoing monitoring and evaluation: Regularly monitoring and evaluating the performance, impacts, and ethical implications of ML applications in urban ecology is essential for ensuring that these tools are used responsibly and effectively (Bhatti 2022b; Bhatti 2022c; Bhatti 2023a; Bhatti 2023b; Bhatti 2023c; Bhatti 2023d; Bhatti 2023e; Ullah 2020; Wang 2023). This may involve tracking the social, environmental, and economic outcomes of ML-driven interventions, as well as conducting audits or impact assessments to identify and address potential ethical concerns.

Capacity building and education: Building capacity and raising awareness among researchers, practitioners, and decision-makers about the ethical considerations associated with ML in urban ecology is crucial for promoting responsible and equitable use of these technologies (Di Vaio et al., 2020). This may involve providing training, resources, or support to help stakeholders navigate the ethical dimensions of ML applications.

By adopting these strategies, researchers and practitioners can address the ethical challenges associated with the use of ML in urban ecology, ensuring that these powerful tools are used in a responsible and equitable manner that benefits all stakeholders and promotes sustainable urban environments.

10.7.5 Climate Change and Urban Ecology

As climate change increasingly impacts urban environments, ML can indeed play a crucial role in understanding and adapting to these changes. Future research should focus on developing ML models that can predict the impacts of climate change on urban ecosystems and support the development of adaptive urban planning and management strategies. Some potential applications of ML in this context include the following:

Climate change impact prediction: ML models can be trained on historical climate data, urban land-use patterns, and environmental variables to predict future changes in temperature, precipitation, and extreme weather events (Madzokere et al., 2020; Janizadeh et al., 2021). These predictions can help urban planners identify areas that are particularly vulnerable to climate change and prioritize adaptation measures accordingly.

Urban heat island effect assessment: The urban heat island (UHI) effect refers to the increased temperature in densely populated urban areas compared to surrounding rural areas (Imhoff et al., 2010). ML algorithms can analyze land-use patterns, building materials, and green space distribution to assess the severity of the UHI effect in specific locations and suggest targeted interventions, such as increasing green spaces or implementing cool roof technologies.

Flood risk modeling: ML models can be used to predict areas of increased flood risk due to climate change-induced increases in precipitation or sea level rise (Elmqvist et al., 2015). By identifying vulnerable areas, urban planners can develop strategies to mitigate flood risk, such as through the construction of green infrastructure, improved stormwater management, or enhanced coastal defenses.

Biodiversity conservation and urban ecology: Climate change can significantly impact biodiversity and ecological processes in urban areas. ML models can be used to identify important habitat corridors, predict the distribution of species under different climate scenarios, and inform the design of urban green spaces that promote biodiversity and ecosystem resilience (Marselle et al., 2021).

Assessing the effectiveness of adaptation measures: ML models can be used to evaluate the success of implemented climate change adaptation strategies. By monitoring changes in environmental variables, such as temperature or flood risk, over time, researchers can determine which interventions are most effective in mitigating climate change impacts and inform future planning efforts (Gohari et al., 2017).

Public health impacts: Climate change can have wide-ranging effects on public health in urban areas, from increased heat-related illnesses to the spread of vector-borne diseases. ML algorithms can help identify populations at risk and inform targeted public health interventions, such as early warning systems or vaccination campaigns (Tambo et al., 2021).

Machine learning has the potential to play a vital role in understanding and adapting to the impacts of climate change on urban environments (Balogun et al., 2020). Future research should focus on developing ML models that can predict climate change impacts on urban ecosystems and support the development of adaptive urban planning and management strategies. By leveraging the power of ML, urban planners and policymakers can make more informed decisions and build more resilient, sustainable cities for future generations (Allam & Dhunny, 2019; Bibri, 2021).

By addressing these challenges and exploring future directions, ML has the potential to significantly contribute to the advancement of urban ecology research and practice, ultimately promoting more sustainable, resilient, and biodiverse urban environments.

10.8 CONCLUSION

The application of ML in urban ecology offers promising opportunities to enhance our understanding of complex urban ecosystems and contribute to more sustainable, resilient, and inclusive urban environments. By harnessing the power of ML techniques, researchers and practitioners can analyze and model the intricate relationships between biotic, abiotic, and anthropogenic factors within urban socio-ecological systems, ultimately informing more effective urban planning, design, and management strategies. Throughout this book, we have explored various applications of ML in urban ecology, including data pre-processing, the assessment and monitoring of urban ecosystem services, landscape planning and design, and the analysis of socio-ecological systems. We have also discussed the challenges and future directions for the field, highlighting the importance of data quality, model interpretability, cross-disciplinary collaboration, ethical considerations, and climate change adaptation. As we move forward, it is essential to continue refining and expanding the use of machine learning techniques in urban ecology, fostering cross-disciplinary collaboration, and addressing the ethical and practical challenges associated with these applications. By doing so, we can harness the full potential of ML to support the development of sustainable, resilient, and biodiverse urban environments that enhance the well-being of both human societies and the ecosystems they inhabit.

REFERENCES

Albani Rocchetti, G., Armstrong, C. G., Abeli, T., Orsenigo, S., Jasper, C., Joly, S., ... & Vamosi, J. C. (2021). Reversing extinction trends: New uses of (old) herbarium specimens to accelerate conservation action on threatened species. *New Phytologist*, 230(2), 433–450.

Allam, Z., & Dhunny, Z. A. (2019). On big data, artificial intelligence and smart cities. *Cities*, 89, 80–91.

Angione, C., Silverman, E., & Yaneske, E. (2022). Using machine learning as a surrogate model for agent-based simulations. *PloS one*, 17(2), e0263150.

Anguelovski, I. (2013). New directions in urban environmental justice: Rebuilding community, addressing trauma, and remaking place. *Journal of Planning Education and Research*, 33(2), 160–175.

Annan-Diab, F., & Molinari, C. (2017). Interdisciplinarity: Practical approach to advancing education for sustainability and for the Sustainable Development Goals. *The International Journal of Management Education*, 15(2), 73–83.

Arora, R., Pahwa, P., & Gupta, D. (2017). Data quality improvement in data warehouse: A framework. *International Journal of Data Analysis Techniques and Strategies*, 9(1), 17–33.

Arsenault, K. R., Kumar, S. V., Geiger, J. V., Wang, S., Kemp, E., Mocko, D. M., ... & Peters-Lidard, C. D. (2018). The Land surface Data Toolkit (LDT v7. 2)–a data fusion environment for land data assimilation systems. *Geoscientific Model Development*, 11(9), 3605–3621.

Arulkumaran, K., Deisenroth, M. P., Brundage, M., & Bharath, A. A. (2017). Deep reinforcement learning: A brief survey. *IEEE Signal Processing Magazine*, 34(6), 26–38.

Aviso, K. B., Mayol, A. P., Promentilla, M. A. B., Santos, J. R., Tan, R. R., Ubando, A. T., & Yu, K. D. S. (2018). Allocating human resources in organizations operating under crisis conditions: A fuzzy input-output optimization modeling framework. *Resources, Conservation and Recycling*, 128, 250–258.

Ayodele, T. O. (2010). Types of machine learning algorithms. *New Advances in Machine Learning*, 3, 19–48.

Azevedo, R. (2015). Defining and measuring engagement and learning in science: Conceptual, theoretical, methodological, and analytical issues. *Educational Psychologist*, 50(1), 84–94.

Bai, X., Surveyer, A., Elmqvist, T., Gatzweiler, F. W., Güneralp, B., Parnell, S., ... & Webb, R. (2016). Defining and advancing a systems approach for sustainable cities. *Current Opinion in Environmental Sustainability*, 23, 69–78.

Balaji, T. K., Annavarapu, C. S. R., & Bablani, A. (2021). Machine learning algorithms for social media analysis: A survey. *Computer Science Review*, *40*, 100395.

Balogun, A. L., Marks, D., Sharma, R., Shekhar, H., Balmes, C., Maheng, D., ... & Salehi, P. (2020). Assessing the potentials of digitalization as a tool for climate change adaptation and sustainable development in urban centres. *Sustainable Cities and Society*, *53*, 101888.

Balogun, A. L., Tella, A., Baloo, L., & Adebisi, N. (2021). A review of the inter-correlation of climate change, air pollution and urban sustainability using novel machine learning algorithms and spatial information science. *Urban Climate*, *40*, 100989.

Bergen, K. J., Johnson, P. A., de Hoop, M. V., & Beroza, G. C. (2019). Machine learning for data-driven discovery in solid Earth geoscience. *Science*, *363*(6433), eaau0323.

Bhatti, U. A., Zeeshan, Z., Nizamani, M. M., Bazai, S., Yu, Z., & Yuan, L. (2022a). Assessing the change of ambient air quality patterns in Jiangsu Province of China pre-to post-COVID-19. *Chemosphere*, *288*, 132569.

Bhatti, U. A., Nizamani, M. M., & Mengxing, H. (2022b). Climate change threatens Pakistan's snow leopards. *Science*, *377*(6606), 585–586.

Bhatti, U. A., Yu, Z., Chanussot, J., Zeeshan, Z., Yuan, L., Luo, W., ... & Mehmood, A. (2022c). Local similarity-based spatial–spectral fusion hyperspectral image classification with deep CNN and Gabor filtering. *IEEE Transactions on Geoscience and Remote Sensing*, *60*, 1–15.

Bhatti, U. A., Tang, H., Wu, G., Marjan, S., & Hussain, A. (2023a). Deep learning with graph convolutional networks: An overview and latest applications in computational intelligence. *International Journal of Intelligent Systems*, *2023*, 1–28.

Bhatti, U. A., Marjan, S., Wahid, A., Syam, M. S., Huang, M., Tang, H., & Hasnain, A. (2023b). The effects of socioeconomic factors on particulate matter concentration in China's: New evidence from spatial econometric model. *Journal of Cleaner Production*, *417*, 137969.

Bhatti, U. A., Masud, M., Bazai, S. U., & Tang, H. (2023c). Investigating AI-based smart precision agriculture techniques. *Frontiers in Plant Science*, *14*, 1237783.

Bhatti, U. A., Hashmi, M. Z., Sun, Y., Masud, M., & Nizamani, M. M. (2023d). Artificial intelligence applications in reduction of carbon emissions: Step towards sustainable environment. *Frontiers in Environmental Science*, *11*, 1183620.

Bhatti, U. A., Huang, M., Neira-Molina, H., Marjan, S., Baryalai, M., Tang, H., ... & Bazai, S. U. (2023e). MFFCG–Multi feature fusion for hyperspectral image classification using graph attention network. *Expert Systems with Applications*, *229*, 120496.

Bibri, S. E. (2021). Data-driven smart sustainable cities of the future: Urban computing and intelligence for strategic, short-term, and joined-up planning. *Computational Urban Science*, *1*, 1–29.

Bibri, S. E., & Krogstie, J. (2020). The emerging data–driven Smart City and its innovative applied solutions for sustainability: The cases of London and Barcelona. *Energy Informatics*, *3*, 1–42.

Biesbroek, R., Badloe, S., & Athanasiadis, I. N. (2020). Machine learning for research on climate change adaptation policy integration: An exploratory UK case study. *Regional Environmental Change*, *20*(3), 85.

Blanco, E., Pedersen Zari, M., Raskin, K., & Clergeau, P. (2021). Urban ecosystem-level biomimicry and regenerative design: Linking ecosystem functioning and urban built environments. *Sustainability*, *13*(1), 404.

Bolund, P., & Hunhammar, S. (1999). Ecosystem services in urban areas. *Ecological Economics*, *29*(2), 293–301.

Buyantuyev, A., & Wu, J. (2010). Urban heat islands and landscape heterogeneity: Linking spatiotemporal variations in surface temperatures to land-cover and socioeconomic patterns. *Landscape Ecology*, *25*, 17–33.

Cai, W., Wang, J., Jiang, P., Cao, L., Mi, G., & Zhou, Q. (2020). Application of sensing techniques and artificial intelligence-based methods to laser welding real-time monitoring: A critical review of recent literature. *Journal of Manufacturing Systems*, 57, 1–18.

Caldow, C., Monaco, M. E., Pittman, S. J., Kendall, M. S., Goedeke, T. L., Menza, C., ... & Costa, B. M. (2015). Biogeographic assessments: A framework for information synthesis in marine spatial planning. *Marine Policy*, 51, 423–432.

Caniglia, B. S., & Mayer, B. (2021). Socio-ecological systems. *Handbook of Environmental Sociology*, 517–536.

Celino, I. (2020). Who is this explanation for? Human intelligence and knowledge graphs for eXplainable AI. In *Knowledge Graphs for eXplainable Artificial Intelligence: Foundations, Applications and Challenges* (pp. 276–285). IOS Press.

Cerreta, M., Mele, R., & Poli, G. (2020). Urban Ecosystem Services (UES) Assessment within a 3D virtual environment: A methodological approach for the Larger Urban Zones (LUZ) of Naples, Italy. *Applied Sciences*, 10(18), 6205.

Cha, Y., Shin, J., Go, B., Lee, D. S., Kim, Y., Kim, T., & Park, Y. S. (2021). An interpretable machine learning method for supporting ecosystem management: Application to species distribution models of freshwater macroinvertebrates. *Journal of Environmental Management*, 291, 112719.

Chaki, S., Routray, A., & Mohanty, W. K. (2018). Well-log and seismic data integration for reservoir characterization: A signal processing and machine-learning perspective. *IEEE Signal Processing Magazine*, 35(2), 72–81.

Chapman, J. M., & Schott, S. (2020). Knowledge coevolution: Generating new understanding through bridging and strengthening distinct knowledge systems and empowering local knowledge holders. *Sustainability Science*, 15(3), 931–943.

Chen, J., Huang, G., & Chen, W. (2021). Towards better flood risk management: Assessing flood risk and investigating the potential mechanism based on machine learning models. *Journal of Environmental Management*, 293, 112810.

Chen, Y., Sanesi, G., Li, X., Chen, W. Y., & Lafortezza, R. (2021). Remote sensing and urban green infrastructure: A synthesis of current applications and new advances. *Urban Remote Sensing: Monitoring, Synthesis, and Modeling in the Urban Environment*, 447–468.

Cheng, H. (2022). Contemporary urban space philosophy in China using lightweight deep learning model-under ecological ethics. *Computational Intelligence and Neuroscience*, 2022.

Cheng, X. L., Nizamani, M. M., Jim, C. Y., Balfour, K., Da, L. J., Qureshi, S., ... & Wang, H. F. (2020). Using SPOT Data and FRAGSTAS to analyze the relationship between plant diversity and green space landscape patterns in the tropical coastal city of Zhanjiang, China. *Remote Sensing*, 12(21), 3477.

Dai, D. (2011). Racial/ethnic and socioeconomic disparities in urban green space accessibility: Where to intervene?. *Landscape and Urban Planning*, 102(4), 234–244.

Darvishi, A., Yousefi, M., Dinan, N. M., & Angelstam, P. (2022). Assessing levels, trade-offs and synergies of landscape services in the Iranian province of Qazvin: Towards sustainable landscapes. *Landscape Ecology*, 1–23.

Deilami, K., Kamruzzaman, M., & Liu, Y. (2018). Urban heat island effect: A systematic review of spatio-temporal factors, data, methods, and mitigation measures. *International Journal of Applied Earth Observation and Geoinformation*, 67, 30–42.

Di Vaio, A., Palladino, R., Hassan, R., & Escobar, O. (2020). Artificial intelligence and business models in the sustainable development goals perspective: A systematic literature review. *Journal of Business Research*, 121, 283–314.

Díaz, S., Demissew, S., Carabias, J., Joly, C., Lonsdale, M., Ash, N., ... & Zlatanova, D. (2015). The IPBES Conceptual Framework—connecting nature and people. *Current Opinion in Environmental Sustainability*, 14, 1–16.

Ding, Y., Ma, J., & Luo, X. (2022). Applications of natural language processing in construction. *Automation in Construction, 136*, 104169.

Eini, M., Kaboli, H. S., Rashidian, M., & Hedayat, H. (2020). Hazard and vulnerability in urban flood risk mapping: Machine learning techniques and considering the role of urban districts. *International Journal of Disaster Risk Reduction, 50*, 101687.

Elias, M. J., Zins, J. E., & Weissberg, R. P. (1997). *Promoting Social and Emotional Learning: Guidelines for Educators*. Ascd.

Elmqvist, T., Zipperer, W. C., & Güneralp, B. (2015). Urbanization, habitat loss and biodiversity decline: Solution pathways to break the cycle. In *The Routledge Handbook of Urbanization and Global Environmental Change* (pp. 163–175). Routledge.

ElShawi, R., Sherif, Y., Al-Mallah, M., & Sakr, S. (2021). Interpretability in healthcare: A comparative study of local machine learning interpretability techniques. *Computational Intelligence, 37*(4), 1633–1650.

Eslamirad, N., Malekpour Kolbadinejad, S., Mahdavinejad, M., & Mehranrad, M. (2020). Thermal comfort prediction by applying supervised machine learning in green sidewalks of Tehran. *Smart and Sustainable Built Environment, 9*(4), 361–374.

Frank, B., Delano, D., & Caniglia, B. S. (2017). Urban systems: A socio-ecological system perspective. *Sociol. Int. J, 1*(1), 1–8.

Franklin, J., Serra-Diaz, J. M., Syphard, A. D., & Regan, H. M. (2016). Global change and terrestrial plant community dynamics. *Proceedings of the National Academy of Sciences, 113*(14), 3725–3734.

Garzon, M. B., Blazek, R., Neteler, M., De Dios, R. S., Ollero, H. S., & Furlanello, C. (2006). Predicting habitat suitability with machine learning models: The potential area of Pinus sylvestris L. in the Iberian Peninsula. *Ecological Modelling, 197*(3–4), 383–393.

Gebbert, S., & Pebesma, E. (2014). A temporal GIS for field based environmental modeling. *Environmental Modelling & Software, 53*, 1–12.

Gohari, A., Mirchi, A., & Madani, K. (2017). System dynamics evaluation of climate change adaptation strategies for water resources management in central Iran. *Water Resources Management, 31*, 1413–1434.

Gomez, A., Diez, G., Salazar, A., & Diaz, A. (2016, December). Animal identification in low quality camera-trap images using very deep convolutional neural networks and confidence thresholds. In *Advances in Visual Computing: 12th International Symposium, ISVC 2016, Las Vegas, NV, USA, December 12-14, 2016, Proceedings, Part I* (pp. 747–756). Cham: Springer International Publishing.

Gosal, A. S., Geijzendorffer, I. R., Václavík, T., Poulin, B., & Ziv, G. (2019). Using social media, machine learning and natural language processing to map multiple recreational beneficiaries. *Ecosystem Services, 38*, 100958.

Green, A. G., Abdulai, A. R., Duncan, E., Glaros, A., Campbell, M., Newell, R., ... & Fraser, E. D. (2021). A scoping review of the digital agricultural revolution and ecosystem services: implications for Canadian policy and research agendas. *Facets, 6*(1), 1955–1985.

Gudivada, V., Apon, A., & Ding, J. (2017). Data quality considerations for big data and machine learning: Going beyond data cleaning and transformations. *International Journal on Advances in Software, 10*(1), 1–20.

Gulshad, K., Wang, Y., Li, N., Wang, J., & Yu, Q. (2022). Likelihood of Transformation to Green Infrastructure Using Ensemble Machine Learning Techniques in Jinan. China. *Land, 11*(3), 317.

Harvey, A. S. (1993). Guidelines for time use data collection. *Social Indicators Research, 30*, 197–228.

He, B. J., Wang, J., Zhu, J., & Qi, J. (2022). Beating the urban heat: Situation, background, impacts and the way forward in China. *Renewable and Sustainable Energy Reviews, 161,* 112350.

Hernandez-Santin, C., Amati, M., Bekessy, S., & Desha, C. (2023). Integrating biodiversity as a non-human stakeholder within urban development. *Landscape and Urban Planning, 232,* 104678.

Heymans, A., Breadsell, J., Morrison, G. M., Byrne, J. J., & Eon, C. (2019). Ecological urban planning and design: A systematic literature review. *Sustainability, 11*(13), 3723.

Hidayat, A. A., Cenggoro, T. W., & Pardamean, B. (2021). Convolutional neural networks for scops owl sound classification. *Procedia Computer Science, 179,* 81–87.

Himanen, L., Geurts, A., Foster, A. S., & Rinke, P. (2019). Data-driven materials science: Status, challenges, and perspectives. *Advanced Science, 6*(21), 1900808.

Hira, Z. M., & Gillies, D. F. (2015). A review of feature selection and feature extraction methods applied on microarray data. *Advances in Bioinformatics, 2015.*

Hohman, F., Park, H., Robinson, C., & Chau, D. H. P. (2019). Summit: Scaling deep learning interpretability by visualizing activation and attribution summarizations. *IEEE Transactions on Visualization and Computer Graphics, 26*(1), 1096–1106.

Huang, X., Wang, Y., Li, J., Chang, X., Cao, Y., Xie, J., & Gong, J. (2020). High-resolution urban land-cover mapping and landscape analysis of the 42 major cities in China using ZY-3 satellite images. *Science Bulletin, 65*(12), 1039–1048.

Imhoff, M. L., Zhang, P., Wolfe, R. E., & Bounoua, L. (2010). Remote sensing of the urban heat island effect across biomes in the continental USA. *Remote sensing of environment, 114*(3), 504–513.

Janevic, M. R., Mathur, V. A., Booker, S. Q., Morais, C., Meints, S. M., Yeager, K. A., & Meghani, S. H. (2022). Making pain research more inclusive: Why and how. *The Journal of Pain, 23*(5), 707–728.

Janizadeh, S., Pal, S. C., Saha, A., Chowdhuri, I., Ahmadi, K., Mirzaei, S., … & Tiefenbacher, J. P. (2021). Mapping the spatial and temporal variability of flood hazard affected by climate and land-use changes in the future. *Journal of Environmental Management, 298,* 113551.

Kesavan, R., Muthian, M., Sudalaimuthu, K., Sundarsingh, S., & Krishnan, S. (2021). ARIMA modeling for forecasting land surface temperature and determination of urban heat island using remote sensing techniques for Chennai city, India. *Arabian Journal of Geosciences, 14*(11), 1016.

Khalil, U., Aslam, B., Azam, U., & Khalid, H. M. D. (2021). Time series analysis of land surface temperature and drivers of urban heat island effect based on remotely sensed data to develop a prediction model. *Applied Artificial Intelligence, 35*(15), 1803–1828.

Kim, D., Kang, Y., Park, Y., Kim, N., & Lee, J. (2020). Understanding tourists' urban images with geotagged photos using convolutional neural networks. *Spatial Information Research, 28,* 241–255.

Kingsland, S. E. (2019). Urban Ecological Science in America. *Science for the sustainable city: Empirical insights from the Baltimore school of urban ecology, 24.*

Klein, L. J., Marianno, F. J., Albrecht, C. M., Freitag, M., Lu, S., Hinds, N., … & Hamann, H. F. (2015, October). PAIRS: A scalable geo-spatial data analytics platform. In *2015 IEEE International Conference on Big Data (Big Data)* (pp. 1290–1298). IEEE.

Klemas, V. (2011). Remote sensing techniques for studying coastal ecosystems: An overview. *Journal of Coastal Research, 27*(1), 2–17.

Koh, Y. F., Loc, H. H., & Park, E. (2022). Towards a "City in nature": Evaluating the cultural ecosystem services approach using online public participation GIS to support urban green space management. *Sustainability, 14*(3), 1499.

Labenski, P., Ewald, M., Schmidtlein, S., & Fassnacht, F. E. (2022). Classifying surface fuel types based on forest stand photographs and satellite time series using deep learning. *International Journal of Applied Earth Observation and Geoinformation, 109*, 102799.

Labib, S. M. (2019). Investigation of the likelihood of green infrastructure (GI) enhancement along linear waterways or on derelict sites (DS) using machine learning. *Environmental Modelling & Software, 118*, 146–165.

Lausch, A., Erasmi, S., King, D. J., Magdon, P., & Heurich, M. (2017). Understanding forest health with remote sensing-part II—A review of approaches and data models. *Remote Sensing, 9*(2), 129.

Leal Filho, W., Barbir, J., Sima, M., Kalbus, A., Nagy, G. J., Paletta, A., ... & Bonoli, A. (2020). Reviewing the role of ecosystems services in the sustainability of the urban environment: A multi-country analysis. *Journal of Cleaner Production, 262*, 121338.

Lee, H. C., & Chang, C. T. (2018). Comparative analysis of MCDM methods for ranking renewable energy sources in Taiwan. *Renewable and Sustainable Energy Reviews, 92*, 883–896.

Lee, K. A., Lee, J. R., & Bell, P. (2020). A review of Citizen Science within the Earth Sciences: Potential benefits and obstacles. *Proceedings of the Geologists' Association, 131*(6), 605–617.

Li, P., Xu, T., Wei, S., & Wang, Z. H. (2022). Multi-objective optimization of urban environmental system design using machine learning. *Computers, Environment and Urban Systems, 94*, 101796.

Linkov, I., Satterstrom, F. K., Kiker, G., Batchelor, C., Bridges, T., & Ferguson, E. (2006). From comparative risk assessment to multi-criteria decision analysis and adaptive management: Recent developments and applications. *Environment International, 32*(8), 1072–1093.

Liu, D. (2022). Application of Modern Urban Landscape Design Based on Machine Learning Model to Generate Plant Landscaping. *Scientific Programming, 2022*.

Lu, Y., Yang, J., Peng, M., Li, T., Wen, D., & Huang, X. (2022). Monitoring ecosystem services in the Guangdong-Hong Kong-Macao Greater Bay Area based on multi-temporal deep learning. *Science of the Total Environment, 822*, 153662.

Ma, J., Ding, Y., Cheng, J. C., Jiang, F., Tan, Y., Gan, V. J., & Wan, Z. (2020). Identification of high impact factors of air quality on a national scale using big data and machine learning techniques. *Journal of Cleaner Production, 244*, 118955.

Madzokere, E. T., Hallgren, W., Sahin, O., Webster, J. A., Webb, C. E., Mackey, B., & Herrero, L. J. (2020). Integrating statistical and mechanistic approaches with biotic and environmental variables improves model predictions of the impact of climate and land-use changes on future mosquito-vector abundance, diversity and distributions in Australia. *Parasites & Vectors, 13*, 1–13.

Maes, M. J., Jones, K. E., Toledano, M. B., & Milligan, B. (2019). Mapping synergies and trade-offs between urban ecosystems and the sustainable development goals. *Environmental science & policy, 93*, 181–188.

Marando, F., Heris, M. P., Zulian, G., Udías, A., Mentaschi, L., Chrysoulakis, N., ... & Maes, J. (2022). Urban heat island mitigation by green infrastructure in European Functional Urban Areas. *Sustainable Cities and Society, 77*, 103564.

Marselle, M. R., Lindley, S. J., Cook, P. A., & Bonn, A. (2021). Biodiversity and health in the urban environment. *Current Environmental Health Reports, 8*(2), 146–156.

Mauree, D., Naboni, E., Coccolo, S., Perera, A. T. D., Nik, V. M., & Scartezzini, J. L. (2019). A review of assessment methods for the urban environment and its energy sustainability to guarantee climate adaptation of future cities. *Renewable and Sustainable Energy Reviews, 112*, 733–746.

Maurya, K., Mahajan, S., & Chaube, N. (2021). Remote sensing techniques: mapping and monitoring of mangrove ecosystem—a review. *Complex & Intelligent Systems, 7*, 2797–2818.

McIntyre, N. E., Knowles-Yánez, K., & Hope, D. (2008). Urban ecology as an interdisciplinary field: differences in the use of "urban" between the social and natural sciences. *Urban Ecology: An International Perspective on the Interaction Between Humans and Nature*, 49–65.

McKay, A. J., & Johnson, C. J. (2017). Identifying effective and sustainable measures for community-based environmental monitoring. *Environmental Management, 60*, 484–495.

Meerow, S. (2019). A green infrastructure spatial planning model for evaluating ecosystem service tradeoffs and synergies across three coastal megacities. *Environmental Research Letters, 14*(12), 125011.

Mehrabi, N., Morstatter, F., Saxena, N., Lerman, K., & Galstyan, A. (2021). A survey on bias and fairness in machine learning. *ACM Computing Surveys (CSUR), 54*(6), 1–35.

Mosavi, A., Ozturk, P., & Chau, K. W. (2018). Flood prediction using machine learning models: Literature review. *Water, 10*(11), 1536.

Munawar, H. S., Hammad, A. W., & Waller, S. T. (2021). A review on flood management technologies related to image processing and machine learning. *Automation in Construction, 132*, 103916.

Nizamani, M. M., Cubino, J. P., Harris, A. J., Guo, L. Y., & Wang, H. F. (2023). Spatial patterns and drivers of plant diversity in the tropical city of Sanya, China. *Urban Forestry & Urban Greening, 79*, 127818.

Nizamani, M. M., Harris, A. J., Cheng, X. L., Zhu, Z. X., Jim, C. Y., & Wang, H. F. (2021). Positive relationships among aboveground biomass, tree species diversity, and urban greening management in tropical coastal city of Haikou. *Ecology and Evolution, 11*(17), 12204–12219.

O'connor, S., Hanlon, P., O'donnell, C. A., Garcia, S., Glanville, J., & Mair, F. S. (2016). Understanding factors affecting patient and public engagement and recruitment to digital health interventions: A systematic review of qualitative studies. *BMC medical informatics and decision making, 16*, 1–15.

Pachouly, J., Ahirrao, S., Kotecha, K., Selvachandran, G., & Abraham, A. (2022). A systematic literature review on software defect prediction using artificial intelligence: Datasets, Data Validation Methods, Approaches, and Tools. *Engineering Applications of Artificial Intelligence, 111*, 104773.

Plumb, G., Al-Shedivat, M., Cabrera, Á. A., Perer, A., Xing, E., & Talwalkar, A. (2020). Regularizing black-box models for improved interpretability. *Advances in Neural Information Processing Systems, 33*, 10526–10536.

Polk, M. (2015). Transdisciplinary co-production: Designing and testing a transdisciplinary research framework for societal problem solving. *Futures, 65*, 110–122.

Pouya, S., & Aghlmand, M. (2022). Evaluation of urban green space per capita with new remote sensing and geographic information system techniques and the importance of urban green space during the COVID-19 pandemic. *Environmental Monitoring and Assessment, 194*(9), 633.

Quackenbush, J. (2002). Microarray data normalization and transformation. *Nature Genetics, 32*(4), 496–501.

Rahman, M., Chen, N., Islam, M. M., Mahmud, G. I., Pourghasemi, H. R., Alam, M., … & Dewan, A. (2021). Development of flood hazard map and emergency relief operation system using hydrodynamic modeling and machine learning algorithm. *Journal of Cleaner Production, 311*, 127594.

Recio-García, J. A., Díaz-Agudo, B., & Pino-Castilla, V. (2020). CBR-LIME: A case-based reasoning approach to provide specific local interpretable model-agnostic explanations. In *Case-Based Reasoning Research and Development: 28th International Conference, ICCBR 2020, Salamanca, Spain, June 8–12, 2020, Proceedings 28* (pp. 179–194). Springer International Publishing.

Reif, M. K., & Theel, H. J. (2017). Remote sensing for restoration ecology: Application for restoring degraded, damaged, transformed, or destroyed ecosystems. *Integrated Environmental Assessment and Management*, 13(4), 614–630.

Rivasplata, C. R. (2013). Congestion pricing for Latin America: Prospects and constraints. *Research in Transportation Economics*, 40(1), 56–65.

Rolnick, D., Donti, P. L., Kaack, L. H., Kochanski, K., Lacoste, A., Sankaran, K., ... & Bengio, Y. (2022). Tackling climate change with machine learning. *ACM Computing Surveys (CSUR)*, 55(2), 1–96.

Samal, K. K. R., Panda, A. K., Babu, K. S., & Das, S. K. (2021). An improved pollution forecasting model with meteorological impact using multiple imputation and fine-tuning approach. *Sustainable Cities and Society*, 70, 102923.

Santos, R. N., Yamouni, S., Albiero, B., Vicente, R., A Silva, J., FB Souza, T., ... & Lei, Z. (2021). Gradient boosting and Shapley additive explanations for fraud detection in electricity distribution grids. *International Transactions on Electrical Energy Systems*, 31(9), e13046.

Sarker, I. H. (2021). Machine learning: Algorithms, real-world applications and research directions. *SN Computer Science*, 2(3), 160.

Schmeller, D. S., Böhm, M., Arvanitidis, C., Barber-Meyer, S., Brummitt, N., Chandler, M., ... & Belnap, J. (2017). Building capacity in biodiversity monitoring at the global scale. *Biodiversity and conservation*, 26, 2765–2790.

Schuwirth, N., Borgwardt, F., Domisch, S., Friedrichs, M., Kattwinkel, M., Kneis, D., ... & Vermeiren, P. (2019). How to make ecological models useful for environmental management. *Ecological Modelling*, 411, 108784.

Song, X. P., Richards, D. R., & Tan, P. Y. (2020). Using social media user attributes to understand human–environment interactions at urban parks. *Scientific Reports*, 10(1), 1–11.

Tambo, E., Djuikoue, I. C., Tazemda, G. K., Fotsing, M. F., & Zhou, X. N. (2021). Early stage risk communication and community engagement (RCCE) strategies and measures against the coronavirus disease 2019 (COVID-19) pandemic crisis. *Global Health Journal*, 5(1), 44–50.

Tan, C. N. L. (2016). Enhancing knowledge sharing and research collaboration among academics: the role of knowledge management. *Higher Education*, 71, 525–556.

Tehrany, M. S., Jones, S., Shabani, F., Martínez-Álvarez, F., & Tien Bui, D. (2019). A novel ensemble modeling approach for the spatial prediction of tropical forest fire susceptibility using LogitBoost machine learning classifier and multi-source geospatial data. *Theoretical and Applied Climatology*, 137, 637–653.

Tekouabou, S. C. K., Diop, E. B., Azmi, R., Jaligot, R., & Chenal, J. (2022). Reviewing the application of machine learning methods to model urban form indicators in planning decision support systems: Potential, issues and challenges. *Journal of King Saud University-Computer and Information Sciences*, 34(8), 5943–5967.

Teutschbein, C., & Seibert, J. (2012). Bias correction of regional climate model simulations for hydrological climate-change impact studies: Review and evaluation of different methods. *Journal of Hydrology*, 456, 12–29.

Toivonen, T., Heikinheimo, V., Fink, C., Hausmann, A., Hiippala, T., Järv, O., ... & Di Minin, E. (2019). Social media data for conservation science: A methodological overview. *Biological Conservation*, 233, 298–315.

Trivedi, S., Aloufi, A. A., Ansari, A. A., & Ghosh, S. K. (2016). Role of DNA barcoding in marine biodiversity assessment and conservation: An update. *Saudi Journal of Biological Sciences*, 23(2), 161–171.

Ullah, Z., Al-Turjman, F., Mostarda, L., & Gagliardi, R. (2020). Applications of artificial intelligence and machine learning in smart cities. *Computer Communications*, 154, 313–323.

Van Herzele, A., & Wiedemann, T. (2003). A monitoring tool for the provision of accessible and attractive urban green spaces. *Landscape and Urban Planning*, 63(2), 109–126.

Vetrò, A., Torchiano, M., & Mecati, M. (2021). A data quality approach to the identification of discrimination risk in automated decision making systems. *Government Information Quarterly, 38*(4), 101619.

Voelkel, J., Hellman, D., Sakuma, R., & Shandas, V. (2018). Assessing vulnerability to urban heat: A study of disproportionate heat exposure and access to refuge by socio-demographic status in Portland, Oregon. *International Journal of Environmental Research and Public Health, 15*(4), 640.

Wang, C., Yu, Q., Law, K. H., McKenna, F., Stella, X. Y., Taciroglu, E., ... & Cetiner, B. (2021). Machine learning-based regional scale intelligent modeling of building information for natural hazard risk management. *Automation in Construction, 122*, 103474.

Wang, H. F., Cheng, X. L., Nizamani, M. M., Balfour, K., Da, L., Zhu, Z. X., & Qureshi, S. (2020). An Integrated approach to study spatial patterns and drivers of land cover within urban functional units: A multi-city comparative study in China. *Remote Sensing, 12*(14), 2201.

Wang, J., Liu, J., Wang, H., & Mei, C. (2020). Approaches to multi-objective optimization and assessment of green infrastructure and their multi-functional effectiveness: A review. *Water, 12*(10), 2714.

Wang, Shiyong, Khan, Asad, Lin, Ying, Jiang, Zhuo, Tang, Hao, Alomar, Suliman Yousef, Sanaullah, Muhammad, & Bhatti, Uzair Aslam (2023). Deep reinforcement learning enables adaptive-image augmentation for automated optical inspection of plant rust. Frontiers in Plant Science, 14. 10.3389/fpls.2023.1142957.

Watson, R., Baste, I., Larigauderie, A., Leadley, P., Pascual, U., Baptiste, B., ... & Mooney, H. (2019). Summary for policymakers of the global assessment report on biodiversity and ecosystem services of the Intergovernmental Science-Policy Platform on Biodiversity and Ecosystem Services. *IPBES Secretariat: Bonn, Germany*, 22–47.

Wu, A. N., & Biljecki, F. (2021). Roofpedia: Automatic mapping of green and solar roofs for an open roofscape registry and evaluation of urban sustainability. *Landscape and Urban Planning, 214*, 104167.

Wu, J. (2014). Urban ecology and sustainability: The state-of-the-science and future directions. *Landscape and Urban Planning, 125*, 209–221.

Xia, Y., Yabuki, N., & Fukuda, T. (2021). Development of a system for assessing the quality of urban street-level greenery using street view images and deep learning. *Urban Forestry & Urban Greening, 59*, 126995.

Xiao, S., Dong, H., Geng, Y., Tian, X., Liu, C., & Li, H. (2020). Policy impacts on Municipal Solid Waste management in Shanghai: A system dynamics model analysis. *Journal of Cleaner Production, 262*, 121366.

Xie, L., Feng, X., Zhang, C., Dong, Y., Huang, J., & Liu, K. (2022). Identification of urban functional areas based on the multimodal deep learning fusion of high-resolution remote sensing images and social perception data. *Buildings, 12*(5), 556.

Ye, Y., Richards, D., Lu, Y., Song, X., Zhuang, Y., Zeng, W., & Zhong, T. (2019b). Measuring daily accessed street greenery: A human-scale approach for informing better urban planning practices. *Landscape and Urban Planning, 191*, 103434.

Ye, Y., Zeng, W., Shen, Q., Zhang, X., & Lu, Y. (2019a). The visual quality of streets: A human-centred continuous measurement based on machine learning algorithms and street view images. *Environment and Planning B: Urban Analytics and City Science, 46*(8), 1439–1457.

Yigitcanlar, T., Desouza, K. C., Butler, L., & Roozkhosh, F. (2020). Contributions and risks of artificial intelligence (AI) in building smarter cities: Insights from a systematic review of the literature. *Energies, 13*(6), 1473.

Yousefi, S., Avand, M., Yariyan, P., Goujani, H. J., Costache, R., Tavangar, S., & Tiefenbacher, J. P. (2021). Identification of the most suitable afforestation sites by Juniperus excels specie using machine learning models: Firuzkuh semi-arid region, Iran. *Ecological Informatics, 65*, 101427.

Yuan, B., & Li, J. (2019). The policy effect of the general data protection regulation (GDPR) on the digital public health sector in the european union: An empirical investigation. *International Journal of Environmental Research and Public Health, 16*(6), 1070.

Yuan, F. (2008). Land-cover change and environmental impact analysis in the Greater Mankato area of Minnesota using remote sensing and GIS modelling. *International Journal of Remote Sensing, 29*(4), 1169–1184.

Yuan, Q., Shen, H., Li, T., Li, Z., Li, S., Jiang, Y., ... & Zhang, L. (2020). Deep learning in environmental remote sensing: Achievements and challenges. *Remote Sensing of Environment, 241*, 111716.

Zhai, Z., Martínez, J. F., Beltran, V., & Martínez, N. L. (2020). Decision support systems for agriculture 4.0: Survey and challenges. *Computers and Electronics in Agriculture, 170*, 105256.

Zhang, H. L., Cubino, J. P., Nizamani, M. M., Harris, A. J., Cheng, X. L., Da, L., ... & Wang, H. F. (2022). Wealth and land use drive the distribution of urban green space in the tropical coastal city of Haikou, China. *Urban Forestry & Urban Greening, 71*, 127554.

Zhang, Q., Wu, S., Wang, X., Sun, B., & Liu, H. (2020). A PM2. 5 concentration prediction model based on multi-task deep learning for intensive air quality monitoring stations. *Journal of Cleaner Production, 275*, 122722.

Zhong, S., Zhang, K., Bagheri, M., Burken, J. G., Gu, A., Li, B., ... & Zhang, H. (2021). Machine learning: New ideas and tools in environmental science and engineering. *Environmental Science & Technology, 55*(19), 12741–12754.

Application of Machine Learning in Urban Land Use

Haili Zhang and Qin Zhou

Hainan Key Laboratory for Sustainable Utilization of Tropical Bioresources, Hainan University, Haikou, China

11.1 INTRODUCTION

11.1.1 Briefly Introduce the Concept of Machine Learning and Urban Land Use

As we witness unprecedented urbanization across the globe, urban planners and policymakers face the ever-growing challenge of creating sustainable and resilient cities (He et al., 2016). The efficient allocation and management of land resources play a crucial role in this endeavor. Urban land use encompasses various aspects of urban planning, including zoning, transportation, housing, and public amenities, all of which significantly impact the quality of life for city dwellers. Traditional methods of urban land use planning, such as static data analysis and rule-based models, often fall short in addressing the complexity and dynamism of modern urban environments. Consequently, there is an increasing need for innovative solutions that can tackle these challenges and ensure the sustainable growth of our cities. At the same time, the world of technology has made remarkable strides in recent years, with artificial intelligence (AI) and machine learning (ML) emerging as transformative forces across diverse domains (Chaturvedi et al., 2021). Machine learning, a subfield of AI, involves the development of algorithms that can learn from data and improve their performance over time without explicit programming. These algorithms have the potential to revolutionize various aspects of urban land use by processing vast amounts of data, identifying patterns, making predictions, and adapting to new information (Mao et al., 2020).

This introduction aims to provide a brief overview of the concept of machine learning and urban land use, highlighting their synergistic potential in promoting sustainable urban development. Urban land use is a multifaceted domain that involves the allocation, regulation, and management of land resources within a city. Several key factors must be considered to ensure that urban areas remain functional, livable, and environmentally sustainable. These factors include the following:

DOI: 10.1201/9781032646268-11

1. Population Growth: Rapid population growth in urban areas demands the efficient allocation of land for housing, amenities, and public services (Meyer and Turner, 1992).

2. Economic Development: A city's economic prosperity hinges on the effective utilization of land resources for commercial, industrial, and infrastructural purposes (Deng et al., 2010).

3. Transportation Networks: Efficient and sustainable transportation systems are essential for connecting different parts of a city and reducing congestion, pollution, and greenhouse gas emissions (Okeke et al., 2021).

4. Environmental Impacts: Sustainable urban development requires the careful assessment of environmental impacts associated with land use changes, such as air quality, water resources, and ecosystems (Augustijn-Beckers et al., 2011).
   Machine Learning: A Powerful Tool for Urban Land Use

Machine learning offers a range of capabilities that can significantly enhance various aspects of urban land use planning and management (Hagenauer et al., 2019). These capabilities include the following:

1. Large-Scale Data Processing: ML algorithms can process vast amounts of data from diverse sources, such as satellite imagery, GIS, census data, and social media. This enables planners to make more informed decisions based on accurate and up-to-date information (Cao et al., 2019).

2. Pattern Recognition and Prediction: ML models can identify patterns and trends in urban land use data, allowing planners to anticipate future changes and develop proactive strategies.

3. Adaptability: ML algorithms can learn from new data and adapt to changing conditions, making them particularly suited to the dynamic nature of urban environments.

4. Automation: ML can automate complex and time-consuming tasks, such as land use classification and transportation network analysis, streamlining the urban planning process and increasing efficiency.

The integration of machine learning in urban land use planning holds immense potential for sustainable urban development. Some key applications include the following:

1. Land Use Classification and Monitoring: ML algorithms can analyze satellite and aerial imagery to accurately classify land use types and monitor changes over time, enabling planners to assess the effectiveness of land use policies and make data-driven decisions.

2. Urban Growth Modeling and Prediction: By analyzing historical and real-time data, ML-based models can predict future land use changes and inform the development of strategic growth plans, infrastructure investments, and zoning regulations that support sustainable urban development (Zhang et al., 2018; Hu et al., 2007).

3. Transport Planning and Optimization: ML algorithms can be used to analyze traffic patterns, public transit usage, and other transportation-related data to optimize transportation networks and reduce congestion. This information can be used to design more efficient and sustainable transport systems, encouraging alternative modes of transport and reducing greenhouse gas emissions.

4. Environmental Impact Assessment: ML can help quantify and predict the impacts of urban growth on air quality, water resources, and ecosystems. By integrating these insights into the planning process, decision makers can develop land use strategies that minimize negative environmental effects and promote the long-term health of urban environments (Foley et al., 2005).

Despite these challenges, the potential benefits of machine learning in urban land use planning are immense, and the opportunities for innovation and growth are vast. By leveraging the power of machine learning, urban planners and policymakers can make more informed decisions, develop proactive strategies, and ultimately create more sustainable, resilient, and livable cities. In conclusion, the synergistic intersection of machine learning and urban land use presents a promising avenue for sustainable urban development. As our cities continue to grow and evolve, embracing innovative solutions like machine learning will be crucial to ensuring the efficient allocation and management of land resources. By understanding the potential applications, benefits, and challenges associated with machine learning in urban land use planning, we can work towards creating cities that are not only economically prosperous but also environmentally sustainable and socially equitable.

11.1.2 Explain the Significance of Integrating Machine Learning in Urban Planning and Management

The rapid urbanization of the twenty-first century presents both opportunities and challenges for cities worldwide. With over 68% of the global population projected to live in urban areas by 2050, urban planners and managers face increasing pressure to build and maintain resilient, sustainable, and efficient cities that can accommodate this growth (United Nations, 2018). As urban environments become more complex, it is essential to explore innovative approaches and tools that can support data-driven decision making, enhance efficiency, and promote sustainable practices in urban planning and management. One such promising technology is machine learning (ML), an integral component of artificial intelligence (AI), which has demonstrated great potential to revolutionize various aspects of urban life (Hain et al., 2023). Machine learning is a computational approach that enables computers to learn from data, identify patterns, and make predictions or decisions without explicit programming. In recent years, the increased availability of vast data sets, advancements in computing power, and the development of sophisticated algorithms have propelled ML to the forefront of technology innovation. As a result, ML is being leveraged across a wide range of applications, from healthcare (Kanevsky et al., 2016) and finance to transportation and agriculture (Sharma et al., 2020). Integrating machine learning into urban planning and management holds significant promise for addressing the complex challenges posed by urbanization. By harnessing the power of ML, planners and managers can gain valuable insights from data, optimize urban infrastructure, and improve overall livability for the growing urban population (Milusheva et al., 2021). This essay will delve into the significance of integrating machine learning in urban planning and management, exploring its potential applications and benefits, as well as the associated ethical considerations and potential pitfalls.

First, we will examine how machine learning can be used to analyze and interpret the vast amounts of data generated by urban environments. This includes data from sensors and Internet of Things (IoT) devices, social media, satellite imagery, and other sources. By processing and analyzing this data, ML algorithms can uncover patterns and trends that would be difficult, if not impossible, for humans to discern, providing valuable insights for urban planning and management. Next, we will explore the potential applications of machine learning in various urban planning and management domains. These include transportation and traffic management, energy and resource optimization, environmental monitoring and sustainability, public safety and security, and land use planning. We will discuss how ML can be harnessed to optimize urban infrastructure, enhance decision-making processes, and promote more sustainable practices in these domains. In addition, we will address the ethical considerations and potential pitfalls associated with integrating machine learning in urban planning and management. This includes issues related to privacy and data security, algorithmic bias and fairness, and the potential displacement of human expertise. We will consider how these challenges can be mitigated through responsible and transparent practices, as well as the development of policies and guidelines to govern the use of ML in urban contexts. Finally, we will conclude with a discussion of the future prospects of integrating machine learning in urban planning and management. As the technology continues to advance and evolve, it is essential for urban planners and managers to stay informed about the latest developments and explore new ways to harness the power of ML for the betterment of cities and their inhabitants. By embracing the potential of machine learning, we can move towards a more sustainable, resilient, and efficient urban future.

"Application of Machine Learning in Urban Land Use" is a comprehensive guide that explores the integration of ML techniques in urban land use planning and management. The book aims to provide a thorough understanding of the potential applications, challenges, and benefits of using machine learning in land use analysis, decision making, and policy implementation. It is structured into several chapters, each focusing on a specific aspect of machine learning in urban land use, as well as case studies that demonstrate real-world applications and successes.

11.2 BACKGROUND: UNDERSTANDING URBAN LAND USE AND MACHINE LEARNING

11.2.1 Discuss the Basics of Urban Land Use, Including its Importance, Challenges, and Traditional Methods Used in Planning

Urban land use is a critical aspect of urban planning and development, as it determines the allocation of land resources within a city for various purposes, such as residential, commercial, industrial, recreational, and transportation (Ma and Zhou, 2018; Xu et al., 2018; Zhang et al., 2021). The efficient and sustainable management of urban land use is crucial to promoting economic growth, social equity, and environmental protection. This discussion aims to provide an overview of the basics of urban land use, highlighting its importance, challenges, and traditional methods used in planning. Urban land use plays a vital role in promoting economic development by ensuring that land resources are optimally allocated for various economic activities, such as commercial and industrial development (Deng et al., 2010; He et al., 2014; Seto et al., 2011; Ding et al., 2011). A well-planned urban land use pattern can attract investments, generate employment opportunities, and contribute to the overall economic growth of a city. Urban land use planning is essential for addressing social equity concerns by ensuring that all residents have access to adequate housing, education, healthcare, and other essential services (Soltani et al., 2019; Kelobonye et al., 2019; Becker et al., 2019; Ullah et al., 2016). A well-balanced land use pattern can prevent the concentration of poverty and promote social integration within a city. Sustainable urban land use planning is necessary for minimizing the environmental impacts of urbanization, such as air pollution, water pollution, and loss of natural habitats (Thinh et al., 2002; Pauleit et al., 2005; Pauleit et al., 2000). By promoting compact urban development, preserving open spaces, and encouraging the use of environmentally friendly transportation modes, urban land use planning can contribute to the overall environmental sustainability of a city. The rapid urbanization experienced by cities worldwide has placed immense pressure on urban land resources, leading to challenges such as urban sprawl, traffic congestion, inadequate infrastructure, and loss of agricultural land (Yin et al., 2011; Chen et al., 2007; Yu et al., 2019; Rukmana et al., 2018). Urban planners and policymakers must grapple with these issues to ensure the sustainable management of urban land use. Urban land use planning often involves balancing competing demands for land resources, such as the need for housing, commercial development, and environmental conservation. Addressing these conflicting demands requires a comprehensive understanding of the social, economic, and environmental implications of various land use patterns.Land tenure and property rights are critical factors that influence urban land use patterns. In many cities, particularly in developing countries, insecure land tenure and unclear property rights can hinder the effective implementation of urban land use policies and lead to informal settlements and land disputes.

Land use zoning is a widely used planning tool that involves dividing a city into various zones, each with a specific set of allowable land uses and development regulations. Zoning helps to ensure the orderly development of a city by separating incompatible land uses, such as residential and industrial areas, and by controlling the density and scale of development (Talen, 2005; Rossi-Hansberg et al., 2004; Geneletti et al., 2013; Qian et al., 2010; McMillen et al., 1999). Master planning is a long-term, comprehensive planning approach that involves developing a vision and strategic framework for the future growth and development of a city. Master plans typically include detailed land use plans, transportation plans, infrastructure plans, and other elements that guide urban development over a specified time horizon (Waddell, 2002; Zhu et al., 2004). Site-specific planning involves the detailed planning and design of individual development projects within a city, taking into consideration the unique characteristics and constraints of each site. Site-specific planning typically involves the preparation of site plans, architectural drawings, and other documents that guide the development process. Public participation and consultation are essential components of the urban land use planning process, as they enable planners and policymakers to understand the needs and preferences of local communities and to involve stakeholders in decision making. Public consultation can take various forms, such as community meetings, surveys, and focus groups.

Understanding the basics of urban land use is crucial for urban planners, policy-makers, and other stakeholders involved in shaping the urban environment. The effective management of urban land use is essential for promoting economic development, social equity, and environmental sustainability in cities (Arefi, 2004; Liu et al., 2014). However, urban planners face several challenges, including rapid urbanization, conflicting land use demands, and land tenure and property rights issues. Traditional methods in urban land use planning, such as land use zoning, master planning, site-specific planning, and public participation and consultation, have been widely used to address these challenges and guide the orderly development of cities. However, as urban environments become increasingly complex, there is a growing need for innovative approaches and tools that can support more efficient, data-driven, and sustainable urban land use planning and management. Recent advancements in technologies, such as machine learning and artificial intelligence, offer promising opportunities to revolutionize urban land use planning by harnessing the power of data and analytics (Helber et al., 2019; Parente et al., 2019). By integrating these technologies into the planning process, urban planners can gain valuable insights, optimize land use patterns, and address the complex challenges posed by urbanization more effectively. In conclusion, urban land use planning is a critical aspect of sustainable urban development, and understanding its fundamentals is essential for addressing the diverse challenges faced by cities worldwide. By combining traditional planning methods with innovative technologies and approaches, urban planners can create more resilient, inclusive, and sustainable urban environments for future generations.

11.2.2 Introduce Machine Learning and Its Key Concepts, Including Algorithms, Training, and Validation

Machine learning (ML) is a subfield of artificial intelligence (AI) that focuses on the development of algorithms and techniques that enable computers to learn from data, identify patterns, and make predictions or decisions without explicit programming (Carleo et al., 2019; Bell et al., 2022). ML has become increasingly popular in recent years, driven by advancements in computing power, the availability of large data sets, and the development of sophisticated algorithms. This introduction aims to provide an overview of the key concepts and principles of machine learning, including algorithms, training, and validation.

Supervised learning is the most common form of machine learning, in which an algorithm is trained on a labeled data set, meaning the input data is accompanied by the correct output. The goal of supervised learning is for the algorithm to learn a mapping between the inputs and the outputs, which can then be used to make predictions on new, unseen data (Saravanan and Sujatha, 2018; Rashidi et al., 2021). Examples of supervised learning tasks include classification, in which an algorithm is trained to categorize data into distinct classes, and regression, in which an algorithm is trained to predict a continuous value.

Unsupervised learning is a type of machine learning where the algorithm is not provided with labeled data, and must instead discover patterns, relationships, or structures within the data on its own (Saravanan and Sujatha, 2018; Zaadnoordijk et al., 2022). Unsupervised learning is often used for tasks such as clustering, which involves grouping similar data points together, and dimensionality reduction, which involves reducing the number of variables in the data while preserving its essential structure.

Reinforcement learning is a type of machine learning in which an algorithm, called an agent, learns to make decisions by interacting with an environment and receiving feedback in the form of rewards or penalties. The goal of reinforcement learning is for the agent to learn a policy, which is a mapping from states to actions, that maximizes the cumulative reward over time. Reinforcement learning has been successfully applied to a variety of complex tasks, such as game playing, robotics, and autonomous vehicle control (Mahmud et al., 2018; Coronato et al., 2020).

Machine learning algorithms are the mathematical models and computational techniques used to learn from data and make predictions or decisions. There are numerous ML algorithms available, each with its own strengths and weaknesses, and the choice of algorithm depends on the specific problem and data set at hand (Mahesh, 2020; Alzubi et al., 2018). Some of the most widely used machine learning algorithms include linear regression, logistic regression, decision trees, support vector machines, neural networks, and deep learning.

Features are the variables or attributes used to represent data in machine learning algorithms. In many cases, the quality and representation of the features can have a significant impact on the performance of the algorithm. Feature engineering is the process of selecting, transforming, or creating new features from the raw data to improve the algorithm's ability to learn and make predictions. Techniques used in feature engineering include normalization, scaling, and the extraction of relevant information from text, images, or other complex data types.

Training and validation are essential steps in the machine learning process that involve using a data set to evaluate and refine the performance of an algorithm.

11.2.2.1 Training Data

Training data is the portion of the data set used to train a machine learning algorithm. The algorithm learns from the training data by adjusting its parameters in order to minimize the error between its predictions and the actual outputs. The process of training typically involves iteratively updating the algorithm's parameters, using techniques such as gradient descent, until a desired level of performance is achieved (Batista et al., 2004; Nasteski et al., 2017).

11.2.2.2 Validation Data

Validation data is the portion of the data set used to evaluate the performance of a machine learning algorithm during training. The validation data is not used to update the algorithm's parameters and is instead used to provide an unbiased estimate of the algorithm's performance on unseen data. Validation is essential for preventing overfitting, which occurs when an algorithm becomes too specialized to the training data and performs poorly on new, unseen data.

11.2.2.3 Cross-Validation

Cross-validation is a technique used to assess the performance of a machine learning algorithm more reliably by partitioning the data set into multiple smaller subsets, or folds. In a common method called k-fold cross-validation, the data set is divided into k equally sized folds. The algorithm is trained on k-1 folds and tested on the remaining fold, with this process repeated k times, with each fold being used as the validation set once. The performance of the algorithm is then averaged across the k iterations to provide a more robust estimate of its performance (Tougui et al., 2021; A. Ramezan et al., 2019).

Evaluation metrics are quantitative measures used to assess the performance of machine learning algorithms. The choice of evaluation metric depends on the specific problem and the objectives of the analysis. For example, in classification tasks, common evaluation metrics include accuracy, precision, recall, F1-score, and area under the receiver operating characteristic (ROC) curve. In regression tasks, common evaluation metrics include mean squared error (MSE), mean absolute error (MAE), and R-squared.

Hyperparameters are the parameters of a machine learning algorithm that are not learned from the data but are set by the user before training begins. Examples of hyperparameters include the learning rate, the number of layers in a neural network, and the depth of a decision tree. Hyperparameter tuning is the process of selecting the optimal values for these parameters to maximize the algorithm's performance. Techniques for hyperparameter tuning include grid search, random search, and Bayesian optimization.

Machine learning is a powerful and versatile tool that has the potential to transform various aspects of our lives, from healthcare and finance to transportation and urban planning. Understanding the key concepts and principles of ML, such as algorithms, training, and validation, is essential for harnessing its potential and applying it effectively to real-world problems. As the field continues to advance and evolve, it is crucial for practitioners, researchers, and policymakers to stay informed about the latest developments and explore new ways to leverage the power of ML for the betterment of society.

11.3 MACHINE LEARNING TECHNIQUES FOR URBAN LAND USE

11.3.1 Describe Various Machine Learning Techniques and Their Relevance to Urban Land Use Applications, Such as Classification, Regression, and Clustering Algorithms

Machine learning has become an indispensable tool for urban planners and researchers in recent years, as it allows for the analysis of complex urban systems and the development of data-driven solutions for land use management. This essay will describe various machine learning techniques, including classification, regression, and clustering algorithms, and their relevance to urban land use applications (Ahuja et al., 2020; Ray et al., 2019).

11.3.1.1 Classification Algorithms

Classification algorithms are supervised learning techniques that categorize input data into distinct classes or categories. They are often used to identify patterns in land use and to predict future land use changes. Some popular classification algorithms include the following:

a. Decision Trees: Decision trees are a hierarchical structure that recursively splits the input data into subsets based on the features' values. The goal is to minimize the impurity of each subset. In urban land use applications, decision trees can be used to classify land parcels based on features such as zoning, accessibility, and environmental constraints.

b. Support Vector Machines (SVMs): SVM is a powerful classification technique that aims to find the best hyperplane separating different classes. This method is particularly useful for urban land use applications when dealing with high-dimensional data, such as satellite imagery, to identify various land use classes, like residential, commercial, and industrial areas (Tang, 2013; Rodriguez-Galiano et al., 2015).

c. Random Forests: Random forests are an ensemble of decision trees that work together to improve classification accuracy. They can handle large data sets and reduce overfitting, making them suitable for land use classification tasks, such as predicting land conversion or identifying the most suitable locations for urban expansion.

11.3.1.2 Regression Algorithms

Regression algorithms are another category of supervised learning techniques that aim to predict a continuous output variable based on input features. These algorithms are relevant in urban land use applications for modeling and predicting land values, rent prices, and land use intensities. Some common regression algorithms are:

a. Linear Regression: Linear regression is a simple yet powerful technique that models the relationship between input features and a continuous output variable. In urban land use, linear regression can be used to predict land prices or rent based on features such as proximity to amenities, population density, and transportation access.

b. Ridge and Lasso Regression: These techniques are extensions of linear regression that incorporate regularization to prevent overfitting. They are useful in urban land use applications to select the most important features affecting land values or land use intensity (Muthukrishnan and Rohini, 2016; Yang et al., 2018).

c. Neural Networks: Neural networks are versatile machine learning models that can approximate complex relationships between input features and output variables. They can be used to model nonlinear relationships in urban land use, such as predicting land values or estimating the impact of land use policies on urban development.

11.3.1.3 Clustering Algorithms

Clustering algorithms are unsupervised learning techniques that group data points based on similarity. In urban land use applications, clustering can help identify patterns and trends in land use, detect anomalies, and discover similarities between urban areas. Some popular clustering algorithms include the following:

a. K-means: K-means is a simple and efficient clustering algorithm that aims to partition the data into K distinct clusters based on similarity. In urban land use, K-means can be used to identify homogeneous land use zones or group neighborhoods with similar land use characteristics.

b. DBSCAN: Density-based spatial clustering of applications with noise (DBSCAN) is a robust clustering algorithm that groups data points based on their density. This method is useful for detecting spatial patterns in urban land use, such as identifying areas with concentrated development or highlighting irregular land use patterns (Deng, 2020; Kumar et al., 2016).

c. Hierarchical Clustering: Hierarchical clustering is an algorithm that builds a tree-like structure to represent the nested grouping of data points based on similarity. In urban land use applications, hierarchical clustering can help uncover the hierarchical organization of urban areas or identify clusters of similar land use types (Nunez-Iglesias et al., 2013).

In conclusion, ML techniques, such as classification, regression, and clustering algorithms, play a significant role in understanding and managing urban land use. These methods provide valuable insights into patterns, trends, and relationships within urban systems, allowing for data-driven decision making in land use planning and policy development. Classification algorithms, including decision trees, support vector machines, and random forests, are crucial for identifying different land use types and predicting land use changes. These techniques help urban planners to allocate resources effectively and guide urban expansion in a sustainable manner. Regression algorithms, such as linear regression, ridge and lasso regression, and neural networks, are essential for predicting continuous variables related to land use, such as land values, rent prices, and land use intensities. By understanding the factors that influence these variables, urban planners can make informed decisions and implement policies to promote equitable development and efficient land use. Clustering algorithms, like K-means, DBSCAN, and hierarchical clustering, help in identifying patterns and trends in land use, detecting anomalies, and discovering similarities between urban areas. These insights can inform urban planning policies, identify areas in need of intervention, and support the development of targeted strategies for sustainable urban growth. As urbanization continues to accelerate globally, ML techniques offer valuable tools to address the challenges associated with land use management. By leveraging these techniques, urban planners and researchers can develop data-driven solutions that promote sustainable urban development and ensure the efficient use of scarce land resources.

11.3.2 Explain How Specific Algorithms, Like Convolutional Neural Networks and Support Vector Machines, can be Employed in Urban Land Use Planning

Urban land use planning is a crucial aspect of sustainable city development, ensuring that various land uses, such as residential, commercial, and recreational areas, are optimally allocated to meet the needs of citizens and promote environmental sustainability. Advanced algorithms, such as convolutional neural networks (CNNs) and support vector machines (SVMs), can enhance the planning process by enabling planners to analyze complex spatial data, extract relevant features, and classify urban areas based on their land use characteristics.

CNNs are a type of deep learning algorithm specifically designed for image analysis and recognition (Wäldchen and Mäder, 2018; Aamir et al., 2019). They consist of multiple layers, including convolutional, pooling, and fully connected layers, which work together to detect patterns and features in images. CNNs can be employed to classify satellite and aerial imagery of urban areas into different land use categories. By training a CNN model with labeled land use data, the algorithm can identify features and patterns associated with various land uses and categorize them accordingly. This enables planners to create detailed land use maps, which can inform zoning decisions and land allocation. Using CNNs to analyze time-series satellite images can help detect changes in land use patterns and monitor urban growth. This information can be crucial for urban planners in identifying areas with rapid expansion, land use conflicts, and potential environmental issues. It can also inform policies aimed at controlling urban sprawl and promoting sustainable growth. CNNs can be used to predict future land use patterns based on historical data and trends. By training the model with historical data, it can learn to identify trends and predict the likelihood of land use changes in specific areas. This information can help planners make more informed decisions regarding land use allocation and urban development strategies. SVMs are a type of ML algorithm used for classification and regression tasks. They work by finding the optimal hyperplane that separates different classes in a high-dimensional feature space.

Similar to CNNs, SVMs can be employed for land use classification in satellite and aerial images. By training an SVM model with labeled land use data, the algorithm can identify the optimal decision boundary between different land use classes (Abdullah and Abdulazeez, 2021). The SVM model's ability to handle nonlinear relationships between features can provide more accurate classification results compared to traditional methods. SVMs can also be used to detect changes in land use patterns over time by comparing historical and current land use classifications. By identifying areas that have undergone significant changes, planners can take appropriate measures to address any resulting issues, such as land use conflicts, urban sprawl, or environmental degradation. SVMs can be used to model urban growth patterns by analyzing socioeconomic, demographic, and environmental factors that influence land use changes (Lamine et al., 2018). By identifying the relationships between these factors and land use, planners can better understand the driving forces behind urban growth and design strategies to manage it sustainably. Urban planners can leverage the strengths of both CNNs and SVMs to improve land use planning. This integration can enhance decision making, optimize land use, and predict future developments.

Combining the outputs of CNNs and SVMs can yield more accurate and comprehensive land use classifications. CNNs can be used to extract relevant features from satellite and aerial imagery, while SVMs can leverage these features to classify the land use types. This fusion of algorithms can improve the overall accuracy and reliability of land use classification results. By integrating CNNs and SVMs in scenario planning and simulation, urban planners can analyze different land use policies and their potential impacts on urban growth and sustainability. By simulating various policy scenarios, planners can identify the most effective strategies for managing urban growth and land use allocation (Rana and Suryanarayana, 2020). Incorporating CNNs and SVMs into decision support systems can provide urban planners with valuable insights and recommendations based on data-driven analyses. These systems can help planners visualize and assess the implications of various land use decisions, ultimately leading to more informed and sustainable choices. While CNNs and SVMs offer promising solutions for urban land use planning, several challenges need to be addressed.

High-quality, up-to-date, and labeled satellite and aerial imagery are essential for training and implementing these algorithms. Obtaining such data can be expensive and time-consuming, potentially limiting the applicability of these methods in some contexts. The complexity of CNNs and SVMs can make it difficult for planners to understand and interpret the underlying relationships between features and land use classes. Developing more interpretable models and visualization tools can help bridge this gap and improve decision making. Integrating CNNs and SVMs into traditional urban land use planning processes can be challenging, as it requires planners to adapt to new methods and technologies. Ensuring effective communication and collaboration between urban planners, data scientists, and other stakeholders is critical for successful implementation.

Convolutional neural networks and support vector machines offer significant potential for improving urban land use planning by enabling the analysis of complex spatial data, extracting relevant features, and classifying urban areas based on their land use characteristics. By integrating these algorithms into the planning process, urban planners can make more informed decisions, optimize land use allocation, and predict future developments. However, addressing the challenges related to data quality, model interpretability, and integration with traditional planning methods is crucial for realizing the full potential of these technologies in urban land use planning.

11.4 KEY APPLICATIONS OF MACHINE LEARNING IN URBAN LAND USE

11.4.1 Land Use Classification and Monitoring

Urban land use is a complex and dynamic system that involves the management of land, buildings, infrastructure, and transportation networks in urban areas. Understanding the patterns and changes in urban land use is critical for urban planning, environmental management, and sustainable development. In recent years, the use of machine learning (ML) for classification and monitoring of urban land use has gained significant attention due to its ability to analyze large amounts of data and extract valuable insights.

11.4.1.1 Machine Learning

Machine learning is a subfield of artificial intelligence (AI) that involves developing algorithms that can learn from data and make predictions or decisions based on that data. ML algorithms can be trained on large data sets and can automatically identify patterns and relationships in the data that may not be apparent to human observers. There are several types of ML algorithms, including supervised learning, unsupervised learning, and reinforcement learning (Jordan and Mitchell, 2015).

11.4.1.2 Classification

Classification is a type of supervised learning in which the ML algorithm is trained to predict the class or category of a new observation based on its characteristics (Kotsiantis et al., 2006). In the context of urban land use, classification can be used to identify different types of land use, such as residential, commercial, industrial, and recreational. Classification algorithms can be trained using various sources of data, including satellite imagery, aerial photographs, and ground-based sensors. The accuracy of the classification model depends on the quality and quantity of the training data, as well as the choice of the algorithm and its parameters.

11.4.1.3 Monitoring

Monitoring is the process of regularly observing and recording changes in a system over time. In the context of urban land use, monitoring can be used to track changes in land use patterns and identify areas of urban growth or decline. ML algorithms can be trained on historical data to detect changes in land use over time, and these algorithms can be used to forecast future changes in land use. Monitoring can also be used to identify areas that are at risk of environmental degradation, such as areas that are prone to flooding or soil erosion (Ghannam and Techtmann, 2021).

ML algorithms can be used to classify different types of land use in urban areas. This information can be used for urban planning, environmental management, and infrastructure development. For example, classification can be used to identify areas of high population density, which can be used to plan for public transportation and other infrastructure needs. ML algorithms can be used to analyze the growth of urban areas over time. This information can be used to forecast future growth patterns and identify areas that are at risk of overdevelopment or environmental degradation. For example, urban growth analysis can be used to identify areas that are prone to flooding, which can be used to plan for flood control measures.

ML algorithms can be used to monitor environmental changes in urban areas, such as changes in vegetation cover, water quality, and air pollution levels. This information can be used to identify areas that are at risk of environmental degradation and develop strategies to mitigate these risks. For example, environmental monitoring can be used to identify areas that are at risk of soil erosion, which can be used to plan for erosion control measures. ML algorithms can be used to plan for infrastructure development in urban areas. For example, ML algorithms can be used to predict traffic flow patterns, which can be used to plan for new roads and public transportation systems. ML algorithms can also be used to identify areas that are in need of new infrastructure, such as areas that lack access to clean water or sanitation facilities.

The accuracy of ML algorithms depends on the quality and quantity of the training data Collecting high-quality data for urban land use can be challenging, as it requires integrating data from various sources, such as satellite imagery, aerial photographs, and ground-based sensors (Zhou et al., 2020). In some cases, data may be outdated, incomplete, or inconsistent, which can affect the performance of the ML algorithms. Machine learning models can be complex and difficult to interpret, especially for non-experts. This can make it challenging for urban planners and policymakers to understand and trust the predictions and recommendations generated by the ML algorithms. Developing more interpretable and explainable models can help address this challenge. Using ML for urban land use monitoring can raise privacy and ethical concerns, as it may involve collecting and analyzing sensitive data about individuals and their properties. Ensuring that the data is collected and used responsibly and with proper consent is essential for addressing these concerns.

Machine learning algorithms can provide more accurate and up-to-date information about urban land use, which can help urban planners and policymakers make better-informed decisions. This can lead to more efficient and sustainable urban development, as well as improved environmental management.

Machine learning algorithms can help identify areas that are at risk of environmental degradation or overdevelopment, allowing for early intervention and mitigation measures (Torabi Haghighi et al., 2021). This can help prevent or reduce the negative impacts of urban growth, such as increased pollution, loss of green spaces, and increased risk of flooding. Machine learning can help optimize the allocation of resources for urban land use management, such as the deployment of inspectors or maintenance crews. This can lead to more efficient use of resources and improved outcomes for urban residents.

The use of ML for urban land use can help facilitate collaboration between different stakeholders, such as urban planners, environmental agencies, and local communities. By providing a common platform for data analysis and decision making, ML can help bridge the gap between these stakeholders and promote more effective and coordinated urban land use management.

Machine learning for classification and monitoring in urban land use is a promising approach that can help address the complex and dynamic challenges of urban development and environmental management. By leveraging the power of ML algorithms, urban planners and policymakers can gain valuable insights into land use patterns, identify areas at risk, and optimize resource allocation for more sustainable and efficient urban growth. While there are challenges to overcome, such as data quality and privacy concerns, the potential benefits of using ML for urban land use are significant and offer exciting opportunities for improving the quality of life in urban areas around the world.

11.4.2 Urban Growth Modeling and Prediction

As the world's population continues to increase and urbanize, understanding the patterns and processes of urban growth is becoming increasingly essential for urban planners, policymakers, and other stakeholders. Urban growth modeling and forecasting are critical tools that help inform decision-making, enabling sustainable and efficient urban development. Urban growth refers to the expansion of urban areas, primarily characterized by increases in population density, land use changes, and infrastructure development. Rapid urban growth can lead to several challenges, including increased demand for resources, strains on infrastructure, loss of agricultural land, and environmental degradation. Understanding the dynamics of urban growth is crucial for planning and managing urban areas, as well as for mitigating negative impacts on social, economic, and environmental systems.

Urban growth modeling refers to the quantitative representation of the processes and factors that drive urban growth (Li and Gong, 2016). These models aim to explain and predict the patterns of urban expansion by considering various factors, such as demographic trends, economic conditions, land use policies, transportation infrastructure, and environmental constraints. Urban growth models can be broadly classified into four categories:

a. Cellular Automata (CA) Models: These models are based on a grid system, where each cell represents a spatial unit with specific attributes, such as land use or population density. CA models simulate urban growth by applying a set of rules that determine the changes in cell states based on their attributes and the surrounding neighborhood conditions.

b. Agent-Based Models (ABM): ABM represent urban growth processes through the interactions of various agents, such as individuals, households, or firms, who make decisions based on specific rules and objectives. These models can capture the complex and dynamic nature of urban growth by considering the heterogeneity and adaptability of the agents (Crooks and Heppenstall, 2011).

c. Spatial Econometric Models: These models are rooted in economic theories, focusing on the relationships between urban growth and economic factors, such as labor markets, land prices, and accessibility to amenities. Spatial econometric models can be used to estimate the impact of policy interventions or investment strategies on urban growth patterns.

d. Land-Use and Transport Interaction (LUTI) Models: LUTI models integrate land use and transportation components to simulate the mutual effects of urban growth and transportation systems. These models can be used to evaluate the impacts of transportation infrastructure investments or land use policies on urban development and mobility patterns (Wegener, 2021).

Data and Methods in Urban Growth Modeling. Various data sources and methods are used in urban growth modeling, depending on the model type and the research objectives. Common data sources include census data, remote sensing imagery, land use maps, and transportation networks. Geographical information systems (GISs) play a crucial role in handling and analyzing spatial data, facilitating the visualization and interpretation of urban growth patterns. Statistical and machine learning techniques, such as regression analysis, neural networks, and decision trees, are often employed to identify the relationships between urban growth and its driving factors, as well as to develop predictive models.

Urban growth forecasting involves the application of urban growth models to project future urban expansion patterns. Accurate forecasts can provide valuable insights for urban planners and policymakers, allowing them to make informed decisions regarding land use, infrastructure, and resource allocation. There are two main approaches to urban growth forecasting:

a. Deterministic Forecasting: This approach involves the use of urban growth models that rely on specific assumptions and parameters to produce a single, deterministic projection of urban growth. Deterministic forecasts are often criticized for their limited ability to account for the uncertainties and complexities inherent in urban growth processes.

b. Probabilistic Forecasting: This approach addresses the limitations of deterministic forecasting by incorporating uncertainties and variability into the urban growth models. Probabilistic forecasts generate multiple potential urban growth scenarios, providing a range of possible outcomes that account for the inherent uncertainties in the driving factors and processes.

Despite the advancements in urban growth modeling and forecasting, several uncertainties and limitations persist:

a. Data Quality and Availability: The accuracy and reliability of urban growth forecasts depend on the quality and availability of input data. In many cases, data sources may be outdated, incomplete, or inconsistent, which can affect the robustness of the models and the forecasts.

b. Model Calibration and Validation: Ensuring the accuracy of urban growth models requires rigorous calibration and validation processes. This involves comparing the model outputs with observed data and adjusting the model parameters accordingly. However, the calibration and validation processes can be challenging due to the complexity of urban growth dynamics and the lack of comprehensive historical data.

c. Representation of Complex Processes: Urban growth models may not fully capture the complex and nonlinear interactions among various driving factors, leading to oversimplification of the urban growth processes. This can result in biased or inaccurate forecasts.

d. Incorporating Stakeholder Input: The effectiveness of urban growth forecasting can be improved by involving stakeholders in the modeling and decision-making processes. This can help to ensure that the forecasts reflect local knowledge and address the concerns and priorities of different stakeholders.

Urban growth modeling and forecasting have several practical applications in urban planning and policymaking:

a. Land Use Planning: Urban growth forecasts can inform land use planning by identifying areas with high potential for urban expansion or redevelopment. This can guide the allocation of land resources for various uses, such as housing, commercial, industrial, or recreational purposes.

b. Infrastructure Investment: Urban growth models can be used to evaluate the impacts of different infrastructure investments on urban growth patterns. This can help policymakers to prioritize and allocate resources for transportation, utilities, and other critical infrastructure.

c. Environmental Impact Assessment: By simulating the spatial patterns of urban growth, models can be used to assess the potential environmental impacts of urban expansion, such as habitat fragmentation, loss of agricultural land, or increased greenhouse gas emissions. This can inform the development of strategies to mitigate or avoid negative environmental consequences.

d. Scenario Analysis and Policy Evaluation: Urban growth models can be used to analyze the potential impacts of various policy interventions or development scenarios on urban growth patterns. This can support decision-making by providing insights into the trade-offs and consequences associated with different policy options.

Urban growth modeling and forecasting are indispensable tools for understanding and managing the complex and dynamic processes of urban expansion. By providing valuable insights into the patterns and drivers of urban growth, these models can inform decision-making processes and contribute to the development of more sustainable, efficient, and equitable urban environments. However, it is essential to recognize and address the uncertainties and limitations inherent in urban growth modeling and forecasting to ensure their effective and responsible application in urban planning and policymaking.

11.4.3 Transport Planning and Optimization

Urbanization, the process of population concentration in cities and towns, is a major driving force behind the development of modern societies. As cities grow, so do their infrastructural needs, with transportation being a key component of their functionality. Efficient and sustainable transport systems are essential for the economic growth, environmental protection, and overall quality of life in urban areas. Consequently, transport planning and optimization have become critical components of urban land use management. Transport planning in urban land use involves the development and implementation of policies, plans, and strategies aimed at improving the accessibility, safety, efficiency, and sustainability of urban transportation systems. It encompasses various modes of transportation, such as walking, cycling, public transit, and private vehicles, as well as the integration of these modes to create a seamless, multi-modal transportation network.

Economic Growth: Efficient transport systems are vital for the economic growth of urban areas, as they facilitate the movement of goods and people, enhance connectivity, and promote commerce. Improved transport infrastructure attracts businesses and investments, leading to job creation and increased productivity.

Environmental Protection: Sustainable transport planning helps to minimize the negative environmental impacts of urban transportation systems, such as air pollution, noise pollution, and greenhouse gas emissions. By promoting public transit, non-motorized transport, and clean energy vehicles, cities can reduce their ecological footprint and contribute to global efforts to combat climate change.

Quality of Life: A well-planned and optimized transport system enhances the quality of life for urban residents by reducing traffic congestion, improving air quality, promoting physical activity through walking and cycling, and providing equitable access to essential services and opportunities.

Challenges in Transport Planning and Optimization. Rapid Urbanization: The unprecedented rate of urbanization, particularly in developing countries, puts enormous pressure on existing transportation infrastructure and demands proactive planning to accommodate future growth. Limited Resources: The scarcity of financial and human resources in many urban areas, especially in developing countries, poses a significant challenge to the implementation of effective transport planning and optimization initiatives. Inadequate Data and Information: A lack of reliable and up-to-date data on transport systems, travel patterns, and land use often hampers the development of evidence-based transport policies and plans. Technological Change: Emerging technologies, such as autonomous vehicles and shared mobility platforms, present both opportunities and challenges for urban transport planning and optimization, requiring planners to adapt and incorporate these innovations into their strategies. Social and Political Factors: Transport planning and optimization efforts may face resistance from various stakeholders, such as local communities, businesses, and political entities, due to conflicting interests and priorities.

Tools and Methodologies for Transport Planning and Optimization. Land Use and Transportation Integration: Integrating land use and transportation planning is essential for achieving sustainable urban development (Geerlings and Stead, 2003). This involves coordinating land use policies, zoning regulations, and transportation investments to create compact, mixed-use, and transit-oriented development patterns that reduce the need for private vehicle use and promote sustainable modes of transport. Multi-modal Transportation Planning: A multi-modal approach to transportation planning considers all modes of transport – walking, cycling, public transit, and private vehicles – and their integration into a seamless network. This involves the development of high-quality pedestrian and cycling infrastructure, efficient and accessible public transit systems, and context-sensitive road designs that accommodate all users.

11.5 DATA ACQUISITION, PROCESSING, AND INTEGRATION

11.5.1 Discuss the Importance of Quality Data for Effective Machine Learning Applications

In the era of rapid technological advancements, machine learning (ML) has emerged as a transformative force, driving innovation across diverse industries such as healthcare, finance, transportation, and retail (Agarwal et al., 2022). The crux of ML lies in its ability to automatically learn patterns and insights from data, enabling businesses and researchers to make better predictions and decisions (Pramod et al., 2021). However, the effectiveness of ML applications hinges on the quality of the data they are built upon. Without high-quality data, even the most sophisticated ML algorithms would be rendered useless, producing inaccurate predictions and negatively affecting decision-making processes (Longo et al., 2020). This article delves into the importance of quality data for effective ML applications, examining the consequences of poor data quality, the factors that contribute to quality data, and the best practices for ensuring data quality in ML project.

11.5.1.1 Consequences of Poor Data Quality

The phrase "garbage in, garbage out" aptly describes the relationship between data quality and ML outcomes. When poor quality data is fed into ML algorithms, the resulting predictions and insights are likely to be flawed or unreliable (Zeevi et al., 2015). Several consequences of poor data quality in ML applications include the following:

Inaccurate Predictions: Low-quality data, which might be incomplete, inconsistent, or noisy, can lead to incorrect insights and predictions. For instance, a recommendation system trained on inaccurate or irrelevant data may suggest inappropriate products or content to users, undermining the user experience and potentially harming the reputation of the business (Crawford et al., 2015).

Biased Models: Inadequate representation of certain groups or variables in the data set can result in biased ML models that perpetuate existing prejudices and stereotypes. Such biases may have grave implications, especially in critical domains like healthcare, finance, and law enforcement, where they can lead to unfair treatment of certain individuals or communities.

Increased Costs: Poor data quality can lead to wasted resources, as developers and data scientists may need to invest additional time and effort to clean and preprocess the data. Moreover, inaccurate predictions may necessitate costly interventions, such as product recalls or public relations campaigns, to mitigate the negative impact on businesses (Munappy et al., 2019).

To build effective ML applications, it is crucial to understand the factors that contribute to quality data. These factors can be broadly classified into four categories:

Accuracy: Accurate data is free from errors and inconsistencies, reflecting the true state of the underlying phenomenon. Ensuring data accuracy requires meticulous data collection, proper data entry, and thorough validation processes.

Completeness: Complete data includes all relevant observations and features necessary for the ML application (Colquhoun et al., 2020). Missing data can lead to gaps in understanding and may result in biased or incomplete models. Data completeness can be achieved by adopting comprehensive data collection strategies and imputing missing values using appropriate techniques (Liew et al., 2011).

Relevance: Relevant data contains the necessary information to address the problem at hand. Collecting irrelevant data not only increases the complexity of the ML model but may also reduce its predictive power. Identifying relevant data requires a deep understanding of the problem domain and the relationships between different variables (Queirós et al., 2017).

Representativeness: A representative data set captures the diversity of the population or phenomenon under study. Ensuring representativeness involves stratified sampling, oversampling underrepresented groups, or using synthetic data generation techniques to create balanced data sets that avoid biases.

11.5.1.2 Best Practices for Ensuring Data Quality

To maximize the effectiveness of ML applications, businesses and researchers must prioritize data quality throughout the entire project life cycle. The following best practices can help ensure data quality in ML projects:

Develop a Data Quality Plan: Establish a data quality plan that outlines the data collection, validation, and preprocessing procedures (Fox et al., 2018). This plan should include data quality metrics, such as accuracy, completeness, relevance, and representativeness, to measure and track data quality throughout the project (Batini et al., 2009).

Use Multiple Data Sources: Leverage multiple data sources to ensure a comprehensive and diverse data set. Cross-referencing and merging data from various sources can help fill gaps, improve accuracy, and increase the representativeness of the data set (Song et al., 2013).

Perform Data Cleaning and Preprocessing: Rigorously clean and preprocess the data to remove errors, inconsistencies, and outliers. Use appropriate techniques, such as data imputation, normalization, and feature engineering, to ensure that the data is accurate, complete, and suitable for the ML algorithm (Huyghues-Beaufond et al., 2020).

Implement Data Validation Techniques: Employ data validation techniques, such as cross-validation and holdout validation, to assess the performance of the ML model on unseen data. This helps identify potential issues with the data, such as overfitting, underfitting, or biases, and guides further improvements in data quality.

Address Class Imbalance: In case of class imbalance, use techniques like oversampling, undersampling, or synthetic data generation to create balanced data sets (Douzas et al., 2018). This helps ensure that the ML model does not favor any particular class, thus reducing biases and improving prediction accuracy.

Monitor and Update Data: Continuously monitor and update the data to ensure that it remains accurate, relevant, and representative over time. Regular data updates help the ML model adapt to changing circumstances and maintain its predictive power.

Foster a Culture of Data Quality: Encourage a culture of data quality within the organization by involving all stakeholders, such as data scientists, domain experts, and decision makers, in the data quality process (McGilvray et al., 2021). This collaborative approach helps identify potential issues, share expertise, and promote a shared understanding of the importance of quality data for ML applications.

Quality data is the lifeblood of effective machine learning applications. Ensuring data accuracy, completeness, relevance, and representativeness is critical to the success of ML projects, as it directly impacts the accuracy and reliability of the resulting predictions and insights. By adopting best practices for data collection, validation, and preprocessing, businesses and researchers can mitigate the risks associated with poor data quality and harness the full potential of ML technology to drive innovation, improve decision making, and create value across various industries (Wang et al., 2006).

11.5.2 Explain Various Data Sources Relevant to Urban Land Use, Such as Satellite Imagery, GIS, and Open Data Platforms

Urban land use is a complex and multidimensional concept, encompassing a variety of spatial, social, and economic factors. Understanding how land is used in urban areas is critical for urban planning, infrastructure development, environmental sustainability, and socioeconomic analysis (Surya et al., 2020). A variety of data sources are available for examining urban land use, including satellite imagery, geographic information systems (GISs), and open data platforms. This in-depth introduction will guide you through these various data sources, highlighting their unique characteristics, relevance, and potential applications (Burrough et al., 2015).

Satellite imagery is a rich source of spatial data that allows for the monitoring and analysis of urban land use patterns (Henderson et al., 1997). High-resolution images captured by satellites provide a comprehensive view of Earth's surface, capturing crucial details such as land cover, vegetation, and built-up areas (Roy et al., 2019). Satellite imagery is particularly useful for observing large-scale changes in urban land use over time, as well as for identifying smaller-scale variations within a city (Mathieu et al., 2007). There are numerous satellite platforms that offer varying levels of spatial resolution, spectral resolution, and temporal frequency. Some well-known satellite systems include Landsat, Sentinel, and WorldView (Zhao et al., 2022). These systems offer different advantages and limitations, depending on the specific requirements of a project. For example, Landsat images have a 30-meter spatial resolution and are available every 16 days, while WorldView images have a sub-meter resolution and are available more frequently. One of the main advantages of satellite imagery is its ability to provide consistent, unbiased, and objective data (Rivas Casado et al., 2015). This data can be used to analyze urban land use changes over time and across different geographic areas, making it possible to identify trends and patterns that might not be evident through other data sources. Additionally, satellite imagery is particularly valuable in regions where ground-based data collection is limited or unavailable.

Geographic information systems (GISs) are powerful tools that enable the management, analysis, and visualization of spatial data. GIS software can integrate various types of data, such as satellite imagery, vector data, and attribute data, to create comprehensive and dynamic representations of urban land use (Burrough et al., 2015). GIS has become an indispensable tool in urban planning and land use analysis, as it allows for a better understanding of complex spatial relationships and interactions. GIS data can be acquired through various sources, including government agencies, non-governmental organizations, academic institutions, and private companies (Thornton et al., 2002). This data often comes in the form of vector layers, which represent geographic features like points, lines, or polygons, and can be attributed with additional information. Common types of GIS data relevant to urban land use include land cover, land use zoning, transportation networks, and demographic data (Zhong et al., 2020). The versatility of GIS enables it to be used in a wide range of applications related to urban land use, from identifying suitable locations for new development to analyzing the impact of land use policies on environmental sustainability (Javadian et al., 2011). Furthermore, GIS can be combined with other data sources, like remote sensing and statistical data, to create comprehensive and robust analyses of urban land use patterns and trends.

Open data platforms are online repositories that provide free access to a wide range of data sets, including those related to urban land use. These platforms are typically maintained by government agencies, research institutions, or non-profit organizations and can be valuable resources for urban planners, policymakers, and researchers. Examples of open data platforms that offer urban land use data include the following:

a. USGS EarthExplorer: The U.S. Geological Survey's EarthExplorer provides access to satellite imagery, aerial photography, and other geospatial data sets, including land use and land cover information (Faundeen et al., 2002).

b. European Space Agency's (ESA) Copernicus Programme: The Copernicus Programme provides free and open access to satellite imagery from the Sentinel satellites, which can be used for various land use analysis applications, such as monitoring urban growth, detecting land use changes, and assessing environmental impacts (Castro Gomez et al., 2017).

c. OpenStreetMap (OSM): OpenStreetMap is a community-driven, editable map of the world that contains rich information about land use, infrastructure, and points of interest. OSM data can be integrated with other geospatial data sets in GIS for a comprehensive analysis of urban land use patterns (Haklay et al., 2008).

d. World Bank's World Development Indicators (WDI): The WDI database provides access to a wealth of economic, social, and environmental indicators, including data on urbanization and land use (World Bank et al., 2005). This data can be used to analyze the relationships between land use patterns and various socioeconomic factors.

e. Global Human Settlement Layer (GHSL): Developed by the European Commission's Joint Research Centre, the GHSL provides global data on human settlements, including population density and land use patterns (Melchiorri et al., 2019). This data can be used to study the spatial distribution of urban areas and their relationship with land use.

By combining data from satellite imagery, GIS, and open data platforms, it is possible to create a holistic understanding of urban land use patterns and their underlying drivers. This integrated approach allows for a more nuanced analysis of the complex interactions between social, economic, and environmental factors in urban areas (Tahir et al., 2013). For example, satellite imagery can be used to identify land use changes over time, while GIS can be employed to analyze the spatial distribution of these changes in relation to infrastructure and population density. Open data platforms can provide additional context, such as socioeconomic indicators or environmental data, to help explain why certain land use patterns are occurring.

In conclusion, a variety of data sources, including satellite imagery, GIS, and open data platforms, play a crucial role in urban land use analysis. Each data source offers unique insights and capabilities, making it essential for researchers, planners, and policymakers to understand their strengths and limitations. By integrating these data sources, it is possible to create a more comprehensive understanding of urban land use patterns and inform sustainable urban planning and development strategies.

11.5.3 Describe Data Pre-Processing Techniques, Including Cleaning, Normalization, and Feature Extraction

Data pre-processing is an indispensable step in the data mining process, as it ensures that raw data is transformed into a format that can be easily understood and analyzed by ML algorithms. The primary goal of data preprocessing is to convert raw, unstructured data into a structured format that is more suitable for data analysis and modeling. This process includes data cleaning, normalization, and feature extraction (Arora et al., 2019). These techniques are essential to obtain reliable and accurate results from data-driven models, as the quality of the input data directly impacts the performance of the model.

Data cleaning is the process of detecting, correcting, and removing errors and inconsistencies in the raw data to improve its quality. Data cleaning techniques can be classified into three main categories: error detection and correction, missing value imputation, and noise reduction. Errors in data can be a result of human input, system glitches, or data transmission (Choi et al., 2022). To identify and correct these errors, the following methods are commonly used:

a. Data Auditing: This process involves the examination of data to identify inconsistencies and errors. Data auditing typically involves the use of data profiling tools and algorithms to automatically detect data anomalies (Kandel et al., 2011).

b. Data Validation: This technique involves checking data for errors by applying predefined rules or constraints. For example, a rule could be that the age of a person must be a positive integer. If the data fails to meet the specified criteria, it is flagged as erroneous (Frawley et al., 1992).

c. Data Editing: Once errors are identified, they must be corrected. This can be done manually by a data curator or automatically using data editing tools. The choice of method depends on the complexity and size of the data set (Freitas et al., 2016).

Missing values are a common issue in real-world data sets, and they can significantly impact the performance of a model. Several techniques can be employed to handle missing values:

a. Deletion: This method involves removing instances with missing values from the data set. This approach is suitable when the percentage of missing values is small, and their removal does not significantly impact the data set's representativeness (Penone et al., 2014).

b. Imputation: Imputation involves estimating missing values based on other available data points. Common imputation techniques include mean or median imputation, regression-based imputation, and nearest neighbor imputation (Jadhav et al., 2019). Noise refers to random errors or variations in the data that hinder the extraction of meaningful information.

Noise reduction techniques aim to remove these errors and improve data quality. Some common methods include:

a. Binning: Binning involves grouping data into intervals or categories to reduce noise. This can be done by equal-width binning, equal-frequency binning, or clustering-based binning (Patra et al., 2015).

b. Data Smoothing: Data smoothing techniques, such as moving average, exponential smoothing, and Savitzky-Golay filtering, are used to reduce noise by averaging or filtering out random fluctuations in the data (Al-Mbaideen et al., 2019).

Data normalization is the process of transforming data to a common scale or range, which allows for meaningful comparisons between data points. Normalization is crucial when dealing with data sets that have attributes with different scales or units. Some popular normalization techniques include min-max scaling. This technique scales the data into a specified range, typically [0, 1], by subtracting the minimum value and dividing by the range of the attribute. Z-score normalization, also known as standardization, scales the data by subtracting the mean and dividing by the standard deviation, resulting in a data set with a mean of 0 and a standard deviation of 1 (Mohamad et al., 2013). Log transformation is used to reduce the effect of outliers and skewness in the data by taking the logarith

11.6 FUTURE TRENDS AND OPPORTUNITIES

11.6.1 Explore the Future of Machine Learning in Urban Land Use, Including Advances in AI Technology, New Data Sources, and Interdisciplinary Collaboration

The rapid expansion of urban areas and the increasing complexity of urban systems necessitate innovative approaches to managing land use (Wilbanks et al., 2014). Machine learning (ML), a subset of artificial intelligence (AI), offers promising solutions to tackle the challenges associated with urban land use. In this in-depth exploration, we will discuss the future of ML in urban land use, focusing on advancements in AI technology, new data sources, and interdisciplinary collaboration.

11.6.1.1 Advances in AI Technology

11.6.1.1.1 Deep Learning and Neural Networks   Deep learning, a subset of ML, has shown great potential in land use classification and analysis. Convolutional neural networks (CNNs) and recurrent neural networks (RNNs) are two popular deep learning architectures that have been successfully applied to urban land use analysis (Pelletier et al., 2019). These networks can automatically learn and extract relevant features from high-dimensional data, such as satellite images, improving land use classification accuracy.

11.6.1.1.2 Generative Adversarial Networks (GANs)   GANs have gained attention for their ability to generate realistic images from random noise. In the context of urban land use, GANs can be used to generate plausible urban growth scenarios, helping city planners identify potential land use conflicts and make informed decisions about land allocation (Chaturvedi et al., 2021).

11.6.1.1.3 Reinforcement Learning (RL)   RL techniques have been applied to optimize land use allocation and urban planning. In these applications, an agent learns optimal actions to take in a given environment, with the goal of maximizing some long-term objective (e.g., economic growth or environmental sustainability) (Barbier et al., 1987). RL can be used to explore various land use policies, balancing trade-offs between competing objectives.

11.6.1.2 New Data Sources

11.6.1.2.1 Remote Sensing and Earth Observation Data   High-resolution satellite imagery has become an essential data source for urban land use analysis. The increasing availability of open-access satellite data, such as from the Copernicus program and Landsat, enables ML algorithms to identify and monitor urban land use patterns at unprecedented spatial and temporal resolutions (Lefebvre et al., 2016).

11.6.1.2.2 Social Media and Crowdsourced Data   Social media platforms and crowdsourcing initiatives provide valuable, real-time data on human activity and perceptions of urban spaces. These data sources can be used to enrich land use classification, monitor urban changes, and evaluate the impact of land use policies on residents (Harris et al., 1995).

11.6.1.2.3 Internet of Things (IoT) and Smart Cities   IoT devices and sensors have the potential to generate vast amounts of data on urban land use and human activities. This data can be integrated into ML models to improve land use predictions, monitor compliance with zoning regulations, and optimize resource allocation.

11.6.1.3 Interdisciplinary Collaboration

11.6.1.3.1 Urban Planning and Geospatial Science   Collaboration between urban planners and geospatial scientists is crucial for the development of effective ML models for land use analysis. Geospatial scientists provide expertise in data processing and spatial analysis, while urban planners contribute domain knowledge and practical insights into the urban land use context (Malczewski et al., 2004).

11.6.1.3.2 Environmental and Social Sciences   The integration of environmental and social sciences into ML research is essential for understanding the complex relationships between urban land use and ecosystem services, as well as the social and economic implications of land use decisions (Liu et al., 2022). This interdisciplinary approach can help ensure that ML models are grounded in real-world contexts and reflect the diverse values and priorities of urban residents.

11.6.1.3.3 Public-Private Partnerships   Public-private partnerships can facilitate the development of innovative ML solutions for urban land use management. Governments and academic institutions can provide access to data and domain expertise, while private companies contribute technical expertise and resources for ML model development and implementation (Asad et al., 2022).

11.7 CONCLUSION

11.7.1 Summarize the Key Takeaways from this Chapter

Key takeaways from this chapter includethe following:

   Importance of urban land use: Understanding and managing urban land use is crucial for sustainable city development, environmental conservation, and improved quality of life for residents (Suzuki et al., 2013).

Machine learning and its potential: Machine learning, a subfield of artificial intelligence, offers the potential to revolutionize urban land use by providing more accurate predictions, detecting patterns, and facilitating decision-making processes.

Data-driven approaches: The chapter emphasizes the importance of incorporating diverse data sources, such as satellite imagery, demographic information, and social media, to create more comprehensive and accurate models for urban land use (Bibri et al., 2022).

Common machine learning techniques: The chapter introduces various machine learning algorithms used in urban land use applications, such as supervised learning (e.g., regression, classification), unsupervised learning (e.g., clustering), and deep learning (e.g., convolutional neural networks).

Case studies and applications: Several real-world examples and case studies demonstrate the effectiveness of machine learning techniques in addressing urban land use challenges, such as predicting land use changes, detecting urban sprawl, and optimizing land allocation for different purpose.

Challenges and limitations: The chapter highlights potential limitations and challenges in implementing machine learning techniques, including data quality and availability, computational resources, and the need for interdisciplinary collaboration among urban planners, data scientists, and policymakers.

Future directions: The chapter discusses emerging trends and potential future research directions, such as incorporating new data sources, integrating machine learning with traditional urban planning methods, and using machine learning to inform policy decisions and drive sustainable urban development.

11.7.2 Reiterate the Significance of Machine Learning in Urban Land Use Planning and Management

Urban planning and land use management play critical roles in shaping the future of cities around the world. In today's rapidly urbanizing world, ensuring efficient land use and sustainable urban development is becoming increasingly important. With the advancements in technology and data science, machine learning (ML) has emerged as a powerful tool in various fields, including urban planning and land use management (Sun et al., 2019). This essay reiterates the significance of machine learning in urban land use planning and management, highlighting the advantages and potential applications it brings to the field.

Machine learning refers to the process through which computer algorithms improve their performance over time by learning from data. This ability allows ML models to uncover complex patterns and relationships within large data sets, making it particularly relevant to urban planning, where vast amounts of data are often available (Tai et al., 2019). The incorporation of machine learning into urban land use planning and management can provide numerous benefits, including increased efficiency, better decision making, and enhanced sustainability. Efficiency is a key consideration in urban planning, as resources are often limited, and decisions can have long-lasting impacts on the built environment. Machine learning can help optimize land use planning by enabling planners to quickly analyze and interpret large data sets, making data-driven decisions faster and more accurate. For instance, ML algorithms can be used to forecast future land use demands and urban growth patterns, allowing for more efficient allocation of resources and infrastructure investments (Chaturvedi et al., 2021). Another significant advantage of machine learning in urban planning is its ability to support better decision making. Through the analysis of historical data, ML models can identify trends and patterns that might not be apparent to human analysts. This can lead to more informed decision-making and improved land use strategies. For example, ML algorithms can help identify areas prone to flooding or other environmental risks, enabling planners to make informed decisions about land use restrictions and mitigation measures (Chaturvedi et al., 2021). Machine learning can also help enhance the sustainability of urban development by providing insights into the environmental and social impacts of land use decisions. By analyzing data on various environmental factors, such as air quality, water usage, and energy consumption, ML algorithms can help planners identify the most sustainable land use options. Additionally, machine learning can aid in the development of more equitable urban environments by analyzing socioeconomic data to ensure that land use decisions do not disproportionately impact vulnerable populations (Lukanov et al., 2019). There are several potential applications of machine learning in urban land use planning and management, including land use classification, urban growth modeling, and scenario analysis. These applications can help address various challenges faced by urban planners, such as the need for accurate land use data, understanding the dynamics of urban growth, and evaluating the potential impacts of different development scenarios.

Land use classification is a critical aspect of urban planning, as it provides the foundation for decision making and policy development. Machine learning can be used to automate the classification process by analyzing high-resolution satellite imagery and other geospatial data. This can result in more accurate and up-to-date land use maps, which are essential for effective planning and management (Abdikan 2016; Bhatti 2021; Bhatti 2022a; Bhatti 2022b; Bhatti 2023a; Bhatti 2023b; Fei 2022; Wang 2023; Wu 2022). Urban growth modeling is another area where machine learning can make a significant contribution. By analyzing historical urban growth patterns and various socio-economic and environmental factors, ML algorithms can help predict future urban expansion and inform land use planning strategies. This can help planners allocate resources more efficiently, minimize urban sprawl, and promote sustainable development. Scenario analysis is a critical component of the planning process, as it allows planners to evaluate the potential impacts of different land use options and development scenarios. Machine learning can be used to create more sophisticated and realistic simulations, providing valuable insights into the potential consequences of various policy decisions. This can enable planners to make more informed choices, taking into consideration the long-term implications of their decisions on the environment, economy, and society.

11.7.3 Encourage Readers to Explore and Implement Machine Learning Solutions to Promote Sustainable Urban Development

As the world's urban population continues to grow rapidly, cities are faced with the daunting challenge of ensuring sustainable development. The pressure on resources, infrastructure, and the environment has reached critical levels, demanding innovative solutions that can help us create a better future for generations to come. Machine learning, a cutting-edge technology with transformative potential, presents an extraordinary opportunity to address these challenges head-on. This article aims to encourage you, the reader, to explore and implement machine learning solutions to promote sustainable urban development.

11.7.3.1 Tackling Environmental Challenges with Machine Learning

One of the most pressing concerns for sustainable urban development is the mitigation of environmental issues such as air pollution, waste management, and energy consumption. Machine learning can play a vital role in addressing these challenges through the following methods:

a. Air Quality Prediction and Monitoring: By analyzing vast amounts of historical and real-time data on air pollution levels, machine learning algorithms can accurately predict air quality and identify pollution hotspots. This information can then be used by policymakers to devise strategies for reducing emissions and improving air quality.

b. Smart Waste Management: Machine learning algorithms can optimize waste collection routes, predict waste generation patterns, and even help identify waste sorting errors. This results in more efficient waste management systems that save resources, reduce emissions, and contribute to a cleaner urban environment.

c. Energy Efficiency: By analyzing consumption patterns and predicting demand, machine learning models can enable smarter energy management in buildings and across cities. This can lead to significant reductions in energy use and carbon emissions, driving us closer to a sustainable future.

Urban mobility is a critical factor in sustainable development, with congestion, pollution, and inefficient transportation systems contributing to numerous negative consequences. Machine learning offers powerful solutions in this area:

a. Traffic Management: By analyzing traffic data in real-time, machine learning models can predict congestion patterns and suggest optimal traffic light timings, resulting in smoother traffic flow and reduced emissions.

b. Public Transportation Optimization: Machine learning can help improve public transportation systems by predicting demand, suggesting optimal routes, and even identifying areas that lack access to public transit. This results in more efficient and equitable transportation networks that are better suited to meet the needs of urban residents.

c. Autonomous Vehicles: As the technology behind self-driving cars advances, machine learning will be critical to their safe and efficient operation. Autonomous vehicles have the potential to revolutionize urban transportation, reducing congestion and emissions while improving safety and accessibility.

11.7.3.2 Strengthening Urban Resilience Through Predictive Analytics

As climate change continues to threaten our world, it is essential to build resilient cities that can withstand and adapt to extreme weather events and other environmental hazards. Machine learning can help achieve this by including the following:

a. Flood Prediction: By analyzing historical flood data and real-time weather conditions, machine learning algorithms can predict potential flood risks and provide early warnings to authorities and residents. This enables cities to take preventive measures and minimize the impact of floods.

b. Infrastructure Maintenance: Machine learning can help monitor the structural health of buildings, bridges, and other infrastructure, identifying signs of wear and tear before they lead to catastrophic failures. This allows for proactive maintenance and reduces the likelihood of expensive and disruptive repairs.

c. Disaster Response: In the aftermath of a natural disaster, machine learning can help emergency responders by analyzing satellite imagery and social media data to identify the hardest-hit areas and prioritize relief efforts.

As we have seen, ML holds tremendous potential for promoting sustainable urban development. By leveraging the power of data and advanced algorithms, we can create cities that are more efficient, resilient, and environmentally friendly, ultimately enhancing the quality of life for all urban dwellers. Now is the time to explore and implement machine learning solutions in our pursuit of sustainable urban development. By embracing this technology, we can unlock new pathways to a greener, more prosperous future for our cities and their inhabitants. So, dive into the fascinating world of ML, and play your part in shaping the sustainable cities of tomorrow.

REFERENCES

Aamir, Muhammad, Rahman, Ziaur, Ahmed Abro, Waheed, Tahir, Muhammad, & Mustajar Ahmed, Syed (2019). An Optimized Architecture of Image Classification Using Convolutional Neural Network. *International Journal of Image, Graphics and Signal Processing*, 11, 30–3910.5815/ijigsp.2019.10.05.

Abdikan, S., Sanli, F. B., Ustuner, M., & Calò, F. (2016, July). Land cover mapping using sentinel-1 SAR data. In *The International Archives of the Photogrammetry, Remote Sensing and Spatial Information Sciences* (Volume XLI-B7). 2016 XXIII ISPRS Congress.

Abdullah, D. M., & Abdulazeez, A. M. (2021). Machine learning applications based on SVM classification a review. *Qubahan Academic Journal*, 1(2), 81–90. 10.48161/qaj.v1n2a50

Agarwal, P., Swami, S., & Malhotra, S. K. (2022). Artificial intelligence adoption in the post COVID-19 new-normal and role of smart technologies in transforming business: A review. *Journal of Science and Technology Policy Management*.

Ahuja, R., Chug, A., Gupta, S., Ahuja, P., & Kohli, S. (2020). Classification and clustering algorithms of machine learning with their applications. *Nature-Inspired Computation in Data Mining and Machine Learning*, 225–248. 10.1007/978-3-030-28553-1_11

Al-Mbaideen, A. A. (2019). Application of moving average filter for the quantitative analysis of the NIR spectra. *Journal of Analytical Chemistry*, 74, 686–692.

Alzubi, J., Nayyar, A., & Kumar, A. (2018, November). Machine learning from theory to algorithms: an overview. In *Journal of physics: conference series* (Vol. 1142, p. 012012). IOP Publishing. 10.1088/1742-6596/1142/1/012012

Arefi, M. (2004). An asset-based approach to policymaking: Revisiting the history of urban planning and neighborhood change in Cincinnati's West End. *Cities*, 21(6), 491–500. 10.101 6/j.cities.2004.08.003

Arora, M., & Kansal, V. (2019). Character level embedding with deep convolutional neural network for text normalization of unstructured data for Twitter sentiment analysis. *Social Network Analysis and Mining*, 9, 1–14.

Asad, M. M., Rind, A. A., & Abdulmuhsin, A. A. (2022). The effect of knowledge management in educational settings: A study of education management organizations (EMOs) schools of Pakistan. *International Journal of Organizational Analysis*, 30(5), 1156–1171.

Augustijn-Beckers, E. W., Flacke, J., & Retsios, B. (2011). Simulating informal settlement growth in Dar es Salaam, Tanzania: An agent-based housing model. *Computers, Environment and Urban Systems*, 35(2), 93–103. 10.1016/j.compenvurbsys.2011.01.001

Barbier, E. B. (1987). The concept of sustainable economic development. *Environmental Conservation*, 14(2), 101–110.

Batini, C., Cappiello, C., Francalanci, C., & Maurino, A. (2009). Methodologies for data quality assessment and improvement. *ACM Computing Surveys (CSUR)*, 41(3), 1–52.

Batista, G. E., Prati, R. C., & Monard, M. C. (2004). A study of the behavior of several methods for balancing machine learning training data. *ACM SIGKDD Explorations Newsletter*, 6(1), 20–29. 10.1145/1007730.1007735

Becker, D. A., Browning, M. H., Kuo, M., & Van Den Eeden, S. K. (2019). Is green land cover associated with less health care spending? Promising findings from county-level Medicare spending in the continental United States. *Urban Forestry & Urban Greening*, 41, 39–47. 10.1 016/j.ufug.2019.02.012

Bell, J. (2022). What is machine learning?. *Machine Learning and the City: Applications in Architecture and Urban Design*, 207–216. 10.1002/9781119815075.ch18

Bhatti, Uzair Aslam, Yan, Yuhuan, Zhou, Mingquan, Ali, Sajid, Hussain, Aamir, Qingsong, Huo, Yu, Zhaoyuan, & Yuan, Linwang (2021). Time Series Analysis and Forecasting of Air Pollution Particulate Matter ($PM_{2.5}$): An SARIMA and Factor Analysis Approach. *IEEE Access*, 9, 41019–41031. 10.1109/access.2021.3060744.

Bhatti, Uzair, Wu, Guilu, Bazai, Sibghat Ullah, Ali Nawaz, Saqib, Baryalai, Mehmood, Bhatti, Mughair Aslam, Hasnain, Ahmad, & Nizamani, Mir Muhammad (2022a). A Pre- to Post-COVID-19 Change of Air Quality Patterns in Anhui Province Using Path Analysis and Regression. *Polish Journal of Environmental Studies*, 31, 4029–404210.15244/pjoes/148065.

Bhatti, Uzair Aslam, Yu, Zhaoyuan, Chanussot, Jocelyn, Zeeshan, Zeeshan, Yuan, Linwang, Luo, Wen, Nawaz, Saqib Ali, Bhatti, Mughair Aslam, Ain, Qurat Ul, & Mehmood, Anum (2022b). Local Similarity-Based Spatial–Spectral Fusion Hyperspectral Image Classification With Deep CNN and Gabor Filtering. *IEEE Transactions on Geoscience and Remote Sensing*, 60, 1–1510.1109/tgrs.2021.3090410.

Bhatti, Uzair Aslam, Huang, Mengxing, Neira-Molina, Harold, Marjan, Shah, Baryalai, Mehmood, Tang, Hao, Wu, Guilu, & Bazai, Sibghat Ullah (2023a). MFFCG – Multi feature fusion for hyperspectral image classification using graph attention network. *Expert Systems with Applications*, 229, 12049610.1016/j.eswa.2023.120496.

Bhatti, Uzair Aslam, Masud, Mehdi, Bazai, Sibghat Ullah, & Tang, Hao (2023b). Editorial: Investigating AI-based smart precision agriculture techniques. *Frontiers in Plant Science*, 1410.3389/fpls.2023.1237783.

Bibri, S. E. (2022). Eco-districts and data-driven smart eco-cities: Emerging approaches to strategic planning by design and spatial scaling and evaluation by technology. *Land Use Policy*, 113, 105830.

Burrough, P. A., McDonnell, R. A., & Lloyd, C. D. (2015). *Principles of geographical information systems*. Oxford University Press.

Cao, C., Dragićević, S., & Li, S. (2019). Land-use change detection with convolutional neural network methods. *Environments*, 6(2), 25. 10.3390/environments6020025

Carleo, G., Cirac, I., Cranmer, K., Daudet, L., Schuld, M., Tishby, N., & Zdeborová, L. (2019). Machine learning and the physical sciences. *Reviews of Modern Physics*, 91(4), 045002. 10.1103/RevModPhys.91.045002

Castro Gomez, M. G. (2017). *Joint use of Sentinel-1 and Sentinel-2 for land cover classification: A machine learning approach*. Lund University GEM thesis series.

Chaturvedi, V., & de Vries, W. T. (2021). Machine learning algorithms for urban land use planning: A review. *Urban Science*, 5(3), 68. 10.3390/urbansci5030068

Chen, J. (2007). Rapid urbanization in China: A real challenge to soil protection and food security. *Catena*, 69(1), 1–15. 10.1016/j.catena.2006.04.019

Choi, J., Lee, I. W., & Cha, S. W. (2022). Analysis of data errors in the solar photovoltaic monitoring system database: An overview of nationwide power plants in Korea. *Renewable and Sustainable Energy Reviews*, 156, 112007.

Colquhoun, D. A., Shanks, A. M., Kapeles, S. R., Shah, N., Saager, L., Vaughn, M. T., … & Mathis, M. R. (2020). Considerations for integration of perioperative electronic health records across institutions for research and quality improvement: The approach taken by the Multicenter Perioperative Outcomes Group. *Anesthesia and Analgesia*, 130(5), 1133.

Coronato, A., Naeem, M., De Pietro, G., & Paragliola, G. (2020). Reinforcement learning for intelligent healthcare applications: A survey. *Artificial Intelligence in Medicine*, 109, 101964. 10.1016/j.artmed.2020.101964

Crawford, M., Khoshgoftaar, T. M., Prusa, J. D., Richter, A. N., & Al Najada, H. (2015). Survey of review spam detection using machine learning techniques. *Journal of Big Data*, 2(1), 1–24.

Crooks, A. T., & Heppenstall, A. J. (2011). Introduction to agent-based modelling. In *Agent-based models of geographical systems* (pp. 85–105). Dordrecht: Springer Netherlands. 10.1007/978-90-481-8927-4_5

Deng, D. (2020, September). DBSCAN clustering algorithm based on density. In *2020 7th International Forum on Electrical Engineering and Automation (IFEEA)* (pp. 949–953). IEEE. 10.1109/IFEEA51475.2020.00199

Deng, X., Huang, J., Rozelle, S., & Uchida, E. (2010). Economic growth and the expansion of urban land in China. *Urban Studies*, 47(4), 813–843. 10.1177/0042098009349770

Ding, C., & Lichtenberg, E. (2011). Land and urban economic growth in China. *Journal of Regional Science*, 51(2), 299–317. 10.1111/j.1467-9787.2010.00686.x

Douzas, G., Bacao, F., & Last, F. (2018). Improving imbalanced learning through a heuristic oversampling method based on k-means and SMOTE. *Information Sciences*, 465, 1–20.

Faundeen, J. L., Kanengieter, R. L., & Buswell, M. D. (2002). US geological survey spatial data access. *Journal of Geospatial Engineering*, 4(2), 145–145.

Fei, Sun, Wagan, Raja Asif, Hasnain, Ahmad, Hussain, Aamir, Bhatti, Uzair Aslam, & Elahi, Ehsan (2022). Spatiotemporal impact of the COVID-19 pandemic lockdown on air quality pattern in Nanjing, China. *Frontiers in Environmental Science*, 10. 10.3389/fenvs.2022.952310.

Foley, J. A., DeFries, R., Asner, G. P., Barford, C., Bonan, G., Carpenter, S. R., & Snyder, P. K. (2005). Global consequences of land use. *Science*, 309(5734), 570–574. 10.1126/science.1111772

Fox, F., Aggarwal, V. R., Whelton, H., & Johnson, O. (2018, June). A data quality framework for process mining of electronic health record data. In *2018 IEEE International Conference on Healthcare Informatics (ICHI)* (pp. 12–21). IEEE.

Frawley, W. J., Piatetsky-Shapiro, G., & Matheus, C. J. (1992). Knowledge discovery in databases: An overview. *AI magazine*, 13(3), 57-57.

Freitas, A., & Curry, E. (2016). Big data curation. *New Horizons for a Data-Driven Economy: A Roadmap for Usage and Exploitation of Big Data in Europe*, 87–118.

Geerlings, H., & Stead, D. (2003). The integration of land use planning, transport and environment in European policy and research. *Transport Policy*, 10(3), 187–196. 10.1016/S0967-070X(03)00020-9

Geneletti, D. (2013). Assessing the impact of alternative land-use zoning policies on future ecosystem services. *Environmental Impact Assessment Review*, 40, 25–35. 10.1016/j.eiar.2012.12.003

Ghannam, R. B., & Techtmann, S. M. (2021). Machine learning applications in microbial ecology, human microbiome studies, and environmental monitoring. *Computational and Structural Biotechnology Journal*, 19, 1092–1107. 10.1016/j.csbj.2021.01.028

Hagenauer, J., Omrani, H., & Helbich, M. (2019). Assessing the performance of 38 machine learning models: The case of land consumption rates in Bavaria, Germany. *International Journal of Geographical Information Science*, 33(7), 1399–1419. 10.1080/13658816.2019.1579333

Hain, D., Jurowetzki, R., Lee, S., & Zhou, Y. (2023). Machine learning and artificial intelligence for science, technology, innovation mapping and forecasting: Review, synthesis, and applications. *Scientometrics*, 128(3), 1465–1472. 10.1007/s11192-022-04628-8

Haklay, M., & Weber, P. (2008). Openstreetmap: User-generated street maps. *IEEE Pervasive Computing*, 7(4), 12–18.

Harris, P. M., & Ventura, S. J. (1995). The integration of geographic data with remotely sensed imagery to improve classification in an urban area. *Photogrammetric Engineering and Remote Sensing*, 61(8), 993–998.

He, C., Chen, T., Mao, X., & Zhou, Y. (2016). Economic transition, urbanization and population redistribution in China. *Habitat International*, 51, 39–47. 10.1016/j.habitatint.2015.10.006

He, C., Huang, Z., & Wang, R. (2014). Land use change and economic growth in urban China: A structural equation analysis. *Urban Studies*, 51(13), 2880–2898. 10.1177/0042098013513649

Helber, P., Bischke, B., Dengel, A., & Borth, D. (2019). Eurosat: A novel data set and deep learning benchmark for land use and land cover classification. *IEEE Journal of Selected Topics in Applied Earth Observations and Remote Sensing*, 12(7), 2217–2226. 10.1109/JSTARS.2019.2918242

Henderson, F. M., & Xia, Z. G. (1997). SAR applications in human settlement detection, population estimation and urban land use pattern analysis: A status report. *IEEE Transactions on Geoscience and Remote Sensing*, 35(1), 79–85.

Hu, Z., Lo, C. P. (2007). Modeling urban growth in Atlanta using logistic regression. *Computers, Environment and Urban Systems*, 31(6), 667–688. 10.1016/j.compenvurbsys.2006.11.001

Huyghues-Beaufond, N., Tindemans, S., Falugi, P., Sun, M., & Strbac, G. (2020). Robust and automatic data cleansing method for short-term load forecasting of distribution feeders. *Applied Energy*, 261, 114405.

Jadhav, A., Pramod, D., & Ramanathan, K. (2019). Comparison of performance of data imputation methods for numeric data set. *Applied Artificial Intelligence*, 33(10), 913–933.

Javadian, M., Shamskooshki, H., & Momeni, M. (2011). Application of sustainable urban development in environmental suitability analysis of educational land use by using AHP and GIS in Tehran. *Procedia Engineering*, 21, 72–80.

Jordan, M. I., & Mitchell, T. M. (2015). Machine learning: Trends, perspectives, and prospects. *Science*, 349(6245), 255–260. 10.1126/science.aaa8415

Kandel, S., Heer, J., Plaisant, C., Kennedy, J., Van Ham, F., Riche, N. H., ... & Buono, P. (2011). Research directions in data wrangling: Visualizations and transformations for usable and credible data. *Information Visualization*, 10(4), 271–288.

Kanevsky, J., Corban, J., Gaster, R., Kanevsky, A., Lin, S., & Gilardino, M. (2016). Big data and machine learning in plastic surgery: A new frontier in surgical innovation. *Plastic and reconstructive surgery*, 137(5), 890e–897e. 10.1097/PRS.0000000000002088

Kelobonye, K., McCarney, G., Xia, J. C., Swapan, M. S. H., Mao, F., & Zhou, H. (2019). Relative accessibility analysis for key land uses: A spatial equity perspective. *Journal of Transport Geography*, 75, 82–93. 10.1016/j.jtrangeo.2019.01.015

Kotsiantis, S. B., Zaharakis, I. D., & Pintelas, P. E. (2006). Machine learning: A review of classification and combining techniques. *Artificial Intelligence Review*, 26(3), 159–190. 10.1007/s1 0462-007-9052-3

Kumar, K. M., & Reddy, A. R. M. (2016). A fast DBSCAN clustering algorithm by accelerating neighbor searching using Groups method. *Pattern Recognition*, 58, 39–48. 10.1016/j.patcog.2 016.03.008

Lamine, S., Petropoulos, G. P., Singh, S. K., Szabó, S., Bachari, N. E. I., Srivastava, P. K., & Suman, S. (2018). Quantifying land use/land cover spatio-temporal landscape pattern dynamics from Hyperion using SVMs classifier and FRAGSTATS®. *Geocarto international*, 33(8), 862–878. 10.1080/10106049.2017.1307460

Lefebvre, A., Sannier, C., & Corpetti, T. (2016). Monitoring urban areas with Sentinel-2A data: Application to the update of the Copernicus high resolution layer imperviousness degree. *Remote Sensing*, 8(7), 606.

Li, X., & Gong, P. (2016). Urban growth models: Progress and perspective. *Science bulletin*, 61(21), 1637–1650. 10.1007/s11434-016-1111-1

Liew, A. W. C., Law, N. F., & Yan, H. (2011). Missing value imputation for gene expression data: Computational techniques to recover missing data from available information. *Briefings in Bioinformatics*, 12(5), 498–513.

Liu, M., Wei, H., Dong, X., Wang, X. C., Zhao, B., & Zhang, Y. (2022). Integrating land use, ecosystem service, and human well-being: A systematic review. *Sustainability*, 14(11), 6926.

Liu, Y., Fang, F., & Li, Y. (2014). Key issues of land use in China and implications for policy making. *Land Use Policy*, 40, 6–12. 10.1016/j.landusepol.2013.03.013

Longo, L., Goebel, R., Lecue, F., Kieseberg, P., & Holzinger, A. (2020, August). Explainable artificial intelligence: Concepts, applications, research challenges and visions. In *Machine Learning and Knowledge Extraction: 4th IFIP TC 5, TC 12, WG 8.4, WG 8.9, WG 12.9 International Cross-Domain Conference, CD-MAKE 2020, Dublin, Ireland, August 25–28, 2020, Proceedings* (pp. 1–16). Cham: Springer International Publishing.

Lukanov, B. R., & Krieger, E. M. (2019). Distributed solar and environmental justice: Exploring the demographic and socio-economic trends of residential PV adoption in California. *Energy Policy*, 134, 110935.

Ma, C., & Zhou, M. (2018). A GIS-based interval fuzzy linear programming for optimal land resource allocation at a city scale. *Social Indicators Research*, 135, 143–166. 10.1007/s11205-016-1476-1

Mahesh, B. (2020). Machine learning algorithms-a review. *International Journal of Science and Research (IJSR).[Internet]*, 9, 381–386. 10.21275/ART20203995

Mahmud, M., Kaiser, M. S., Hussain, A., & Vassanelli, S. (2018). Applications of deep learning and reinforcement learning to biological data. *IEEE Transactions on Neural Networks and Learning Systems*, 29(6), 2063–2079. 10.1109/TNNLS.2018.2790388

Malczewski, J. (2004). GIS-based land-use suitability analysis: A critical overview. *Progress in Planning*, 62(1), 3–65.

Mao, W., Lu, D., Hou, L., Liu, X., & Yue, W. (2020). Comparison of machine-learning methods for urban land-use mapping in Hangzhou city, China. *Remote Sensing*, 12(17), 2817. 10.33 90/rs12172817

Mathieu, R., Aryal, J., & Chong, A. K. (2007). Object-based classification of Ikonos imagery for mapping large-scale vegetation communities in urban areas. *Sensors*, 7(11), 2860–2880.

McGilvray, D. (2021). *Executing data quality projects: Ten steps to quality data and trusted information (TM)*. Academic Press.

McMillen, D. P., & McDonald, J. F. (1999). Land use before zoning: The case of 1920's Chicago. *Regional Science and Urban Economics*, 29(4), 473–489.10.1016/S0166-0462(99)00004-6

Melchiorri, M., Pesaresi, M., Florczyk, A. J., Corbane, C., & Kemper, T. (2019). Principles and applications of the global human settlement layer as baseline for the land use efficiency indicator—SDG 11.3. 1. *ISPRS International Journal of Geo-Information*, 8(2), 96.

Meyer, W. B., Turner, B. L. (1992). Human population growth and global land-use/cover change. *Annual Review of Ecology and Systematics*, 23(1), 39–61. 10.1146/annurev.es.23.110192. 000351

Milusheva, S., Marty, R., Bedoya, G., Williams, S., Resor, E., & Legovini, A. (2021). Applying machine learning and geolocation techniques to social media data (Twitter) to develop a resource for urban planning. *PloS one*, 16(2), e0244317. 10.1371/journal.pone.0244317

Mohamad, I. B., & Usman, D. (2013). Standardization and its effects on K-means clustering algorithm. *Research Journal of Applied Sciences, Engineering and Technology*, 6(17), 3299–3303.

Munappy, A., Bosch, J., Olsson, H. H., Arpteg, A., & Brinne, B. (2019, August). Data management challenges for deep learning. In *2019 45th Euromicro Conference on Software Engineering and Advanced Applications (SEAA)* (pp. 140–147). IEEE.

Muthukrishnan, R., & Rohini, R. (2016, October). LASSO: A feature selection technique in predictive modeling for machine learning. In *2016 IEEE international conference on advances in computer applications (ICACA)* (pp. 18–20). IEEE. 10.1109/ICACA.2016.7887916

Nasteski, V. (2017). An overview of the supervised machine learning methods. *Horizons. b*, 4, 51–62. 10.20544/HORIZONS.B.04.1.17.P05

Nunez-Iglesias, J., Kennedy, R., Parag, T., Shi, J., & Chklovskii, D. B. (2013). Machine learning of hierarchical clustering to segment 2D and 3D images. *PloS one*, 8(8), e71715. 10.1371/journal.pone.0071715

Okeke, F. O., Gyoh, L., & Echendu, F. I. (2021). Impact of land use morphology on urban transportation. *Civil Engineering Journal*, 7(10), 1753–1773. 10.28991/cej-2021-03091758

Parente, L., Taquary, E., Silva, A. P., Souza Jr, C., & Ferreira, L. (2019). Next generation mapping: Combining deep learning, cloud computing, and big remote sensing data. *Remote Sensing*, 11(23), 2881. 10.3390/rs11232881

Patra, S., Modi, P., & Bruzzone, L. (2015). Hyperspectral band selection based on rough set. *IEEE Transactions on Geoscience and Remote Sensing*, 53(10), 5495–5503.

Pauleit, S., & Duhme, F. (2000). Assessing the environmental performance of land cover types for urban planning. *Landscape and Urban Planning*, 52(1), 1–20. 10.1016/S0169-2046(00)00109-2

Pauleit, S., Ennos, R., & Golding, Y. (2005). Modeling the environmental impacts of urban land use and land cover change—a study in Merseyside, UK. *Landscape and Urban Planning*, 71(2–4), 295–310. 10.1016/j.landurbplan.2004.03.009

Pelletier, C., Webb, G. I., & Petitjean, F. (2019). Temporal convolutional neural network for the classification of satellite image time series. *Remote Sensing*, 11(5), 523.

Penone, C., Davidson, A. D., Shoemaker, K. T., Di Marco, M., Rondinini, C., Brooks, T. M., … & Costa, G. C. (2014). Imputation of missing data in life-history trait data sets: Which approach performs the best?. *Methods in Ecology and Evolution*, 5(9), 961–970.

Pramod, A., Naicker, H. S., & Tyagi, A. K. (2021). Machine learning and deep learning: Open issues and future research directions for the next 10 years. *Computational analysis and deep learning for medical care: Principles, methods, and applications*, 463–490.

Qian, Z. (2010). Without zoning: Urban development and land use controls in Houston. *Cities*, 27(1), 31–41. 10.1016/j.cities.2009.11.006

Queirós, A., Faria, D., & Almeida, F. (2017). Strengths and limitations of qualitative and quantitative research methods. *European Journal of Education Studies.*

Ramezan, C. A., Warner, T. A., & Maxwell, A. E. (2019). Evaluation of sampling and cross-validation tuning strategies for regional-scale machine learning classification. *Remote Sensing*, 11(2), 185. 10.3390/rs11020185

Rana, V. K., & Suryanarayana, T. M. V. (2020). Performance evaluation of MLE, RF and SVM classification algorithms for watershed scale land use/land cover mapping using sentinel 2 bands. *Remote Sensing Applications: Society and Environment*, 19, 100351. 10.1016/j.rsase.2020.100351

Rashidi, H. H., Tran, N., Albahra, S., & Dang, L. T. (2021). Machine learning in health care and laboratory medicine: General overview of supervised learning and Auto-ML. *International Journal of Laboratory Hematology*, 43, 15–22. 10.1111/ijlh.13537

Ray, S. (2019, February). A quick review of machine learning algorithms. In *2019 International conference on machine learning, big data, cloud and parallel computing (COMITCon)* (pp. 35–39). IEEE. 10.1109/COMITCon.2019.8862451

Rivas Casado, M., Ballesteros Gonzalez, R., Kriechbaumer, T., & Veal, A. (2015). Automated identification of river hydromorphological features using UAV high resolution aerial imagery. *Sensors*, 15(11), 27969–27989.

Rodriguez-Galiano, V., Sanchez-Castillo, M., Chica-Olmo, M., & Chica-Rivas, M. J. O. G. R. (2015). Machine learning predictive models for mineral prospectivity: An evaluation of neural networks, random forest, regression trees and support vector machines. *Ore Geology Reviews*, 71, 804–818. 10.1016/j.oregeorev.2015.01.001

Rossi-Hansberg, E. (2004). Optimal urban land use and zoning. *Review of Economic Dynamics*, 7(1), 69–106. 10.1016/S1094-2025(03)00056-5

Roy, A., & Inamdar, A. B. (2019). Multi-temporal Land Use Land Cover (LULC) change analysis of a dry semi-arid river basin in western India following a robust multi-sensor satellite image calibration strategy. *Heliyon*, 5(4), e01478.

Rukmana, D. (2018, March). Rapid urbanization and the need for sustainable transportation policies in Jakarta. In *IOP Conference Series: Earth and Environmental Science* (Vol. 124, No. 1, p. 012017). IOP Publishing. 10.1088/1755-1315/124/1/012017

Saravanan, R., & Sujatha, P. (2018, June). A state of art techniques on machine learning algorithms: A perspective of supervised learning approaches in data classification. In *2018 Second International Conference on Intelligent Computing and Control Systems (ICICCS)* (pp. 945–949). IEEE. 10.1109/ICCONS.2018.8663155

Seto, K. C., Fragkias, M., Güneralp, B., & Reilly, M. K. (2011). A meta-analysis of global urban land expansion. *PLoS one*, 6(8), e23777. 10.1371/journal.pone.0023777

Sharma, A., Jain, A., Gupta, P., & Chowdary, V. (2020). Machine learning applications for precision agriculture: A comprehensive review. *IEEE Access*, 9, 4843–4873. 10.1109/ACCESS.2020.3048415.

Soltani, A., Balaghi, R., Rezaei, M., & Riyabi, M. A. (2019). Spatial analysis and urban land use planning with emphasis on hospital site selection, case study: Isfahan city. Bulletin of Geography. *Socio-economic Series*, (43), 71–89. 10.2478/bog-2019-0005

Song, J., Yang, Y., Yang, Y., Huang, Z., & Shen, H. T. (2013, June). Inter-media hashing for large-scale retrieval from heterogeneous data sources. In *Proceedings of the 2013 ACM SIGMOD international conference on management of data* (pp. 785–796).

Sun, A. Y., & Scanlon, B. R. (2019). How can Big Data and machine learning benefit environment and water management: A survey of methods, applications, and future directions. *Environmental Research Letters*, 14(7), 073001.

Surya, B., Ahmad, D. N. A., Sakti, H. H., & Sahban, H. (2020). Land use change, spatial interaction, and sustainable development in the metropolitan urban areas, South Sulawesi Province, Indonesia. *Land*, 9(3), 95.

Suzuki, H., Cervero, R., & Iuchi, K. (2013). *Transforming cities with transit: Transit and land-use integration for sustainable urban development.* World Bank Publications.

Tahir, M., Imam, E., & Hussain, T. (2013). Evaluation of land use/land cover changes in Mekelle City, *Ethiopia using Remote Sensing and GIS. Computational Ecology and Software*, 3(1), 9.

Tai, A. M., Albuquerque, A., Carmona, N. E., Subramanieapillai, M., Cha, D. S., Sheko, M., ... & McIntyre, R. S. (2019). Machine learning and big data: Implications for disease modeling and therapeutic discovery in psychiatry. *Artificial Intelligence in Medicine*, 99, 101704.

Talen, E. (2005). Land use zoning and human diversity: Exploring the connection. *Journal of Urban Planning and Development*, 131(4), 214–232. 10.1061/(ASCE)0733-9488(2005)131:4(214)

Tang, Y. (2013). Deep learning using linear support vector machines. arXiv preprint arXiv:1306.0239. 10.48550/arXiv.1306.0239

Thinh, N. X., Arlt, G., Heber, B., Hennersdorf, J., & Lehmann, I. (2002). Evaluation of urban land-use structures with a view to sustainable development. *Environmental Impact Assessment Review*, 22(5), 475–492. 10.1016/S0195-9255(02)00023-9

Thornton, P. (2002). *Mapping poverty and livestock in the developing world* (Vol. 1). ILRI (aka ILCA and ILRAD).

Torabi Haghighi, A., Darabi, H., Karimidastenaei, Z., Davudirad, A. A., Rouzbeh, S., Rahmati, O., & Klöve, B. (2021). Land degradation risk mapping using topographic, human-induced, and geo-environmental variables and machine learning algorithms, for the Pole-Doab watershed, Iran. *Environmental Earth Sciences*, 80, 1–21. 10.1007/s12665-020-09327-2

Tougui, I., Jilbab, A., & El Mhamdi, J. (2021). Impact of the choice of cross-validation techniques on the results of machine learning-based diagnostic applications. *Healthcare Informatics Research*, 27(3), 189–199. 10.4258/hir.2021.27.3.189

Ullah, K. M., & Mansourian, A. (2016). Evaluation of land suitability for urban land-use planning: Case study D haka City. *Transactions in GIS*, 20(1), 20–37.

United Nations, The Sustainable Development Goals Report, 2018. https://unstats.un.org/sdgs/report/2018/overview/

Waddell, P. (2002). UrbanSim: Modeling urban development for land use, transportation, and environmental planning. *Journal of the American Planning Association*, 68(3), 297–314. 10.1 080/01944360208976274

Wäldchen, J., & Mäder, P. (2018). Machine learning for image based species identification. *Methods in Ecology and Evolution*, 9(11), 2216–2225. 10.1111/2041-210X.13075

Wang, R. Y., Ziad, M., & Lee, Y. W. (2006). *Data quality* (Vol. 23). Springer Science & Business Media.

Wang, Shiyong, Khan, Asad, Lin, Ying, Jiang, Zhuo, Tang, Hao, Alomar, Suliman Yousef, Sanaullah, Muhammad, & Bhatti, Uzair Aslam (2023). Deep reinforcement learning enables adaptive-image augmentation for automated optical inspection of plant rust. *Frontiers in Plant Science*, 1410.3389/fpls.2023.1142957.

Wegener, M. (2021). Land-use transport interaction models. *Handbook of regional science*, 229–246. 10.1007/978-3-662-60723-7_41

Wilbanks, T. J., & Fernandez, S. (2014). *Climate change and infrastructure, urban systems, and vulnerabilities: Technical report for the US Department of Energy in support of the national climate assessment.* Island Press.

World Bank. (2005). *World development indicators 2005.* The World Bank.

Wu, Guilu, Sahabuddin, Md, Bhatti, Uzair, Nawaz, Saqib Ali, Hasnain, Ahmad, Bhatti, Mughair Aslam, Fahim, Asmaa, Kaleri, Asif, & Kaleri, Arif Hussain (2022). COVID-19 and Air Pollution: Air Quality Impact in 13 Cities of the Jiangsu Province of China. *Polish Journal of Environmental Studies*, 31, 4907–491610.15244/pjoes/149714.

Xu, L., Huang, Q., Ding, D., Mei, M., & Qin, H. (2018). Modelling urban expansion guided by land ecological suitability: A case study of Changzhou City, China. *Habitat international*, 75, 12–24. 10.1016/j.habitatint.2018.04.002

Xu, R., & Wunsch, D. (2005). Survey of clustering algorithms. *IEEE Transactions on Neural Networks*, 16(3), 645–678. 10.1109/TNN.2005.845141

Yang, X., & Wen, W. (2018). Ridge and lasso regression models for cross-version defect prediction. *IEEE Transactions on Reliability*, 67(3), 885–896. 10.1109/TR.2018.2847353

Yin, J., Yin, Z., Zhong, H., Xu, S., Hu, X., Wang, J., & Wu, J. (2011). Monitoring urban expansion and land use/land cover changes of Shanghai metropolitan area during the transitional economy (1979–2009) in China. *Environmental Monitoring and Assessment*, 177, 609–621. 10.1007/s10661-010-1660-8

Yu, Z., Yao, Y., Yang, G., Wang, X., & Vejre, H. (2019). Strong contribution of rapid urbanization and urban agglomeration development to regional thermal environment dynamics and evolution. *Forest Ecology and Management*, 446, 214–225. 10.1016/j.foreco.2019.05.046

Zaadnoordijk, L., Besold, T. R., & Cusack, R. (2022). Lessons from infant learning for unsupervised machine learning. *Nature Machine Intelligence*, 4(6), 510–520. 10.1038/s42256-022-00488-2

Zeevi, D., Korem, T., Zmora, N., Israeli, D., Rothschild, D., Weinberger, A., ... & Segal, E. (2015). Personalized nutrition by prediction of glycemic responses. *Cell*, 163(5), 1079–1094.

Zhang, C., Wang, P., Xiong, P., Li, C., & Quan, B. (2021). Spatial pattern simulation of land use based on FLUS model under ecological protection: A case study of hengyang city. *Sustainability*, 13(18), 10458. 10.3390/su131810458

Zhang, P., Ke, Y., Zhang, Z., Wang, M., Li, P., & Zhang, S. (2018). Urban land use and land cover classification using novel deep learning models based on high spatial resolution satellite imagery. *Sensors*, 18(11), 3717. 10.3390/s18113717

Zhao, Q., Yu, L., Du, Z., Peng, D., Hao, P., Zhang, Y., & Gong, P. (2022). An overview of the applications of Earth observation satellite data: Impacts and future trends. *Remote Sensing*, 14(8), 1863.

Zhong, Y., Su, Y., Wu, S., Zheng, Z., Zhao, J., Ma, A., ... & Zhang, L. (2020). Open-source data-driven urban land-use mapping integrating point-line-polygon semantic objects: A case study of Chinese cities. *Remote Sensing of Environment*, 247, 111838.

Zhou, Q., Lu, S., Wu, Y., & Wang, J. (2020). Property-oriented material design based on a data-driven machine learning technique. *The Journal of Physical Chemistry Letters*, 11(10), 3920–3927. 10.1021/acs.jpclett.0c00665

Zhu, J. (2004). From land use right to land development right: Institutional change in China's urban development. *Urban Studies*, 41(7), 1249–1267. 10.1080/0042098042000214770

Application of GIS and Remote-Sensing Technology in Ecosystem Services and Biodiversity Conservation

Mir Muhammad Nizamani[1], Qian Zhang[1],
Ghulam Muhae-Ud-Din[1], Muhammad Awais[2],
Muhammad Qayyum[3], Muhammad Farhan[1],
Muhammad Jabran[4], and Yong Wang[1]

[1]*Department of Plant Pathology, Agricultural College, Guizhou University, Guiyang, China*
[2]*Institute of Plant Sciences, Faculty of Natural Sciences, University of Sindh,*
 Jamshoro, Pakistan
[3]*School of Economics and Statistics, Guangzhou University, Guangzhou, China*
[4]*State Key Laboratory for Biology of Plant Diseases, Institute of Plant Protection,*
 Chinese Academy of Agricultural Sciences, Beijing, China

12.1 INTRODUCTION

12.1.1 Overview of Ecosystem Services and Biodiversity Conservation

Ecosystem services are indispensable to human life, supporting our well-being, driving economic growth, and contributing to environmental sustainability (Summers et al., 2012). These services stem from the intricate web of biodiversity that exists on our planet, encompassing the vast array of species, genetic diversity, and the ecosystems they inhabit. Recognizing the significance of ecosystem services is key to making informed decisions about conserving and managing our natural resources and ecosystems, thereby fostering a healthier and more sustainable future for all (Tallis & Polasky, 2009).

Ecosystem services can be divided into four primary groups: Provisioning services encompass the tangible resources that ecosystems provide for human use, such as food, water, raw materials, and medicines (Layke, 2009). These resources are essential for human survival, livelihoods, and economic growth. Regulating services pertain to the vital role

DOI: 10.1201/9781032646268-12

ecosystems play in controlling various natural processes that maintain environmental balance, such as climate regulation, air quality, water purification, waste decomposition, pollination, and natural pest control. These services help create stable conditions for human life and well-being. Cultural services involve the contributions of ecosystems to our cultural, spiritual, and recreational experiences, including aesthetic beauty, cultural heritage, artistic and literary inspiration, spiritual fulfillment, and opportunities for recreation and ecotourism. These services enrich our lives and contribute to our overall quality of life. Finally, supporting services consist of the fundamental processes that underpin other ecosystem services, like nutrient cycling, soil formation, and primary production. Although humans do not directly consume or utilize these services, they are vital for maintaining the provision of other essential ecosystem services (Daily, 2003).

Biodiversity, or the variety of life on Earth, is the foundation of ecosystem services. A diverse array of species and habitats is necessary for maintaining the resilience and stability of ecosystems, which in turn ensures the continuous provision of vital services to human society. By prioritizing the conservation of biodiversity, we can protect the invaluable ecosystem services that are integral to human well-being and a sustainable future for generations to come.

12.1.2 Importance of GIS and Remote Sensing in Ecosystem Services and Biodiversity Conservation

Geographic information systems (GISs) and remote-sensing technologies have indeed become essential tools for ecosystem services assessment and biodiversity conservation (Tahri et al., 2021). These advanced tools offer valuable spatial and temporal data, enabling scientists, policymakers, and practitioners to analyze, monitor, and make informed decisions about ecological processes, threats, and conservation strategies. GIS and remote-sensing technologies facilitate the efficient mapping, monitoring, and management of ecosystems and their services across various spatial and temporal scales, providing several key benefits:

1. Detailed spatial analysis: GIS allows for the integration, analysis, and visualization of spatial data from diverse sources (Yue et al., 2010). This enables the identification of patterns and relationships between various environmental factors, such as land use, habitat distribution, and species richness. This information is crucial for understanding the dynamics of ecosystems and assessing the provision of ecosystem services.

2. Improved monitoring: Remote-sensing technologies, including satellite imagery and aerial photography, provide consistent and up-to-date information on land cover, vegetation, and changes in ecosystems (Giri, 2016). This allows for timely detection of habitat loss, degradation, and fragmentation, as well as the monitoring of species populations and the effectiveness of conservation measures.

3. Enhanced decision making: GIS and remote-sensing technologies facilitate data-driven decision making in biodiversity conservation and ecosystem management

(McCarthy et al., 2017). By providing accurate and timely information, these tools support the development of targeted conservation strategies, the evaluation of potential impacts of land use changes on ecosystems, and the identification of priority areas for restoration and protection.

4. Comprehensive assessments: Combining GIS and remote-sensing data enables the quantification and mapping of ecosystem services, such as carbon sequestration, water purification, and pollination (Cord et al., 2017). This information is essential for assessing the value of ecosystems, understanding trade-offs between different land uses, and promoting sustainable management practices.

5. Increased collaboration: GIS and remote-sensing technologies promote inter-disciplinary collaboration among researchers, practitioners, and policymakers working in the fields of ecology, geography, environmental science, and conservation (Acevedo, 2011). This fosters the exchange of ideas, data, and expertise, leading to more effective and informed conservation efforts.

Overall, the integration of GIS and remote-sensing technologies has revolutionized the fields of ecosystem services assessment and biodiversity conservation. These tools provide a wealth of spatial and temporal information, enabling a deeper understanding of ecosystems and their services and promoting informed, data-driven decision making for more effective conservation and sustainable management practices.

12.1.3 Scope of the Chapter

This chapter will explore the application of GIS and remote-sensing technologies in ecosystem services and biodiversity conservation. It will introduce the fundamental concepts of GIS and remote sensing, discuss their application in assessing ecosystem services, and illustrate how these technologies can be employed to support biodiversity conservation efforts. The chapter will also present case studies and real-world applications, highlighting the importance of integrating GIS and remote sensing in decision-making processes related to ecosystem services and biodiversity conservation (Figure 12.1). Finally, the chapter will identify challenges and future prospects in this field, offering insights for researchers, practitioners, and policymakers.

12.2 FUNDAMENTALS OF GIS AND REMOTE SENSING

12.2.1 Geographic Information Systems (GISs)

12.2.1.1 Definition and Basic Concepts

Geographic information systems (GISs) are computer-based tools used to capture, store, manipulate, analyze, and visualize spatial or geographic data (Reddy, 2018). GIS integrates various types of data, such as raster, vector, and attribute data, to represent and model the real world. It allows users to perform spatial analysis, overlay multiple data layers, and create maps to facilitate decision-making processes related to environmental management, urban planning, and natural resource management.

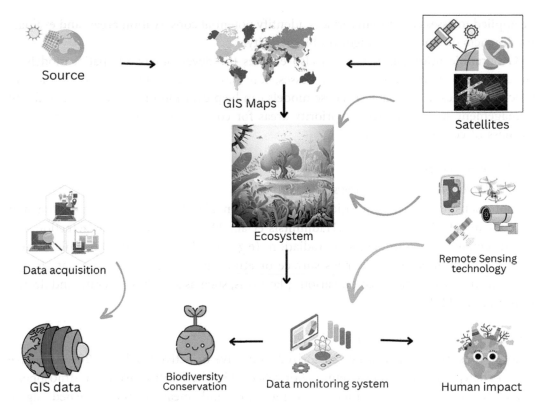

Source

GIS Maps

Satellites

Ecosystem

Data acquisition

Remote Sensing technology

GIS data

Biodiversity Conservation

Data monitoring system

Human impact

FIGURE 12.1   Application of machine learning to urban ecology.

12.2.1.2 Components and Data Structures

A GIS consists of five main components: hardware, software, data, users, and procedures. The hardware includes the computers and peripheral devices used for data input, storage, and output. The software includes the programs and applications that enable spatial data manipulation and analysis. The data consists of spatial (e.g., geographic coordinates) and attribute (e.g., population, land use) information (Bhat et al., 2011; Al-Quraishi et al., 2019). The users are the people who interact with the system, while the procedures refer to the methodologies and techniques employed in data analysis.

Spatial data in a GIS can be represented using two primary data structures: raster and vector. Raster data consists of a grid of cells or pixels, where each cell represents a specific geographic area and contains a value that represents a particular attribute (e.g., elevation, land cover) (Peuquet, D. J., & Duan, 1995). Vector data, on the other hand, uses points, lines, and polygons to represent discrete geographic features such as locations, roads, and administrative boundaries (Crooks, 2010).

12.2.1.3 Spatial Analysis and Modeling

Spatial analysis is a core function of GIS, allowing users to explore patterns, relationships, and trends in geographic data (Bailey et al., 1994). It includes a wide range of techniques such as buffering, overlay, proximity analysis, and network analysis. These techniques can be applied to assess ecosystem services, identify potential conservation areas, and evaluate the impacts of land-use changes on biodiversity.

Geographic information systems also enables the development of spatial models to simulate and predict ecological processes, land-use changes, and the distribution of species (Vanacker et al., 2003). These models can help decision makers evaluate different management scenarios, identify priority areas for conservation, and monitor the effectiveness of conservation actions.

12.2.2 Remote Sensing

12.2.2.1 Definition and Principles

Remote sensing is the acquisition of information about an object or phenomenon without direct physical contact (Hadjimitsis et al., 2013). It involves the detection and measurement of electromagnetic radiation (e.g., visible light, infrared, microwave) reflected or emitted by the Earth's surface or atmosphere. Remote-sensing data is collected using sensors mounted on various platforms, such as satellites, aircraft, and drones (Sozzi et al., 2021).

12.2.2.2 Sensors and Platforms

Remote sensing sensors can be categorized as passive or active (Tedesco, 2015). Passive sensors detect natural radiation emitted or reflected by the Earth's surface or atmosphere, while active sensors emit their own radiation and measure the returned signal (Lettenmaier et al., 2015). Examples of passive sensors include multispectral and hyperspectral sensors, while active sensors include radar and lidar.

The choice of platform depends on factors such as the desired spatial, temporal, and spectral resolution, as well as the cost and accessibility of the data. Satellites are the most common platforms for remote sensing, offering global coverage and consistent data acquisition. Aircraft and drones provide higher spatial resolution and flexibility, making them suitable for local-scale studies and rapid response applications (Pádua et al., 2017).

12.2.2.3 Image Acquisition, Processing, and Interpretation

Remote-sensing data is acquired in the form of digital images, which can be processed and analyzed to extract valuable information about the Earth's surface and atmosphere (Richards & Richards, 2022). Image processing techniques include radiometric and geometric corrections, image enhancement, and classification (Sowmya et al., 2017). Image interpretation involves the identification of features and patterns in the imagery, either through visual analysis or using automated algorithms (Quackenbush, 2004).

Remote-sensing data, when integrated with GIS, can provide valuable insights into ecosystem services and biodiversity conservation (Gong et al., 2021). For example, land cover classification using remote-sensing images can help identify different ecosystems and their extent, enabling the assessment of the distribution and status of ecosystem services (Murray et al., 2018). In addition, time-series analysis of remote-sensing data can help monitor changes in ecosystems and biodiversity, providing valuable information for conservation planning and management (Alleaume et al., 2018).

Remote-sensing data can also be combined with other spatial and non-spatial data (e.g., climate, topography, and species occurrence records) in GIS to create species distribution models, which can predict the potential distribution of species under different environmental conditions. These models can inform conservation strategies, such as the identification of priority areas for habitat protection and restoration, or the assessment of the impacts of climate change on biodiversity (Brown et al., 2017).

Geographic information systems and remote sensing are fundamental tools in the study and management of ecosystem services and biodiversity conservation. These technologies provide a wealth of spatial and temporal data, enabling researchers, practitioners, and policymakers to make informed decisions regarding the sustainable management of natural resources and the protection of our planet's biodiversity.

12.3 ASSESSING ECOSYSTEM SERVICES USING GIS AND REMOTE SENSING

12.3.1 Provisioning Services

12.3.1.1 Food and Water Resources

Geographic information systems and remote sensing are valuable tools for monitoring and assessing the availability and distribution of food and water resources (Ceccato et al., 2005). By combining different types of data and utilizing various analysis techniques, researchers, governments, and organizations can make more informed decisions about resource management and allocation. Here are some of the ways GIS and remote sensing can be employed for this purpose:

1. Land Cover Classification: Using remote-sensing data, such as satellite images, researchers can classify land cover types, including agricultural lands, forests, and water bodies (Rwanga & Ndambuki, 2017). This information is crucial for understanding where potential food and water sources are located.

2. Soil Quality Analysis: GIS can be used to analyze soil quality data, which can help determine the suitability of specific areas for agriculture (AbdelRahman et al., 2016). Soil quality directly influences crop productivity, and understanding it can help inform decisions about land use and agricultural practices.

3. Topographic Analysis: Using GIS, topographic data can be analyzed to identify areas prone to flooding or drought, as well as to determine optimal locations for water storage and distribution infrastructure (Alwan et al., 2020). Topography plays a critical role in water availability and agricultural productivity.

4. Climate Analysis: GIS can be used to analyze climate data, such as precipitation, temperature, and evapotranspiration (Fu et al., 2007). This information can be used to identify areas with favorable conditions for agriculture and water availability, as well as to forecast potential impacts of climate change on food and water resources.

5. Vegetation Health Monitoring: Remote-sensing data, such as NDVI, can be used to monitor the health and productivity of vegetation (Kureel et al., 2022). This information can provide early warning signs of drought, disease, or other factors impacting crop productivity, allowing for timely interventions and resource management decisions.

6. Water Resource Assessment: By combining remote-sensing data with GIS analysis, researchers can assess the availability of surface and groundwater resources (Liu et al., 2023). This information can help inform decisions about water allocation, infrastructure development, and conservation efforts.

7. Food Security Analysis: By integrating data on food production, population, and socioeconomic factors, GIS can be used to identify areas at risk of food insecurity (Tiwari & Joshi, 2012). This information can help guide targeted interventions to improve food access and distribution.

8. Disaster Risk Assessment: GIS and remote sensing can be used to assess the vulnerability of food and water resources to natural disasters, such as floods, droughts, and storms (Van Westen, 2013). This information can help inform disaster risk reduction strategies and preparedness measures.

Overall, the integration of GIS and remote-sensing technologies provides a powerful toolset for monitoring and assessing food and water resources. By leveraging these tools, stakeholders can make more informed decisions about resource management, ultimately improving food and water security for communities worldwide.

12.3.1.2 Raw Materials

Remote sensing and GIS are indeed invaluable tools for identifying, mapping, and monitoring the distribution of natural resources. By employing these technologies, researchers and decision makers can gain a better understanding of the availability and distribution of resources, facilitating sustainable management and reducing environmental impacts. Here are some examples of how remote sensing and GIS can be applied in this context:

1. Forest Biomass Estimation: Remote-sensing techniques, such as LiDAR (light detection and ranging) and radar, can be employed to estimate forest biomass and monitor changes over time (Messinger et al., 2016). These data can be used to assess the sustainability of logging practices and inform forest management strategies.

2. Deforestation Monitoring: Satellite imagery can be used to detect and monitor deforestation, logging activities, and land cover changes (Kamlun et al., 2016). Combining this data with GIS allows for the analysis of spatial patterns and trends, providing essential information for developing sustainable forest management policies.

3. Mineral Resource Mapping: Remote-sensing data, such as hyperspectral imagery, can be used to identify and map the spatial distribution of mineral resources (Booysen et al., 2022). GIS can then be employed to analyze the distribution of these resources in relation to other factors, such as infrastructure, protected areas, and population centers.

4. Environmental Impact Assessment: GIS can be utilized to assess the potential environmental impacts of mining operations and other extractive industries (Werner et al., 2019). By integrating data on factors such as land use, hydrology, and biodiversity, researchers can identify areas of concern and develop strategies to mitigate potential impacts.

5. Land Reclamation Monitoring: Remote sensing and GIS can be used to monitor the progress of land reclamation efforts following mining or logging activities (Ali et al., 2022). This information can help ensure that reclamation efforts are effective and that the land is restored to its original state or repurposed for other uses.

6. Wildlife Habitat Analysis: GIS and remote sensing can be employed to analyze the impacts of resource extraction on wildlife habitats (Mallegowda et al., 2015). By identifying critical habitat areas and monitoring changes in land cover, decision makers can develop strategies to protect and restore habitats affected by resource extraction.

7. Resource Management and Planning: Combining remote sensing and GIS data allows for more informed decision making in resource management and planning (Hellegers et al., 2010). For example, data on resource distribution, land use, and environmental factors can be used to identify suitable locations for new extraction sites, minimizing conflicts with other land uses and reducing potential environmental impacts.

8. Monitoring and Enforcement: Remote sensing and GIS can be used to monitor compliance with regulations related to resource extraction, such as logging quotas and mining permits (Neeff et al., 2020). This information can help authorities identify and address illegal activities and ensure that industries operate in a sustainable manner.

Remote sensing and GIS technologies offer numerous applications for identifying, mapping, and monitoring the distribution of natural resources. By integrating these tools into resource management and planning processes, stakeholders can make more informed decisions and promote sustainable practices, minimizing the environmental impacts of resource extraction.

12.3.1.3 Genetic Resources

Geographic information systems and remote sensing can indeed play a significant role in assessing and conserving genetic resources. Genetic diversity is crucial for maintaining the resilience of agricultural systems and ensuring food security in the face of changing environmental conditions and emerging pests and diseases. By mapping the distribution of crop varieties, wild relatives, and their habitats, researchers can better understand patterns of genetic diversity and identify areas in need of conservation. Here are some ways GIS and remote sensing can contribute to the conservation of genetic resources:

1. Distribution Mapping: Remote-sensing data, such as satellite imagery, can be used to map the distribution of crop varieties and their wild relatives (Tuanmu et al., 2010). GIS can then be employed to analyze the spatial patterns of genetic diversity, helping researchers to identify areas with high levels of diversity.

2. Habitat Monitoring: Remote-sensing data can be used to monitor changes in the habitats of crop varieties and wild relatives, providing early warning signs of habitat loss or degradation (Nagendra et al., 2013). This information can help inform conservation efforts and guide the development of strategies to protect these valuable genetic resources.

3. Climate Change Impact Assessment: GIS can be used to analyze the potential impacts of climate change on the distribution and habitats of crop varieties and wild relatives (Jarvis et al., 2008). This information can help researchers and policy-makers to develop strategies for conserving genetic resources in the face of changing environmental conditions.

4. Identification of Conservation Priorities: By combining data on the distribution of genetic resources with information on land use, protected areas, and threats such as habitat loss and climate change, GIS can be used to identify priority areas for conservation efforts (Stralberg et al., 2020). This information can help guide the allocation of resources for in situ (in their natural habitats) and ex situ (in gene banks or other conservation facilities) conservation strategies.

5. Protected Area Planning: GIS can be used to assess the effectiveness of existing protected areas in conserving genetic resources and to identify gaps in the protected area network (Hoveka et al., 2020). This information can help inform the estab-lishment of new protected areas or the expansion of existing ones to better conserve genetic resources.

6. Landscape Connectivity Analysis: GIS can be used to analyze landscape connec-tivity, which is important for maintaining gene flow and genetic diversity in crop varieties and wild relatives (Ross et al., 2020). By identifying areas with high con-nectivity, researchers and policymakers can prioritize these areas for conservation and restoration efforts.

7. Crop Breeding and Improvement: Information on the distribution of genetic resources and their habitats can be used to inform crop breeding and improvement efforts (Halewood et al., 2018). By identifying areas with high genetic diversity, breeders can target these regions for the collection of germplasm (plant genetic

material) to develop new crop varieties with improved traits, such as pest and disease resistance or climate adaptability.

In GIS and remote-sensing technologies can significantly contribute to the assessment and conservation of genetic resources. By providing valuable information on the distribution, habitat, and threats facing these resources, these tools can help inform more effective conservation strategies, ultimately safeguarding the resilience of agricultural systems and supporting food security.

12.3.2 Regulating Services

12.3.2.1 Climate Regulation

Remote sensing and GIS are powerful tools for studying ecosystems' role in climate regulation, including carbon sequestration and temperature regulation (Avtar et al., 2017). By analyzing satellite data and integrating spatial information, researchers can better understand how ecosystems contribute to climate regulation and inform effective climate change mitigation strategies.

1. Carbon sequestration:

   a. Estimating carbon storage: Remote-sensing data can be used to estimate the amount of carbon stored in various ecosystems, particularly in forests. Satellite imagery can provide information on forest structure, biomass, and species composition, allowing for the calculation of carbon stocks. Techniques such as LiDAR (light detection and ranging) and radar can provide accurate estimations of forest biomass, while multispectral and hyperspectral imagery can be used to differentiate between tree species and age classes, both of which influence carbon storage capacity (Rodríguez-Veiga et al., 2017).

   b. Monitoring forest cover changes: Remote sensing allows for the continuous monitoring of changes in forest cover, such as deforestation, afforestation, and reforestation. By analyzing changes in forest cover over time, researchers can estimate the carbon fluxes associated with these processes and assess the effectiveness of forest conservation and management strategies (Estoque et al., 2021).

2. Temperature regulation:

   a. Analyzing land cover and land-use changes: Land cover and land-use changes can significantly impact local and regional climate patterns by altering surface albedo, evapotranspiration rates, and the distribution of vegetation. Remote-sensing data can be used to map and monitor land cover changes, while GIS can help analyze the spatial relationships between land cover, land-use, and climate variables (Rogan & Chen, 2004).

   b. Urban heat island effect: The urban heat island (UHI) effect refers to the phenomenon where urban areas experience higher temperatures than their surrounding rural areas due to factors such as reduced vegetation cover, increased impervious surfaces, and the release of waste heat from human activities. Remote-sensing data, particularly thermal infrared imagery, can be used to map the spatial distribution of surface temperatures and identify UHI patterns. GIS can then be employed to analyze the relationship between land cover, land-use, and temperature patterns, guiding urban planning and mitigation strategies (Schweighofer et al., 2021).

c. Ecosystem-based adaptation and mitigation: Remote sensing and GIS can also be used to assess the potential of ecosystem-based adaptation and mitigation strategies, such as reforestation, afforestation, and the restoration of wetlands (Dhyani et al., 2018). By modeling the effects of these strategies on carbon sequestration, temperature regulation, and other ecosystem services, decision makers can prioritize and implement cost-effective, sustainable interventions to combat climate change.

Remote sensing and GIS provide valuable insights into the role of ecosystems in climate regulation, including carbon sequestration and temperature regulation. By monitoring and analyzing changes in land cover, land use, and other factors, these tools can contribute to the development and implementation of effective climate change mitigation and adaptation strategies.

12.3.2.2 Water Regulation

The use of GIS and remote-sensing technologies indeed plays a significant role in understanding how ecosystems regulate water quantity and quality. By collecting and analyzing spatial data, these tools can provide valuable insights into the dynamics of water resources and help develop effective water management strategies.

1. Monitoring surface water and wetlands:

   a. Surface water mapping: Remote-sensing data, such as satellite imagery and radar, can be used to map and monitor surface water bodies, including lakes, rivers, and reservoirs. These data allow for the assessment of changes in water extent, volume, and flow patterns, providing essential information for water resource management (Huang et al., 2018).

   b. Wetland mapping and monitoring: Wetlands play a crucial role in maintaining water quality and quantity by filtering pollutants, storing floodwater, and recharging groundwater. Remote-sensing data can be used to map wetland extent, monitor changes over time, and assess the health and functionality of these ecosystems. Techniques such as multispectral and hyperspectral imaging, as well as radar and LiDAR, can provide detailed information on wetland vegetation, hydrology, and topography (Jie et al., 2021).

2. Modeling the impacts of land-use changes on water flow and quality:

   a. Hydrological modeling: GIS can be employed to integrate various data sources, such as remote-sensing data, topography, land cover, and soil information, to create hydrological models that simulate water flow and transport processes (Miller et al., 2002). These models can help identify the impacts of land-use changes, such as urbanization and deforestation, on water flow patterns and the availability of water resources.

   b. Water quality modeling: GIS can also be used to model the impacts of land-use changes on water quality by analyzing the relationships between land cover, land-use, and water quality parameters, such as nutrient concentrations and sediment loads (Preetha et al., 2021). This information can help identify potential sources of pollution, assess the effectiveness of conservation measures, and guide the development of water quality management strategies.

3. Supporting water resource management strategies:

   a. Watershed management: Remote sensing and GIS can be used to delineate watersheds, identify critical areas for conservation or restoration, and evaluate the effectiveness of watershed management practices (Wang et al.., 2016b). By integrating spatial data on land cover, land use, and hydrology, these tools can help prioritize interventions and allocate resources more effectively.

   b. Flood risk assessment and mitigation: Remote sensing and GIS can be employed to model flood risk and develop mitigation strategies. By integrating data on topography, land cover, and precipitation, these tools can help identify flood-prone areas, assess the potential impacts of flooding, and guide the implementation of flood management measures, such as floodplain zoning and the construction of flood protection infrastructure (Franci, et al., 2016).

   c. Groundwater management: Remote-sensing data, such as satellite-based gravity measurements, can provide information on changes in groundwater storage, while GIS can help analyze the relationships between land use, recharge rates, and groundwater availability (Safari et al., 2023). This information is crucial for the sustainable management of groundwater resources, particularly in regions facing water scarcity.

Geographic information systems and remote-sensing technologies can significantly enhance our understanding of how ecosystems regulate water quantity and quality. By monitoring changes in surface water, wetlands, and land use, and modeling the impacts of these changes on water flow and quality, these tools can provide crucial information for the development and implementation of effective water resource management strategies.

12.3.2.3 Pest and Disease Control

Geographic information systems and remote-sensing technologies can indeed contribute significantly to the assessment and management of ecosystem services related to pest and disease control. By collecting and analyzing spatial data, these tools can help monitor and predict the spread of pests and diseases and evaluate the effectiveness of various control measures. Here are some ways in which GIS and remote sensing can be utilized in this context:

1. Monitoring vegetation distribution and abundance:

   a. Habitat mapping: Remote-sensing data can be used to map the distribution and abundance of vegetation types, which can serve as habitats for pest predators and hosts for pests and diseases (Richard et al., 2018). Multispectral and hyperspectral satellite imagery can provide detailed information on vegetation health, structure, and species composition, allowing for the identification of areas at risk of pest and disease outbreaks.

   b. Detection of pest and disease symptoms: Remote-sensing technologies can also be used to detect early signs of pest and disease infestations by identifying changes in vegetation health, such as reduced photosynthetic activity or leaf area (Zhang et al., 2019). Techniques such as thermal and hyperspectral imaging can help detect plant stress caused by pests and diseases, enabling timely intervention and control measures.

2. Modeling the spread of pests and diseases:

   a. Spatial analysis: GIS can be employed to analyze the spatial patterns of pest and disease outbreaks and identify factors that may contribute to their spread, such as landscape connectivity, climate, and land-use practices (Ostfeld et al., 2005). This information can help predict the risk of future outbreaks and guide the implementation of preventive measures.

   b. Species distribution modeling: GIS can also be used to model the potential distribution of pests and diseases based on environmental factors, such as temperature, precipitation, and habitat availability (Bradie & Leung, 2017). These models can help identify areas at risk of invasion and inform surveillance efforts and management strategies.

3. Evaluating the effectiveness of control measures:

   a. Natural enemies: GIS can be used to assess the effectiveness of biological control agents, such as predatory insects and parasitoids, in suppressing pest populations (Roubos et al., 2014). By analyzing the spatial relationships between pests, their natural enemies, and environmental factors, researchers can better understand the factors influencing biological control success and guide the release and conservation of natural enemies.

b. Pesticide applications: GIS can help evaluate the effectiveness and potential environmental impacts of pesticide applications by integrating data on pesticide use, pest distribution, and environmental variables (Wang et al., 2019). This information can inform the development of integrated pest management strategies that minimize pesticide use and promote sustainable agricultural practices.

4. Decision support tools:

a. Integrated pest management (IPM): GIS and remote sensing can be used to develop decision support tools that help farmers and land managers implement effective IPM strategies (Damos, 2015). By integrating real-time and historical data on pest and disease distribution, environmental factors, and control measures, these tools can provide recommendations on when and where to apply control measures, such as the release of natural enemies or the targeted application of pesticides.

Geographic information systems and remote-sensing technologies can play a vital role in the assessment and management of ecosystem services related to pest and disease control. By monitoring vegetation distribution and abundance, modeling the spread of pests and diseases, and evaluating the effectiveness of control measures, these tools can help inform the development and implementation of sustainable pest and disease management strategies.

12.3.3 Cultural Services

12.3.3.1 Recreation and Ecotourism

Geographic information systems and remote-sensing technologies can indeed play a significant role in supporting the planning and management of recreational and ecotourism activities. By providing valuable spatial information and allowing for the monitoring of environmental changes, these tools can help ensure that recreational and ecotourism resources are managed sustainably and efficiently. Here are some ways in which GIS and remote sensing can be applied in this context:

1. Identifying and mapping recreational and ecotourism resources:

a. Resource inventory: GIS can be employed to compile an inventory of recreational and ecotourism resources, such as trails, parks, wildlife viewing areas, and cultural heritage sites (Cetin & Sevik, 2016). By integrating various data sources, such as land cover, topography, and infrastructure, GIS can help identify and map these resources, providing a basis for planning and decision making.

b. Accessibility analysis: GIS can be used to analyze the accessibility of recreational and ecotourism resources, taking into account factors such as distance, terrain, and transportation infrastructure (Talebi, et al., 2019). This information can help identify underserved areas, prioritize investments in infrastructure, and guide the development of new recreational and ecotourism opportunities.

2. Monitoring changes in land cover and habitat quality:

a. Land cover mapping: Remote-sensing data can be used to map and monitor changes in land cover, such as deforestation, urbanization, and habitat fragmentation (Curtis et al., 2018). By tracking these changes over time, land managers can assess the impacts of human activities on recreational and ecotourism resources and implement measures to protect and restore these resources.

b. Habitat quality assessment: Remote-sensing technologies, such as multispectral and hyperspectral imaging, can provide detailed information on vegetation health and habitat quality (Klemas, 2016). This information can help identify areas with high biodiversity or scenic value, which are of particular interest for ecotourism, as well as areas where habitat degradation may threaten the viability of recreational and ecotourism activities.

3. Supporting planning and management:

a. Visitor capacity analysis: GIS can be used to estimate the carrying capacity of recreational and ecotourism sites, taking into account factors such as visitor demand, resource availability, and environmental sensitivity (Sobhani et al., 2022). This information can help land managers develop strategies to manage visitor use and minimize the impacts of tourism on natural and cultural resources.

b. Impact assessment: GIS and remote sensing can be employed to assess the environmental and socioeconomic impacts of recreational and ecotourism activities, such as habitat disturbance, pollution, and changes in local livelihoods (Rai & Singh, 2020). By integrating spatial data on tourism infrastructure, visitor use, and environmental variables, these tools can help identify potential conflicts and guide the development of sustainable management strategies.

c. Decision support tools: GIS and remote-sensing technologies can be used to develop decision support tools that help land managers and planners evaluate the trade-offs between different recreational and ecotourism development scenarios (Rezvani et al., 2022). By integrating spatial data on resource availability, visitor demand, and environmental constraints, these tools can provide insights into the potential benefits and impacts of different management options and guide the planning and decision-making process.

GIS and remote sensing can provide valuable support for the planning and management of recreational and ecotourism activities. By identifying and mapping resources, monitoring changes in land cover and habitat quality, and supporting decision making, these tools can help ensure the sustainable and efficient management of recreational and ecotourism resources.

12.3.3.2 Aesthetic and Spiritual Values

The aesthetic and spiritual values of ecosystems can also be assessed and monitored using GIS and remote sensing (Vaz et al., 2019). For example, remote-sensing data can be employed to evaluate the visual quality of landscapes, while GIS can be used to map the distribution of culturally and spiritually significant sites, such as sacred groves or archaeological sites.

12.3.3.3 Educational and Scientific Values

Geographic information systems and remote sensing can contribute to the assessment and preservation of ecosystems' educational and scientific values. Remote-sensing data can be utilized to monitor changes in ecosystems, providing valuable information for research and education (Rose et al., 2015). GIS can be employed to create educational materials, such as interactive maps and virtual field trips, which can enhance the understanding of ecosystem services and biodiversity conservation among students and the general public.

12.3.4 Supporting Services

12.3.4.1 Soil Formation

Geographic information systems and remote sensing can help in understanding and monitoring the processes of soil formation, which underpin many provisioning and regulating services (Pettorelli et al., 2016). For instance, remote-sensing data can be used to assess the distribution and health of vegetation, which influences soil development through processes such as organic matter accumulation and root penetration. GIS can be employed to analyze the relationships between soil formation processes and environmental factors, such as climate, topography, and land use.

12.3.4.2 Nutrient Cycling

Remote sensing and GIS can contribute to the assessment of nutrient cycling in ecosystems, which is essential for the maintenance of ecosystem functions and services (Radeva et al., 2018). For example, remote sensing can be used to monitor the distribution and productivity of vegetation, which plays a critical role in nutrient cycling. GIS can be employed to model nutrient fluxes within ecosystems, allowing for the evaluation of the impacts of land-use changes and management practices on nutrient cycling processes.

12.3.4.3 Primary Production

Geographic information systems and remote sensing can be applied to study primary production, the conversion of solar energy into organic matter through photosynthesis, which forms the basis of food webs and supports various ecosystem services (Cavicchioli et al., 2019). Remote-sensing data, such as the NDVI, can be used to estimate primary productivity and monitor changes in vegetation health and growth. GIS can be employed to analyze the spatial distribution of primary production and its relationship with environmental factors, such as climate and land use.

In GIS and remote-sensing technologies offer significant potential for assessing and monitoring ecosystem services across various spatial and temporal scales. By integrating these tools with other data sources and analytical methods, researchers, practitioners, and policymakers can gain valuable insights into the status and trends of ecosystem services, informing the development of effective strategies for their sustainable management and conservation.

12.4 BIODIVERSITY CONSERVATION THROUGH GIS AND REMOTE SENSING

12.4.1 Habitat Mapping and Monitoring

12.4.1.1 Land Cover Classification

Remote-sensing data, such as satellite imagery, can be used to classify land cover types, providing essential information on the distribution and extent of different habitats. Land cover classification can be achieved through various techniques, such as supervised and unsupervised classification, object-based image analysis, and machine learning algorithms. GIS can be employed to analyze land cover data, allowing for the identification of critical habitats, the assessment of habitat fragmentation, and the evaluation of habitat quality (Lucas et al., 2007).

12.4.1.2 Habitat Fragmentation and Connectivity Analysis

Geographic information systems can be used to assess habitat fragmentation and connectivity, which are essential factors for biodiversity conservation. Habitat fragmentation can be quantified using metrics such as patch size, shape, and isolation. Habitat connectivity can be assessed through techniques like least-cost path analysis and circuit theory, which model the movement potential of species across the landscape (Andronache et al., 2019). These analyses can inform the design of conservation strategies, such as the establishment of ecological corridors and the prioritization of areas for habitat restoration.

12.4.2 Species Distribution Modeling

12.4.2.1 Predictive Modeling Techniques

Geographic information systems and remote-sensing data can be combined with species occurrence records and environmental variables to develop species distribution models (SDMs) (Vila-Viçosa et al., 2020). These models can predict the potential distribution of species under different environmental conditions, such as current and future climate scenarios. Various modeling techniques can be employed, including regression-based models, machine learning algorithms, and ensemble modeling approaches.

12.4.2.2 Applications in Conservation Planning

Species distribution models can be used to support conservation planning by identifying priority areas for species conservation, assessing the impacts of land-use changes and climate change on species distributions, and evaluating the effectiveness of protected area networks (Marshall et al., 2014). By integrating SDMs with other conservation planning tools, such as systematic conservation planning and decision support systems, practitioners can develop more effective and targeted conservation strategies.

12.4.3 Monitoring and Assessing Biodiversity Change

12.4.3.1 Deforestation and Reforestation

Remote-sensing data can be used to monitor deforestation and reforestation activities, providing crucial information for biodiversity conservation. For instance, time-series analysis of satellite imagery can be employed to detect changes in forest cover and assess the effectiveness of forest conservation and restoration efforts (DeVries et al., 2016). GIS can be used to analyze the spatial patterns of deforestation and reforestation, allowing for the identification of drivers and potential mitigation measures.

12.4.3.2 Invasive Species Detection

Remote sensing and GIS can contribute to the detection and monitoring of invasive species, which pose significant threats to native biodiversity (Kattenborn et al., 2019). Remote-sensing data, such as hyperspectral imagery, can be used to detect the presence of invasive species based on their unique spectral signatures. GIS can be employed to model the potential distribution of invasive species and assess their impacts on native ecosystems.

12.4.3.3 Climate Change Impacts on Biodiversity

Geographic information systems and remote sensing can be used to study the impacts of climate change on biodiversity by monitoring changes in species distributions, phenology, and community composition (Randin et al., 2020). For example, remote-sensing data can be employed to track changes in the timing of vegetation phenology, which can provide insights into the responses of species to climate change. GIS can be used to model the potential impacts of climate change on species distributions, informing the development of climate change adaptation strategies for biodiversity conservation. GIS and remote-sensing technologies play a critical role in biodiversity conservation by providing valuable data and tools for habitat mapping and monitoring, species distribution modeling, and the assessment of biodiversity change. By integrating these technologies with other data sources and conservation planning tools, researchers, practitioners, and policymakers can develop more effective strategies for conserving the Earth's biodiversity and sustaining the ecosystem services it provides.

12.5 CASE STUDIES AND APPLICATIONS

12.5.1 Monitoring Forest Loss and Fragmentation in the Amazon Rainforest

The Amazon rainforest, a biodiversity hotspot, has experienced significant deforestation due to logging, agriculture, and infrastructure development (Trancoso et al., 2009). Remote sensing and GIS have been used to monitor forest loss and fragmentation, providing crucial information for conservation efforts. For instance, satellite imagery from Landsat and Sentinel-2 has been employed to track deforestation over time, quantify forest fragmentation, and identify deforestation hotspots. This information has informed the establishment and management of protected areas and the development of policies aimed at reducing deforestation.

12.5.2 Assessing the Impacts of Land-Use Change on Wetland Ecosystems

Wetlands provide critical ecosystem services, such as water purification and flood regulation, but are threatened by land-use changes, including agriculture and urbanization (Zorrilla-Miras et al., 2014). Remote sensing and GIS have been used to study the impacts of land-use change on wetland ecosystems in various regions. For example, satellite imagery has been used to map wetland extent and monitor changes in wetland cover over time. GIS has been employed to analyze the relationships between wetland loss and land-use changes, providing valuable information for the development of wetland conservation and restoration strategies.

12.5.3 Predicting the Impacts of Climate Change on Mountain Biodiversity

Mountain ecosystems are highly vulnerable to climate change, which can result in shifts in species distributions and the loss of unique biodiversity (Tse-Ring et al., 2010). Remote sensing and GIS have been employed to study the impacts of climate change on mountain biodiversity in regions such as the European Alps and the Andes (Hotaling et al., 2017; Verrall & Pickering, 2020). For example, species distribution models have been developed to predict the potential impacts of climate change on the distributions of plant and animal species. This information has informed the design of climate change adaptation strategies, such as the establishment of climate corridors and the management of protected area networks.

12.5.4 Identifying Priority Areas for Coral Reef Conservation

Coral reefs are among the most biodiverse ecosystems on Earth, but they face numerous threats, including climate change, overfishing, and pollution (Keller et al., 2009; Hoegh-Guldberg et al., 2018). Remote sensing and GIS have been employed to identify priority areas for coral reef conservation. For instance, satellite imagery has been used to map the distribution and health of coral reefs, while GIS has been employed to analyze factors such as human pressures and reef resilience. These analyses have informed the design of marine protected areas and the development of integrated coastal management plans.

12.5.5 Monitoring the Spread of Invasive Species in the Great Lakes Region

The Great Lakes region in North America has experienced significant impacts from invasive species, such as the zebra mussel and the Eurasian watermilfoil (Buchan & Padilla, 2000; Escobar et al., 2018). Remote sensing and GIS have been used to detect and monitor the spread of invasive species in the region. For example, aerial and satellite imagery has been employed to identify the presence of invasive species based on their spectral signatures. GIS has been utilized to model the potential distribution of invasive species and assess their impacts on native ecosystems. This information has informed the development of invasive species management strategies, such as early detection and rapid response programs.

These case studies illustrate the diverse applications of GIS and remote-sensing technologies in ecosystem services assessment and biodiversity conservation. By providing timely and spatially explicit information, these tools enable researchers, practitioners, and policymakers to develop more effective and targeted strategies for conserving the Earth's ecosystems and the services they provide.

12.6 CHALLENGES AND FUTURE PROSPECTS

12.6.1 Challenges

Despite the significant potential of GIS and remote-sensing technologies in ecosystem services assessment and biodiversity conservation, several challenges remain:

12.6.1.1 Data Quality and Availability

Data quality and availability play a crucial role in ensuring accurate and reliable analyses in various fields, including remote sensing, ecology, and environmental sciences. Several factors can impact the quality and usefulness of remote-sensing data, and the availability of supplementary data sources can be limited, particularly in remote or under-studied regions. In this context, it is essential to understand the challenges and limitations of remote-sensing data, ground truth data, species occurrence records, and environmental variables.

1. Remote-Sensing Data Quality:

   a. Cloud cover: Clouds can obstruct the view of satellite sensors, leading to incomplete or unreliable data (Dong & Menzel, 2016). Cloud cover is especially problematic in tropical and humid regions where persistent cloudiness is common. Techniques like cloud masking, compositing, and using data from different dates can help mitigate this issue to some extent.

   b. Sensor noise: Sensor noise refers to errors in measurements due to instrument limitations or external factors such as atmospheric conditions (Maisonneuve et al., 2010). This noise can distort the true values of remote-sensing data, leading to inaccuracies in the analysis. Calibration, noise reduction algorithms, and data correction techniques can be employed to minimize these errors.

   c. Spatial resolution: Spatial resolution refers to the size of the smallest object that can be detected by a remote-sensing system (Chen et al., 2018). Low spatial resolution can limit the ability to distinguish between different land cover types or detect small-scale features. Using high-resolution sensors or data fusion techniques can help overcome this limitation.

   d. Temporal resolution: Temporal resolution is the frequency at which remote-sensing data is collected (Xie et al., 2016). Low temporal resolution may not capture seasonal or short-term changes in the environment, which can be crucial for some applications. Utilizing multiple data sources with complementary temporal resolutions or deploying more frequent satellite passes can help address this issue.

2. Data Availability:

a. Ground truth data for validation: Ground truth data, collected through in-situ measurements, is essential for validating remote-sensing-derived information (Wang et al., 2016a). However, collecting ground truth data can be labor-intensive, expensive, and logistically challenging, especially in remote or inaccessible areas. This limitation can be addressed by utilizing alternative data sources, such as crowdsourced data, citizen science projects, or leveraging machine learning algorithms that require less ground truth data for training.

b. Species occurrence records: Accurate species distribution modeling relies on the availability of species occurrence records, which can be sparse or biased in under-studied regions (Reside et al., 2019). Collaborating with local researchers, promoting citizen science, and integrating data from various sources, such as museum collections and online databases, can help improve the availability and quality of species occurrence data.

c. Environmental variables: Environmental variables, such as temperature, precipitation, and soil characteristics, are vital for understanding ecosystems and species distributions (Thammanu et al., 2021). However, these variables can be difficult to obtain or measure, particularly in remote regions. Remote-sensing data, reanalysis data sets, and global climate models can provide proxies for these variables, helping to fill gaps in data coverage.

Ensuring high-quality remote-sensing data and the availability of supplementary information is vital for accurate and reliable analyses. Understanding the limitations of remote-sensing data and addressing data availability issues through various methods, such as data fusion, collaboration, and utilizing alternative data sources, can significantly improve the outcomes of environmental and ecological studies.

12.6.1.2 Scale Mismatch

The mismatch between the spatial and temporal scales of remote sensing and GIS data and the scales relevant for ecological processes and conservation planning can pose significant challenges. However, there are various approaches that can help in addressing these issues:

1. Multi-scale analysis: Integrating data from different spatial and temporal resolutions can provide a more comprehensive understanding of ecological processes (McGarigal et al., 2016). Multi-scale analysis involves combining fine-scale data (e.g., high-resolution satellite imagery, LiDAR) with coarse-scale data (e.g., lower

resolution satellite imagery, climate data) to capture both local and regional patterns and processes.

2. Data fusion: Data fusion techniques can be used to combine information from different sources, such as satellite imagery, aerial photography, and ground-based surveys, to create a more complete picture of the study area (Cucchiaro et al., 2020). For example, pan-sharpening techniques can be employed to enhance the spatial resolution of multispectral images using higher-resolution panchromatic images.

3. Downscaling and upscaling: Downscaling involves the use of statistical or empirical models to predict fine-scale patterns based on coarse-scale data, while upscaling involves aggregating fine-scale data to a coarser resolution (Rasera et al., 2020). Both approaches can help in bridging the gap between the scales of remote-sensing data and ecological processes.

4. Spatial and temporal aggregation: Aggregating data over space or time can help in capturing the patterns and processes relevant for conservation planning (Higgins et al., 2005). For instance, calculating averages, medians, or other summary statistics can provide useful information on habitat quality, species distribution, and other ecological variables.

5. Incorporating expert knowledge: Expert knowledge can be invaluable in guiding the integration of data across different scales (Bennett et al., 2017). Ecologists, conservation practitioners, and local stakeholders can provide insights into the spatial and temporal scales relevant for the study species, ecosystems, and conservation objectives.

6. Dynamic modeling: Dynamic models, such as agent-based models, cellular automata, and system dynamics models, can help in understanding how ecological processes and human actions interact across different spatial and temporal scales (Liu et al., 2020). These models can be informed by remote sensing and GIS data, as well as field observations and expert knowledge.

By employing these approaches, researchers and conservation practitioners can better integrate data across different scales, enabling more effective conservation planning and decision making.

12.6.1.3 Uncertainty and Model Validation

Uncertainty is indeed a crucial aspect to consider in remote sensing and GIS analyses, especially when it comes to making informed conservation decisions. To address these uncertainties and improve the reliability of the results, several steps can be taken:

1. Quantifying uncertainty: It is important to quantify uncertainty through the use of various statistical methods and techniques, such as error propagation analysis, Monte Carlo simulations, and fuzzy logic (Abdo & Flaus, 2016). These methods can help in estimating the degree of uncertainty associated with the data and results.

2. Communicating uncertainty: Properly communicating uncertainty is key for decision makers to understand the limitations of the data and analyses (Ramos et al., 2010). Visualization techniques, such as error bars, confidence intervals, and probability maps, can be employed to convey the uncertainty in the data and results.

3. Model validation: Validating the models with independent data sets is essential to assess their accuracy and reliability (Tropsha et al., 2003). This can be done through cross-validation, where a portion of the data is set aside for testing the model, or by comparing the model's predictions with ground truth data obtained from field surveys or other independent sources.

4. Rigorous preprocessing: Ensuring that the input data is of high quality by performing rigorous preprocessing can help reduce uncertainty (Chen et al., 2004). This may include geometric and radiometric corrections, atmospheric corrections, and normalization of multi-temporal data.

5. Selection of appropriate methods: Choosing the appropriate methods and algorithms for the analysis, based on the nature of the data and the research question, can help in minimizing uncertainties (Teng et al., 2017). Additionally, using ensemble techniques, where multiple models or algorithms are combined, can provide more reliable results.

6. Documentation and transparency: Providing detailed documentation of the methodologies, assumptions, and uncertainties involved in the analysis is crucial for transparency and reproducibility (Aguinis & Solarino, 2019). This enables other researchers and decision-makers to understand the strengths and limitations of the results and make informed decisions accordingly.

By following these steps, the uncertainties in remote sensing and GIS analyses can be better managed and communicated, ultimately leading to more informed conservation decision making.

12.6.1.4 Integration of Social and Ecological Data

Integrating social and ecological data is essential for providing a comprehensive understanding of the relationships between human activities, ecosystem services, and biodiversity. This integrated approach allows for better decision making and policy development aimed at sustainable resource management and conservation efforts. However, there are several challenges in incorporating social data into GISs (geographic information systems) and remote-sensing analyses.

1. Data formats: Social data often comes in diverse formats such as text, tables, or surveys, whereas ecological data is typically available as raster or vector layers in GIS (Jones, 2014). Converting and harmonizing these different data formats to

make them compatible for analysis can be time-consuming and may require advanced technical skills.

2. Spatial scales: Social and ecological data can be collected at different spatial scales, ranging from local to global (Ottelin et al., 2019). Integrating data with varying spatial resolutions can be challenging, as the mismatch in scale can lead to inaccurate or incomplete analyses.

3. Temporal scales: Social and ecological processes may occur at different time scales. While some ecological processes are slow and continuous, social processes can be dynamic and rapidly changing (Sivapalan & Blöschl, 2015). Aligning these different temporal scales can be challenging in order to establish relationships between the two sets of data.

4. Confidentiality issues: Social data often contains sensitive information, such as personal or household-level information, which raises concerns about privacy and data protection (Popescul & Genete, 2016). Ensuring that the analysis and sharing of social data comply with ethical guidelines and legal regulations is essential to protect individual privacy.

5. Data quality and reliability: The accuracy, consistency, and completeness of social and ecological data are crucial for meaningful analysis (Cai & Zhu, 2015). However, data quality can vary widely, and researchers need to be cautious when combining data from different sources.

6. Integration techniques: Different statistical methods and techniques can be employed to integrate social and ecological data, such as spatial regression, multivariate analysis, and network analysis (Anselin, et al., 2009). Selecting the appropriate method for a specific study requires expertise and a clear understanding of the research objectives.

7. Interdisciplinary collaboration: Integrating social and ecological data requires expertise from different disciplines, such as social sciences, ecology, and geospatial science (Bardosh et al., 2020). Collaborating across disciplines can be challenging due to differences in terminology, methods, and perspectives.

Despite these challenges, recent advances in GIS and remote-sensing technology, data processing, and interdisciplinary research have made it increasingly possible to integrate social and ecological data for a more comprehensive understanding of human-environment interactions. By addressing these challenges and fostering collaboration among various disciplines, researchers can better inform sustainable resource management and conservation efforts.

12.6.2 Future Prospects
Despite these challenges, the future of GIS and remote sensing in ecosystem services assessment and biodiversity conservation is promising.

12.6.2.1 Technological Advances

Advances in remote-sensing technology and GIS software have indeed opened up new possibilities for ecological analyses. The development of high-resolution sensors, unmanned aerial vehicles (UAVs), hyperspectral imaging, and LiDAR (light detection and ranging) has provided more detailed and accurate data, while advancements in GIS software and computing power have enabled more sophisticated analyses and modeling approaches. These innovations are transforming the way we study and manage ecosystems, as well as monitor biodiversity and environmental changes.

Some key advancements and their implications for ecological analyses include the following:

1. High-resolution sensors: The availability of high-resolution satellite imagery allows for more detailed observations and mapping of land cover, vegetation, and habitat types (Gairola et al., 2013). This enables more accurate assessments of ecosystem services, biodiversity, and land-use changes, and can inform better conservation and management strategies.

2. Unmanned aerial vehicles (UAVs): UAVs, or drones, provide an affordable and flexible platform for collecting high-resolution aerial imagery and other remote-sensing data (Yao et al., 2019). They can be used to monitor wildlife populations, assess vegetation health, and map habitats in areas that are difficult to access or cover with traditional remote-sensing methods.

3. Hyperspectral imaging: Hyperspectral sensors capture data across a wide range of wavelengths, providing detailed information about the composition and properties of the observed objects (Tasseron et al., 2021). This technology can be used to identify and map plant species, assess vegetation health, and detect signs of stress or disturbance in ecosystems.

4. LiDAR imaging: LiDAR uses laser pulses to measure the distance between the sensor and the Earth's surface, creating high-resolution, three-dimensional representations of terrain and vegetation structure (Swatantran et al., 2016). This technology can be used to map forest canopy height, biomass, and habitat complexity, as well as to model the distribution of species that depend on specific habitat characteristics.

5. Advancements in GIS software: The continuous development of GIS software enables more sophisticated spatial analyses and modeling techniques, such as machine learning and agent-based models (de Paula Ferreira et al., 2022). These tools can help researchers understand the drivers of ecological processes, predict species distributions, and simulate the impacts of land-use and climate change on ecosystems and biodiversity.

6. Increased computing power: The growth in computing power allows for the processing and analysis of large and complex data sets, such as high-resolution satellite

imagery or LiDAR data (Sohn & Dowman, 2007). This enables researchers to conduct more detailed and accurate ecological analyses, as well as to develop and refine predictive models.

These advancements in remote sensing technology and GIS tools offer new opportunities for ecological research and environmental management. By providing more detailed and accurate data, as well as enabling more sophisticated analyses, these innovations can significantly improve our understanding of ecosystems and biodiversity, inform more effective conservation strategies, and support better decision making for sustainable development.

12.6.2.2 Integration of Big Data and Machine Learning

The integration of big data and machine learning techniques, including deep learning and artificial intelligence (AI), has indeed revolutionized remote sensing and GIS analyses. By leveraging large data sets and advanced computational methods, these techniques can significantly improve the accuracy and efficiency of various tasks related to land cover classification, species distribution modeling, and the detection of changes in ecosystems and biodiversity.

Some key applications of big data and machine learning in remote sensing and GIS include the following:

1. Land cover classification: Machine learning algorithms can analyze high-resolution satellite imagery and automatically classify different land cover types, such as forests, urban areas, and water bodies (Ghorbanian et al., 2020). This enables the generation of accurate and up-to-date land cover maps, which are crucial for monitoring changes in land use and informing land management decisions.

2. Species distribution modeling: Machine learning models can predict the distribution of species based on environmental variables, such as temperature, precipitation, and vegetation cover (Amiri et al., 2020). These predictions can help identify suitable habitats and potential threats to species, guiding conservation planning and management efforts.

3. Change detection: Machine learning techniques, such as deep learning-based convolutional neural networks (CNNs), can analyze time-series satellite imagery to detect and monitor changes in ecosystems, such as deforestation, urbanization, and land degradation (Xie & Niculescu, 2021). This information can be used to track the impacts of human activities on ecosystems and biodiversity and inform conservation policies.

4. Ecosystem services assessment: By integrating remote-sensing data with other geospatial data sources, machine learning models can estimate the value of ecosystem services, such as carbon sequestration, water purification, and pollination

(Tavares et al., 2019). This information can support decision-making processes and promote the sustainable management of natural resources.

5. Biodiversity monitoring: Machine learning algorithms can analyze remote-sensing data to identify and monitor critical habitats, such as wetlands and protected areas, and assess the impacts of human activities on these habitats (Zhang et al., 2022). This can help prioritize conservation actions and inform the design of protected area networks.

6. Climate change modeling: Machine learning techniques can be used to downscale global climate models and predict the impacts of climate change on ecosystems and biodiversity at regional and local scales (Rolnick et al., 2022). This information can help inform climate change adaptation and mitigation strategies.

7. Disaster management: Machine learning models can analyze remote-sensing data to predict and assess the impacts of natural disasters, such as floods, landslides, and wildfires (Bhatti 2021; Bhatti 2022a; Bhatti 2022b; Bhatti 2023a; Bhatti 2023b; Fei 2022; Hasnain 2022; He 2021; Wang 2023; Wu 2022). This can inform disaster risk reduction strategies and support emergency response efforts.

The integration of big data and machine learning techniques in remote sensing and GIS analyses holds immense potential for improving our understanding of ecosystems and biodiversity and informing more effective conservation and management strategies. However, it is essential to ensure the quality and representativeness of the data used and to validate the models' predictions through ground-truthing and expert knowledge to maximize the reliability and utility of these techniques.

12.6.2.3 Citizen Science and Crowdsourcing

Citizen science and crowdsourcing initiatives are invaluable tools that enable the general public to contribute to scientific research, data collection, and analysis (Welvaert & Caley, 2016). By engaging non-experts in the collection of ground truth data, species occurrence records, and environmental variables, these initiatives can significantly improve data quality and availability while also promoting public engagement in ecosystem services assessment and biodiversity conservation.

Some key benefits of citizen science and crowdsourcing initiatives include:

1. Scalability: By involving a large number of people in data collection and observation, these initiatives can cover more ground and collect data at a much larger scale than would be possible through traditional scientific methods (Jabłoński, 2016).

2. Cost-effectiveness: Citizen science projects often require lower financial resources compared to traditional research methods, making them more accessible and allowing for the allocation of funds to other crucial areas of research and conservation (Aceves-Bueno et al., 2015).

3. Real-time monitoring: Engaging the public in data collection can enable real-time monitoring of environmental changes and events, such as pollution incidents or invasive species outbreaks, allowing for faster and more efficient responses (Quansah et al., 2010).

4. Public engagement and awareness: Involving the general public in scientific research helps increase awareness and understanding of the importance of ecosystem services and biodiversity conservation. This can lead to more informed decision making and greater support for conservation efforts (Elsawah et al., 2019).

5. Education and skill development: Participation in citizen science projects can help individuals develop new skills and knowledge in various scientific disciplines, fostering a lifelong interest in learning and scientific exploration (Bonney et al., 2016).

6. Data validation and quality control: When properly designed and managed, citizen science projects can incorporate quality control measures to ensure the data collected is accurate and reliable (McKinley et al., 2017).

7. Networking and collaboration: These initiatives can foster collaboration between scientists, researchers, and the general public, leading to new partnerships and innovative solutions to complex environmental problems (O'Donnell et al., 2018).

8. Policy and decision-making support: High-quality data generated through citizen science initiatives can inform policy and decision-making processes, leading to more effective conservation efforts and better environmental management (Newman et al., 2017).

To maximize the benefits of citizen science and crowdsourcing initiatives, it is crucial to provide participants with adequate training, tools, and support to ensure data accuracy and reliability. Moreover, maintaining clear communication between researchers and participants is essential to foster a sense of ownership and responsibility, ultimately enhancing the impact of these initiatives on ecosystem services assessment and biodiversity conservation.

12.6.2.4 Interdisciplinary Collaboration

Interdisciplinary collaboration between various experts, such as ecologists, remote-sensing specialists, GIS specialists, social scientists, and other stakeholders, is essential for developing holistic and integrated approaches to ecosystem services assessment and biodiversity conservation (Berg et al., 2016). When these professionals work together, they can leverage their unique knowledge and skills to create more robust methodologies and strategies. Such collaborative efforts can lead to the improved incorporation of social data, which is crucial for understanding the human dimensions of conservation issues. Social scientists can help identify the values, beliefs, and attitudes of local communities, which can inform the design of conservation policies and programs that better address local needs and concerns (Bennett et al., 2017).

Additionally, interdisciplinary collaboration can enhance the applicability of research findings in conservation decision making. By incorporating insights from multiple disciplines, decision makers can develop more effective, context-specific, and socially acceptable conservation strategies. Collaborative projects can also foster capacity building among stakeholders, as they have the opportunity to learn from one another's expertise. This can lead to more effective communication and coordination among various actors, ultimately improving the overall success of conservation efforts. Moreover, interdisciplinary collaboration can help identify new research questions, innovative methods, and novel solutions. By considering the perspectives of different disciplines, researchers can gain a broader understanding of complex conservation issues and develop more effective ways to address them. Interdisciplinary collaboration is vital for enhancing ecosystem services assessment and biodiversity conservation. By working together, experts from various fields can create more comprehensive and integrated approaches that account for social data, improve the applicability of research findings, foster capacity building, and drive innovation. Such collaborative efforts can ultimately contribute to more effective and sustainable conservation strategies. Addressing the challenges associated with GIS and remote-sensing technologies and harnessing the opportunities offered by technological advances, big data, and interdisciplinary collaboration will enable researchers, practitioners, and policymakers to develop more effective strategies for ecosystem services assessment and biodiversity conservation in the future.

12.7 CONCLUSION

Geographic information systems and remote-sensing technologies have emerged as essential tools for ecosystem services assessment and biodiversity conservation. These technologies offer valuable data and analytical capabilities for habitat mapping and monitoring, species distribution modeling, and the assessment of biodiversity change. Case studies from around the world demonstrate the diverse applications of these tools in various ecosystems and conservation contexts. However, challenges remain, including data quality and availability, scale mismatch, uncertainty and model validation, and the integration of social and ecological data. Future prospects for the field are promising, with ongoing technological advances, the integration of big data and machine learning techniques, the growth of citizen science and crowdsourcing initiatives, and interdisciplinary collaboration. By addressing these challenges and capitalizing on emerging opportunities, researchers, practitioners, and policymakers can continue to harness the power of GIS and remote sensing technologies to improve our understanding of ecosystem services and biodiversity, inform conservation decision making, and ultimately contribute to the sustainable management and preservation of our planet's precious natural resources.

REFERENCES

AbdelRahman, M. A., Natarajan, A., & Hegde, R. (2016). Assessment of land suitability and capability by integrating remote sensing and GIS for agriculture in Chamarajanagar district, Karnataka, India. *The Egyptian Journal of Remote Sensing and Space Science, 19*(1), 125–141.

Abdo, H., & Flaus, J. M. (2016). Uncertainty quantification in dynamic system risk assessment: A new approach with randomness and fuzzy theory. *International Journal of Production Research*, *54*(19), 5862–5885.

Acevedo, M. F. (2011). Interdisciplinary progress in food production, food security and environment research. *Environmental conservation*, *38*(2), 151–171.

Aceves-Bueno, E., Adeleye, A. S., Bradley, D., Tyler Brandt, W., Callery, P., Feraud, M., ... & Tague, C. (2015). Citizen science as an approach for overcoming insufficient monitoring and inadequate stakeholder buy-in in adaptive management: Criteria and evidence. *Ecosystems*, *18*, 493–506.

Aguinis, H., & Solarino, A. M. (2019). Transparency and replicability in qualitative research: The case of interviews with elite informants. *Strategic Management Journal*, *40*(8), 1291–1315.

Ali, N., Fu, X., Ashraf, U., Chen, J., Thanh, H. V., Anees, A., ... & Ahmed, A. (2022). Remote sensing for surface coal mining and reclamation monitoring in the Central Salt Range, Punjab, Pakistan. *Sustainability*, *14*(16), 9835.

Alleaume, S., Dusseux, P., Thierion, V., Commagnac, L., Laventure, S., Lang, M., ... & Luque, S. (2018). A generic remote sensing approach to derive operational essential biodiversity variables (EBVs) for conservation planning. *Methods in Ecology and Evolution*, *9*(8), 1822–1836.

Al-Quraishi, A. M. F., & Negm, A. M. (2019). *Environmental remote sensing and GIS in Iraq*. Springer-Water, Springer, Cham.

Alwan, I. A., Aziz, N. A., & Hamoodi, M. N. (2020). Potential water harvesting sites identification using spatial multi-criteria evaluation in Maysan Province, Iraq. *ISPRS International Journal of Geo-Information*, *9*(4), 235.

Amiri, M., Tarkesh, M., Jafari, R., & Jetschke, G. (2020). Bioclimatic variables from precipitation and temperature records vs. remote sensing-based bioclimatic variables: Which side can perform better in species distribution modeling?. *Ecological informatics*, *57*, 101060.

Andronache, I., Marin, M., Fischer, R., Ahammer, H., Radulovic, M., Ciobotaru, A. M., ... & Peptenatu, D. (2019). Dynamics of forest fragmentation and connectivity using particle and fractal analysis. *Scientific Reports*, *9*(1), 12228.

Anselin, L., Syabri, I., & Kho, Y. (2009). GeoDa: An introduction to spatial data analysis. In *Handbook of applied spatial analysis: Software tools, methods and applications* (pp. 73–89). Berlin, Heidelberg: Springer Berlin Heidelberg.

Avtar, R., Kumar, P., Oono, A., Saraswat, C., Dorji, S., & Hlaing, Z. (2017). Potential application of remote sensing in monitoring ecosystem services of forests, mangroves and urban areas. *Geocarto International*, *32*(8), 874–885.

Bailey, T. C., Fotheringham, S., & Rogerson, P. (1994). A review of statistical spatial analysis in geographical information systems. *Spatial Analysis and GIS*, 13–44.

Bardosh, K. L., de Vries, D. H., Abramowitz, S., Thorlie, A., Cremers, L., Kinsman, J., & Stellmach, D. (2020). Integrating the social sciences in epidemic preparedness and response: A strategic framework to strengthen capacities and improve global health security. *Globalization and Health*, *16*, 1–18.

Bennett, N. J., Roth, R., Klain, S. C., Chan, K., Christie, P., Clark, D. A., ... & Wyborn, C. (2017). Conservation social science: Understanding and integrating human dimensions to improve conservation. *biological conservation*, *205*, 93–108.

Berg, C., Rogers, S., & Mineau, M. (2016). Building scenarios for ecosystem services tools: Developing a methodology for efficient engagement with expert stakeholders. *Futures*, *81*, 68–80.

Bhat, M. A., Shah, R. M., & Ahmad, B. (2011). Cloud Computing: A solution to Geographical Information Systems(GIS). *International Journal on Computer Science and Engineering*, *3*(2), 594–600.

Bhatti, U. A., Yan, Y., Zhou, M., Ali, S., Hussain, A., Qingsong, H., ... & Yuan, L. (2021). Time Series Analysis and Forecasting of Air Pollution Particulate Matter ($PM_{2.5}$): an SARIMA and Factor Analysis Approach. *IEEE Access, 9,* 41019–41031.

Bhatti, U. A., Nizamani, M. M., & Mengxing, H. (2022a). Climate change threatens Pakistan's snow leopards. *Science, 377*(6606), 585–586.

Bhatti, U. A., Wu, G., Bazai, S. U., Nawaz, S. A., Baryalai, M., Bhatti, M. A., ... & Nizamani, M. M. (2022b). A Pre- to Post-COVID-19 Change of Air Quality Patterns in Anhui Province Using Path Analysis and Regression. *Polish Journal of Environmental Studies, 31*(5), 4029–4042.

Bhatti, U. A., Huang, M., Neira-Molina, H., Marjan, S., Baryalai, M., Tang, H., ... & Bazai, S. U. (2023a). MFFCG–Multi feature fusion for hyperspectral image classification using graph attention network. *Expert Systems with Applications, 229,* 120496.

Bhatti, U. A., Masud, M., Bazai, S. U., & Tang, H. (2023b). Investigating AI-based smart precision agriculture techniques. *Frontiers in Plant Science, 14,* 1237783.

Bonney, R., Phillips, T. B., Ballard, H. L., & Enck, J. W. (2016). Can citizen science enhance public understanding of science? *Public understanding of science, 25*(1), 2–16.

Booysen, R., Lorenz, S., Thiele, S. T., Fuchsloch, W. C., Marais, T., Nex, P. A., & Gloaguen, R. (2022). Accurate hyperspectral imaging of mineralised outcrops: An example from lithium-bearing pegmatites at Uis, Namibia. *Remote Sensing of Environment, 269,* 112790.

Bradie, J., & Leung, B. (2017). A quantitative synthesis of the importance of variables used in MaxEnt species distribution models. *Journal of Biogeography, 44*(6), 1344–1361.

Brown, J. L., Bennett, J. R., & French, C. M. (2017). SDMtoolbox 2.0: The next generation Python-based GIS toolkit for landscape genetic, biogeographic and species distribution model analyses. *PeerJ, 5,* e4095.

Buchan, L. A., & Padilla, D. K. (2000). Predicting the likelihood of Eurasian watermilfoil presence in lakes, a macrophyte monitoring tool. *Ecological Applications, 10*(5), 1442–1455.

Cai, L., & Zhu, Y. (2015). The challenges of data quality and data quality assessment in the big data era. *Data science journal, 14.*

Cavicchioli, R., Ripple, W. J., Timmis, K. N., Azam, F., Bakken, L. R., Baylis, M., ... & Webster, N. S. (2019). Scientists' warning to humanity: Microorganisms and climate change. *Nature Reviews Microbiology, 17*(9), 569–586.

Ceccato, P., Connor, S. J., Jeanne, I., & Thomson, M. C. (2005). Application of geographical information systems and remote sensing technologies for assessing and monitoring malaria risk. *Parassitologia, 47*(1), 81–96.

Cetin, M., & Sevik, H. (2016). Assessing potential areas of ecotourism through a case study in Ilgaz Mountain National Park. *Tourism-from empirical research towards practical application, 190,* 81–110.

Chen, C., Fu, J., Gai, Y., Li, J., Chen, L., Mantravadi, V. S., & Tan, A. (2018). Damaged bridges over water: Using high-spatial-resolution remote-sensing images for recognition, detection, and assessment. *IEEE Geoscience and Remote Sensing Magazine, 6*(3), 69–85.

Chen, J., Jönsson, P., Tamura, M., Gu, Z., Matsushita, B., & Eklundh, L. (2004). A simple method for reconstructing a high-quality NDVI time-series data set based on the Savitzky–Golay filter. *Remote sensing of Environment, 91*(3-4), 332–344.

Cord, A. F., Brauman, K. A., Chaplin-Kramer, R., Huth, A., Ziv, G., & Seppelt, R. (2017). Priorities to advance monitoring of ecosystem services using earth observation. *Trends in ecology & evolution, 32*(6), 416–428.

Crooks, A. T. (2010). Constructing and implementing an agent-based model of residential segregation through vector GIS. *International Journal of Geographical Information Science, 24*(5), 661–675.

Cucchiaro, S., Fallu, D. J., Zhang, H., Walsh, K., Van Oost, K., Brown, A. G., & Tarolli, P. (2020). Multiplatform-SfM and TLS data fusion for monitoring agricultural terraces in complex topographic and landcover conditions. *Remote Sensing, 12*(12), 1946.

Curtis, P. G., Slay, C. M., Harris, N. L., Tyukavina, A., & Hansen, M. C. (2018). Classifying drivers of global forest loss. *Science, 361*(6407), 1108–1111.

Daily, G. (2003). What are ecosystem services. *Global environmental challenges for the twenty-first century: Resources, consumption and sustainable solutions,* 227–231.

Damos, P. (2015). Modular structure of web-based decision support systems for integrated pest management. A review. *Agronomy for sustainable development, 35*(4), 1347–1372.

de Paula Ferreira, W., Armellini, F., de Santa-Eulalia, L. A., & Thomasset-Laperrière, V. (2022). Extending the lean value stream mapping to the context of Industry 4.0: An agent-based technology approach. *Journal of Manufacturing Systems, 63,* 1–14.

DeVries, B., Pratihast, A. K., Verbesselt, J., Kooistra, L., & Herold, M. (2016). Characterizing forest change using community-based monitoring data and Landsat time series. *PLoS one, 11*(3), e0147121.

Dhyani, S., Lahoti, S., Khare, S., Pujari, P., & Verma, P. (2018). Ecosystem based Disaster Risk Reduction approaches (EbDRR) as a prerequisite for inclusive urban transformation of Nagpur City, India. *International journal of disaster risk reduction, 32,* 95–105.

Dong, C., & Menzel, L. (2016). Producing cloud-free MODIS snow cover products with conditional probability interpolation and meteorological data. *Remote Sensing of Environment, 186,* 439–451.

Elsawah, S., Filatova, T., Jakeman, A. J., Kettner, A. J., Zellner, M. L., Athanasiadis, I. N., Hamilton, S. H., Axtell, R. L., Brown, D. G., Gilligan, J. M., Janssen, M. A., Robinson, D. T., Rozenberg, J., Ullah, I. I. T., & Lade, S. J. (2020). Eight grand challenges in socio-environmental systems modeling. *Socio-Environmental Systems Modelling, 2,* 16226. https://doi.org/10.18174/sesmo.2020a16226

Escobar, L. E., Mallez, S., McCartney, M., Lee, C., Zielinski, D. P., Ghosal, R., ... & Phelps, N. B. (2018). Aquatic invasive species in the Great Lakes Region: An overview. *Reviews in Fisheries Science & Aquaculture, 26*(1), 121–138.

Estoque, R. C., Johnson, B. A., Gao, Y., DasGupta, R., Ooba, M., Togawa, T., ... & Nakamura, S. (2021). Remotely sensed tree canopy cover-based indicators for monitoring global sustainability and environmental initiatives. *Environmental Research Letters, 16*(4), 044047.

Fei, S., Wagan, R. A., Hasnain, A., Hussain, A., Bhatti, U. A., & Elahi, E. (2022). Spatiotemporal impact of the COVID-19 pandemic lockdown on air quality pattern in Nanjing, China. *Frontiers in Environmental Science, 10.* .10.3389/fenvs.2022.952310

Franci, F., Bitelli, G., Mandanici, E., Hadjimitsis, D., & Agapiou, A. (2016). Satellite remote sensing and GIS-based multi-criteria analysis for flood hazard mapping. *Natural Hazards, 83,* 31–51.

Fu, G., Charles, S. P., & Chiew, F. H. (2007). A two-parameter climate elasticity of streamflow index to assess climate change effects on annual streamflow. *Water Resources Research, 43*(11).

Gairola, S., Procheş, Ş., & Rocchini, D. (2013). High-resolution satellite remote sensing: A new frontier for biodiversity exploration in Indian Himalayan forests. *International Journal of Remote Sensing, 34*(6), 2006–2022.

Ghorbanian, A., Kakooei, M., Amani, M., Mahdavi, S., Mohammadzadeh, A., & Hasanlou, M. (2020). Improved land cover map of Iran using Sentinel imagery within Google Earth Engine and a novel automatic workflow for land cover classification using migrated training samples. *ISPRS Journal of Photogrammetry and Remote Sensing, 167,* 276–288.

Giri, C. (2016). Observation and monitoring of mangrove forests using remote sensing: Opportunities and challenges. *Remote Sensing, 8*(9), 783.

Gong, J., Cao, E., Xie, Y., Xu, C., Li, H., & Yan, L. (2021). Integrating ecosystem services and landscape ecological risk into adaptive management: Insights from a western mountain-basin area, China. *Journal of Environmental Management, 281*, 111817.

Hadjimitsis, D. G., Agapiou, A., Themistocleous, K., Alexakis, D. D., & Sarris, A. (2013). Remote sensing for archaeological applications: Management, documentation and monitoring. *Remote Sensing of Environment-Integrated Approaches*, 57–95.

Halewood, M., Chiurugwi, T., Sackville Hamilton, R., Kurtz, B., Marden, E., Welch, E., ... & Powell, W. (2018). Plant genetic resources for food and agriculture: Opportunities and challenges emerging from the science and information technology revolution. *New Phytologist, 217*(4), 1407–1419.

Hasnain, A., Sheng, Y., Hashmi, M. Z., Bhatti, U. A., Hussain, A., Hameed, M., Marjan, S., Bazai, S. U., Hossain, M. A., Sahabuddin, M., Wagan, R. A., & Zha, Y. (2022). Time series analysis and forecasting of air pollutants based on prophet forecasting model in Jiangsu province, China. *Frontiers in Environmental Science, 10*. 10.3389/fenvs.2022.945628

He, Q., Jiang, Z., Wang, M., & Liu, K. (2021). Landslide and wildfire susceptibility assessment in southeast asia using ensemble machine learning methods. *Remote Sensing, 13*(8), 1572.

Hellegers, P. J., Soppe, R., Perry, C. J., & Bastiaanssen, W. G. (2010). Remote sensing and economic indicators for supporting water resources management decisions. *Water Resources Management, 24*, 2419–2436.

Higgins, J. V., Bryer, M. T., Khoury, M. L., & Fitzhugh, T. W. (2005). A freshwater classification approach for biodiversity conservation planning. *Conservation Biology, 19*(2), 432–445.

Hoegh-Guldberg, O., Kennedy, E. V., Beyer, H. L., McClennen, C., & Possingham, H. P. (2018). Securing a long-term future for coral reefs. *Trends in Ecology & Evolution, 33*(12), 936–944.

Hotaling, S., Finn, D. S., Joseph Giersch, J., Weisrock, D. W., & Jacobsen, D. (2017). Climate change and alpine stream biology: Progress, challenges, and opportunities for the future. *Biological Reviews, 92*(4), 2024–2045.

Hoveka, L. N., van der Bank, M., & Davies, T. J. (2020). Evaluating the performance of a protected area network in South Africa and its implications for megadiverse countries. *Biological Conservation, 248*, 108577.

Huang, C., Chen, Y., Zhang, S., & Wu, J. (2018). Detecting, extracting, and monitoring surface water from space using optical sensors: A review. *Reviews of Geophysics, 56*(2), 333–360.

Jabłoński, A. (2016). Scalability of sustainable business models in hybrid organizations. *Sustainability, 8*(3), 194.

Jarvis, A., Lane, A., & Hijmans, R. J. (2008). The effect of climate change on crop wild relatives. *Agriculture, Ecosystems & Environment, 126*(1-2), 13–23.

Jie, W. H., Xiao, C. L., Zhang, C., Zhang, E., Li, J. Y., Wang, B., ... & Dong, S. F. (2021). Remote sensing-based dynamic monitoring and environmental change of wetlands in southern Mongolian Plateau in 2000–2018. *China Geology, 4*(2), 353–363.

Jones, C. B. (2014). *Geographical information systems and computer cartography*. https://doi.org/10.4324/9781315846231.

Kamlun, K. U., Arndt, R. B., & Phua, M. H. (2016). Monitoring deforestation in Malaysia between 1985 and 2013: Insight from South-Western Sabah and its protected peat swamp area. *Land Use Policy, 57*, 418–430.

Kattenborn, T., Lopatin, J., Förster, M., Braun, A. C., & Fassnacht, F. E. (2019). UAV data as alternative to field sampling to map woody invasive species based on combined Sentinel-1 and Sentinel-2 data. *Remote sensing of environment, 227*, 61–73.

Keller, B. D., Gleason, D. F., McLeod, E., Woodley, C. M., Airamé, S., Causey, B. D., ... & Steneck, R. S. (2009). Climate change, coral reef ecosystems, and management options for marine protected areas. *Environmental management, 44*, 1069–1088.

Klemas, V. V. (2016). Remote sensing of submerged aquatic vegetation. *Seafloor mapping along continental shelves: Research and techniques for visualizing benthic environments*, 125–140.

Kureel, N., Sarup, J., Matin, S., Goswami, S., & Kureel, K. (2022). Modelling vegetation health and stress using hypersepctral remote-sensing data. *Modeling Earth Systems and Environment*, 1–16.

Layke, C. (2009). Measuring nature's benefits: A preliminary roadmap for improving ecosystem service indicators. *World Resources Institute: Washington*, 1–36.

Lettenmaier, D. P., Alsdorf, D., Dozier, J., Huffman, G. J., Pan, M., & Wood, E. F. (2015). Inroads of remote sensing into hydrologic science during the WRR era. *Water Resources Research*, 51(9), 7309–7342.

Liu, D., Zheng, X., & Wang, H. (2020). Land-use Simulation and Decision-Support system (LandSDS): Seamlessly integrating system dynamics, agent-based model, and cellular automata. *Ecological Modelling*, 417, 108924.

Liu, Z., Xu, J., Liu, M., Yin, Z., Liu, X., Yin, L., & Zheng, W. (2023). Remote sensing and geostatistics in urban water-resource monitoring: A review. *Marine and Freshwater Research*.

Lucas, R., Rowlands, A., Brown, A., Keyworth, S., & Bunting, P. (2007). Rule-based classification of multi-temporal satellite imagery for habitat and agricultural land cover mapping. *ISPRS Journal of Photogrammetry and Remote Sensing*, 62(3), 165–185.

Maisonneuve, N., Stevens, M., & Ochab, B. (2010). Participatory noise pollution monitoring using mobile phones. *Information polity*, 15(1-2), 51–71.

Mallegowda, P., Rengaian, G., Krishnan, J., & Niphadkar, M. (2015). Assessing habitat quality of forest-corridors through NDVI analysis in dry tropical forests of south India: implications for conservation. *Remote Sensing*, 7(2), 1619–1639.

Marshall, C. E., Glegg, G. A., & Howell, K. L. (2014). Species distribution modelling to support marine conservation planning: The next steps. *Marine Policy*, 45, 330–332.

McCarthy, M. J., Colna, K. E., El-Mezayen, M. M., Laureano-Rosario, A. E., Méndez-Lázaro, P., Otis, D. B., … & Muller-Karger, F. E. (2017). Satellite remote sensing for coastal management: A review of successful applications. *Environmental management*, 60, 323–339.

McGarigal, K., Wan, H. Y., Zeller, K. A., Timm, B. C., & Cushman, S. A. (2016). Multi-scale habitat selection modeling: a review and outlook. *Landscape ecology*, 31, 1161–1175.

McKinley, D. C., Miller-Rushing, A. J., Ballard, H. L., Bonney, R., Brown, H., Cook-Patton, S. C., … & Soukup, M. A. (2017). Citizen science can improve conservation science, natural resource management, and environmental protection. *Biological Conservation*, 208, 15–28.

Messinger, M., Asner, G. P., & Silman, M. (2016). Rapid assessments of Amazon forest structure and biomass using small unmanned aerial systems. *Remote Sensing*, 8(8), 615.

Miller, S. N., Kepner, W. G., Mehaffey, M. H., Hernandez, M., Miller, R. C., Goodrich, D. C., … & Miller, W. P. (2002). Integrating landscape assessment and hydrologic modeling for land cover change analysis 1. *JAWRA Journal of the American Water Resources Association*, 38(4), 915–929.

Murray, N. J., Keith, D. A., Simpson, D., Wilshire, J. H., & Lucas, R. M. (2018). Remap: An online remote sensing application for land cover classification and monitoring. *Methods in Ecology and Evolution*, 9(9), 2019–2027.

Nagendra, H., Lucas, R., Honrado, J. P., Jongman, R. H., Tarantino, C., Adamo, M., & Mairota, P. (2013). Remote sensing for conservation monitoring: Assessing protected areas, habitat extent, habitat condition, species diversity, and threats. *Ecological Indicators*, 33, 45–59.

Neeff, T., Steel, E. A., Kleinn, C., Hung, N. D., Bien, N. N., Cerutti, P. O., & Moutinho, P. (2020). How forest data catalysed change in four successful case studies. *Journal of Environmental Management*, 271, 110736.

Newman, G., Chandler, M., Clyde, M., McGreavy, B., Haklay, M., Ballard, H., … & Gallo, J. (2017). Leveraging the power of place in citizen science for effective conservation decision making. *Biological Conservation*, 208, 55–64.

O'Donnell, E. C., Lamond, J. E., & Thorne, C. R. (2018). Learning and Action Alliance framework to facilitate stakeholder collaboration and social learning in urban flood risk management. *Environmental Science & Policy, 80*, 1–8.

Ostfeld, R. S., Glass, G. E., & Keesing, F. (2005). Spatial epidemiology: An emerging (or re-emerging) discipline. *Trends in Ecology & Evolution, 20*(6), 328–336.

Ottelin, J., Ala-Mantila, S., Heinonen, J., Wiedmann, T., Clarke, J., & Junnila, S. (2019). What can we learn from consumption-based carbon footprints at different spatial scales? Review of policy implications. *Environmental Research Letters, 14*(9), 093001.

Pádua, L., Vanko, J., Hruška, J., Adão, T., Sousa, J. J., Peres, E., & Morais, R. (2017). UAS, sensors, and data processing in agroforestry: A review towards practical applications. *International Journal of Remote Sensing, 38*(8-10), 2349–2391.

Pettorelli, N., Owen, H. J. F., & Duncan, C. (2016). How do we want Satellite Remote Sensing to support biodiversity conservation globally? *Methods in Ecology and Evolution, 7*(6), 656–665.

Peuquet, D. J., & Duan, N. (1995). An event-based spatiotemporal data model (ESTDM) for temporal analysis of geographical data. *International Journal of Geographical Information Systems, 9*(1), 7–24.

Popescul, D., & Genete, L. D. (2016). Data security in smart cities: Challenges and solutions. *Informatica Economică, 20*(1).

Preetha, P. P., Al-Hamdan, A. Z., & Anderson, M. D. (2021). Assessment of climate variability and short-term land use land cover change effects on water quality of Cahaba River Basin. *International Journal of Hydrology Science and Technology, 11*(1), 54–75.

Quackenbush, L. J. (2004). A review of techniques for extracting linear features from imagery. *Photogrammetric Engineering & Remote Sensing, 70*(12), 1383–1392.

Quansah, J. E., Engel, B., & Rochon, G. L. (2010). Early warning systems: A review. *Journal of Terrestrial Observation, 2*(2), 5.

Radeva, K., Nedkov, R., & Dancheva, A. (2018). Application of remote sensing data for a wetland ecosystem services assessment in the area of Negovan village. *Remote Sensing for Agriculture, Ecosystems, and Hydrology XX.* https://doi.org/10.1117/12.2325767.

Rai, P. K., & Singh, J. S. (2020). Invasive alien plant species: Their impact on environment, ecosystem services and human health. *Ecological indicators, 111*, 106020.

Ramos, M. H., Mathevet, T., Thielen, J., & Pappenberger, F. (2010). Communicating uncertainty in hydro-meteorological forecasts: Mission impossible? *Meteorological Applications, 17*(2), 223–235.

Randin, C. F., Ashcroft, M. B., Bolliger, J., Cavender-Bares, J., Coops, N. C., Dullinger, S., ... & Payne, D. (2020). Monitoring biodiversity in the Anthropocene using remote sensing in species distribution models. *Remote Sensing of Environment, 239*, 111626.

Rasera, L. G., Gravey, M., Lane, S. N., & Mariethoz, G. (2020). Downscaling images with trends using multiple-point statistics simulation: An application to digital elevation models. *Mathematical Geosciences, 52*(2), 145–187.

Reddy, G. O. (2018). Geographic information system: Principles and applications. *Geospatial Technologies in Land Resources Mapping, Monitoring and Management*, 45–62.

Reside, A. E., Critchell, K., Crayn, D. M., Goosem, M., Goosem, S., Hoskin, C. J., ... & Pressey, R. L. (2019). Beyond the model: Expert knowledge improves predictions of species' fates under climate change. *Ecological Applications, 29*(1), e01824.

Rezvani, M., Nickravesh, F., Astaneh, A. D., & Kazemi, N. (2022). A risk-based decision-making approach for identifying natural-based tourism potential areas. *Journal of Outdoor Recreation and Tourism, 37*, 100485.

Richard, K., Abdel-Rahman, E. M., Mohamed, S. A., Ekesi, S., Borgemeister, C., & Landmann, T. (2018). Importance of remotely-sensed vegetation variables for predicting the spatial distribution of African citrus triozid (Trioza erytreae) in Kenya. *ISPRS International Journal of Geo-Information, 7*(11), 429.

Richards, J. A., & Richards, J. A. (2022). *Remote sensing digital image analysis* (Vol. 5). New York: Springer.

Rodríguez-Veiga, P., Wheeler, J., Louis, V., Tansey, K., & Balzter, H. (2017). Quantifying forest biomass carbon stocks from space. *Current Forestry Reports, 3,* 1–18.

Rogan, J., & Chen, D. (2004). Remote sensing technology for mapping and monitoring land-cover and land-use change. *Progress in Planning, 61*(4), 301–325.

Rolnick, D., Donti, P. L., Kaack, L. H., Kochanski, K., Lacoste, A., Sankaran, K., … & Bengio, Y. (2022). Tackling climate change with machine learning. *ACM Computing Surveys (CSUR), 55*(2), 1–96.

Rose, R. A., Byler, D., Eastman, J. R., Fleishman, E., Geller, G., Goetz, S., … & Wilson, C. (2015). Ten ways remote sensing can contribute to conservation. *Conservation Biology, 29*(2), 350–359.

Ross, S., Costanzi, J. M., Al Jahdhami, M., Al Rawahi, H., Ghazali, M., & Senn, H. (2020). First evaluation of the population structure, genetic diversity and landscape connectivity of the Endangered Arabian tahr. *Mammalian Biology, 100,* 659–673.

Roubos, C. R., Rodriguez-Saona, C., & Isaacs, R. (2014). Mitigating the effects of insecticides on arthropod biological control at field and landscape scales. *Biological Control, 75,* 28–38.

Rwanga, S. S., & Ndambuki, J. M. (2017). Accuracy assessment of land use/land cover classification using remote sensing and GIS. *International Journal of Geosciences, 8*(04), 611.

Safari, S., Sharghi, S., Kerachian, R., & Noory, H. (2023). A market-based mechanism for long-term groundwater management using remotely sensed data. *Journal of Environmental Management, 332,* 117409.

Schweighofer, J. A., Wehrl, M., Baumgärtel, S., & Rohn, J. (2021). Calculating energy and its spatial distribution for a subsurface urban heat island using a GIS-approach. *Geosciences, 11*(1), 24.

Sivapalan, M., & Blöschl, G. (2015). Time scale interactions and the coevolution of humans and water. *Water Resources Research, 51*(9), 6988–7022.

Sobhani, P., Esmaeilzadeh, H., Sadeghi, S. M. M., & Marcu, M. V. (2022). Estimation of eco-tourism carrying capacity for sustainable development of protected areas in Iran. *International Journal of Environmental Research and Public Health, 19*(3), 1059.

Sohn, G., & Dowman, I. (2007). Data fusion of high-resolution satellite imagery and LiDAR data for automatic building extraction. *ISPRS Journal of Photogrammetry and Remote Sensing, 62*(1), 43–63.

Sowmya, D. R., Deepa Shenoy, P., & Venugopal, K. R. (2017). Remote sensing satellite image processing techniques for image classification: A comprehensive survey. *International Journal of Computer Applications, 161*(11), 24–37.

Sozzi, M., Kayad, A., Gobbo, S., Cogato, A., Sartori, L., & Marinello, F. (2021). Economic comparison of satellite, plane and UAV-acquired NDVI images for site-specific nitrogen application: Observations from Italy. *Agronomy, 11*(11), 2098.

Stralberg, D., Carroll, C., & Nielsen, S. E. (2020). Toward a climate-informed North American protected areas network: Incorporating climate-change refugia and corridors in conservation planning. *Conservation Letters, 13*(4), e12712.

Summers, J. K., Smith, L. M., Case, J. L., & Linthurst, R. A. (2012). A review of the elements of human well-being with an emphasis on the contribution of ecosystem services. *Ambio, 41,* 327–340.

Swatantran, A., Tang, H., Barrett, T., DeCola, P., & Dubayah, R. (2016). Rapid, high-resolution forest structure and terrain mapping over large areas using single photon lidar. *Scientific Reports, 6*(1), 28277.

Tahri, M., Kaspar, J., Vacik, H., & Marusak, R. (2021). Multi-attribute decision making and geographic information systems: Potential tools for evaluating forest ecosystem services. *Annals of Forest Science, 78*(2), 1–19.

Talebi, M., Majnounian, B., Makhdoum, M., Abdi, E., Omid, M., Marchi, E., & Laschi, A. (2019). A GIS-MCDM-based road network planning for tourism development and management in Arasbaran forest, Iran. *Environmental Monitoring and Assessment, 191*, 1–15.

Tallis, H., & Polasky, S. (2009). Mapping and valuing ecosystem services as an approach for conservation and natural-resource management. *Annals of the New York Academy of Sciences, 1162*(1), 265–283.

Tasseron, P., Van Emmerik, T., Peller, J., Schreyers, L., & Biermann, L. (2021). Advancing floating macroplastic detection from space using experimental hyperspectral imagery. *Remote Sensing, 13*(12), 2335.

Tavares, P. A., Beltrão, N., Guimarães, U. S., Teodoro, A., & Gonçalves, P. (2019). Urban ecosystem services quantification through remote sensing approach: A systematic review. *Environments, 6*(5), 51.

Tedesco, M. (2015). Remote sensing and the cryosphere. *Remote Sensing of the Cryosphere*, 1–16.

Teng, J., Jakeman, A. J., Vaze, J., Croke, B. F., Dutta, D., & Kim, S. J. E. M. (2017). Flood inundation modelling: A review of methods, recent advances and uncertainty analysis. *Environmental Modelling & Software, 90*, 201–216.

Thammanu, S., Marod, D., Han, H., Bhusal, N., Asanok, L., Ketdee, P., … & Chung, J. (2021). The influence of environmental factors on species composition and distribution in a community forest in Northern Thailand. *Journal of Forestry Research, 32*, 649–662.

Tiwari, P. C., & Joshi, B. (2012). Natural and socio-economic factors affecting food security in the Himalayas. *Food Security, 4*, 195–207.

Trancoso, R., Carneiro Filho, A., Tomasella, J., Schietti, J., Forsberg, B. R., & Miller, R. P. (2009). Deforestation and conservation in major watersheds of the Brazilian Amazon. *Environmental Conservation, 36*(4), 277–288.

Tropsha, A., Gramatica, P., & Gombar, V. K. (2003). The importance of being earnest: validation is the absolute essential for successful application and interpretation of QSPR models. *QSAR & Combinatorial Science, 22*(1), 69–77.

Tse-Ring, K., Sharma, E., Chettri, N., & Shrestha, A. B. (2010). *Climate change vulnerability of mountain ecosystems in the Eastern Himalayas.* International centre for integrated mountain development (ICIMOD). http://lib.riskreductionafrica.org/bitstream/handle/123456789/485/climate%20change%20vulnerability%20of%20mountain%20ecosystems%20in%20the%20Eastern%20Himalayas.pdf?sequence=1. Accessed 30 Apr 2023

Tuanmu, M. N., Viña, A., Bearer, S., Xu, W., Ouyang, Z., Zhang, H., & Liu, J. (2010). Mapping understory vegetation using phenological characteristics derived from remotely sensed data. *Remote Sensing of Environment, 114*(8), 1833–1844.

Van Westen, C. J. (2013). Remote sensing and GIS for natural hazards assessment and disaster risk management. *Treatise on Geomorphology, 3*(15), 259–298.

Vanacker, V., Vanderschaeghe, M., Govers, G., Willems, E., Poesen, J., Deckers, J., & De Bievre, B. (2003). Linking hydrological, infinite slope stability and land-use change models through GIS for assessing the impact of deforestation on slope stability in high Andean watersheds. *Geomorphology, 52*(3-4), 299–315.

Vaz, A. S., Gonçalves, J. F., Pereira, P., Santarém, F., Vicente, J. R., & Honrado, J. P. (2019). Earth observation and social media: Evaluating the spatiotemporal contribution of non-native trees to cultural ecosystem services. *Remote Sensing of Environment, 230*, 111193.

Verrall, B., & Pickering, C. M. (2020). Alpine vegetation in the context of climate change: A global review of past research and future directions. *Science of the Total Environment, 748*, 141344.

Vila-Viçosa, C., Arenas-Castro, S., Marcos, B., Honrado, J., García, C., Vázquez, F. M., … & Gonçalves, J. (2020). Combining satellite remote sensing and climate data in species distribution models to improve the conservation of iberian white oaks (Quercus L.). *ISPRS International Journal of Geo-Information, 9*(12), 735.

Wang, S., Khan, A., Lin, Y., Jiang, Z., Tang, H., Alomar, S. Y., Sanaullah, M., & Bhatti, U. A. (2023). Deep reinforcement learning enables adaptive-image augmentation for automated optical inspection of plant rust. *Frontiers in Plant Science, 14.* 10.3389/fpls.2023.1142957.

Wang, S., Li, X., Ge, Y., Jin, R., Ma, M., Liu, Q., ... & Liu, S. (2016a). Validation of regional-scale remote sensing products in China: From site to network. *Remote Sensing, 8*(12), 980.

Wang, G., Mang, S., Cai, H., Liu, S., Zhang, Z., Wang, L., & Innes, J. L. (2016b). Integrated watershed management: evolution, development and emerging trends. *Journal of Forestry Research, 27,* 967–994.

Wang, R., Yuan, Y., Yen, H., Grieneisen, M., Arnold, J., Wang, D., ... & Zhang, M. (2019). A review of pesticide fate and transport simulation at watershed level using SWAT: Current status and research concerns. *Science of the Total Environment, 669,* 512–526.

Welvaert, M., & Caley, P. (2016). Citizen surveillance for environmental monitoring: combining the efforts of citizen science and crowdsourcing in a quantitative data framework. *SpringerPlus, 5,* 1–14.

Werner, T. T., Bebbington, A., & Gregory, G. (2019). Assessing impacts of mining: Recent contributions from GIS and remote sensing. *The Extractive Industries and Society, 6*(3), 993–1012.

Wu, G., Sahabuddin, M., Bhatti, U., Nawaz, S. A., Hasnain, A., Bhatti, M. A., Fahim, A., Kaleri, A., & Kaleri, A. H. (2022). COVID-19 and Air Pollution: Air Quality Impact in 13 Cities of the Jiangsu Province of China. *Polish Journal of Environmental Studies, 31,* 4907–4916. 10.15244/pjoes/149714.

Xie, D., Zhang, J., Zhu, X., Pan, Y., Liu, H., Yuan, Z., & Yun, Y. (2016). An improved STARFM with help of an unmixing-based method to generate high spatial and temporal resolution remote-sensing data in complex heterogeneous regions. *Sensors, 16*(2), 207.

Xie, G., & Niculescu, S. (2021). Mapping and monitoring of land cover/land use (LCLU) changes in the Crozon Peninsula (Brittany, France) from 2007 to 2018 by machine learning algorithms (support vector machine, random forest, and convolutional neural network) and by post-classification comparison (PCC). *Remote Sensing, 13*(19), 3899.

Yao, H., Qin, R., & Chen, X. (2019). Unmanned aerial vehicle for remote sensing applications—A review. *Remote Sensing, 11*(12), 1443.

Yue, P., Gong, J., Di, L., Yuan, J., Sun, L., Sun, Z., & Wang, Q. (2010). GeoPW: Laying blocks for the geospatial processing web. *Transactions in GIS, 14*(6), 755–772.

Zhang, J., Huang, Y., Pu, R., Gonzalez-Moreno, P., Yuan, L., Wu, K., & Huang, W. (2019). Monitoring plant diseases and pests through remote sensing technology: A review. *Computers and Electronics in Agriculture, 165,* 104943.

Zhang, L., Hu, Q., & Tang, Z. (2022). Using Sentinel-2 imagery and machine learning algorithms to assess the inundation status of Nebraska conservation easements during 2018–2021. *Remote Sensing, 14*(17), 4382.

Zorrilla-Miras, P., Palomo, I., Gómez-Baggethun, E., Martín-López, B., Lomas, P. L., & Montes, C. (2014). Effects of land-use change on wetland ecosystem services: A case study in the Doñana marshes (SW Spain). *Landscape and Urban Planning, 122,* 160–174.

## CHAPTER 13

From Data Quality to Model Performance

Navigating the Landscape of Deep Learning Model Evaluation

Muhammad Akram, Wajid Hassan Moosa, and Najiba

Faculty of Information and Communication Technology, Balochistan University of Information Technology, Engineering and Management Sciences, Quetta, Pakistan

13.1 INTRODUCTION

The development and evaluation of deep learning models rely heavily on the quality and diversity of the data sets used to train them. Benchmarks are crucial for evaluating the performance of these models, while validations ensure that they are performing as intended. The importance of these topics cannot be overstated, as they are essential for the successful application of deep learning to a wide range of problems in multimedia analysis.

13.2 IMPORTANCE OF DATA SETS, BENCHMARKS, AND VALIDATIONS

In recent years, deep learning technologies have made significant strides in multimedia analysis, including natural language processing, visual data analytics, and audio recognition. However, the success of these technologies' hinges on the quality of the data sets used to train them. Without diverse and high-quality data sets, deep learning models are unable to capture the full range of features in multimedia data.

The choice of the data set can have a significant impact on the performance of deep learning models. A data set should be representative of the problem domain, contain a diverse range of examples, and provide sufficient coverage of the features of interest. Furthermore, the data set should be large enough to capture the complexity of the problem and provide enough training examples for the deep learning model to learn the underlying patterns.

However, developing high-quality data sets can be challenging, particularly for complex problems with many features. Data collection can be expensive and time-consuming,

DOI: 10.1201/9781032646268-13

and the process of labeling data can be subjective and error prone. To address these challenges, researchers have developed strategies for curating data sets, such as transfer learning and data augmentation, which we will see in this chapter, that enables the use of smaller data sets or reduce the amount of labeled data required.

Benchmarks play a vital role in evaluating the performance of deep learning models. Benchmarks provide a standard for evaluating the accuracy and efficiency of these models, as well as a basis for comparison with other models. Without benchmarks, it is challenging to determine how well a deep learning model is performing relative to state-of-the-art models or the expectations of the problem domain.

Benchmark data sets should be representative of the problem domain and contain a diverse range of examples. Furthermore, the benchmarks should provide a standardized evaluation protocol, including metrics and evaluation criteria, to enable fair comparisons across models. Researchers often use popular benchmark data sets such as ImageNet, COCO, and MS-COCO, which provide standardized evaluations for image and object recognition.

Validations ensure that deep learning models are performing as intended. Validations help to uncover biases in the data, identify overfitting, and ensure that the model's performance generalizes to new data. Without proper validation, deep learning models may perform well on the training data set but poorly on new data, leading to unreliable results and incorrect conclusions.

Validation techniques include cross-validation, hold-out validation, and leave-one-out validation. These techniques evaluate the model's performance on a subset of the data set and provide estimates of its performance on new data. Additionally, techniques such as adversarial validation can help identify cases where the training and testing data come from different distributions, highlighting potential issues with the model's generalization performance.

Given the importance of data sets, benchmarks, and validations in the development and evaluation of deep learning models, this chapter aims to provide an in-depth discussion of these topics. The chapter will cover popular data sets used in deep learning research, characteristics of a good data set, popular benchmarks used in deep learning research, and common validation techniques. Additionally, the chapter will discuss the challenges associated with developing and using data sets, benchmarks, and validations in deep learning research, including issues with data bias and overfitting. Finally, the chapter will outline future directions for improving these techniques, such as developing more comprehensive benchmark data sets and developing techniques for automated data labeling and validation.

13.3 DATA SETS FOR DEEP LEARNING

13.3.1 What is a Data Set and Why is it Important in AI?

A data set is a collection of data points that are used to train a machine learning model. In the context of deep learning, data sets are used to train neural networks to recognize patterns and make predictions. These data sets can come in different formats, including text, images, videos, and audio.

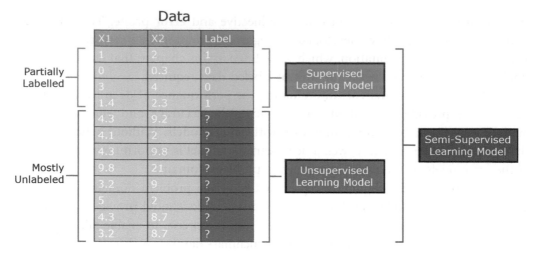

FIGURE 13.1   Types of data in machine learning: supervised, unsupervised, and semi-supervised.

There are primarily two types of data sets for deep learning: supervised and unsupervised. Supervised learning involves training a model on labeled data, meaning that each data point is associated with a corresponding label or output. The goal of supervised learning is to learn a mapping between the input data and its corresponding output. Examples of supervised learning data sets include the MNIST data set for handwritten digit recognition and the CIFAR-10 data set for object recognition.

On the other hand, unsupervised learning involves training a model on unlabeled data, where there are no corresponding output labels. The goal of unsupervised learning is to discover patterns and structures within the data itself. Examples of unsupervised learning data sets include the *ImageNet* data set for image classification and clustering and the *Text8* data set for natural language processing.

Another type of data set used in deep learning is semi-supervised learning, which involves a combination of labeled and unlabeled data as shown in Figure 13.1 (Bishirian, 2021). This approach is often used when labeling data is expensive or time-consuming. The model is first trained on a small amount of labeled data, and then on a larger amount of unlabeled data. Examples of semi-supervised learning data sets include the LabelMe data set for object recognition and the CoNLL-2003 data set for named entity recognition.

Deep learning models can also be trained on transfer learning (Karl Weiss, 2016) data sets, where the model is pre-trained on a large data set before being fine-tuned on a smaller, task-specific data set. This approach is often used when the target data set is small or when there is limited access to labeled data. If the problem you are solving is related to image classification and you do not have sufficient data, then you can use any pre-trained model such as ResNet and apply transfer learning using your data.

The process involves taking the pre-trained model, which has already learned to recognize certain features in images, and re-training it on a new data set with a different set of labels. By doing this, the model can quickly learn to identify new objects without requiring a large amount of labeled data. In this case, the model was able to adapt to

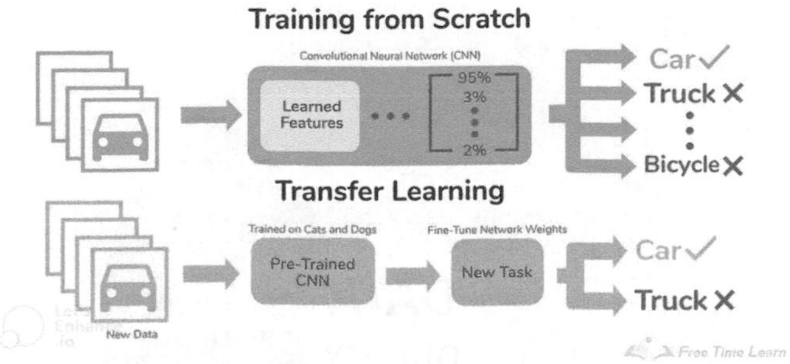

FIGURE 13.2 The figure shows a neural network model that was originally trained on a data set of cats and dogs. The model was then fine-tuned using transfer learning techniques to detect cars and trucks in images.

detect cars and trucks by leveraging the knowledge it had already gained from the original training on cats and dogs as shown in Figure 13.2 (Deep Learning Interview Questions). This approach can be particularly useful in scenarios where labeled data is scarce, as it allows for the effective utilization of existing pre-trained models to perform new tasks.

Data sets can also be classified based on their characteristics such as size, diversity, quality, bias, and balance. These characteristics play a crucial role in the success of the deep learning models trained on them. It is important to carefully select and prepare data sets to ensure that they are appropriate for the task at hand and that the models trained on them can generalize well to new, unseen data.

13.3.2 The Impact of Data Quality on Deep Learning Model Performance

The quality of data used to train deep learning models has a significant impact on the model's performance. If the data is of poor quality, the model may learn incorrect patterns, leading to poor predictions and classifications. In this section, we will discuss the impact of data quality on deep learning model performance.

First, let's define data quality. Data quality refers to the accuracy, completeness, consistency, and timeliness of data, as shown in Figure 13.3 (McDonald, 2021). Accurate data is data that is free from errors, while complete data includes all necessary information. Consistent data is data that is uniform in format, and timely data is up-to-date data.

The impact of data quality on deep learning model performance is significant. Poor data quality can lead to poor model performance and inaccurate predictions. For example, if a data set used to train a deep learning model is incomplete, the model may not have enough information to accurately classify new data. Similarly, if the data is inconsistent, the model may learn incorrect patterns, leading to poor predictions.

Data quality also affects the generalization of a deep learning model. If a model is trained on a small, biased data set, it may not generalize well to new, unseen data. This is because the model has not learned enough about the target population and is overfitting the training data. Overfitting (Shaeke Salman, 2019) occurs when the model is too complex and trained on a small data set, leading to poor generalization.

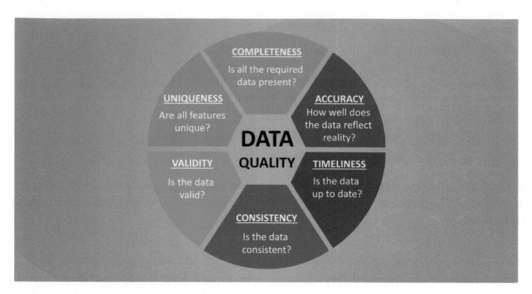

FIGURE 13.3 Six common characteristics of data quality. Image created by the Author (McDonald, 2021) The picture above illustrates the six qualities that data should ideally possess to be considered high quality.

One way to improve data quality is through data pre-processing. Data pre-processing involves cleaning and transforming the data before it is used to train the model. This can include removing missing or incorrect data, normalizing the data, and transforming the data into a suitable format.

Another way to improve data quality is through data augmentation (Luis Perez, 2017).

Data augmentation involves artificially increasing the size of the data set by creating new, synthetic data. This can help to address issues with data set size and diversity, which are important characteristics of a good data set for deep learning.

In addition to improving data quality through pre-processing and augmentation, it is also important to carefully select the data set used to train the model. The data set should be large enough to capture the variability of the target population and should be diverse enough to capture different patterns and features. The data set should also be labeled accurately to ensure that the model is learning the correct patterns.

13.3.3 Overview of Popular Data Sets for Deep Learning Models

The development of deep learning models has been fueled by the availability of large, high-quality data sets. These data sets are essential for training and evaluating deep learning models, as they provide the necessary input data and ground truth labels for supervised learning tasks. In recent years, several popular data sets have emerged that have become the de facto standards for evaluating deep learning models in various domains. In this chapter, we will discuss some of the most popular data sets used in deep learning research, including ImageNet, COCO, and CIFAR.

ImageNet is perhaps the most well-known data set used in deep learning research, particularly in the field of computer vision. ImageNet consists of over 14 million

COCO 2020 Panoptic Segmentation Task

FIGURE 13.4   The figure illustrates the COCO data set.

images, each labeled with one of over 20,000 categories. The data set was first introduced in 2009 and has since become the standard benchmark for image classification tasks. The development of deep learning models for image classification, such as convolutional neural networks (CNNs) (Keiron O'Shea, 2015) has been heavily influenced by the ImageNet data set. The annual ImageNet large-scale visual recognition challenge (ILSVRC) has become a major event in the deep learning community, where researchers from around the world compete to achieve the best results on a standardized set of test images.

The common objects in context (COCO) data set is another popular data set in the computer vision community, as shown in Figure 13.4 (Solawetz, 2020). COCO consists of over 320,000 images, each labeled with object annotations, key points, and captions. The data set was first introduced in 2014 and has since become the standard benchmark for object detection, segmentation, and captioning tasks. The COCO data set is known for its challenging and diverse set of images, with objects in various sizes, poses, and occlusions. Deep learning models trained on the COCO data set have achieved state-of-the-art performance on a range of computer vision tasks.

The CIFAR data sets are a series of image classification data sets that have become popular benchmarks in the deep learning community. CIFAR-10 consists of 60,000 32 × 32 color images in ten classes, while CIFAR-100 consists of 60,000 images in 100 classes, as shown in Figure 13.5 (cifar10). The data sets were first introduced in 2009 and have since become widely used for evaluating deep learning models for image classification tasks. The CIFAR data sets are known for their relatively small size and simple structure, which make them ideal for benchmarking new deep learning models.

In addition to these data sets, there are several other popular data sets used in deep learning research, including the MNIST data set for handwritten digit recognition, the Pascal VOC data set for object detection, and the Berkeley DeepDrive data set for

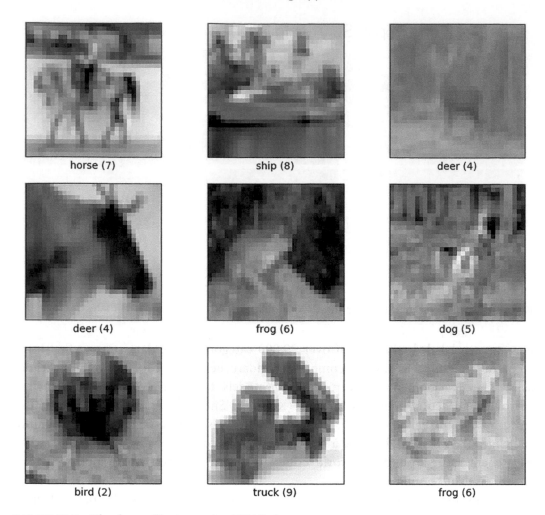

FIGURE 13.5   The figure illustrates the CIFAR data set.

autonomous driving. These data sets have become the standard benchmarks for evaluating deep learning models in their respective domains, and many research papers and projects use them as a starting point for developing and testing new deep learning models.

The availability of high-quality data sets is essential for the development and evaluation of deep learning models. The data sets discussed in this chapter, including ImageNet, COCO, and CIFAR, have become the de facto standards for evaluating deep learning models in various domains. The popularity of these data sets has led to intense competition among researchers to develop better models and achieve state-of-the-art performance. As the field of deep learning continues to evolve, new data sets will likely emerge that will become the new benchmarks for evaluating deep learning models.

Voice and text data sets are also important in deep learning research. These data sets are used in natural language processing (NLP) tasks such as speech recognition, language translation, and sentiment analysis.

One example of a popular voice data set is the common voice data set, which is an open-source, multi-language data set of human speech. It was created by Mozilla to improve speech recognition technology by collecting voice samples from people worldwide. The data set currently includes over 9,000 hours of speech from over 60 languages.

The Google Speech Commands data set is another widely used data set for speech recognition tasks. It includes over 100,000 utterances of 35 different commands, such as "stop," "go," and "yes."

For text data sets, the Penn Treebank data set is a popular choice for NLP tasks such as language modeling and part-of-speech tagging. It consists of over 4.5 million words of annotated text from various sources, including newswire articles and academic papers.

Another popular text data set is the Stanford Sentiment Treebank, which contains over 10,000 movie reviews with sentiment annotations. It is commonly used for sentiment analysis tasks, such as predicting whether a given review is positive or negative.

Voice and text data sets play a critical role in advancing deep learning research in the area of NLP. By providing high-quality and diverse data for training and validation, these data sets enable researchers to develop more accurate and robust deep learning models for speech and language-related tasks.

13.3.4 Advantages and Limitations of Using Publicly Available Data Sets

Deep learning has rapidly gained popularity in recent years, and one of the reasons for its success is the availability of publicly available data sets. These data sets are readily accessible and provide researchers and developers with a means to train and test their models on a wide variety of real-world data. However, while the use of publicly available data sets has several advantages, it also has limitations that must be considered.

Advantages of Using Publicly Available Data Sets:
   1. *Cost-effectiveness*: One of the significant advantages of using publicly available data sets is that they are cost-effective. As these data sets are already available, researchers and developers do not need to spend time and resources in collecting data. This can be especially beneficial for small research groups or startups with limited resources.

   2. *Standardization*: Publicly available data sets are typically well-organized and standardized. This can save researchers and developers time and effort in data preprocessing, cleaning, and labeling. Standardization can also make it easier for researchers to compare their results with others in the field.

   3. *Diversity*: Publicly available data sets are often large and diverse, providing researchers with a wide variety of data to work with. This can help to improve the robustness and generalization of deep learning models.

   4. *Accessibility*: Publicly available data sets are often made accessible to the wider research community. This can help to promote collaboration and can accelerate research progress.

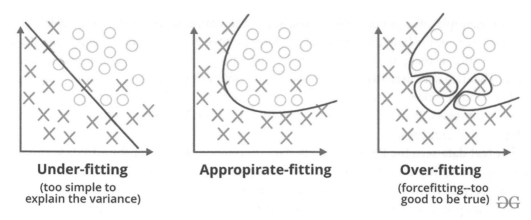

Under-fitting
(too simple to
explain the variance)

Appropirate-fitting

Over-fitting
(forcefitting--too
good to be true)

FIGURE 13.6   The figure illustrates the concepts of overfitting, underfitting, and appropriate fitting in machine learning.

Limitations of Using Publicly Available Data Sets:

1. *Quality*: The quality of publicly available data sets can be variable, and not all data sets are suitable for every use case. It is essential to carefully evaluate data sets before using them to ensure that they meet the requirements of the problem being solved.

2. *Bias* (Eirini Ntoutsi, 2020): Publicly available data sets can also be biased, either due to the selection of samples or labeling. Biased data sets can lead to inaccurate or unfair results, which can have significant consequences.

3. *Privacy*: Publicly available data sets may contain sensitive information, such as personal data, that must be protected. It is essential to ensure that the data is anonymized before using it for research purposes.

4. *Overfitting* (Shaeke Salman, 2019): Publicly available data sets may have been used extensively in previous research, making it easier for models to overfit. Overfitting occurs when a model becomes too specialized to the training data and performs poorly on new, unseen data as shown in Figure 13.6 (dewangNautiyal, 2023).

13.3.5 Best Practices for Data Set Creation and Curation

Creating and curating high-quality data sets is critical to achieving accurate and robust deep-learning models. In this section, we will discuss some best practices for data set creation and curation.

1. *Define the task and data requirements*: Before starting to collect data, it's essential to define the problem you are trying to solve and the data requirements for the model. This involves determining what type of data is needed, how much data is required, and what features or labels are needed. It's also essential to identify any potential biases or data quality issues that might affect the performance of the model.

2. *Collect diverse data:* Diverse data can help the model to generalize better and perform well on unseen data. It's important to collect data from different sources, environments, and conditions to ensure that the model can handle variations and adapt to new situations. For example, if you are training an image classification model, it's important to collect images with different lighting conditions, backgrounds, and viewpoints.

3. *Label data accurately:* Labeling is a critical aspect of data set creation, and it's important to ensure that the labels are accurate and consistent. Labeling errors can lead to a biased or inaccurate model, which can have serious consequences in real-world applications. It's important to have multiple people label the data and have a process to resolve any disagreements.

4. *Clean and preprocess data:* Data cleaning and pre-processing are essential steps to ensure that the data is of high quality and ready for model training. This involves removing duplicate or irrelevant data, handling missing values, and transforming the data into a format that the model can handle. It's important to document these steps and ensure that they are reproducible.

5. *Validate and test the data set:* Validation and testing are critical steps to ensure that the data set is of high quality and suitable for model training. This involves checking for data quality issues, such as missing values or mislabeled data, and assessing the data set's suitability for the intended task. It's important to have a process for validating and testing the data set and to document the results.

6. *Document the data set:* Documentation is critical for ensuring that the data set is usable and understandable by others. This involves providing detailed information about the data set, such as the data collection process, data format, and any pre-processing steps. It's also essential to include any relevant metadata, such as the source of the data and any licensing information.

7. *Update and maintain the data set:* Data Sets can become outdated or no longer relevant over time, and it's important to have a process for updating and maintaining the data set. This involves monitoring the data set for any changes or issues and updating the documentation and pre-processing steps as needed.

13.3.6 Techniques for Ensuring Data Set Diversity and Balance

In deep learning, having a diverse and balanced data set is crucial for achieving high performance. A diverse data set allows the model to learn from different types of data, while a balanced data set ensures that the model does not become biased toward a particular class or category. In this section, we will discuss techniques for ensuring data set diversity and balance.

1. *Augmentation Techniques:* Data augmentation is a technique used to increase the size and diversity of a data set by creating new training examples from the existing

ones. Augmentation can be done by applying various transformations to the original data, such as cropping, flipping, rotating, and changing the brightness and contrast levels. This technique can be especially useful when dealing with small data sets, as it helps to increase the amount of training data and makes the model more robust to variations in the input.

2. *Ensemble Learning:* (M.A. Ganaie, 2021) Ensemble learning is a technique used to combine multiple models to improve overall performance. In the context of data set diversity and balance, ensemble learning can be used to combine models trained on different subsets of the data set. By training multiple models on different parts of the data set, the resulting ensemble model can be more robust to variations in the input, and less prone to overfitting or underfitting.

3. *Stratified Sampling:* (Kevin Lang, June 2016) Stratified sampling is a technique used to ensure that each class or category in the data set is represented proportionally in the training and testing sets. This technique can be useful when dealing with imbalanced data sets, where some classes have significantly fewer examples than others. By ensuring that each class is represented proportionally, the model can learn to recognize each class equally well.

4. *Data Collection and Curation Ensuring:* data set diversity and balance start with the collection and curation of the data. When collecting data, it is important to ensure that it represents the target population accurately. This can be done by collecting data from multiple sources and ensuring that the data covers a wide range of scenarios and variations. When curating data, it is important to ensure that the data is labeled accurately and consistently and that any bias in the labeling process is minimized.

5. *Regularization Techniques:* (Jan Kukačka, 2017) Regularization techniques are used to prevent overfitting of the model on the training data. In the context of data set diversity and balance, regularization techniques can be used to ensure that the model does not become biased toward a particular class or category. For example, L1 and L2 regularization can be used to penalize the model for weights that are too large, which can help prevent the model from becoming overly biased toward a particular feature or class.

13.3.7 The Role of Data Augmentation in Improving Data Set Quality

Data augmentation is the process of creating new data by applying transformations to the existing data set. It is a popular technique in deep learning for improving the quality of the data set and preventing overfitting. By applying various transformations, such as rotations, translations, and flipping, the data set can be diversified, resulting in a larger and more varied data set.

Data augmentation is especially important for image data sets. Augmenting the data set can help in creating variations of images that may not have been present in the original data set. This can lead to better training of the deep learning models, as the model can learn to recognize the object regardless of the orientation or position.

There are several ways to apply data augmentation to image data sets. One popular method is to randomly crop a portion of the image and resize it to the original size. This can help the model learn to recognize the object even when it is partially visible or occluded. Another common technique is to apply random rotations, translations, and scaling to the images. This can help in generating variations of the same object, which can lead to better generalization of the model.

Data augmentation is also useful for text data sets. In natural language processing, data augmentation can be used to create variations of the original text by applying various transformations, such as synonym replacement, word deletion, and word reordering. By augmenting the text data set, the model can be trained to recognize the same meaning expressed in different ways shown in Figure 13.7 (Kumar, 2019). This can lead to better generalization and performance of the model.

However, it is important to note that data augmentation can also have limitations. One limitation is that the transformations applied to the data set should not significantly alter the meaning or context of the original data. Otherwise, the model can be trained on misleading or incorrect data, which can result in poor performance. Additionally, data augmentation can also increase the computational cost of training the deep learning model, as it requires additional processing power and memory.

To ensure that data augmentation is applied effectively, it is important to follow best practices for data set creation and curation. This includes ensuring that the original data set is of high quality, diverse, and balanced. Additionally, it is important to carefully

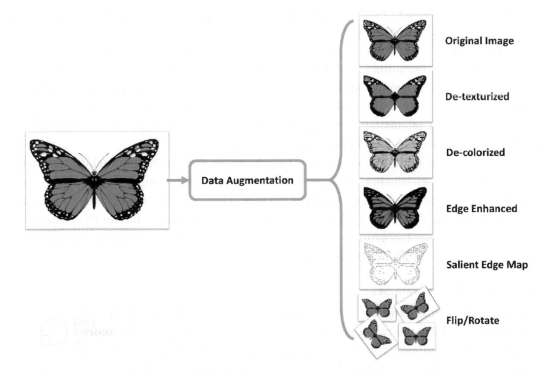

FIGURE 13.7   The figure illustrates an example of data augmentation on the image of a butterfly.

select the transformations to be applied to the data set to ensure that they are appropriate for the task at hand.

13.3.8 Techniques for Labeling Data Sets Accurately and Efficiently

Labeling data sets accurately and efficiently is crucial for training deep learning models. The accuracy of labels determines how well the model can recognize and classify patterns, while efficiency ensures that the model is trained within a reasonable time frame. In this section, we will discuss some techniques for labeling different types of data sets accurately and efficiently, including image, text, spatial, and audio data sets.

Image data sets: For image data sets, several labeling techniques can be used, including manual labeling, semi-automatic labeling, and fully automatic labeling. Manual labeling involves a human annotator manually marking the relevant regions in the image, which can be time-consuming but provides accurate labeling. Semi-automatic labeling involves a combination of manual labeling and automated tools, such as object detection algorithms, which can speed up the labeling process while maintaining accuracy. Fully automatic labeling uses computer vision algorithms to label the images automatically, which is efficient but may not always be accurate.

Text data sets: For text data sets, the most common labeling technique is manual labeling, where human annotators read and label the text data based on predefined categories or tags. This process can be time-consuming and subjective, as different annotators may label the same text differently. However, the use of inter-annotator agreement measures, such as Kappa statistics (Andrew Rosenberg, 2004), can help ensure consistency in labeling. Another technique is using pre-trained models for labeling, which can help speed up the labeling process.

Spatial data sets: For spatial data sets, such as satellite imagery, labeling can be done using manual or semi-automatic techniques. Manual labeling involves human annotators marking the relevant regions on the imagery, which can be time-consuming but provides accurate labeling. Semi-automatic labeling uses machine learning algorithms, such as object detection or segmentation, to automatically label the imagery, which can speed up the labeling process but may not always be accurate.

Audio data sets: For audio data sets, labeling can be done using manual or automatic techniques. Manual labeling involves human annotators listening to the audio and labeling it based on predefined categories or tags. This process can be time-consuming and subjective, as different annotators may label the same audio differently. Automatic labeling uses speech recognition algorithms to label the audio automatically, which is efficient but may not always be accurate.

13.3.9 Quality of Data Set

Size: The size (Philip Woodall, 2014) of a data set is a critical factor in deep learning as it affects the model's ability to generalize. A larger data set provides more variability, making it more representative of the target population. For instance, a data set with only a few samples may not capture the variability of the target population, leading to poor generalization. However, a larger data set requires more computational resources and longer training time, which may not be feasible in some cases.

For example, in natural language processing, the Common Crawl data set is a vast collection of web pages that have been crawled and archived. The data set contains over 4.6 billion web pages, making it one of the largest publicly available data sets. The data set has been used to train language models such as GPT-3/3.5, which has achieved state-of-the-art performance in various natural language processing tasks.

Diversity: A diverse data set should contain samples with different attributes and characteristics to capture the variability of the target population. A more diverse data set can help improve the model's performance by enabling it to recognize patterns that may be missed in a more homogeneous data set. For example, in image classification tasks, a data set with images of different sizes, backgrounds, and perspectives is more diverse and can help improve the model's ability to generalize to new data.

The Open Images Data Set, which contains over 9 million images and annotations, is an example of a diverse data set used in deep learning research. The data set includes images with different sizes, backgrounds, and perspectives, making it more representative of real-world scenarios.

Quality: (Sylvaine Picard, 2020) the quality of a data set is essential as it affects the model's ability to learn the correct patterns. A high-quality data set should be labeled accurately, ensuring that the model learns the correct patterns. Inaccurate labeling can lead to poor performance of the model, which can result in incorrect predictions or classifications.

For example, the ImageNet data set, which contains over 14 million labeled images, is a high-quality data set used in image classification tasks. The data set has been labeled accurately, ensuring that the models trained on the data set achieve state-of-the-art performance in various image classification tasks.

Bias: Bias in a data set can occur due to various factors, such as the selection of samples or labeling. A good data set should be free from any form of bias to ensure that the model learns the right patterns. Bias in a data set can lead to poor performance of the model, especially when the model is deployed in the real world.

For example, facial recognition technology has been criticized for being biased toward certain demographics due to the lack of diversity in the training data sets. To address this issue, more diverse data sets are being used to train facial recognition models, which can lead to more accurate and less biased models.

Balance: A balanced data set should contain an equal number of samples for each class or category. Imbalanced data sets can lead to poor performance of the model, as it tends to be biased towards the majority class. A balanced data set can help the model learn the correct patterns and achieve better performance.

For example, in medical image analysis, a data set with an equal number of samples for each category can help the model learn the correct patterns and achieve better performance. An imbalanced data set, such as a data set with more healthy patients than patients with diseases, can lead to poor performance of the model in detecting diseases.

13.4 BENCHMARKING FOR DEEP LEARNING MODEL

13.4.1 Importance of Benchmarks in Evaluating the Performance of Deep Learning Models

(Jeyan Thiyagalingam, 2021) In the field of deep learning, the development of new algorithms and architectures is often accompanied by the need for an objective evaluation of their performance. This is where benchmarks come in, providing a standardized and well-defined set of tasks and metrics for measuring the quality and efficiency of deep learning models.

One of the primary advantages of using benchmarks is that they enable researchers and engineers to compare the performance of different models on the same set of tasks and data. This helps to establish a baseline for the state of the art in a particular domain and allows researchers to gauge the relative performance of their models against existing approaches. This, in turn, enables researchers to identify areas where further improvements are needed and to develop new techniques for addressing these challenges.

Benchmarks also play a critical role in promoting transparency and reproducibility in deep learning research. By providing a standardized set of tasks and metrics, benchmarks allow researchers to compare their results with those of other researchers, facilitating the sharing of knowledge and promoting collaboration. This can help to accelerate progress in the field and improve the quality of research outcomes.

Another important aspect of benchmarks is that they can serve as a reference point for the development of new deep-learning applications. By providing a well-defined set of tasks and metrics, benchmarks can help to establish the feasibility of using deep learning models for a particular application, providing a foundation for further research and development.

They can also help to identify the strengths and weaknesses of different models. By evaluating a range of models on the same set of tasks and metrics, benchmarks can highlight the areas in which models excel and those in which they struggle. This can help to guide further research and development, enabling researchers to identify promising avenues for improving the performance of their models.

They also play a critical role in advancing the practical applications of deep learning. By providing standardized and well-defined tasks and metrics, benchmarks enable researchers and developers to evaluate the real-world performance of their models, providing insights into the potential of these models for real-world applications. This can help to drive innovation and improve the efficiency and effectiveness of deep learning solutions for a range of applications.

13.4.2 Metrics Used for Benchmarking

(Kathrin Blagec, 2021) In deep learning, benchmarks are used to evaluate the performance of models and compare them to other models or state-of-the-art methods. Metrics are used to quantify the model's performance and provide objective measures for comparison. There are several popular metrics used in benchmarks for deep learning models, some of which are discussed below.

1. *Accuracy*: Accuracy is one of the most commonly used metrics for evaluating classification models. It measures the proportion of correctly classified instances out of the total number of instances in the data set. However, accuracy alone can be misleading if the data set is imbalanced, where one class has significantly more instances than others. In such cases, accuracy can be high even if the model is not performing well in the minority classes.

2. *Precision and Recall*: Precision and recall are two important metrics used for evaluating classification models, especially when dealing with imbalanced data sets. Precision measures the proportion of true positives (instances classified as positive that are positive) out of all instances classified as positive. Recall measures the proportion of true positives out of all actual positive instances. A model with high precision and recall is desirable for tasks such as fraud detection or medical diagnosis, where the cost of false positives or false negatives can be significant.

3. *F1-Score*: F1-score is a combination of precision and recall and is used as a measure of the overall performance of a classification model. It is the harmonic mean of precision and recall and ranges from 0 to 1, where 1 represents perfect precision and recall. F1-score is a more robust metric than accuracy, especially when dealing with imbalanced data sets.

4. *Mean Squared Error (MSE)*: MSE is a commonly used metric for evaluating regression models. It measures the average of the squared differences between the predicted and actual values. A lower MSE indicates a better model fit.

5. *Root Mean Squared Error (RMSE)*: RMSE is similar to MSE but takes the square root of the MSE to put the error metric back in the same units as the original data. It is a useful metric for comparing the magnitudes of the errors across different models.

6. *Area Under the Receiver Operating Characteristic Curve (AUC-ROC)*: AUC-ROC is a commonly used metric for evaluating binary classification models. It measures the performance of the model across all possible classification thresholds and provides a measure of the model's ability to distinguish between positive and negative classes.

7. *Intersection over Union (IoU)*: IoU is a metric commonly used in object detection tasks. It measures the overlap between the predicted bounding box and the ground truth bounding box. A higher IoU indicates a better model performance.

8. *Mean Average Precision (mAP)*: mAP is a metric used to evaluate the performance of object detection models. It considers both the precision and recall of the model across different IoU thresholds and provides a single number to represent the overall performance of the model.

In addition to the above metrics, there are several domain-specific metrics used in benchmarks for deep learning models, such as the BLEU score for machine translation, perplexity for language models, and the Dice score for medical image segmentation. The choice of metrics depends on the task and the domain-specific requirements.

13.4.3 Famous Benchmarks

Deep learning research relies on the evaluation of models against well-defined benchmarks. These benchmarks can be used to compare different models, algorithms, and techniques, as well as to track progress in the field. Here are some examples of popular benchmarks used in deep learning research:

1. *Image Classification*: ImageNet is a well-known benchmark data set for image classification tasks. It consists of over 1 million images and has been used as a benchmark for many deep learning models, including AlexNet, VGG, and ResNet.

2. *Object Detection*: The COCO (Common Objects in Context) data set is widely used as a benchmark for object detection tasks. It contains over 330,000 images and more than 2.5 million object instances and has been used to evaluate models such as Faster R-CNN, YOLO, and RetinaNet.

3. *Semantic Segmentation*: The Cityscapes (Marius Cordts, 2016) data set is a popular benchmark for semantic segmentation tasks. It contains high-quality street-level images from 50 cities, with detailed pixel-level annotations for object classes such as cars, pedestrians, and buildings. Models such as PSPNet, Deeplab, and FCN have been evaluated on this data set.

4. *Speech Recognition*: The LibriSpeech (Panayotov, Chen, Povey, & Khudanpur, 2015) data set is a benchmark for speech recognition tasks. It contains over 1,000 hours of read speech and has been used to evaluate models such as DeepSpeech, Wav2Letter, and Listen Attend and Spell.

5. *Natural Language Processing*: The GLUE (General Language Understanding Evaluation) (Alex Wang, 2018) benchmark is a collection of data sets for natural language processing tasks. It includes tasks such as question answering, sentiment analysis, and textual entailment, and has been used to evaluate models such as BERT, RoBERTa, and GPT-2.

6. *Reinforcement Learning*: The Atari (Games) game benchmark is a popular benchmark for reinforcement learning tasks. It consists of a set of Atari games and has been used to evaluate models such as DQN, A3C, and PPO.

7. *Recommender Systems:* The Movielens data set is a benchmark for recommender systems tasks. It contains a set of user ratings for movies and has been used to evaluate models such as Matrix Factorization, DeepFM, and Neural Collaborative Filtering.

13.4.4 Considerations for Selecting and Designing Benchmarks for Deep Learning Models

(Ling Liu, 2018) The selection and design of a benchmark can have a significant impact on the quality of the results obtained from benchmarking experiments. In this section, we will discuss the considerations that should be taken into account when selecting and designing benchmarks for deep learning models.

13.4.4.1 Relevance to Real-World Applications

One of the most important considerations when selecting and designing benchmarks for deep learning models is their relevance to real-world applications. Benchmarks should be designed to mimic real-world scenarios as closely as possible. This ensures that the models evaluated on these benchmarks perform well in real-world applications.

13.4.4.2 Difficulty Level

Benchmarks should be designed to be challenging enough to provide meaningful insights into the performance of the models evaluated on them. However, they should not be so difficult that the models are unable to perform well on them.

13.4.4.3 Diversity

Benchmarks should be diverse, covering a wide range of scenarios and data types. This ensures that the models evaluated on them are robust and can generalize well to different types of data.

13.4.4.4 Reproducibility

Benchmarks should be designed to be reproducible, with clear instructions on how to obtain and pre-process the data, as well as how to evaluate the models. This ensures that the results obtained from benchmarking experiments are reliable and can be reproduced by other researchers.

13.4.4.5 Standardization

Benchmarks should be designed with standardization in mind. This includes using standard evaluation metrics, ensuring that the data is in a standard format, and providing standard pre-processing instructions. Standardization ensures that the results obtained from benchmarking experiments are comparable across different models and data sets.

13.4.4.6 Scalability

Benchmarks should be scalable, meaning that they can be used to evaluate the performance of models of different sizes and complexities. This ensures that the benchmarks remain relevant even as new, more complex models are developed.

13.4.4.7 Openness

Benchmarks should be designed with openness in mind. This means that the data and evaluation metrics should be publicly available, and the benchmarks should be open to contributions from the research community. This ensures that the benchmarks remain relevant and up to date as new models and data sets are developed.

13.4.4.8 Ethical Considerations

Benchmarks should be designed with ethical considerations in mind. This includes ensuring that the data used in the benchmarks are obtained ethically and that the benchmarks do not perpetuate biases or discrimination.

13.4.4.9 Benchmarking Tools

it is important to consider the availability and suitability of benchmarking tools when selecting and designing benchmarks for deep learning models. The benchmarking tools should be easy to use and capable of evaluating models quickly and accurately.

Selecting and designing benchmarks for deep learning models is a critical step in evaluating their performance. When selecting and designing benchmarks, it is important to consider their relevance to real-world applications, difficulty level, diversity, reproducibility, standardization, scalability, openness, ethical considerations, and benchmarking tools. By considering these factors, researchers can design benchmarks that provide meaningful insights into the performance of deep learning models and help advance the field of artificial intelligence.

13.4.5 Challenges in Interpreting Benchmarks for Deep Learning Models in the Context of Specific Problems

Benchmarks provide a standardized way to compare different models and algorithms on a common set of tasks, allowing researchers to identify the most effective approaches for specific problems. However, benchmarks also have limitations that must be considered when interpreting the results.

One limitation of benchmarks is that they may not accurately reflect the complexity and variability of real-world data. The tasks and data sets used in benchmarks are often simplified and may not capture the full range of challenges that deep learning models may face when applied to real-world problems. For example, image classification benchmarks typically use well-lit and clear images with simple backgrounds, while real-world images may have complex backgrounds, occlusions, or other challenges that make classification more difficult. As a result, a model that performs well on a benchmark may not necessarily perform well on real-world data.

Another limitation of benchmarks is that they may not capture the full range of performance metrics that are important for a particular problem. Benchmarks typically focus on a small number of metrics, such as accuracy or F1-score, that may not fully capture the needs of a particular application. For example, a model that achieves high accuracy on a benchmark may still be unsuitable for use in a medical application if it frequently misclassifies rare but important cases.

Benchmarks may not fully capture the diversity of use cases and scenarios for which deep learning models may be applied. A model that performs well on a benchmark for one specific task or data set may not necessarily perform well on other related tasks or data sets. As a result, researchers must be cautious when extrapolating the results of benchmarks to other applications or domains.

Another important consideration when interpreting benchmark results is the potential for overfitting. Deep learning models are capable of fitting complex patterns in data and may perform well on a benchmark by overfitting the particular data set used in the benchmark. This can result in models that are not generalizable to new data and may perform poorly on real-world problems. To avoid overfitting, researchers must carefully design benchmarks that test the generalization ability of models and use appropriate techniques such as cross-validation to evaluate performance.

Despite these limitations, benchmarks remain an important tool for evaluating the performance of deep learning models. To ensure that benchmarks accurately reflect real-world challenges and needs, researchers must carefully design benchmarks that are representative of the problem domain and use a range of evaluation metrics that capture the full range of performance needs. Additionally, benchmarks should be used in combination with real-world testing to ensure that models are suitable for deployment in practical applications.

13.5 VALIDATIONS OF DEEP LEARNING MODELS

(Farhad Maleki, 2020) Validation is a crucial step in the development and deployment of deep learning models. It involves assessing the performance of the model on a separate data set that was not used during training. The purpose of validation is to ensure that the model is not overfitting, which means that it is not simply memorizing the training data and failing to generalize to new, unseen data.

The importance of validation cannot be overstated, as failing to validate a model can lead to poor performance on new data and even incorrect predictions in real-world scenarios. A model that is overfitting will have high accuracy on the training data but will perform poorly on new data. Validation helps to ensure that the model is not overfitting and is capable of generalizing to new data.

There are several techniques used for validating deep learning models, such as hold-out validation, k-fold cross-validation, and leave-one-out cross-validation. Hold-out validation involves randomly splitting the data set into a training set and a validation set, and then training the model on the training set and evaluating its performance on the validation set. K-fold cross-validation involves dividing the data set into k equal-sized folds and training the model k times, each time using a different fold as the validation set and the remaining folds as the training set. Leave-one-out cross-validation is similar to k-fold cross-validation but involves leaving out one sample at a time as the validation set. We will discuss each.

Validation also involves selecting appropriate metrics to measure the performance of the model. These metrics should be chosen based on the specific problem being addressed and should provide a meaningful measure of the model's performance. As discussed, common metrics used in deep learning include accuracy, precision, recall, F1-score, and AUC-ROC.

It is important to note that validation is not a one-time step but rather an ongoing process throughout the development of the model. As the model is improved and refined, it should be revalidated to ensure that it continues to perform as intended.

However, there are some limitations and challenges associated with validating deep learning models. One of the main challenges is the need for large amounts of labeled data for both training and validation. This can be particularly difficult in fields such as healthcare, where acquiring labeled data can be time-consuming and expensive.

Another limitation is the potential for bias in the validation process. The choice of validation data set and the metrics used to evaluate the model can introduce bias into the process. For example, if the validation data set is not representative of the population being studied, the model may not generalize well to new data. Similarly, if the metrics used to evaluate the model are not appropriate for the problem being addressed, the model's performance may be misleading.

The validation process can be time-consuming and computationally expensive, particularly for large data sets and complex models. This can make it difficult to perform multiple rounds of validation and can slow down the development of the model.

To conclude, (Zheng, 2013) validating deep learning models is a critical step in ensuring that they are performing as intended and can generalize to new, unseen data. It involves selecting appropriate validation techniques and metrics, as well as ongoing revalidation as the model is refined. However, there are limitations and challenges associated with the validation process, such as the need for large amounts of labeled data and the potential for bias. As such, it is important to approach validation with care and to interpret results in the context of the specific problem being addressed.

13.5.1 Popular Validation Techniques Used in Deep Learning Research

Validation is an important step in the process of building deep learning models. It involves testing the trained model on a separate set of data to evaluate its performance and ensure it is working as intended. In this section, we will discuss some of the popular validation techniques used in deep learning research.

1. *Cross-Validation*: Cross-validation is a popular technique used for model validation in deep learning research. It involves splitting the data set into multiple subsets or folds. The model is trained on all but one of the folds and tested on the remaining fold. This process is repeated multiple times, with each fold used as the validation set once. The results are then averaged to obtain a final performance metric. Cross-validation is useful when the data set is small, and we want to make the most of the limited data available.

2. *Hold-out Validation*: Hold-out validation is a simple technique used for model validation in deep learning research. It involves splitting the data set into two sets, a training set, and a validation set. The model is trained on the training set and evaluated on the validation set. The advantage of hold-out validation is that it is easy to implement, and it is useful when the data set is large.

3. *Bootstrapping*: Bootstrapping is a technique used for model validation in deep learning research that involves resampling the data set with replacement. The resampled data set is then used to train the model, and the performance is evaluated on the original data set. This process is repeated multiple times, and the results are averaged to obtain a final performance metric. Bootstrapping is useful when we have a small data set and want to estimate the uncertainty associated with the performance metric.

4. *Leave-One-Out Cross-Validation*: Leave-one-out cross-validation (LOOCV) is a technique used for model validation in deep learning research that involves leaving out one data point from the data set and training the model on the remaining data points. The model is then tested on the left-out data point. This process is repeated for each data point in the data set. LOOCV is useful when we have a small data set and want to make the most of the limited data available.

5. *K-Fold Cross-Validation*: K-fold cross-validation is a technique used for model validation in deep learning research that involves dividing the data set into K equal parts or folds. The model is trained on K-1 folds and tested on the remaining fold. This process is repeated K times, with each fold used as the validation set once. The results are then averaged to obtain a final performance metric. K-fold cross-validation is useful when we have a small data set and want to make the most of the limited data available.

6. *Stratified Sampling*: Stratified sampling is a technique used for model validation in deep learning research that involves dividing the data set into subsets or strata based on some criteria, such as class labels or feature values. The model is trained on each subset and tested on the remaining data. This process is repeated multiple times, and the results are averaged to obtain a final performance metric. Stratified sampling is useful when we have imbalanced data sets, and we want to ensure that each class or subset is adequately represented in the training and validation sets.

7. *Shuffle-Split Cross-Validation*: Shuffle-split cross-validation is a technique used for model validation in deep learning research that involves randomly shuffling the data set and then splitting it into training and validation sets. This process is repeated multiple times, and the results are averaged to obtain a final performance metric. Shuffle-split cross-validation is useful when we have a large data set and want to make the most of the limited computational resources available.

13.5.2 Interpreting Validation Results in the Context of Specific Problems

Interpreting validation results in the context of the specific problem being addressed is critical in deep learning research. It is essential to understand that a model's performance on a specific data set does not necessarily translate to its effectiveness in the real world. Therefore, it is essential to consider the context in which the model is intended to be used and interpret the validation results accordingly.

One of the key considerations in interpreting validation results is the bias-variance trade-off. The bias-variance trade-off is the tradeoff between a model's ability to fit the training data and its ability to generalize to new, unseen data. A model with high bias has underfit the training data and is unable to capture the underlying patterns in the data. On the other hand, a model with high variance has overfit the training data and has captured noise and random fluctuations in the data. In general, a model with a moderate level of complexity is more likely to have the best balance between bias and variance and generalize well to new data.

Another important consideration in interpreting validation results is the distribution of the data. In real-world applications, the data may have a different distribution than the training data, and the model may perform poorly on such data. Therefore, it is essential to validate the model on a test data set that has a similar distribution as the real-world data. It is important to consider the potential biases in the training and test data sets, as biased data can result in a biased model.

it is also important to consider the metrics used to evaluate the model's performance in the specific problem being addressed. For example, in medical image analysis, sensitivity and specificity are critical metrics, as false positives and false negatives can have severe consequences. In contrast, in natural language processing, metrics such as precision and recall may be more appropriate. Therefore, it is essential to choose the right metrics that are relevant to the specific problem being addressed and interpret the validation results accordingly.

The engineer or researcher must consider the impact of hyperparameters on the model's performance. Hyperparameters are parameters that are not learned from the data but are set before training. Examples of hyperparameters include learning rate, regularization strength, and network architecture. The choice of hyperparameters can have a significant impact on the model's performance, and it is essential to tune them appropriately. Therefore, it is important to validate the model with different hyperparameter settings and interpret the validation results accordingly.

13.6 CHALLENGES AND FUTURE DIRECTIONS

Deep learning has gained popularity in recent years, with breakthroughs in many applications such as image recognition, speech recognition, natural language processing, and more. However, as with any technology, there are challenges associated with the development and use of data sets, benchmarks, and validations in deep learning research. In this section, we will discuss some of the major challenges faced by researchers and practitioners in the field, as well as the potential future directions for addressing these challenges.

1. *Bias and Fairness*

   One of the major challenges in deep learning research is the issue of bias and fairness. Bias can occur in data sets when the data used to train the model is not representative of the real-world population or contains inherent biases. This can lead to models that are not fair or accurate in their predictions, particularly for underrepresented or marginalized groups. Addressing bias and fairness in deep learning requires careful consideration and data curation to ensure that the data used to train models is representative of the target population and does not contain any inherent biases.

2. *Data Privacy*

Another significant challenge in deep learning is data privacy. Deep learning models require large amounts of data to be trained effectively, and this data often includes personal and sensitive information. The use of this data for training models raises ethical privacy concerns, particularly when the data is sourced from individuals who have not consented to its use. Addressing data privacy concerns in deep learning research requires the development of ethical guidelines and regulatory frameworks that ensure the protection of individuals' privacy while still enabling research progress.

3. *Generalization*

A major goal of deep learning research is to develop models that can generalize well to new, unseen data. However, deep learning models often suffer from overfitting, where they perform well on the training data but poorly on new data. Addressing this challenge requires the use of regularization techniques such as dropout and weight decay, as well as the development of new algorithms that can improve generalization performance.

4. *Interpretability*

Another challenge in deep learning research is the lack of interpretability in many models. Deep learning models are often considered black boxes, making it difficult to understand how they arrive at their predictions. This lack of interpretability can make it challenging to diagnose errors or biases in models and can limit their adoption in fields such as healthcare and finance, where transparency is critical. Addressing the interpretability challenge requires the development of new techniques for understanding and interpreting deep learning models, such as feature visualization, saliency mapping, and attention mechanisms.

5. *Scalability*

Finally, the scalability of deep learning models remains a significant challenge. Deep learning models require significant computational resources to train, particularly for large data sets. This can limit the use of deep learning in applications with limited resources, such as edge devices and embedded systems. Addressing the scalability challenge requires the development of new hardware and software architectures that can accelerate deep learning computations while minimizing energy consumption.

While deep learning has shown tremendous promise in many applications, it is not without its challenges. Addressing these challenges will require careful consideration and collaboration between researchers, practitioners, and policymakers. With continued research and development, deep learning has the potential to revolutionize many industries and improve our understanding of complex systems.

13.6.1 Examples of Current Challenges

The rapid development of deep learning has enabled significant advancements in various fields, from computer vision to natural language processing. However, the use of deep learning models also presents several challenges, particularly in the development and use of data sets, benchmarks, and validations. Some of the current challenges faced by the deep learning community include bias and overfitting.

Bias in deep learning refers to the systematic errors that can occur when training a model on a biased data set. For example, if a data set contains more images of light-skinned individuals than dark-skinned individuals, a deep learning model trained on that data set may struggle to recognize individuals with darker skin tones. This can have significant real-world consequences, such as in facial recognition systems used by law enforcement agencies. Additionally, bias can be introduced through the design of the model itself or the selection of hyperparameters. To address this challenge, researchers are exploring methods for mitigating bias, such as developing more diverse data sets, using data augmentation techniques, and incorporating fairness metrics into model training.

Overfitting is another challenge in deep learning, where a model learns the training data set too well and becomes unable to generalize to new, unseen data. This can occur when a data set is too small or when the model is too complex, leading to over-parameterization. Overfitting can result in poor model performance and limit the model's ability to be used in real-world applications. To address this challenge, researchers are exploring techniques such as regularization, early stopping, and dropout to prevent overfitting and improve model generalization.

Another challenge in deep learning is the lack of transparency and interpretability in model predictions. Deep learning models are often considered black boxes, where it is difficult to understand how the model arrived at its prediction. This lack of interpretability can limit the adoption of deep learning models in high-stakes applications such as healthcare and finance. Researchers are exploring methods for improving the interpretability of deep learning models, such as developing attention mechanisms and feature visualization techniques.

The scalability of deep learning models is also a significant challenge, particularly as the size of data sets and models continues to grow. Large models such as GPT-3 have millions of parameters and require significant computational resources to train and run. This can limit the accessibility of deep learning to smaller organizations and individuals without access to powerful computing resources. Researchers are exploring methods for improving the scalability of deep learning models, such as model pruning, knowledge distillation, and federated learning.

The ethical implications of using deep learning models also present a significant challenge. As deep learning is increasingly used in applications such as surveillance, autonomous vehicles, and healthcare, questions around privacy, accountability, and fairness arise. For example, facial recognition systems can be used to identify individuals without their consent, and autonomous vehicles may prioritize the safety of the vehicle's occupants over pedestrians. Researchers are exploring ethical considerations and developing guidelines and frameworks for the responsible use of deep learning models.

13.6.2 Future Directions for Improving the Development and Use of Data Sets, Benchmarks, and Validations in Deep Learning Research

It is important to consider the future directions for improving the development and use of data sets, benchmarks, and validations in deep learning research. In this section, we will discuss some potential future directions.

13.6.2.1 Improved Data Collection and Labeling

One of the biggest challenges in deep learning research is the collection and labeling of high-quality data sets. There is a need for improved techniques for collecting data and labeling it consistently and accurately. This could involve the use of crowdsourcing platforms or the development of automated labeling techniques. Additionally, efforts should be made to ensure that data sets are diverse and representative of the populations they are intended to serve.

13.6.2.2 Addressing Bias and Fairness

Bias and fairness are critical issues in deep learning research. There is a need for better tools and techniques for detecting and addressing bias in data sets and models. Additionally, efforts should be made to ensure that models are fair and equitable across different groups. This could involve the development of new metrics and benchmarks for measuring fairness, as well as the use of techniques like adversarial training.

13.6.2.3 Addressing Overfitting and Generalization

Overfitting is a common problem in deep learning research, where models become too specialized to the training data and fail to generalize to new data. There is a need for improved techniques for addressing overfitting and improving generalization. This could involve the use of regularization techniques, better optimization algorithms, or the development of new architectures that are more robust to overfitting.

13.6.2.4 Developing Better Metrics and Benchmarks

The development of better metrics and benchmarks is critical for advancing deep learning research. There is a need for metrics that are more robust to imbalanced data sets and that can better capture the nuances of real-world problems. Additionally, benchmarks should be designed with a clear understanding of the problem being addressed and should be representative of the intended use case.

13.6.2.5 Automated Machine Learning

Automated machine learning (AutoML) is an emerging field that aims to automate the process of building machine learning models. AutoML techniques have the potential to streamline the process of developing and validating deep learning models. This could involve the development of tools that can automatically select the best architecture, hyperparameters, and optimization algorithms for a given problem.

13.6.2.6 Interdisciplinary Collaboration

Finally, there is a need for more interdisciplinary collaboration in deep learning research. The development of high-quality data sets, benchmarks, and validations requires expertise in a variety of fields, including computer science, statistics, and domain-specific knowledge. By bringing together experts from different fields, we can develop better solutions to the challenges facing deep learning research.

REFERENCES

Alex Wang, A. S. (2018). GLUE: A Multi-Task Benchmark and Analysis Platform for Natural Language Understanding. *arXiv, 3*, 20.

Andrew Rosenberg, E. B. (2004). Augmenting the kappa statistic to determine interannotator reliability. 77–80.

Bishirian, M. (2021). *Introduction to Semi-Supervised Learning.* Retrieved Mar 26, 2023, from morioh.com: https://morioh.com/p/f711f42a6c93

cifar10. (n.d.). Retrieved Mar 26, 2023, from www.tensorflow.org: https://www.tensorflow.org/datasets/catalog/cifar10

Deep Learning Interview Questions. (n.d.). Retrieved Mar 26, 2023, from https://www.freetimelearning.com: https://www.freetimelearning.com/software-interview-questions-and-answers.php?Explain-transfer-learning-in-the-context-of-deep-learning.&id=4184

dewangNautiyal. (2023, Feb 20). *ML | Underfitting and Overfitting.* Retrieved Mar 26, 2023, from www.geeksforgeeks.org: https://www.geeksforgeeks.org/underfitting-and-overfitting-in-machine-learning/

Eirini Ntoutsi, P. F.-E.-K. (2020). Bias in Data-driven AI Systems - An Introductory Survey. *arXiv, 19.*

Farhad Maleki, N. M. (2020). Machine Learning Algorithm Validation. *ResearchGate.*

Games, A. (n.d.). *atari-games-on-atari-2600-venture.* Retrieved Mar 26, 2023, from paperswithcode.com: https://paperswithcode.com/sota/atari-games-on-atari-2600-venture

Jan Kukačka, V. G. (2017). Regularization for Deep Learning: A Taxonomy. *arXiv, 23.*

Jeyan Thiyagalingam, M. S. (2021). Scientific Machine Learning Benchmarks. *arXiv, 21.*

Karl Weiss, T. M. (2016). A survey of transfer learning. *SpringerOpen, 40.*

Kathrin Blagec, G. D. (2021). A critical analysis of metrics used for measuring progress in artificial intelligence. *arXiv, 28.*

Keiron O'Shea, R. N. (2015). An Introduction to Convolutional Neural Networks. *arXiv, 10.*

Kevin Lang, E. L. (June 2016). Stratified sampling meets machine learning. *Proceedings of the 33rd International Conference on International Conference on Machine Learning, 48*, pp. 2320–2329.

Ling Liu, Y. W. (2018). Benchmarking Deep Learning Frameworks: Design Considerations, Metrics and Beyond. *IEEE 38th International Conference on Distributed Computing Systems (ICDCS).*

Luis Perez, J. W. (2017). The Effectiveness of Data Augmentation in Image Classification using Deep Learning. *arXiv, 8.*

M.A. Ganaie, M. H. (2021). Ensemble deep learning: A review. *arXiv, 47.*

Marius Cordts, M. O. (2016). The Cityscapes Data Set for Semantic Urban Scene Understanding. *arXiv, 2.*

McDonald, A. (2021, Oct 7). Data Quality Considerations for Machine Learning Models. *ResearchGate.*

Panayotov, V., Chen, G., Povey, D., & Khudanpur, S. (2015). Librispeech: An ASR corpus based on public domain audio books. *IEEE International Conference on Acoustics, Speech and Signal Processing (ICASSP).*

Philip Woodall, A. B. (2014). An Investigation of How Data Quality is Affected by Data Set Size in the Context of Big Data Analytics. *International Conference on Information Quality.* China.

Shaeke Salman, X. L. (2019). Overfitting Mechanism and Avoidance in Deep Neural Networks. *arXiv, 8.*

Solawetz, J. (2020, Oct 18). *An Introduction to the COCO Data Set.* Retrieved Mar 26, 2023, from blog.roboflow.com: https://blog.roboflow.com/coco-dataset/

Sylvaine Picard, C. C. (2020). Ensuring Data Set Quality for Machine Learning Certification. *arXiv, 8.*

what-is-data-augmentation-in-deep-learning. (2022, May 21). Retrieved Mar 26, 2023, from insights.daffodilsw.com: https://insights.daffodilsw.com/blog/what-is-data-augmentation-in-deep-learning

Zheng, H. W. (2013). Model Validation, Machine Learning. In *Encyclopedia of Systems Biology* (p. 2).

## CHAPTER 14

Deep Learning for the Turnover Intention of Industrial Workers

Evidence from Vietnam

Nguyen Ngoc Long, Nguyen Ngoc Lam, and Bui Huy Khoi

Industrial University of Ho Chi Minh City, Ho Chi Minh City, Vietnam

14.1 INTRODUCTION

The employees leaving a job in the fields of industrial production makes a great impact on the stability and development of enterprises[1] that have to spend an amount equivalent to one-fifth of an old employee's annual income on training new ones, and this cost gets more expensive for the training of good employees.[2] It is proven that the resignation of employees affects many systems of human resources for enterprises and the behavior of organizations.[3] It has implications for various aspects of the business of the enterprises such as increased cost of employee training and development,[2] reduction of creativity,[4] limitation of company's competitiveness and reputation,[5] reduced labor productivity, and reduced attachment in organizations.[6] Therefore, both academics and human resource managers need to clearly understand factors that influence employees' turnover intention.

According to a survey report from an investment journal in Vietnam, the rate of employees leaving their job in Vietnam in 2019 is very worrying, at 29%.[7] A high rate of resignation in industries makes managers increasingly more concerned about labor costs, and it is very important to understand the factors that motivate workers to have a strong attachment to their organization for a long time. In many certain industries, the job-hopping situation of industrial employees is relatively common, especially those who are skilled in the industries of textile, electronics, and construction. In the forums of human resources (for example, hrlink.vn, hrvn.com.vn, hrvn.com. vn, vnhr.vn), people often discuss a lot about the reasons for leaving and how to minimize this situation. However, independent studies on employee turnover intentions are rare. Most studies on employees' intention to leave only focus on the behavior of employees or the management

DOI: 10.1201/9781032646268-14

without referring to job-hopping because this situation in this area seems to be under-valued. There are only a few relatively old studies on employees' intention of leaving a particular unit. Though these studies also presented the status of employees leaving jobs, their scope is limited and the work context has also changed after many years of publication, which shows the necessity to have a thorough understanding of the intention to leave industrial employees. This study was conducted to meet the above needs and is expected to understand the key factors influencing the turnover intention for employees in a variety of industries.

Previous studies have shown that unfairness is the main cause of many conflicts in organizations,[8] and many of them have been concerned about perceptions of unfairness,[9,10] but very few studies on the influence of unfairness on industrial employees' turnover intentions were conducted. Unfairness in behavior makes employees act opposite to expectations of the organization such as secret concealment,[11] decreased working motivation,[12] emotional change at work,[13] working dissatisfaction,[14] and especially leading to employee behavior leaving.[15] The studies mentioned above have also shown that the enhancement of justice in organizations is key to handling problems from unfairness. However, there are many other aspects of the influence of unfairness in the organization on employee turnover that require attention.

This study was conducted to simultaneously review many aspects, including competitiveness of the work environment, justice factors in the organization, and chief roundabout work impedance with individual life and turnover expectation for modern representatives. As suggested by Shapoval,[13] there are differences in the factors influencing the justice of part-time, hourly, and full-time employees. According to Khattak et al.[16] and Barclay et al.,[17] the studies on factors influencing employees' negative emotions in relationships with colleagues should be expanded. This study evaluated the influence of interpersonal justice, informational justice, and work interference with personal life on industrial employees' turnover intention. This review is in response to the call of previous studies by Gim and Ramayah[18] on the expansion of investigation objects and the factors influencing employees' turnover intention in different professions.

The next sections of this study include the presentation of the theoretical basis of the research model, research method, research results, and finally discussion of relevant governance implications. Finally, the study also shows some limitations for other authors to note in conducting related studies in the future. We use the PLS algorithm for the turnover aim of modern laborers in Ho Chi Minh City.

14.2 LITERATURE REVIEW

14.2.1 Justice in an Organization and Work Interference with Personal Life and Turnover Intention

According to the theory of conservation of resources (COR) of Hobfoll,[19] people tend to conserve existing resources and keep searching for new ones for their prosperity. Failure to satisfy the needs or failure to preserve and develop resources can lead to employee turnover intention.[9] According to Takase,[20] the turnover intention is indicated as a process in which an employee leaves his or her current job and is ready to leave the current organization. Another definition by Akgunduz and Eryilmaz,[21] turnover intention refers to an employee's perception or thinking about leaving their current job. Meanwhile, the turnover intention is an intention an employee has before officially leaving the job including willingness, ability, and planning to leave the job.[22] Intention to leave is also considered as an orientation of employees who are about to leave their organization and as a prediction about an employee's official leaving.[23] Although the turnover intention is not a fact, the organization can rely on studies on turnover intention to have a better understanding and prediction about employees' actual behavior to leave, which is a basis for the organization to arrange and restructure personnel as well as offer countermeasures after clearly identifying the factors influencing the employee's turnover intention.

Turnover intention is influenced by many different factors such as work environment (both internal and external), organizational culture, organizational behavior, justice in the organization, leadership style, and others. Justice in the organization is considered as an individual's perception of how fair the organization gives them and behavior followed by that perception.[3] Many previous studies have acknowledged the factors in the scale for justice in the organization of Colquitt[24] as an effective tool to assess the influences on employees' perception of justice on job and turnover intention. Accordingly, the fairness factors based on the psychological mechanism of employees in the organization consist of distributive justice,[25] procedural justice,[26] and justice in personal relationships and interactions.[23] In particular, distributive justice is the fairness in dividing the output for people in the same organization or society,[27] and procedural justice of the organization is fairness in formulating and promulgating regulations as a basis for decision making without favoritism for members of the organization,[26] and interpersonal justice emphasizes the importance of the quality of relationships and behavior of members with each other in the organization.[24] Besides, Colquitt et al.[24] also indicated that justice in relation together with another factor informational justice are two basic factors of behavior in the organization, in which, informational justice refers to the completeness and honesty perceived from the release of information by the most senior leaders to their employees. Many studies have proved that the factors of justice in the organization – including distributive justice, procedural justice, interpersonal justice, and informational justice – are associated with employees' turnover intention.[3,18] Many other studies also imply that justice in the organization with equivalent names such as treatment in relation, to communication at work, also has an impact on negative attitudes of employees, thereby driving employee turnover intention; or the lower the procedural justice is, the more job safety reduces and increasingly accelerates the employee's turnover intention.[28] These studies also demonstrated that when employees believe they are treated fairly, they tend to get higher performance, better work attitudes, and lower stress.

Another study by Gim and Ramayah[18] showed that distributive justice, interpersonal justice, and competitive working climate are associated with work interference with personal life (work interference with personal life–WIPL), while WIPL was found to be positively related to employee turnover intention.[18] WIPL is understood as interference in personal life by work-related issues and drives employees' turnover intention by a powerful influence on work or personal life and vice versa.[29] A lot of previous studies also have referred to the balance or contradiction of the relationship between work and family.[29] In addition, more and more people today decide to choose a single life or life without children, and there is a relatively sizable difference between the number of these objects and those who have to take care of their families and children apart from working. Therefore, considering how the WIPL factor affects turnover intention is very necessary. We also took the achievements and the limitations in the study of Hsieh et al.[30] and Wang et al.[29] into consideration to decide on assessment of the relation of work interference with personal life on employees' turnover intention.

14.2.2 Research Model and Hypothesis

14.2.2.1 Competitive Working Climate (KKLV)

A competitive working atmosphere is a manifestation of employees' awareness of how the organization recognizes and rewards their efforts compared to the others in the same organization.[31] A competitive environment can promote working performance when the tasks are simple and mechanical, with little help from colleagues.[32] However, for a task that requires teamwork, the competitive environment, now, no longer promotes higher performance.[31] In the industrial production environment, teamwork, working lines, or coordination of departments are often prioritized to accomplish goals. The high competitiveness in the organization will require an exchange of information from senior managers to employees to be accurate, honest, and timely. If the exchange of information between senior managers and employees is limited, a competitive workplace increases the likelihood that employees may leave the organization.[33] A study conducted in the United States[34] pointed out that when an employee regularly works with another employee whose capacity and performance are better, he is more likely to leave the company. The reason for this is that inferior people rarely open up and discuss with colleagues and friends their weaknesses at work. Another study[35] also showed that when employees in an organization self-evaluate their competitiveness with each other, they often have less work effort and leave the job because they feel that information shared by their peers is unreliable. Our hypothesis is that:

Hypothesis (H1): *The competitive working climate has a positive impact on informational justice.*

14.2.2.2 Procedural Salary Justice (CBCS)

The word "procedural justice" describes how policies that determine rewards or outcomes are seen as being fair.[24] According to the previously mentioned studies of Spell and Arnold,[36] procedural justice focuses on procedures used to determine salaries and bonuses. Leventhal[37] conceptualized six principles of policy as a guide to creating justice in organizational policies, including consistency must be at every time, everywhere; appointment decisions must be centralized without favoritism; decisions are made based on accurate information; modification is possible if no longer appropriate; parties involved in a decision can make an influence on the decision, and decisions are made following moral and ethical values. Also, according to the research results of Gori et al.,[28] justice in policies and procedures has a positive impact on justice in income distribution. Folger and Martin[38] showed that procedural salary justice and distributive justice are two independent concepts that interact with each other. Greenberg[39] also found an important linkage between justice in policy and justice in income distribution. When organizations pay employees a high salary, they will have no concern about procedural salary justice because they believe it is appropriate. For a low salary, employees will be very interested in the details of the policy, and procedural salary justice has a powerful impact on distributive justice.

Accordingly, hypothesis H2 is stated as follows:

Hypothesis (H2): *Procedural salary justice has a positive impact on distributive justice.*

14.2.2.3 Distributive Justice (CBPP)

Distributive justice refers to the fairness of rewards or outcomes including salary.[24] Fairness in distribution is derived from Adams' equity theory, where an employee compares his performance-based outcome with that of another employee to ensure that such an outcome is fair for his contribution. Similar to the approach of previous researchers such as Spell and Arnold,[36] distributive justice focuses on employees' subjective perceptions of their salary. Once employees suppose that their salary is not commensurate with what they are paid, they will assume a poor relationship with and non-respect from senior managers,[28] leading to a tendency to leave the organization. Alsaraireh et al.[40] also pointed out that, when an employee's income is not commensurate with their efforts for a long enough time, that person can be stressed and their attachment to the organization will be worse, especially when people around them have a higher income than them despite lower performance. Hypothesis H3 is stated:

Hypothesis (H3): *Distributive justice has a positive impact on interpersonal justice.*

14.2.2.4 Informational Justice (CBTD)

Informational justice refers to the perceived sufficiency and truthfulness of the information provided by senior managers to employees, which is a fair interaction in terms of communication between senior managers and employees in the organization.[24] According to the Equity Theory of Adams,[41] individuals are more interested in the fairness of information under uncertain conditions, they get complete and accurate information, trust in the relationship is strengthened, and the quality of the relationship will be improved. Besides, the concept of motivated perception also pointed out that people who change their jobs will receive less information from the new organization than what they got from the old organization. It is the reason they often work hard to change the perception of fairness in their relationship with what they want to come true,[42] in this case, interpersonal equity in the new organization is higher than that of where they left the job. Meanwhile, according to Gori et al.,[28] informational justice positively affects interpersonal justice at work. Informational justice refers to the extent to which employees perceive that their managers have been forthright in communication, and have explained policies thoroughly, specifically, and promptly. The employees who perceive this from senior managers feel more secure about their good and fair relationships in the organization. In addition, they will not hesitate to discuss questions, making the attachment between them and the organization strong.[43] In the past, many studies have discussed the influence of organizational equity on turnover intention, but the number of studies focusing separately on the impact of each fairness factor on turnover intention, especially for industrial employees, is quite small. This study was conducted to evaluate how two factors fairness in exchange and relational equity affect turnover intention as suggested by Kim et al.[3] and Mengstie.[15]

From there, hypotheses H4 and H5 are stated as follows:

Hypothesis (H4): *Informational justice has a positive impact on interpersonal justice.*

Hypothesis (H5): *Informational justice has a positive impact on turnover intention.*

14.2.2.5 Interpersonal Justice (CBQH)

Interpersonal justice is the extent to which employees perceive respect for their dignity from senior managers in the organization for its execution of policies.[24] It is the attitude when senior managers treat their employees in the organization with courtesy, honesty, respect, or tact in making comments. When employees feel treated with respect, they feel more confident and contribute more to the organization, thereby improving productivity and retaining more loyal customers.[44] In previous studies, interpersonal justice (as described above) is an integral factor with informational justice and is integrated under a common name as interaction fairness as suggested by Bies.[45] Then, Greenberg and Cropanzano[16] separated the interaction between interpersonal justice and informational justice. From there, four factors, distributive justice, procedural justice, informational justice, and interpersonal justice, have been considered for their impact on turnover intention in various fields.

Another study by Camerino et al.,[47] demonstrated that interpersonal justice at work and effective communication are related to the profession, thereby establishing measures to prevent risks and ensure the safety and health of employees, as well as reducing work interference with family (WIF). Work interference with personal life (WIPL) is an extension of WIF.[48] It refers to work interference with matters in one's personal life. When interpersonal justice is perceived as lacking, inadequate, or a risk to other resources, including time and energy spent by the individual,[49] it can cause employees distress and increase the risk of work interference with personal life. A few previous studies have examined the impact of organizational justice on work interference with family (WIF)[50,51] while WPIL is an extension of WIF, so WPIL can completely influence employees' turnover intention.

Therefore, hypotheses H6 and H7 are stated as follows:

Hypothesis (H6): *Interpersonal justice has a negative impact on turnover intention.*

Hypothesis (H7): *Interpersonal justice has a negative impact on work interference with personal life.*

14.2.2.6 Work Interference with Personal Life (SXP)

The research results of Hsieh et al.[30] supposed that WIPL also has a positive relation to turnover intention. Once the work interference with personal life increases, the turnover intention will arise if there are no measures to cope and intervene. The COR theory suggests that individuals are more likely to find a new balance rather than try to create resources[19] and that's why employees often give up their stressful jobs to preserve their resources from further loss when their personal lives have interfered, on the other hand, if WIPL level is low, employees are likely to perceive that their time and energy are adequate, which will prevent them from leaving the organization. Accordingly, hypothesis H8 is stated as follows:

Hypothesis (H8): *Work interference with personal life has a positive impact on turnover intention.*

14.3 METHOD

14.3.1 Sample

A formal survey was shown after changing the questionnaire according to the views of industrial employees during the pilot survey. The employees are directly surveyed in industrial parks and export processing zones. This chapter was carried out in Ho Chi Minh City for the convenience of the sampling technique. Respondents initially answered questions correlated to demographics, then questions associated with fairness, working climate, work interference with personal life, and turnover intention at their job. The survey lasted from September 10, 2022, to October 30, 2022, with 250 questionnaires distributed. After the removal of invalid questionnaires, a sum of 226 legitimate surveys were examined to evaluate the dependability, legitimacy, and significance of the speculations.

14.3.2 Scale

The scale is inherited from the scales of previous studies, as presented in Table 14.1. The previous questions were all in English, so the research team translated them into Vietnamese at the request of Brislin,[52] and then the questionnaire was given to familiar respondents for trial to make necessary adjustments based on suggestions, provided that the original meaning of the questions remains. The final version was translated by final-year English students who are interns within the research team's organization to ensure the original meaning of the questionnaires. Details on how to do this are as follows.

The scale of organizational justice is updated from the scales of Colquitt,[24] with four variables for each scale. In the industrial production environment, the author uses the

TABLE 14.1   Measurement Model

Factors and items		Standard loadings
CBCS1	The efforts I put in at work are exactly reflected in my salary.	0.792
CBCS2	My pay is commensurate with the work I've done.	0.822
CBCS3	My pay is completely in line with what I have given to the business.	0.861
CBCS4	My salary is reasonable based on my work results.	0.878
CBPP1	I can express my point of view on salary policies.	0.927
CBPP2	The salary policies are applied consistently.	0.898
CBPP3	The salary policies have no favoritism.	0.937
CBPP4	The salary policies are based on transparent public information.	0.927
CBQH1	Senior managers treat employees politely.	0.896
CBQH2	Senior managers treat employees honestly.	0.934
CBQH3	Senior managers treat employees with respect.	0.940
CBQH4	Senior managers are tactful in giving comments to subordinates.	0.915
CBTD1	Senior managers are honest in communication with employees	0.803
CBTD2	Senior managers explain income policies	0.920
CBTD3	Senior managers explain income policies	0.931
CBTD4	Senior managers explain income policies.	0.904
KKLV1	My superiors often compare my work results with my colleagues.	0.839
KKLV2	My superiors rely on the comparison of my work results with that of others for recognition.	0.795
KKLV3	Every member of the company is interested in top performance.	0.708
KKLV4	My colleagues always compare their work results with mine.	0.808
SXP1	I usually feel too tired after coming home from work.	0.839
SXP2	My work affects my personal life a lot.	0.795
SXP3	I often have to skip my personal needs to fulfill my work.	0.708
SXP4	I often miss important personal activities because of work.	0.808
YDNV1	I am actively considering another job.	0.923
YDNV2	I will leave this company as soon as I catch a better job.	0.817
YDNV3	I'm seriously thinking about leaving my job.	0.866
YDNV4	I often think about leaving this company.	0.806

term "salary" to measure the outcome of justice, while the term "the most senior management" is used to measure the origin of justice. As for the concept of a competitive working climate, and work interference with personal life, they are inherited in the study of Gim and Ramayah.[18] Finally, four variables about turnover intention, based on the study of Bothma et al.,[53] were used in this study. The pilot survey was conducted on September 10, 2022, to October 30, 2022, to evaluate the structure and content of the questionnaire. Since Ho Chi Minh City is the biggest and most developed city in Vietnam, workers in its industrial production zones were chosen for data gathering. After completing all the instructions-required questions, respondents were asked to comment on the overall structure and the clarity of the questions. A survey of 30 industrial employees showed that they almost agreed with most of the questions, but the content of some questions is still unclear. The questions of measuring fairness in income distribution, salary policy, and working relations were adjusted to conform employees from different localities in Vietnam. Data for pilot studies were not included in the major study.

14.3.3 Demographics of Respondents

The segment attributes of the exploration test were analyzed. The proportion of males accounts for 42.9% and this for females was 57.1%. The gender ratio of respondents is like the demographic characteristics of Vietnam (General Statistics Office of Vietnam 2020). The surveyed age ranges from 18 to over 36 years old, of which the age group from 22 to 25 accounted for the highest proportion, with 38.9%. Most of the respondents completed high school and university education. The number of respondents between the ages of 18 to 35 accounts for 90.7%. This is the major labor force working in a variety of industries and industrial production zones in Ho Chi Minh City, many of which require specialized qualifications. Therefore, the ratio of respondents graduating from college–university is necessary. Finally, the income from 6 to 10 million VND accounts for the highest proportion of 57.1%.

In the previous studies, though demographic factors such as education, income, and age, etc. influence intention to leave,[54] the respondents all have similar ages and income as well as qualifications, accounting for the majority of the survey samples, so they can represent the young industrial workforce in Vietnam.

14.4 RESULTS

14.4.1 Measurement Model

The partial least squares (PLS) algorithm was used to test the model and hypotheses that were presented.[55,56] The measurement model was confirmed by evaluating the internal consistency, convergent and discriminant validity, as well as the dependability of the various indicators through their loadings (Table 14.1) (Table 14.2). It should be mentioned that multicollinearity forced the removal of some items from various constructs from the measurement model.

As shown in Table 14.1, all the questionnaire items in this study feature factor loadings greater than 0.7, satisfying the certification criterion.[57]

TABLE 14.2 Measurement Model

Reliability and validity			Fornell-Larcker criterion						
	CR	AVE	CBCS	CBPP	CBQH	CBTD	KKLV	SXP	YDNV
CBCS	0.905	0.704	0.839						
CBPP	0.958	0.851	0.570	0.922					
CBQH	0.957	0.849	0.436	0.417	0.921				
CBTD	0.939	0.794	0.559	0.461	0.611	0.891			
KKLV	0.868	0.622	0.185	0.148	0.220	0.288	0.789		
SXP	0.904	0.703	−0.201	−0.251	−0.033	−0.089	0.018	0.838	
YDNV	0.915	0.729	−0.128	−0.218	−0.132	0.024	−0.070	0.338	0.854

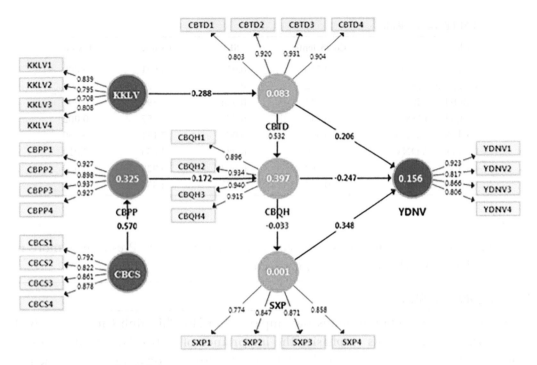

FIGURE 14.1 PLS algorithm.

14.4.2 Estimation and Evaluation of the Structural Model

Composite reliability (CR) overtakes in terms of internal consistency and convergent validity (Table 14.2); 0.7 was proposed by Nunnally and Bernstein[58] as a good benchmark for reasonable reliability. All items are accepted.

All of the constructs meet the AVE criterion put forth by Fornell and Larcker[59] in terms of convergent validity by higher than the cut-off point of 0.5; each construct accounts for at least 50% of the variance of the assigned indicators. The significant corner to corner values' square foundation of the difference between the form and its markers (AVE) surpasses the relationships between each development and some other build, demonstrating that the conditions for discriminant validity are also met (the rest of the matrix).

The structural model's estimation and validation are displayed in Figure 14.1. A 5,000-sample bootstrap approach was used to estimate the parameters once it was determined that there was no multicollinearity (VIF 5 for all indicators). The parameters were significant in all cases (p 0.05), except for the direction in which they were related.[60] About 15.6% of industrial workers' (YDNV) intentions are impacted by three factors.

14.4.3 Hypothesis Testing

Table 14.3 shows that respondents' intentions toward industrial workers (YDNV) have a positive impact on three variables (= −0.247, 0.348; p 0.05) but have no effect on one (= 0.206; discarded because positive). With a P-value of 0.05, these hypotheses can be

TABLE 14.3 Path

Path	Coefficients	SE	t-value	P-value
CBCS -> CBPP	0.570	0.054	10.521	0.000
CBPP -> CBQH	0.172	0.059	2.929	0.004
CBQH -> SXP	−0.033	0.084	0.390	0.697
CBQH-> YDNV	−0.247	0.078	3.157	0.002
CBTD -> CBQH	0.532	0.075	7.131	0.000
CBTD -> YDNV	0.206	0.084	2.455	0.014
KKLV -> CBTD	0.288	0.073	3.929	0.000
SXP -> YDNV	0.348	0.072	4.854	0.000

accepted because six routes are statistically important. Since the P-esteem is more noteworthy than 0.05, Hypothesis 7 is not rejected.

14.5 CONCLUSIONS

For the turnover intention of industrial employees in Ho Chi Minh City, we apply the PLS algorithm. The results emphasize the importance of justice factors in an organization, working environment, and interference with personal life for influencing industrial employees' turnover intention in Vietnam. It pointed out that industrial employees' intention to leave is negatively affected by relational equity according to the study of Smith and Sweet.[44] Turnover intention is positively influenced by WIPL, which is consistent with previous studies on Hobfoll.[19] In addition, the research results also show that interpersonal justice is positively affected by informational justice and distributive justice; procedural salary justice has a positive impact on distributive justice, all three results are consistent with the study of Gori et al.,[28] besides the positive influence of competitive working climate, on informational justice. Factors such as informational justice and distributive justice have an influence on interpersonal justice, in which informational justice affects interpersonal justice, while the factors of interpersonal justice, WIPL, and informational justice significantly influence turnover intention. An interesting thing in the result is that informational justice has a positive effect on turnover intention, which is in contrast to the study of Hussain and Khan.[43] This can also be explained that when employees get full information about their jobs and working conditions, they easily compare it with other jobs outside. In particular, when employees know each other's salary, they will be easily affected negatively (when their income is not commensurate with others, no matter how they work harder), or feel embarrassed (when their income is higher than others but working less), as explained by Case.[61]

The working environment of industrial employees is getting more and more competitive, requiring more attention from the enterprises to the employee for their attachment. The enterprises need to pay attention to the factors leading to employees leaving their jobs to promulgating policies to minimize this situation, avoiding damage to the organization's resources.

REFERENCES

1. Bao L, Xing Z, Xia X, Lo D, Li S. Who will leave the company?: A large-scale industry study of developer turnover by mining monthly work report. Paper presented at: 2017 IEEE/ACM 14th International Conference on Mining Software Repositories (MSR). 2017.
2. Memon MA, Sallaeh R, Baharom MNR, Nordin SM, Ting H. The relationship between training satisfaction, organisational citizenship behaviour, and turnover intention: A PLS-SEM approach. *Journal of Organizational Effectiveness: People and Performance.* 2017.
3. Kim S, Tam L, Kim J-N, Rhee Y. Determinants of employee turnover intention: Understanding the roles of organizational justice, supervisory justice, authoritarian organizational culture and organization-employee relationship quality. *Corporate Communications: An International Journal.* 2017.
4. Tongchaiprasit P, Ariyabuddhiphongs V. Creativity and turnover intention among hotel chefs: The mediating effects of job satisfaction and job stress. *International Journal of Hospitality Management.* 2016;55:33–40.
5. Deniz S. The relationship between perception of corporate reputation and turnover intention: Results from Turkey. *Journal of Health Management.* 2020;22(1):103–113.
6. Moynihan DP, Landuyt N. Explaining turnover intention in state government: Examining the roles of gender, life cycle, and loyalty. *Review of Public Personnel Administration.* 2008;28(2):120–143.
7. Nghi, X. Why 77% Why 77% of young employee change jobs. 2021; https://vneconomy.vn/vi-sao-77-nguoi-tre-nhay-viec-2019041910211.
8. Nyarko K, Ansah Nyarko M, Sempah D. Organisational injustice and interpersonal conflict on counterproductive work behaviour. *European Journal of Business and Management.* 2014;6(21):117–123.
9. Gouveia-Pereira M, Vala J, Correia I. Teachers' legitimacy: Effects of justice perception and social comparison processes. *British Journal of Educational Psychology.* 2017;87(1):1–15.
10. Kennedy DB, Homant RJ, Homant MR. Perception of injustice as a predictor of support for workplace aggression. *Journal of Business and Psychology.* 2004;18(3):323–336.
11. Jahanzeb S, De Clercq D, Fatima T. Organizational injustice and knowledge hiding: The roles of organizational dis-identification and benevolence. *Management Decision.* 2020.
12. Lotfi MH, Pour MS. The relationship between organizational justice and job satisfaction among the employees of Tehran Payame Noor University. *Procedia-Social and Behavioral Sciences.* 2013;93:2073–2079.
13. Shapoval V. Organizational injustice and emotional labor of hotel front-line employees. *International Journal of Hospitality Management.* 2019;78:112–121.
14. Ozel A, Bayraktar CA. Effect of organizational justice on job satisfaction. *Industrial Engineering in the Industry 4.0 Era*: Springer; 2018:205–218.
15. Mengstie MM. Perceived organizational justice and turnover intention among hospital healthcare workers. *BMC Psychology.* 2020;8(1):1–11.
16. Khattak MN, Khan MB, Fatima T, Shah SZA. The underlying mechanism between perceived organizational injustice and deviant workplace behaviors: Moderating role of personality traits. *Asia Pacific Management Review.* 2019;24(3):201–211.
17. Barclay SP, Barclay, LJ, Skarlicki, DP, Pugh, SD. Exploring the role of emotions in injustice perceptions and retaliation. *Journal of Applied Psychology.* 2005; 90(4):629–643.
18. Gim GC, Ramayah T. Predicting turnover intention among auditors: Is WIPL a mediator? *The Service Industries Journal.* 2020;40(9–10):726–752.
19. Hobfoll SE. Conservation of resources: A new attempt at conceptualizing stress. *American psychologist.* 1989;44(3):513.

20. Takase M. A concept analysis of turnover intention: Implications for nursing management. *Collegian.* 2010;17(1):3–12.

21. Akgunduz Y, Eryilmaz G. Does turnover intention mediate the effects of job insecurity and co-worker support on social loafing? *International Journal of Hospitality Management.* 2018;68:41–49.

22. James L, Charles W. A causal model of turnover for nurse. *Academy of Management Journal.* 1981;24(3):543–565.

23. Cropanzano R, Goldman BM, Benson III L. Organizational justice. *Handbook of Work Stress.* 2005;6:63–87.

24. Colquitt JA, Conlon DE, Wesson MJ, Porter CO, Ng KY. Justice at the millennium: A meta-analytic review of 25 years of organizational justice research. *Journal of Applied Psychology.* 2001;86(3):425.

25. Adams JS. Inequity in social exchange. *Advances in Experimental Social Psychology.* Vol 2: Elsevier; 1965:267–299.

26. Diamond SS, Zeisel H. *Procedural Justice: A Psychological Analysis.* JSTOR; 1978.

27. Roemer JE. *Theories of Distributive Justice.* Harvard University Press; 1996.

28. Gori A, Topino E, Palazzeschi L, Di Fabio A. How can organizational justice contribute to job satisfaction? A chained mediation model. *Sustainability.* 2020;12(19):7902.

29. Wang I-A, Lee B-W, Wu S-T. The relationships among work-family conflict, turnover intention and organizational citizenship behavior in the hospitality industry of Taiwan. *International Journal of Manpower.* 2017.

30. Hsieh Y-C, Pearson TE, Kline SF. The moderating effects of job and personal life involvement on the relationship between work–personal life conflict and intention to quit. *Journal of Human Resources in Hospitality & Tourism.* 2008;8(1):1–14.

31. Brown SP, Cron WL, Slocum Jr JW. Effects of trait competitiveness and perceived intraorganizational competition on salesperson goal setting and performance. *Journal of Marketing.* 1998;62(4):88–98.

32. Johnson DW, Johnson RT. Instructional goal structure: Cooperative, competitive, or individualistic. *Review of Educational Research.* 1974;44(2):213–240.

33. Dalton DR, Hill JW, Ramsay RJ. Women as managers and partners: Context specific predictors of turnover in international public accounting firms. *Auditing.* 1997;16(1):29.

34. Arhab A, Houston J, Kolla V, Lucker J. Are star performers leaving you? Workforce analytics can help you determine why, and what to do about it. *Human Resource Executive Online.* 2013.

35. Barankay I. Rankings and social tournaments: Evidence from a field experiment. *University of Pennsylvania Mimeo.* 2010;15.

36. Spell CS, Arnold TJ. A multi-level analysis of organizational justice climate, structure, and employee mental health. *Journal of Management.* 2007;33(5):724–751.

37. Leventhal GS. What should be done with equity theory? *Social Exchange.* Springer; 1980:27–55.

38. Folger R, Martin C. Relative deprivation and referent cognitions: Distributive and procedural justice effects. *Journal of Experimental Social Psychology.* 1986;22(6):531–546.

39. Greenberg J. Reactions to procedural injustice in payment distributions: Do the means justify the ends? *Journal of Applied Psychology.* 1987;72(1):55.

40. Alsaraireh F, Quinn Griffin MT, Ziehm SR, Fitzpatrick JJ. Job satisfaction and turnover intention among J ordanian nurses in psychiatric units. *International Journal of Mental Health Nursing.* 2014;23(5):460–467.

41. Adams JS. Towards an understanding of inequity. *The Journal of Abnormal and Social Psychology.* 1963;67(5):422.

42. Elovainio M, van den Bos K, Linna A, et al. Combined effects of uncertainty and organizational justice on employee health: Testing the uncertainty management model of fairness judgments among Finnish public sector employees. *Social Science & Medicine.* 2005;61(12):2501–2512.

43. Hussain M, Khan MS. Organizational justice and turnover intentions: probing the Pakistani print media sector. Paper presented at: Evidence-based HRM: a Global Forum for Empirical Scholarship. 2019.

44. Smith CM, Sweet J. Analyzing the relationship between Maslow's hierarchy of needs and consumer spending patterns. *Journal of Financial Service Professionals.* 2021;75(4).

45. Bies RJ. Interactional justice: Communication criteria of fairness. *Research on Negotiation in Organizations.* 1986;1:43–55.

46. Greenberg J, Cropanzano R. The social side of fairness: Interpersonal and informational classes of organizational justice. *Justice in the Workplace: Approaching Fairness in Human Resource Management.* Hillsdale, NJ: Lawrence Erlbaum Associates; 1993.

47. Camerino D, Sandri M, Sartori S, Conway PM, Campanini P, Costa G. Shiftwork, work-family conflict among Italian nurses, and prevention efficacy. *Chronobiology International.* 2010;27(5):1105–1123.

48. Fisher GG, Bulger CA, Smith CS. Beyond work and family: A measure of work/nonwork interference and enhancement. *Journal of Occupational Health Psychology.* 2009;14(4):441.

49. Ghosh D, Sekiguchi T, Gurunathan L. Organizational embeddedness as a mediator between justice and in-role performance. *Journal of Business Research.* 2017;75:130–137.

50. Kinnunen* U, Geurts S, Mauno S. Work-to-family conflict and its relationship with satisfaction and well-being: A one-year longitudinal study on gender differences. *Work & Stress.* 2004;18(1):1–22.

51. Kyei-Poku IA. Linking interactional justice to work-to-family conflict: The mediating role of emotional exhaustion. *Organization Management Journal.* 2014;11(2):74–83.

52. Brislin RW. Cross-cultural research methods. *Environment and Culture.* Springer; 1980:47–82.

53. Bothma CF, Roodt G. The validation of the turnover intention scale. *SA Journal of Human Resource Management.* 2013;11(1):1–12.

54. Giao HNK, Vuong BN, Huan DD, Tushar H, Quan TN. The effect of emotional intelligence on turnover intention and the moderating role of perceived organizational support: Evidence from the banking industry of Vietnam. *Sustainability.* 2020;12(5):1857.

55. Khoi BH, An PTH, Van Tuan N. Applying the PLS-SEM Model for the Loyalty of Domestic Travelers. Paper presented at: International Econometric Conference of Vietnam. 2021.

56. Mai D, Hai P, Cuong D, Khoi B. PLS-SEM algorithm for the decision to purchase durian milk with seeds. Paper presented at: Journal of Physics: Conference Series. 2021.

57. Henseler J, Ringle CM, Sarstedt M. A new criterion for assessing discriminant validity in variance-based structural equation modeling. *Journal of the Academy of Marketing Science.* 2015;43(1):115–135.

58. Nunnally JC, Bernstein I. The assessment of reliability. *Psychometric Theory.* 1994;3(1):248–292.

59. Fornell C, Larcker DF. Structural equation models with unobservable variables and measurement error: Algebra and statistics. *Journal of Marketing Research.* 1981:382–388.

60. Ngan NT, Khoi BH. Using PLS-SEM algorithm for Choice of University in Vietnam. Paper presented at: Journal of Physics: Conference Series. 2021.

61. Case J. When salaries aren't secret. *Harvard Business Review.* 2001;79(5):37–39, 42.

## CHAPTER 15

Deep Learning for Multimedia Analysis

Hafiz Gulfam Ahmad Umar

Department of Computer Science & IT, Ghazi University, Dera Ghazi Khan, Pakistan

15.1 INTRODUCTION

The extraction of useful information from various types of multimedia data, such as photographs, videos, and audio, is referred to as multimedia analysis. With the exponential growth of multimedia data in recent years, the necessity for automated systems to analyze and comprehend such data has grown. Deep learning has emerged as a potent technique for multimedia analysis, producing cutting-edge findings in image identification, speech recognition, and video analysis [1]. We present a detailed overview of recent achievements in deep learning for multimedia analysis in this paper, outlining its strengths and drawbacks and analyzing some of the important difficulties and prospects in this field [2].

15.1.1 Overview of Deep Learning

A machine learning method is deep learning. subfield that employs deep using neural networks to learn big data sets. Deep in neural networks are made up of numerous layers of connectedness neurons that can learn complex data representations. Backpropagation, which includes changing the neurons' weights and biases. It is often used to train these networks to decrease the gap between predicted and actual output [3].

One of the main benefits of deep learning is its capacity to automatically learn characteristics from raw data. Feature extraction is often conducted manually in traditional machine learning algorithms, which can be time-consuming and error-prone [4]. Deep learning learns features automatically from data, which can result in greater performance and more accurate outcomes [1].

15.1.2 Applications of Deep Learning in Multimedia Analysis

Deep learning applications perform a variety of multimedia analysis such as semantic segmentation, picture classification, object identification, video summarization, and audio recognition. Object detection has made use of deep learning. to automatically recognize and localize items in pictures and videos [5]. The use of deep learning may be

DOI: 10.1201/9781032646268-15

seen in image classification to classify photos into several categories such as animals, automobiles, and buildings. The use of deep learning is semantic segmentation the process of giving each pixel in a picture, allowing for more exact item recognition [6].

A variety of fields, including video summarizing to automatically construct a summary of a long film, emphasizing the most significant parts. Deep learning has been applied in speech recognition to transcribe spoken words into text, enabling for more accurate and efficient communication [3,4].

15.1.3 Recent Advances in Analysis of Multimedia Using Deep Learning

Recent research in the analysis of multimedia using deep learning has focused on improving the accuracy and efficiency of deep neural networks and tackling some of the major problems in this region. Recurrent neural networks, convolutional neural networks, and other innovative deep neural network designs are examples of this and generative adversarial networks (GANs) have been one field of research [7]. CNNs have been very useful for image and video analysis, whereas RNNs have been employed for processing natural language and voice. GANs have been used to produce realistic photos and videos, as well as to enhance the quality of existing multimedia data [8].

Another area of research has been the development of new training techniques for deep neural networks, such as transfer learning and reinforcement learning. Transfer learning entails using a previously trained neural network as a starting point for a new task, which can reduce the quantity of training data necessary while improving network performance. Reinforcement learning involves training a neural network to learn from its own actions, which can lead to more adaptive and intelligent behavior [9].

15.2 LITERATURE REVIEW

Alex Krizhevsky, Ilya Sutskever, and Geoffrey Hinton published "ImageNet Classification with Deep Convolutional Neural Networks" in the *Journal of Neural Information Processing Systems* in 2012.

Method: The authors introduced the AlexNet architecture, which consisted of multiple convolutional layers and achieved recent findings on the ImageNet data set for image classification.

"Going Deeper with Convolutions" by Christian Szegedy et al., published in 2015.

Method: The authors proposed the inception architecture, which utilized several convolutional layers and filters sizes to improve the efficiency and accuracy of deep neural networks.

Kaiming He et al.'s article, 2016, saw the publication of "Deep Residual Learning for Image Recognition" at the IEEE Conference on Computer Vision & Pattern Recognition.

Method: The scientists presented the ResNet architecture, which employed residual connections to train very deep neural networks and produced modern performance on a range of image identification tasks.

Jeff Donahue et al. published in 2015 the article "Long-term Recurrent Convolutional Networks for Visual Recognition &Description" from the IEEE Conference on Computer Vision &Pattern Recognition was presented.

Method: (LRCN) architecture was proposed by the authors, which integrated CNN and recurrent neural networks to recognize objects in films and provide natural language descriptions of the videos.

"Deep Semantic Role Labeling: What Works & What's Next" by Emma Strubell et al., was published in the Proceedings of the Association for Computational Linguistics' 56th Annual Meeting in 2018.

Method: The authors presented a deep learning strategy for semantic role labeling that includes predicting predicate-argument structures as well as semantic role labels simultaneously.

"Multimodal Deep Learning" by Shih-Fu Chang et al., was published in 2017 in the Proceedings of the IEEE.

Method: The authors provided an overview of multimodal deep learning, which involves integrating multiple types of sensory data (e.g., visual, audio, text) to enhance deep neural network performance.

In 2019, Yue Zhao and colleagues published "Deep Reinforcement Learning for Multimedia In the ACM Transactions on Multimedia Computing, Communications" in an article titled "Data Analytics: A Survey, & Applications."

Method: The authors provided a survey of deep reinforcement learning techniques for multimedia data analytics, which involve training agents to interact with multimedia data and perform tasks such as video summarization and speech recognition.

15.3 IN-DEPTH LEARNING

A machine learning method is deep learning, a subfield that uses artificial neural network networks. Deep neural networks, which are made up of numerous layers of interconnected nodes, or artificial neurons, are used to learn patterns and features from enormous amounts of data; there are several disciplines, including robotics, computer vision, natural language processing, and speech recognition by deep learning [10].

Deep learning is predicated on the principle of learning hierarchical representations of data by passing it through numerous layers of nonlinear transformations. The neural network's layers extract higher-level features from the input data, which are subsequently transferred to the following layer for processing. The last layer's output represents the learnt features or class labels for the incoming data [11].

The most common kind of deep neural network is an input layer, one or more hidden layers, an output layer, and the feedforward neural network. The raw input data is received by the input layer, while the hidden layers take input and extract features through nonlinear transformations [12]. The output layer generates the network's final output, which could be a prediction or classification of the incoming data.

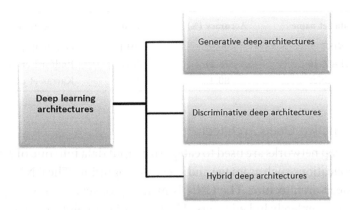

FIGURE 15.1   Deep learning architectures.

Deep neural networks are trained using the backpropagation process. It entails calculating the difference between the network's expected and actual output and then changing the network's weights to minimize the error. This process is performed several times until the network finds a set of weights that produces accurate predictions on a validation set of data (Figure 15.1).

15.3.1 Generative Deep Architectures

For modeling probability distributions over input data, generative deep architectures are utilized. These architectures are commonly used for picture and text generation. The GAN is a typical type of generative deep architecture. The GAN is made up of two networks: one for the generator and one for the discriminator. The generator network receives random noise as input. vector and outputs a sample from the desired data distribution [13]. The discriminator network accepts a sample from either the real or created data distribution as input and returns a binary output, indicating whether the sample is real or artificial. The network of generators is taught to generate samples that are difficult to differentiate from actual data, but the discriminator network has been programmed to accurately categorize the samples as real or fake.

15.3.1.1 Mathematical Equation for GAN
The loss function for the GAN is characterized as:

$$L(G, D) = E[\log(D(x))] + E[\log(1 - D(G(z)))]$$

where G stands for the generator network, D for the discriminator network, x represents a sample from the real data distribution, z represents a random noise vector, and E[] is the expected value over the corresponding distribution. The first term in the loss function assesses the capability of the discriminator network to accurately categorize real samples, while the second term measures the capability of the generating network to make samples that deceive the discriminator network.

Data set name	Accuracy (%)	Year	Authors
MNIST	99.52	2014	Goodfellow et al.
CIFAR-10	73.21	2014	Radford et al.
ImageNet	80.4	2016	Karras et al.

15.3.2 Discriminative Deep Architectures

Discriminative deep networks are used to categorize input data into one of several predefined categories in applications such as image and speech recognition. The CNN is a typical type of discriminative deep architecture. The CNN is made up of several convolutional layers that have one or more completely linked layers. The layers of convolution retrieve characteristics of the input data, whereas completely interconnected layers classify it. The last layer produces a probability distribution over all potential categories [14].

15.3.2.1 Mathematical Equation for CNN

In a CNN, the output of the last layer may be expressed as:

$$y = \text{softmax}(Wx + b)$$

where y represents the output probability distribution, W represents the weight matrix, x represents the input data, b represents the bias vector, and softmax represents the softmax function that normalizes the output to sum to one.

Data set name	Accuracy (%)	Year	Authors
MNIST	99.79	2018	Wan et al.
CIFAR-10	96.53	2016	He et al.
ImageNet	88.0	2019	Tan & Le

15.3.3 Hybrid Deep Architectures

To improve performance on certain tasks, hybrid deep architectures mix generative and discriminative deep architectures. The variational autoencoder (VAE) is a typical sort of hybrid deep architecture. The VAE is made up of two networks: an encoder network and a decoder network. The encoder network transforms the input data into a low-dimensional latent space, while the decoder network transforms the latent space back into the input space. The VAE is trained to minimize the decoder network's reconstruction error while also including a regularization term that promotes the latent space to follow a given distribution, such as a Gaussian distribution [15]. The resulting model can be used to generate images and text, as well as compress data and extract features.

15.3.3.1 Mathematical Equation for VAE

The loss function for the VAE can be defined as:

Data set name	Accuracy (%)	Year	Authors
MNIST	99.79	2018	Chollet et al.
CIFAR-10	97.53	2015	Srivastava et al.
ImageNet	92.0	2018	Huang et al.

$$L(x, z) = -E[\log(p(x|z))] + KL(q(z|x)\|p(z))$$

where x represents the input data, z represents the $p(x|z)$, a latent variable represents the likelihood of the given hidden variable, the input data, $q(z|x)$ represents the latent variable's posterior distribution given the input data, $p(z)$ represents the prior distribution of the latent variable, E[] represents the expected value over the corresponding distribution, and KL() represents the Kullback-Leibler divergence between two distributions.

Deep learning has the automated learning of characteristics from data, eliminating the need for manual feature engineering. This is especially helpful for assignments where the underlying features are unclear or difficult to extract using traditional methods. Numerous applications have successfully used deep learning, including picture and speech recognition, natural language processing, autonomous vehicles, and drug discovery [16] (Table 15.1).

A solid foundation in linear algebra, calculus, and probability theory is required to master intense learning. Having knowledge of deep learning frameworks such as Use PyTorch or TensorFlow, as well as programming skills in a high-level language such as Python, are also required. Many online courses and tutorials for deep learning are available, including free resources such as the online book *Deep Learning* by Yoshua Bengio, Aaron Courville, and Ian Goodfellow, as well as popular online courses on Coursera & Udacity. There are also several research publications and annual conferences on neural information processing systems (NeurIPS) and the international conference on learning representations (ICLR) are devoted to deep learning (Figure 15.2).

15.3.4 CNN

A type of neural network is a deep convolutional neural network (CNN) used for image and video recognition. A CNN is made up of numerous convolutional and accumulating layers, and then one or more fully linked layers. The pooling layers downsample the feature maps after the convolutional layers collect features from the input picture. Classification is accomplished by the use of completely connected layers.

15.3.4.1 Mathematical Equation for CNN

A convolutional layer's output may be expressed as follows:

$$z\_i = f(W\_ix + b\_i)$$

where z_i represents the output feature map at position i, W_i represents the convolutional x stands for the input data, b_i for the bias term, and f() for the activation function in the kernel. The output of a pooling layer may be expressed as:

TABLE 15.1 Summarizing Various Studies on Deep Learning for Multimedia Analysis

Study	Accuracy	Method	Time	Data set	Journal	Authors
"Deep Convolutional Neural Networks for ImageNet Classification"	84.7%	CNN	5–6 days	ImageNet	Neural Information Processing Systems	Alex Krizhevsky, Ilya Sutskever, & Geoffrey Hinton
"Delving Deeper into Convolutions"	89.0%	CNN	7 days	ImageNet	IEEE Conference on Pattern Recognition & Computer Vision	Christian Szegedy et al.
"Image Recognition Using Deep Residual Learning"	96.53%	CNN	20–30 days	ImageNet	IEEE Conference on Pattern Recognition & Computer Vision	Kaiming He et al.
"Visual Recognition and Description Using Long-term Recurrent Convolutional Networks" is the title of a paper published in the journal Nature.	67.0%	CNN + RNN	-	MSR-VTT	IEEE Computer Vision & Pattern Recognition Conference	Jeff Donahue et al.
"What Works & What's Next in Deep Semantic Role Labeling"	81.5%	Dp	-	CoNLL 2012 Shared Task	Proceedings of the Association for Psychological Science's 56th Annual Meeting Computational Linguistics	Emma Strubell et al.
"Multimodal Deep Learning"	-	Dp	-	-	Proceedings of the IEEE	Shih-Fu Chang et al.
"A Deep Ocean Survey Reinforcement Understanding Multimedia Data Analytics"	-	Deep reinforcement l	-	-	Transactions on Multimedia Computing, Communications, & Applications published by ACM.	Yue Zhao et al.

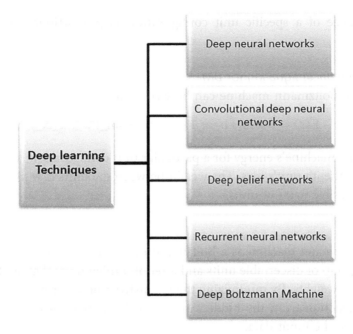

FIGURE 15.2   Deep learning techniques.

$$y\_j = g(\max(z\_j))$$

where y_j represents the output of the pooling layer at position j, z_j represents the input feature map, max() represents the maximum operation, and g() represents the activation function.

15.3.5 DNN

A DNN is a form of neural network made up of several layers of neural connections. Every neuron receives input from the layer before it and calculates a weighted total of the inputs, which is then processed by using an activation mechanism to produce the neuron's output. DNNs are frequently used for speech and text recognition, as well as image categorization.

15.3.5.1 Mathematical Equation for DNN
One way to express a neuron's output is as follows:

$$y = f(Wx + b)$$

where y is the neuron's output, x is its input vector, W is its weight matrix, b is its bias vector, and f() is its activation function.

15.3.6 BM

A Boltzmann machine is a sort of unsupervised learning generative model. It is made up of a collection of binary units that are linked together using symmetric weights. The Boltzmann machine's energy is defined by the state of the units and the weights between them. The chance of a specific unit configuration is proportional to the Boltzmann distribution.

15.3.6.1 Mathematical Equation for BM

The energy of a Boltzmann machine can be written as:

$$E(x) = -\text{sum\_i } b\_i x\_i - \text{sum\_i sum\_j } w\_ij x\_i x\_j$$

where $E(x)$ is the machine's energy for a particular unit configuration, x_i is the ith unit's state, and b_i is the ith unit's bias. The weight between the units is w_ij, and sum() is the sum over all possible pairs of units.

15.3.7 RBM

A restricted Boltzmann machine is a Boltzmann machine used for feature learning. It is made up of a group of discernible units and a set of hidden units that are linked together using symmetric weights. By minimizing the reconstruction error between the input data and its reconstruction from the hidden units, the RBM is trained to learn a compact representation of the input data.

15.3.7.1 Mathematical Equation for RBM

The probability of a visible state given a hidden state can be written as:

$$p(x|h) = \text{prod\_i } p(x\_i|h)$$

where $p(x\_i|h)$ is the probability of the ith visible unit being on given the state of the hidden units. The probability of a hidden state given a visible state can be stated as:

$$p(h|x) = \text{prod\_j } p(h\_j|x)$$

where $p(h\_j|x)$ is the probability of the jth hidden unit being on given the state of the visible units (Table 15.2).

TABLE 15.2 Comparison Table between Different Method

Deep learning model	Data set name	Accuracy	Year	Author
Deep Convolutional Network (CNN)	MNIST	99.79%	2012	Alex Krizhevsky, Ilya Sutskever, & Geoffrey Hinton
Deep Neural Network (DNN)	CIFAR-10	96.53%	2012	Dan Ciresan, Ueli Meier, & Jürgen Schmidhuber
Boltzmann Machine (BM)	MNIST	96.4%	2007	Ruslan Salakhutdinov & Geoffrey Hinton
Restricted Boltzmann Machine (RBM)	MNIST	98.2%	2006	Geoffrey Hinton
Deep Belief Network (DBN)	MNIST	98.3%	2006	Geoffrey Hinton
Deep Auto-encoder	MNIST	98.1%	2011	Yoshua Bengio, Nicolas Le Roux, & Pascal Vincent

15.4 MULTIMEDIA CONTENT USING DEEP LEARNING APPLICATIONS

Deep learning for multimedia content analysis is an active research area that has made substantial development in recent years. Deep learning models have been effectively applied to image classification, object detection, speech recognition, and video segmentation, among other tasks in multimedia analysis. The capacity of deep learning models to automatically learn features and representations from raw data without manual feature engineering is their primary advantage.

The convolutional neural network (CNN) is one of the most often used deep learning architectures for multimedia analysis. CNNs are specifically intended for image and video data processing, and they can learn features that are translation, rotation, and scale insensitive. Convolutional layers, pooling layers, and fully linked layers make up CNNs. Convolutional layers extract local features from an input image using a set of filters, pooling layers reduce the spatial resolution of the feature maps, and fully connected layers classify the input into one of several output categories. The arithmetic equation for a rudimentary CNN architecture is as follows:

$$Y = f(WX + b)$$

where Y is the output, X denotes the input, W denotes the weight matrix, b denotes the bias, and f denotes the activation function.

The deep belief network (DBN) is another prominent deep learning model for multimedia analysis. DBNs are probabilistic graphical models made up of many layers of hidden units. Undirected edges connect the hidden units, and the model is taught using a layer-by-layer unsupervised learning approach. DBNs have been utilized for image classification, speech recognition, and video segmentation, among other tasks in multimedia analysis. The arithmetic equation for a simple DBN architecture is as follows:

$$P(v) = 1/Z_* \sum \text{hexp}(\ E(v, h))$$

where $P(v)$ represents the probability distribution over the visible units, h represents the set of hidden units, Z represents the partition function, and $E(v,h)$ represents the energy function.

In conclusion, deep learning models have transformed multimedia content analysis by providing strong and adaptable tools for autonomously learning features and representations from raw data. Deep learning is predicted to continue driving advancements in multimedia analysis applications as large-scale multimedia data sets and computational resources become more widely available.

Here are some possible points to explain the methods used in multimedia content using deep learning applications:

15.4.1 Convolutional Neural Networks

(CNNs) are widely utilized in image and video analysis because of their ability to extract high-level features from raw pixel data. CNNs are often made up of numerous convolutional layers, which are then followed by pooling and fully connected layers.

15.4.2 Recurrent Speech and Natural Language Processing

Tasks are frequently performed using recurrent neural networks (RNNs). RNNs can analyze variable-length data sequences and detect temporal connections. RNNs that can handle long-term dependencies and prevent vanishing gradients include LSTM and GRU.

15.4.3 Autoencoders are Neural Networks

That can re-create compressed representations of input data from a lower-dimensional latent space. Autoencoders that may create fresh samples from the learnt latent space include variational autoencoders (VAEs) and GANs.

15.4.4 Transfer Learning

Is a strategy for improving performance on smaller data sets by leveraging pre-trained models on large data sets. This is especially beneficial in multimedia applications where labeled data.

15.4.5 Reinforcement Learning

Is a technique for teaching agents to make decisions in difficult situations. It entails creating a reward function that the agent tries to maximize and learn the optimal policy through trial and error. Reinforcement learning has been used in a variety of multimedia applications, including video game play and content suggestion.

15.4.6 Bayesian Deep Learning

Is a method for modeling uncertainty and making probabilistic predictions that blends deep learning and Bayesian inference. This is useful in multimedia applications where data is noisy or missing.

15.5 CHALLENGES AND FUTURE DIRECTIONS

Here are some challenges and future directions of deep learning for multimedia analysis:

15.5.1 Challenges

15.5.1.1 Lack of Labeled Data

For training, in order to use deep learning models, a significant amount of labeled data. Labeling data for multimedia analysis, on the other hand, can be time-consuming and costly.

15.5.1.2 Complexity

Multimedia data, such as images, movies, and audio, can be complicated and high-dimensional, making deep learning models challenging to handle and analyze.

15.5.1.3 Interpretability

Reading deep learning models may be challenging, making it difficult to grasp how they make decisions and produce results.

15.5.1.4 Generalization

Deep learning models might overfit specific data, making generalization to new, previously unknown data problematic.

15.5.1.5 Scalability

As multimedia data continues to grow in size and complexity, deep learning models need to be scalable to handle this increase in data.

15.5.2 Future Directions

15.5.2.1 Improving Interpretability

Developing methods to increase deep learning's interpretability models for multimedia analysis, making it easier to understand how they arrive at their decisions and results.

15.5.2.2 Incorporating Domain Knowledge

Incorporating domain knowledge into deep learning models can improve their performance and make them more adaptable to different domains.

15.5.2.3 Transfer Learning

Transfer learning can help alleviate the problem of limited labeled data by allowing pre-trained models to be used as a starting point for new tasks with limited labeled data.

15.5.2.4 Multimodal Analysis

Integrating multiple sources of multimedia data such as images, videos, and audio, can improve the accuracy of deep learning models and enable more comprehensive analysis.

15.5.2.5 Developing New Architectures

Creating fresh deep learning architectures to address the complexity of multimedia data more effectively, while also improving interpretability and scalability.

15.6 CONCLUSIONS

Medical imaging applications of machine learning include computer-assisted image-guided surgery, image segmentation, registration, and fusion treatment., annotation, and image database retrieval. Deep learning techniques are a class of machine learning algorithms that try to automatically detect different levels of abstraction and representation in order to aid with data interpretation. To properly apply and develop the methods, it is vital to know and carefully evaluate the properties of deep learning approaches. In comparison to more classic techniques when compared to other machine learning and feature engineering approaches, deep learning has the advantage of potentially offering a solution to the data analysis and learning issues brought on by huge amounts of input data approaches. To be more precise, it helps with the automated extraction of intricate data models from vast quantities of unsupervised data. It is therefore a vital tool for big data analytics, which involves processing information from vast volumes of unstructured, unsupervised raw data. The hierarchical learning and extraction of various complex data abstraction levels provided by deep learning simplifies some big data analytics tasks, particularly those involving the analysis of large volumes of data, semantic indexing, information retrieval, data tagging, and discriminative tasks like classification and prediction. When conducting tasks like classification, denoising, and compression, feature hierarchies offer a time- and space-efficient breakdown of the inputs. It was unclear how feature hierarchies may be taught for a very long period. We spoke about the difficulties in learning the various local minima and gradient dilutions. By resolving a string of straightforward shallow problems, deep learning acquires feature hierarchies. Deep techniques gain new information about the distribution of input data with each iteration as they learn a new level of features [17–28].

REFERENCES

1. Costello, V. (2016). *Multimedia foundations: Core concepts for digital design*. CRC Press.
2. Kennedy, L. (2009). Advanced techniques for multimedia search: Leveraging cues from content and structure (Doctoral dissertation, Columbia University).
3. Roy, P., Goswami, S., Chakraborty, S., Azar, A. T., & Dey, N. "Image segmentation using rough set theory: A review", *International Journal of Rough Sets & Data Analysis (IJRSDA), IGI Global*. 1(2):62–74.
4. Pal, G., Acharjee, S., Rudrapaul, D., Ashour, A. S., & Dey, N. "Video segmentation using minimum ratio similarity measurement", *International Journal of Image Mining (Inderscience)*. 1(1).
5. Samanta, S., Dey, N., Das, P., Acharjee, S., & Chaudhuri, S. S. "Multilevel threshold based gray scale image segmentation using Cuckoo search", *International Conference on Emerging Trends in Electrical, Communication & Information Technologies-ICECIT*, Dec 12-23, 2012.
6. Bose, S., Mukherjee, A., Madhulika, Chakraborty, S., Samanta, S., & Dey, N. (2013). "Parallel image segmentation using multi-threading & K-means algorithm", *IEEE International Conference on Computational Intelligence & Computing Research(ICCIC)*, Madurai, Dec 26-28 2013.
7. Dey, N., & Ashour, A. eds. (2016). "Classification & clustering in biomedical signal processing", *Advances in Bioinformatics & Biomedical Engineering (ABBE) book series, IGI*.
8. Karaa, W. B. A., Ashour, A. S., Sassi, D. B., Roy, P., Kausar, N., & Dey, N. (2015). "MEDLINE text mining: An enhancement genetic algorithm based approach for document clustering, applications of intelligent optimization in biology & medicine: Current trends & open problems".
9. Chakraborty, S., Dey, N., Samanta, S., Ashour, A. S., & Balas, V. E. (2016). "Firefly algorithm for optimized non-rigid demons registration", will be published in "Bio-Inspired Computation & Applications in Image Processing", Editors: X. S. Yang & J. P. Papa.
10. Mohamed, A., Dahl, G., & Hinton, G. (January 2012). "Acoustic modeling using deep belief networks", *IEEE Transactions on Audio, Speech, & Language Processing* 20(1).
11. Hinton, G. E., Osindero, S., & Teh, Y. W. (2006). "A fast learning algorithm for deep belief nets", *Neural Computation*, 18(7):1527–1554.
12. Deng, L. (2014). "A tutorial survey of architectures, algorithms, and applications for deep learning", *APSIPA Transactions on Signal & Information Processing*. 3:e2.
13. Ackley, D. H., Hinton, G. E., & Sejnowski, T. J. (1985). "A learning algorithm for boltzmann machines*", *Cognitive Science*. 9(1):147–169.
14. Salakhutdinov, R., & Hinton, G. E. (2009). "Deep Boltzmann machines". In *AISTATS*, pages 448–455.

15. Salakhutdinov, R., Mnih, A., & Hinton, G. E. (2007). "Restricted boltzmann machines for collaborative filtering". In *ICML*, pages 791–798.
16. Hinton, G. E.,Osindero, S., & Teh, Y. W. (2006). "A fast learning algorithm for deep belief nets", *Neural Computation.* 18(7):1527–1554.
17. Hinton, G., Deng, L., Yu, D., Dahl, G. E., Mohamed, A.-R., Jaitly, N., Senior, A., Vanhoucke, V., Nguyen, P., Sainath, T. N., et al. (2012). "Deep neural networks for acoustic modeling in speech recognition: The shared views of four research groups", *Signal Processing Magazine, IEEE.* 29(6):82–97.
18. Ciresan, D. C., Giusti, A., Gambardella, L. M., & Schmidhuber, J. (2012). "Deep neural networks segment neuronal membranes in electron microscopy images". In *NIPS*, pages 2852–2860.
19. Dean, J., Corrado, G., Monga, R., Chen, K., Devin, M., Le, Q. V., Mao, M. Z., Ranzato, M., Senior, A. W., Tucker, P. A., Yang, K., & Ng, A. Y. (2012). "Large scale distributed deep networks". In *NIPS*, pages 1232–1240.
20. Krizhevsky, A., Sutskever, I., & Hinton, G. E. (2012). "Imagenet classification with deep convolutional neural networks". In *NIPS*, pages 1106–1114.
21. LeCun, Y., Bottou, L., Bengio, Y., & Haffner, P. (1998). "Gradient-based learning applied to document recognition", *Proceedings of the IEEE.* 86(11):2278–2324.
22. Razavian, A. S., Azizpour, H., Sullivan, J., & Carlsson, S. (2014). "CNN features off-the-shelf: An astounding baseline for recognition". In *Computer Vision & Pattern Recognition Workshops (CVPRW)*, 2014 IEEE Conference on IEEE, pages 512–519.
23. Denil, M., Bazzani, L., Larochelle, H., & de Freitas, N. (2012). "Learning where to attend with deep architectures for image tracking", *Neural Computation.* 24(8):2151–2184.
24. Larochelle, H., & Hinton, G. E. (2010). "Learning to combine foveal glimpses with a third-order Boltzmann machine", *Advances in Neural Information Processing Systems.* 23:1243–1251.
25. Dahl, G., Ranzato, M., Mohamed, A., & Hinton, G. (2010). "Phone recognition with the mean-covariance restricted Boltzmann machine", *Proc. NIPS.* 23:469–477.
26. Guan, Yurong, Aamir, Muhammad, Hu, Zhihua, Dayo, Zaheer Ahmed, Rahman, Ziaur, Abro, Waheed Ahmed, & Soothar, Permanand (2021). An Object Detection Framework Based on Deep Features and High-Quality Object Locations. *Traitement du Signal*, 38, 719–730. 10.18280/ts.380319.
27. Aamir, Muhammad, Rahman, Ziaur, Ahmed Abro, Waheed, Tahir, Muhammad, & Mustajar Ahmed, Syed (2019). An Optimized Architecture of Image Classification Using Convolutional Neural Network. *International Journal of Image, Graphics and Signal Processing*, 11, 30–39. 10.5815/ijigsp.2019.10.05.
28. Guan, Yurong, Aamir, Muhammad, Hu, Zhihua, Abro, Waheed Ahmed, Rahman, Ziaur, Dayo, Zaheer Ahmed, & Akram, Shakeel (2021). A Region-Based Efficient Network for Accurate Object Detection. *Traitement du Signal*, 38, 481–494. 10.18280/ts.380228.

## CHAPTER 16

Challenges and Techniques to Improve Deep Detection and Recognition Methods for Text Spotting

Anuj Abraham[1,*] and Shitala Prasad[2,*]

[1]*Technology Innovation Institute, Abu Dhabi, United Arab Emirates*
[2]*Computer Science & Engineering, School of Mathematics & Computer Science, Indian Institute of Technology Goa, Goa, India*

16.1 INTRODUCTION

Over the few years, the detection of text contents on images and presentation slides has attracted several researchers due to its potential applications, such as in video lecture and conference summarization, document analysis, robot assistance in stationery stores and shopping malls, forensic linguistics with text reading, vehicle number plate tracking, to assist Google web crawler's prediction search, etc. Although there has been substantial contribution in text detection and recognition, it remains a challenge due to the large variation of text patterns, complicated background, and extensive computational cost and with the usage of machine learning (ML) and artificial intelligence (AI) techniques will play a significant role to improve network performances [1].

Recently, Google tested and launched a new feature of the video chapter concept in YouTube player.[1] This feature will help the YouTube user no longer wait in the player by watching a lengthy video, instead, it will allow users to go to any part of a video that is of most interest, using just the slider. Seemingly, YouTube's "Video Chapter" segments a video into sections marked by timestamps and changes them into various segments, which are visible on the slider (see Figure 16.1). This can be done by pressing or clicking the chapter marker, or by selecting the relevant timestamp of the video segment.

---

[*] Both authors contributed equally to this work.

DOI: 10.1201/9781032646268-16

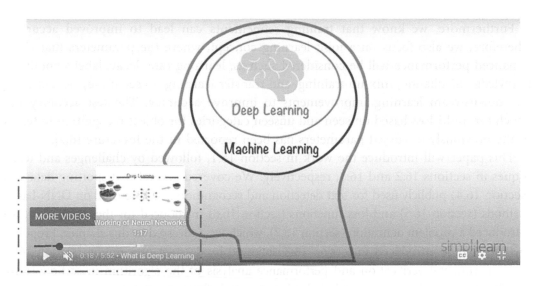

FIGURE 16.1 YouTube's "Video Chapter" with timestamps.

Meanwhile, researchers from the computer vision (CV) community are more focused on extracting valuable information from images with the usage of semantic-based text spotting algorithms, which have been extensively used for prediction. In addition, detection of scene text and text recognition are also performed with convolutional neural network (CNN) and long short-term memory (LSTM) [2]. The development of deep learning (DL) methods has provided new ideas and methods for the research and application for CV tasks. A solution to sequence recognition problem caused by variable length sequence data or labels was achieved by using a deep neural network (DNN) with an attention model [3]. This helps to recognize scene text with the least number of parameters.

The loss function design is very important in deep learning methods, which highly influences network performance. Compared to a single-loss function, a multi-loss function training strategy (otherwise known as final-loss) is the weighted sum of each loss, which will converge the network faster [3–5]. A progressive multi-view learning approach was introduced by Prasad et al. [3] that utilizes multi-loss view-invariant stochastic solution to improve and minimize the recognition accuracy at different viewpoints.

In the above-mentioned work, the authors have attempted a new learning strategy for object recognition, and in future work addressed to apply the concept to advanced CV tasks such as segmentation and prediction. Therefore, in our proposed method, we inherit the concept of a multi-loss classroom (CR) learning strategy for detection and segmentation tasks. The additional benefit of such methods is that we do not need to modify the base model architecture in the baseline work proposed by Slidin' Videos AI-5G Challenge, organized in 2022 (click link for more information: https://challenge.aiforgood.itu.int/match/matchitem/74). Here, our main task and contribution are in the development of an optimization method that minimizes the final loss errors using the same architecture without any extensive computational cost. Our methodology is focused on modifying the learning strategy used based on multi-loss functions to improve text detection and segmentation [6].

Furthermore, we know that training refinements can lead to improved accuracy. Therefore, we also focus on a joint learning concept, where the parameters that allow enhanced performance will be considered such as, learning rate decay, label smoothing, knowledge distillation, mix-up training, and transfer learning, to see if they benefit from any downstream learning improvements to improve accuracy. The test accuracy per epoch for multi-loss based on seen and unseen categories for object recognition in terms of the previously discussed parameters has been reported in the literature [6,7].

This paper will introduce the work in section 16.1, followed by challenges and techniques in sections 16.2 and 16.3, respectively. We covered several text spotting data sets (section 16.4) publicly used for text detection and recognition and discussed on DNN-based methods (section 16.5) and loss functions (section 16.6) introduced for the same. Next, we introduced a problem definition (section 16.7), which we addressed in this chapter. Proposed methodology is introduced in section 16.8, followed by data set preparation (section 16.9) and experimental verification and performance analysis of the algorithm in section 16.10. Finally, in section 16.11, we concluded this paper with future works.

16.2 CHALLENGES IN TEXT SPOTTING

In this chapter, we address a few most important challenges and techniques involved in text spotting using deep learning.

16.2.1 Variable Text Size and Orientation

Text in images can vary in size, font, orientation, and perspective, making it difficult to accurately detect and recognize the text; see Figure 16.2(a). One solution to this problem is to use multi-scale detection methods, which apply the text detector at multiple scales to capture different sizes of text. Another solution is to use data augmentation techniques, such as rotation and scaling, to train the model on various text orientations and sizes.

16.2.2 Occlusion

Text can be occluded by other objects or partially visible, making it difficult to recognize; see Figure 16.2(b). One approach to handling occlusion is to use context information to infer the missing text. An attention mechanism is another approach that allows the model to selectively focus on relevant regions of the image.

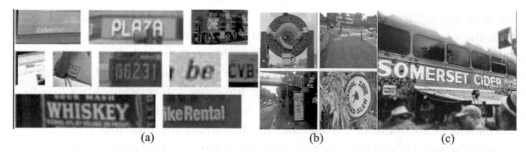

FIGURE 16.2   A few challenging images from the text data set: (a) varying text size and resolution. (b) text occlusion. (c) vocabularies.

16.2.3 Low-Quality Images

Text spotting performance can be affected by low-quality images, such as those with low resolution or compression artifacts; see Figure 16.2(a). One approach to improve the quality of the images before feeding them into the model is to use image enhancement techniques, such as denoising and sharpening.

16.2.4 Large Vocabulary

Text spotting models must be able to recognize a large vocabulary of words and characters; see Figure 16.2(c). One approach is to use a lexicon, which limits the set of possible words that the model can recognize. Another approach is to use language models, which incorporate contextual information to improve recognition accuracy.

16.2.5 Training Data

Models for text spotting require a large amount of training data to generalize well to new images. Here, one way to address the data scarcity problem is to use transfer learning. In this process, it involves pre-training of the considered model on a large data set. Then, fine-tune the processed model on a smaller target data set. Another approach is to use synthetic data generation techniques, such as text rendering, to generate additional training data.

In summary, text spotting using deep learning is a challenging task that requires over coming various challenges related to text size, orientation, occlusion, image quality, vocabulary, and training data. Techniques such as multi-scale detection, attention mechanisms, image enhancement, lexicons, language models, transfer learning, and synthetic data generation can be used to address these challenges and improve text spotting performance.

16.3 DEEP LEARNING IN TEXT SPOTTING

DL-based methods have the main ability to learn features from input data automatically and is extensively accepted for text spotting. Here, we describe some of the deep learning methods commonly used in text spotting.

16.3.1 Convolutional Neural Networks (CNNs)

CNNs are a type of deep learning method that uses neural network architecture and have been widely used for image analysis tasks, including text spotting. CNNs are capable of automatically learning features from the input images, making them well suited for text spotting.

16.3.2 Recurrent Neural Networks (RNNs)

RNNs are a type of DL neural network that is commonly used for text recognition. RNNs can process sequences of input data, making them well suited for recognizing sequences of characters in text.

16.3.3 Convolutional Recurrent Neural Networks (CRNNs)

CRNNs combine the advantages of CNNs and RNNs. Here, in this architecture, a CNN will extract features from the input images and a RNN is used to process the extracted features. Moreover, CRNNs have been shown to achieve state-of-the-art (SOTA) performance result in text spotting tasks.

16.3.4 Attention Mechanisms

Attention mechanisms let the target model selection on a relevant section of the input image, improving recognition accuracy. Attention mechanisms can be incorporated into CNNs, RNNs, and CRNNs [8].

16.3.5 Transfer Learning

The main tasks involved in the process of transfer learning are pre-training a model on a large data set and then fine-tuning it on a smaller target data set. It can be used to address the data scarcity problem in text spotting by leveraging pre-trained models to improve recognition accuracy.

16.3.6 Lexicons

Lexicons can be used to limit the set of possible words that the model can recognize, improving recognition accuracy. Lexicons can be incorporated into CNNs, RNNs, and CRNNs.

16.3.7 Language Models

Language models incorporate contextual information to improve recognition accuracy. Language models can be incorporated into RNNs and CRNNs to improve recognition accuracy.

In summary, deep learning methods such as CNNs, RNNs, CRNNs, attention mechanisms, transfer learning, lexicons, and language models have been widely used in text spotting tasks to improve recognition accuracy. Figure 16.3 shows a few DL-based methods for text spotting.

16.4 TEXT SPOTTING DATA SETS

Text spotting requires large and diverse data sets to train and evaluate the model performance. Here are some of the commonly used data sets for text spotting.

16.4.1 COCO-Text

COCO-Text contains over 63,000 images with 173,589 text instances and is a large-scale data set. The data set includes both regular and irregular text, as well as text in various orientations and languages.

16.4.2 SynthText

SynthText is a data set consisting of synthesized text images designed for text recognition and spotting. The data set contains over 800,000 images with over 8 million words in total, covering a wide range of fonts, colors, and backgrounds.

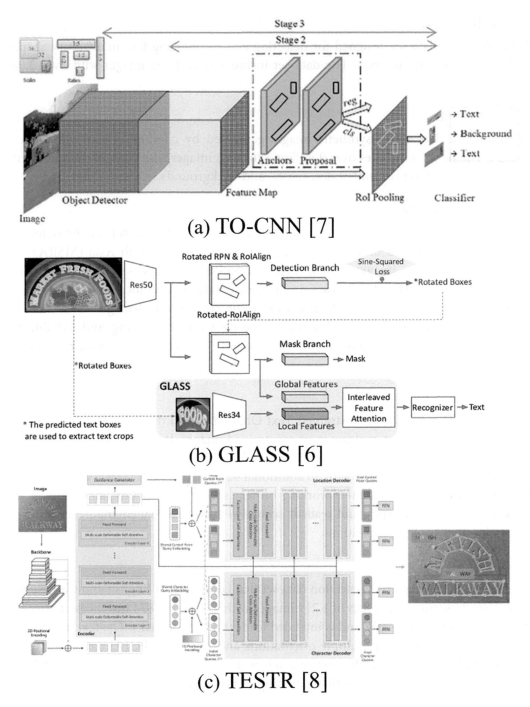

(a) TO-CNN [7]

(b) GLASS [6]

(c) TESTR [8]

FIGURE 16.3 Few popular DL-based methods for text spotting.

16.4.3 Street View Text

The Street View Text data set comprises text instances in street view images captured by Google Street View. The data set includes over 647,000 images with over 1.7 million text instances, covering various languages, orientations, and font styles.

16.4.4 Total-Text

Total-Text is a data set designed for detecting and recognizing text in arbitrary shapes, such as curves and polygons. The data set includes over 1,550 images with over 3,000 annotated text instances.

16.4.5 MJSynth

MJSynth is a data set of synthetic images generated by combining text with natural images. The data set includes over 9 million synthetic images with over 90 million words, covering a wide range of font styles, colors, and backgrounds.

16.4.6 MSRA-TD500

The MSRA-TD500 data set is a commonly used benchmark data set for the detection of text and recognition tasks. It was made by Microsoft Research Asia (MSRA) and contains 500 natural images with a total of 3,555 text instances. The text instances in the MSRA-TD500 data set vary in size, orientation, and location. They can be horizontal, oriented, or curved, and can occur on various backgrounds, such as cluttered, textured, or blurry. This makes the data set challenging and suitable for evaluating the robustness and generalization ability of text detection and recognition algorithms.

16.4.7 NTU-UTOI

The NTU-UTOI (NTU Unconstrained Text Object Images) data set [9] is a large-scale data set designed for text spotting in unconstrained images. It was created by researchers from Nanyang Technological University (NTU) and contains over 22,000 images with more than 227k text instances with an additional 42 objects. The NTU-UTOI data set is a valuable resource for researchers working on text spotting in unconstrained images. Its large size, diverse text types, and realistic scenarios make it a challenging benchmark for evaluating text spotting algorithms.

16.4.8 FORU

The FORU data set is a text detection data set that comprises of English and Chinese text in real-world scenes. It consists of 1,219 images with a total of 3,874 instances of text. The data set was released in 2017 and is intended for text detection tasks. The text instances in the images may appear in multiple orientations and sizes. The FORU data set is open-sourced and generally available for research works and can be seen in the mentioned GitHub link: https://github.com/jiangxiluning/FORU_data set.

16.4.9 ICDAR'19 MLT

The ICDAR 2019 MLT (multi-lingual text) data set is a benchmark data set for multi-lingual text detection and recognition. It contains 10,000 images with text instances in multiple languages, including Chinese, Japanese, Korean, Arabic, and English. The data set was released in 2019 and is designed for both tasks. The text instances in the images differ with font, size, orientation, and background complexity, making the data set challenging for both detection and recognition. The ICDAR 2019 MLT data set is available online for research works and can be downloaded from the mentioned link: https://rrc.cvc.uab.es/?ch=15.

16.4.10 Inverse-Text

The Inverse-Text data set is a recently proposed data set that focuses on arbitrary-shaped scene text, where approximately 40% of text instances have inverse-like shapes. The data set contains 500 testing images and is aimed to evaluate the performance task of text detection approaches on challenging scenarios with irregular text shapes. In the paper referenced, the authors tested their method on this data set using a model trained on the Total-Text data set. The Inverse-Text data set is available online for research works and can be downloaded from the mentioned GitHub link: https://github.com/BADAMO/Inverse-Text.

In summary, there are various data sets available for text spotting, ranging from large-scale real-world data sets to synthetic data sets designed for specific text spotting tasks. These data sets enable researchers to develop and evaluate text spotting models that can perform well in real-world scenarios. More details are summarized in Table 16.1, below.

There are some evaluation metrices used to compare the accuracy of text spotting models. Comparing the accuracy of deep learning models for text spotting can be challenging, as there are many factors that can affect performance, such as the size and complexity of the data set, the quality of the annotations, and the specific evaluation metrics used. However, there are several commonly used evaluation metrics that can be used to compare the accuracy of text spotting models:

TABLE 16.1   Text Spotting Data Sets Summarization

Data set name	Number of images	Annotation type	Language	Image type	Real/ Synthetic	Additional properties
ICDAR 2013[2]	229	Bounding boxes	English	Scene text	Real	-
ICDAR 2015 Incidental Scene Text[3]	1,500	Bounding boxes	Multiple	Scene text	Real	Background clutter
MSRA-TD500[4]	500	Bounding boxes	Chinese	Scene text	Real	Perspective distortion
COCO-Text[5]	63,686	Polygonal regions	Multiple	Scene text	Real	Variety of text instances
Total-Text[6]	1,255	Quadrilaterals	English	Scene text	Real	Curved and multi-oriented text
SynthText[7]	800,000	Word-level annotations	Multiple	Synthetic	Synthetic	Large-scale synthetic data set
CTW1500[8]	1,000	Bounding boxes	Chinese	Scene text	Real	Long and curved text
SCUT-CTW1500[9]	1,000	Bounding boxes	Chinese	Scene text	Real	Large scale and diverse
CUTE80[10]	80	Quadrilaterals	English	Scene text	Real	Small-scale data set

- *Precision and Recall*: Precision is the measure of proportion of true positives (i.e., correctly identified text instances) among all identified instances, while recall is another measure of the proportion of true positives, but among all actual text instances in the image. Higher precision and recall imply better text spot functioning.

- *F1-score*: The F1-score is another evaluation metric or summary metric used for text spotting accuracy. It is defined as the harmonic mean of precision and recall measure.

- *Word Accuracy*: Word accuracy measures the proportion of correctly recognized words among all words in the image. This metric is often used in text recognition tasks and can be used to evaluate the accuracy of the recognition component of a text spotting system.

- *Mean Average Precision (mAP)*: mAP is a common evaluation parameter used in detection tasks and can be adapted for text spotting. It measures the average precision of text instances detected at different confidence thresholds and provides an overall measure of text spotting performance.

- *Intersection over Union (IoU)*: It is defined as the measure of overlap between the predicted bounding box and its ground truth bounding box of a text instance. Higher IoU values indicate better text spotting accuracy.

It's worth noting that different evaluation metrics can be more appropriate for different text spotting tasks and data sets. Therefore, it is important to carefully consider the evaluation metrics when comparing the accuracy of deep learning models for text spotting.

16.5 DL MODELS USED IN TEXT SPOTTING

CNNs have an important advantage of their ability to extract main feature concerned from input images and is a popular choice for text spotting tasks. Here are some commonly used CNN backbones in text spotting.

16.5.1 VGG

The VGG (visual geometry group) architecture is a deep CNN with up to 19 layers. It is widely used in various computer vision related tasks, especially text spotting. VGG is known for its simplicity and high accuracy [8].

16.5.2 ResNet

ResNet (residual network) is a deep CNN architecture that introduced residual connections to address the vanishing gradient problem. ResNet is highly effective at extracting features from images with many layers and has been used successfully in text spotting tasks [9].

16.5.3 Inception

Inception is a CNN architecture that uses multi-scale convolutional filters to extract features from images. The original Inception architecture was highly complex, but later versions, such as Inception V3, are more streamlined and efficient [10].

16.5.4 DenseNet

DenseNet is a CNN architecture that uses densely connected layers to extract features from images. DenseNet is highly effective at extracting features from images with many layers and has been used successfully in text spotting tasks [11].

16.5.5 EfficientNet

EfficientNet uses CNN architectures that are optimized for both accuracy and computational efficiency. It does this by using a compound scaling method to balance the model size, resolution, and depth. EfficientNet has been shown to outperform other CNN architectures in various computer vision tasks, including text spotting [12].

16.5.6 MobileNet

MobileNet is also used successfully in various computer vision related tasks, especially for text spotting. MobileNet has the potential to achieve high accuracy while reducing the computational complexity of the system. It can be particularly helpful for mobile and embedded devices by using this architecture as the backbone of a text spotting system. One example of using MobileNet for text spotting is the MobileTextSpotter system proposed by researchers from the University of Surrey. The system uses a modified version of the MobileNet architecture as the backbone and includes additional modules for text detection, recognition, and correction [13].

16.5.7 SSD

The SSD (single shot detector) architecture is a popular detection framework of objects which uses a single neural network structure to directly predict bounding boxes of objects and class probabilities from the input images. SSD has been extended to various CV-related tasks, including text spotting [14]. To apply SSD to text spotting, the SSD architecture can be modified to output bounding boxes for text instances instead of general objects. This can be done by adding additional layers to the network to predict the size and position of text instances. One example of using SSD for text spotting is the TextBoxes [15] system proposed by researchers from Huazhong University of Science and Technology. While performing their experiments, the researchers found that TextBoxes achieved SOTA performance results on several text spotting data sets, especially the ICDAR 2015 and MSRA-TD500 data sets [16,17].

These are just a few of the many CNN backbones that can be used for text spotting. The choice of backbone depends on the specific text spotting task, the size and complexity of the data set, and the available computational resources. Table 16.2 shows a few comparisons of deep learning methods for text spotting on COCO-Text data set.

TABLE 16.2 Comparison of Different Methods for Text Spotting

Methods	Backbone	Pre-training data set	#Param.	val AP	test AP
Soft-Teacher [18]	Swin-L	IN22k + O365 + COCO (unlabeled)	284M	60.7	61.3
BEiT-3 [19]	ViT-g [20]	merged data + O365	1.9B	-	63.7
Co-Deformable-DETR [21]	MixMIM-g [21]	IN-1K + O365	1.0B	64.4	64.5
EVA-02 [22]	EVA-02	merged-38M	304M	64.1	64.5
Focal-Stable-DINO [23]	FocalNet-Huge [24]	IN-22K + O365	689M	64.6	64.8
TO-CNN [8]	VGG-16	COCO train	230M	-	0.47

***Note:** IN is for Imagenet and the number associated with it is the size while O365 is a 1.7M image data in total and merged-38M is a set of IN-22K (14M) + CC12M + ADE20K + CC3M + COCO + Objects365 + Image-Text (35M) + OpenImage whereas merged data is a set of IN-22K (14M) + Text (160GB) only.

16.6 LOSS FUNCTIONS USED IN TEXT SPOTTING

There are several loss functions available in literature that can be used in text spotting, that depend on the specific task and architecture of the system. Here, we discuss some of the commonly used loss functions to spot text.

16.6.1 Binary Cross-Entropy Loss

Binary cross-entropy loss function is generally used in text detection tasks where the aim is to predict whether a pixel or region contains text or not. It measures the difference between the predicted probability of a pixel or region being text and the true label (0 for non-text and 1 for text). Refer to TO-CNN [8].

16.6.2 L1 or L2 Loss

These loss functions are commonly used in text recognition tasks where the goal is to predict the correct text string given an input image. L1 loss function is the measure of absolute difference between the predicted and actual text, while L2 loss function is the measure of the squared differences of the text embeddings. Refer to TO-CNN [8].

16.6.3 Connectionist Temporal Classification (CTC) Loss

CTC loss function is generally used in text recognition relevant tasks where the input image has a classification of characters that need to be identified. CTC loss allows for variable-length outputs and does not require explicit alignment between the input and output sequences. It is defined as the difference between the predicted probability distribution over all possible output sequences and the actual or true label.

16.6.4 Multi-Task Loss

Multi-task loss function is widely used in text spotting relevant tasks where the goal is to simultaneously detect and recognize text in an image. It combines multiple losses to form a total loss function, such as binary cross-entropy and L1 or L2 loss, into a single objective function that is optimized jointly.

16.6.5 Focal Loss

Focal loss function is an alternative of the binary cross-entropy loss function that is proposed to address the class imbalance problem in text detection tasks. It assigns higher weights to hard examples that are misclassified or difficult to classify, which can improve the overall accuracy of the system. These loss functions can be combined or modified in terms of specific requirements of the text spotting task and the architecture of the system.

16.7 PROBLEM DEFINITION FOCUSED

In this problem statement of Slidin' Videos AI-5G Challenge on *"Slide Transition Detection and Title Extraction in Lecture Videos"*, the main task for us is to develop the best AI model for slide transitions by:

- Detecting the start and end frames of each slide in the video.

- Obtaining the apparent titles of each slide.

- All videos were recorded at 25 *fps*.

For this study, a compilation of 140+ video presentations of the scientific community, entrepreneurs, and standardization experts were performed from the recordings of 100 "AI for Good" (https://aiforgood.itu.int/) webinars.

While the AI challenge is a slide annotation problem, the data set contains some complex features. Cases of presenters demonstrating real-world footage amid the slide-show or minimizing PowerPoint and opening another program should be treated as non-slide content.

To distinguish slide content from everything else in predictions, we utilize the *"is_slide"* column. It is set to "0" (zero) for any video fragment that is not a slide, and to "1" (one) otherwise. Non-slide content can be identified in videos through tracking pixels refresh ratio (a typical slide fragment will have simple and discrete visual changes unlike real-world footage) or through an advanced image recognition model trained specifically for this task. Existing evaluation metric will focus on how accurate slide content/slide transitions were predicted in the video without taking into consideration other types of content.

The representation of frames extracted from a screenshare at 25 fps is illustrated in Figure 16.4. Similarly, Figure 16.5 demonstrates the Excel file listing of all ground truth slides available in the video.

The structure information in the Excel file named *"groundtruth.csv"* is as follows:

a. *starting_frame1, starting_frame2:* A range of possible starting frame numbers of the slide

- If slide appearance is animated, this range will match the duration of the animation.

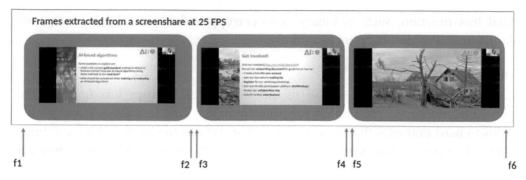

Frames extracted from a screenshare at 25 FPS
AI-based algorithms
Get involved!
f1
f2 f3
f4 f5
f6
frame_start, frame_end, is_slide, title
f1, f2, 1, "AI-based algorithms"
f3, f4, 1, "Get involved!"
f5, f6, 1, "NO_TITLE"
where f1, f2, f3, f4, f5, f6 - are frame numbers,
f2 is adjacent to f3, f4 is adjacent to f5

FIGURE 16.4 Expected annotation workflow.

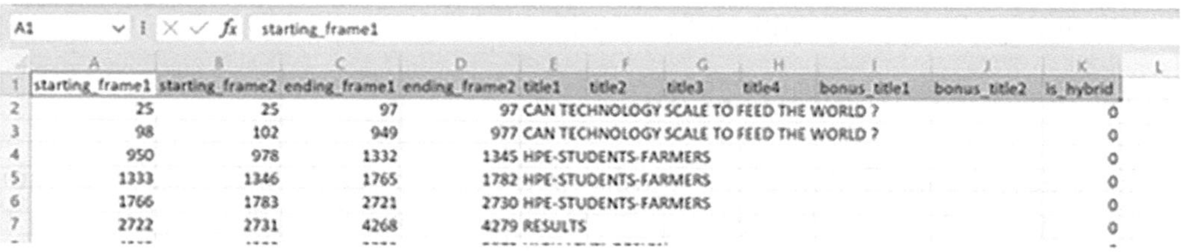

	A	B	C	D	E	F	G	H	I	J	K
1	starting_frame1	starting_frame2	ending_frame1	ending_frame2	title1	title2	title3	title4	bonus_title1	bonus_title2	is_hybrid
2	25	25	97	97	CAN TECHNOLOGY SCALE TO FEED THE WORLD ?						0
3	98	102	949	977	CAN TECHNOLOGY SCALE TO FEED THE WORLD ?						0
4	950	978	1332	1345	HPE-STUDENTS-FARMERS						0
5	1333	1346	1765	1782	HPE-STUDENTS-FARMERS						0
6	1766	1783	2721	2730	HPE-STUDENTS-FARMERS						0
7	2722	2731	4268	4279	RESULTS						0

FIGURE 16.5 "Ground_truth.csv".

- Predicting any frame within this range as a starting point of a slide will be correct.
- If slide appearance is not animated, "*starting_frame_1*" will be equal to "*starting_frame2.*"

b. *ending_frame1, ending_frame2*: A range of possible ending frames of the slide.

c. *title1, title2, title3, title4*: One or more optional titles of the slide

- If only "title1" is specified, a solution should predict it as a slide title.
- If "*title2*"/"*title3*"/"*title4*" are specified, a solution can predict any of the specified titles.

d. *bonus_title1, bonus_title2*: Bonus point answers.

- If "*bonus_title1*" is specified, a solution will be granted double points for predicting this title.

- If *"bonus_title1"* and *"bonus_title2"* are specified, a solution will be granted double points for predicting both titles.

e. *is_hybrid*: "hybrid" slides

- Some slides have video elements and are labeled as "hybrid" (*is_hybrid*=1)

- These slides are optional prediction: if a hybrid slide will be part of a prediction output it will not be considered a mistake.

- No points will be given for predicting hybrid slides, but you can use them to enhance your training.

16.8 PROPOSED SOLUTION ARCHITECTURE

This paper proposes a solution that is based on modifying the learning strategy and development of multi-loss function to improve the text detection and segmentation. The basic block diagram of the methodology used in our work is illustrated in Figure 16.6. We do not modify the deep feature extractor block in this work. In literature, it is seen that if we use more complex architectures, models will be better, but results in extensive computational cost.

16.8.1 ResNet Architecture

ResNet architecture is a conventional neural network for CV relevant tasks. The proposed model in ResNet was the winner of the ImageNet challenge in 2015. To solve the

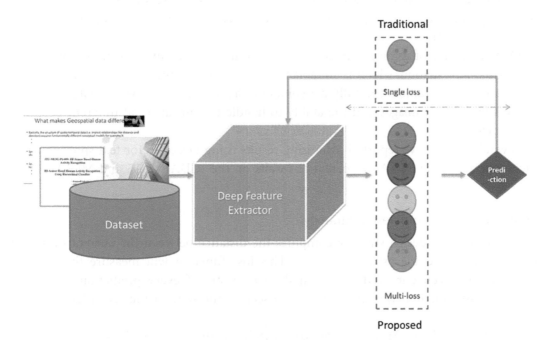

FIGURE 16.6 Proposed solution based on learning strategy.

vanishing gradient problem, residual neural networks (RNN) are introduced. The key advantages of using ResNet are as follows:

i. It allows us to train deep neural networks with more than 150 layers.

ii. The problem of vanishing gradients is resolved.

iii. It is a pre-trained CNN model and aids to train the model with CV task.

The most used architectures are Resnet 18, Resnet 50, and Resnet 101. Reset 18 has around 11 million trainable parameters. It will have only two pooling layers (one at the beginning and another at the end). It follows 3×3 CONV layers. It also follows a batch normalization process at every layer where the inputs will be normalized for each batch, if every batch resembles the normal distribution characteristics of the entire sample.

For simpler data sets, where the classes are easily distinguishable, or where the features are easier to identify and classify, a Resnet 50 will be a better fit; it's smaller, faster to train, and easier to use and deploy. In our work, we use *createDeepLabv3 ResNet 101* as the backbone network.

To adapt DeepLab for text spotting tasks, the architecture can be modified to output a heatmap of the text probability in the input image. The heatmap can be generated by adding a classification layer to the end of the DeepLab network that generates a binary prediction for each pixel, indicating whether it belongs to a text region or not. This can be trained with the usage of a binary cross-entropy loss function.

Once the heatmap is generated, text instances can be detected by applying a connected-component analysis to a group of adjacent text pixels into text regions. The text recognition can then be performed on each detected text region using a separate text recognition module.

One advantage of using DeepLab for text spotting is its ability to capture multi-scale contextual information, which is suitable for text instance detection of varying sizes and orientations. In addition, the fully convolutional nature of the network enables efficient processing of large images and the ability to handle text instances at different positions and scales.

Several studies have reported promising results using DeepLab for text spotting tasks, including achieving SOTA performance results on the ICDAR 2015 and MSRA-TD500 data sets.

16.8.2 Loss Function Design Strategy

The loss function design strategy computes the distance between the current output of the algorithm and the expected output. This loss function will measure the absolute difference between our prediction and the true value of every prediction. There are different loss function types of classification seen in the state of the art as follows:

i. *Regression Types*: Mean Square Error (MSE)/Quadratic loss/L2 loss, Mean Absolute Error (MAE)/Mean Square Logarithm Error (MSLE), L1 loss, Smooth Mean

Absolute Error/Huber loss, Log-Cosh loss (logarithm of the hyperbolic cosine), Quantile loss, Mean Bias Error, Likelihood loss.

ii. *Classification types*: Log loss/Binary Cross-Entropy loss, Hinge loss.

We used MAE, MSE, MSLE, and variations of Huber loss functions for our simulated experiments.

16.9 DATA SET PREPARATION

Since Slidin' Videos AI-5G Challenge data set has video as the input source, we needed to extract frames from these video files for feeding the deep model. Therefore, for data set preparation, we used the following steps:

i. The videos fps is 25.

ii. Use video files to extract images, 25 frames per second video.

iii. That is, if the video is of X length, the total number of frames will be: X(minute) * 60(second) * 25(fps).

iv. Once the images are extracted, they are categorized into training and validation sets.

v. There are three types of images: no title, same title, and new title slides.

16.9.1 Data Set Formulation

The steps involved in the preparation of data sets for creating training and validation sets are as follows:

i. From the ground truth CSV file, we extracted the number of frames with the same titles by using starting and ending frame numbers.

ii. Split the computed frame number by 80%–20%.

iii. Using the frame number, split the data set.

Then the main task is to detect the title from the slides. We have from the baseline of the ground truth data set with titles. Hence, we have extracted frames from these video files for feeding a deep model with title and no title slides, as illustrated in Figure 16.7 and Figure 16.8, respectively.

On average, we assume that titles are seen on the top of the slides. So, from each slide frame, we assume that 1/3 of the portion represents the probability of title search and used for training, whereas the remaining 2/3 represents the no title slide. The standard slide masking based on the threshold for title search is illustrated in Figure 16.8. In order to distinguish them, we create a mask (white = 1 or black = 0) with a threshold for title search line represented in red color, as shown in Figure 16.9. Rather than annotation, we create a mask, which is easy logic to implement.

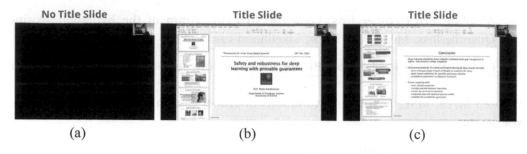

(a)   (b)   (c)

FIGURE 16.7   (a)-(c) Title and no title slide data extraction.

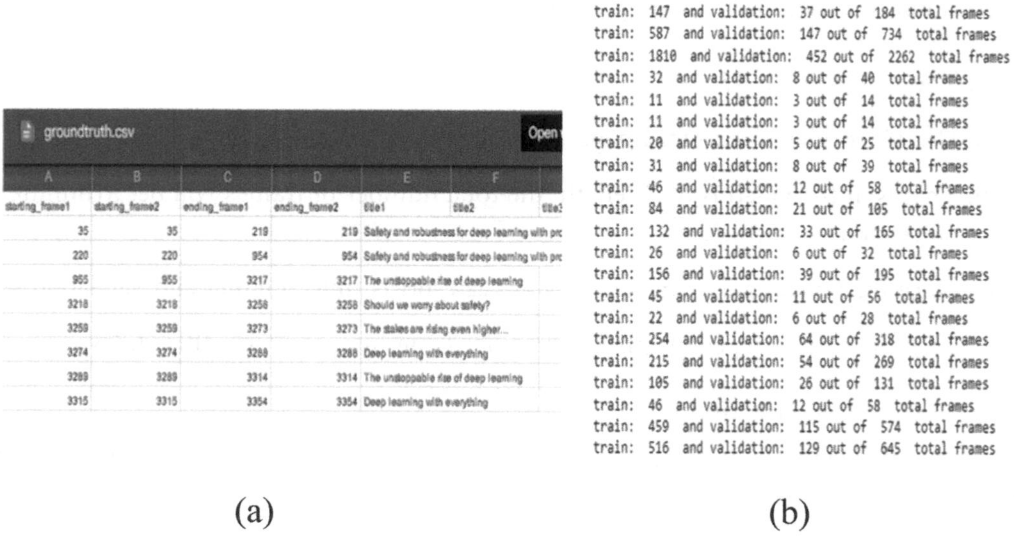

```
train:  147  and validation:  37 out of  184  total frames
train:  587  and validation:  147 out of  734  total frames
train:  1810 and validation:  452 out of  2262 total frames
train:  32   and validation:  8 out of  40   total frames
train:  11   and validation:  3 out of  14   total frames
train:  11   and validation:  3 out of  14   total frames
train:  20   and validation:  5 out of  25   total frames
train:  31   and validation:  8 out of  39   total frames
train:  46   and validation:  12 out of  58  total frames
train:  84   and validation:  21 out of  105 total frames
train:  132  and validation:  33 out of  165 total frames
train:  26   and validation:  6 out of  32   total frames
train:  156  and validation:  39 out of  195 total frames
train:  45   and validation:  11 out of  56  total frames
train:  22   and validation:  6 out of  28   total frames
train:  254  and validation:  64 out of  318 total frames
train:  215  and validation:  54 out of  269 total frames
train:  105  and validation:  26 out of  131 total frames
train:  46   and validation:  12 out of  58  total frames
train:  459  and validation:  115 out of  574 total frames
train:  516  and validation:  129 out of  645 total frames
```

(a)   (b)

FIGURE 16.8   (a)-(b) Illustration of training and validation sets of data sets in *"data set.part01"*.

(a)   (b)

FIGURE 16.9   (a)-(b) Slide masking based on the threshold for title search.

16.9.2 Parameter Settings

The following parameter settings were considered while performing training and testing procedures:

i. Trainable parameters: 60996202

ii. Training time: 8.6 minutes / epoch X 10 @ Nvidia GeForce GTX 1080Ti GPU × 2, RAM-11GB, Batch size: 4 images, Train model weight size: 235MB

iii. Training set: 2528, Validation set: 506,

iv. Total: 2528 ground truth slides.

16.10 EXPERIMENTAL RESULTS AND ANALYSIS

This section covers the experimental verification of results and performance analysis of the algorithm with a comparative study of baseline vs. proposed multi-loss in terms of performance metrices.

16.10.1 Environment

This paper discusses the software and hardware requirements and various environment library packages installed to perform our tasks on Linux ubuntu 18.04 LTS with Python – 3.9.13, PyTorch, Sklearn, and Cuda – 11.6 software on Nvidia GeForce GTX 1080Ti GPU × 2, RAM-11GB.

16.10.2 Comparison Study

A comparative study of baseline vs. proposed multi-loss (4) is tabulated in Table 16.3. It is observed that there is a significant improvement observed in the test F1 measure and AUROC for the proposed multi-loss function (4) when compared with the baseline work.

16.10.3 Ablation Study

We compared our methods with several settings, which are shown below. The first experiment shows that the multi-loss concept helps the network boost the performance without much computational overhead. Figure 16.9 shows a bar graph

TABLE 16.3 Comparative Study of Baseline vs. Proposed Multi-Loss

Metrics	Baseline	Proposed multi-loss (4)
Epochs	10	10
Train Loss	0.00279	0.00192
Train F1	0.853	0.911
Train AUROC	0.993	0.99
Test Loss	0.0241	0.02
Test F1	0.764	0.812
Test AUROC	0.925	0.949

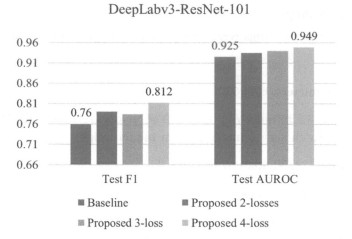

FIGURE 16.10 Simulation results of Test F1 and AUROC.

comparison with several loss functions of the students in the classroom of learning. We see that the multi-loss with four students outperforms the baseline method with roughly 5%, which is really a significant number. That means there are different losses that can recognize different title captions at different times of feature representations. This learning strategy reduces the computational cost and instead of several epochs, our model converges much faster. The cost cut is roughly 37.2%, as given in Figure 16.10.

Numerical calculation for boost in performance of F1 = $(0.812 - 0.76) \times 100 = 5.2\%$.

In addition, AUROC is the cost difference of accuracy between the ROC curve for the baseline and proposed. Basically, it is an area under the curve.

Numerical calculation for boost in performance of AUROC = $(0.949 - 0.925) \times 100 = 1.9\%$.

There is a significant improvement from the baseline work observed in the F1-score and AUROC, respectively, as illustrated in Figure 16.11.

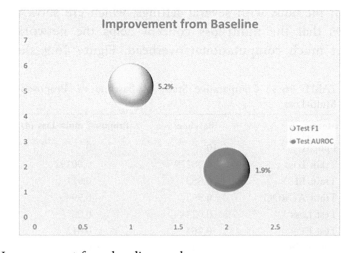

FIGURE 16.11 Improvement from baseline work.

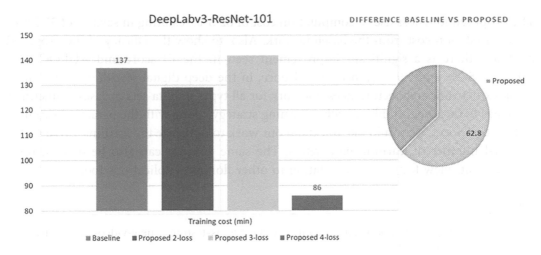

FIGURE 16.12   Simulation results in terms of computational cost.

From the ablation study in terms of computation, we observe that not all loss is suitable for this challenge task. We had tried for a 5-6-7 loss, but not much improvement was seen. Also, there is no point in simply using all loss functions without knowing their purposes. We observed that the best computational results were obtained at four-loss functions.

Therefore, the proposed four-loss classroom-based learning strategy uses a computation cost of $86/137 * 100 = 62.8\%$, resulting in a savings of 37.2% of computation cost compared to the baseline work, as described in Figure 16.12.

16.10.4 Key Contribution and Advantages

The main contribution and advantages of the proposed method, which is a joint learning approach for deep detection and segmentation, are as follows:

   i. Model used ResNet101 (createDeepLabv3),

   ii. No architectural changes,

   iii. Negligible model computation cost (equivalent to the original),

   iv. The proposed training strategy converges the network much faster and gives a significant performance boost of ~5%.

16.11 CONCLUSION AND FUTURE WORK

This paper proposes a joint learning approach for text segmentation and prediction. The proposed method boosts the network learning capability and converges the network much faster with a significant performance improvement. Our work enhances the learning power of the existing models without adding any additional changes to the network architecture. Classroom learning inherits various loss functions as students learn the same feature representation and use the best student to compute the backpropagation gradient. The classroom learning approach consistently outperforms the SOTA methods.

The proposed four-loss uses a computation cost of 62.8%, resulting in savings of 37.2% of the computation cost from the baseline work. Also, to show the efficacy of the proposed methods, there is a significant improvement seen in the F1-score and AUROC with values of 5.2% and 1.9%, respectively. Hence, in the deep digital world, only creating a complex network architecture does not work for all types of data sets or tasks. Sometimes there has to be proper thinking with a learning strategy, along with the parameters tuning.

In future work, we would like to extend our work to optimize the learning curve with a minimal number of learning parameters. The same concept can also be used in optimizing multi-view feature representation to other domain applications too.

NOTES

1. [online] https://www.phonearena.com/news/Google-is-testing-a-new-video-chapter-feature-in-YouTube_id123841
2. Online: http://dagdata.cvc.uab.es/icdar2013competition/?ch=2&com=downloads
3. Online: http://rrc.cvc.uab.es/?ch=4&com=downloads
4. Online: http://www.iapr-tc11.org/~/MSRA_Text_Detection_500_Database_(MSRA-TD500)
5. Online: http://vision.cornell.edu/se3/coco-text/
6. Online: https://github.com/cs-chan/Total-Text-Dataset
7. Online: http://www.robots.ox.ac.uk/~vgg/data/scenetext/
8. Online: https://ctwdata set.github.io/
9. Online: https://github.com/Yuliang-Liu/Curve-Text-Detector
10. Online: http://cs-chan.com/downloads_CUTE80_data set.html

REFERENCES

[1] Zhai, G., Zhou, J., Yang, H., An, P., Yang, X., (eds). Convolutional-Block-Attention Dual Path Networks for Slide Transition Detection in Lecture Videos. In: *Digital TV and Wireless Multimedia Communication. IFTC 2019. Communications in Computer and Information Science*, vol. 1181. Springer, Singapore, 2019.
[2] Haurilet, M., Al-Halah, Z., Stiefelhagen, R. SPaSe - Multi-Label Page Segmentation for Presentation Slides, Winter Conference on Applications of Computer Vision.
[3] Prasad, S., Chai, T., Li, J., Zhang, Z. CR Loss: Improving Biometric Using ClassRoom Learning Approach, *The Computer Journal*, 2022, bxac134, https://doi.org/10.1093/comjnl/bxac134
[4] Prasad, S., Tang, C., Zhang, Y., Wang, B. FAV-Net: A Simple Single-Shot Self-attention Based ForeArm-Vein Biometric. In *Computer Vision and Image Processing: 7th International Conference, CVIP 2022, Nagpur, India, November 4–6, 2022, Revised Selected Papers, Part II* (pp. 443–457). Cham: Springer Nature Switzerland. 2023, May.
[5] Prasad, S., Chai, T. Multi-Scale Arc-Fusion Based Feature Embedding for Small-Scale Biometrics, *Neural Processing Letters*, 2023, pp.1–18.
[6] Prasad, S., Li, Y., Lin, D., Dong, S., Nwe, M.T.L. A Progressive Multi-View Learning Approach for Multi-Loss Optimization in 3D Object Recognition, *IEEE Signal Processing Letters*, 2021, 29, pp.707–711.
[7] Yan, Z.H.O.U., Qinbin, W.E.I., Junwei, L.I.A.O., Fanzhi, Z.E.N.G., Wenjie, F.E.N.G., Xiangyu, L.I.U., Yuexia, Z.H.O.U. Natural Scene Text Detection and End-to-End Recognition: Deep Learning Methods, *Journal of Frontiers of Computer Science & Technology*, 2023, 17(3), p.577.

[8] Ronen, R., Tsiper, S., Anschel, O., Lavi, I., Markovitz, A., Manmatha, R. Glass: Global to Local Attention for Scene-Text Spotting. In *Computer Vision–ECCV 2022: 17th European Conference, Tel Aviv, Israel, October 23–27, 2022, Proceedings, Part XXVIII* (pp. 249–266). Cham: Springer Nature Switzerland, 2022, October.

[9] Prasad, S., Kong, A.W.K. Using Object Information for Spotting Text. In *Proceedings of the European Conference on Computer Vision (ECCV)* (pp. 540–557). 2018.

[10] Chowdhury, T., Shivakumara, P., Pal, U., Lu, T., Raghavendra, R., Chanda, S. DCINN: Deformable Convolution and Inception Based Neural Network for Tattoo Text Detection Through Skin Region. In *Document Analysis and Recognition–ICDAR 2021: 16th International Conference, Lausanne, Switzerland, September 5–10, 2021, Proceedings, Part II 16* (pp. 335–350). Springer International Publishing. 2021.

[11] Behzadi, M., Safabakhsh, R. Text detection in natural scenes using fully convolutional densenets. In *2018 IEEE 4th Iranian Conference on Signal Processing and Intelligent Systems (ICSPIS)* (pp. 11–14). 2018, December.

[12] Wang, P., Zhang, C., Qi, F., Liu, S., Zhang, X., Lyu, P., Han, J., Liu, J., Ding, E., Shi, G. Pgnet: Real-time arbitrarily-shaped text spotting with point gathering network. In *Proceedings of the AAAI Conference on Artificial Intelligence* (Vol. 35, No. 4, pp. 2782–2790). 2021, May.

[13] Hassan, E. Scene Text Detection Using Attention with Depthwise Separable Convolutions, *Applied Sciences*, 2022, 12(13), p.6425.

[14] Gao, F., Li, S., You, H., Lu, S., Xiao, G. Text Spotting for Curved Metal Surface: Clustering, Fitting, and Rectifying, *IEEE Transactions on Instrumentation and Measurement*, 2020, 70, pp. 1–12.

[15] Liao, M., Shi, B., Bai, X., Wang, X., Liu, W. Textboxes: A fast text detector with a single deep neural network. In *Proceedings of the AAAI conference on artificial intelligence* (Vol. 31, No. 1). 2017, February.

[16] Zhang, X., Su, Y., Tripathi, S., Tu, Z. Text spotting transformers. In *Proceedings of the IEEE/CVF Conference on Computer Vision and Pattern Recognition* (pp. 9519–9528). 2022.

[17] Liu, J., Huang, X., Liu, Y., Li, H. MixMIM: Mixed and Masked Image Modeling for Efficient Visual Representation Learning. *arXiv preprint arXiv:2205.13137*. 2022.

[18] Xu, M., Zhang, Z., Hu, H., Wang, J., Wang, L., Wei, F., Bai, X., Liu, Z. End-to-End Semi-Supervised Object Detection with Soft Teacher. In *Proceedings of the IEEE/CVF International Conference on Computer Vision* (pages 3060–3069). 2021.

[19] Wang, W., Bao, H., Dong, L., Bjorck, J., Peng, Z., Liu, Q., Aggarwal, K., Mohammed, O.K., Singhal, S., Som, S., et al. Image as a Foreign Language: BEiT Pretraining for All Vision and Vision-Language Tasks. *arXiv preprint arXiv:2208.10442*. 2022.

[20] Zhai, X., Kolesnikov, A., Houlsby, N., Beyer, L. Scaling Vision Transformers. In *Proceedings of the IEEE/CVF Conference on Computer Vision and Pattern Recognition* (pages 12104–12113). 2022.

[21] Zong, Z., Song, G., Liu, Y. DETRs with Collaborative Hybrid Assignments Training. *arXiv preprint arXiv:2211.12860*. 2022.

[22] Fang, Y., Sun, Q., Wang, X., Huang, T., Wang, X., Cao, Y. EVA-02: A Visual Representation for Neon Genesis. *arXiv preprint arXiv:2303.11331*. 2023.

[23] Ren, T., Yang, J., Liu, S., Zeng, A., Li, F., Zhang, H., Li, H., Zeng, Z., Zhang, L. A Strong and Reproducible Object Detector with Only Public Datasets. *arXiv preprint arXiv:2304.13027*. 2023.

[24] Yang, J., Li, C., Dai, X., Gao, J. Focal Modulation Networks, *Advances in Neural Information Processing Systems*, 2022, 35, 4203–4217.

## CHAPTER 17

Leaf Classification and Disease Detection Based on R-CCN Deep Learning Approach

Tayyab Rehman[1], Muhammad Sajid Khan[2], and Noshina Tariq[1]

[1]Institute of Avionics Engineering, Air University, Islamabad, Pakistan
[2]Wales Institute for Digital Information, University of South Wales, Cardiff, United Kingdom

17.1 INTRODUCTION

The role of plants in our atmosphere is vital. Without plants, there will not be any existence in the world's ecosystem. Despite this action, many different plant species face extinction. The paper describes the background and motivation for our research and the innovations in the field and the framework for accurate and straightforward detection of plant pests and diseases. It will contribute to developing a remedy while reducing economic losses significantly. The primary aim is to identify plants from a leaf image before our suggested Leaf Identification and Diseases Detection solution with Raspberry Pi [1,2]. This research suggests a new method for extending the shape context method for identifying species from images of leaves. The data set's image categorizes plant diseases and identification [3]. The proposed research developed a method for automatically identifying leaf species by examining shape and color features from captured photos of their leaf. Subsequently matching against the data set, the system provides information about the leaf family name, leaf name, and whether the leaf is defecated. The commercial importance of such a smart, intelligent system and the effort needed to carry out precise identification and diagnostics reinforce the need for such a system. Knowing agriculture disease detection identification and diagnosis using image analysis utilizing human expertise is necessary for all this [4].

Image-based preliminary screening is a helpful method for identifying and measuring plant diversity. Commercial models that make regular photo gatherings simple are

DOI: 10.1201/9781032646268-17

typically prohibitively expensive. It can produce additional goods in that order. One should employ inexpensive digital technology and cameras that can be used to gather plant image data to make high-quality data and data collection procedures more widely available. Convolutional neural networks are the core deep learning tool used in cutting-edge work (CNNs), particularly by the advancement of computing systems in recent ages. Vision processing units, integrated processors, and machine learning–related artificially intelligent applications have grown exponentially, resulting in the creation of novel approaches and models that have given rise to a new class; deep learning is the main characteristic that sets them apart, and it is their capacity for supervised learning training. Through this procedure, neural networks remain "trained" to represent almost all systems using current data that contains definite matchings of the system's inputs and results [5]. These are a collection of specific characteristics that must be carefully considered, especially when applying this framework to leaf species. In this kind of circumstance, the proposed approach is kind-hearted in viewing higher fields of harvesting. Also, when the plant leaves are increasingly denser, automated disease identification by sensing the indicators on the plant leaves is increasingly simple.

This object recognition with all bracing to smoothly image predicated designed critical process inspection [6]. This research looks at leaf identification as well as disease recognition. The suggested method relies on technology for image processing and extensively uses MATLAB employing the primary processing implementation. Digital image processing, scientific statistics, biology, and further related sciences are examples of this. Manually monitoring plant diseases is difficult. It requires much work, expertise in plant diseases, and a prolonged processing period. As a result, image processing is utilized to diagnose plant diseases. Image processing serves as the most effective method for detecting and diagnosing illnesses. Detecting diseases includes image acquisition, segmentation, feature extraction, and classification. In particular, the paper addresses methods and extraction functions for detecting plant illnesses in our suggested model. Compared to conventional image recognition, there are several advancements in picture segmentation and system architecture. To meet their specifications, people can enhance illness segmentation in several ways. The linear regression method can also be applied to several different plant diseases. A leaf can be used to identify a disease; it was identified after researching the suggested techniques. It suggests the way forward for future research into the progress and improvement of the current system. Our proposed research consists of both hardware and software bases.

The proposed is developed in MATLAB and proposed hardware integration in Python. It utilizes up to 10,000 images from the leaf data set. The system records the leaf using the Pi camera in real time and compares it to the data collection. Upon identification, it reveals the outcome. The faster RCNN is implemented to create the framework in our proposed research. The proposed research project focuses on creating a framework and a trained model that can identify the names and diseases of plants from pictures as input and then consolidating the model into the application with feature order to identify particular plant diseases. This application can be used on any smartphone and web app.

17.2 LITERATURE REVIEW

Identification of plant diseases has been a significant study area in the agricultural industry, motivated by the necessity for generating nutritious food. Many ways have been established and widely used over the years. CNN for image recognition and classification, as well as deep learning system image classifier, are examples of existing studies that focused on implementing specific DL models and direct observations. It is divided into three stages. The generated pictures are segmented in the first phase through the K-means and leaf transformation algorithms. In the second stage, segmented pictures remain sent and determined before the neural network. The proposed system is made up of about three primary components: Color extracted from a simple backdrop. The color for illness is extracted from the leaf in the second section. Finally, leaf identification and disease categorization are performed. It presents cutting-edge research in both plant and disease identification. A system is needed to create computational methods for auto- matically identifying and classifying illness using leaf pictures. Unfortunately, there are significant restrictions to removing intriguing color pixels from the image's backdrop. Nevertheless, the technique shows promising results for any plant or leaf examination [7]. The extraction characteristics for leaf categorization are addressed in four funda- mental processes. The initial step in getting diseases and leaves from fields or gardens to use in the RCCN Object Detection method. After pre-processing the image to eliminate noise from the infected leaf, the mean filtering method enhances the image quality.

In the third stage, the left transformation approach was employed to extract the image's contaminated region. The segmentation results generated radial color distribu- tion vectors that are employed as the vector feature in the final step. It uses the results to support the view clustering approach based on color pixels clustered for leaf categori- zation and defect detection. The merger is then limited to a set number of areas and independent of color, despite incorrect segmentation. As a result, separate power is generated in various regions of the picture.

Nevertheless, in our method, image processing employs the presented transforma- tion technique and our own data set to improve image processing [8]. The color and intensity of the disease on the plant leaf vary. The sickness spot appears when a threshold is placed on a grayscale in a based image. Therefore, only disease spots on the leaf must be found and not the vein. Before segmentation, the RGB picture needs to be color converted. The color component's threshold is used to detect illness spots cor- rectly. Three color RGB models are compared in this research [9,10]. This proposed research involves gathering photographs of various diseased, healthy, and potentially contaminated leaves. The picture is subsequently analyzed, and "deep learning and image processing" determines which plant leaves are impacted. Area, border, area ratio, rectangle, rotation, and the contrasting, correlations, and contrast moment of a channel-based texture [11,12]. Thus, constructing a hardware-based machine is man- datory to handle leaf information and increase output productivity. MatLab and Raspberry Pi were used for feature and image extraction and recognition in our research project. The extraction of leaf images is essential for extracting the element from that image [13].

The proposed research suggested a problem in identifying plants using leaf photos before employing "Leaf detection and disease detection by Raspberry Pi" to uncover distinguishing characteristics that can discriminate between plants and disease detectors. Color, shape, length, and edges were among the characteristics used to distinguish plant species. The novel technique in our proposed system extends the form context method for identifying plants based on leaf photos. The data set's photos identify the leaf and illnesses [14]. The proposed approach detects a method that enables us to automatically separate the various types of color features from the digital images of the leaf after combining the form characteristics from the data set. The surname, facility name, and authorization have all been reserved. The commercial interest in developing such a smart system and the work necessary for proper diagnosis justifies its development. In this, leaf plant diseases in field crops are identified and diagnosed using an image processing method created by experts on humans. Additional critical aspects include the system's reaction time, safety, and dependability [15]. Our research aims to create a "Leaf identification and illness detector using Raspberry Pi" utilizing a deep learning method. This technique is intended to produce more accurate and exact outcomes. It is widely accessible for fast and accurate categorization. The precision this approach found in selections is analogous to the recent works. Plant class identification is an essential topic researched in various fields. It is not easy to design and construct an automated plant recognition system.

The suggested approach, implemented at the start of the classification, is based on pretreatment, character extraction, and weighted normalization. It analyzed new technologies and chose the most significant characteristics based on their investigation. The normalization of weighted features is frequently employed in data extraction, and so this procedure is applied to this operation to increase classification accuracy. The suggested approach ensures an extra 90% rotation. It aims to use mature a reliable method for classifying plant species [16]. According to the different research techniques, image analysis technology to identify agricultural diseases has many advantages over simple and older methods in providing immediate and direct results. Sadly, only a few plant diseases were addressed, and the techniques were often inappropriate. Plant infections have become a severe problem, affecting the leaves, stems, and even sections of the roots. Because disease symptoms differ from plant to plant, and illnesses must be predicted more correctly, this research will examine and employ several training samples of leaf diseases [17]. Automation of disease recognition by machine learning generates much excitement in the agriculture industry worldwide [18].

17.3 PROPOSED MODEL AND TECHNIQUES

17.3.1 Proposed Model

By building a rapid and truthful model for identifying leaf illnesses that could be employed on devices supplied with the images, food insecurity may become less of a problem. While using deep learning, it is cautionary to minimize false suppositions. The model must undergo considerable training to obtain high reliability in the learning experience, which calls for using robust computer systems (Figure 17.1).

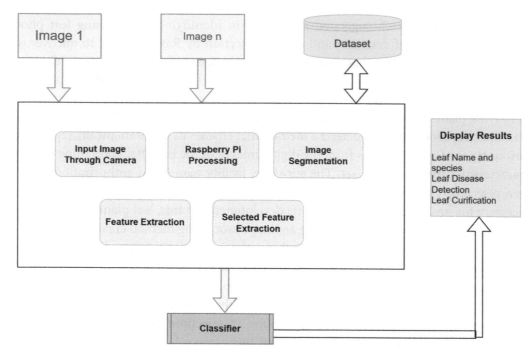

FIGURE 17.1   Proposed architecture of the system to enhance usability.

It is the method of recognizing a plant based on an image of a single leaf. For segmentation, pre-processing, and recognition, employ concurrent phases. The suggested approach incorporates a diverse set of form, aspect, and color properties. Several of them appear to be plant-specific. The following are the objectives of our suggested system: Improve plant resistance while decreasing expenses; color, style, leaf shape, and sickness detection may all be accomplished using our proposed method; and improve the efficiency of the industry (Figure 17.2).

17.3.2 Data Pre-Processing

A large data set of images is used to assess and train deep learning models. To classify and diagnose plant illness on photos that the model has not previously seen, we trained a deep learning framework using images of plant leaves in this study. Filtering, edge detection, form detection, and morphological procedures are common pre-processing activities in image processing. The proposed research image was captured using a PI digital camera. Plant categorization has garnered particular interest in the field of machine vision due to its crucial implications in the realm of farm automation and environmental protection. It significantly advances by using pictures to diagnose illnesses and increases image quality and clarity.

In comparison to the original photograph, a treatment plan was developed. Most of the time, you distinguish pixels with green colors. The proposed technique is a site identification procedure based on the test findings. The big training data set contains around 10,000 tagged photos of various plant parts. Flower labels, fruit labels, leaf labels,

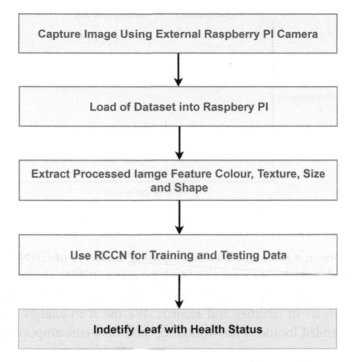

FIGURE 17.2 The proposed technique for monitoring the health of leaves.

and stem labels are some examples. Because these data sets are complex, numerous photographers have gathered images from various places utilizing diverse backdrops, poses, colors, and illumination [19]. Image segmentation is a method for making an image's representation more pertinent and understandable. The fundamental technique for processing digital images is called image segmentation, and it forms the basis for feature extraction and pattern recognition.

17.3.3 Leaf Transformation Algorithm for Training Data Set

In this proposed research, we used the plant challenge data to evaluate the performance of deep neural networks. It appears that transfer training is an ML technique in which the model established in one activity is used as the foundation for the model created in the following. This popular deep learning technique accounts for the processing power and time needed to develop computational solutions for specific problems to explore how computers and people understood language at the dawn of technology, such as before a model was utilized.

The aspects of transfer that can improve learning are shown in Figure 17.3. An example of the transfer learning algorithm is provided in this [20].

17.3.4 RCCN Model

The recognition network and the orientation categorization system are the two components of the R-CNN model. Both are constructed using the well-liked RCNN VGG-Net methodology. The R-CNN model extracts picture characteristics successfully using CNN. However, the primary problem is that it is prolonged. You can provide thousands

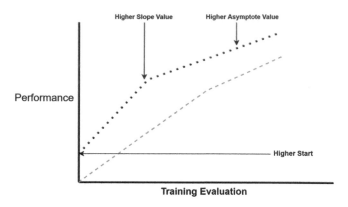

FIGURE 17.3   Proposed system throughput graph.

of proposed regions in a picture, necessitating using numbers of CNN front-end objects to find items. In this study, we applied a deep learning RCNN approach to extract leaf characteristics more accurately [21,22]. Initial (R-CNN) training typically involves identifying image nets in facilities and records. We use it to analyze this network and send it to the intended locations for workgroup and data consumption improvements.

17.3.5 Convolutional Neural Network

CNN has gained popularity in machine learning, particularly in recent years, due to its superior performance in different trained models. A novel approach for identifying viral plant diseases is proposed. DL is one of the techniques for machine learning and is regarded as a distinct learning approach in CNN [23]. The CNN with R-CCN classifications method is suggested as a model for identifying healthy leaves. Our accuracy ranged from 81.0% to 92% for various tests, with an average accuracy of 86.3%, using approximately 10,000 images in the data sets [24].

17.3.6 Advancements in Technologies

As the proposed research began and progressed towards its aim, and to ensure the correctness of the models again for research, including the compatibility with a web application [25]. Deep learning is a branch of machine learning that trains robots to learn from experience, just like people do naturally. Machine learning algorithms employ mathematical techniques to "learn" data-related information instead of using pre-existing equations as models. Image recognition, essential for problem solving in areas like image recognition, motion sensors, and various sophisticated safety technologies like autonomous vehicles, area sensing, conventional detection, and impartial technologies, is especially suited to deep learning. Deep learning algorithms sometimes outperform experts regarding object classification accuracy [26,27].

17.3.7 Hardware Equipment

The Raspberry Pi 3 in the United Kingdom created a series of inexpensive single-board computers to promote fundamental computer science instruction in schools and

FIGURE 17.4   Raspberry Pi 3 device.

developing nations. In addition to the primary demographic for robot usage, the initial model sold more than expected, neglecting peripherals such as a mouse and keyboard or housing. However, specific attachments are packaged in both formal and informal ways. The Raspberry Pi organization is split into two sections. The very first two models were built with Raspberry Pi. The Raspberry Pi Trading Foundation is in charge of technological development. Raspberry Pi Trading Foundation is an educational organization that supports elementary and secondary learning in computing and schools in impoverished republics [28] (Figure 17.4).

17.3.8 Micro USB Power Cable, Power Supply

The Raspberry Pi III card requires a small standard USB linked with a power production of 2.5 A to control. Instead of a rechargeable power supply, a power cord is used (Figure 17.5).

FIGURE 17.5   5 V 2.5 A switching power supply with 20 awg micro USB cable.

17.3.9 Python Script

Python is a powerful language commonly utilized in microcontroller boards due to its ease of reading and writing. Python's syntax is clean and uses Standard English idioms to make it easier to read.

17.4 EXPERIMENT AND RESULTS

17.4.1 Experiment Process

To complete the proposed research with a plant disease detector and diagnosis system that can localize and detect disease-affected regions of the plant leaf and provide causes and methods for controlling each specific disease or how it can be diagnosed to prevent it from spreading. All tests were carried out in MATLAB using Raspberry Pi and PI cameras and Python Sigling. The fully accessible deep learning framework serves as the model's foundation. Compared to traditional classification systems, the data pre-processing for deep learning approaches is significantly more straightforward. Figure 17.7 depicts (the GUI) outcomes of healthy and ill plants. The most active and quickest method for identifying leaf and disease detection is employed in this research study. It is regarded as a successful effort since the result is gratifying and rewarding [29]. This research integrates a variety of innovative methodologies in image processing and visual and color identification of an image shot. We compared the precision of our method to other broad categorization techniques. The fundamental learning rate is initially set at 0.001 during several early training sessions, gradually declining with each epoch. The momentum factor is 0.9, while the maturity value is 10-6. With improved experimental performance and precision, the new system delivered superior results (Figure 17.6).

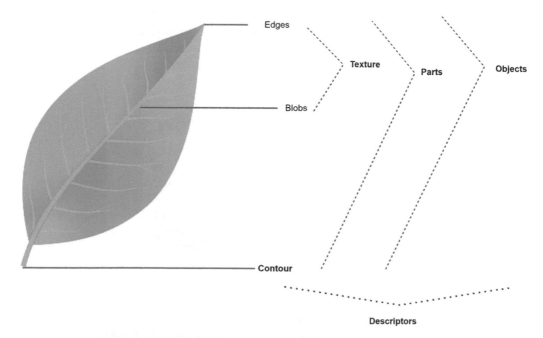

FIGURE 17.6   Scheme for feature extraction proposed.

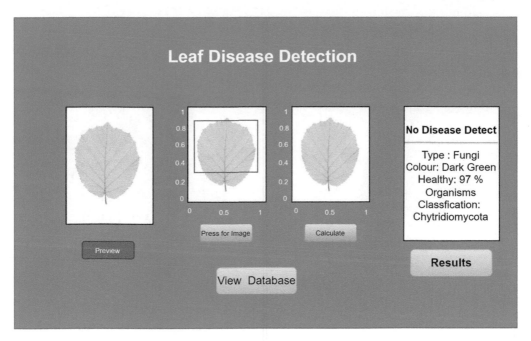

FIGURE 17.7 Experimental measurements of leaves in the frequency range results.

17.4.2 Results and Analysis

The extraction techniques are used to identify essential elements from a photo that has been provided. Texture feature extraction methods are used to extract texture characteristics from snapshots. The most popular texture extraction strategies are explained. To build this data set, we photographed the leaves with a PI camera and saved the images in JPEG format. We photographed around 8,000 distinct plant leaves. This data set was created to deal with a challenging environment. Almost 8,000 real-time leaf photos were included in this collection, with several leaf forms. For simple identification of leaves, we labeled all the photographs using Image Label. After evaluating the leaf into images in the data set, it used a learning model to recognize the current image of the leaf. It determined whether the leaf was normal, sick, or unhealthy [30] (Figure 17.8).

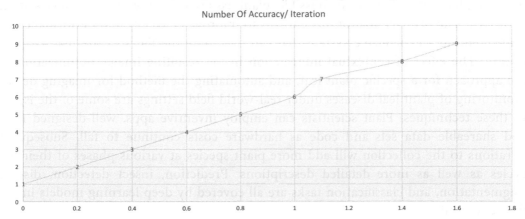

FIGURE 17.8 Accuracy acquired using the proposed framework.

FIGURE 17.9   Different leaf with several angles for results.

This research uses MATLAB and Python image processing for efficient and accurate plant disease detection method-based approaches [31]. The MATLAB software package is appropriate for image processing [32,33]. The leaf transformation algorithm, RCNN, and CNN achieve higher accuracy while consuming less processing time (Figure 17.9).

17.5 CONCLUSION

This research strongly suggests using it to detect plant identification and sickness by leaf evaluation rapidly. Captured images are produced to determine the composition of each plant. It will identify possible plant issues by using the leaf recognition approach. The primary goal of this effort is to improve efficiency and performance by implementing a dependable system that can overcome the flaws of the manual procedure. The effect of contextual information in the resulting image, optimization of the approach for a specific plant leaf, and automating the method for imaging device monitoring of plant leaf diseases under real-world field settings are some of the issues in these techniques. Plant scientists can employ inventive apps, well-designed files, and shareable data sets and code as hardware costs continue to fall. Subsequent iterations to the collection will add more plant species at various phases of their life cycles as well as more detailed descriptions. Prediction, insect detection, disease fragmentation, and classification tasks are all covered by deep learning models in the future as well.

REFERENCES

[1] Thakur, P.S., Khanna, P., Sheorey, T. and Ojha, A. 2022. Trends in vision-based machine learning techniques for plant disease identification: A systematic review. *Expert Systems with Applications*, p.118117.

[2] Singh, M.M. and Singh, T.R. 2021 Jul 28. A Survey on different methods for medicinal plants identification and classification system. *Revista Geintec-gestao Inovacao e Tecnologias*, 11(4), pp.3191–3202.

[3] Jagtap, S.B. and Hambarde, M.S.M. 2014. Agricultural plant leaf disease detection and diagnosis using image processing based on morphological feature extraction. *IOSR J. VLSI Signal Process*, 4(5), pp.24–30.

[4] Ferentinos, K.P. 2018. Deep learning models for plant disease detection and diagnosis. *Computers and electronics in agriculture*, 145, pp.311–318.

[5] Banzi, J. and Abayo, T. 2021. Plant species identification from leaf images using deep learning models (CNN-LSTM architecture). *Tanzania Journal of Forestry and Nature Conservation*, 90(3), pp.93–103.

[6] Singh, V. and Misra, A.K. 2015, March. Detection of unhealthy regions of plant leaves using image processing and genetic algorithm. In 2015 International Conference on Advances in Computer Engineering and Applications (pp. 1028–1032). IEEE.

[7] Nair, R.R., Adsul, S.S., Khabale, N.V., Kawade, V.S. and More, A.S. 2015. Analysis and detection of infected fruit part using improved K-means clustering and segmentation techniques. *IOSR Journal of Computer Engineering (IOSR-JCE)*, 3741.

[8] Chaudhary, P., Chaudhari, A.K., Cheeran, A.N. and Godara, S. 2012. Colour transform-based approach for disease spot detection on a plant leaf. *International Journal of Computer Science and Telecommunications*, 3(6), pp.65–70.

[9] Aamir, M., Pu, Y. F., Abro, W. A., Naeem, H. and Rahman, Z. 2019. A hybrid approach for object proposal generation. In The Proceedings of the International Conference on Sensing and Imaging (pp. 251–259). Springer International Publishing.

[10] Aamir, M., Pu, Y.F., Rahman, Z., Tahir, M., Naeem, H. and Dai, Q. 2018. A framework for automatic building detection from low-contrast satellite images. *Symmetry*, 11(1), 3.

[11] Jhuria, M., Kumar, A. and Borse, R. 2013 Dec 9. Image processing for smart farming: Detection of disease and fruit grading. In 2013 IEEE second international conference on image information processing (ICIIP-2013) (pp. 521–526). IEEE.

[12] Rathod, A.N., Tanawal, B. and Shah, V. 2013 Nov. Image processing techniques for detection of leaf disease. *International Journal of Advanced Research in Computer Science and Software Engineering*, 3(11).

[13] Aamir, M., Rahman, Z., Pu, Y.F., Abro, W.A. and Gulzar, K. (2019). Satellite image enhancement using wavelet-domain based on singular value decomposition. *International Journal of Advanced Computer Science and Applications*, 10(6). Ferentinos, Konstantinos P. "Deep learning models for plant disease detection and diagnosis. Computers and Electronics in Agriculture." (2018): 311–318.

[14] Kumar, S.S. and Raghavendra, B.K. 2019 Mar 15. Diseases detection of various plant leaf using image processing techniques: A review. In2019 5th International Conference on Advanced Computing & Communication Systems (ICACCS) (pp. 313–316). IEEE.

[15] Aamir, M., Pu, Y.F., Rahman, Z., Abro, W.A., Naeem, H., Ullah, F. and Badr, A.M. 2018. A hybrid proposed framework for object detection and classification. *Journal of Information Processing Systems*, 14(5), 1176–1194.

[16] Reyalat, M., Al Hiary, B., Ahmad, B. and Rahamneh, Z. 2017 Mar. Fast and accurate plant disease detection and classification. *International Journal of Computer Applications*, 17(1). (0975-8887)

[17] Kaboli, M. 2017. A review of transfer learning algorithms.

[18] Girshick, R., Donahue, J., Darrell, T. and Malik, J. 2015 May 25. Region-based convolutional networks for accurate object detection and segmentation. *IEEE Transactions on Pattern Analysis and Machine Intelligence*, 38(1), 142–158.

[19] Gerasimchuk, M. and Uzhinskiy, A. 2022 Oct. R-CCN plant diseases detector using triples loss and siamese neural networks. *Physics of Particles and Nuclei Letters*, 19(5), 570–573.

[20] Abade, A., Ferreira, P.A. and de Barros Vidal, F. 2021 Jun 1. Plant diseases recognition on images using convolutional neural networks: A systematic review. *Computers and Electronics in Agriculture*, 185, 106125.

[21] Nandhini, S. and Ashokkumar, K. 2021 Mar 25. Analysis on prediction of plant leaf diseases using deep learning. In2021 International Conference on Artificial Intelligence and Smart Systems (ICAIS) (pp. 165–169). IEEE.

[22] Aamir, M., Rahman, Z., Dayo, Z.A., Abro, W.A., Uddin, M.I., Khan, I., ... and Hu, Z. 2022. A deep learning approach for brain tumour classification using MRI images. *Computers and Electrical Engineering*, 101, 108105.

[23] Quoc Bao, T., Tan Kiet, N.T., Quoc Dinh, T. and Hiep, H.X. 2020. Plant species identification from leaf patterns using histogram of oriented gradients feature space and convolution neural networks. *Journal of Information and Telecommunication*, 4(2), 140–150.

[24] Guan, Y., Aamir, M., Hu, Z., Dayo, Z.A., Rahman, Z., Abro, W.A. and Soothar, P. 2021. An object detection framework based on deep features and high-quality object locations. *Traitement du Signal*, 38(3), 719–730.

[25] Coleman, G., Salter, W. and Walsh, M. 2021. OpenWeedLocator (OWL): An open-source, low-cost device for fallow weed detection. AgriRxiv, (2021), 20210317449.

[26] Guan, Y., Aamir, M., Hu, Z., Abro, W.A., Rahman, Z., Dayo, Z.A. and Akram, S. 2021. A region-based efficient network for accurate object detection. *Traitement du Signal* 38(2), 481–494.

[27] Uthpala, T.G.G. and Navaratne, S.B. 2021. Acmella oleracea plant; identification, applications and use as an emerging food source–review. *Food Reviews International*, 37(4), 399–414.

[28] Işik, Ş. and Özkan, K. 2021. Overview of handcrafted features and deep learning models for leaf recognition. *Journal of Engineering Research*, 9(1).

[29] Guan, Y., Aamir, M., Rahman, Z., Ali, A., Abro, W.A., Dayo, Z.A., Bhutta, M.S. and Hu, Z. 2021. A framework for efficient brain tumour classification using MRI images. *Mathematical Biosciences and Engineering*, 18(5), 5790–5815. doi: 10.3934/mbe.2021292

[30] Aamir, M., Rahman, Z., Abro, W.A., Tahir, M. and Ahmed, S.M. 2019. An optimized architecture of image classification using a convolutional neural network. *International Journal of Image, Graphics and Signal Processing*, 10(10), 30.

[31] Aamir, M., Rehman, Z., Pu, Y.F., Ahmed, A. and Abro, W.A. 2019, December. Image enhancement in varying light conditions based on wavelet transform. In 2019 16th International Computer Conference on Wavelet Active Media Technology and Information Processing (pp. 317–322). IEEE.

[32] Xiong, J., Yu, D., Liu, S., Shu, L., Wang, X. and Liu, Z. 2021. A review of plant phenotypic image recognition technology based on deep learning. *Electronics*, 10(1), 81.

[33] Ravindar, L.C., et al. 2022. Detection of Bullet Impact using Mask RCCN in Silhouettes. 2022 6th International Conference on Computing Methodologies and Communication (ICCMC). IEEE.

## CHAPTER 18

Multimedia Analysis with Deep Learning

Advancements & Challenges

Ahmed Mateen Buttar[1], Muhammad Anwar Shahid[2], Muhammad Nouman Arshad[1], and Irfan Ali[1]

[1]*Department of Computer Science, University of Agriculture Faisalabad, Faisalabad, Pakistan*
[2]*Univeristy of Windsor, Windsor, Canada*

18.1 INTRODUCTION

18.1.1 Background

The term "deep learning for multimedia analysis" describes the use of DL methods to examine and comprehend information included in various forms of multimedia content. To get insights from unstructured data, DL, a branch of ML, employs multi-layered artificial neural networks.

Classifying images, finding objects in photos, adding captions, summarizing videos, sorting music, and gauging viewer emotions are all part of the multimedia analysis process. Due to their superior capacity to automatically create hierarchical representations from data, deep learning models have shown significant presentation in several domains [1].

Convolutional neural networks (CNNs): CNNs are particularly effective for analyzing images and have been widely used in tasks such as image arrangement and object discovery. They leverage convolutional layers to extract local features and pooling layers to capture spatial relationships within images.

Recurrent neural networks (RNNs): Sequential data, such as films and audio, are ideal for RNNs. In order to capture temporal dependencies, they use recurrent connections. Two common RNN variations that help deal with the vanishing gradient problem and model long-term dependencies are long short-term memory (LSTM) and gated recurrent units (GRUs).

Transfer learning: Applying deep learning models that have been experts on comprehensive data sets, like ImageNet, to new problems with less labeled data is what transfer learning is all about. By transferring knowledge from the pre-trained models, transfer learning enables effective training of deep learning models even with limited data.

Generative adversarial networks (GANs): It is used for generating new multimedia content, such as realistic images or videos, by training a generative network against an adversarial network (discriminator). GANs have been used for tasks like image synthesis, image-to-image translation, and video generation.

Attention mechanisms: Attention mechanisms enhance the ability of deep learning models to focus on relevant regions or frames within multimedia data. They allow the model to appear to different parts of the input, emphasizing the most important information for the task at hand.

Multimodal fusion: Multimedia analysis often involves combining information from different modalities, such as images and text or audio and video. Multimodal fusion techniques integrate and model the interactions between different modalities, enabling joint analysis and better understanding of the multimedia data.

Deep reinforcement learning: With the use of both deep learning and RL, an agent can learn to respond in a given environment in order to maximize a reward signal. It has been applied to multimedia analysis tasks such as video game playing, interactive systems, and personalized recommendation systems.

18.1.2 Purpose of the Study

The purpose of studying deep learning for multimedia analysis can be manifold and can vary depending on the specific research or application context. However, some common purposes and objectives of such studies include:

Improve accuracy and performance: Deep learning techniques have shown exceptional performance in analyzing multimedia data compared to traditional approaches. The purpose of studying deep learning for multimedia analysis is often to further improve the accuracy, efficiency, and overall performance of algorithms and models in tasks like image classification, object detection, video analysis, and audio recognition.

Enhance understanding of multimedia data: Multimedia data is rich in information, and deep learning models can uncover complex patterns and representations within this data. Studying deep learning for multimedia analysis aims to enhance our understanding of multimedia data by developing models that can effectively extract and interpret meaningful information from images, videos, audio, and associated text.

Develop new applications and technologies: Deep learning for multimedia analysis drives the growth of new tenders and technologies that can leverage the insights gained from analyzing multimedia data. For example, it can lead to advancements in areas such as content-based image retrieval, video surveillance, automated video editing, augmented reality, natural language processing for multimedia content, and personalized recommendation systems [2].

Enable multimodal analysis: Multimedia data often involves multiple modalities, such as images, text, and audio, which are interrelated. Studying deep learning for multimedia analysis enables the development of techniques to effectively fuse and analyze these multimodal data sources, enabling a richer and more comprehensive analysis of multimedia content.

Address real-world challenges: Deep learning for multimedia analysis aims to address real-world challenges and problems related to multimedia content. This can include tasks like identifying and categorizing visual content in large-scale image or video databases, detecting and recognizing objects or events in surveillance footage, sentiment analysis of user-generated multimedia content, or understanding and summarizing complex multimedia data.

Support automation and decision making: Deep learning models for multimedia analysis have the potential to automate labor-intensive tasks, assist decision-making processes, and improve the efficiency and accuracy of multimedia-related workflows. By studying deep learning for multimedia analysis, researchers and practitioners aim to develop intelligent systems and tools that can assist in tasks like automated content tagging, recommendation systems, content filtering, and real-time analysis of multimedia data [2].

18.1.3 Research Questions

Research questions in the field of deep learning for multimedia analysis can focus on various aspects and challenges of analyzing multimedia data using deep learning techniques. Here are some research questions that can be explored in this area:

- How can state-of-the-art performance be achieved when using DL models for applications like image classification, object detection, video analysis, and audio recognition?

- How can transfer learning be utilized to improve the performance of deep learning models in multimedia analysis tasks, especially in scenarios with limited labeled data?

- What are the most effective architectures and techniques for multimodal fusion in deep learning models, enabling the integration of information from multiple modalities such as images, text, and audio?

- How can attention mechanisms be effectively utilized in deep learning models for multimedia analysis to enhance the model's ability to focus on relevant regions, frames, or segments within the multimedia data?

- How can deep learning models be utilized to generate realistic multimedia content, such as images, videos, or audio, with applications in areas like image synthesis, video generation, or music composition?

- How can deep learning models be leveraged to analyze and understand the sentiment, emotions, or subjective aspects of text associated with multimedia content, enabling a deeper understanding of user-generated multimedia data?

- How can deep reinforcement learning techniques be employed to enhance multimedia analysis tasks, such as interactive video analysis, personalized recommendation systems, or adaptive multimedia content generation?

- How can deep learning models be optimized for efficient processing and analysis of large-scale multimedia data sets, considering the computational and memory constraints?

- What are the ethical and privacy considerations associated with deep learning for multimedia analysis, and how can these challenges be addressed to ensure responsible and fair use of multimedia data?

- How can deep learning models be made more interpretable and explainable in the context of multimedia analysis, enabling better understanding and trust in the decisions made by these models?

18.1.4 Chapter Objectives

- Learn about deep learning, its principles, and how it differs from typical machine learning.

- Show how deep learning is used in multimedia analysis, including photos, videos, audio, and text. Learn how deep learning models like CNNs, RNNs, and GANs are used for image identification, sentiment analysis, and text production.

- Explore multimedia deep learning applications in entertainment, healthcare, advertising, and surveillance. Show how these technologies can transform.

- List the main obstacles to using deep learning for multimedia analysis, such as big data sets, high computational demands, and model interpretability limitations.

- Evaluate deep learning in multimedia analysis and anticipate future trends, taking into account ongoing research and technical breakthroughs.

18.1.5 Chapter Organization

The chapter opens with "Introduction to Deep Learning," which explains how deep learning methods differ from typical machine learning methods and their benefits. Convolutional neural networks (CNNs), recurrent neural networks (RNNs), and generative adversarial networks (GANs) are introduced in this segment. The second section, "Applications in Multimedia Analysis," examines photos, videos, audio, and text. It uses deep learning models for image identification, sentiment analysis, and autonomous text production. The "Real-World Use Cases" section shows how deep learning is applied in entertainment, healthcare, advertising, and surveillance. It explains these technologies' practical applications and transformational possibilities. The "Challenges" section discusses the challenges of using deep learning for multimedia analysis. Large data sets, computational resources, and model interpretability are these obstacles. "Future Directions," based on current research and state of the art, finishes the chapter. This section predicts deep learning's multimedia analysis evolution.

18.2 LITERATURE REVIEW

18.2.1 Traditional Multimedia Analysis Approaches

Traditional multimedia analysis approaches and deep learning for multimedia analysis represent two different paradigms in the field. Here's a comparison between the two.

18.2.1.1 Traditional Multimedia Analysis Approaches

Handcrafted Features: Traditional approaches frequently rely on manually devising and extracting multimedia data features. These characteristics can be based on color, texture, shape, or sound. Engineering features require domain expertise and prior knowledge of the problem domain.

Model Design: Typically, traditional methods entail the development of specific models or algorithms for various tasks. For instance, support vector machines (SVMs) or decision trees may be used for classification tasks, while edge detection or template matching may be used for image processing.

Task-Specific Methods: Traditional methods are frequently task-specific and may necessitate customized algorithms for various analysis tasks. This can lead to a fragmented strategy with separate algorithms for image processing, audio analysis, and video comprehension.

Limited Generalization: Traditional methods may lack generalization capabilities due to their reliance on handcrafted characteristics and task-specific designs. They may have difficulty adapting to new information or handling variations in real-world scenarios.

18.2.1.2 Deep Learning for Multimedia Analysis

End-to-End Learning: The goal of deep learning techniques is to directly learn hierarchical representations from unprocessed multimedia data. Deep neural networks autonomously learn feature representations in lieu of handcrafted features, reducing the need for manual feature engineering [2].

Representation Learning: Abstract representations of multimedia data are learned hierarchically by deep learning models. This enables them to recognize intricate patterns and relationships, resulting in enhanced performance across a variety of duties.

Transfer Learning: Deep learning models can leverage pre-trained models on comprehensive data sets to initialize or perfect their parameters for specific tasks. Transfer learning enables effective training even with limited labeled data, and learned representations can be transferred across different tasks.

Multimodal Fusion: Deep learning allows for the effective fusion of information from multiple modalities, such as combining image features with text or audio features. This enables joint analysis and a better understanding of multimedia data.

Scalability: Deep learning models can handle large-scale data sets and parallel computations efficiently. With advancements in hardware and distributed computing, deep learning has enabled scalable analysis of multimedia data.

Improved Performance: Deep learning has achieved advanced performance in many multimedia analysis tasks, such as image classification, object detection, and speech recognition. It has significantly pushed the boundaries of accuracy and achieved break-throughs in various domains [3].

18.2.2 Deep Learning in Multimedia Analysis

Deep learning has made significant advancements in the field of multimedia analysis, revolutionizing the way we analyze and understand multimedia data. Here are some key areas where DL techniques have been successfully applied:

Image Classification: In the field of image classification, DL models, and in particular CNNs, have shown amazing accuracy. They can take raw picture data and automatically learn hierarchical representations, allowing them to categorize photos into different classifications.

Object Detection and Recognition: For object detection and recognition in images and videos, deep learning models, such as region-based CNNs and single-shot detectors, are extensively employed. These models can precisely identify and locate objects of interest in complex scene environments.

Semantic Segmentation: Semantic segmentation tasks have been accomplished using deep learning techniques such as fully convolutional networks (FCN) and U-Net architectures. They are capable of pixel-level image segmentation, designating each pixel to a specific class or group.

Video Analysis: For video analysis tasks, including action recognition, video summarization, and video captioning, deep learning models have been implemented. RNNs and 3D CNNs are frequently utilized to extract temporal dependencies and spatio-temporal patterns from video data.

Speech and Audio Analysis: In speech recognition, speaker identification, music genre classification, and environmental sound classification, DL models, such as RNNs and CNNs, have demonstrated significant advancements.

Text Analysis in Multimedia: Text associated with multimedia data has been analyzed using deep learning techniques, such as sentiment analysis, text-based image and video captioning, and text-based recommendation systems. RNNs and attention mechanisms are frequently used to model the relationships between text and visual or auditory data [4].

Generative Models: Realistic multimedia content has been produced using DL-based generative models, such as GANs and VAEs. These models enable applications such as image synthesis, video generation, and music composition by producing images, videos, and audio that closely resemble the training data.

Multimodal Fusion: Deep learning techniques enable the integration and fusion of information from multiple modalities, such as the combination of image and text or auditory features. Multimodal fusion enables the joint analysis of multimedia data, thereby improving tasks such as image captioning, cross-modal retrieval, and multimodal sentiment analysis, as depicted in Figure 18.1 [5].

18.2.3 Multimodal Learning and Cross-Modal Retrieval

Deep multimedia analysis uses multimodal learning and cross-modal retrieval. These concepts include the following.

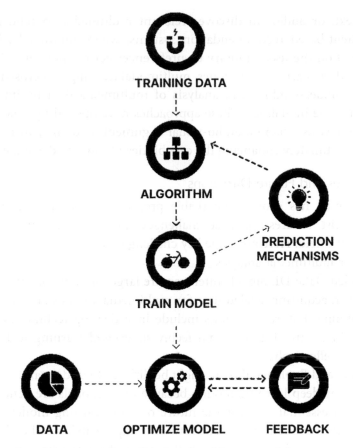

FIGURE 18.1 Proposed data workflow diagram of predictive model.

18.2.3.1 Multimodal Learning

DL analyzes multimodal data by combining images, text, and audio to understand multimodal data.

Multimodal deep learning models study multimodal data. Multimodal models can match images and descriptions. Semantic linkages across modalities improve picture captioning, video summarization, and multimedia sentiment analysis [6].

Cross-modal Retrieval: Cross-modal retrieval, also known as multimodal retrieval, is the retrieval of pertinent data from one modality in response to a query from another modality. Cross-modal retrieval aims, for instance, to retrieve pertinent textual descriptions or audio clips associated with an image.

Learning joint representations of data from multiple modalities enables cross-modal retrieval through techniques of deep learning. The models are taught to map data from one modality into a shared embedding space, where similar information from different modalities is closer together. This shared embedding space facilitates the retrieval and matching of data from various modalities.

Cross-modal retrieval has multiple domain-specific applications. It can be used, for instance, in multimedia search engines where users can query using different modalities (e.g., images, text, or audio) to discover relevant multimedia content. It can also be applied to content-based recommendation systems, where multimedia items are recommended based on the user's inquiry or preferences across modalities [7].

By leveraging deep learning techniques, multimodal learning and cross-modal retrieval enable a deeper understanding and analysis of multimedia data by integrating information from multiple modalities. These approaches have opened up new possibilities in tasks like image-text association, audio-visual alignment, and efficient retrieval of multimedia content, ultimately enhancing the capabilities of multimedia analysis systems [8].

18.2.4 Challenges and Future Directions

While deep learning has shown remarkable progress in multimedia analysis, several challenges still exist. Addressing these challenges and exploring future directions can further advance the field. Here are some key challenges and potential future directions in deep learning for multimedia analysis:

Limited Labeled Data: DL models often require large amounts of categorized data for training. However, acquiring labeled data for multimedia analysis tasks can be expensive and time-consuming. Future directions include investigating techniques such as semi-supervised learning, active learning, and feebly supervised learning to leverage limited labeled data more effectively.

Interpretability and Explainability: It might be difficult to understand and interpret the judgments made by deep learning models because these models are generally viewed as "black boxes." An essential goal for the future of deep learning models in multimedia analysis is to improve their interpretability and explainability. The decision-making process can be better understood through the study of approaches including attention mechanisms, visualization techniques, and model explanations [9].

Multimodal Fusion: Integrating information from multiple modalities, such as images, text, and audio, remains a challenging task. Future directions involve exploring advanced multimodal fusion techniques that can effectively combine and utilize information from different modalities, enabling more robust and accurate analysis of multimedia data.

Real-Time Processing: Real-time analysis of multimedia data is crucial for applications such as video surveillance, live streaming, and autonomous systems. Future directions involve developing efficient and scalable deep learning models that can process multimedia data in real time, considering the computational constraints of resource-limited devices or platforms.

Ethical and Privacy Concerns: DL models trained on large-scale multimedia data sets raise concerns regarding privacy, bias, and fairness. Future directions involve addressing these ethical considerations by developing techniques for privacy-preserving deep learning, algorithmic fairness, and bias mitigation in multimedia analysis applications.

Domain-Specific Challenges: Different domains have their specific challenges in multimedia analysis. For instance, in healthcare, handling medical imaging data and ensuring the interpretability of deep learning models is crucial. Future directions involve domain-specific research to address challenges in areas such as healthcare, entertainment, surveillance, and social media analysis.

Transfer Learning and Generalization: Generalizing deep learning models to new domains or unseen data remains a challenge. Future directions involve exploring transfer learning techniques that can effectively transfer knowledge from pre-trained models to new tasks or domains, enabling better generalization and adaptation to novel data.

Robustness to Adversarial Attacks: Deep learning models are susceptible to adversarial attacks, where carefully crafted unrests can fool the models into making incorrect predictions. Future directions involve developing robust deep learning models that can resist adversarial attacks, ensuring the reliability and security of multimedia analysis systems [10].

Lifelong Learning and Continual Adaptation: Deep learning models should be able to continually adapt and learn from evolving multimedia data over time. Future directions involve investigating lifelong learning approaches that can handle concept drift, incremental learning, and dynamic environments, enabling models to adapt and improve with new data.

Multi-Domain and Multi-Task Learning: Multi-domain deep learning is promising. Sharing knowledge and dependencies aids multimedia analysis systems.

Deep learning for multimedia analysis improves model correctness, interpretability, efficiency, and scalability, enabling additional multimedia data applications and real-world effects [11].

18.3 METHODOLOGY

18.3.1 Data Set Description

Multimedia analysis deep learning requires data sets for model training and evaluation. Multimedia deep learning data sets have several significant traits:

Data Set Size: Missions determine data set size. Small data sets have hundreds or thousands of samples; large databases have millions. Data set size affects model generalization and robustness.

Modalities of Data: Multimedia data sets include images, text, audio, and video. Text and voice can accompany images and videos. Data may include image labels and video timestamps. Annotations provide labels or ground truth for multimedia data, thereby facilitating supervised learning. Annotations can include image-level or pixel-level labels, bounding boxes for object detection, sequence labels for action recognition, and textual descriptions for image captioning, among others, depending on the task. Unsupervised or weakly supervised data sets may contain fewer annotations or rely on alternative supervision sources [12].

Diversity and Variability: For training robust and generalizable deep learning models, a diverse data set is essential. It should encompass a vast array of variations, such as various object categories, viewpoints, lighting conditions, background noise, and audio characteristics. The data set should capture the variability of the actual world to ensure that models can handle a variety of scenarios and perform well with unobserved data.

Data Split: It is common practice to split data sets into training, validation, and test sets when assessing a deep learning model's efficacy. Models are constructed utilizing the training set, validated utilizing the validation set, and then evaluated utilizing the test set. Correctly dividing the data permits objective testing and extrapolation of the model's results.

Dataset Origins: It is possible to obtain data sets for multimedia analysis from various sources. They can be curated for a specific task or application, such as ImageNet or COCO benchmark data sets for image classification and object detection, respectively. Real-world multimedia data can also be collected from online platforms such as social media platforms and video-sharing websites. It is crucial to consider the data sources and any inherent biases [13].

Data Pre-Processing: Pre-processing steps are applied to prepare the data set for deep learning. This can include resizing images or videos to a standard size, normalizing pixel values, applying data augmentation techniques to increase data diversity, or encoding text into numerical representations, among other preprocessing steps specific to the task at hand.

Data Availability and Accessibility: The availability and accessibility of the data set are important considerations for research and reproducibility. Openly available data sets facilitate the comparison of results and the advancement of the field. Proper documentation and data distribution ensure that researchers can access and utilize the data set effectively.

18.3.2 Deep Learning Architectures

DL designs used in multimedia analysis leverage neural network models to process and analyze multimedia data. Here are some popular deep learning architectures commonly employed in multimedia analysis:

Convolutional Neural Networks (CNNs): In the realm of image and video analysis, CNNs see extensive use. Their visual feature representations are learned in a hierarchical fashion over several convolutional layers. In a variety of computer vision applications, including image classification, object recognition, and picture segmentation, CNNs have excelled.

Recurrent Neural Networks (RNNs): For sequential data processing, such as in speech recognition, language modeling, and video captioning, RNNs are frequently utilized. By including feedback links that permit information flow through time, RNNs are able to manage sequential dependencies. Two well-known RNN versions are the LSTM and the GRU.

Transformer Networks: Recent years have seen a rise in the use of transformer networks for NLP and other multimodal applications. They rely on the model's attention mechanism, which zeroes down the most important bits of an input sequence. Machine translation, visual question answering, and image captioning are just a few of the areas where transformers have shown to be effective.

Generative Adversarial Networks (GANs): Two neural networks, called a "generator" and a "discriminator," make up GANs, making them a type of generative model. New samples of data that are similar to the training data can be generated using GANs. They have been applied to tasks like image synthesis, video generation, and audio generation [7].

Autoencoders: Autoencoders are unsupervised learning models utilized in data compression and representation learning. They are made up of an encoder network, which transforms data into a representation in a low-dimensional latent space, and a decoder network, which uses this representation to reconstruct the original data. Image denoising, anomaly detection, and dimensionality reduction are only a few of the applications of autoencoders.

Siamese Networks: Siamese networks are used for similarity-based tasks, such as face recognition and image retrieval. They consist of two or more identical subnetworks that share weights. Siamese networks are taught to embed input samples into a common space where the similarity or dissimilarity between samples can be measured.

Multimodal Fusion Networks: Multimodal fusion networks use audio, video, and text. Deep learning analyzes multimodal data collaboratively. Early, late, and attention-based fusion exist.

Graph Neural Networks (GNNs): GNNs process social networks, knowledge graphs, and 3D point clouds. GNNs record graph dependencies for social network analysis, recommendation systems, and 3D object recognition.

18.3.2.1 Convolutional Neural Networks (CNNs)

CNNs have revolutionized multimedia analysis by attaining cutting-edge performance on a variety of tasks. CNNs are particularly well suited for processing grid-like data such as images and videos. Here's how CNNs are used in deep learning for multimedia analysis:

Image Classification: CNNs are widely employed for image classification tasks. They can learn to automatically extract hierarchical representations of visual features from raw image pixels. By stacking multiple convolutional layers, CNNs can capture low-level features like edges and textures and gradually learn high-level features like shapes and objects. The final layers of the network classify the image into different categories.

Object Detection: Object detection, which employs CNNs, entails locating and categorizing items in a picture. The object bounding boxes and objects within them can be identified and classified using CNN-based object detection models such region-based CNNs (R-CNN), fast R-CNN, and faster R-CNN, which use region proposal methods and convolutional layers.

Image Segmentation: For image segmentation jobs where semantic labels for individual pixels are needed, CNNs are frequently used. U-Net topologies and fully convolutional networks (FCNs) are frequently employed for picture segmentation. FCNs utilize upsampling and skip connections to generate pixel-wise segmentation maps, while U-Net architectures use an encoder-decoder structure to capture detailed local information.

Image Generation: CNNs are utilized for image generation tasks, where the goal is to generate new images that resemble the training data. Generative adversarial networks (GANs) employ CNNs as generators and discriminators to generate realistic images. Variational autoencoders (VAEs) also use CNN-based encoders and decoders to generate images from a learned latent space.

Style Transfer: CNNs are used for artistic style transfer, where the style of one image is applied to the content of another image. CNN-based models, such as neural style

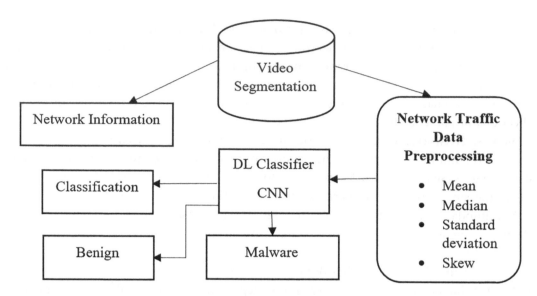

FIGURE 18.2   Proposed diagram of the CNN model.

transfer, learn to separate the content and style representations of images and transfer the style to new images, creating visually appealing artistic compositions.

Video Analysis: CNNs are applied to video analysis tasks, such as action recognition and video captioning. 3D CNNs extend the 2D convolutional operations to the temporal dimension, enabling the modeling of spatiotemporal patterns in videos. Recurrent neural networks (RNNs) combined with CNNs can capture temporal dependencies in videos for tasks like action recognition and video captioning [14].

Transfer Learning: CNNs trained on large-scale data sets, such as ImageNet, have learned rich and generic visual representations. Transfer learning leverages these pre-trained CNN models as a starting point for new tasks with limited data. By fine-tuning or extracting features from pre-trained CNNs, multimedia analysis tasks can benefit from the learned representations and improve performance, as shown in Figure 18.2 [15].

Multimodal Fusion: CNNs are utilized for multimodal fusion tasks that involve combining information from multiple modalities, such as images, text, and audio. CNNs are employed to process the visual modality, while other DL models, like RNNs or transformers, handle other modalities. The fused representations from different modalities can enhance tasks such as image captioning, cross-modal retrieval, or multimodal sentiment analysis [16].

18.3.3 Recurrent Neural Networks (RNNs)

Speech recognition, video captioning, and sentiment analysis are just a few examples of sequential data types that significantly benefit from the application of recurrent neural networks (RNNs) in deep learning for multimedia analysis. RNNs maintain a state that remembers the context of prior inputs in order to process sequential data. RNNs are utilized as follows for multimedia analysis:

Speech Recognition: RNNs are frequently used for speech recognition tasks where the ultimate goal is to convert audio to text. RNNs interpret audio signals as sequential data in order to identify temporal dependencies in the spoken stream. LSTM and GRU networks are two prominent RNN variants utilized in voice recognition due to their ability to effectively simulate long-range dependencies.

Video Captioning: RNNs are utilized for video captioning, which generates textual descriptions or captions for videos. An RNN-based model encapsulates the visual information of an input video using CNNs and then uses an RNN, such as an LSTM, to generate a sequence of words that form a coherent caption. The RNN's concealed state captures temporal dependencies and video frame context.

Sentiment Analysis: RNNs classify text and multimedia emotions. RNNs can record sequential data and attach emotion to context when processing text or voice. RNNs enable sentiment analysts to assess long-term dependencies and context.

Action Recognition: RNNs recognize and classify actions in video frames. RNNs sequentially process video frames to capture temporal dynamics and interframe interactions for precise action and activity recognition.

Video Generation: RNNs are used with GANs to generate videos. RNN-based generators encode the temporal dependencies and structure of training films to generate new video sequences.

Temporal Modeling: RNNs model multimedia temporal analysis well. They exhibit long-term interconnectedness and temporal dynamics. RNNs analyze multimedia motion, temporal context, and sequential links.

Multimodal Fusion: RNNs are utilized for multimodal fusion tasks involving the combination of textual, visual, and auditory data, for example. RNNs are capable of processing sequential data from various modalities, thereby encoding temporal relationships and dependencies. By combining the RNNs' hidden states, the models can produce joint representations for multimodal analysis tasks.

Language Modeling: RNNs, especially LSTM and GRU variants, are extensively employed in language modeling. RNN-trained language models can predict the next word in a sequence based on the preceding context. Multimedia analysis requires language models for duties such as machine translation, text generation, and speech synthesis. Figure 18.3 [17] demonstrates that RNNs flourish at capturing sequential information and modeling temporal dependencies in multimedia analysis tasks. Their ability to maintain concealed states and record context over time makes them useful instrument for controlling the processing and acceptance of sequential data. However, RNNs have limitations such as vanishing gradients and limited memory, which has led to the development of more sophisticated architectures, such as transformer networks [18].

18.3.4 Transformers

Transformers have emerged as a potent architecture for deep learning in multimedia analysis, especially for tasks involving sequential and contextual data. Transformers were initially developed for natural language processing but have since been effectively applied

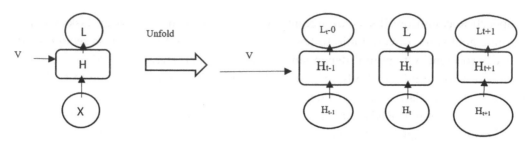

FIGURE 18.3   Proposed diagram of the RNN model.

to a variety of multimedia analysis tasks. Here is how transformers are used for multimedia analysis in deep learning:

Image and Video Captioning: Image and video captioning tasks have utilized transformers. Utilizing a combination of self-attention mechanisms and feed-forward networks, transformers can effectively recognize global dependencies and contextual information in images and videos. They are able to generate captions by focusing on germane visual characteristics and composing cogent textual descriptions.

Machine Translation: In machine translation tasks, such as multimodal translation, transformers have demonstrated significant progress. Transformers capture contextual information from both source and target languages using self-attention mechanisms, enabling accurate translation between different modalities, such as translating image descriptions to text or vice versa.

Speech Recognition: Transformers help sequential audio speech recognition. Transformers accurately transcribe audio signals by analyzing long-range dependencies and context.

Cross-Modal Retrieval: Cross-modal retrieval answers cross-modal questions. Transformer-based models can translate image searches into text. Transformers identify semantic parallels and linkages for cross-modal memory.

Visual Question Answering: Transformers have been utilized for visual question answering tasks in which the model must respond to image-based inquiries. Transformers can encode both the image features and the textual question, enabling the model to heed pertinent visual and textual information in order to generate accurate answers.

Video Action Recognition: Transformers have been extended to video action recognition tasks. By modeling spatiotemporal relationships in videos, transformers can capture long-term dependencies and contextual information across video frames. They have shown promising results in recognizing complex actions and activities.

Image Generation: Transformers have been used for image generation tasks, such as generating realistic images from scratch or completing missing parts of an image. By learning the distribution of image features and capturing global dependencies, transformers can generate high-quality images with fine-grained details.

Pretraining and Transfer Learning: Transformers have proven to be effective in pretraining models on large-scale data sets, such as self-supervised learning or language modeling. Pretrained transformers capture rich contextual representations, which can be transferred to downstream multimedia analysis tasks with limited labeled data, improving performance and efficiency.

Transformers excel at capturing long-range dependencies, contextual information, and global relationships in multimedia data. Their self-attention mechanism allows them to attend to relevant parts of the input, enabling effective modeling of complex relationships across modalities and sequences. Transformers have revolutionized multimedia analysis, pushing the boundaries of performance in various tasks and paving the way for advancements in understanding and processing multimedia content [19].

18.3.5 Experimental Setup

Models' efficacy in deep learning for multimedia analysis can be judged using a number of different measures. Metrics used for testing and measuring performance should be tailored to the job at hand and the information available. Common metrics used for assessment in multimedia analysis include:

Accuracy: In a classification task, accuracy is the percentage of occurrences that were properly labeled. Image classification, object detection, and emotion analysis are all typical applications. The accuracy of a prediction system is measured by how many of those forecasts came true.

Precision and Recall: In binary classification tasks like object detection and image segmentation, precision and recall are often employed metrics. Precision is the percentage of anticipated positive occurrences that were actually positive, whereas recall is the percentage of true positive instances that were accurately detected. If you're working with skewed data, you'll find these metrics especially helpful [20].

Intersection over Union (IoU): Object detection and picture segmentation are two common applications of IoU, which measures the degree to which anticipated and ground-truth regions coincide. It is determined by comparing the area of the anticipated and ground-truth regions and the area of the union of the two regions. When the IoU is high, the localization precision is also high.

$$IoU = \frac{TP}{(TP + FP + FN)} \tag{18.1}$$

Mean Average Precision (mAP): mAP is usually used to assess object detection models. It procedures the accuracy at different levels of recall by considering multiple detection thresholds. The mAP is the average of the AP (average precision) values across different classes or object categories.

$$MAP = \frac{1}{n} \sum_{k=1}^{k=n} AP_k \tag{18.2}$$

Mean Squared Error (MSE): MSE is often used in regression tasks, such as image super-resolution or depth estimation. It measures the average squared difference between predicted and ground truth values. Lower MSE values indicate better accuracy in regression tasks.

$$MSE = \frac{1}{n} \sum_{i=1}^{n} (Yi - \acute{Y}i)^2 \qquad (18.3)$$

Mean Absolute Error (MAE): MAE is similar to MSE but procedures the average absolute difference between expected and ground truth values. It is also used in regression tasks and provides a more interpretable measure compared to MSE.

$$MAE = \frac{1}{n} \sum_{i=1}^{n} |Yi - \acute{Y}i| \qquad (18.4)$$

Mean Opinion Score (MOS): MOS is commonly used in multimedia quality assessment tasks, such as image or video quality assessment. It is obtained through subjective human ratings, where observers rate the quality of multimedia content. The MOS is calculated as the average rating across different observers.

$$MOS = \frac{\sum_{n=1}^{N} R_n}{N} \qquad (18.5)$$

Retrieval-Based Metrics: In tasks like cross-modal retrieval or image/video search, retrieval-based metrics are used. These include metrics like precision, recall, mean average precision, and standardized discounted cumulative gain (NDCG), which measure the relevance and ranking accuracy of retrieved results.

18.4 RESULTS AND DISCUSSION

18.4.1 Performance of Deep Learning Models

Deep learning models have demonstrated remarkable performance in various multimedia analysis tasks, including image classification, object detection, image segmentation, video understanding, and speech recognition. Here are some notable examples of their performance in different multimedia analysis domains:

Image Classification: DL, particularly CNNs, have achieved remarkable accuracy in image classification tasks. For instance, models like ResNet, Inception, and DenseNet have achieved top-1 accuracy of over 90% on benchmark data sets such as ImageNet, which contains millions of labeled images across thousands of classes.

Object Detection: Deep learning models have significantly advanced object detection performance. Models like faster R-CNN, YOLO (you only look once), and SSD (single shot multiBox detector) have achieved high accuracy in detecting and localizing objects within images or videos. These models provide real-time or near real-time inference speed while maintaining competitive accuracy [21].

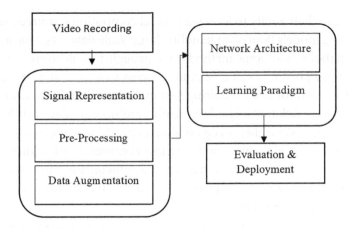

FIGURE 18.4   Workflow diagram of the video segmentation.

Image Segmentation: DL models, such as U-Net, Mask R-CNN, and DeepLab, have made substantial progress in image segmentation tasks. These models can accurately segment and classify individual pixels or regions within images, enabling applications like medical image analysis, autonomous driving, and semantic scene understanding.

Video Understanding: Deep learning models have been applied to video understanding tasks, including action recognition, video summarization, and video captioning. Recurrent neural networks (RNNs), 3D CNNs, and attention mechanisms have been employed to capture spatiotemporal features and temporal dependencies in video data. These models have achieved state-of-the-art performance in large-scale video data sets such as Kinetics and ActivityNet.

Speech Recognition: RNNs, LSTMs, and transformer models changed speech recognition. LAS, DeepSpeech, and transformer-based models accurately transcribe spoken language, improving voice assistants, transcription services, and automated speech recognition.

Cross-modal Analysis: Deep learning models caption photos, fuse audio-visuals, and synthesize text-to-images. Deep learning algorithms may find important relationships and create sophisticated multimedia from images, words, and audio. These models create captions and graphics from text, as shown in Figure 18.4 [22].

18.4.2 Comparison with Traditional Methods

Deep learning methods have shown significant advantages over traditional methods in multimedia analysis tasks. Here are some key areas where deep learning outperforms traditional approaches:

Feature Learning: Traditional methods frequently rely on handcrafted features created by domain specialists. These features require manual engineering and may not effectively capture complex data forms. In contrast, deep learning models can autonomously learn hierarchical data representations, allowing them to discover and exploit intricate features from unprocessed data. This end-to-end learning process frequently results in superior performance and eliminates the requirement for manual feature engineering.

Scalability: Due to their ability to leverage parallel computing resources, such as GPUs or TPUs, deep learning models flourish at handling large-scale data sets. Due to computational and memory limitations, traditional methods may struggle to scale to enormous quantities of data. Deep learning algorithms can efficiently process vast quantities of multimedia data, making them well suited for tasks requiring vast quantities of training data.

Complex Nonlinear Relationships: Frequently, multimedia data exhibits intricate and nonlinear relationships. With their deep architectures and nonlinear activation functions, deep learning models can effectively capture these complex relationships. They can learn intricate patterns and representations that may be difficult for conventional methods to capture. This benefit is especially evident in tasks like image classification, object detection, and speech recognition.

Transfer Learning: Pre-trained DL models on massive data sets can be fine-tuned for less labeled data workloads. Knowledge transfer helps when collecting and annotating massive amounts of data for each activity is impractical. Traditional methods require extensive re-engineering and parameter tweaking for different data sets or applications.

End-to-End Learning: Deep learning models learn directly from the raw input data, enabling end-to-end learning without the need for manual feature extraction or pre-processing steps. Traditional methods often involve multiple stages of processing, including feature extraction, dimensionality reduction, and classification. Deep learning's ability to learn useful representations directly from raw data simplifies the overall workflow and reduces human effort [23].

Despite these advantages, there are scenarios where traditional methods may still be relevant and competitive:

Limited Data Availability: DL models typically involve large amounts of labeled data for effective training. In cases where labeled data is scarce or costly to obtain, traditional methods with domain-specific knowledge and feature engineering techniques may perform better.

Interpretable Results: Deep learning models are often considered black boxes, as the complex architectures and high-dimensional representations make it challenging to interpret their decision-making process. Traditional methods, with their explicit feature engineering, may provide more interpretable results, which can be crucial in certain domains, such as medical diagnosis or legal applications.

Computation and Memory Efficiency: Deep learning models, particularly large-scale architectures, can be computationally expensive and memory-intensive. Traditional methods, with their lightweight algorithms and simpler models, may offer faster inference times and require fewer computational resources.

It's important to carefully consider the specific requirements, constraints, and characteristics of the multimedia analysis task at hand when choosing between deep learning and traditional methods. In many cases, deep learning has demonstrated superior performance and is the preferred choice due to its ability to learn complex representations and leverage large-scale data. However, traditional methods may still be relevant in certain scenarios, depending on the available data, interpretability requirements, and computational constraints [24].

18.4.3 Insights and Analysis

Deep learning for multimedia analysis has provided numerous insights and advancements in various domains. Here are some key insights and analyses resulting from deep learning in multimedia analysis:

Improved Accuracy: Deep learning models have suggestively advanced the high-tech accuracy in multimedia analysis tasks. They have achieved remarkable performance in image classification, object detection, image segmentation, video understanding, and speech recognition. Deep learning's ability to learn intricate patterns and exploit complex relationships in data has led to breakthroughs in accuracy, surpassing traditional methods.

Feature Extraction: Deep learning models have demonstrated the power of automatic feature extraction from raw data. Instead of relying on handcrafted features, deep learning algorithms learn hierarchical representations that capture essential features and patterns directly from the data. This feature learning capability has improved the performance and robustness of multimedia analysis models, eliminating the need for manual feature engineering.

Transfer Learning and Generalization: Transfer learning helps multimedia analysis with pre-trained deep learning models. Big data set trained models can be fine-tuned or used as feature extractors for applications with less labeled data. Models can compete with smaller labeled data sets via transfer learning.

Handling Large-Scale Data: DL's large data set management has changed multimedia analysis. GPUs and TPUs analyze large multimedia data to train and infer deep learning models. Scalable deep learning models thrive in image categorization, object detection, and video understanding.

Multimodal Fusion: Deep learning analyzes images, words, and noises. Multimodal models aid picture captioning, audio-visual fusion, and text-to-image synthesis. Deep learning's multimodal data management improves multimedia comprehension and generation.

Interpretability and Explainability Challenges: With their complex architectures and high-dimensional representations, deep learning models frequently lack interpretability and explainability. Understanding the decision-making process and providing human-interpretable explanations for deep learning models continue to be active areas of study. In domains where transparency, accountability, and interpretability are crucial, such as healthcare and legal applications, addressing these challenges is essential [25].

Robustness to Variability: Various forms of variability in multimedia data, such as viewpoint changes, occlusions, variations in illumination, and background noise, have been shown to have little effect on deep learning models. The capacity of deep learning models to learn abstract and invariant representations from large and diverse data sets has enhanced their performance in complex real-world scenarios.

Real-Time and Interactive Applications: Models of deep learning have enabled real-time and interactive multimedia analysis applications. With advances in model architectures, hardware acceleration, and optimization techniques, deep learning models can provide quick and responsive results, enabling applications like real-time object detection, live video analytics, and interactive voice assistants.

Transferability Across Domains: DL models trained on one domain are frequently transferable or adaptable to related domains with minimal modifications. This transferability has accelerated research and applications in multimedia analysis across multiple domains, such as medical imaging, autonomous driving, surveillance, entertainment, and human-computer interaction.

Ethical Considerations: Deep learning's impact on multimedia analysis raises ethical considerations, including privacy, bias, fairness, and accountability. As deep learning models increasingly become part of critical decision-making processes, ensuring transparency, fairness, and responsible deployment of these models is crucial.

18.5 CASE STUDIES

18.5.1 Case Study 1: Image Classification

Deep learning has made remarkable strides in the area of image categorization, a fundamental issue in multimedia analysis. DL models, in particular CNNs, have revolutionized image categorization by outperforming baseline methods and attaining state-of-the-art performance. The following are some of the most essential features of deep learning for image classification based on multimedia analysis:

Convolutional Neural Networks (CNNs): CNNs serve a crucial role in the classification of images in deep learning. These designs are intended to capture the spatial relationships and hierarchical nuances of images. CNN consists of multiple layers, including convolutional, pooling, and entirely connected. While convolutional layers are responsible for learning neighborhood-specific patterns and characteristics, pooling layers then sample these characteristics while preserving context. Finally, these characteristics are combined in completely interconnected layers for categorization.

End-to-End Learning: Deep learning models for image categorization no longer require manual feature extraction because they can learn directly from the raw pixel values of images. This full-stack learning approach teaches models the characteristics and representations that will enable them to perform the classification task with the utmost accuracy. The effectiveness and accuracy of image categorization systems have benefited tremendously from this characteristic.

Transfer Learning: Transfer learning has benefited deep learning for image categorization tremendously. By training on large-scale image data sets such as ImageNet, CNN models such as VGGNet, ResNet, and Inception have acquired extensive and generalized picture representations. These models have been trained and can be used as feature extractors for novel tasks or refined using domain-specific data sets. Transfer learning serves to train and improve the performance of image classification models when only a small amount of labeled data is available.

Data Augmentation: In order to increase the diversity and quantity of training data, data augmentation techniques are frequently employed in deep learning models for image classification. Enhancement techniques include randomly rotating, translating, scaling, inverting, or adding noise to images. Data augmentation helps enhance the model's generalization to unknown data and reduces overfitting by exposing the model to diverse variants of the training data.

Loss Functions: Deep learning models for image classification use appropriate loss functions to guide the training process. Commonly used loss functions include categorical cross-entropy and softmax loss. These loss functions compare the predicted probabilities of the model with the ground truth labels, penalizing incorrect predictions and updating the model's parameters accordingly during the training process [26].

Optimization and Regularization Techniques: Various optimization techniques and regularization methods are employed to improve the training process and prevent overfitting. Techniques such as stochastic gradient descent (SGD) with momentum, adaptive optimization algorithms (e.g., Adam), and learning rate schedules are used to optimize the model's parameters effectively. Regularization techniques like failure, batch normalization, and weight deterioration help stop overfitting and increase generalization.

Evaluation Metrics: Evaluation of image classification models involves assessing their performance using appropriate metrics. Common evaluation metrics include accuracy, precision, recall, F1-score, and top-k accuracy. Accuracy measures the percentage of correctly classified images, while top-k accuracy accounts for correct predictions within the top-k predicted labels, allowing for partial correctness in multi-label scenarios.

Large-Scale Data Sets: Deep learning models for image classification are often trained and evaluated on large-scale benchmark data sets like ImageNet, CIFAR-10, or COCO. These data sets contain millions of labeled images across multiple categories, providing a diverse and challenging set of examples for training and evaluation. Large data sets guarantee that models can discover robust and generalizable representations.

Deep learning has revolutionized image classification in multimedia analysis, enabling models to achieve exceptional accuracy and generalize well to data that has never been seen. Combining CNN architectures, end-to-end learning, transfer learning, data augmentation, and optimization techniques has propelled deep learning models to the vanguard of image classification tasks, thereby establishing their dominance.

18.5.2 Case Study 2: Video Analysis

Video analysis is a difficult and crucial task in multimedia analysis, and deep learning has made significant contributions to this field. Deep learning models have shown extraordinary performance in a variety of video analysis tasks, including action recognition, video segmentation, video captioning, and video summarization. Here are several of the most crucial facets of deep learning for video analysis in multimedia analysis:

Modeling Spatiotemporal Data: Models for video analysis that utilize deep learning capture both spatial and temporal information in order to comprehend the dynamics and movements within videos. Commonly used to derive spatiotemporal features from video frames are convolutional neural networks (CNNs) enhanced with 3D convolutions or two-stream architectures. These models can learn to recognize patterns and actions by analyzing appearance and motion information across successive frames.

Action Recognition: Action recognition seeks to identify and categorize specific actions or activities conducted in videos. Significant advancements have been made by deep learning models in this domain. On benchmark action recognition data sets such as UCF101 and Kinetics, two-stream networks, I3D (Inflated 3D ConvNet), and TSN (Temporal Segment Networks) models have achieved state-of-the-art performance. These models can capture temporal dependencies and subtle motion indicators for accurate action recognition and classification.

Video Segmentation: Deep learning has contributed to tasks involving the segmentation of videos into distinct regions or objects of interest. Models like 3D U-Net, temporal convolutional networks (TCNs), and mask R-CNN have been applied to video segmentation, enabling pixel-level or object-level segmentation in videos. These models exploit both spatial and temporal information to provide accurate and temporally consistent segmentation results.

Video Captioning: Deep learning models have been employed for video captioning, which involves generating natural language descriptions or captions for videos. Models like encoder-decoder architectures with attention mechanisms, such as show, attend, and tell (SAT) or transformer-based models, have shown promising results in generating coherent and descriptive captions for videos. These models learn to attend to relevant video frames and generate captions based on the learned spatiotemporal context.

Video Summarization: Deep learning models have been used for video summarization, aiming to condense long videos into shorter summaries that capture the key moments or highlights. Recurrent neural networks (RNNs) or reinforcement learning–based approaches have been applied to extract salient frames or select representative video segments. These models learn to identify important content or events within videos and generate informative summaries as shown in Table 18.1 [27].

Temporal Action Localization: Deep learning models have been developed for temporal action localization, which involves localizing and classifying actions in videos at the temporal level. Models like TAL-Net, BMN (boundary-matching network), or TSN with temporal action proposals enable accurate action localization, identifying the temporal boundaries and class labels for specific actions within videos. These models consider the temporal context and discriminative features to precisely locate actions.

Large-Scale Video Datasets: Deep learning models for video analysis are often trained and evaluated on large-scale video data sets like Kinetics, ActivityNet, or THUMOS. These data sets contain thousands of videos with diverse action categories, providing a rich and challenging training and evaluation environment. Large-scale video data sets facilitate the training of deep learning models to learn discriminative spatiotemporal representations and generalize well to unseen videos.

Real-Time Video Analysis: Deep learning models have made real-time video analysis feasible by leveraging hardware acceleration and optimization techniques. Efficient model

TABLE 18.1   Traditional versus Deep Learning Methods

	Proposal-generation, refinement and merging for video object segmentation	
Year	Description1	Description2
2012	• GMM-background subtraction • (Zivkovic et al., 2006) • NN-background subtraction	• (Culibrk et al., 2007) • Level set-based propagation (Chockalingan et al., 2009)
2015	• Point track-based • VOS • (Brox et al., 2010b)	• Object proposal- based VOS (Lee et al, 2011) • MRF-based propagation (Tai et al., 2012)
2017	• Saliency-based VOS (Wang et al., 2015)	
2018	• Deep network-based VOS (FusionSeg) (Jain et al., 2017) • Online fine-tuning (OSVOS) (Calles et al., 2017)	• Mask Propagation (MaskTrack) (Perazzi et al., 2017)
2019	• Bi-directional propagation (Dyenet) (Li et al., 2018)	• Long-term spatial-temporal prop. (S2S) (Plu et al., 2018)
2020	• Co-attention-based VOS (COSNet) (Lu et al., 2019)	• Memory-based VOS (STM) (Oh et al, 2019)
2021	• Visual attention-based • UVOS (AGS) (Wang et al., 2020)	• Discriminative target model-based VOS (FRTM) (Robinson et al., 2020)
2022	• Transformers for VOS (AOT) (Yang et al., 2021a)	• Space-time com. • net (STCN) (Chang et al., 2001)

architectures, model compression, and deployment on specialized hardware, such as GPUs or TPUs, enable fast inference times, allowing real-time video analysis applications like surveillance, autonomous driving, or live video analytics [28].

18.5.3 Case Study 3: Multimodal Learning

Multimodal learning is a powerful approach in deep learning for multimedia analysis that aims to leverage and fuse information from multiple modalities, such as images, texts, audio, or sensor data. By combining information from different modalities, multimodal learning enables a richer and more comprehensive understanding and analysis of multimedia data. Here are some key aspects of multimodal learning in deep learning for multimedia analysis:

Modality Fusion: Multimodal learning focuses on effectively fusing information from different modalities to create a unified representation. Various fusion techniques can be employed, including early fusion, where modalities are combined at the input level, late fusion, where modalities are combined at higher layers and intermediate fusion, where fusion occurs at intermediate layers. Fusion methods can range from simple concatenation or weighted averaging to more complex attention mechanisms or graph-based fusion [15].

Cross-Modal Representation Learning: Multimodal learning involves learning joint representations that capture the correlations and dependencies between different modalities. Deep learning models can learn shared representations by training on multimodal data, allowing them to encode and capture relevant information from each modality. This joint representation learning facilitates tasks such as cross-modal retrieval, where one modality can be used to query and retrieve information from another modality.

Multimodal Fusion Architectures: Deep learning architectures for multimodal learning include multimodal neural networks (MNNs), multimodal recurrent neural networks (MRNNs), and graph-based models. MNNs combine separate networks for each modality, which are then fused at different levels to learn joint representations. MRNNs extend recurrent neural networks to model temporal dependencies across modalities. Graph-based models capture interactions and relationships between modalities using graph structures [29].

Multimodal Tasks: Multimodal learning addresses various tasks in multimedia analysis. These tasks include multimodal sentiment analysis, where emotions or sentiments are inferred from text and associated images or videos. Other tasks include multimodal machine translation, where translation occurs between languages using both textual and visual information, and multimodal image captioning, where descriptions are generated for images using both visual and textual modalities.

Data Acquisition and Pre-Processing: Multimodal learning often requires multimodal data sets that provide labeled examples for different modalities. Data acquisition can involve collecting and annotating data from various sources, including images, texts, audio recordings, or sensor data. Pre-processing steps are required to normalize and align data across modalities, ensuring that they can be effectively fused and processed by the multimodal learning models.

Transfer Learning in Multimodal Settings: Transfer learning plays a crucial role in multimodal learning, similar to unimodal deep learning. Pre-trained models on large-scale unimodal data sets such as image or text data sets can be utilized as feature extractors for specific modalities in multimodal tasks. These pre-trained models capture general knowledge and features, which can be leveraged to learn multimodal representations with limited labeled multimodal data.

Challenges in Multimodal Learning: Multimodal learning poses several challenges, including data alignment, modality imbalance, and heterogeneity. Aligning data from different modalities and ensuring consistent annotations can be complex and time-consuming. Modalities can also have varying amounts of available data, leading to imbalanced learning scenarios. Furthermore, heterogeneity in data distribution, noise levels, or modal interactions can affect the performance of multimodal learning models.

Applications of Multimodal Learning: Multimodal learning finds applications in various domains. In healthcare, multimodal learning can integrate medical images, patient records, and clinical notes to enhance diagnosis and treatment. In autonomous driving, fusion of visual, lidar, and radar sensor data enables robust perception and understanding of the environment. Multimodal learning is also employed in human-computer interaction and multimedia retrieval, as shown in Figure 18.5 [30].

Machine Learning Use Case

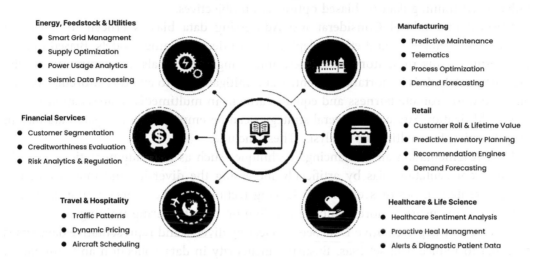

Energy, Feedstock & Utilities
- Smart Grid Managment
- Supply Optimization
- Power Usage Analytics
- Seismic Data Processing

Financial Services
- Customer Segmentation
- Creditworthiness Evaluation
- Risk Analytics & Regulation

Travel & Hospitality
- Traffic Patterns
- Dynamic Pricing
- Aircraft Scheduling

Manufacturing
- Predictive Maintenance
- Telematics
- Process Optimization
- Demand Forecasting

Retail
- Customer Roll & Lifetime Value
- Predictive Inventory Planning
- Recommendation Engines
- Demand Forecasting

Healthcare & Life Science
- Healthcare Sentiment Analysis
- Proactive Heal Managment
- Alerts & Diagnostic Patient Data

FIGURE 18.5 Proposed diagram of the ML use cases.

18.6 CHALLENGES AND LIMITATIONS

18.6.1 Data Bias

Data bias is an important consideration in deep learning for multimedia analysis. Bias can arise in various forms and can significantly impact the performance and fairness of the models. Here are some key aspects of data bias in deep learning for multimedia analysis:

Data Set Bias: Data set bias refers to the presence of systematic and unintended biases within the training data. These biases can stem from various sources, including the data collection process, annotation process, or inherent societal biases. For example, if a data set predominantly consists of images of certain demographics or cultural contexts, the trained model may exhibit biases towards those groups, leading to unfair or inaccurate predictions [29].

Label Bias: Label bias occurs when the annotations or labels in the training data are themselves biased. Annotators may have subjective judgments or implicit biases when labeling the data, leading to inconsistencies or unfairness. Label bias can propagate through the training process, affecting the model's predictions and reinforcing the biases present in the data.

Representation Bias: Representation bias arises when the training data does not adequately represent the diversity and distribution of the real-world data. If certain classes or scenarios are underrepresented in the training data, the model may struggle to generalize well to unseen examples, leading to biased or inaccurate predictions. Representation bias can result from various factors, including data collection procedures, sample selection, or inherent biases in the data sources.

Algorithmic Bias: Deep learning models can also introduce bias through the learning process itself. Biases can emerge if the model is trained on data that reflects or amplifies existing societal biases. The model may learn to make predictions that align with these biases, perpetuating discrimination or unfairness. Algorithmic bias can also occur due to imbalanced training data or biased optimization objectives.

Fairness and Ethical Considerations: Addressing data bias is crucial for ensuring fairness, accountability, and ethical deployment of deep learning models. Biased models can result in discriminatory outcomes, impacting individuals or communities disproportionately. It is important to identify and mitigate bias to avoid reinforcing societal biases and to promote fairness and equal treatment in multimedia analysis applications.

Bias Mitigation Strategies: Several strategies can be employed to mitigate data bias in deep learning for multimedia analysis. These include:

Data Augmentation and Balancing: Techniques such as data augmentation can help address representation bias by artificially increasing the diversity and quantity of underrepresented classes or scenarios. Balancing techniques, like oversampling or undersampling, can ensure a more equitable distribution of data during training.

Diverse and Representative Data Sets: Collecting diverse and representative data sets is essential to reduce data set bias. Ensuring inclusivity in data collection and annotation processes can help mitigate biases related to demographics, cultures, or perspectives.

Bias-Aware Training: Training models with explicit consideration of fairness and bias can help reduce algorithmic bias. Incorporating fairness metrics or regularization terms in the training process can encourage models to make unbiased predictions and avoid discriminatory behaviors.

Post-Processing and Calibration: Post-processing techniques, such as threshold adjustment or calibration, can be applied to adjust the model's outputs to align with desired fairness objectives. These techniques can help correct bias introduced during the training process.

Transparency and Auditability: Providing transparency in the training pipeline and making the decision-making process of the models interpretable can enable external audits and facilitate the identification and mitigation of biases.

Addressing data bias in deep learning for multimedia analysis is an ongoing research area. It requires a multi-faceted approach involving careful data collection, annotation, model training, and evaluation to ensure fair and unbiased outcomes.

18.6.2 Interpretability

Interpretability in deep learning for multimedia analysis refers to the ability to understand and explain the decision-making process and underlying factors of deep learning models. Deep learning models, particularly deep neural networks, are often considered black boxes due to their complex architectures and large number of parameters. However, interpretability is crucial for building trust, understanding model behavior, and ensuring ethical deployment [31]. Here are some aspects of interpretability in deep learning for multimedia analysis:

Model Visualization: Visualization techniques can provide insights into the internal workings of deep learning models. For example, visualizing the activation maps or feature maps at different layers of a convolutional neural network (CNN) can help understand what visual patterns or features the model focuses on during classification or object recognition tasks. Techniques like Grad-CAM can highlight regions of input images that contribute most to the model's decision.

Attention Mechanisms: Attention mechanisms play a vital role in interpreting deep learning models. They allow the model to focus on specific regions or elements of the input data that are relevant to the task at hand. Attention mechanisms provide a form of interpretability by highlighting essential regions or by providing weights indicating the contribution of various parts of the input, such as particular image regions or words.

Saliency Maps: Saliency maps show image prediction. The model's output gradients relative to the input image exhibit saliency maps. Saliency maps explain the model's logic and forecast picture.

Feature Attribution: Inputs determine the model's decision. These algorithms detect color, texture, and geometry model prediction. LIME and integrated gradients favor multimedia.

Rule Extraction: Deep learning models learn human-understandable rules or decision boundaries. These rules clarify the model's behavior and predictions. Decision trees and symbolic rule extraction can comprehend deep learning model rules [32].

Model Compression: The development of effective model architectures is a fundamental aspect of computational efficiency. Model architectures can be optimized by reducing the number of parameters, network depth, or network girth. Techniques such as network pruning, quantization, and knowledge distillation can be used to reduce model size and computational needs without sacrificing performance significantly.

Counterfactual Explanations: Counterfactual explanations aim to provide explanations by showing how changing the input data would lead to different model predictions. By generating alternative inputs that would result in different outcomes, counterfactual explanations help understand the factors or attributes that have the most impact on the model's decisions. These explanations can be particularly useful in multimedia analysis tasks, such as image classification or recommendation systems.

Ethical Considerations: Interpretability in deep learning for multimedia analysis also has ethical implications. Transparent and interpretable models enable accountability, fairness, and bias detection. It allows stakeholders to identify and rectify biases, address ethical concerns, and ensure that the models are making decisions in an explainable and fair manner [33].

Interpretability techniques in deep learning for multimedia analysis are an active research area. They aim to bridge the gap between the complex nature of deep learning models and the need for understanding and trust in their decision-making process [25].

18.6.3 Computational Efficiency

Computational efficiency is a crucial consideration in deep learning for multimedia analysis, especially when dealing with large-scale data sets and complex models. Efficient algorithms and architectures are essential for practical deployment, real-time processing, and scalability. Here are some aspects of computational efficiency in deep learning for multimedia analysis:

Model Architecture Optimization: Designing efficient model architectures is a key aspect of computational efficiency. Model architectures can be optimized by reducing the number of parameters, depth, or width of the network. Techniques like network pruning, quantization, and knowledge distillation can be employed to reduce model size and computational requirements without significant loss in performance.

Parallelization and Distributed Computing: Models based on deep learning can benefit from parallel computing techniques that increase computational efficiency. GPUs and specialized hardware such as TPUs are utilized extensively to accelerate deep learning computations. Using parallelization techniques such as data parallelism or model parallelism, the burden can be distributed across multiple devices or machines, resulting in faster training and inference times.

Model Compression: The objective of model compression techniques is to reduce the size of deep learning models, thereby increasing computational efficiency. Pruning, which eliminates unnecessary connections or filters, and quantization, which reduces the precision of weights and activations, are techniques that can substantially reduce model size and computational requirements. Compressed models are deployable on devices with limited resources and can be processed more efficiently in cloud environments.

Efficient Training Strategies: It can be computationally intensive to train deep learning models on massive multimedia data sets. Mini-batch training, gradient accumulation, and asynchronous training are examples of effective training strategies that can be used to reduce the memory footprint and increase training performance. Transfer learning and pretraining on large unimodal data sets can also be used to leverage existing knowledge and accelerate the training of multimodal tasks.

Approximation Techniques: Approximation techniques aim to strike a balance between model accuracy and computational efficiency. Techniques like low-rank approximation, tensor decomposition, or knowledge distillation can be used to approximate complex models or replace computationally expensive operations with more efficient alternatives. These techniques help reduce the computational cost while maintaining reasonable performance levels.

Hardware Acceleration: Deep learning for multimedia analysis can benefit from specialized hardware acceleration. GPUs, TPUs, or dedicated AI chips are designed to accelerate deep learning computations and provide significant speed-ups compared to traditional CPUs. Leveraging hardware acceleration can lead to faster training and inference times, enabling real-time or near-real-time multimedia analysis applications [34].

Model Parallelism for Large-Scale Models: Creation of efficient model architectures is a crucial element of computational efficiency. It is possible to optimize model architectures by reducing the number of parameters, network depth, and network circumference.

Quantitative Trade-Offs: There are frequent trade-offs between computational efficiency and other performance metrics, such as model accuracy or memory requirements. It is essential to quantify these trade-offs and discover the optimal balance for the multimedia analysis task. Techniques such as model profiling and resource-aware training can aid in the analysis and optimization of the computational efficiency of deep learning models, taking into account the intended performance metrics.

Effective deep learning for multimedia analysis requires a combination of algorithmic optimization, hardware acceleration, and intelligent engineering techniques. By resolving computational efficiency, deep learning models can be deployed in environments with limited resources, enable real-time multimedia analysis, and promote scalability for large-scale applications.

18.7 CONCLUSION

18.7.1 Key Findings

Significant advancements and optimistic findings in a variety of fields have resulted from the use of deep learning for multimedia analysis. Key findings in deep learning for multimedia analysis include the following:

Improved Image Classification: In image classification tasks, deep learning models, particularly CNNs, have attained remarkable performance. Models such as AlexNet, VGGNet, GoogLeNet, and ResNet have outperformed traditional methods on benchmark data sets such as ImageNet. Deep learning models have demonstrated superior learning of discriminative features from images, facilitating accurate and robust image classification.

Object Detection and Localization: Deep learning has transformed the detection and localization of objects in images. Techniques such as region-based CNNs (R-CNN), faster R-CNN, and you only look once (YOLO) have significantly enhanced the detection and localization of objects within images. These models utilize deep convolutional networks to efficiently identify objects with high precision and recall, facilitating autonomous driving, surveillance, and visual search applications.

Image Segmentation: Significant progress has been made by deep learning models in image segmentation, the process of dividing an image into meaningful regions. Fully convolutional networks (FCNs) and U-Net architectures have shown impressive efficacy in segmenting objects and comprehending the spatial context of images. This has medical imaging, semantic segmentation, and scene comprehension applications [35].

Video Analysis and Action Recognition: Deep learning has advanced video analysis by enabling accurate action recognition and video understanding. RNNs and 3D convolutional neural networks (3D CNNs) have been employed to model temporal dependencies and capture spatio-temporal features in videos. Deep learning models have demonstrated state-of-the-art performance in action recognition, video captioning, and video summarization tasks.

Multimodal Fusion: Deep learning has significantly contributed to multimodal fusion, which involves combining information from multiple modalities such as images, texts, and audio. Multimodal architectures, including multimodal neural networks (MNNs) and graph-based models, have been developed to learn joint representations and enable cross-modal tasks like image-text retrieval, video captioning, and sentiment analysis. Deep learning models have showcased the ability to leverage complementary information from different modalities, leading to improved performance in multimodal analysis [36].

Generative Models: Deep learning has introduced powerful generative models, such as GANs and VAEs, for generating realistic multimedia content. GANs have been used to generate high-quality images, videos, and even audio samples, while VAEs enable controlled generation and manipulation of multimedia content.

Generative models have applications in content creation, data augmentation, and synthetic data generation.

Transfer Learning and Pre-Training: Deep learning has demonstrated the effectiveness of transfer learning and pre-training techniques. Pre-training large-scale models on extensive data sets, such as ImageNet, and fine-tuning them on specific tasks has become a common practice. Transfer learning allows leveraging learned representations from pre-training to improve performance on smaller or domain-specific data sets, reducing the need for large amounts of labeled data.

Ethical and Bias Considerations: Deep learning for multimedia analysis has highlighted the ethical implications and challenges related to bias, fairness, and interpretability. Biases present in training data can propagate to deep learning models, leading to biased predictions and unfair outcomes. Researchers have recognized the importance of addressing biases, ensuring fairness, and developing interpretable models to mitigate these concerns.

These key findings in deep learning for multimedia analysis demonstrate the significant advancements and potential of deep learning techniques in understanding and analyzing multimedia content. Continued research and innovation in this field hold the promise of further enhancing the capabilities and applications of multimedia analysis in various domains.

18.7.2 Recommendations for Future Research

Future research in deep learning for multimedia analysis can focus on several areas to further advance the field and address emerging challenges. Here are some recommendations:

Explainable and Interpretable Models: Developing methods for improving the interpretability of deep learning models in multimedia analysis tasks is a crucial direction for future research. Techniques that can provide meaningful explanations for model predictions and highlight important features or regions in multimedia data would enhance transparency, trust, and accountability.

Multimodal Fusion and Cross-Modal Understanding: Further exploration of multimodal fusion techniques and models that can effectively leverage information from multiple modalities (images, texts, audio, etc.) is essential. Developing advanced architectures and learning algorithms that can model complex interactions and dependencies between modalities would improve tasks like multimodal retrieval, captioning, and sentiment analysis [37].

Adversarial Robustness and Security: Investigating methods to improve the robustness of deep learning models against adversarial attacks in multimedia analysis tasks is an important research direction. Adversarial attacks on multimedia data can pose significant security risks, and developing models that are resilient to such attacks would be valuable.

Lifelong and Continual Learning: Exploring lifelong and continual learning approaches for deep learning in multimedia analysis can enable models to learn continuously from new data and adapt to changing environments. Developing techniques that allow models to retain previously learned knowledge while efficiently incorporating new information would be beneficial for long-term multimedia analysis tasks.

Federated Learning for Privacy-Preserving Analysis: Exploring the use of federated learning approaches for privacy-preserving multimedia analysis can be valuable. Federated learning enables models to be trained on distributed data without the need for data sharing, ensuring privacy protection. Investigating efficient algorithms and techniques for federated learning in the context of multimedia analysis can unlock new possibilities while addressing privacy concerns.

Data Bias and Fairness: Continuing research on addressing data bias and ensuring fairness in multimedia analysis is critical. Methods that can detect and mitigate biases in training data, develop fairness-aware models, and promote ethical considerations in multimedia analysis applications would be instrumental in creating fair and unbiased systems [38].

Resource-Efficient and Edge Computing: Investigating resource-efficient deep learning techniques and architectures suitable for edge computing environments is an important direction. Efficient model compression, quantization, and distributed learning methods can enable deep learning models to be deployed on resource-constrained devices or at the edge, facilitating real-time multimedia analysis in edge computing scenarios.

Few-Shot and Zero-Shot Learning: Exploring techniques for few-shot and zero-shot learning in multimedia analysis can enhance the generalization capabilities of deep learning models. Developing models that can learn from limited labeled data or even perform inference on unseen classes would reduce the reliance on large annotated data sets and enable more flexible and adaptable systems.

Domain-Specific Multimedia Analysis: Conducting research that focuses on domain-specific challenges in multimedia analysis, such as medical imaging, remote sensing, or surveillance, can lead to tailored solutions that address specific needs and requirements in these domains. Customized architectures, specialized data augmentation techniques, and transfer learning approaches can be explored to tackle domain-specific challenges effectively.

Ethical Considerations and Societal Impact: Investigating the societal impact and ethical implications of deep learning in multimedia analysis is crucial. Research should address issues related to bias, privacy, accountability, and fairness, ensuring that deep learning models are developed and deployed in a responsible and ethical manner.

By pursuing these research directions, the field of deep learning for multimedia analysis can continue to advance, addressing key challenges and expanding the capabilities and impact of multimedia analysis in various domains.

REFERENCES

[1] S. Manikandan, P. Dhanalakshmi, K. C. Rajeswari, and A. Delphin Carolina Rani, "Deep Sentiment Learning for Measuring Similarity Recommendations in Twitter Data," *Intell. Autom. Soft Comput.*, vol. 34, no. 1, pp. 183–192, 2022, doi: 10.32604/iasc.2022.023469.

[2] S. Suganyadevi, V. Seethalakshmi, and K. Balasamy, "A Review on Deep Learning in Medical Image Analysis," *Int. J. Multimed. Inf. Retr.*, vol. 11, no. 1, pp. 19–38, 2022, doi: 10.1007/s13735-021-00218-1.

[3] J. Naskath, G. Sivakamasundari, and A. A. S. Begum, "A Study on Different Deep Learning Algorithms Used in Deep Neural Nets: MLP SOM and DBN," *Wirel. Pers. Commun.*, vol. 128, no. 4, pp. 2913–2936, 2023, doi: 10.1007/s11277-022-10079-4.

[4] A. Jeya Christy and K. Dhanalakshmi, "Content-Based Image Recognition and Tagging by Deep Learning Methods," *Wirel. Pers. Commun.*, vol. 123, no. 1, pp. 813–838, 2022, doi: 10.1007/s11277-021-09159-8.

[5] Rapidops, "Use Cases of Machine Learning in Retail," 2022, [Online]. Available: https://www.rapidops.com/blog/how-is-machine-learning-used-in-retail/

[6] P. Saranya, R. Pranati, and S. S. Patro, "Detection and Classification of Red Lesions from Retinal Images for Diabetic Retinopathy Detection Using Deep Learning Models," *Multimed. Tools Appl.*, 2023, doi: 10.1007/s11042-023-15045-1.

[7] M. A. Akbar *et al.*, "Prioritization Based Taxonomy of DevOps Challenges Using Fuzzy AHP Analysis," *IEEE Access*, vol. 8, pp. 202487–202507, 2020, doi: 10.1109/ACCESS.2020.3035880.

[8] S. R. Waheed, M. S. M. Rahim, N. M. Suaib, and A. A. Salim, "CNN Deep Learning-Based Image to Vector Depiction," *Multimed. Tools Appl.*, pp. 20283–20302, 2023, doi: 10.1007/s11042-023-14434-w.

[9] D. Garg, G. K. Verma, and A. K. Singh, "A Review of Deep Learning Based Methods for Affect Analysis Using Physiological Signals," *Multimed. Tools Appl.*, 2023, doi: 10.1007/s11042-023-14354-9.

[10] A. Mughaid *et al.*, "Improved Dropping Attacks Detecting System in 5G Networks Using Machine Learning and Deep Learning Approaches," *Multimed. Tools Appl.*, pp. 13973–13995, 2022, doi: 10.1007/s11042-022-13914-9.

[11] M. Şah and C. Direkoğlu, "Review and Evaluation of Player Detection Methods in Field Sports: Comparing Conventional and Deep Learning Based Methods," *Multimed. Tools Appl.*, pp. 13141–13165, 2021, doi: 10.1007/s11042-021-11071-z.

[12] D. P. Tobón, M. S. Hossain, G. Muhammad, J. Bilbao, and A. El Saddik, "Deep Learning in Multimedia Healthcare Applications: A Review," *Multimed. Syst.*, vol. 28, no. 4, pp. 1465–1479, 2022, doi: 10.1007/s00530-022-00948-0.

[13] V. Ravi, H. Narasimhan, C. Chakraborty, and T. D. Pham, "Deep Learning-Based Meta-Classifier Approach for COVID-19 Classification Using CT Scan and Chest X-Ray Images," *Multimed. Syst.*, vol. 28, no. 4, pp. 1401–1415, 2022, doi: 10.1007/s00530-021-00826-1.

[14] G. Chenais *et al.*, "Deep Learning Transformer Models for Building a Comprehensive and Real-Time Trauma Observatory: Development and Validation Study," *Jmir Ai*, vol. 2, p. e40843, 2023, doi: 10.2196/40843.

[15] Explainer, "Jay Wang, Robert Turko, Omar Shaikh, Haekyu Park," 2023, [Online]. Available: https://poloclub.github.io/cnn-explainer/

[16] J. Faritha Banu *et al.*, "Modeling of Hyperparameter Tuned Hybrid CNN and LSTM for Prediction Model," *Intell. Autom. Soft Comput.*, vol. 33, no. 3, pp. 1393–1405, 2022, doi: 10.32604/iasc.2022.024176.

[17] F. Omrane, "RNN," 2019, [Online]. Available: https://ai.stackexchange.com/questions/4683/what-is-the-fundamental-difference-between-cnn-and-rnn

[18] B. Suh *et al.*, "Interpretable Deep-Learning Approaches for Osteoporosis Risk Screening and Individualized Feature Analysis Using Large Population-Based Data: Model Development and Performance Evaluation," *J. Med. Internet Res.*, vol. 25, 2023, doi: 10.2196/40179.

[19] J. M. Vala and U. K. Jaliya, "Deep Learning Network and Renyi-Entropy Based Fusion Model for Emotion Recognition Using Multimodal Signals," *Int. J. Mod. Educ. Comput. Sci.*, vol. 14, no. 4, pp. 67–84, 2022, doi: 10.5815/ijmecs.2022.04.06.

[20] S. K. B. Sangeetha, M. S. Kumar, K. Deeba, H. Rajadurai, V. Maheshwari, and G. T. Dalu, "An Empirical Analysis of an Optimized Pretrained Deep Learning Model for COVID-19 Diagnosis," *Comput. Math. Methods Med.*, vol. 2022, 2022, doi: 10.1155/2022/9771212.

[21] X. Li and S. Ding, "Interpersonal Interface System of Multimedia Intelligent English Translation Based on Deep Learning," *Sci. Program.*, vol. 2022, 2022, doi: 10.1155/2022/8027003.

[22] J. Abeßer, "A Review of Deep Learning Based Methods for Acoustic Scene Classification," *Appl. Sci.*, vol. 10, no. 6, 2020, doi: 10.3390/app10062020.

[23] H. Li, J. Wang, N. Xiong, Y. Zhang, A. V. Vasilakos, and X. Luo, "A Siamese Inverted Residuals Network Image Steganalysis Scheme Based on Deep Learning," *ACM Trans. Multimed. Comput. Commun. Appl.*, pp. 1–22, 2023, doi: 10.1145/3579166.

[24] S. Jabeen, X. Li, M. S. Amin, O. Bourahla, S. Li, and A. Jabbar, "A Review on Methods and Applications in Multimodal Deep Learning," *ACM Trans. Multimed. Comput. Commun. Appl.*, vol. 19, no. 2s, pp. 1–41, 2023, doi: 10.1145/3545572.

[25] A. Anand and A. Kumar Singh, "A Comprehensive Study of Deep Learning-Based Covert Communication," *ACM Trans. Multimed. Comput. Commun. Appl.*, vol. 18, no. 2, 2022, doi: 10.1145/3508365.

[26] Z. Lv, Z. Yu, S. Xie, and A. Alamri, "Deep Learning-Based Smart Predictive Evaluation for Interactive Multimedia-Enabled Smart Healthcare," *ACM Trans. Multimed. Comput. Commun. Appl.*, vol. 18, no. 1s, pp. 1–20, 2022, doi: 10.1145/3468506.

[27] M. Gao, F. Zheng, J. J. Q. Yu, C. Shan, G. Ding, and J. Han, *Deep Learning for Video Object Segmentation: A Review*, vol. 56, no. 1. Springer Netherlands, 2023. doi: 10.1007/s10462-022-10176-7.

[28] S. Liu and Q. Chen, "College Sports Multimedia Network Based on Wireless Communication and Deep Learning Network Environment," *Wirel. Commun. Mob. Comput.*, vol. 2022, 2022, doi: 10.1155/2022/3267639.

[29] M. Hammad, A. M. Iliyasu, I. A. Elgendy, and A. A. A. El-Latif, "End-to-End Data Authentication Deep Learning Model for Securing IoT Configurations," *Human-Centric Comput. Inf. Sci.*, vol. 12, 2022, doi: 10.22967/HCIS.2022.12.004.

[30] SlideTerm, "Machine Learning Use Cases," 2023, [Online]. Available: https://www.slideteam.net/machine-learning-use-cases-ppt-powerpoint-presentation-professional-gallery.com

[31] Y. Wang *et al.*, "A Survey on Deploying Mobile Deep Learning Applications: A Systemic and Technical Perspective," *Digit. Commun. Networks*, vol. 8, no. 1, pp. 1–17, 2022, doi: 10.1016/j.dcan.2021.06.001.

[32] A. Gutub, M. K. Shambour, and M. A. Abu-Hashem, "Coronavirus Impact on Human Feelings during 2021 Hajj Season via Deep Learning Critical Twitter Analysis," *J. Eng. Res.*, vol. 11, no. 1, p. 100001, 2023, doi: 10.1016/j.jer.2023.100001.

[33] H. N. Noura, J. Azar, O. Salman, R. Couturier, and K. Mazouzi, "A Deep Learning Scheme for Efficient Multimedia Iot Data Compression," *Ad Hoc Netw.*, vol. 138, no. December 2021, p. 102998, 2023, doi: 10.1016/j.adhoc.2022.102998.

[34] S. K. Prabhakar and S. W. Lee, "Holistic Approaches to Music Genre Classification Using Efficient Transfer and Deep Learning Techniques," *Expert Syst. Appl.*, vol. 211, no. August 2022, p. 118636, 2023, doi: 10.1016/j.eswa.2022.118636.

[35] P. Singhal, A. Verma, P. K. Srivastava, V. Ranga, and R. Kumar, *Image Processing and Intelligent Computing Systems*, 2022. doi: 10.1201/9781003267782.

[36] Z. Ahmad, R. Jindal, N. S. Mukuntha, A. Ekbal, and P. Bhattachharyya, "Multi-Modality Helps in Crisis Management: An Attention-Based Deep Learning Approach of Leveraging Text for Image Classification," *Expert Syst. Appl.*, vol. 195, no. November 2019, p. 116626, 2022, doi: 10.1016/j.eswa.2022.116626.

[37] J. Liu, Z. Xiao, S. Lu, D. Che, M. Dong, and C. Bai, "Infrastructure-Level Support for GPU-Enabled Deep Learning in DATAVIEW," *Futur. Gener. Comput. Syst.*, vol. 141, pp. 723–737, 2023, doi: 10.1016/j.future.2022.12.014.

[38] A. M. Buttar, U. Ahmad, A. H. Gumaei, A. Assiri, M. A. Akbar, and B. F. Alkhamees, "Deep Learning in Sign Language Recognition: A Hybrid Approach for the Recognition of Static and Dynamic Signs," *Mathematics.*, vol. 11, no. 17, p. 3729, 10.3390/math11173729.

Index

Note: Bold page numbers refer to tables and italic page numbers refer to figures.